A FINE AND PLEASANT MISERY

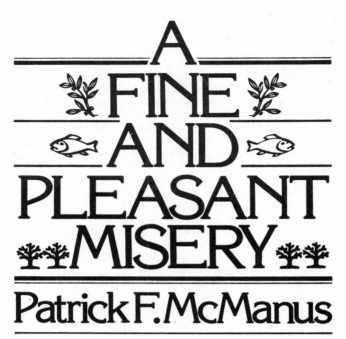

Patrick F. McManus

Edited and with an Introduction by
J ACK S AMSON

An Owl Book

Henry Holt and Company
New York

Copyright © 1968, 1969, 1970, 1971, 1972, 1973, 1974, 1975, 1976,
1977, 1978 by Patrick F. McManus.
Published by Henry Holt and Company, Inc.,
115 West 18th Street, New York, New York 10011.
Published in Canada by Fitzhenry & Whiteside Limited,
195 Allstate Parkway, Markham, Ontario L3R 4T8.

Library of Congress Cataloging-in-Publication Data
McManus, Patrick F.
A fine and pleasant misery.
1. Outdoor life—Anecdotes, facetiae, satire, etc.
2. Camping—Anecdotes, facetiae, satire, etc.
3. Fishing—Anecdotes, facetiae, satire, etc.
4. Hunting—Anecdotes, facetiae, satire, etc.
I. Samson, Jack. II. Title.
GV191.6.M32 1981   799   80-24733
ISBN 0-8050-0166-2
ISBN 0-8050-0032-1 (An Owl book: pbk.)

Henry Holt books are available at special discounts
for bulk purchases for sales promotions, premiums,
fund-raising, or educational use. Special editions
or book excerpts can also be created to specification.

For details contact:
Special Sales Director
Henry Holt and Company, Inc.
115 West 18th Street
New York, New York 10011

First published in hardcover by Holt, Rinehart and
Winston in 1978.

First Owl Book Edition—1981

All stories in this book originally appeared in *Field & Stream*.
The title story, "A Fine and Pleasant Misery," was first published
as "The Misery Kit."

Designer: Joy Chu

Printed in the United States of America
23   25   27   29   30   28   26   24

A Fine and Pleasant Misery

Also by Patrick F. McManus

Kid Camping From Aaaaiii! to Zip
They Shoot Canoes, Don't They?
Never Sniff a Gift Fish
The Grasshopper Trap
Rubber Legs and White Tail-Hairs

To Darlene and Mom

CONTENTS

Acknowledgments

I WOULD LIKE to acknowledge my debt to Jack Samson, editor of *Field & Stream,* who is largely responsible for bringing this book into existence; to Clare Conley, former editor of *Field & Stream,* who first detected some faint promise in me as a writer and whose encouragement and direction sustained me in the early years; to my mother, as an inexpendable source of wit and good humor; to my sister (The Troll) for provoking me into writing; to my wife, who corrects my spelling, grammar and taste; to my friend and colleague Dick Hoover, who daily endures the indignities of close association with a humorist; and to my friends Lloyd Humphrey and Vern Schultz, who have lived many of these stories.

Introduction

I GUESS Pat McManus sort of sneaked up on me. I had been editing his stories for a couple of years—from back around 1970—and I really didn't *read* Pat that much. Sometimes an editor is too busy editing to settle down and really enjoy the material.

Oh, I knew he was good and everyone on the staff kept telling me how funny he was. And there was the constant flow of reader mail demanding more of McManus in *Field & Stream*. A typical reader letter would go something like: "My husband and son have been subscribing to your magazine for years because they are both ardent hunters and fishermen, but I never read it because I am a golfer. But the other day I happened to read a story in *Field & Stream* by Patrick McManus. He is really funny! I think he is a riot! Now when the magazine comes in I look for McManus before I give the magazine to my husband or son. More! [Signed] Mrs. . . ."

Then one day one of Pat's stories came in and

I was not bogged down in some administrative chore; I put my feet up on the desk and began to read. The story was called "A Dog for All Seasons," and by the time I had gotten to the third page I was, literally, doubled over. My secretary said she had never—in all those years—heard me laugh so hard—or for so long. The more I read the funnier McManus became.

The damned dog, which he had as a kid and which you will read about in this collection of his best stories, was called Strange. His name in the beginning had been Stranger, wrote McManus, in the faint hope that he was just passing through when they first saw him. Strange was that most wonderful of all dogs: a mutt. A mutt with no redeeming features.

According to Pat, the dog had only two chores around his house: to attack prowlers, especially those whose character bore the slightest resemblance to his own, and to protect the chickens. On the second point, Strange always thought it was the other way around. He was also constantly making snide remarks about Pat's grandmother's cooking.

He insisted on following McManus when he went hunting or fishing—something Pat claims he tried to prevent.

"An army of Cossacks could have bivouacked on our front lawn for the night without his knowing a thing about it," McManus wrote, "but he could hear the sound of a shotgun shell being dropped into a flannel shirt pocket at a hundred yards."

Strange made slightly less noise going through the woods than an armored division through a bamboo jungle. Nevertheless, says Pat, they usually managed to get a few birds, apparently because the birds thought that anything that made that much noise couldn't possibly be hunting!

"My dog," says McManus of Strange, "believed

in a mixed bag: grouse, ducks, pheasants, rabbits, squirrels, chipmunks, gophers, skunks and porcupines. If we saw a cow or a horse, he would shout 'There's a big one! Shoot! Shoot!' "

Well, by now I am sure you see what I mean about McManus and his sneaking up on you. I quickly did three things: wiped the tears from my eyes; called Pat at his home in Spokane, Washington; and offered him a full-time job as an associate editor of *Field & Stream*. I have never been sorry, and I am delighted the editors of my competing outdoor magazines were just enough dumber than I was about how funny Pat is. No, I did four things, come to think of it. I dug up all the back issues I could find in the office for which Pat had written and took them all home with me that night. I read every one of them, and my wife was so annoyed at me for completely ignoring her that she went to have dinner with her sister. I never knew she was gone until she returned home at about midnight to find me sleeping on the den couch—a delighted smile still on my face.

A number of you reading this will remember the great American humorist Robert Benchley. You younger readers may not, but you sure missed a funny man if you never read anything he wrote. He used to write for all sorts of magazines, especially the *New Yorker*. He also wrote books, and I guess a lot of his talent was inherited by his kids because a couple of them also write—including his son Peter who wrote *Jaws*.

Well, Pat McManus is the Bob Benchley of the outdoors. When I heard my close friend and associate Ed Zern say he thought Pat was one of the funniest writers he had ever read I knew we had a winner, because Ed—of "Exit Laughing" fame in *Field & Stream*—has got to be one of the deans of outdoor humor.

We all have our favorite McManus stories and I guess mine (along with "A Dog for All Seasons") is "The Modified Stationary Panic"—also found in this collection which I have had the pleasure and privilege of editing. Pat was off on his own cloud nine about how easy it is to get lost in the woods and how the experts on survival caution everyone not to panic. Pat disagrees with this theory. He feels if one gets lost he or she should, especially if they are a panicker as is Pat, get the panic out of the system all at once. He claims that holding panic in may cause severe psychological disorders and even stomach cramps and baldness. Over the years, Pat says, he has been involved in several dozen panics, usually as a participant, sometimes simply as an observer.

"Most of my panics have been of a solitary nature," he says, "but on several occasions I have organized and led group panics, one of which involved twenty-some people. In that instance, a utility company took advantage of the swath we cut through the forest and built a power line along it."

Pat says back in the earlier days of his panicking he utilized what he refers to as the Full Bore Linear Panic (FBLP). This is where you run flat out in a straight line until the course of your panic is deflected by a large rock or tree, after which you get up and sprint off in the new direction.

"One time when we were kids," says Pat, "my friend Retch and I panicked right through a logging crew and the loggers dropped what they were doing and ran along with us under the impression we were being pursued by something. When they found out all we were doing was panicking, they fell back, cursing, and returned to their work."

Nowadays, Pat says, he will advise against undertaking a Full Bore Linear Panic unless, of course, one is equipped with a stout heart, a three-day supply of food, and a valid passport.

Only McManus could have thought up "The Great Cow Plot"—also contained in this collection. All of us have been harassed by cows while fly fishing for trout, but nobody but Pat could have realized the cows had gotten together and planned the war against us. Biologists and science-fiction buffs have speculated about the earth's takeover by the insect world, but Pat suggests perhaps the bovine species poses a far greater threat. Even when he plans a fishing trip forty miles back into the wilderness, he says, a herd of cows usually will get wind of it and go on a forced march to get there before Pat does.

"If I was on the nineteenth floor of a department store and stopped to net a guppy out of an aquarium," he says, "a cow would get off the elevator and rush over to offer advice."

Beginning to see what I am talking about? McManus is not only funny, there are more than a few suspicions around the *Field & Stream* editorial offices that just maybe Pat ain't wrapped all that tight! But if he *has* come unglued let us all hope he stays that way!

There is altogether too little humor in the outdoor field. What with all the protectionists telling us we are responsible for every endangered species from the Arizona pupfish to the California condor, we could use a few laughs—those of us who love the outdoors.

Like a great many fine writers Pat went into newspaper work upon graduation from Washington State University in 1956. Also, he has been a television reporter and later an English teacher. He earned an M.A. in English from his alma mater in 1962 and now teaches at Eastern Washington University—with the rank of professor.

But it is early life that prepared him for his

outdoor writing. He was born and raised in Idaho where his mother was a schoolteacher. He grew up on a small farm with a creek running through it—like the creek running through so many of his stories. He writes about the outdoors well because he has done a number of things in it besides fish, camp and hunt. He has been in heavy construction work, a truck driver, high scaler, grease monkey, and a groundman for a power line construction crew.

You will never forget his cast of characters—from his boyhood pal Retch; his mentor, old Rancid Crabtree; Grogan, of war surplus fame; Grandma; and least of all Strange, the dog with no redeeming features.

Look out world. Here comes Pat McManus!

Jack Samson, Editor
Field & Stream

A Fine and
Pleasant Misery

A Fine and Pleasant Misery

MODERN TECHNOLOGY has taken most of the misery out of the outdoors. Camping is now aluminum-covered, propane-heated, foam-padded, air-conditioned, bug-proofed, flip-topped, disposable, and transistorized. Hardship on a modern camping trip is blowing a fuse on your electric underwear, or having the battery peter out on your Porta-Shaver. A major catastrophe is spending your last coin on a recorded Nature Talk and then discovering the camp Comfort & Sanitation Center (featuring forest green tile floors and hot showers) has pay toilets.

There are many people around nowadays who seem to appreciate the fact that a family can go on an outing without being out. But I am not one of them. Personally, I miss the old-fashioned misery of old-fashioned camping.

Young people just now starting out in camping

probably have no idea that it wasn't but a couple of decades ago that people went camping expecting to be miserable. Half the fun of camping in those days was looking forward to getting back home. When you did get back home you prolonged the enjoyment of your trip by telling all your friends how miserable you had been. The more you talked about the miseries of life in the woods, the more you wanted to get back out there and start suffering again. Camping was a fine and pleasant misery.

A source of much misery in old-fashioned camping was the campfire, a primitive contrivance since replaced by gas stoves and propane heaters. It is a well-known fact that your run-of-the-mill imbecile can casually flick a soggy cigar butt out of a car window and burn down half a national forest. The campfire, on the other hand, was a perverse thing that you could never get started when you needed it most. If you had just fallen in an icy stream or were hopping around bare-footed on frosted ground (uncommon now but routine then), you could not ignite the average campfire with a bushel of dry tinder and a blowtorch.

The campfire was of two basic kinds: the Smudge and the Inferno. The Smudge was what you used when you were desperately in need of heat. By hovering over the Smudge the camper could usually manage to thaw the ice from his hands before being kippered to death. Even if the Smudge did burst into a decent blaze, there was no such thing as warming up gradually. One moment the ice on your pants would show slight signs of melting and the next the hair on your legs was going up in smoke. Many's the time I've seen a blue and shivering man hunched over a crackling blaze suddenly eject from his boots and pants with a loud yell and go bounding about in the snow, the front half of him the color of boiled lobster, the back half still blue.

The Inferno was what you always used for cooking. Experts on camp cooking claimed you were supposed to cook over something called "a bed of glowing coals." But what everyone cooked over was the Inferno. The "bed of glowing coals" was a fiction concocted by experts on camp cooking. Nevertheless the camp cook was frequently pictured, by artists who should have known better, as a tranquil man hunkered down by a bed of glowing coals, turning plump trout in the frying pan with the blade of his hunting knife. In reality the camp cook was a wildly distraught individual who charged through waves of heat and speared savagely with a long sharp stick at a burning hunk of meat he had tossed on the grill from a distance of twenty feet.

The rollicking old fireside songs originated in the efforts of other campers to drown out the language of the cook and prevent it from reaching the ears of little children. Meat roasted over a campfire was either raw or extra well done, but the cook usually came out medium rare.

The smoke from the campfire always blew directly in the eyes of the campers, regardless of wind direction. No one minded much, since it prevented you from seeing what you were eating. If a bite of food showed no signs of struggle, you considered this a reasonable indication that it came from the cook pot and was not something just passing through.

Aluminum foil was not used much in those days, and potatoes were simply thrown naked into the glowing coals, which were assumed to lie somewhere at the base of the Inferno. After about an hour the spuds were raked out with a long stick. Most of the potatoes would be black and hard as rocks, and some

of them would be rocks, but it didn't make much difference either way. Successive layers of charcoal would
be cracked off until a white core of potato was uncov-
ered, usually the size of a walnut or maybe a pea. This
would be raw. Sometimes there would be no white core
at all, and these potatoes were said to be "cooked
through." Either that or they were rocks.

There were other fine sources of camping misery besides campfires. One of the finest was the old-
fashioned bedroll. No matter how well you tucked in
the edges of the bedroll it always managed to spring a
leak in the middle of the night. A wide assortment of
crawly creatures, driven by a blast of cold air, would
stream in through the leak. Efforts to close the gap
merely opened new leaks, and finally you just gave up
and lay there, passing the time until sunrise—approximately thirty-seven hours—by counting off insects one
by one as they froze to death on your quivering flesh.

My bedroll, made from one of my grandmoth-
er's patchwork quilts, was an oven compared to the first
"sleeping bag" I ever spent a night in. My inconstant
boyhood companion, "Stupe" Jones, told me one
September day that I would not need my bedroll on
our outing that night because he had discovered an
honest-to-goodness sleeping bag in the attic of his house
and it was big enough for both of us to sleep in. Now
when I saw what a compact little package a real sleeping
bag could be folded up into, I became immediately
ashamed of my own cumbersome bedroll, which rolled
up into a bundle the size of a bale of hay. I was glad
that I had not marred the esthetics of our little camping
trip by toting the gross thing along. That night we
spread the sleeping bag out on a sandy beach alongside
Sand Creek, stripped to our shorts (we had both been
taught never to sleep with our clothes on), and hopped
into the bag. The effect was much like plunging

through thin ice into a lake. Not wishing to insult my friend or his sleeping bag, I stifled a shrill outcry with a long, deep gasp disguised in turn as a yawn. Stupe said through chattering teeth that the sleeping bag was bound to warm up, since it was, after all, a sleeping bag, wasn't it? No two lovers ever clung to each other with such tenacity as did those two eight-year-old boys through that interminable night. Later we discovered that some sleeping bags come in two parts, one a nice padded liner and the other a thin canvas cover. What we had was the latter.

One of the finest misery-producing camping trips I've ever been on occurred when I was about fourteen. Three friends and I were hiking to a lake high up in the Idaho Rockies. What had been a poor, struggling drizzle when we left home worked its way up and became a highly successful blizzard in the mountains. Before long our climbing boots (called "tennis shoes" in more prosperous parts of the world) were caked with ice. The trail was slowly being erased before our very eyes, and I was beginning to write news stories in my head: "The futile search for four young campers lost in a snowstorm has been called off. . . ." As we clawed our way up the side of the mountain, one of the frailer souls—never ask me who—suggested that the better part of valor or even of stark madness might be to turn back. But he was shouted down with such cries as, "When I come this far to fish, I am going to fish!" and "Who knows which way is *back*?"

Eventually we came to the tiny cabin of a trapper, who had either been a midget or had crawled around on his knees all day, for the structure was only four feet from dirt floor to log ceiling. We tidied the place up by evicting a dead porcupine, split up enough wood to last a

month, and started a fire in a little makeshift stove. The
stovepipe was a foot short of the roof and this resulted
in the minor inconvenience of having the roof catch fire
every once in a while, but nobody really minded.

On the second day Kenny and I fought our way
up to the lake, where he carried out his vow to fish, and
then we stumbled back to the cabin. We stripped off
our sopping clothes and sat down side by side on the
woodpile next to the stove, whose glowing pipe was
sending out soothing waves of heat from the flames
howling up through it. Now as was our practice in those
days, we had carried enough grub with us to feed a
regiment of lumberjacks for a week of full-time eating,
and Norm, a rather plump kid, decided to take the edge
off his boredom by shooting "baskets" with an excess of
hardboiled eggs he had discovered. The opening at the
top of the stovepipe served as the "basket." Kenny and I
watched in fascinated horror, as they say, as one of the
rim shots lodged on the edge of the glowing pipe and
the whole contraption began to topple toward our
naked laps. Now both of us worked up a sizable amount
of activity, but because of the cramped quarters, it was
insufficient to move us clear of the descending pipe. In
order to avoid incurrence of potentially worse damage
to our anatomies we caught the stove pipe in our hands.
For two or three hundredths of a second we passed the
glowing cylinder back and forth between us, all the
while calmly contemplating the best course of action,
since neither one of us could manage to accumulate
enough free time or leverage to get up from the woodpile. At last it occurred to us to simply drop the pipe on
the floor, both of us wondering why we hadn't thought
of such an obvious solution sooner. At the time it seemed
that we had juggled the stovepipe for approximately
two hours, but in retrospect, I doubt that the total
time was more than half a second.

Smoke, true to its nature, had in the meantime filled the cabin to overflowing and the four of us rolled out through the tiny door hole as a single choking ball of adolescent humanity. The storm outside, particularly to those not wearing any clothes, was refreshing and seemed to call for some strenuous exercise. What followed, as Vern remarked later, was something you don't see every day: two naked and enraged people chasing an hysterical fat kid up the side of a mountain in the middle of a blizzard.

In terms of misery, that camping trip was very fine.

I once launched my family on a program designed to toughen them up, on the assumption that the more misery they could endure the more they would enjoy hunting, fishing, and camping. Whenever anyone skinned a knee or thumped his "crazy bone," he was to reply in answer to inquiries about the extent of his pain: "A mere detail." Thus my children were expected to ignore the minor miseries encountered in the acquisition of outdoor knowledge and experience, and to make little of mosquito bites, burned fingers, and that vast assortment of natural projectiles known as "stickers."

As it turned out, though, I had to abandon the program. One day on a family camping trip, I picked up a large branch for firewood and discovered an outlaw band of yellow jackets waiting in ambush. A running battle ensued. I finally outdistanced the little devils, as I called them, but not before several of them had inflicted some terrible wounds on various parts of my person. My family watched as I flitted like a nymph through the woods, careening off of boulders and leaping mammoth moss-covered logs. Fortunately, as my wife said later, most of my shouts were inaudible and the children were saved from traumas that might have wrought psychological havoc. When I finally lunged back into camp, still sweating and snarling, my littlest girl consoled me with the words, "Details, Daddy, mere details."

Well I decided right then and there if a kid can't distinguish between *real* pain and a little old skinned knee, then I had better call off the whole program, and that is what I did. I mean you don't want your children to grow up to be totally insensitive.

But camping misery is a thing of the past. Like most of my fellow outdoorsmen, having gathered unto the camper the fruits of technology, I am protected from cold by propane, from hardness by foam rubber, and from the insect world by a bug bomb. Still, sometimes I have a nostalgic yearning for some of that old-fashioned misery, and it came to me that what we need nowadays is a misery kit. I think it would find a market, especially among older campers, who might enjoy a bit of instant misery on a camping trip so they would have something to tell the folks back home about. There could be an aerosol can for spraying a blast of cold air down your back every once in a while, another for spraying smoke in your eyes. There might even be a pair of refrigerated boots that you could stick your feet into for a few minutes each morning. A rock or a pine cone could be included for slipping under the fitted sheet of a camper bunk. Everyone, of course, would want a pre-charred spud. There might even be a box of mixed insects—yellow jackets, mosquitoes, ticks, jiggers, and deer flies—but maybe that would be carrying misery a bit far.

A Dog for All Seasons

ONE OF THESE DAYS they'll probably come out with a mechanical bird dog that locates pheasants with a special scent detector and radar. A small on-dog computer will record and analyze all available information and give the hunter a report: two roosters and five hens in stubble field—253 feet. A pointer on the dog's back would indicate the exact direction.

There would be luxury models, of course, with built-in stereo and FM sets, a special compartment for lunches, a cooler for beverages. The dog's nose would be a cigarette lighter.

The really high-priced jobs would not only retrieve the bird but pluck it, dress it, wrap it in foil, and quick-freeze it. By the time the bird got back to the hunter it would be neat and trim as a TV dinner.

Since no self-respecting hunter would want to be seen carrying his dog around by a handle, all but the cheapest models would be designed to look like nifty attaché cases. If you passed by some good hunting ground on your way home from work, you could get out and let your attaché case nose around in a thicket or two.

There would be minor inconveniences ("We'll have to go back, Harry. I thought I had my bird dog but it's just a bag of briefs."), but on the whole, the mechanical bird dog would have many advantages over the standard makes most of us have now.

Still, I'm something of a traditionalist, and if the mechanical bird dog were to go on the market tomorrow I'd probably stick with my old ready-made hound, such as he is. His eyes don't light up much anymore, let alone his tubes, and you can't light a cigarette on the end of his nose. The sounds that come out of him are not stereo (fortunately) and he has never been much on fidelity any way you look at it. But I would keep him nevertheless. There was a time in my youth, however, when I would have swapped my dog for a mechanical job and thrown in my T-shirt decorated with bottle caps to boot.

Take the flaws of character you find in all dogs and most human beings, roll them up in the hide of a sickly wart hog, and you would have a reasonable facsimile of my dog Stranger, who was dirty, lazy, bigoted, opinionated, gluttonous, conceited, ill-tempered, and an incorrigible liar.

An old man once summed up Stranger's character succinctly. "He's a prevert!" he said. I didn't know what preverts were but had no doubt Stranger was one of them.

We had called the dog Stranger out of the faint hope he was just passing through. As it turned out, the name was most inappropriate since he stayed on for nearly a score of years, all the while biting the hands that fed him and making snide remarks about my grandmother's cooking. Eventually the name was abbreviated to "Strange," which was shorter and much more descriptive.

My mother used to say that Strange was like one of the family. Then my grandmother would bawl her out and say that was no way to talk about my uncle George. That was one of Mom's favorite jokes and was probably the reason she allowed the dog to stay on the place. At least nobody ever thought of another reason.

I used to beg for a decent dog—a Labrador retriever, an Irish setter, or just a regular old mongrel like most of the other guys had—but with no success. We just weren't a two-dog family, and since no one in his right mind would take Strange and Mom wouldn't take advantage of anyone who revealed his low mentality by offering to take Strange, I was stuck with him.

Strange didn't even make good as a criminal. In our part of the country the worst crime a dog can commit is to run deer. As soon as Strange found this out, he rushed out into our clover field and tried to run the deer that grazed there. They would have none of it. They looked at the wildly yapping creature dancing around them and went back to their munching.

Strange had only two chores, but he could never get them straight. He was supposed to attack prowlers, especially those whose character bore the slightest resemblance to his own, and to protect the chickens. He always thought it was the other way around.

Whenever he was caught assaulting a chicken he would come up with some cock-and-bull story about how the chicken had been about to set fire to the house when he, Strange, happened along and prevented arson. "Bad enough we have a dog that attacks chickens, we have to have one that lies about it besides!" Mom would say. (It should be understood that Strange did not actually speak in words, or at least that anyone ever heard, but with his eyes and gestures with feet, tail, and ears.)

As for prowlers, Strange would go out and invite tramps in off the road for a free meal. While the dog was out in the yard apologizing to the tramp for my grandmother's cooking, the womenfolk would peek out through the curtains and try to determine whether the fellow was dangerous. If so, they would wait until he had just about finished his meal and then my sister would bellow, "Do you want the gun, Ma? Do you want the gun?" This usually would bring the tramp to his feet and send him at a fast walk toward the nearest cover, the ditch on the far side of the road. Even had the gun been real, which it wasn't, the tramp would have been in no danger—unless of course he happened to step between Mom and the dog.

As soon as I was old enough to hunt I would borrow a shotgun and sneak out to the woods in search of grouse. I had to sneak, not because Mom disapproved of my hunting, but because Strange would insist upon going along and contributing his advice and services. An army of Cossacks could have bivouacked on our front lawn for the night without his knowing a thing about it, but he could hear the sound of a shotgun shell being dropped into a flannel shirt pocket at a hundred yards.

Just as I would be easing my way out the door, he would come staggering out of the woodshed, his eyes bloodshot and bleary from a night of carousing, and say, "My suggestion is that we try Schultz's woods first and then work our way up Stagg's hill and if we don't get anything there we can stop by the Haversteads and shoot some of their chickens."

Strange made slightly less noise going through the woods than an armored division through a bamboo jungle. Nevertheless, we usually managed to get a few birds, apparently because they thought that anything that made that much noise couldn't possibly be hunting.

My dog believed in a mixed bag: grouse, ducks, pheasants, rabbits, squirrels, chipmunks, gophers, skunks, and porcupines. If we saw a cow or horse, he would shout, "There's a big one! Shoot! Shoot!"

Fortunately, Strange tired of hunting after about an hour. "Let's eat the lunch now," he would say. If he had been particularly disgusting that day, I would lie and tell him that I had forgotten to bring a lunch, knowing that it was against his principle—he only had one—to ever be caught more than an hour's distance away from a food supply. He would immediately strike off for home with the look of a man who has suddenly been deposited in the middle of the Mojave Desert.

Thus it went through most of the years of my youth, until finally Strange's years totaled what we supposed to be about a dozen. He sensed death approaching—probably the first thing in his life he ever did sense approaching—and one day staggered to a window, looked out and said, "A dog like me should live for a thousand years!" Then he died.

Everyone wept and said he hadn't been such a bad dog after all. Everyone except my grandmother, who simply smiled to herself as she stirred the gravy.

That night at dinner I said, "This sure is lumpy gravy," and "This pie crust sure is tough." It seemed the least I could do for Strange.

As I say, there was a time when I would have traded a dog like Strange in an instant for a mechanical bird dog. But now? Well, let me think about that for a while.

The Modified Stationary Panic

EVERY SO OFTEN I read an article on how to survive when lost in the wilds, and I have to laugh. The experts who write these pieces know everything about survival but next to nothing about getting lost. I am an expert on getting lost. I have been lost in nine different countries, forty-three cities, seven national forests, four national parks, countless parking lots, and one Amtrak passenger train. My wife claims I once got lost riding an elevator in a tall building, but that is an unwarranted exaggeration based on my momentary confusion over the absence of a thirteenth floor. (If you are a person with an inherent fear of heights, you want to make certain that all the floors are right where they are supposed to be, and you're not about to listen to a lot of lame excuses for any empty space between the twelfth and fourteenth floors.)

Since I have survived all of these experiences

of being lost, it follows that I am also something of an expert on survival. Consequently, out of my identification with and concern for that portion of humanity that frequently finds itself in the predicament of not knowing its way home from its left elbow, I have been motivated to publish the following compilation of field-tested tips on how to get lost. I have also included information on how to survive, and, of equal interest, how to pass the time if you don't.

The most common method for getting lost starts with telling a hunting partner, "I'll just cut down over the hill here and meet you on the first road." Nine times out of ten, the next road in the direction you choose is the Trans-Canada Highway. That is, of course, unless you are in Canada, in which case it may well be a supply route to a Siberian reindeer farm.

Another good method for getting lost in a quick and efficient manner is to rely on a companion who claims to have infallible sense of direction. Spin him around any time, any place in the world, according to him, and he will automatically point toward home. Your first clue that his sense of direction is somewhat overrated comes when he says something like, "Hey, now that's weird! The sun is setting in the east!" There is, of course, an appropriate response to such a statement. Unfortunately, it may result in a long jail term.

My favorite method for getting lost is daydreaming. I'll be trailing a deer whose tracks are so old pine seedlings will have sprouted in them. When I have to count the growth rings on a tree to determine how fresh a set of tracks is, my interest in the hunt begins to wane. Pretty soon I'm daydreaming. I imagine myself shooting a trophy buck. Then I unsheath my knife, dress him out, and drag him back to camp, where my hunting companions go wild with envy and astonishment.

"Would ya look at the size of that buck ol' Pat got!"

"Man, where did you ever get a beauty like that?"

"Just tracked him down," I say. "He was a smart one too, but every so often he made the mistake of bending a blade of grass the wrong way. The wind changed and spooked him though, and I had to drop him on a dead run at nine hundred yards and . . ."

And I'll look around and I'll be lost. The last time I had looked, I was hunting in a pine woods on a mountain. Now I'll be so deep in a swamp the wildlife is a couple of stages back on the scale of evolution. (It's bad enough being lost without having to put up with a bunch of feathered lizards learning to fly.)

Undoubtedly, the surest way to get lost is to venture into the woods as a member of a group. Sooner or later one of the boys, on a pretext of offering up a riddle, says, "Hey, guys, I bet none of you can tell me which direction the car is in. Heh heh." (The "heh heh" is tacked on to imply that he knows the right direction, but truth is he couldn't tell it from a kidney stone.) Everyone now points firmly and with great authority in a different direction. In every such case, the most forceful personality in the group gets his way. The effectiveness of this method arises out of the fact that the most forceful personality usually turns out to rank on intelligence scales somewhere between sage hens and bowling balls. He is also an accomplished magician. With a wave of his arm and the magic words "the car's just over that next rise" he can make the whole bunch of you vanish for three days.

While the process of becoming lost is usually a lot of fun, the entertainment value diminishes rapidly once the act is accomplished. The first small twinges of fear, however, do not last long, and are soon replaced by waves of terror. There is also a sense of general disorientation, the first symptom of which is confusion about which side of your head your face is on. Two questions immediately occur to the lost outdoorsman: "What shall I do now?" and "Why didn't I stick with golf?"

I disagree sharply with most survival experts on what the lost person should do first. Most of them start out by saying some fool thing like, "The first rule of survival is DON'T PANIC!" Well, anyone who has ever been lost knows that kind of advice is complete nonsense. They might as well tell you "DON'T SWEAT!" or "DON'T GET GOOSE BUMPS ALL OVER YOUR BODY!"

Survival experts are apparently such calm, rational people themselves that they assume a lost person spends considerable time deliberating the question of whether he should panic: "Let's see, the first thing I'll do is panic, and then I'll check to see on which side of the trees the moss is growing." It doesn't work that way.

First of all, one is either a panicker or one isn't, and the occasion of being lost is no time to start fretting about a flaw in one's character. My own theory holds that it is best, if one is a panicker, to get the panic out of the system as quickly as possible. Holding panic in may cause severe psychological disorders and even stomach cramps and baldness. Also, the impacted panic may break loose at a later date, if there is a later date, and cause one to sprint across a shopping mall yelling "Help! Help!" at the top of his lungs. Shopping malls being what they are, no one would probably notice but it might be embarrassing anyway.

Over the years I've been involved in several dozen panics, usually as a participant, sometimes simply as an observer. Most of my panics have been of a solitary nature, but on several occasions I have organized and led group panics, one of which involved twenty-some people. In that instance a utility company took advantage of the swath we cut through the forest and built a power line along it.

Back in the earlier days of my panicking I utilized what is known technically as the Full Bore Linear Panic (FBLP). This is where you run flat out in a straight line until the course of your panic is deflected by a large rock or tree, after which you get up and sprint off in the new direction. The FBLP is also popularly referred to as the ricochet or pinball panic or sometimes simply as "going bananas." Once an FBLP is underway there is no stopping it. It gains momentum at every stride, and the participants get so caught up in it they forget the reason for holding it in the first place. They'll panic right out of the woods, onto a road, down the road, through a town, and back into the woods, all the time picking up momentum. One time when we were kids my friend Retch and I panicked right through a logging crew and the loggers dropped what they were doing and ran along with us under the impression we were being pursued by something. When they found out all we were doing was panicking, they fell back, cursing, and returned to their work. This tendency of panic to feed upon itself gives it ever-increasing momentum and occasionally indigestion.

Although it will do absolutely no good, I must advise against undertaking a Full Bore Linear Panic unless, of course, one is equipped with a stout heart, a three-day supply of food, and a valid passport. Instead, I recommend the Stationary or Modified Panic. It offers the same therapeutic effect and subsides after a few minutes with none of the FBLP's adverse side effects, such as making your life insurance company break out in a bad rash.

The Stationary Panic first came to my attention one time when a large but harmless snake slithered across a trail a couple of yards ahead of my wife. She made a high-pitched chittering sound and began jumping up and down and flailing the air with her arms. It was a most impressive performance, particularly since each jump was approximately a foot high and her backpack happened to be the one with the tent on it. The only adverse side effect to the Stationary Panic was that the lone witness to the spectacle could not help laughing every time he thought about it, a reaction quickly remedied, however, by his sleeping most of the night outside the tent in a driving rainstorm.

Although I immediately perceived the advantage of this form of panic, I could not imagine myself bouncing up and down, flailing my arms and chittering like an angry squirrel, particularly in front of the rough company with whom I usually find myself in a predicament requiring a panic. Thus it came about that I invented the Modified Stationary Panic, or MSP.

The key to the MSP is not to bounce up and down in a monotonous fashion but to vary the steps so that it appears to be a sort of folk dance. You can make up your own steps but I highly recommend throwing in a couple of Russian squat kicks. The chittering sound should be replaced by an Austrian drinking song, shouted out at the top of your voice. The MSP is particularly appropriate for group panics. There are few sights so inspiring as a group of lost hunters, arms entwined, dancing and singing for all they are worth as night closes in upon them.

Once you have established the fact that you are

indeed lost and have performed the perfunctory Modified Panic, you should get started right away on the business of surviving. Many survival experts recommend that you first determine on which side of the trees the moss is growing. I'm not sure why this is, but I suppose it it because by the time you get hungry enough to eat moss you will want to know where to find it in a hurry.

If you think you may have to spend the night in the woods, you may wish to fashion some form of temporary shelter. For one night, a tree with good thick foliage will serve the purpose. Thick foliage will help keep the rain off, and reduces the chance of falling out of the tree.

After a day or two, it is probably a good idea to build a more permanent shelter, such as a lean-to. A very nice lean-to can be made out of large slabs of bark, pried from a dead cedar, pine or tamarack, and leaned against the trunk of an upright tree. If you have a tendency to walk in your sleep, the lean-to should not be more than fifteen feet from the ground. After a couple of weeks, it might be a good idea to add some simple furnishings and pictures.

Each day you are lost should be recorded by carving a notch on some handy surface. (This procedure should be skipped by anyone lost at sea in a rubber life raft.) I've known people lost only a few hours and already they had carved half a notch. The reason for the notches is that you may write a book on your experience and sell it to the movies. As is well known, a film about being lost is absolute zilch without an ever-increasing string of notches. The best film treatment of notches that I've seen was in a TV movie about a couple whose plane had crashed in the Yukon. They painted the notches on the plane's fuselage with a set of oil paints. It was a great touch and added a lot of color to the drama. I for one never go out into the woods anymore without a set of oil paints, just in case I'm lucky enough to be lost long enough to interest a film producer.

Many survival experts are of the opinion that lost persons have little to fear from wild animals. I disagree. It is true that bear and cougar will almost always do their best to avoid contact with human beings, but how about squirrels and grouse? On several occasions the sound of a squirrel charging through dry leaves has inflicted partial paralysis on my upper ganglia, erasing from my consciousness the knowledge that one has nothing to fear from bear or cougar. Having a grouse blast off from under one's feet can cause permanent damage to one's psyche. The first-aid recommended for restoring vital bodily functions after such occurrences is simply to pound your chest several times with a large rock. On the other hand, if the jolt has been sufficient to lock your eyelids in an open position, it is best to leave them that way. This will prevent you from dozing off during the night and falling out of your tree.

The excitement of being lost wears off rather quickly, and after a few days boredom sets in. It is then that one may wish to turn to some of the proven techniques for getting one's self found. Building a large smoky fire is always good. During fire season, this will almost always attract attention and it won't be long before a team of smoke-jumpers will be parachuted in to put out the fire. They may be a little angry about having their poker game back at camp interrupted but can usually be persuaded to take you out of the woods with them anyway. (The term "survival tip," by the way, originated from the practice of giving smoke-jumpers five dollars each for not leaving the fire-builder behind.) There is always the possibility that a bomber may just fly over and dump a load of fire retardant on you and your fire and you will have to turn to other measures.

Scooping water up in your hat and pouring it down a badger hole is good, if you are fortunate enough to have both a hat and a badger hole handy. Someone is bound to show up to ask you why you are doing such a fool thing. If this person isn't afraid of associating with a madman, he will probably show you the way home.

Similarly, you can try your hand at catching some large fish. If you're successful, three anglers will immediately emerge from the brush and ask you what bait you're using. In case you don't have a valid fishing license, one of the three will be a game warden who will place you under arrest as soon as he has caught his own limit. But at least you'll be found.

When everything else fails and you are really desperate, you can always resort to taking off all your clothes. Even when lost, I've never known this technique to fail in attracting a large crowd of people, no matter how far back in the wilderness I happened to be. Here's an example:

My friend Retch and I had been fishing a high mountain stream at least three miles from the nearest road.

We hadn't seen a sign of human life all day. The fish had stopped biting and we were hot and sticky and decided to take a dip in a pool beneath a small waterfall.

We took off our clothes and dove into the water, the temperature of which instantly proved to be somewhere between damn cold and ice. As we popped to the surface, and started flailing wildly toward the ledge from which we had dived, approximately twelve members of a mushroom club rounded a bend in the trail and headed straight for us. I would like to be able to tell you that modesty forced us to remain submerged in that liquid ice until they had passed, their pleasant outing unblemished by nothing more lascivious than a patch of morel mushrooms. Unfortunately, that would not be the truth. The startling spectacle of two grown men lunging out of the water, snatching up their clothes and racing off through a thicket of devil's club was at least mitigated by the fact that most of the ladies in the group apparently thought we were wearing blue leotards. I was also relieved that a particularly bad twelve-letter word had frozen on Retch's lower lip and didn't thaw out until we were in the car driving home.

Perhaps the most important thing to remember when lost is to accept the experience in a philosophical manner. Whenever I start becoming slightly confused over which is my elbow and which the way home and night is tightening its noose upon me in some primordial swamp, I never fail to recall the folksy wisdom spoken to me under similar circumstances by the old woodsman Rancid Crabtree. Rancid spat out his chaw of tobacco and in that comical, bug-eyed way of his said, "JUMPIN' GOSH ALMIGHTY, WHERE IN HELL IS WE?!" Somehow those words always seem a fitting introduction to a lively folk dance and a rousing rendition of an Austrian drinking song.

Grogan's
War Surplus

My old camping buddy Retch, his eyes dreamy and wet with nostalgia, leaned forward and stirred the fire under our sizzling pan of trout with a stick. I could tell he was getting deep into his cups because that's the only time he turns sloppily sentimental. Also, we were cooking on a propane camp stove.

"You know," he said, "it seems like only yesterday that you and me was crouched in the mud in some Godforsaken place using our bayonets to roast a couple hunks of Spam over some canned heat."

"Yeah, and heatin' our water in a steel helmet," I said, sinking suddenly into the morass of reminiscence. "And lyin' awake night after night in a pup tent, listenin' for the first sound of attack . . ."

". . . and half our gear riddled with bullet holes," Retch put in, shaking a tear off the end of his mustache.

"Yep," I said, "we really had some great campin'

when we were kids. It's just too damn bad kids nowadays don't have some of those old-time war surplus stores around to sell them their campin' gear."

Retch forked a small, crisp trout out of the pan and munched it down tail first. "Say, what was it that was always attackin' us in those days?"

"I'm not sure what they were called," I said, glancing out into the surrounding darkness, "but they were always big and hairy and had red eyes, and teeth the size of railroad spikes. I haven't seen one of them since I was twelve years old." I leaned over and stopped Retch from throwing a log on the fire. "Not when I was sober, anyway."

"Say," Retch said suddenly. "You remember ol' Grogan's War Surplus store?"

Did I remember Grogan's War Surplus store! Why, the mere sound of that melodious name made my heart dance the Light Fantastic. Grogan's War Surplus. Ah, how could I ever forget!

Immediately after World War II, Grogan had remodeled an old livery stable and feed store in the style now referred to in architectural textbooks as "war surplus modern," a decor that attempts to emulate the aesthetic effects of a direct hit on an army ordnance depot.

The store front itself was elegantly festooned with gerry cans, yellow life rafts, landing nets, ammo boxes, and other assorted residue of recent history. On the lot behind the store, the plundered wreckage of a dozen or so military vehicles had been cleverly arranged in such a manner as to conceal what had once been an unsightly patch of wild flowers. But all the really precious stuff was kept inside the store itself, illuminated by a few naked light bulbs and the watchful eyes of Henry P. Grogan.

The great thing about Grogan's War Surplus

was not only did it sell every conceivable thing that might possibly be used for camping, but it was cheap. With a few dollars and a sharp eye for a bargain, you could go into Grogan's and outfit yourself with at least the bare essentials for the routine overnight camping trip—a sleeping bag, pup tent, canteen, cook kit, entrenching shovel, paratrooper jump boots, leggings, packboard, packsack, web belt, ammo pouches, medic kit, machete, bayonet, steel helmet, fiber helmet liner, .45 automatic holster (empty), G.I. can opener, and the other basic necessities.

Then if you had any change left, you might pick up a few luxury items, things you had no idea what they might be used for but were reasonably sure you would think of something—ammo box, camouflage net, G.I. soap, parachute harness, and the like.

Naturally, you never took all of this gear with you on a simple overnight trip. Nine times out of ten you forgot the soap and probably the can opener, too.

Since one of the rules of backpacking requires that all nonessentials be omitted from the pack, we strained our imaginations to bring every last piece of beloved war surplus into the realm of our necessities.

Take the bayonet, for example. It was needed for cutting and spearing things. Frequently, it cut and speared things we didn't want cut and speared, but this drawback was more than made up for by its otherwise benign service as a cooking spit, paring knife, or even use as a tent stake.

The machete was needed anytime you had to slash out your own trail. This necessity arose more often than a person who is not a kid with a machete might think. Sometimes you had to walk several miles out of your way in order for that particular necessity to arise but time was of no consequence when you were in search of necessity. Over the years we slashed out literally hundreds of trails through the wilderness. The longest of these was The Great Rocky Mountain Divide Trail. It was never used much by backpackers, but the mother of a friend of mine, who lived at the jumping-off point, later put up a post at each end of the trail and strung a clothesline between them. The other trails we built, of course, were not nearly so impressive as this one.

We had learned from war movies that steel helmets could be used for boiling things in. On hot summer days, we found out what—our heads. The helmets could also be used for pillows. If you went to sleep, your head would slip off the helmet and bonk on the ground. Bonking your boiled head on the ground kept you awake all night, which was one of the reasons for using a helmet for a pillow in the first place.

Filling up a .45 automatic holster was always a challenge, particularly since our parents had indicated they would just as soon we didn't buy any .45 automatics. About the only thing you could do with the holster was stuff a sardine-cheese-pickle-onion sandwich in it to be quickdrawn anytime you got hungry. Actually, a .45 automatic probably would have been safer than some of our sandwiches.

You had to be a shrewd shopper not to get taken by Henry P. Grogan. We realized that some of the war surplus was brand-spanking-new. Other merchandise had obviously seen combat; it was cracked, tarnished, stained, ripped, riddled, rotten, rusty, and moldy. Frequently, Henry P. would try to pawn off some of the new stuff on us but we weren't to be fooled. We held out for the authentic war surplus. Ah, you can't imagine how old Henry P. would roll his eyes and gnash his teeth every time one of us kids outwitted him like that. He'd get very angry.

The real treasure, of course, was any item with a bullet hole in it. For a long time you practically never came across anything with a bullet hole in it, and then one day Larry Swartze found a canteen with what looked like an honest-to-goodness bullet hole drilled through it. Henry P. himself had to break up the fight to see who was going to get the perforated canteen. Immediately after that incident, all sorts of war surplus turned up with bullet holes in it, and we kept ourselves broke trying to buy it all. Then it occurred to us that maybe old Henry P. was going around at night with a hammer and large spike, counterfeiting bullet holes. The bottom subsequently dropped out of the bullet-hole market at Henry P's.

Shrewd as I was, Henry P. managed to take even me a few times. One of the worst things he did was to sell me what he called "one of the down bags used by Arctic troops to keep them comfortable in 70-below weather." The bags turned out to be a secret weapon of the War Department, designed to be dropped behind the lines in hopes that enemy troops would attempt to sleep in them and either freeze or break out in an itch that would occupy both hands scratching for the duration of the war. The stuffing consisted not of down but chicken feathers with, if the size of the lumps in the bag was any indication, several of the chickens still attached. But the worst feature of the bag was triggered by its getting even slightly wet. Any time it rained on one of our camping trips, I went home smelling like high tide at the local chicken and turkey farm.

Another time, Henry P. induced me to buy a

two-man mountain tent, so called, I later discovered, because it was heavy as a mountain and took two men to set it up. The roof of the tent looked like it had been made out of dried batskin, and was impervious to everything but wind, rain, and heavy dew. A tubular air vent extended from each end of the tent, an effect which, combined with the batskin roof, gave it the appearance of a creature dropped in from outer space. It frequently gave us quite a start when we returned to camp late in the evening and glimpsed the pterodactylous wings of the roof flapping in the breeze and the vent tubes bobbing about. I remember one occasion when a brave kid named Kenny stood at a distance and threw rocks, trying to drive our tent out of camp.

The tent was designed to sleep two grown men, providing they were both Pygmies and on exceptionally good terms with each other. We managed to crowd four of us into it, after drawing straws to see who got to have their heads by the air vents. The losers had to suck their air through bullet holes. If a loud sound suddenly reminded us of unfinished business at home, there was always a big traffic jam at the exit. Sometimes we would be about halfway home and still not out of the tent yet.

As a result of these drawbacks to the mountain tent, I was constantly on the lookout for some kind of portable shelter that would afford me a bit more comfort and protection. One day, poking around Grogan's War Surplus, I found it. After sorting through the ever-present snarl of nylon rope, I discovered a canvas tube attached to dried batskin and mosquito netting. The mosquito netting on one side had a zipper running the full length of it.

"What is it?" I asked Grogan.

"That, my boy, is a jungle hammock," he said. "This canvas is the hammock part, the mosquito netting is the walls, and then this tough and very attractive fabric here is the roof."

Not having any jungles readily available, I inquired as to how it would work in our part of the world.

"Just fine," he said. "For example, there's some folks who don't much care for slimy, crawly ol' snakes sneakin' into their nice, cozy 70-below down sleepin' bags to get warm, and they like this here jungle hammock because it keeps 'em outta reach of the poisonous critters."

I didn't let on in the slightest to Grogan that he had just made reference to my kind of people. He nevertheless came to that conclusion because he scooped up the jungle hammock and carried it toward the checkout counter.

"How is it for bears?" I asked in a tone of complete indifference, following along behind him.

"Bears? Oh, it's fine on bears. In bear country you just hitch it a little higher in the trees—say, about fifteen feet."

The roof of the jungle hammock had some bad cracks in it, several of the ropes were frayed, the mosquito netting had small tears in it, and the canvas looked as if it were being attacked by at least four varieties of exotic mold. Grogan didn't seem to notice though and let me have it for not much more than he would have charged for a new one.

I lost no time in getting the jungle hammock home and suspended between two trees in our backyard for a trial run. It looked so secure suspended up there in the air—a modest ten feet from the ground—that I decided I would spend the night there.

The family came out that evening to cheer me on as I climbed the stepladder to launch myself on my maiden voyage in the hammock. After they had retreated back into the house, muttering enviously I thought, I zipped up the mosquito netting, wiggled into my chicken-down sleeping bag, and lay back to contemplate the closing in of my ancient enemy, darkness.

After four or five hours of this contemplation, an unnerving thought occurred to me. I had not remembered to have the stepladder removed! It continued to connect ground and hammock like a boarding ramp for any ravenous beast that happened along. I leaned over to kick the ladder. As I did so the hammock flipped on its side, sending me like a shot through the mosquito netting, still encased in my sleeping bag.

As bad luck would have it, my crotchety old dog, Strange, had a short while before staggered in from a night of carousing and collapsed on the target area. Nothing in his experience, of course, had taught him to expect me even to be out at night let alone suspended in the air ten feet above him. Consequently, when a large, screeching shape wrapped in chicken feathers plummeted down on him out of the darkness, it was certainly reasonable for him to assume that he had fallen prey to some huge, carnivorous bird of the night. I, for my part, fully expected to be greeted by a hairy beast with fast, snapping jaws, an expectation that did not go unfulfilled. Within ten seconds we had fought ourselves to a state of total exhaustion, perhaps not surprising when you consider the fact that we had gone fully around the yard three times, failed in our attempts to climb several trees and a lilac bush, battered open the door to the house, and finally collapsed in a single panting heap on the kitchen floor. Both of us smelled of wet chicken feathers for days afterwards, and it was a full week before I could brush the taste of dog off my teeth.

After I had recovered from that night though, I couldn't help chuckling over how I had put one over on ol' Grogan. If Henry P. had known the mosquito netting on that jungle hammock was eaten plumb through with jungle rot he would have charged me twice the price that he did.

"Do I remember Henry P. Grogan's War Surplus store?" I said to Retch. "Wasn't his that high-class place with the sign that said SHIRTS AND SHOES MUST BE WORN ON THESE PREMISES?"

But he didn't hear me. He was too busy blowing on the fire.

The Big Trip

WHEN I WAS VERY YOUNG and the strange wild passion for mountains was first upon me, I wrote, produced, and directed for myself a magnificent, colossal, 3-D, Technicolor, Wide-Screen, Stereophonic fantasy—the fantasy of the Big Trip.

Whenever the jaws of tedium gnawed too harshly on my bones, I simply turned down the lights on the murk and grind of the world outside and projected the fantasy on the backsides of my eyeballs, each of which was equipped with a Silver Screen.

The fantasy was primarily an adventure story set in the vast wilderness of the Selkirk mountains. It starred You Know Whom, who bore a striking resemblance to a four-foot-eight-inch Gregory Peck. The basic plot was that the hero, a pack on his back, hiked far back into these beautiful mountains, endured great hardships, overcame terrible obstacles, and occasionally even rescued from perilous distress a beautiful red-haired lady. It was strictly a G-rated fantasy. (The R- and X-rated fantasies came later.) But I enjoyed it. In fact, with time, the Big Trip began to gain a strange sort of dominance over my life.

Several times the fantasy prevented my perishing from a loathsome childhood affliction: school. Once in a seventh-grade English class I stumbled into a nest of dangling participles. Had I not been able to get my fantasy going in time, those slimy, leechlike creatures would have drained me dry as a puffball in five minutes.

On occasion, Mr. Rumsdale, our seventh-grade English teacher, would unexpectedly break through the thick and buttressed walls of our indifference and start throwing parts of speech in all directions. Several of my friends were knocked silly by flying objects of the preposition, but long before there was any threat to my own cherished ignorance, the old fantasy would carry me to safety. I would be roasting a fresh-caught trout on the rocky shore of some high and distant stream, or maybe just striding along under the sweet weight of a good pack, and it would be morning in the mountains, with the sun rising through the trees.

Mr. Rumsdale once lowered the battering ram he used for a voice and told me that I had better stop this constant dreaming. Otherwise, he predicted, both he and I would probably die as old men in seventh-grade English.

Even I knew by then that the Big Trip, for all its utility as an antidote to boredom, could not endure forever simply as fantasy. One day I would have to turn it into the real thing. I would have to take the Big Trip back into the mountains and face great hardship and overcome terrible obstacles. To that end, I began serving an apprenticeship in the out-of-doors.

I practiced "sleeping out alone" in the backyard, my ears ever alert to the approaching footpad of some hairy terror, until at last I conquered my over-powering fear of the dark and the ghastly things that flourished there. I learned to build fires, using nothing more than a few sticks, a couple of newspapers, and a box and a half of kitchen matches. I studied the art of camp cookery, and soon could serve up a hearty meal of flaming bacon, charred potatoes, three-pound pancakes, and butterscotch pudding with gnat topping. After a longer time, I even taught myself to eat these things. Through practical experience, I learned that it is best not to dry wet boots over a fire with your feet still in them. I learned that some sleeping bags are stuffed with the same filler used in dynamite fuse and that it is best not to let sparks land on one of them, particularly when it is occupied by your body. Thus did the Big Trip shape my life and give meaning even to its failures and disasters.

As I grew older, I went off with friends on numerous lengthy trips into the mountains, thinking each time that perhaps at last I was making the Big Trip. But I never was. These were pleasant, amiable excursions, occasionally distinguished by a crisis or two, but I was always disappointed by the realization that they fell far short of the Big Trip of my aging fantasy. So one day in the summer that I turned seventeen, I decided I would at last, once and for all, plan and exe-cute, or be executed by, the Big Trip.

When I announced and elaborated on my plans for the benefit of my mother and stepfather, there was great wailing and a gnashing of teeth already well gnashed from my previous and much lesser excursions into the wilderness. From then until the day I left, my mother could scarcely take time out from climbing the walls to make the beds and cook our meals.

The plans were indeed formidable, and in my

unsure moments they even caused me to wail and gnash a little. The terrain I planned to cross looked on a topographical map like the scribblings of a mildly demented chimpanzee and spanned a distance of some thirty miles as the crow flies. If the crow walked, as they say, it was more like fifty. The area was unmarred by roads or trails. It contained plenty of tracks, though, some of which belonged to grizzlies. And as everyone knows, a grizzly, if he happens along at the right moment, can transform a quiet walk to a privy into a memorable experience.

Preparations for the Big Trip were remarkably simple, since by this time I knew that nothing destroys a Big Trip quicker than a surplus of comforts or a dearth of hardships. And a Big Trip is defined by its hardships.

These hardships, of course, could not be left to mere chance. A number of them had to be prepared in advance and taken along in the pack, so to speak, to be trotted out any time the going got easy. The basic formula for creating hardships is to take no nonessentials and only a few of the essentials.

One of the essentials you leave behind is most of the food. My stock of grub consisted of pancake flour, a slab of bacon, dried fruit, butter, sugar, and salt. For emergency rations, I took a bag of dehydrated chicken noodle soup, enough, it turned out, to feed an army of starving Cossacks for upwards of three weeks.

About the only gear I took was a sleeping bag, a knife, and a rifle. I carried along the rifle in case I ran into a grizzly, since my idea of hardships did not include getting eaten by a bear. Although I knew a .32 Special couldn't stop a charging grizzly, I took comfort in the notion that I might be able to take the edge off his appetite on his way to the table. In the early days of my fantasy, I had conceived of building a stockade each night as protection against bears, but when you have a grizzly coming for you, no matter how much encouragement and incentive he might offer, it is difficult to get a stockade up in time to do much good. So I was taking the rifle.

At practically the last moment, I decided to take along a companion. In light of the other meticulous preparations for the Big Trip, it seems incongruous now that I should have selected my traveling companion so casually. Retch, as he will be known here, had just moved to town recently and was probably the only person of my acquaintance who had not heard of the Big Trip. This gap in his knowledge may be the reason that he was the only person I could find who was ready and willing to accompany me on the expedition. Perhaps in my last-minute desperation for companionship I skipped a few details and did not impress upon him the full magnitude of the trip.

"How would you like to go on a camping trip?" I asked him. "Spend a few days hiking around in the mountains, catch some fish, cook out?"

Retch said he thought he would like that. Somehow he got the impression we were going on an extended fishing trip and marshmallow roast. Later, under somewhat harsher circumstances, he was to reveal to me that never in his whole life had he nourished any fantasies about a Big Trip. I was appalled that a human life could be so sterile, so devoid of splendor.

Even by the time my parents were driving us to the jumping-off spot, Retch still did not fully comprehend the full portent of the Big Trip. My stepfather's funereal air, my mother's quivering lips, and my own grim silence, however, began to undermine his confidence.

"It isn't as though we're going to be gone forever," he would say, attempting to console my mother. She would reply with a low, quavering moan. By the time we disembarked from the car, Retch was convinced that we were going to be gone forever.

As things turned out, he was nearly right.

For two pleasant days, the Big Trip did seem as if it were going to be nothing more than an ordinary camping trip, and therefore not a Big Trip at all. The sky was an impeccable blue, the firewood dry and fragrant, the trout in the lakes fat and hungry, the huckleberries sweet. I could scarcely conceal my disappointment at the good time we were having.

On the third morning I was awakened by a howl of anguish from Retch. "The deer got into our packs and ate everything but the bacon and chicken noodle soup," he yelled.

My heart laughed up. This, finally, was a real hardship.

"Don't worry," I said. "We can always live off the country." Then I looked around. The country didn't seem to be very edible. Perhaps the trip would be harder than even I expected.

Later that same day, we came across what we thought must be fresh grizzly tracks. Concluding that where there are fresh grizzly tracks, there are likely to be fresh grizzlies, we quickened our pace. Near the top of the next mountain, we slowed to a dogtrot, which we maintained for the rest of the day.

That night we camped on a barren ridge without water, and ate fried bacon and soup for supper. The soup, which wasn't much good with water, was even worse without it. (The fact that the deer had not touched the chicken noodle soup proved to me once and for all that deer are animals of good sense and discriminating taste.) After dinner, we sat around the fire picking the bacon out of our teeth with noodles.

"I've got an idea," Retch said.

"What?" I said.

"Let's quit," he said.

Our quitting then would have been like a sky-diver's quitting halfway to the ground. "Don't worry," I said. "It will be a lot easier from now on."

Storm clouds were rising in the west when we crawled into our sleeping bags. Soon the heavy, black thunderheads were over us. Lightning licked the peak of our mountain a few times and then started walking down the ridge toward us. When it struck close enough to bounce us off the ground, I predicted, breathlessly, "It's going to pass over the top of us. Next time it will strike down below . . ."

By the time I was this far along in my prophecy, it was evident that I didn't have much future as a prophet. It didn't seem as if I even had much future.

When you see lightning hit from a distance, it appears that the bolt zaps into the ground and that's it, but when you are occupying the ground the bolt zaps into, it's not that way at all. First, a terrible bomb goes off and you're inside the bomb, and then streams of fire are going every which way and you're going every which way, and the brush lights up like neon signs in Chinatown, and there are pools of fire on the ground and high voltage sings in the air. Then it's dark again, black, sticky dark, and the rain hits like a truckful of ice.

The first thing I noticed, upon regaining consciousness, was that I was running to beat hell down the side of the mountain. I was wearing only my shorts. I do not know if I was fully dressed or not when the lightning hit.

Something was bounding like a deer through the brush ahead of me, and I hoped it was a deer and not a grizzly, because I was gaining on it. Then I saw that it was just a pair of white shorts, or reasonably white shorts, also running down the mountain. I yelled at the white shorts that I thought there was a cliff up ahead. The white shorts gave a loud yelp and vanished.

I found Retch sorting and counting his bones at the bottom end of a ten-foot drop. He said he might have been hurt worse, but some rocks cushioned his fall.

"You didn't happen to bring an aspirin, did you?" he said.

"No," I said.

"I didn't think so," he said.

While we were draining out sleeping bags (it was raining, remember), I made one last attempt at prophecy.

"Well, Retch," I said, "think of it this way—things just can't get any worse than they are right now."

In the days that followed we were to look back upon that moment as a time of great good fortune and decadent high living.

The driving, ice-cold rain continued through the night. The next morning we crawled out of our sleeping bags, stirred around in the mud until we found our clothes, put them on, and with an absolute minimum of jovial banter, spent an unsuccessful hour trying to start a fire. For breakfast we stirred up some chicken noodle soup in muddy water. The muddy water improved the flavor and texture of the soup considerably, and by drinking it through our teeth we could strain out the larger pebbles and even some of the noodles.

On all sides of us, as far as a bloodshot eye could see, was a vast, raging storm of mountains. Our soggy map told us we were ten miles from the end of the nearest trail, more than twenty miles from the nearest road. Retch and I stared at each other across the pile of steaming sticks that represented our aborted effort at fire-building, and I could see a reflection of my own misery and despair swirling in his eyes. "What do we do now?" I thought.

Then I remembered a sure-fire remedy for predicaments of this sort. It was recommended to me by a fierce, old man who knew the mountains well and knew what they can do to a person. "When everything else has failed, there is only one thing to do," he said. "You tough it out."

So that is what we did. We toughed it out. We went down mountains, up mountains, around mountains, lunged over windfalls, through swamps, across rainswollen streams, and we ate handfuls of chicken noodle mush, and then surged on across more mountains, streams, and windfalls. Had we run across a grizzly we would have eaten him raw on the spot and strung his claws for necklaces. There was nothing now, perhaps not even a beautiful red-haired lady in perilous distress, that could have interrupted our relentless march.

And then one day—or was it night?—we walked out of the mountains. There were cars going by on the highway, people zipping comfortably along through their lives at a mile a minute, looking out at us in mild amusement and wondering what muddy, bloody fools were these. We had triumphed over the mountains and over ourselves and over the Big Trip, but nobody knew or cared what we had done. We limped along the road in search of a farmhouse with a phone, our clothes torn, bodies aching, jaws clenched on the bullet, and the last dehydrated chicken noodle soup we would ever eat in our lives still matting our wispy beards.

Then I heard a strange, small sound in the

empty air. I glanced over at Retch to see if he heard it too, and he did, and there was this little pained smile on his cracked lips. As we slogged along the sound grew in volume, swelling up and filling the silence and emptiness, until it reached a great thundering crescendo.

It was the sound of applause and cheering—the sound of a standing ovation.

The Theory and Application of Old Men

EVERY KID SHOULD HAVE an old man. I don't mean just a father. Fathers are all right and I'm not knocking them, since I'm one myself, but from a kid's point of view they spend entirely too much time at a thing called the office or some other equally boring place of work. If you're a kid, what you need is someone who can take you out hunting or fishing or just poking around in the woods anytime you feel the urge. That's an old man. Doing things like that is what old men were designed for.

If you've never had an old man of your own before, you may not know what to look for or how to use one once you find him. I am something of an expert on the subject, having studied under some of the best old men in the business. Someday I hope to get into the field myself. In any case, I am eminently qualified to advise you on getting and caring for your first old man.

First off, let us consider the problem of identifying old men in the field. All old men are male. This is important to remember, and even then one can make a mistake. Occasionally, on hunting trips I have discovered that what I thought were men turned out to be old women. Had they turned out to be young women, I would have been a good deal less disappointed, but that turn of circumstance almost never happens to me.

Here is a good basic description of an old man: He is a male person with white hair, a stubbly beard, wrinkled hide, bifocals, long underwear, chewing tobacco, and the disposition of a bull walrus with a bad case of the shingles. If you find a female person with these basic characteristics, she would probably work just as well.

Old men come in various vintages. The sixties are good, the seventies are excellent, and the eighties are prime. Nineties are fine too, but there is always the risk they won't make it to the punchline on a good story.

Every youngster should be properly trained in the safe handling of an old man before he is allowed to take one out alone. One good bit of advice is to treat every old man as if he were loaded. If a kid accidentally triggers an old man, he is liable to get his vocabulary peppered with colorful expressions that will send his mother into shock the first time one tumbles off his tender lips. As a boy, I once addressed a piece of malfunctioning machinery in the appropriately descriptive language of my own old man. Quick as lightning my grandmother struck, deftly boxing my ears in a one-two combination. Fortunately for me, she used a small box.

"You been hangin' out with that blinkety-blank old Rancid Crabtree agin," she said. "He jist ain't the sort for a blinkety-blank young boy always to be traipsin' after, and I'll tell him so next time I lay eyes on the blinkety-blank!" ("Blinkety-blank," by the way, was one of Mr. Crabtree's favorite words.) The very next time the old man was in our kitchen, ol' Gram lit into him, and he grinned like a shaggy old dog, sitting there dunking a big sugar cookie in his coffee. He was very good at concealing his fear of Gram.

Mr. Crabtree, by the way, had a definite aura about him, a presence that seemed to linger on in the house long after he had gone home. Frequently, my mother would comment on it. "Throw open the windows!" she would shout.

Let us next consider the proper technique for starting an old man. When you are older, you can start an old man simply by loading him or, in the more common expression, "getting him loaded." While you're still a kid, however, you will have to use empty old men, who are a good deal harder to start. The best technique for starting an empty old man is called "priming." You say something like this to your O.M.: "Mr. Jenkins, I'll bet fishing is sure a lot better nowadays than when you were a kid." That bit of priming should not only get him started but keep him going for a couple of hours.

A kid may come across an old man who gambles, drinks, lies, cusses, chews 'n' spits, and hates to shave and take baths, but there's also a chance that he will run into one with a lot of bad habits. There are two kinds of old men in particular that he wants to watch out for—the Sleeper and the Drifter.

Once you've gone to all the trouble of getting the Sleeper started, he will set you up something like this:

"So, that ol' sow b'ar shooshes her cubs up a tree, an' then she comes fer me. I can see she's got her heart set on turnin' my bride into a widder woman. Wall, I ups with my twenty-two single-shot . . ."

"Yes, yes?" you say. "Go on."

"Snort, mimph, wheeze, snore," he says. Sleepers will drop off like that every time, and you want to avoid them like the plague.

The Drifter is just as bad as the Sleeper and maybe even worse. Keep in mind that most old men are masters of the art of digression. They will start off something like this: "I recollect the time a bobcat got loose in Poke Martin's plane. Funniest thing I ever seen! Ol' Poke, he was flyin' supplies into Pat Doyle's camp at Terrible Crick—Terrible Crick, that's whar I caught a twenty-pound char one time on a piece of bacon rind. Ha! Ol' Shorty Long an' me was runnin' a trapline that winter, about the coldest winter since I got my tongue stuck on the pump handle when I was a youngun. Back in those days . . ." In this fashion the average old man will digress back to about the time the earth's crust was beginning to harden and then will work his way back to the original topic, touching every base as he goes. A brief anecdote is somehow transformed into the history of western civilization, but it is all entertaining and enlightening. The Drifter, however, just leaves you back there in the mists of time, the two of you looking about, wondering what it was you had come for.

"But what about the bobcat?" you ask, hoping to jog the Drifter's memory.

"Bobcat?" he says. "What bobcat?"

My own luck with old men over the years has been exceptionally good. I still keep a stable of them around to remind me of a time when men (and women, too) were measured not by whether their look was wet or dry but whether they possessed a mysterious quality called "grit." When I was a youngster, grit was the chief remedy for a variety of ailments. "What that boy needs," an old man would prescribe, "is more grit." A deficiency in grit was considered more serious than a shortage of Vitamin B. It was generally felt that you couldn't live without it. Grit, I've learned over the years, is one of the best things an old man has to offer a kid. That and fine lying, and maybe the proper use of the language.

Most of my early language training was attended to by old men. The first person to truly appreciate the value of this linguistic tutoring was my Freshman Composition teacher in college. He called me into his office and told me that my composition papers were filled with the most outrageous lies ever inflicted on the consciousness of a civilized and rational mind (meaning his) and that my spelling, grammar, and syntactical monstrosities approached the absolute in illiteracy. I was embarrassed. I just wasn't used to compliments like that. I thanked him, though, and said I realized I could write pretty good all right, but I reckoned I could do even better if I put my mind to it. Well, he was dumbfounded to hear that I might even surpass my previous literary efforts. As he gently shoved me out of his office, uttering over and over, "I don't *believe* it! I don't *believe* it!" I could tell he wasn't a man who knew anything about grit, or old men either.

For a long while when I was growing up, I didn't have an old man of my own, and had to borrow one belonging to a friend of mine. The old man was my friend's grandfather, which seemed to me like just about the most convenient arrangement a kid could ask for. Then my friend moved away and left the old man in his entirety to me alone. It was a fine stroke of luck. In the easy informality of the day, the old man called me "Bub" and I called him "Mr. Hooker." He didn't seem to mind the familiarity.

Mr. Hooker was a prime old man. One of the first things a kid learns about prime old men is that they don't put up with any kind of nonsense. Included in the vast store of things that Mr. Hooker considered nonsense were complaints, all of which he defined as "whining" or maybe on occasion "bawling like a calf." Consequently, when Mr. Hooker would take me out on cold winter days to check his trapline along Sand Creek, I would keep my complaints corked up until I could stand it no longer. Then I would articulate them in the form of a scientific hypothesis.

"I wonder what happens when a person's toes freeze plumb solid?" I would say.

"Wall, when they gets warm again, they jist thaws out," Mr. Hooker would reply, splattering a square yard of snow with tobacco juice. "Then they falls off."

I would respond to this news in a manner of appropriate indifference, as though I were unacquainted with anyone whose toes were at that moment in just such a predicament. Then Mr. Hooker would abruptly change the subject. "Say, Bub," he would ask me, "I ever show you how to build a fahr in the snow?"

"A couple of times," I would reply. "But I certainly wouldn't mind seeing it again."

Then Mr. Hooker would make a few magical motions with his feet and hands, and there would be a bare spot on the ground with a pile of sticks on it. He would snap the head of a kitchen match with his thumbnail, and before I knew what was happening we would be warming ourselves over a roaring fire, eating dried apricots, and talking of crows.

I couldn't begin to relate all the things I learned from Mr. Hooker, but maybe one will suffice. Even though he was in his late seventies and early eighties during the time that I knew him, he always insisted on climbing to the top of the mountain in back of our place to pick huckleberries. He taught me that the best huckleberries always grow on the top of the mountain. They weren't any bigger or sweeter or more plentiful up there than huckleberries growing at lower elevations. They were the best because they grew on top of the mountain. Some people may not understand that. If they don't, it's because they never had an old man to teach it to them.

The winter I was a senior in high school, Mr. Hooker almost died. It made him pretty damn mad, too, because he still had some things he wanted to do. I could imagine Death coming timidly into Mr. Hooker's hospital room and the old man giving him a tongue lashing. "You gol-durn ol' fool, you've come too soon! I ain't even used it all up yet!" He lived to greet another spring run of cutthroat trout up Sand Creek.

I was away at college the following winter when I got word that Mr. Hooker had at last used it all up. By the time I got home, the funeral was over and the relatives had come and gone, paying their last respects and dividing up among themselves his meager belongings.

"It would have been nice if they could have given you one of his fishing rods or a knife or something," my mother said. "I know he would liked to have left you something."

I decided to snowshoe out into the woods for a while, just to get away from people and hear what the crows had to say about the passing of Mr. Hooker. My eight-year-old nephew, Delbert, wanted to go along and try out his Christmas skis. Since I didn't consider him a people, I said, "All right, come on."

After we had tracked nearly the full length of the old trapline, Delbert raised an interesting point.

"What do you s'pose happens when a person's toes freeze plumb solid?" he said.

"Wall," I said, "they jist thaws out when they gets warm agin. Then they falls off. Say, Bub, I ever show you how to build a fahr in the snow?"

The
Two-Wheeled
ATV

My FIRST all-terrain vehicle was a one-wheel drive, and it could take you anywhere you had nerve and guts enough to peddle it.

Most of the other kids around had decent, well-mannered bicycles of distinct makes and models. Mine was a balloon-tired monster born out of wedlock half-way between the junkyard and the secondhand store. Some local fiend had built it with his own three hands and sold it to my mother for about the price of a good milk cow.

For two cents or even a used jawbreaker, I would have beaten it to death with a baseball bat, but I needed it for transportation. And transportation, then as now, was the name of the game.

You could walk to some good fishing holes, all right, but when the guys you were with all rode bikes, you had to walk pretty fast.

Perhaps the worst thing about the Bike, as I called it within hearing range of my mother, was that you simply could not ride it in a manner that allowed you to retain any sense of dignity let alone savoir-faire. The chief reason for this was that the seat was permanently adjusted for a person about six-foot-four. I was a person about five-foot-four. The proportions of the handlebars suggested strongly that they had been stolen from a tricycle belonging to a four-year-old midget. The result of this unhappy combination was that wherever I went on the Bike my rear was always about three inches higher than my shoulder blades.

I tried never to go any place on the Bike where girls from school might see me, since it was difficult if not impossible in that position to maintain the image I was cultivating among them of a dashing, carefree playboy.

The seat on the Bike was of the kind usually found on European racing bikes. The principle behind the design of this seat is that the rider goes to beat hell the sooner to get off of it. The idea for heel-and-toe walking races was conceived by someone watching the users of these particular seats footing it back home after a race.

To get the proper effect of one of these seats, you might spend a couple of hours sitting balanced on the end of a baseball bat—the small end. Put a doily on it for cushioning.

Whatever the other guys thought of my appearance on the Bike, they had respect for me. I was the fastest thing around on two wheels, thanks to that seat.

The Bike had a couple of little tricks it did with its chain that the Marquis de Sade would have envied. One was that it would wait until you had just started down a long, steep, curving hill and then reach up with its chain and wind your pant leg into the sprocket. This move was doubly ingenious, since the chain not only prevented you from putting on the coaster brakes, it also shackled you to a hurtling death-machine. Many was the time that a streamlined kid on a bike streaked silently past cars, trucks, and motorcycles on grades where a loose roller skate could break the sound barrier.

The Bike's other favorite trick was to throw the chain off when you needed it most. This usually happened when you were trying to outrun one of the timber wolves the neighbors kept for watchdogs. You would be standing up pedaling for all you were worth, leaving a trail of sweat and burned rubber two inches wide on the road behind you. The wolf would be a black snarl coming up fast to your rear. Then the chain would jump its sprocket and drop you with a crunch on the crossbar, the pedals still spinning furiously under your feet. The wolf gnawed on you until you got the chain back on the sprocket or until he got tired and went home.

The standard method for getting off the Bike was to spring clear and let it crash. If it got the chance, it would grab you by the pant leg at the moment of ejection and drag you along to grim destruction.

The Bike would sometimes go for weeks without the front wheel bouncing off. This was to lure you into a false sense of security. You would be rattling hell-bent for home past the neighbors, and for a split second you would see the front wheel pulling away from you. Then the fork would hit the ground and whip you over the handlebars. Before you had your breath back, the wolf was standing on your belly reading the menu.

I spent half my waking moments repairing the Bike and the other half repairing myself. Until I was old enough to drive, I went around looking like a commercial for Band-Aids and mercurochrome. I hated to stop the Bike along the highway long enough to pick up an empty beer bottle for fear people would stop their cars and try to rush me to a doctor. Even on one of its good days, the Bike looked like an accident in which three people had been killed.

Much as I hated the Bike, I have to admit that it was one of the truly great all-terrain vehicles. It could navigate streams, cross fallen logs, smash through brush, follow a mountain trail, and in general do just about anything but climb trees. Several times it did try to climb trees but the damage to both of us was sufficient to make continued efforts in that direction seem impractical and unrewarding.

Our bicycles in those days were the chief mode of transportation for 90 percent of our camping trips. Occasionally even today I see people use bicycles for camping. They will be zipping along the road on ten-speed touring bikes, their ultralight camping gear a neat little package on the rear fender. When we went camping on our one-speed bikes, it looked as if we had a baby elephant on the handlebars and the mother on behind.

Loading a bicycle for a camping trip was not simply a remarkable feat of engineering, it was a blatant defiance of all the laws of physics. First of all, there may have been ultralight camping gear in those days, but we didn't own any of it. Our skillet alone weighed more than one of today's touring bikes, and a bedroll in cold weather, even without the feather bed, was the weight and size of a bale of straw. The tent was a tarp that worked winters as a haystack cover. A good portion of our food was carried in the quart jars our mothers had canned it in. Then there were all the axes, hatchets, saws, machetes, and World War II surplus bayonets without which no camping trip was complete. And, of course, I could never leave behind my jungle hammock, the pride of my life, just in case I happened to come across a jungle.

The standard packing procedure was to dump most of your stuff into the center of the tarp, roll the tarp up into a bundle, tie it together with half a mile of rope, and then find nine boys and a man to lift it to the back fender of the Bike. Anything left over was rolled up in the jungle hammock and tied to the diminutive handlebars. The hardware was distributed evenly around the outside of the two massive bundles, just in case you had sudden need for an ax or a bayonet.

Then you sprang onto the saddle and pedaled with all the fury you could generate from ninety-eight pounds of bone and muscle. The Bike would howl in rage, the twin humps of camp gear would shudder and sway like a sick camel, and slowly, almost imperceptibly, the whole catastrophe would move out of the yard and wobble off down the road on some incredible journey.

Sometimes during the winter now, when the cold awakens in my bones and flesh the ache of a thousand old injuries, I suddenly will recall in vivid detail the last few terrifying moments of the Bike's existence as a recognizable entity.

A ragged gypsy band of us had just begun another trip into the mountains on our camel-humped ATVs. As usual, I was far out in the lead, the hatchet-head bicycle seat urging me on.

There was a hill about three miles from my home called Sand Creek Hill, a name deceptive in its lack of color and description. By rights the hill should have been called Deadman's Drop or Say Goodby Hill. Loggers drove their trucks down it with one foot on the running board and one hand clutching a rosary—even the atheists.

Just as I crested the hill and started my descent, whom should I notice coming up it but one of our neighbors' wolves, apparently returning home after a hard night of killing elk in the mountains. From fifty yards away I could see his face brighten when he caught sight of me hurtling toward him like doom on two wheels. He crouched expectantly, his eyes happily agleam.

The chain, not to be outdone, chose that moment to eat my pant leg half way up to the knee. I expected to be abandoned by the front wheel any second. The washboard road rattled my bones; axes, saws, and bayonets filled the air on all sides; and the great straining mass of the rear pack threatened to collapse on me. With one last great effort, I aimed a quick kick at the wolf, ripped the pant leg free and threw myself into space. I bounced four times to distribute the injuries evenly about my body, and finally, using my nose for a brake, slid to a stop.

The Bike apparently self-destructed shortly after my departure. Probably the front wheel came off, and the two packs took it from there, ripping and tearing, mashing and grinding, until there was nothing left but a streak of assorted rubble stretching off down the hill.

Even the wolf was somewhat shaken by the impact of the crash. He stared at the wreckage in silent awe, almost forgetting my one good leg he held in his slack jaws.

When I was up and around once more, my mother bought me a car, my second ATV. She got it from a local fiend, who had built it with his own three hands, but that's another story.

The Backyard Safari

CITY PLANNERS have shown beyond doubt that old orchards, meadows, and pine woods, which once threatened the outskirts of many of our towns and cities, can be successfully eradicated by constructing a housing development on top of them. To my knowledge there has not been a single recurrence of an old orchard, meadow, or pine woods after one application of a housing development.

Housing developments are a great boon to camping, since they make such fine places to get away from. At the same time, however, many of them are so designed that they are destroying one of the most exotic forms of camping known to man—the backyard safari.

The requirements for a backyard safari are few: a kid, a sleeping bag, and a backyard. The backyard is essential to the sport, and it saddens me that some developers have seen fit to phase it out.

I personally don't sleep out in the backyard much anymore. Oh, occasionally my wife will forget that I'm spending an evening out with the boys and, through some gross oversight, will remove the secret outside key from the geranium pot. An intimate association with slugs, night crawlers, and wandering dogs with terminal halitosis no longer holds the fascination for me it once did, and the ground has become much harder in recent years. Nevertheless there are those persons, mostly under the age of ten, for whom the backyard at night is still wilderness—a Mt. Everest, North Pole, and Amazon all rolled up in a seventy-five-foot-square patch of lilacs and crabgrass.

There are two distinct forms of Sleeping Out: With (Fred, John, etc.) and Alone. Both consist mainly of lying awake all night in the backyard. Otherwise they resemble each other about as much as hunting quail with a 12-gauge does shooting tigers with a blowgun.

At about age seven I gained easy mastery over Sleeping Out With, even though my first attempt was marred by a monumental miscalculation. We decided to sleep out in *his* backyard rather than mine. By daylight, the two backyards were separated by about a quarter mile of countryside laced with barbed-wire fences. At night, the distance was upwards of ten miles, laced with barbed-wire fences and populated by scores of creatures not yet known to science. It should be noted that in the aftermath of the harrowing experience of that first night I could remember distinctly the features of several weird, hairy creatures that flitted past but could not recollect having passed through, over, or under a single barbed-wire fence.

Vern, my camping buddy, and I had snuggled down into our foot-high pile of quilts, comic books, and assorted edibles and were well on our way to spending a pleasantly adventurous night under the stars. Then it got dark. Sometime between 9 P.M. and midnight, I became convinced that the forces of darkness were conspiring to terminate my existence. I emerged from beneath the quilts and prepared to hurl my body out into the abyss of night, informing Vern that I had suddenly recalled some urgent business at home that cried out for my immediate attention. He took the news badly, since he had no experience in Sleeping Out Alone and had no intention of gaining any until he was about forty-seven. His argument for my staying was fierce and brilliant, but it couldn't hold a candle to the pure, hard logic of a wavering screech which at that moment drifted out of the nearby woods. Neighbors said later that they noticed a terrible smell of burned rubber hanging on the air next day, but I think they were exaggerating. Melting the soles off a pair of tennis shoes just doesn't smell that bad.

Sleeping Out With allows for a certain degree of sloppiness and haphazard good fellowship, but Alone is all serious business, fraught with craft, skill, and ritual. Some great writers have suggested that initiation into manhood has something to do with getting your first gun, deer, bear, drink of whiskey, or some other such first, but they are wrong. The true initiation into manhood consists of Sleeping Out Alone in your backyard for the very first time. You can almost always recognize a kid who has just completed this ritual. There will be a slight swagger to his gait, and a new firmness to his jaw —and he will be old and wrinkled and have white hair.

The first step in Sleeping Out Alone is to select just the right spot on which to spend the night. If it is too close to the house you will draw such taunts as, "Albert is spending the night on the back stoop." On the other hand, the sleeping spot should not be so far from the house that the distance cannot be covered in less than two seconds starting from a prone position.

An imaginary straight line extends from the sleeping spot to the back door of the house. This line should be cleared of all obstacles: hoses, lawn chairs, tall blades of grass. If one has a dog, he should be tied or locked up well before night in order to prevent his slipping in under cover of darkness and surreptitiously depositing a new obstacle on the escape route. Dogs have also been known to fall asleep directly on the beeline, as it is sometimes called. Once while traveling at a high rate of speed, I collided with my old dog, Strange, under just such circumstances. The result was multiple bites on the legs, neck, head, and hindquarters, but after a good deal of rest and medication he managed to pull through.

Choice of sleeping gear is largely a matter of preference. Most youngsters prefer to sleep with all their clothes on, although some find it more comfortable to wear only their underwear and shoes. Blankets on an old mattress have the advantage over sleeping bags of being easier to eject from in an emergency. Mummy-type sleeping bags should be avoided, since a stuck zipper may force one to run completely encased in the bag. While by no means impossible, running under such a handicap will cut one's speed nearly in half. Another hazard is that mothers have been known to faint and fathers to screech out strange obscenities at the sight of a mummy bag suddenly bounding into the house.

On a youngster's first attempt at Sleeping Out Alone, the considerate family usually waits up and throws him a little welcoming party shortly before midnight. If the sleeper-out is unprepared for such a reception, he will probably enter the kitchen fully accelerated and wearing the expression of a person possessed of the knowledge that he is being closely pursued by something large and hairy. Under these circumstances it is best if the parents avoid leaping out of hiding places and yelling "Surprise!" The youngster will probably recover from the shock but the kitchen may not. In any case the parents will be creating some distasteful and unnecessary work for themselves.

The eight-year-old who takes it upon himself to sleep alone in the backyard, nine times out of ten, harbors in his heart some hope of one day becoming a mountain man or maybe a cowboy. Everyone knows that the ability to sleep outside alone is a prerequisite for both professions. Also one may wish to squelch once and for all the suspicion among his peers and siblings that he is "chicken." There is nothing that so assaults a man's self-respect as to have an older sister spread the rumor around the neighborhood that her little brother has a gizzard. Thus the sleeper-out who suddenly decides that the better part of valor is to get the hell inside the house as quickly as possible may want to assume some sort of protective coloration, if for no other reason than to hide his ruffled feathers.

The wise youngster, therefore, will decelerate abruptly at the back door, compose himself, and enter his abode with a bearing that exudes dignity, calmness, and self-assurance. He must then be prepared to undergo a certain amount of friendly but mischievous interrogation concerning the reasons for his premature return. Should he be so unsophisticated as to give his actual reasons, he is likely to receive some such response as, "Well, that's strange. I don't recall ever seeing a grizzly bear in the backyard before. A few mountain lion tracks among the azaleas maybe, but no grizzly bear."

Consequently, it is best to have a few plausible answers worked out well in advance, such as, "I thought

I smelled smoke and rushed in to wake the family," or, "I nearly forgot, but I'm expecting an important phone call this evening."

The night that I Slept Out Alone successfully for the first time was probably typical for such undertakings, except it was rather long—about equal in length to the time required for the rise and fall of the Roman Empire. The only part of me that slept at all that night was my right hand, and that only because it was wrapped so tightly around a baseball bat. Several times, off in the distance, an ant coughed. The night dragged on. A pack of wolves circled my camp. Darkness embraced the earth. An ax murderer passed through the yard on his way to work. Where *is* the sun? I thought. It *must* be nearly dawn. A siren sounded faintly in a distant town. The ten o'clock curfew. I had been Sleeping Out Alone for forty-five minutes. I sniffed the air for smoke, hoping that the house might be burning down, and I could rush in and save the family. I was expecting an important telephone call, but we had no phone. Inside the house, I knew my sister, The Troll, lay awake listening for the thunder of my footsteps on the porch. She was sorting and polishing her hoard of "chicken" phrases. I slouched back down into the saddle of my self and grimly rode against the night.

Shooting the Chick-a-nout Narrows

MY LOVE OF RAFTING started in grade school and lasted up until I was thirty years old, or, to be more exact, until about fifteen seconds before my buddy Retch and I became the first persons to shoot the Chick-a-nout Narrows and live.

A teacher by the name of Miss Goosehart got me started on rafting. I was about ten at the time with an academic record that would make a turnip look like an overachiever. One day Miss Goosehart kept me after school and told me she was going to make me literate if it killed her. I said all right I'd do it if she promised not to tell my mother. What she wanted me to litter I had no idea, but I was too smart to let on. Miss Goosehart, her eyes filling with tears, apparently gave up on the idea of forcing me into a life of crime, and instead thrust a book into my hands. "Here," she said. "Read this as soon as you learn how."

The book had pictures in it of this kid and a man floating a raft down a river. They had a little tent

pitched on the raft, and a fishing line trailing behind
in the water. You could tell from looking at their faces
that the two of them were having themselves a fine
time. I sounded out their names. H-u-c-k and J-i-m.
Pretty soon I was overwhelmed by curiosity and started
sounding out the first sentence in the book. I sounded
faster and faster. By the time I had sounded out the
first chapter I knew how to read. Ol' Miss Goosehart
had hooked me on reading. It was a terrible thing to do
to an innocent kid who wanted nothing more out of life
than to fish and hunt and maybe run a trapline in the
off season.

By the time I had finished reading *The Adventures of Huckleberry Finn*, I already had a raft of my
own built. A kid by the name of Harold helped me build
it, but I was the brains behind the project. Since there
weren't many logs to be found lying along the banks of
Sand Creek, we used old cedar fenceposts. We tied the
fenceposts into bundles with rope and baling wire, and
then lashed the bundles of fenceposts to a couple of
rotten planks. The raft was by no means as attractive as
it might appear from this description, but I had little
doubt that it would serve the purpose. The little doubt
I did have moved me to offer some words of advice to
Harold, particularly since Sand Creek was at flood stage
and doing its best to wash out roads, bridges, pump-
houses, and anything else that might offer it some
amusement.

"I bet this raft would hold ten people," I told
Harold proudly.

"I bet it would hold twenty people," Harold
said.

"You're probably right," I said. "But when we
test it, I think only one of us should be on it."

"Good idea," Harold said.

"And," I said, "I think it would be best if you

stand right in the center of the raft so you don't fall overboard when I shove it out into the current."

"I bet it might not even hold one person," Harold said. "And I'm wearing my good pants. You go."

Harold may not have been a great naval architect, but he wasn't dumb. Why hadn't I thought to wear my good pair of pants!

There was nothing to do but make the test float myself. Gingerly I climbed aboard, making a mental note that the raft bobbed about a good deal and that the posts seemed to be spreading apart under my weight. These were not good signs, particularly since the raft was not yet in the water.

Nevertheless, I decided to have a short float. Harold and I first tried christening the raft with a bottle of orange pop, but the bottle refused to break. Since there was every indication we might pound the raft apart before it did so, we drank the pop instead. Then I hopped aboard. Harold pushed the raft out into mid-current and I was on my way. From that moment on, Harold did not refer to his pants as his good pants. He called them his lucky pants.

"How far you going?" Harold shouted.

"Not far," I yelled back. "Just a mile or two."

I must say that I have enjoyed few things in life as much as I did the first ten seconds of my ride on that raft. Then I perceived that the fenceposts were sinking under my feet. Not sinking fast, mind you, but rapidly enough to hold my interest. By the time I rounded the first bend, the raft was completely beneath the surface and the water was lapping at my ankles. Fortunately the raft stabilized at that point, and I continued drifting precariously along, my attention more or less equally divided between retaining some degree of dignity and looking for the first opportunity to disembark.

The spectacle of my apparently standing on the

surface of Sand Creek was not without its rewards. It stimulated a herd of milk cows to race wildly about their pasture in an amusing fashion, sent several dogs slinking for home with their tails between their legs, and brought the Petersons' hired hand to his knees, whether out of laughter, shock, or just reverence I never found out.

Gossips later reported to my mother that I had been seen walking on water and, from observations of the final stage of my journey, floating down Sand Creek with a bundle of fenceposts under each arm. Ol' Mom was furious. She told the gossips I got in enough trouble without folks making up lies about me.

Over the years I built up a couple dozen rafts, all of them vastly superior to that initial effort. My first rafting experience, however, taught me numerous lessons about naval architecture, the most important of which is that when the time comes for the test float to make sure that you are the only one of the crew wearing his good pants. In fact, I have noticed that even when a cost-plus aircraft carrier is launched the people responsible for it are standing around in the best clothes money can buy, and the reason is they started out their careers building fencepost rafts.

Eventually I grew up, a fact that surprised many of our neighbors, some of whom lost good money betting against that likelihood. One of the problems of being a grownup was that I no longer had the time to build log rafts. It occurred to me one day that the next best thing would be a rubber raft. My search for such a raft led me ultimately back to my hometown and to an establishment I had frequented much as a kid—Grogan's War Surplus.

When I emerged from the tunnel of jerrycans, ammo boxes, and landing nets that formed the entrance to the store, Henry P. Grogan, the proprietor, was hunched over a counter pasting little paper swastikas on some battered GI mess kits. I was glad to see he hadn't changed over the years, and was reminded of the long-standing business arrangement we had worked out between ourselves when I had frequented his store as a kid: Grogan would try to sell me every worthless, rotten, rusty piece of junk he couldn't peddle to anyone else. I would buy it. The arrangement seemed equitable enough at the time, and both of us were satisfied with it. Now, of course, I was no longer a kid still wet behind the ears. I chuckled to myself at the thought the old codger might even now try to pull a fast one on me.

When he saw his former associate, Grogan's face erupted into a snaggletoothed grin. He swooped down upon me like a chicken hawk on a Rhode Island red.

"How's business, Mr. Grogan?" I asked after he had extracted from me the history of my life since leaving home.

"Not so good," he said, shaking his head. "It dropped off sharply about the time you went to college. Which reminds me, I'm running a special on some fine parachute harnesses if you're interested."

"Afraid not," I said.

"How about a gen-u-wine antique Nazi mess kit, then? Just happened to come across one in the cellar."

"No," I said. "I still have a dozen left over from the old days. What I am looking for is a surplus seven-man rubber life raft."

Grogan's face clouded over. "Hell, boy, I ain't had one of them in a couple of years."

"What!" I shouted in dismay. "You don't have one?" It was as if a door had slammed shut on an era, and I hadn't heard it. Never in my life had I gone to

Grogan with money in my pocket that he didn't have what I wanted.

"I don't rightly know where you could find one of them rafts anymore," Grogan said, scratching his head as though he too was confused by it all. "Maybe you could find a brand-new raft in one of the sporting-goods stores."

"No," I said. "I've priced them and they're too expensive. All I've managed to save up for a raft is fifty dollars. Well, it sure has been good talking to you again anyway, Mr. Grogan."

"Fif . . . fif . . ." Grogan said, as if about to sneeze. "Ah, hold on there a minute, son, let me ponder this a spell." Then his face split into that old ambergris grin that once had shown down regularly upon my head like the sun at high noon. He scurried out a back door and shortly returned, dragging behind him a greasy yellow amorphous mass.

"What's that?" I asked.

Grogan wiped his hands on his shirt. "This, my boy, is a gen-u-wine seven-man war-surplus rubber life raft I'd forgot. I spread it out over some old jeep trans-missions in the yard a while back to weather a bit. Rubber life rafts like lots of sun and water, ya know. Don't know what suddenly made me remember it."

"That doesn't look to me like it would hold seven men," I said.

"The way the War Department figured these things," Grogan said, "was two men in the raft rowing and five men in the water holdin' on for dear life. That's why they calls it a life raft."

Well, I was absolutely delighted. "How much?"

"Fifty dollars."

I was so elated at having found a raft that I had it home and half inflated before it occurred to me to feel behind my ears. Sure enough, definite signs of moisture.

What Grogan had sold me was not your ordinary seven-man rubber life raft. No. Although I couldn't be certain I was reasonably sure this was the very same raft I had once seen in one of those World War II movies set in the South Pacific. It was the one where the bomber crew has had to ditch in the ocean, and the pilot suddenly yells, "Dang it all to heck, men, the last burst from that Zero riddled our life raft!"

I yelled, too, all the time I was patching up the raft, a task just slightly more complicated than performing abdominal surgery on a hippopotamus. My yells, however, registered a good deal higher than the pilot's on the scale of profanity, and called into question the ancestry of the raft, the War Department, the Zero, and last but not least, Henry P. Grogan.

By the time the raft was finally repaired it looked like some creature from the lower depths that had died of yellow jaundice, bloated and popped to the surface where it had advanced into one of the later stages of decay. Like my first raft, it was not an attractive vessel.

My friend Retch and I would inflate the raft at home with the blower on my wife's vacuum cleaner and then tie it to the top of Retch's small foreign car to haul to a river. Once we were stopped by two highway patrolmen. One of them said he had thought the reason Retch was exceeding the speed limit in a restricted zone was that we were trying to get away from a giant slug that had grabbed our car. I must say it gives the police a bad image when two officers giggle hysterically while one of them is writing you out a ticket.

The raft rekindled in me my old addiction for floating down creeks and rivers. Every spare minute that we could get away from our jobs, Retch and I were either floating down a river or poring over maps to find a good river to float down. We floated streams just deep enough to be called damp. On the other extreme, we floated the Snake and Columbia, both of which had stretches of water that could make a man drunk with fear just looking at photographs of them. Retch and I shot rapids that made our hair stand on end so hard the follicles turned inside out. Sometimes we had to bail the cold sweat out of the raft to keep from swamping. And we called it a whole lot of fun.

"M-m-man," we would say to each other, "that was f-f-fun!"

As we grew older—sometimes on the raft we would age a couple of years in just five seconds—we began to prefer relaxing floats down gentle rivers, maybe catching a few fish or spending a couple of days hunting in a remote area. Once in a while we would be surprised to find ourselves bouncing along over what we called "interesting water," but for the most part these floats were without excitement.

One hunting season Retch and I were going over our maps when we found this river that wound through a thirty-mile stretch of uninhabited country. It looked like just the place for a combined float and deer-hunting trip. On the map the river appeared calm enough, but we decided to ask around and see if we could find someone who had floated it. We talked to several people who said they'd been down the river and they told us about the only thing we had to worry about was that the river would be deep enough to float the raft.

"But watch out for the Narrows," they all said, almost as an afterthought. Then they would describe the horrors of the Narrows, how the river squeezed between these two rock walls, at the same time dropping over a series of waterfalls and making several right angle turns, boiling over rocks the size of houses standing on end, and . . .

"Enough!" we said. "Just tell us where the Narrows are located."

No one seemed exactly sure about their location. "You can't miss 'em, though," one fellow said. "You'll know 'em when you see 'em."

That was what threw us off.

On the first day of the float, Retch and I left our car at the lower end of the river and hired a local rancher to haul us, Retch's dog Smarts, and our raft and gear up to the jumping-off place. You would have thought the rancher had never been confined in a pickup with two madmen before, he was so nervous.

"What for you fellas wanta float that doughnut down the river?" he asked.

"Wanta do some deer hunting," I said.

"Hell," he said. "You could hunt deer on my ranch. Be glad to get rid of a couple of them. Critters are eatin' me right into the poor house."

"Naw," Retch said, "Huntin' that way is too easy. We like to make it as hard as possible."

The rancher didn't say much after that, no doubt fearing for his life. Anyone crazy enough to float a doughnut down a river just to make deer hunting hard might grab you by the throat if you happened to say the wrong thing. After we had unloaded on the bank of the river, he rolled his window down just enough so that a madman couldn't lunge through and grab a person by the throat. "Watch out for the Narrows," he yelled, and then tore off up the road.

Our first day on the river was pleasant enough, almost without incident. Then toward evening Smarts, who had been asleep on the pile of rubberized duffle bags, leaped to his feet and sounded a warning.

Shortly, we too could hear the ominous roar of water off in the distance.

"The Narrows!" I said. "We'd better go ashore and have a look at them."

Well, we had to laugh at the way folks tend to exaggerate. The river did squeeze into a narrow channel between these two big rocks all right, then tumble down a stair-step fall and finally break into a rather modest rapid. "Har, har, har!" we laughed. "So that's the infamous Narrows! Har, har, har!" The only water we took in the raft was tears from laughing so hard.

"Imagine," Retch said, wiping his eyes. "Grown men chickening out from shooting the Narrows!"

"I hereby name them the Chick-a-nout Narrows," I yelled, waving my paddle over the river like a scepter. "The Chick-a-nout Narrows!"

From then on we relaxed and just enjoyed ourselves, our former anxiety over the Chick-a-nout Narrows now merely a source of amusement. We laughed every time one of us mentioned them. "Har, har, har!"

We spent the next day hunting, without success. We started out with the idea of shooting a couple of trophy bucks and finally settled for the possibility of bagging a couple of hamburgers at a drive-in on our way home. When we staggered exhausted into camp that evening, Retch said, "Hey, what's say we throw our gear on the raft and float out of here tonight? After all we don't have to worry about the Chick-a-nout Narrows anymore. Har, har, har!"

"Good idea," I said "Har, har, har!"

As the raft bobbed gently along on the moonlit river, we would take turns dozing. Sometimes we would forget who was supposed to be dozing and we would both doze. On one of these occasions, I awoke with a start and noticed that the momentum of the river had picked up considerably. Also the river was deeper. The reason the river was deeper was that it was flowing through a channel between two sheer rock walls, and the channel was getting—I hate to think of the word—*narrow!*

"Hey, the river is getting narrow!" I yelled.

"Har . . . ?" Retch said, popping up in the raft.

Smarts whimpered. His hair stood out like the quills of a porcupine under attack.

Up ahead the rock walls came together to form a narrow black crack. Occasionally a big glob of foam would spout up into the crack, sparkle for a moment in the moonlight, then drop back into the darkness. Retch and the dog and I all shouted directions to each other but all we could hear was the sound of thunder emanating from the black crack. The three of us churned the river into a froth trying to paddle back upstream. And then the current sucked us into the Narrows.

I will not attempt to tell what shooting the Narrows in the middle of the night was like—about the paddles snapping in our hands like match sticks, about the river wrapping the raft around us like dough around three frightened wieners, the drop-offs, the drop-ups, the part where we were walking horizontally around the walls carrying the raft, the part where the raft was on top of us and the river was on top of the raft, and certainly not about the parts where it got bad. It will suffice to say that when we finally emerged from the Narrows, I was paddling with a boltaction .30-06, Retch was paddling with the dog, and there was no sign to be found of the raft.

Only in recent years has some of the old yearning for rafting returned, but I have no trouble fighting it off. Retch doesn't care much for rafting anymore either, but he has at last reached the point where he can joke about the Chick-a-nout Narrows. He lets on as if he still can't stand the sound of rushing water. If someone turns on a faucet too near him, he pretends to go all white in the face and starts shouting, "Watch out for the Narrows! Watch out for the Narrows!"

The Miracle of the Fish Plate

WHEN I WAS A KID, my family belonged to the landed aristocracy of nothern Idaho: we owned the wall we had our backs to. We were forced to the wall so often that my mother decided she might as well buy the thing to have it handy and not all the time have to be borrowing one.

Part of our standard fare in those days was something my grandmother called gruel, as in "Shut up and eat your gruel!" My theory is that if you called filet mignon "gruel" you couldn't get most people to touch it with a ten-foot pole. They would rather eat the pole. But when you call gruel "gruel," you have a dish that makes starvation look like the easy way out.

My mother shared this opinion. She preferred to call gruel "baked ham" or "roast beef" or "waffles," as in "Shut up and eat your waffles." One Christmas when we were hunched against the wall, she had the

idea of thickening the gruel, carving it, and calling it
"turkey." We were saved from this culinary aberration
by a pheasant that blithely crashed through one of our
windows to provide us with one of the finest Christmas
dinners it has ever been my pleasure to partake of—
pheasant et gruel. Mom said that God had sent us the
pheasant. I figured that if He hadn't actually sent it, He
had at least done His best by cursing the pheasant with
poor eyesight and a bad sense of direction.

In that time and place, wild game was often
looked upon as a sort of divine gift, not just by us but by
many of the poor people, too. Hunting and fishing were
a happy blend of sport, religion, and economics, and
as a result, game was treated with both respect and
reverence. In recent years, my affluence has increased to
the point where I can dine out at Taco Tim's or Burger
Betty's just about anytime I please, so I must admit that
hunting and fishing are no longer economic necessities
to me. To the contrary, they are largely the reasons I
can't afford to dine out at better places, Smilin' John's
Smorgasbord, for example. I still regard the pursuit of
game as primarily a mystical, even religious quest. To
tie into a lunker trout is to enter into communion with
a different dimension, a spiritual realm, something wild
and unknown and mysterious. This theory of mine was
comfirmed by no less an authority than a Catholic
priest with whom I occasionally share fishing water.

"Me lad," he said, "whenever yourself catches
any fish a-tall 'tis a miracle."

I personally would not go so far as to say that my
catching a fish would fall into the category of miracles
. . . except . . . well, yes, there was one time. You might
call it The Miracle of the Fish Plate.

When I was nine years old and the only angler
in our family, my catching a fish was a matter of considerable rejoicing on the part of not only myself but my

mother, sister, and grandmother as well. There was none of that false praise one occasionally sees heaped upon a kid nowadays—"Oh, my goodness, look at the great big fish Johnny caught! Aren't you just a little man!" No, there was none of that nonsense.

"Hey," my sister, The Troll, would yell. "P. F. Worthless caught a fish!"

"Looks like it's worth about three bites," my grandmother would say by way of appraisal. "But it's a dang sight better than nothin'."

"Put it on the fish plate," my mother would order. "Maybe by Sunday he will have caught enough so we can have fish instead of 'baked ham' for dinner."

The concept of the fish plate may require some explanation. My fishing was confined to a small creek that ran through the back of our place. In those far-off times, the legal limit was twenty-one trout. Although I had heard people speak of "limiting out," I never really believed them. It was an achievement beyond comprehension, like somebody running a four-minute mile, or walking on the moon. No one had ever fished with greater persistence and dedication than I, day in and day out, and I knew that it was not humanly possible to catch a limit of twenty-one fish. Six or seven maybe, but certainly not twenty-one!

Days would go by when I would not get even a single tiny nibble. I would send a hundred worms into watery oblivion for every solid bite. But every so often, suddenly, flashing in a silvery arc above my head, would be a caught trout, usually coming to rest suspended by line from a tree branch or flopping forty feet behind me in the brush. The notion of "playing" a fish seemed nearly as ridiculous to me as "limiting out."

Thus, one by one and two by two I would accumulate little six-, seven- and eight-inch trout over a period of several days (reluctantly releasing all fish less than six inches) until there were enough for a fish dinner. The collection place for these fish was a plate we kept for that purpose on the block of ice in the icebox. It was known as the fish plate.

I can say without any exaggeration whatsoever that our family watched the fish plate as intently as any investor ever watched a stock market ticker tape.

The summer of The Miracle of the Fish Plate was rather typical: we were living on gruel and greens; the garden was drying up for lack of rain; my mother was out of work; the wall had been mortgaged and the bank was threatening to foreclose. But good fortune can't last forever, and we soon fell on hard times. It was then that we received a letter from a wealthy relative by the name of Cousin Edna, informing us that she would be traveling in our part of the country and planned to spend a day visiting with us. That letter struck like a bolt of lightning.

The big question was, "What shall we feed Cousin Edna?" Cousin Edna was a cultured person, a lady who in her whole life had never once sat vis-à-vis a bowl of gruel. Certainly, we would not want her to get the impression we were impoverished. After all, we had a reputation to maintain befitting the landed aristocracy of northern Idaho.

After long deliberation, my mother fastened a hard cold eye on me, which I can tell you is just about as disgusting as it sounds. "All we can do is have fish for dinner," she said. "How's the fish plate?"

"It's got two six-inchers on it," I said.

"Pooh!" my grandmother said. "There's no way he's gonna catch enough trout before Cousin Edna gets here. The boy's just slow. And he's got no patience and is just too damn noisy to catch fish. Why his grandfather used to go to the crick and be back in an hour with a bucketful of the nicest trout you could have ever laid eyes on."

As you may have guessed, my grandfather was not one of the country's great conservationists. Although he died before my time, his ghost hovered about, needling me about my angling skills. My grandmother attributed his great fishing success to his patience and silence. Personally, I figured he probably used half a stick of dynamite as a lure.

"Don't tell me we have to depend on P.F. Worthless!" my sister wailed. "We'll be humiliated!"

"I'll catch all the fish we need," I yelled.

"Shut up," Mom said, soothingly. "If worse comes to worst, we'll let Cousin Edna eat the two fish we have and the rest of us will pretend we prefer 'baked ham.'"

"It ain't gonna wash," Gram said. "The best we can hope for is another deranged pheasant."

The gauntlet had been hurled in my face. It was up to me to save the family pride, or die trying.

I dug my worms with special care, selecting only those that showed qualities of endurance, courage, and a willingness to sacrifice themselves to a great cause. By that time of year, I had fished the creek so thoroughly that I had cataloged almost every fish in it, knew them all on a first name basis, and was familiar with their every whim and preference. They, on the other hand, knew all my tricks. It would not be easy enticing them to take a hook but I was determined to do it.

And it was not easy. I knew where a nice eight-inch brookie was holed up under a sunken stump. In the grim cold light of first dawn, when he would not be expecting me, I crawled through the wet brush and stinging nettles just above his hideout. I waited, soaked, teeth chattering quietly, passing the time by studying the waves of goosebumps rippling up and down my arms. As the first rays of morning sun began to descend through the pine trees, I lowered a superb worm, one blessed not only with dauntless courage but intellect as well, into the sluggish current that slid beneath the tangle of naked stump roots. I knew that I could not retrieve the hook without snagging it unless the point was covered by the mouth of a trout. Never was a finer bait presented so naturally, with such finesse. The line slackened, the hook drifting with the currents in the labyrinth of roots. A slight tremor came up the line. I whipped the rod back and the fat little eight-incher came flashing out from under the stump. He threw the hook and landed on the bank ten feet from me. I lunged for him, had him in my grasp. He slipped loose and landed in the water, where he circled frantically in an effort to get his bearings. I plunged in after him hoping to capitalize on his momentary confusion. Unfortunately, the water was much deeper than I expected and closed over my head like the clap of doom. As I dogpaddled my way into the shallows, I realized that filling the fish plate might be even more difficult than I had anticipated the chore would be.

Over the next two days I went up and down the creek like a purse seiner. My total take was two small fish, and Cousin Edna was arriving on the following day. I had become a nine-year-old existentialist, abandoning all faith and hope, driving myself on armed only with simple defiance of despair.

First the fish had abandoned me, then God, and now, on the final day, even the sun had slipped behind the mountains, no doubt sniggering to itself. Before me lay the bleakest, shallowest, most sterile part of the creek. Never in my whole life had I caught a fish there, mostly because it would have been pointless to even try. The water rippled over a bed of white gravel without a single place of concealment for even the smallest trout. Well, possibly there was one place. A small log was buried in the gravel diagonally to the current, and I noticed that at the downstream tip of the log there appeared to be a slight pooling of water. I eased into the stream and crept up to the butt end of the log, whereupon I perceived that the gravel had been washed from under it to form a narrow trough of dark, still water. I lowered my last worm, a pale, haggard, well-traveled fellow, into this trough and let it drift along the log, bumping over gravel, into limbs and knots, until it stopped. "Snagged!" I thought. Furious, I hauled back. My rod doubled over but the hook didn't come loose. Instead, the line began to cut a slow arc through the water, picked up speed, and then, exploding out onto the gravel bar, came what seemed to be a monstrous brook trout.

I cannot tell you how long the ensuing battle lasted because at my first glimpse of the fish, time ceased to exist, and the trout and I became a single pulsating spirit suspended in infinity. When at last we emerged into our separate identities, it was as victor and vanquished. In the dying light, the trout lay clamped between my aching knees on a white gravel beach, and I killed him with a sharp blow of a rock to the back of the head.

As he quivered into stillness, I was filled with unknown joy, unfamiliar sorrow. And I knew. I *knew*. Without the slightest doubt, I knew that under that same log, waiting in that watery darkness, was his twin.

Gently, I removed the hook from those great jaws, repairing the tatters of the heroic worm, threading them as best I could onto the hook, and made my way back to the log for a repeat performance. When you have a miracle going for you, you never want to waste any of it.

The dinner for Cousin Edna was a great success. When it was over and everyone had had his fill, there were still large sections of fried trout on the platter, which I suppose I need not tell you, was the humble fish plate.

"My heavens!" exclaimed Cousin Edna. "I just don't know when I've had a finer meal!"

"It's not over yet," said Gram. And then she served Cousin Edna a heaping bowl of wild strawberries that my sister had picked with her own little troll fingers.

The wild strawberries made Cousin Edna's eyes roll back in her head, they were so good. "Why, I hope you're not giving me all the strawberries," she said suddenly, noting our attentiveness.

"Land sakes," Gram said, "we have them so often we're tired of the little beggars." I looked at Gram in disbelief. It was the first time I'd ever heard her lie.

"We thought we would have some nice pudding instead," my mother said, passing around some bowls. I looked into mine.

"Hey," I said. "This looks like . . . this smells like . . ."

"Hush, dear," my mother said, her voice edged with granite. "And eat your *pudding*."

The Backpacker

STRANGE, THE THINGS that suddenly become fashionable. Take backpacking for instance.

I know people who five years ago had never climbed anything higher than a tall barstool. Now you can scarcely name a mountain within three hundred miles they haven't hoofed up in their Swiss-made waffle-stompers.

They used to complain about the price of sirloin steak. Now they complain about the price of beef jerky (which is about three times that of Maine lobster in Idaho).

Their backpacking is a refined sport, noted for lightness. The gear consists of such things as silk packs, magnesium frames, dainty camp stoves. Their sleeping bags are filled with the down of unborn goose, their tents made of waterproof smoke. They carry two little packets from which they can spread out a nine-course meal. One packet contains the food and the other a freeze-dried French chef.

Well, it wasn't like that back in the old days, before backpacking became fashionable. These latecomers don't know what real backpacking was like.

The rule of thumb for the old backpacking was that the weight of your pack should equal the weight of yourself and the kitchen range combined. Just a casual glance at a full pack sitting on the floor could give you a double hernia and fuse four vertebrae. After carrying the pack all day, you had to remember to tie one leg to a tree before you dropped it. Otherwise, you would float off into space. The pack eliminated the need for any special kind of ground-gripping shoes, because your feet would sink a foot and a half into hard-packed earth, two inches into solid rock. Some of the new breed of backpackers occasionally wonder what caused a swath of fallen trees on the side of a mountain. That is where one of the old backpackers slipped off a trail with a full pack.

My packboard alone met the minimum weight requirement. It was a canvas and plywood model, surplus from the Second World War. These packboards apparently were designed with the idea that a number of them could be hooked together to make an emergency bridge for Sherman tanks. The first time you picked one up you thought maybe someone had forgotten to remove his tank.

My sleeping bag looked like a rolled-up mattress salvaged from a fire in a skid row hotel. Its filling was sawdust, horsehair, and No. 6 bird shot. Some of today's backpackers tell me their sleeping bags are so light they scarcely know they're there. The only time I scarcely knew my sleeping bag was there was when I was in it at 2 A.M. on a cold night. It was freckled from one end to the other with spark holes, a result of my efforts to stay close enough to the fire to keep warm. The only time I was halfway comfortable was when it was ablaze. It was the only sleeping bag I ever heard of which you could climb into in the evening with scarcely a mark on you and wake up in the morning bruised from head to toe. That was because two or three times a night my companions would take it upon themselves to jump up and stomp out my sleeping-bag fires—in their haste neglecting to first evacuate the occupant. Since I was the camp cook, I never knew whether they were attempting to save me from immolation or getting in a few last licks for what they thought might be terminal indigestion.

Our provisions were not distinguished by variety. Dehydrated foods were considered effeminate. A man could ruin his reputation for life by getting caught on a pack trip with a dried apple. If you wanted apples, brother, you carried them with the water still in them. No one could afford such delicacies as commercial beef jerky. What you carried was a huge slab of bacon. It was so big that if the butcher had left on the legs, it could have walked behind you on a leash.

A typical meal consisted of fried bacon, potatoes and onions fried in bacon grease, a pan of beans heated in bacon grease, bacon grease gravy, some bread fried in bacon grease, and cowboy coffee (made by boiling an old cowboy in bacon grease). After meals, indigestion went through our camp like a sow grizzly with a toothache. During the night coyotes sat in nervous silence on surrounding hills and listened to the mournful wailing from our camp.

There were a few bad things, too, about backpacking in the old style, but I loved all of it. I probably would never have thought of quitting if it hadn't been for all those geophysical changes that took place in the Western Hemisphere a few years ago.

The first thing I noticed was a distinct harden-
ing of the earth. This occurred wherever I happened
to spread out my sleeping bag, so I knew that the condition was widespread. (Interestingly enough, my children, lacking their father's scientific training, were
unable to detect the phenomenon.)

A short while later it became apparent to me
that the nights in the mountains had become much
colder than any I could remember in the past. The chill
would sink its fangs into my bones in the pre-dawn
hours and hang on like a terrier until the sun was high.
I thought possibly that the drop in temperature was
heralding a new ice age.

Well, I could put up with the hard and the cold
but then the air started getting thinner. The only way
you could get sufficient oxygen to lug a pack the size of
an adolescent pachyderm was by gasping and wheezing.
(Some of my wheezes were sufficient to strip small pine
trees bare of their needles.) My trail speed became so
slow it posed a dangerous threat to my person. If we
were in fact at the onset of a new ice age, there was a
good chance I might be overtaken and crushed by a
glacier.

The final straw was the discovery that a trail I
had traveled easily and often in my youth had under-
gone a remarkable transformation. In the intervening
years since I had last hiked it, the damn thing had
nearly doubled in length. I must admit that I was puzzled, since I didn't know that trails could stretch or
grow. The fact that it now took me twice as long to hike
it, however, simply did not allow for any other explanation. I asked a couple of older friends about it, and they
said that they had seen the same thing happen. They
said probably the earth shifted on its axis every once in
a while and caused trails to stretch. I suggested that
maybe that was also the cause for the ground getting

harder, the nights colder, and the air thinner. They said that sounded like a plausible theory to them. (My wife had another theory, but it was so wild and far-fetched that I won't embarrass her by mentioning it here.)

Anyway, one day last fall while I was sitting at home fretting about the environment, a couple of friends telephoned and invited me along on a pack trip they were taking into the Cascades. Both of them are of the new school of backpacking, and I thought I owed it to them to go along. They could profit considerably by watching an old trail hand in action.

When I saw the packs R.B. and Charley showed up with I almost had to laugh. Neither pack was large enough to carry much more than a cheese sandwich. I carried more bicarbonate of soda than they had food. I didn't know what they planned to sleep in, but it certainly couldn't be in those tidy little tote bags they had perched on top of their packs. Anyway, I didn't say anything. I just smiled and got out my winch and they each got a pry pole and before you knew it we had my pack out of the car and on my shoulders. As we headed up the trail I knew it was going to be a rough trip. Already a few flakes of snow had fallen on my eyeballs.

The environment on that trip was even harsher than I had remembered. The trails were steeper, the air thinner, the ground harder, the nights colder. Even my trail speed was slower. Several porcupines shot past me like I was standing still.

R.B. and Charley showed obvious signs of relief when I made it into camp that first night.

"You probably thought I wouldn't make it with all the food," I chided them.

"No," R.B. said. "It was just that for a moment

there we didn't recognize you. We thought we were being attacked by a giant snail."

I explained to them that we old-time backpackers made a practice of traveling the last mile or so on our hands and knees in order to give our feet a rest.

It was disgusting to see them sitting there so relaxed and cheerful after a hard day's hike. They didn't seem to have any notion at all what backpacking was about. I could hardly stand it when they whipped out a little stove and boiled up some dried chunks of leather and sponge for supper. It probably would have hurt their feelings if I had got out the slab of bacon, so I didn't mention it. I just smiled and ate their food— four helpings in fact, just to make my act convincing. I never told them, but the Roast Baron of Beef was not quite rare enough for my taste and they had forgotten the cream sauce for the asparagus tips. And I have certainly tasted better Baked Alaska in my day, too.

Well, they can have their fashionable new-school backpacking if they want it. I'm sticking with the old way. Oh, I'm making a few concessions to a harsher environment, but that's all. When I got back from that trip, I did order a new pack frame. It was designed by nine aeronautical engineers, three metallurgists, and a witch doctor, and weighs slightly less than the down of a small thistle. My new sleeping bag weighs nine ounces, including the thermostatic controls. If I want to sleep in, my new cook kit gets up and puts on the coffee. Then I bought a few boxes of that dried leather and sponge. But that's all. I'm certainly not going to be swept along on the tides of fashion.

Great Outdoor Gadgets Nobody Ever Invented

THOUSANDS OF ANGLERS no doubt consider the electronic fish-finder one of the top five achievements of the twentieth century, probably just behind the spinning reel and Einstein's theory of relativity. Personally, I feel the fish-finder is a nice enough gadget, but it is not high on my list of priorities for inventions needed to ease the lot of outdoorspersons. For some unknown reason, inventors specializing in hunting and fishing gadgets have never unleashed their ingenuity on the really tough problems plaguing men, women, and children who participate in outdoor sports.

After some thirty years of research on the subject, I now offer up to the inventors, without any hope or desire for recompense, my own list of inventions that nobody has yet invented.

There are any number of finders much more important than fish-finders, but I will mention only a couple of the more significant ones here.

Take the hunting-partner-finder, for instance. This would be used in situations where you have told your hunting partner, "I'll meet you at the top of that draw in an hour," and with malice aforethought, he immediately contrives to vanish from the face of the earth for the rest of the day. I have two ideas for this invention. One is simply a red balloon, attached to a quarter-mile length of string, that floats along above him. The other is a peanut-butter-seeking mechanical dog that will track him down and clamp a set of iron jaws on that portion of his anatomy adjacent to and slightly below the sack lunch he is carrying in his game pocket. Because you would merely have to stroll leisurely in the direction of the sound emanating from your hunting partner, this finder probably could be considered a sonar device.

Right at the top of my list of invention priorities is the mean-cow-finder. It would be used in this way. Say you want to fish a stream that winds through a cow pasture, which, as almost everyone knows, is the natural habitat of cows. A herd of the beasts will have taken up a good tactical position in the center of the pasture, enabling them to control all access routes to the stream and, more important, shut off the avenues of escape.

Now your average cow is a decent sort of animal, and I can put up with their mooing advice over my shoulder on how to improve my casting technique and choice of fly. I can even ignore their rather casual habits of personal hygiene, at least as long as they conduct their various indiscretions at a reasonable distance from where I am fishing. The problem is that it is almost impossible to distinguish a peace-loving cow from a mean cow, the kind who would swim Lake Erie to get a shot at you. What I have in mind is a simple little electronic gadget that would beep or flash a red light if a herd contained a mean cow. The more elaborate models might have a needle that would point out the malicious beast and maybe even indicate her aggression quotient and rate of acceleration from a standing start. I and a thousand anglers like me would trade in our fish-finders for a mean-cow-finder in a second, or sooner, I bet.

There are numerous gadgets and concoctions on the market for attracting game. What I need is something to repel game. Just last summer, for example, I could have made good use of a bear repellent. My wife and I were asleep in our tent in a remote area of Idaho when suddenly I awoke to the sound of the lid being ripped off our aluminum camp cooler.

"I think a bear just ripped the lid off our camp cooler," I hissed to my wife.

"I heard that," she replied sleepily. "I thought it was you in a hurry to find your pain-killer."

"Very funny," I said, hopping around in the dark in an effort to get my pants on. "Hand me the flashlight. I'm going out there and run the beggar off."

I unzipped the tent flap and switched on the flashlight. There in the beam stood a bear approximately the size of a boxcar; he was making a sandwich out of the camp cooler and appeared somewhat displeased at the interruption.

"HAAAAAYAAAAA!" I yelled. "GET OUTA THERE!"

"Did you run the beggar off?" my wife asked.

"I'M YELLING AT YOU! GET OUT OF THE TENT AND INTO THE CAR! I THINK WE'RE NEXT ON THE MENU!"

Not only would a little bear repellent have saved our camp cooler, it would have saved me the repeated tedium of having to listen to my wife regale my so-called friends with an account, including excessively exaggerated pantomime, of my reaction to the bear.

Inventors have made great strides on the problem of reducing the weight and bulk of backpacking equipment, but they haven't gone far enough. What I would like to see them come up with is a fully loaded backpack that is freeze-dried. When you had hiked into your campsite in the mountains you would merely have to take your backpack out of your pocket, soak it in a little water and, presto, you would have a reconstituted sleeping bag, tent, trail ax, cook kit and, of course, all your food.

When I told a backpacking friend about this idea, he scoffed at it. "Why not a freeze-dried log cabin with a flagstone fireplace?" he suggested, expanding on my concept.

"That's not bad," I told him.

"Hell," he said, "you'd be the first one to complain about missing the weight of a good pack tugging at your shoulders, the soothing, rhythmical squeak-squeak of the frame and harness."

"For the past five years," I told him, "the rhythmical squeak-squeak of the frame and harness has been drowned out by the rhythmical squeak-squeak of my back."

I also have several suggestions for new sleeping-bag designs. One is primarily for use in small two-man tents. This consists primarily of a time-lock on the zipper so that once your tent partner is in his bag he can't get out of it until morning. My friend Retch spends most of the night crawling around, looking for one thing or another. This does not include his answers to nature's call. (On an average night Retch and nature conduct a regular litany between themselves.) Here is a typical verbal exchange he and I had in a tent recently:

"Watch out," I yelled at him. "You're kneeling on my glasses!"

"Sorry," he said. "I thought you still had them on."

"I do, you idiot!"

Another of my sleeping-bag inventions would be primarily for kids who are practicing "sleeping out" in the backyard. The bags would contain leg holes for running. This would save the kid the time required to strip off his sleeping bag in order to sprint for the house. These would be *valuable* seconds saved.

Speaking of children, I would like to see someone invent a small portable lie detector for use on kids while camping in remote wilderness campgrounds where the sole sanitary facility is a privy located at the far end of a quarter-mile trail intersected by logs, several small streams, and a skunk crossing, and frequently occupied with strange creatures that screech murderously at you in the dark. (Usually, these creatures are simply other parents you surprise hauling their tykes down the trail, but you never know.)

The lie detector would work like this: Just before their bedtime I would line the little ones up outside the tent and, one by one, attach them to the anti-fib device.

"Is your name Erin McManus?"

"Yes."

"Do you have a dog named Fergus?"

"Yes."

"Have you gone to the bathroom within the last fifteen minutes?"

"Yes."

"Hah! Hit the trail to the old privy, kiddo!"

Some kind of detector should be developed for the purpose of determining whether camp cooking is fatally poisonous. My own system, far from reliable, is to observe whether the *plat du jour* is killing flies and mosquitoes beyond a fifteen-foot radius. Some kind of chemically treated paper, on the order of litmus, would be perfect and a lot less expensive than seeing if the concoction will dissolve a spoon. I certainly could have used some of this poison detector a while back when Retch whipped up his infamous stew consisting of canned pork and beans, cabbage, beef jerky, and the miscellaneous leavings of a five-day hunting trip. Crammed into a tent with Retch and two other guys, I spent the night moaning in agony and praying for a quick end to it all. I don't know what would have happened to my present or future if I'd been dumb enough to eat any of the stew myself.

There are a number of life preservers for use by stream fishermen on the market now, but like so many other inventions designed for the outdoorsperson, their creators have stopped short of the mark. The basic idea of these life preservers is that if you fall in the water they can be inflated by blowing into a tube. With the kind of water I generally fall into, I don't want to waste any time blowing on some dumb tube. On some of the falls I've taken, I probably could have blown up a seven-man life raft before I hit the water if mere floating had been my chief concern. To hell with floating—what I need in the way of a life preserver is something that really preserves my life. As I see it, this would be a recording device installed in fishing vests. While I was contemplating whether to cross a peeled sapling over a sixty-foot-deep river gorge or possibly to make a running leap to land on a moss-covered rock in the middle of some rapids, the life preserver would activate automatically and shout through two stereo loudspeakers set at full volume, "DON'T TRY IT, YOU FOOL, DON'T TRY IT!"

The Purist

TWELVE-YEAR-OLDS are different from you and me, particularly when it comes to fishing, and most of all when it comes to fishing on Opening Day of Trout Season.

The twelve-year-old is probably the purest form of sports fisherman known to man. I don't know why. Perhaps it is because his passion for fishing is at that age undiluted by the multitude of other passions that accumulate over a greater number of years. Say thirteen.

Now I am reasonably sure that I can catch a limit of trout faster on Opening Day than the average twelve-year-old, but any angler knows that speed and quantity are not true measures of quality when it comes to fishing. It's a matter of style, and here the twelve-year-old beats me hands down. You just can't touch a twelve-year-old when it comes to style.

Preparation is the big part of his secret. If Opening Day of Trout Season is June 5, the twelve-year-old starts his preparation about the middle of March. He knows he should have started earlier, but at that age he likes to put things off. With such a late start, he will be hard pressed to be ready in time.

The first thing he does is to get his tackle out and look at it. He removes from one of his shoe boxes a large snarly ball of lines, hooks, leaders, spinners, flies, plugs, weeds, tree branches, and a petrified frog. He shakes the whole mass a couple of times and nothing comes loose. Pleased that everything is still in good order he stuffs it all back into his shoe box. The next time he will look at it will be on Opening Day Eve, fifteen minutes before he is supposed to go to bed. The tackle snarl will then provide the proper degree of wild, sweaty panic that is so much a part of the twelve-year-old's style.

The next order of business is to check his bait supplies. The best time to do this is in the middle of a blizzard, when it's too cold to be outside without a coat on or to have all the windows in the house open. The large jar of salmon eggs he has stored next to the hot-water pipes that run through his closet seems to look all right, but just to be sure he takes the lid off. He drops the lid on the floor and it rolls under something too large to move. Something must be done immediately, he knows, because uneasy murmurs are rising in distant parts of the house, and besides he won't be able to hold his breath forever. The best course of action seems to be to run the jar through every room in the building, leaving in his wake mass hysteria and the sound of windows being thrown open. Later, standing coatless with the rest of the family in the front yard while a chill north wind freshens up the house, he offers the opinion that he may need a new bottle of salmon eggs for Opening Day.

Occasionally the young angler will do some

work on his hooks. There is, however, some diversity of opinion among twelve-year-olds whether it is better to crack off the crust of last year's worms from the hooks or to leave it on as a little added attraction for the fish. The wise father usually withholds any advice on the subject but does suggest that if his offspring decides to sharpen his hooks on the elder's whetstone, the worm crusts be removed *before-hand*. Nothing gums up a whetstone worse than oiled worm dust.

The twelve-year-old takes extra-special pains in the preparation of his fly rod. He gets it out, looks at it, sights down it, rubs it with a cloth, sights down it again, rubs it some more, and finally puts it away with an air of utter frustration. There is, after all, not much that you can do to a glass rod.

The reel is something else again. A thousand different things can be done to a reel, all of which can be grouped under the general term "taking it apart." The main reason a kid takes his reel apart is to take it apart. But most adults can't understand this kind of reasoning, so the kid has to come up with some other excuse. He says he is taking his reel apart to clean it. No one can deny that the reel needs cleaning. It has enough sand and gravel in it to ballast a balloon. During most of the season it sounds like a miniature rock crusher and can fray the nerves of an adult fisherman at a hundred yards. For Opening Day, however, the reel must be clean.

There are three basic steps used by the twelve-year-old in cleaning a reel. First it is reduced to the largest possible number of parts. These are all carefully placed on a cookie sheet in the sequence of removal. The cookie sheet is then dropped on the floor. The rest of the time between March and the Opening Day of Trout Season is spent looking for these parts. The last one is found fifteen minutes before bedtime on Opening Day Eve.

Some twelve-year-olds like to test their leaders before risking them on actual fish. Nothing is more frustrating to a kid than having a leader snap just as he is heaving a nice fat trout back over his head. Consequently, he is concerned that any weakness in a leader be detected beforehand. There are many methods of doing this, but one of the best is to tie one end of the leader to a rafter in the garage and the other end to a concrete block. The concrete block is then dropped from the top of a stepladder. The chief drawback of this method is the cost involved in replacing cracked rafters.

Eventually the big night comes—Opening Day Eve.

The day is spent digging worms. Early in the season there is a surplus of worms and the young angler can be choosy. The process of worm selection is similar to that used in Spain for the selection of fighting bulls. Each worm is chosen for his size, courage, and fighting ability. One reason kids frequently have poor luck on Opening Day is that their worms can lick the average fish in a fair fight.

Approximately four hundred worms are considered an adequate number. These are placed in a container and covered with moist dirt. The container is then sealed and placed carefully back in the closet by the hotwater pipes, where it is next found during a blizzard the following March.

The twelve-year-old angler really peaks out, however, during that fifteen minutes before bedtime. He discovers that his tackle has become horribly snarled in his tackle box. No one knows how, unless perhaps the house has been invaded by poltergeists. The reel is thrown together with an expertise born of hysteria and panic. Four cogs, six screws, and a worm gear are left over, but the thing works. And it no longer makes that funny little clicking sound!

Finally, all is in readiness and the boy is congratulating himself on having had the good sense to start his preparation three months earlier. As it was, he went right down to the last minutes. Only one major task remains: the setting of the alarm clock.

Naturally, he wants to be standing ready beside his favorite fishing hole at the crack of dawn. The only trouble is he doesn't know just exactly when dawn cracks. He surmises about four o'clock. If it takes him an hour to hike down to the fishing hole, that means he should set the alarm for about three. On the other hand, it may take longer in the dark, so he settles on 2:30. He doesn't have to allow any time for getting dressed since he will sleep with his clothes on.

Once in bed he begins to worry. What if the alarm fails to go off? He decides to test it. The alarm makes a fine, loud clanging sound. After all the shouting dies down and his folks are back in bed, he winds up the alarm again. As a precautionary measure, he decides to set the alarm for two, thus giving himself a half-hour safety margin. He then stares at the ceiling for an hour, visions of five-pound trout dancing in his head. He shakes with anticipation. He worries. What if the alarm fails to awaken him? What if he shuts it off and goes back to sleep? The horror of it is too much to stand.

Midnight. He gets up, puts on his boots, grabs his rod and lunch and brand-new bottle of salmon eggs, and heads out the door.

It's Opening Day of Trout Season, and there's not a minute to spare.

The Outfit

YEARS AGO the Old Wilderness Outfitter started sending me his catalog of surplus outdoor gear: slightly battered canoes, scruffy rucksacks, dulled trail axes, tarnished cook kits, saggy tents, limp snowshoes, and the like. I spent many a fine winter hour thumbing through his catalog. Indeed, such was my enjoyment that occasionally I would lose control of my faculties and actually order some of the stuff. One surplus wilderness tent arrived with authentic wilderness dirt still on the floor, not to mention a few pine needles, a fir cone, a sprinkling of fish scales, and a really nice selection of squashed insects. The Old Wilderness Outfitter never charged for any of these extras, and in numerous other ways revealed himself to be a man of generosity and all-round good character. He put out a fine catalog, too.

The catalog arrived each winter with the same

regularity as the snow, and at about the same time. Then it stopped coming. I thought maybe the Old Wilderness Outfitter had died, or was peeved at me because I had sent a letter telling him I would just as soon furnish my own fish scales and squashed insects, and there was no need to include them with my orders. I hadn't intended to offend him though, and if sending the extras meant that much to him it was all right with me.

A few days ago, I was surprised to find in the mail a new catalog from the Old Wilderness Outfitter. Happily, I licked my thumb and started flipping through the pages. I was flabbergasted. There wasn't a single scruffy rucksack in the thing, let alone a slightly battered canoe. The Old Wilderness Outfitter had filled up his catalog with glossy, color pictures of beautiful people.

Glancing at the prices, I thought at first the beautiful people themselves must be for sale. There was one blonde lady who looked well worth the seventy-five dollars asked, and I would have been interested, too, if I didn't already have one of my own worth almost twice that amount.

Then I determined the prices were for the clothes the beautiful people were wearing! The seventy-five dollars wasn't the price of the blonde lady but what she had on, something described as "a shooting outfit." (I can tell you with absolute certainty that if that lady ever shot anything in her life it was a sultry look across a crowded room.) The men were almost as beautiful as the women, and dressed in a month's wages plus overtime. Their haircuts alone probably cost more than my shooting outfit, if you don't count my lucky sweatshirt with the faded Snoopy on it.

Most of the clothes were trimmed in leather

made from the hides of Spanish cows, which was appropriate, I thought, because most of the catalog copy was American bull.

After about ten minutes of studying the catalog, I could see what had happened. Some unemployed high-fashion clothes designers had got to the Old Wilderness Outfitter and persuaded him to chuck his rucksacks and the like and replace them with fancy clothes. The old codger should have known better. If American outdoorspersons were interested in fancy clothes, outdoor magazines would be written like this:

Doc stood up in the blind and squinted his eyes at the jagged rip of first light beyond the marsh. His closely woven virgin-wool shirt with the full sleeves and deep cape was beaded with rain.

"Hey, Mac," he said, "it's starting to rain. Better hand me my sage-green parka of water-repellent, super-tough eight-ounce cotton canvas duck with the hand-stitched leather flaps."

"Right," I said. "But first I'm going to drop that lone honker, which you'll notice is attractively attired in 100 percent goose down."

The truth is we outdoorspersons just aren't that interested in high fashion. Our preference runs more to low fashion. I myself have turned out a number of outstanding low-fashion designs. There was, for example, my free-form stain made by dropping an open bottle of dry-fly dressing in a shirt pocket. This design should not be confused with the one originating from a leaky peanut butter sandwich. My own favorite is the ripped pant leg laced shut with twenty-pound monofilament line, split-shot sinkers still attached.

Striking as these designs may be, I am just too

old to design really first-rate low fashions. I no longer
have the time, patience, nerves, or stomach for it. As a
matter of fact, low-fashion designers usually reach their
peak about age fourteen. From then on they undergo a
gradual decline until their last shred of self-respect is
gone and they will think nothing of going out wearing,
say (shudder) a brand-spanking-new red felt hat.

You'd never catch a fourteen-year-old wearing
such a monstrosity as a new red felt hat. No sir. The
first thing a fourteen-year-old does with a new hunting
or fishing hat is to redesign it. Immediately upon returning home from the store, he turns the hat over to
his dog. After the dog has exhausted his imagination
and ingenuity on the hat, it is retrieved by the kid and
pounded full of holes with a large spike and hammer.
The edges of the holes are burnt with a match. This
simulates the effect of the kid's having been fired upon
at close range with an elephant gun. (Nobody knows
why this is important to a kid, but it is.) A band of
squirrel, skunk, or muskrat hide, more or less tanned by
the kid himself, is fastened to the crown. Next the brim
is folded up on three sides and pinned with the thigh
bones of a fried chicken or other equally attractive
fasteners. And finally, several tail feathers from a pheasant are artfully arranged about the crown. The hat now
resembles the year-old remains of a high-speed collision
between a large bird and a small mammal.

Not all youngsters, by the way, are born with this talent
for low fashion. Some have to learn it. I recall an incident back in my junior high school days when my
friends Retch and Peewee and I gave Hair Forsyth his
first lesson in low fashion. (The nickname "Hair," by
the way, derived from an observation by Retch, one of
the more scholarly of my companions, that rich kids

who stand to inherit the family fortune are known as "hairs.") Hair had taken to hanging out with us at school, and when it came time for the annual early spring camping trip, we thought we should invite him along. Several bare patches of earth had been reported to us, and we decided this was sufficient evidence that winter was over and camping weather had begun. There was still a bit of a chill in the air, not to mention several inches of snow on the ground, and we thought it likely that Hair would find these sufficient reasons for refusing our invitation. But he said he thought it was a great idea.

Since I lived out in the country at the edge of the Wilderness (sometimes referred to locally as Fergussen's woodlot and north pasture), our farm was selected as the jumping-off place for the weekend expedition. When Hair climbed out of his father's car that day, we regular low-fashion campers nearly burst trying to keep from laughing. Ol' Hair was dressed up just like a dude. He had on these insulated leather boots, special safari pants, a heavy wool shirt, a down jacket, a hat with fur earflaps, and so on. Naturally, we didn't want to hurt his feelings by pointing out how ridiculous he looked. Nevertheless, we thought we should instruct him on the proper attire for a spring camping trip.

"I hate to say this," Retch told Hair, "but you're absolutely gonna roast in all those clothes."

"Yeah," Peewee put in, "and those boots are gonna be awfully heavy for walking. Too bad you don't have tennis shoes like we're wearing."

"Right," I said. "Next time, Hair, why don't you see if you can get some tennis shoes like these, with holes in the canvas so the sweat can drain out."

Hair thanked us for straightening him out and said the next time he would have a better idea how to put together a suitable outfit.

After getting Hair squared away, we loaded up and headed out into the Wilderness. The snow out in the Wilderness was much deeper than any of us had expected. Bit by bit the depth of the snow increased until it was about halfway up to our knees. From time to time we would have to stop and chip the compacted snow off our tennis shoes and try to unplug the drain holes. These stops were occasion for much clowning around by us regulars for the benefit of Hair. Retch and Peewee would pound their feet against trees and make moaning and howling sounds, while I would tear off my tennis shoes and socks and blow on my blue feet in a comical manner. Hair laughed until tears streamed down his cheeks. Indeed, we all had tears streaming down our cheeks.

The wind came up shortly after it started to snow, and pretty soon we were slogging along through what we would have called a blizzard except that this was spring and the first of the good camping weather. Retch came up with the idea that maybe we should try to make it to an old abandoned trapper's cabin a couple of miles away and spend the night there.

"Otherwise, we might freeze to death," Retch joked.

"Heh," Peewee and I laughed.

"Freeze!" Hair cried. "You must be joking. I'm burning up inside of this darn coat. Dang, I hate to ask but, Peewee, could I get you to trade me your shirt for this coat? What do you call that kind of shirt anyway?"

"A t-t-t-t-t-t-tee shirt," Peewee said, thrusting it into Hair's hand.

"Well, I guess I'll just have to leave this wool shirt of mine behind unless I can get one of you fellas to wear it for me," Hair said, taking it off and putting on Peewee's T-shirt over his thick, creamy wool underwear.

I said, "Dang I'll wear it rather than have you leave it behind."

"That underwear's not too hot for you, is it?" asked Retch.

Hair said it wasn't, but that he sure wouldn't mind slipping his boiling feet into a nice cool pair of tennis shoes. So Retch says he has about the coolest pair of tennis shoes a person is likely to find, and he swaps shoes with Hair.

By dark we had made it to the trapper's cabin and had a roaring fire going in the barrel stove and were sitting around roasting ourselves a few marshmallows and listening to the wind howl outside. From then on, Hair was one of the regulars and, as far as I know, nobody ever again mentioned the ridiculous outfit he wore on that first camping trip with us. It was obvious to everyone that he had learned his lesson, and there was no point in hurting his feelings any more than was necessary.

The ultimate in low fashion, at least that I ever saw, was created spontaneously on one of our camping trips by Harold Munster, a tall, gangling, wild-haired youth whose chief claim to fame was an uncanny ability for taking a bad situation and making it worse. Sometimes you would be absolutely certain that a situation couldn't be any worse and then Munster would show up and make it nine times as bad as before.

Back in those days, our camping clothes were referred to by our mothers as "your OLD clothes." A mother would stick her head out the back door and yell at her kids, "Wear your OLD clothes, you hear!" Since all our clothes were old—most of them had been in our families longer than we had—OLD designated the oldest grade. OLD clothes were never discarded, they just faded away. Sometimes they faded away while you were wearing them, and that is what led to Harold Munster's creation of the ultimate in low fashion.

Retch, Peewee, Munster, and I had been backpacking for nearly a week and now were attempting to extricate ourselves from the mountains as expeditiously as possible. In part, this consisted in wild, free-for-all gallops down steep trails, with packs, axes, and iron skillets flailing about on all sides. It was during one of these maniacal charges downhill that Munster, hurtling a windfall, caught his OLD pants on a limb. The pants exploded in midair. Munster landed half naked in a shower of tiny bits of cloth, old patches, buttons, belt loops, and a broken zipper still held shut with a safety pin.

Well, we were all startled, a little embarrassed, and, of course, worried, because here was a bad situation. Nobody knew in what manner Munster would strive to make it worse and which of us might be swept into the vortex of whatever catastrophe he came up with.

The mosquitoes in that area were about the size of piranhas and twice as voracious. As Hemingway might have put it, Munster had been turned into a moveable feast. His expanse of bare skin drew the mosquitoes off the rest of us like a magnet, and, though appreciative of the respite, we became concerned that our unfortunate companion might be eaten alive or, even more likely, slap himself to death.

A small spring issued from the edge of the trail at that point, creating a large muddy bog on the downhill side of the trail. Before we knew what was happening,

Munster had leaped into this bog and begun smearing his lower half with great globs of mud.

"Hey," he yelled up at us. "This really feels great!" We stared down at him with a mounting sense of foreboding, knowing from past experience that this was the beginning of something that would lead to dire consequences.

Not satisfied with coating his lower half with mud, Munster peeled off his OLD shirt and coated his upper half as well. Then he took handfuls of goop and rubbed it in his hair and on his face, all the while ooh-ing and ahhing with relief and saying, "This will take care of those blinkety-blank mosquitoes for a while."

The rest of us divided Munster's load up among ourselves so that his mud coating would not be rubbed off by his pack. Thus unburdened, he took the lead and strolled along light of heart and mosquito-free, oc-casionally whistling a few bars or counting cadence for the rest of us. As we plodded along and the day grew hotter, we noticed that Munster's mud coating was be-ginning to bake into a hard, whitish shell, with webs of tiny cracks spreading out from his joints and seams. Grass, moss, sticks, and small stones protruded from the shell in a rather ghastly manner. Munster began com-plaining about what he described as a blinkety-blank unbearable itch, and occasionally would stop wild-eyed and claw furiously at his mud cast. His claw marks served only to make his overall appearance even more grisly.

Our plan was to intersect a logging road and then try to catch a ride out of the mountains with some gyppo loggers who were working in the area. We en-countered the loggers much sooner than expected. Three of them had hiked back in from the end of the road to eat their lunch by the edge of a small stream. They were now sprawled out resting, smoking, and digging the dirt out from among the calks on their boots. The trail we were on wound around the mountain about a hundred feet above them.

Retch, Peewee, and I had fallen some distance behind Munster, partly because of fatigue and partly because we could no longer endure the sight of him. As we rounded a bend in the trail, we caught sight of the three unsuspecting loggers, languid pools of tobacco smoke hanging in the still air about them. Poised like a silent gargoyle on the lip of the trail directly above this peaceful scene, was Munster, staring down at the loggers. We tried to shout but our tongues were momentarily paralyzed from the sheer horror of the scene before us. And then Peewee found his voice.

"MUNSTER!" he shrieked.

The startled loggers looked up. I could see the lips of one of them, puzzled, silently form the word "monster?"

Then Munster bounded down the hill toward the loggers, waving his arms ecstatically and croaking out his relief at being saved from having to walk the last ten miles home.

Walking the last ten miles home, we attempted to reconstruct the events of the ten seconds following Munster's lunge over the brink of the trail. It was agreed that we had all witnessed superb performances by three of the world's fastest gyppo loggers. Of particular interest was the fact that calked boots traveling at a high rate of speed throw up a fine spray of earth not unlike the plumes of water behind hydroplanes.

Harold Munster and his family moved away from town shortly after the last of his outfit wore off and I haven't seen him since, nor have I seen anything to match his masterpiece of low-fashion design. But if the Old Wilderness Outfitter had a lick of sense left, he would leave no stone unturned in his search for him.

Kid Camping

KIDS STILL DO GO CAMPING by themselves, I don't deny that. They just don't go *kid camping*.

A lot of people think that any camping kids do is kid camping just because kids are doing it. Well that's circular reasoning if I ever heard any. Nothing could be further from the truth. The kind of camping kids do nowadays is just plain adult camping—sans adults.

The kids use the same camp gear and provisions as their parents: featherweight sleeping bags, aluminum cook kits, nylon tents, dehydrated and vacuum-frozen foods, and even little plastic tubes to put their peanut butter and jelly in. The only exception is the family car, and *it* is used to haul the kids to the point of departure. They just don't get to drive.

Why it's enough to make an old-time kid camper roll over in his spaghetti-and-oatmeal omelet!

Properly executed, kid camping was like no other kind of camping known to man. I say "properly executed" because there was a code that governed every move. Any kid camper worth his can of pork 'n' beans knew the code by heart.

The code was not something that you learned, it was something you just *knew*—something you either had or you didn't have. And you never ever went against this thing that you knew. If you did, your camping was no longer kid camping but some other kind, and was divested of some peculiar aura of mystery and adventure.

Kid camping was a thing fairly choked in mystery. Part of the mystery was how a ninety-eight-pound boy who contracted an acute case of exhaustion carrying the dinner scraps out to the garbage pail could lug a four-hundred-pound pack three miles up a mountain trail laced with logs the size of railroad tank cars, and not even be winded. There was also the mystery of how three or four boys could consume every last moldering morsel of a food supply roughly estimated at a quarter ton and return home half starved.

One of the unspoken rules of the code (they were all unspoken) was that preparation for a camping trip should involve absolutely no planning. This, combined with an equal amount of organization, never failed to invest a trip with the proper mood—a deep and abiding sense of insecurity. There was a monumental apprehension that the food would give out an hour before the expedition arrived home and the whole party, fleeing back across the wasteland of the Crabtrees' stump pasture, would perish of starvation.

The only way of combating this dread of starvation was simply to carry enough food to feed Attila and his Huns adequately on an extended foray across Europe. It was assumed that each of the other guys would bring an equal amount.

The code allowed for only one store-bought item, the indispensable pork 'n' beans, which was the basic ingredient for all meals and most of the bad jokes. Wieners and marshmallows could also be purchased if the expedition was to be particularly arduous. These were generally regarded as condiments bearing the taint of Girl Scoutism, since it was known that no true mountain man would have been caught dead rotating a marshmallow over his blazing buffalo chips. The prospect of severe hardship, however, usually provided for a relaxation of the rules and the inclusion of a little morale-booster (the roasted marshmallow is the kid camper's peach brandy). Severe hardship was almost always prospected.

All other provisions had to be culled from the home pantry, cupboards, or refrigerator. This was known as "living off the land." The night before the expedition got underway, the young camper would enter the kitchen, gather his provisions, and depart, skillfully parrying the thrusts of his mother's broom handle with a leg of lamb. He would have tidied up the place to the point where it resembled a delicatessen looted by a Viking raiding party, and it is understandable that he would be surprised to discover that an irate troll had donned ol' Mom's clothes and was attempting to terminate his existence.

Provisioning a kid camping trip was very educational for a youngster. For one thing, it taught him the rudiments of lying. Take a typical situation. The kid would randomly select six or seven eggs from a dozen, boil them for exactly 135 minutes, and replace them randomly in the carton.

"Are you sure you'll be able to tell the boiled from the raw eggs?" his mother would ask.

"Of course," the kid would answer. Now that would be a blatant lie. He wouldn't have the slightest notion how to tell the boiled from the unboiled eggs.

Fortunately, this problem of the eggs always resolved itself. By the time the camper had hauled them over a mountain or two, he could safely assume that all eggs that had not oozed out of the pack and down his backside and legs were the cooked ones.

Kid camping allowed for no such effeminate things as dehydrated or vacuum-frozen foods. It was proof of one's manhood that he carried his food with all the water still in it.

After an hour or so of scrounging about (or "sacking," as some ill-tempered mothers called it) the kitchen, the young camper would have accumulated approximately the following provisions: a loaf of bread, a leg of lamb, a can of condensed cream, nine slices of bacon, a head of lettuce, a dozen eggs, a pint of salad dressing (for the lettuce), a quart jar of cherries, a pint of strawberry jam, three pieces of fried chicken, half a box of corn flakes, five pounds of sugar, ten pounds of flour, seven mealy apples, spaghetti, oatmeal, thirty-seven grapes, a plate of fudge, a jar of peanut butter, thirteen potatoes, a bottle of root beer, and a quart of milk (for the corn flakes).

Once assembled, all the provisions were carefully loaded into a packsack which acquired roughly the size, shape, and weight of an adolescent pachyderm. Then came the moment of truth. The young camper's jeering family would gather around to witness his attempt at raising the pack clear of the sagging floor, a feat that he accomplished with a prolonged grunt which could scarcely be heard by the neighbors three houses away. He would stand there—legs spraddled and beginning to cave, shoulders slowly collapsing into the shape of a folded taco shell—and drill the disbelievers with a disdainful look from his hard, squinty eyes. And it's damned hard to make your eyes squinty when they're bugged way out like that!

Most of the adventure in kid camping came from the cooking of exotic and original dishes. Eating them was even more adventurous. Some of the dishes were undoubtedly fit for human consumption, although the sight and aroma were generally enough to give a starving and unusually indiscriminate hyena a fit of the dry heaves.

There was, of course, that old favorite: fried pork 'n' beans accented with charred potato scraps dislodged from the bottom of the serve-all skillet. This was frequently accompanied by a side order of bacon, either still flaming or recently soused with a bucket of water.

There was the aforementioned spaghetti-and-oatmeal omelet, which made an excellent dessert when topped with catsup. It is true that most of the raw eggs would have leaked away before arrival at the campsite, but usually the bottom of the pack would retain a sizable puddle, which could be augmented by the egg squeezings from the change of underwear and the extra pair of socks. These eggs had the advantage of being prebeaten, something that cannot be said for the dehydrated kind.

It goes without saying that all dishes were

spiced with various curious, careless, and low-flying species of insects.

There was one rule of the code that no one ever mentioned but everyone adhered to, and that was that there was to be absolutely no praying on the camping trip. One time my regular fellow kid campers and I invited along a boy who lied and swore and smoked discarded cigarette butts and generally appeared to be a normal and respectable fellow. We were unutterably embarrassed by his crass display of character when, in the flicker of our dying campfire and the mirthful glow of the last bawdy joke, he knelt down by his sleeping bag, folded his hands, and said his prayers. In one fell swoop, he dealt a death blow to what otherwise showed promise of being a robust and pleasantly vulgar camping trip.

In all honesty, I must confess that I, too, once violated this particular tenet of kid camping. But I at least had the decency to do it discreetly and not in such a way as to unnerve my companions. As it happened, they were already unnerved enough.

In the middle of the night it suddenly came to our attention that a large and obviously famished bear had entered camp under the cover of darkness. He was making a terrible racket, whetting his appetite on our vast store of provisions, prior to getting on to the main course, which lay paralyzed in its sleeping bags and had all but ceased to breathe. The time had come, I realized, to invoke the aid of the Almighty, and immediately set about invoking. The next morning the other guys wrote the whole terrible affair off as a case of mistaken identity. Little did they know that it was due to my inspired efforts in our common behalf that the bear had been changed into a huge black cedar stump. The racket, they supposed, had been caused by a chipmunk assaulting a bag of potato chips. I never bothered to set them right.

Experiences like this provided the educational element in kid camping. For example, we learned that it is merely an old wives' tale that extreme fear will turn your hair snow white all over. Our hair was only a little gray about the temples, and that returned to its normal color four days later. I distinctly remember, because it was a short while after I got my voice back and just before the shaking died down to where it couldn't even be noticed from more than ten feet away.

Kid camping undoubtedly is a thing of the past, but perhaps somewhere back in the hinterlands there are a few rugged lads who practice the sport in its pure form. If there are, I must say they're mighty lucky— mighty lucky if they avoid ptomaine poisoning, permanent curvature of the spine, or growing into adults who break out in a purple rash and hysteria at the mere glimpse of a can of pork 'n' beans.

How to Fish
a Crick

THERE IS MUCH CONFUSION in the world today concerning creeks and cricks. Many otherwise well-informed people live out their lives under the impression that a crick is a creek mispronounced. Nothing could be farther from the truth. A crick is a distinctly separate entity from a creek, and it should be recognized as such. After all, a creek is merely a creek, but a crick is a crick.

The extent of this confusion over cricks and creeks becomes apparent from a glance at almost any map, where you will find that all streams except rivers are labeled as creeks. There are several reasons for this injustice. First, your average run-of-the-mill cartographer doesn't know his crick from his creek. The rare cartographer who does know refuses to recognize cricks in their own right for fear that he will be chastised by one of the self-appointed chaperons of the American language, who, like all other chaperons, are big on purity.

A case in point: One of the maps I possess of the State of Washington labels a small stream as *S. Creek*. Now I don't know for certain but am reasonably sure that the actual name of this stream is not *S*. No. Just by looking at the map one can tell that it is not shaped like an **S**, the only reason I can think of for giving it such a name. *S*. therefore must not be the full name but an abbreviation. Why was the name abbreviated? Was it too long or perhaps too difficult to pronounce? Since the map also contains such stream names as Similkameen and Humptulips and Puyallup, all unabbreviated, one would guess not. This leaves only one other possibility. The cartographers felt that the actual name of the stream was obscene. They did not want it said of them that they had turned out an obscene map, the kind of map sinister characters might try to peddle to innocent school children, hissing at them from an alleyway, "Hey, kid! Wanna buy a dirty map?"

Well, I can certainly sympathize with the cartographers' reluctance to author a dirty map. What irks me is that they use the name *S. Creek*. One does not have to be a mentalist to know that the fellow who named the stream *S*. did not use the word *creek*. He used *crick*. He probably saw right off that this stream he was up was a crick and immediately started casting about for a suitable name. Then he discovered he didn't have a paddle with him. Aha! He would name this crick after the most famous of all cricks, thereby not only symbolizing his predicament but also capturing in a word something of the crick's essential character.

The cartographers in any case chose to ignore this rather obvious origin of the name and its connotations in favor of a discreet *S*. and an effete *Creek*. If they didn't want to come right out and say *crick,* why couldn't they have had the decency just to abbreviate it with a *C.* and let it go at that.

Maybe I can, once and for all, clear up this confusion over cricks and creeks.

First of all a creek has none of the raucous, vulgar, freewheeling character of a crick. If they were people, creeks would wear tuxedos and amuse themselves with the ballet, opera, and witty conversation; cricks would go around in their undershirts and amuse themselves with the Saturday-night fights, taverns, and humorous belching. Creeks would perspire and cricks, sweat. Creeks would smoke pipes; cricks, chew and spit.

Creeks tend to be pristine. They meander regally through high mountain meadows, cascade down dainty waterfalls, pause in placid pools, ripple over beds of gleaming gravel and polished rock. They sparkle in the sunlight. Deer and poets sip from creeks, and images of eagles wheel upon the surface of their mirrored depths.

Cricks, on the other hand, shuffle through cow pastures, slog through beaver dams, gurgle through culverts, ooze through barnyards, sprawl under sagging bridges, and when not otherwise occupied, thrash fitfully on their beds of quicksand and clay. Cows should perhaps be credited with giving cricks their most pronounced characteristic. In deference to the young and the few ladies left in the world whose sensitivities might be offended, I forgo a detailed description of this characteristic. Let me say only that to a cow the whole universe is a bathroom, and it makes no exception of cricks. A single cow equipped only with determination and fairly good aim can in a matter of hours transform a perfectly good creek into a crick.

Now that some of the basic differences between creeks and cricks have been cleared up, I will get down to the business at hand, namely how to fish a crick.

Every angler knows how to fish a creek. He uses relatively light tackle and flies, and his attire consists of waders or hip boots, a fishing vest, creel, lightweight slacks, and a shirt in a tasteful check. The creek is worked artfully, with the fly drifting down like the first flake of winter snow. Everybody knows that's how you fish a creek.

But the crick, as I've pointed out, is an altogether different species of water and demands its own particular approach.

No fancy tackle of any kind is ever used to fish a crick. Since fiberglass rods came on the market, it is difficult to find a good crick pole. The old steel telescope rods were fairly good, but the best crick pole I've ever seen was one I owned as a kid. It consisted of a six-foot section of stiff pipe, with a piece of wire that pulled out from the tip to provide the action. Stores sold it as a fishing pole, but it could also serve fairly well as a lightning rod, fencepost, or a lever for prying a car out of the mud. Rod action, it should be noted, is of little importance in crick fishing, since the crick itself usually provides about all the action one can stand.

Hook size should never be less than No. 4, and leaders, if they are used at all, should be short and test about the same as baling wire. This saves a good deal of time, since if you hook up on an old log, tractor tire, or Model T submerged in the crick, as happens every third cast, you can simply haul it out and not have to bother replacing leader and hook. Sinkers must be large and fat in order not to frighten off the fish. If the splash is large enough, they think it's just another old log, tractor tire, or Model T being dumped in the crick. The reel should be an old bait-caster with the worm gear busted and the handle off. A crick reel, if you don't happen to own one, can be improvised by loaning a perfectly good creek reel to one of your kids for a period of one to five minutes.

The experienced crick fisher never wears hip boots or waders on a crick. Old oxfords with flappy tongues are all right, but tennis shoes in the final stages of decay are the first choice of crick fishers everywhere. Whatever shoes you select, they should have sizable holes both fore and aft. The holes allow for good circulation of the crick water through the shoe and help to cut down on the risk of fermentation of the feet. Another advantage is that the crick fisher can thrust his toes out through the holes and get a good grip on banks of submerged clay, rotting logs, old tractor tires, and Model T's.

The creel is shunned in crick fishing. All fish are carried on a forked stick, which adds immeasurably to the enjoyment of the sport. Most of this enjoyment comes from laying the forked stick down, forgetting it, and then spending several happy hours looking for it. Once the crick fisher tires of this pastime he usually vows to keep the stick in hand at all times. This brings into play the ultimate in crick-fishing skill, since the angler must now land his fish by taking up his slack line with his teeth and one ear, accomplished by a quick, dipping, circular motion of the head.

Flies, of course, are never used on a crick. The crick fish just gaffaw at them. They want real meat—fat, wiggling worms, grasshoppers on the hoof, and, occasionally, toes.

That pretty much covers the technique of crick fishing. Naturally one cannot expect to master it so quickly as creek fishing, unless, of course, he happens to be under the age of fourteen. Eight-year-olds are naturals at crick fishing, and if you have one handy you might take him out to a crick and observe him in action. Despite the opinion of all parents and most behavioral psychologists, eight-year-olds are good for something, and teaching the art of crick fishing is it.

At least once a year I try to fish Sand Crick, the crick of my youth. Admittedly, I have lost a good deal of my technique and most of my stamina but I still manage to have a good time. Usually I come back with a few fish, some good laughs, and a charley horse that extends from my trapezius to my peroneus longus.

Last summer my cousin Buck accompanied me, and I got one of those terrible scares that only crick fishing can give you. We had no more than started when Buck stepped into quicksand. It startled him so badly that he could only manage to get off three or four casts before total panic set in. The quicksand by then was halfway up to his knees.

"Hey," Buck said. "I don't think I'll be able to get out."

A cold chill shot through me. Not only was a lifelong friend and relative in peril but he was carrying the communal worm can.

"Quick," I yelled. "Toss me the worm can!"

"Nothing doing," Buck said. "Not till you drag me out of here."

I wasted a good ten minutes of fishing time getting him out of that quicksand. On the other hand, I probably would have used up more time than that digging a new batch of worms besides having to knock off a little early to tell his wife there was no point in waiting supper on him.

Incidentally, in order to prevent a similar emergency from occurring, I took the precaution of putting a handful of worms in my shirt pocket, where they were eventually discovered by my wife on washday. It is interesting to note that dehydrated worms cannot be reconstituted by even three cycles in an automatic washer. Also of interest is the fact that it is almost as difficult to reconstitute the wife who conducts the experiment. After such an occurrence, the wise though absentminded crick fisher should take care to eat all his meals out for several days, and in the unlikely event that the wife does offer him something to eat, he should first give a bite to the dog and observe the animal carefully for a couple of hours afterwards.

Buck and I fished a couple of miles of Sand Crick together that day, reminiscing every step of the way over our adventures as kids along this same crick. We came upon a half-submerged car, a 1937 Packard that someone had dumped in the crick under the pretext of preventing bank erosion but actually to be rid of a 1937 Packard. Buck drifted his line in through the gaping holes of the front windshield and hooked a fine Eastern brook out of the back seat.

"First time I ever caught anything in the back seat of a 1937 Packard," he said.

"I've never been that lucky," I said enviously, "but I came pretty close once in a '48 Hudson."

The last hole of the day was one known affectionately as The Dead Cow Hole. The particular cow that the hole was named after was one of the most malicious beasts ever to deface the banks of a crick. I don't know what the farmer called his cow but I know some of the names fishermen called her, always preceded by the same presumably accurate adjective. You always knew when a fellow planned on fishing the stretch of crick presided over by the cow, because he carried his fishing pole in one hand and an ax handle in the other. (Usually you could get in at least one good blow each time the cow galloped over the top of you.) Then one day the cow took ill and died, thus, or so I thought, effectively removing herself from action. The news reached me on a sweltering summer day, but nevertheless I made ready immediately to take advantage of the cow's misfortune. I scarcely touched the tops of the withered grass in my rush to get a line in the water.

As I neared the crick, however, I noticed a flock of magpies flying hurriedly in the opposite direction, and several of them, I observed, showed definite signs of nausea. At about the same time a hot, dry gust of wind criminally assaulted my olfactory nerves with such violence as to bring tears to my eyes.

"No!" I thought. "Could it be? Could she actually have been that fiendish?" The question was shortly answered in the affirmative. On peering down from the top of the hill above the crick, I could see her carcass ripening in the summer heat not ten yards from the fishing hole!

Evidently she had seen the end coming and rather than spend her last moments repenting her sins she had, with malice aforethought, used them to drag herself into a strategic position so that, even in death, she would dominate not only the immediate area of the fishing hole but four-hundred yards on all sides.

Several times I took a deep breath and tried to rush the hole but my wind always gave out before I could cover the distance. It was hopeless, at least for me. Cousin Buck did manage to fish Dead Cow Hole that same summer, and with considerable success apparently. He told me about it a week later and I believe he said he caught a couple of good fish. I couldn't be sure because he was still gagging so hard it was difficult to understand him.

That's the nature of crick fishing, though. Some people may not have the heart for it, or even the stomach, but for those who do, it has its rewards. They escape me at the moment, however.

Further Teachings of Rancid Crabtree

GRAM SLICED OFF four great slabs from a loaf of her homemade bread. She spread them with butter, piled on a couple pounds of ham, slices of onions, pickles, cheese, and the leftovers from the previous night's supper. Then she stuffed the sandwiches in a paper bag and thrust them into my hands.

"But I tell you I don't need food," I protested. "Rancid is going to teach me how to live off the land."

"Shoot," my grandmother said, waving a butcher knife at me. "That old fool don't know any more about livin' off the land than he does about workin'. Now take those sandwiches and don't give me any sass."

On my way over to Rancid's cabin, I stuffed the sandwiches down the front of my shirt, hoping he wouldn't notice I was carrying contraband.

"What you hidin' thar?" the old mountain man

said the instant he caught sight of me. "You got a water-melon under yer shart?"

"Naw," I answered, embarrassed. "Gram made me bring along a couple of sandwiches in case I got hungry."

Rancid hooted. "Thet ol' widder woman, when she gonna cut you loose from her apron strings and let you be a man?"

"I don't know," I said. "I told her you were going to teach me how to live off the land, but she pulled a knife and made me take the sandwiches anyway."

"Yup, she's a mean-un, all right," Rancid said. "Wall, them samwiches won't hurt nothin, and might come in handy in case we has an emergency."

I should explain that Gram and Rancid were natural enemies. Gram possessed all the qualities Rancid despised in a person. She was practical, hard-working, neat, clean, methodical, and never smoked, drank, or told lies. "She ain't hoomin," Rancid often complained. Gram claimed Rancid was the only person she had ever known who was totally lacking in charac-ter. By "character" she meant a tendency toward work. A man could rustle cows, steal chickens, and rob banks in his spare time, and Gram would say of him, "Rufus may have some bad ways, but I'll tell you this, he's a *good worker*. He ain't totally no good like some folks by the name of Rancid Crabtree I could mention, but I won't."

To Gram, being a good worker excused a lot of shortcomings, but it wasn't the sort of lifestyle that ap-pealed to me at the age of twelve. Since Rancid was the only person I'd ever known who hadn't once been caught redhanded in an act of holding a job, I figured he must have some secret, and I studied him the way other kids in school studied their arithmetic. Because he didn't work, Rancid always had time to give you, not just little pinched-off minutes but hours and days and even whole weeks. He was a fine example for a kid to pattern himself after.

On this particular day, Rancid and I were going to hike back in the mountains and spend the night in a lean-to we would build ourselves. All we would take with us were some fishline and hooks, some twine and our knives, and, as it turned out, the two four-pound sandwiches. The morning was one of those impeccable specimens found only in early July in the Rocky Mountains, particularly when it is only the twelfth July you have known in your life. That was back in the old days before environment had been discovered, and there were only trees and blue sky and water moving swift and clear. Hiking along behind the lean old woodsman, I listened to the soft humming of summer and paid attention to keeping my toes pointed Indian fashion as I spashed through the shallow pools of sunlight on the trail. It was a very pleasant day to start learning how to live off the land so I would never have to work.

We hiked hard for the first hour to shake off the last lingering shards of civilization, and then slowed our paces as the trail began winding up into the mountains. Far down below in the patchwork of fields, we could see the farmers wrestling with their hay crops. We laughed.

After a while, Rancid started giving me living-off-the-land lessons. The first thing he had me do was to smear my face with mud.

"This hyar mud will keep off the moss-kee-toos," Rancid explained.

I smeared on a copious quantity of mud, because if there was one thing in the world I was interested in keeping off, it was moss-kee-toos. I had heard
plenty about moss-kee-toos from Rancid before. They
were vicious flying creatures that sometimes would
swarm out of the woods and suck the blood from your
body. Since I had spent a good deal of time in the
woods and never seen a moss-kee-too, I hoped they were
merely a figment of Rancid's imagination. (His imagination was crammed with all sorts of weird and interesting
figments.) If moss-kee-toos did exist, the mud did a
good job of keeping them off. It even worked pretty
well on the mosquitoes.

Another rare creature apparently known only
to Rancid was the iggle. He pointed to a large bird circling high above the mountain peak. "Look thar, boy!
Thas a iggle." The bird was too high for me to make
out any of its features, but in the years since, I have
frequently seen high-flying birds that I assumed to be
iggles, so I'm pretty sure they exist. Rancid told me
that iggles were so big they often carried off half-grown
cows in their claws, and as a result were not much loved
by ranchers. "But hell," he said, "iggles got a right to
a livin' too."

Rancid had his own system of ornithological
classification. There were three basic groups of birds:
little birds, medium-sized birds, and big birds. A few
birds were referred to by their common names: ducks,
doves, grouse, pheasants, and iggles. Rancid's system of
ornithology worked just as well on identifying rarer
birds.

"What's that bird?" I would ask Rancid.

"Thet thar is what ya calls yer little black-and-
white bird with a red head," he would tell me authoritatively. I never ceased to marvel at how Rancid knew all

the different kinds of birds. Just by looking at them you could tell he knew what he was talking about.

Along about noon I began to feel the first pangs of hunger. I suggested to Rancid that maybe the time had come for us to knock off the nature study and start living off the land and if it wasn't too much trouble I'd like to take a look at the lunch menu. Rancid looked around the land.

"Ah figured we'd have huckleburries fer lunch, but they's still green. The wild razzburries should be ripe up in the meadows, though. Fer the time bein', whyn't you give me one of them samwiches yer granny packed?"

"Who do you take me for, Mother Nature?" I said angrily. "You're supposed to teach me how to live off the land."

"Don't gitcher tail in a knot," Rancid said. "Livin' off the land takes a powerful lot of thinkin', and ah thinks better if ah'm chompin' on a samwich. Now what did thet ol' widder woman fix us?"

We split one of the sandwiches, and sure enough, Rancid started thinking better. "As soon as we gets done with lunch, we better find us some mushrooms to cook with our game for supper. Thar's a burn up ahead and we kin probably find some mushrooms thar."

I was a bit worried about the mushrooms, since my grandmother had told me Rancid didn't know his fungi from a hole in the ground.

"Gram says one good way to tell if a mushroom ain't poisonous is to see if the deer have been eating them," I offered.

"Thet's the dumbest thing ah ever hear'd tell of," Rancid said with disgust. "Deer don't know much more than yer granny does. Mushrooms is little wrinkled pointy things, and toadstools is all the rest. Deer eat toadstools all the time and it don't bother 'em none. A hoomin bean eat a toadstool, the fust thang he knows he's knockin' on the Parly Gate with one hand and still pickin' his teeth with t' other."

Fortunately, we were unable to find any mushrooms in the burn, although I did happen to come across a patch of little wrinkled pointy things not worth the trouble of calling to Rancid's attention.

The raspberries in the high mountain meadow were ripe, as Rancid had predicted, but not especially plentiful. Nevertheless, I got a keen sense of living off the land from eating them. Rancid explained at considerable length how to pick and eat wild raspberries, and seemed very pleased with himself. "Lots of folks don't know wild razzburries is good to eat," he said. I personally had never encountered anyone who didn't know they were good to eat, but I didn't say anything.

"Gram says even cattails are good to eat," I offered.

"Ha!" Rancid laughed. "Thet silly ol' woman, it's a wonder she's lived to be a hunnert and five, what with all her notions about eatin' pisonous plants."

"I don't think she's that old," I said.

"Thet just goes to show you," Rancid said. "Now don't let me hear no more of thet talk about eatin' cattails."

Next Rancid showed me how to set snares for rabbits, an absolute essential for anyone intending to live off the land. Although I knew the basic principle and technology of snares, I never quite understood how you induced the game to stick his head into the loop and trigger the contraption.

"How do you know the rabbit is going to run

into the snare?" I asked, peering intently over Rancid's shoulder as he worked. "He's got a million other places to run."

"Wall, fust of all, you have to be smarter than the rabbit," he said with a chuckle. "You got to be smarter than the rabbit. Now hep me move these logs and rocks. What we is gonna do is funnel thet ol' rabbit right into our snare, see?"

We dragged rocks and logs and tree limbs and brush and piled them up in a giant open-ended V that pointed right at the snare. By the time the V was finished, both of us were so hot and tired we were staggering, but I didn't complain because I was learning how to live off the land so I would never ever have to work.

After we had rested a while, Rancid said, "Now hyar's what you do. You climb down behind thet thicket over thar and make a racket so that you drive the rabbits into the funnel."

"How come we both don't climb down and make a racket?" I asked.

" 'Cause ah have to sit on thet log up thar and shoosh any rabbits thet come thet way back into the snare."

"Why can't I do that and you drive the rabbits out?"

Rancid thought a moment, mopping the sweat off his face with his shirt sleeve. "You had any experience shooshing wild rabbits?"

"No."

"Wall, thar you are! Now git yerself down in the thicket and start making a racket."

"A half-hour later I emerged from the thicket. Rancid was sitting on the log, his elbows resting on his knees, staring vacantly down at the snare. "How . . . *pant* . . . big a one . . . *pant pant* . . . did we catch?" I asked, sinking to the ground.

Rancid rolled a chaw of tobacco around in his cheek. "Wall, ah kin say one thang about these blankety-blank rabbits. They is powerful smart!"

"You mean to say we didn't catch any?"

"What would you think about chompin' down some nice tender trout roasted over a fahr?" Rancid said brightly. "Don't thet sound good!"

Early in the afternoon we arrived at a little lake tucked away between two mountain peaks. Rancid cut two willow poles and tied fishline to them. Then we started looking around for grubs to bait the hooks with. As Rancid said, you can never find a grub when you really need one. Savagely, we tore apart rotted logs looking for grubs, the essential link between us and a fish supper. I was beginning to think working might be easier than living off the land.

At last we found a small deposit of grubs, tossed them into Rancid's hat and hurried back down to the lake. By the time we got there, the grubs were choking and gagging but otherwise in good shape. The trout brazenly committed grand larceny on most of our bait supply but we managed to land a couple of eight-inchers.

"Now ah'm gonna show you how to build a fahr without matches," Rancid said. He made a little bow-and-stick contraption of the sort I had seen in my Boy Scout handbook. The handbook, however, had not indicated all the good words you were supposed to say in order to get a fire going. Rancid sawed the little bow furiously back and forth on the stick, the spinning of which was supposed to ignite a little pile of shavings. It was all very complicated, and Rancid sweated and panted and swore until his eyes bugged out even more than usual. At last a little curl of smoke drifted up from the shavings. Rancid threw down the bow, dropped on his belly and started blowing on the shavings, whereupon the curl of smoke instantly vanished. He rolled over on his back and crumpled the bow and stick in his hands. "Let this be a lesson to you, boy. Don't never go out in the woods without a fistful of matches."

"That's what Gram told me," I said. "She made me bring a bunch of matches even though I told her we wouldn't be needing them."

"Gol-dang know-it-all ol' woman! Gimmie one of them matches!"

In a second Rancid had a fire going. His hands were shaking from exhaustion and rage as he built a little willow grill to cook our fish on. As the flames licked around the two little trout, Rancid stared moodily into the fire.

"When we gonna build the lean-to?" I asked.

"Don't bother me about no lean-to," he growled. He seemed a bit surly, so I decided not to pursue the subject.

Then the two fish slipped through the grill into the fire. I stepped back, sneaking a glance at Rancid's face. His eyes, widening slightly, stared at the bits of blackened skin on the willow grill. A tiny quiver ran the length of his lower lip.

After a long moment of silence, Rancid said, "We best eat thet last samwich, 'cause we is gonna need lots of energy."

"To build the lean-to?" I asked.

"No," he said. "So we kin walk real fast. Ah figures if we leave now we kin get back to yer house in time for supper."

"Gram said she'd set a couple places for us," I

said, "even though I tried to tell her we'd be gone all night."

"Thet ol' know-it-all," Rancid said. "Ah wonder what's she's fixin' fer supper anyhow. Ah shore hope it ain't gonna be a mess of pisonous cattails!"

The Great Cow Plot

WHEN I CAME IN from fishing the other day, my wife asked, "Have any luck?"

"Great," I said. "I saw only two cows and got away from both of them."

I hadn't caught any fish, but that was beside the point. The success or failure of my fishing trips depends not upon the size of the catch but the number of cows encountered.

Some people do most of their fishing on lakes or the ocean, where cows are seldom if ever encountered. Most of my fishing is done in cow pastures, the natural habitat of cows.

Even when I plan a fishing trip forty miles back into the wilderness a herd of cows will usually get wind of it and go on a forced march to get there before I do and turn the place into a cow pasture. Sometimes the cows get the word a little late, and I'll pass them on the way. Invariably a few of the poor losers will gallop along in front of the car, still trying to get there ahead of me and do what they can on short notice and empty stomachs.

"I've given up hope of finding any place to fish where a cow won't manage to show up and put in her oar. If I was in the pet shop on the nineteenth floor of a department store and stopped to net a guppy out of an aquarium, a cow would get off the elevator and rush over to offer advice.

My wife insists that I've become paranoiac from overexposure to cows. She tries to tell me that the intricate and near-impenetrable patterns of cow spoor laid down around my favorite fishing holes are a result of nothing more than random chance. Even granting high probability from the number of placements per square yard, which is altogether ample, I remain unconvinced that these bovine mine fields are not the product of conspiracy and cunning. There's probably a small island in the Caribbean where cows are given a six-week course in the design and manufacture of mine fields before being turned out to pasture alongside fine trout streams. The whole thing is a plot by Castro to lower our national morale.

All cows are fishing enthusiasts, although their idea of fishing might better be described as "Chase the Fisherman." The object of the sport is to see how many times the fisherman can be made to cross the creek. Five points are earned if he wades across, ten points if he splashes only once, and twenty-five if he hurls himself across without touching the water. The last is achieved by first running him twice around the pasture to pick up momentum and then making a straight shot for the creek. This maneuver is usually good for a score, providing the fisherman can be driven past the other team's goalie.

As fishing enthusiasts, cows can be divided roughly into two groups: participants and *aficionados*. Another grouping I find useful is simply Fast Mean Cows (FMC) and Slow Mean Cows (SMC). The SMC, mediocre athletes at best, are usually content to watch the main events between the FMC and fishermen (thus the expression "contented cows"). They participate only to the extent of doing everything in their power to ruin an otherwise good running turf, apparently in the belief that a slow field improves the spectator sport. The FMC are frequently referred to as "bulls." The term is usually preceded by harsh but accurately descriptive adjectives. It is sometimes argued that "bulls" is not an appropriate term for FMC since some of them are known to give milk. I disagree. Upon hearing the shout "Here comes a ———— bull!" I have yet to see any of my companions wait around to argue over the sex of the beast.

No effective cow repellent has ever been developed for the comfort of fishermen. Simply from the standpoint of size alone, one would think that cow repellent would have priority over mosquito repellent. I don't know if it would work, but someone with a knack for chemistry might try distilling and bottling the aroma of a well-done sirloin.

The only thing that bulls have any respect for at all is the stick, and many knowledgeable cow-pasture fishermen carry one slipped under their belt for easy access in an emergency. This is known as the "bull stick" or sometimes simply "BS." When the bull approaches, the BS is first waved threateningly in the air and then thrown. (This is not to be confused with the BS thrown by hunters.)

A couple of fishermen I know like to brag about their narrow escape from a grizzly bear, *Ursus horribilis,* but I'm not impressed. A man just hasn't done any real escaping until he has escaped from a grizzly cow, *Bovinus horribilis.* I am probably the world's leading authority on the subject, having studied it since my childhood days.

In my mind's eyes, now somewhat astigmatic but Wide Screen and Tru-Color, I see myself as a young boy, fishing pole in one hand, worm can in the other, making my way down to the creek. My phlegmatic and flatulent old dog, Stranger, is close upon my bare heels and close upon his heels is our neighbor's bull, known in those parts as The Bull, and we are all running to beat hell. Stranger, his jaws set in a grim smile, runs between me and The Bull not out of any sense of loyalty or protection but because of old age and a shortness of breath. Arriving at the fence the dog and I hurl ourselves into the sanctuary beyond and The Bull screeches to a stop in a cloud of dust and slobber just short of the wire. Stranger, sweat streaming down his face, pulls himself together long enough to take credit for once again having saved my life—"Well, bailed you out of another bad spot didn't I?"—and then he and The Bull stand on opposite sides of the fence and say cruel and obscene things to each other while I ignore them and get on with the day's fishing.

Why did I risk frequent confrontations with such a malevolent creature as The Bull? The reason is one that perhaps only a trout fisherman would understand. Little Sand Creek was a great trout stream, probably one of the finest in the nation at that time, but with the humility of all the truly great it meandered its regal course through a series of humble and unpretentious—not to say miserable—farms, one of which was ours. The stream was fished with such ardor and love and perseverance by so many anglers that by mid-season any worthwhile trout who had survived the onslaught would strike at nothing that did not show obvious signs of life and then only after taking its pulse. That section of the stream which ran through the farm owned and operated by The Bull, however, remained virtually untouched—except, of course, by me, known affectionately throughout the region as "That Fool Kid."

These sorties across the pasture were not nearly so hazardous as the chance observer might suppose. The Bull's top speed was a good deal faster than mine, no doubt because he didn't have to carry a fishing rod and a can of worms or worry about his dog's heart. But we had the element of surprise on our side, and by the time The Bull caught sight of us we already would be well accelerated. If The Bull closed the gap too quickly, I would jettison rod and worms, and Stranger would jettison everything he could, and we would give it our all, every man for himself, right up to the fence, and hurl ourselves over, under or through the barbed wires. Such instances were rare, however, and most of the time we could get through the fence in a manner that was more dignified and much less painful.

I learned a great deal about plane geometry from these exercises with The Bull. I discovered that the shortest distance between two points is a straight line, an idea that The Bull either could not fathom or he was reading Einsteinian theory in his spare time. At any rate, he almost always ran in a long, arching curve. This resulted from his knowing nothing about leading a moving target; he always held dead on. Consequently, a diagram of our converging lines of motion would show his course as a long curved line intersecting and merging with my short straight line. Successful evasion thus was largely a matter of predicting, given the proper angles, distances, relative speeds, and variable handicaps, the point at which our two converging lines of motion would intersect. As I say, I was a master of such calculations. My talent went wholly unrecognized, however, and people continued to refer to me as "That Fool Kid."

It came to pass that my widowed mother took up with a man and married him, offering the feeble excuse that "the boy needed a father." Both she and I knew that was an out-and-out lie. She had pulled off a clever coup d'etat, designed to deprive me of my place of power and authority over the family, which I had been ruling with a firm but just hand since the age of eight. The mercenary imported to depose me proved to be a tough customer, and I saw that I would have to play it cool and watch for the main chance. It came sooner than I expected. Hank, as he was called, one morning sent a peace feeler in my direction: "Don't know of a spot where we could catch some fish, do you?" he asked.

Well, it seemed like no time at all before the mercenary and I were standing at the fence to The Bull's pasture. I thought it best to warn him. "That ol' cow out there seems to be lookin' our way," I said.

"That ain't no cow," the mercenary said. "That's a bull. But land, boy, you don't have to be afraid of a bull. All you gotta do is show 'im who's boss."

It seemed a comfort to him to see me smile, the first time since being deposed. What he didn't notice was that Stranger and The Bull were smiling too. It became kind of an "in" joke, afterwards. That is, after the mercenary had climbed through the fence and demonstrated to all of us just who was boss. It turned out that the boss was just exactly who I and Stranger and The Bull had known all along was boss.

The mercenary, we smugly observed, wasn't much of a hand at fighting bulls. On the other hand, he proved to be the best broken-field runner ever to hit our county. To this day I have never seen a grown man who could run so fast, even one who wasn't carrying a fishing rod and creel, and wearing hipboots. A kid just had to admire a man who could run like that.

From then on Hank and I and Stranger ran from The Bull together, and we went far afield and ran from other bulls and sometimes cows and even whole herds of cows, and we forgot all about power and authority and the like. We were willing to risk the wrath of any cow who stood guard over a stretch of good fishing water, and it wasn't long before we were being referred to as "That Fool Kid and That Fool Man." But we paid her no mind; she had her hands full, what with being the head of the family and all.

The Mountain Man

MY CHIEF CAREER AMBITION as a youngster was to be a mountain man, but somehow it never worked out. I'm not sure why.

One problem was my family. They were dead set against the idea of my going into the fur trade, and never passed up an opportunity to point out the drawbacks of the profession.

My grandmother had actually known some real mountain men back in the old days, but she had never taken a liking to them. She said they drank and swore and spit tobacco and never took baths and fought and bragged and lied all the time. I don't recall, however, that she ever mentioned what was bad about them.

"There ain't no money in bein' a mountain man," Gram would tell me. She was fond of pointing out that she had never known a mountain man who was the proprietor of the basest vessel of domesticity and personal hygiene. Her exact words escape me at the moment.

I was all for leaving school and getting started in the fur trade as soon as possible, but my mother wouldn't hear of it. She said I would have to wait until I was through the third grade or reached the age of eighteen, whichever came first. "It's the law," she would say. The suggestion was put forth that we might find a loophole in the law if we looked hard enough, but Mom said she didn't think it was proper for a third-grade teacher to be putting forth suggestions like that.

My older sister, who liked to boast that she knew how to turn small boys into frogs and offered me as evidence, was always there to put in her oar and rile the waters of argument.

"You can't be a mountain man," she would say. "You're afraid of the dark."

Well, I certainly didn't see how she knew so much about what mountain men were afraid of and what they weren't. There were probably plenty of mountain men who were afraid of the dark, even though the length of their expeditions into the wilderness may have been somewhat limited by the handicap. One could easily imagine a grizzled old trapper asking, "Any sign of beaver a half-day's ride from the fort?"

In spite of these difficulties, I persisted in preparing myself for a career in the mountain man profession. Every spare moment was spent either in the library extracting the theory from books or out in the woods conducting laboratory experiments.

One thing I learned from the books was that a mountain man had to master three basic skills if he wanted to survive in the wilds. He had to know how to squint his eyes just right, spit through his teeth, and say dry, humorous things anytime he was in pain or danger. (You'd be surprised how difficult it is to think of something dry and humorous to say when, for example, a big furry beast is eating one of your legs.) Much time was spent perfecting squinting and spitting, and I learned that it's easy to say dry if not humorous things after one has spent the day spitting through his teeth.

I had at my disposal about forty-seven rusty traps, which I kept in a neat snarl in our woodshed. From time to time, I would go out and practice setting these traps. It almost never failed that the practice session would end with a trap snapping shut on one portion or another of my anatomy. Now it was part of the mountain man code that you could never cry when caught by one of your own traps, but there was no rule against doing as much loud yelling as you wanted, particularly if you were a mountain man who didn't know how to swear well enough to do a trapped finger much good. Quite often I would become confused on these occasions and go about for some time afterwards squinting my teeth and spitting through my eyes. I could always think of something dry and humorous to say, but it was usually about three days later, and I wasn't sure if that counted.

Besides the traps, I practiced a lot with snares. Since beavers seldom if ever passed through our yard, I impressed my crotchety old dog, Strange, into service. I would rig up a snare outside his house, where he would be sleeping off a night of drunken debauchery. Then I would raise some kind of racket until he staggered out asking for tomato juice and a little peace and quiet, and the snare would close limply around his neck. He would curse me roundly and lunge back into his den of iniquity, dragging the snare with him to be chewed up at his leisure and when his stomach felt better.

The only deadfall I ever constructed utilized an old railroad tie and almost ended the promising career of one of my mother's laying hens. The hen survived the ordeal, but for some time we had the distinction of owning the only flat chicken in the neighborhood. I exhausted my entire supply of ingenuity proposing theories about how a four-pound chicken could manage to crawl under a hundred-pound railroad tie. To this day I'm not sure how she could have triggered the contraption, unless perhaps she was standing under it running tests on the engineering.

One area of information about mountain men that caused me a good deal of confusion was buffalo chips. From my extensive reading on the subject, I knew that mountain men preferred this fuel above all others. The books never came right out and said what buffalo chips were, nor did they give any recommendations about the proper procedure for chipping a buffalo. One thing for certain, it would be dang hard work chipping one of the ornery critters. It was no wonder to me that buffalo were all the time stampeding the way they did, what with mountain men constantly hacking their fuel supply off of them.

When I eventually learned the true nature of buffalo chips, I could scarcely believe it. I had known all along that mountain men were tough but not just how tough.

Most mountain men died off back in the nineteenth century, once again displaying their uncommon good sense but also depriving students of the profession, such as myself, of live models to pattern themselves after. From time to time, someone would attempt to pass himself off to me as a mountain man, but I always found him out. One of these impostors was my older cousin Buck, who was big and husky and had perfected all the mannerisms of the mountain man. He was a good squinter and spitter and spoke mountain man passingly well. He liked to say things like, "Fetch us some water, ol' hoss, and ah'll build us a fahr and bile up some coffee."

For a long time, Buck had me fooled. Then one day we went fishing up Hoodoo Canyon, a place that is spooky even in daylight. We fooled around most of the day, catching a few trout, poking at tracks, studying bent blades of grass, squinting and spitting, saying dry, humorous things, and the like, and before I knew it, I had broken a long-standing promise to myself, which was never to get caught up in Hoodoo Canyon after dark. I comforted myself with the thought that I was in the company of a trained and knowledgeable mountain man. Then I glimpsed Buck's face. I knew without having to ask that he had just broken a long-standing promise to himself.

We started picking our way down the overgrown trail at a pace Buck referred to as a dogtrot, even though I personally have never been acquainted with a dog that could trot that fast. As we dogtrotted along, leaping logs four feet in the air without having to speed up, I began to get the impression we were being followed. Buck received the report of this news with no great enthusiasm, but he stopped to size up the situation. After all, if you are being tracked by something large and hairy, it's a good idea to know how large and how hairy. Every true mountain man knows that the worst thing you can do is let your imagination drive you into a panic. You want to look at your situation coldly and realistically, and that's exactly what Buck and I were doing when a long, cold and very realistic scream drifted down off the mountain above us. As sounds go, it registered right up near the top of the hideous scale.

(The only time I had heard anything like it was when a small, harmless snake managed to sneak into our house and hide in the drawer where my sister kept her underwear.)

"Whazzat?" I asked, attempting to feign idle curiosity.

Buck was silent. Then, drawing upon his vast knowledge, he identified the sound.

. "That was a blinkety-blank *scream!*" he said, thereby confirming my worst suspicions.

No more had this been said than there was the sound of a large animal bolting off down the canyon, snapping off young lodgepole pine like they were matchsticks, bounding over huge logs, smashing its way blindly through thickets, snorting, grunting, and wheezing for all it was worth. It took several seconds before I realized the large animal was Buck.

Although I was fully sympathetic with his motives, I simply could not accept Buck's undignified departure from Hoodoo Canyon as being consistent with the calm, cool manner of a mountain man. His abandoning of his loyal partner in a time of danger was also a serious infraction of the rules. That the loyal partner, despite a late start and short legs, managed to beat him out of the mouth of the canyon by a good forty yards in no way mitigated the offense, at least in my judgment.

My early training as a mountain man has stood me in good stead over all the years I've spent prowling about the wilds on one pretext or another. But in the end, I failed to become a full-time, card-carrying mountain man. The obstacles seemed to increase as the years went by, and there's no question that a mountain man today would have a hard time of it. First of all, he would have difficulty finding a mountain unadorned with ski lodges, condominiums, television towers, and the like. Then he would have to carry a briefcase for all his licenses, registrations, permits, draft and social security cards, health insurances and so on, and that would take a lot of the fun out of it. There would be all the hassles with the fish and game departments, and the Forest Service would be forever flying over and spraying him with one kind of pesticide or another. The USFS recreation officers would probably hound him to use the prepared campsites for his own safety (he might get himself clearcut up on the mountains), and providing he could even find a few buffalo chips to ignite, he would have to run the risk of getting doused with a bomber load of fire retardant.

It's probably just as well that I never became a mountain man. Still, some days on the streets of the city, dodging stampedes of taxis and herds of muggers, squinting my eyes just right against the smog, side-stepping dog chips, and all the time trying to think of something dry and humorous to say, I frequently wonder where I went wrong.

The Rescue

THERE ARE PEOPLE who constantly look as if they are in dire need of help. I am one of them.

Men, women and children, and even scraggly dogs are forever coming up to me to ask if they might be of some assistance. I don't mind if I'm in some sort of real trouble. Usually, though, my predicament is nothing more serious than waiting on a street corner for the light to change, or perhaps trying to look disinterested while the service station attendant tries to remember what he did with the key.

Once I was standing in front of a candy-vending machine, trying to decide between a Nut Crunchy and a Whang-O Bar. A pert young lady came up and asked if she might be of service. I said no, that I had already decided on a Whang-O. You could tell from the look on her face that she was disappointed at having arrived too late to help with the decision. If I'm not mistaken, she went off in a bit of a huff.

Even when I'm at home people are constantly offering me aid and comfort. The other morning I was staring vacantly out the window, a hobby I personally find more entertaining than, say, stamp collecting or golf.

"What's the matter?" my wife asked.

"Nothing," I said. "Why?"

"You're staring vacantly out the window." Her tone suggested that this is an activity engaged in only by persons on the verge of leaping feet first into the garbage disposal. "What's the matter?"

In order to bring a brief but merciful end to the discussion, I made up a mildly risque cock-and-bull story about a premonition, the villain of which was a sadistic crocodile.

"But why do you keep staring out the window like that?" she persisted.

"I'm watching for the SOB!" I told her.

Not only am I not free to stare vacantly out one of my own windows, I'm afraid even to go outside and lie down on my own grass. If I did, one of the neighbors would call an ambulance for me or, worse yet (with a couple of notable exceptions), rush over and try to give me mouth-to-mouth resuscitation.

Now that's the sort of thing that happens to me around my own home, on city streets, and in office buildings. If I wander anywhere off the beaten paths, my would-be rescuers become so numerous they have to circle me in holding patterns in order to await their turns.

When a hunter meets another hunter in the woods, he will usually greet him with some inoffensive remark like, "Any luck?" or "How ya doin'?" and let it go at that. With me, other hunters instantly assume I am lost, injured, or being sought by the Mafia. They launch into intricate directions on how I can make my way to the nearest road, hospital, or hiding place. If I didn't deal somewhat firmly with them, they would boil me a pot of soup, set my leg in a splint, and carry me piggyback to my car.

Even my hunting partners of long years standing are quick to assume that if I'm out of sight, I'm lost. Such an assumption is entirely unfounded. Occasionally I will discover that a road or trail or mountain is not where I last left it, but that is not my fault. If a mountain wishes to change its location, there is nothing I can do to prevent it.

On a hunting trip a few years ago I spent most of the day looking for a road that had mysteriously moved. Upon finding another road, I made my way down to the highway and walked to the nearest diner, where I ordered myself a steak dinner. No sooner had I been served than one of my hunting partners burst into the diner and shouted that he needed some men for a search party to look for some poor devil who was lost in the mountains. I immediately made my steak into a sandwich and stood up to offer my services. It turned out I was the fellow I was supposed to search for. Such incidents are embarrassing.

I should like to make clear here that I am no more incompetent or susceptible to trouble than the average person, no matter what my friends might say. I have managed pretty much on my own to survive a big-league depression, numerous recessions, creeping inflations, and even a couple of phases. I have never been tested in military combat, but I did spend several years teaching English composition to college freshmen. As a police reporter, I had experiences that would give a grave robber goose bumps and a hungry hyena a fit of the dry heaves. I offer this bit of personal history as evi-

dence that I am not totally helpless and inexperienced;
I just look that way.

From years of almost constant rescuing I have arrived
at the firm conviction that if one can possibly avoid
being rescued he should by all means do so. As a rule,
suffering the consequences of one's predicament is
preferable to the risks of being rescued.

One day last summer I had fished a couple of
miles of mountain stream and was just starting to hoof
it back up the road to my car when a pickup truck
pulled up alongside and stopped. Two men and a
woman were in the front seat. A load of firewood was
stacked high in the back of the truck.

"You look plumb wore out," one of them said
despite the fact that I felt quite fresh and vigorous, and
was enjoying the little hike. "Hop onto the wood back
there and we'll give you a lift."

The speaker was one of those burly, broad-
shouldered types—unshaven, voice like a bass drum, and
hard, squinty eyes. The two men weren't exactly cream-
puffs either. I knew they would brook no nonsense about
my declining to be rescued, so I climbed up on top the
firewood. The wood was split into large chunks, each of
which was equipped with an abundance of edges approximately as sharp as the blade of a skinning knife.
I eased myself down on the fewest number possible, attempting through an act of will to keep most of my
weight suspended in air.

Now almost everyone knows that it is impossible to drive a pickup load of firewood sixty miles an
hour over a washboard road. The driver of the truck
proved to be one of the few persons in the world not in
possession of this knowledge. The blocks of wood be-

gan to dance around and I began to dance around with them and sometimes the wood was on top and sometimes I was. One hefty chunk did a nifty little foxtrot along the left side of my rib cage while another practiced the tango with my hip bone. A clownish piece of tamarack went past wearing my hat, and six or seven other chunks were attempting to perform the same trick with my waders and fishing vest. Still, I didn't want to yell out any of the choice phrases blossoming in my head for fear of offending my rescuers. (There is nothing worse than an offended rescuer.) By the time we reached a car ("This is it!" I yelled out.), I felt as though I had spent the day participating in an avalanche.

Some of the minor rescues are only slightly less disastrous. I am perfectly capable of negotiating barbwire fences on my own, and on occasions—particularly in pastures with resident bulls—have done so with considerable speed. Nevertheless it frequently happens that a complete stranger will be standing next to a fence which I must climb through, and he will insist upon holding up the wire for me. It almost never fails that this kindly chap immediately reveals himself to have either exceptionally bad timing, a perverted sense of humor, or a handgrip slightly weaker than that of a deep-fried prawn.

Then there are the direction-givers. I am convinced that there are people who, upon hearing that I am trying to find out how to get to Lost Lake, would climb out of an oxygen tent and run barefooted three miles through the snow for the opportunity of giving me directions to it. Now I would appreciate this sacrifice on their part except for one thing: not only have they never been to Lost Lake in their lives, they didn't even know it existed until they heard I wanted to go there. But I shouldn't be too harsh on these people. Even though I don't find Lost Lake by following their directions I do discover some truly great swamps, vast stretches of country distinguished by a total absence of water, campsites with rock-to-rock rattlesnakes, and sometimes a little mountain valley inhabited only by a family of giant bears, all of whom are suffering from acute irritability.

There are times, of course, when I actually have need of rescue. One of these times occurred last fall on Lake Pend Oreille. Mort Haggard and I had stalled our outboard in the middle of the lake just as we noticed the thin black line of a storm edging toward us. There is only one sensible way to ride out a storm on Lake Pend Oreille and that is astride a barstool in the nearest resort. With this object in mind, we were taking turns flailing away on the pull cord when the damn thing broke. The storm was just about upon us and I got out a can and started bailing as fast as I could. We weren't taking any water over the sides yet, but the bottom of the boat was awash in cold sweat.

There was only one other boat in sight and we hailed it by gesturing with our arms in a fashion that the casual observer might have supposed to be frantic. We also loudly repeated the word "help" at regular intervals of a half second and in a somewhat shrill pitch so as to be heard above the wind.

The two occupants of the other boat responded promptly to these signals, and soon had pulled their rather sleek craft up alongside our rather dumpy one. They were husband and wife, both up in their seventies, lean as lances and deeply tanned. The man was conservatively dressed in bib overalls and his wife wore a long flowery dress. Both of them looked safe enough.

Mort and I immediately made the mistake common to persons being rescued, which is to defer in all matters of logic and common sense to the rescuers, the assumption being that because a person is at this moment displaying a keen sense of goodwill, he is therefore not (a) a madman, (b) an imbecile, or (c) a mugger on vacation. Our rescuers, it turned out, were none of these three. They were something else.

"Can you give us a tow to shore?" I shouted at them.

"Oh not too good," the old man said. "We caught two or three earlier, but they was pretty small."

Mort and I grinned uncomfortably and shot nervous glances at each other and the storm.

"Clifford's a mite hard of hearing," said the woman, whose name, we learned, was Alma. "THEY WANT A TOW TO SHORE!" Alma said to Clifford.

"Fine, fine," Clifford said. "You fellas just grab ahold on the side of our boat and we'll tow you in."

This suggestion did not seem to be one of the ten best ideas I had ever heard.

"Don't you think it would be better to rig up a tow line?" I asked.

"They was all silvers," Clifford said. "But they was small."

Mort and I took another look at the storm and grabbed the side of their boat.

Clifford eased out on the throttle and the two boats began to move. There was a good chop on the water now, and the sky was black. Mort and I clung to the side of the other boat as if it were the brink of an eighty-foot cliff.

Clifford let out on the throttle a bit more, pulling Mort and me over on our sides. We wrapped our legs around the seats and locked our ankles together. Our rib cages began to simulate the action of an accordion in a rock band. Charley horses began to gallop up and down my arms.

Clifford eased out on the throttle a bit more, and Mort began to emit a low, continuous moan, which he politely attempted to disguise as humming. "Hummghh, hummghh," he went.

Clifford eased out on the throttle still a bit more, and the bows of both boats were out of the water. Our fishing lines snapped into the air and trailed out behind us like silver streamers in the wind.

"Hey, Cliff," I yelled through the plume of spray. "How about slowing it down some?"

He smiled down at me. "Yup," he said. "They was all small."

Alma meanwhile had taken a liking to Mort and was attempting to engage him in conversation. She had moved over next to him and was shouting down into his free ear, the one not scrunched into an oarlock.

"Bet you can't guess how long we've lived in these parts, can you, young man?" she asked.

"Yes ma'm," said Mort, always the gentleman. "Hummmgh, hummmgh!"

"You can? How long then?"

"Yes ma'm," Mort said. "Hummmmgh, hummmmgh!"

"We've lived here seventy-odd years now, and let me tell you, we've seen some powerful hard times," Alma said, apparently not realizing that she was seeing one of them right then.

"Yes ma'm," Mort said. "Hummmgh, hummmgh."

We smacked into a huge wave. One moment the other boat was above us, Mort and I holding up there, and the next it was down below, dangling from our aching arms, and all of us still going like sixty. Then the two boats began to go their separate ways. Mort and I wrenched them back together, shouting out a rousing chorus from an old sea chanty frequently sung by sailors as they were being keelhauled.

"Thought we was going to lose you for a minute there," Clifford yelled over at us with a grin.

"Yes ma'm," Mort said. "Hummmmgh, hummmmgh!"

When we were once again standing safely on the dock, which didn't seem like a day over three weeks, Mort turned philosophical about the whole adventure. "Look at it this way," he said. "First of all, we probably never would have survived that storm if we hadn't been rescued. Second, we're standing here on the dock soaking our hands in the lake, and we don't even have to bother to bend down."

"Hummgh, hummgh," I said.

"I'll Never Forget Old 5789-A"

LET ME ADMIT it right off. There was a time not too long ago when I liked my wildlife unadorned. What I mean is, I liked it in the naked. Stark raving raw. In its birthday suit. Nude. Stripped. Bare. Some fur or hair and maybe a set of horns, but otherwise unadorned with so much as an aluminum fig leaf.

The wildlife situation, as I saw it, was becoming grim—sciencewise. The scientists were running all over the place decorating my wild animals with vinyl tags, collars, streamers, flags, patches and jackets. They were putting radio transmitters on grizzly bears and sage grouse and sea turtles. Deer in Idaho were running around in blinking lights, and some falcons of my acquaintance carried so much electronic equipment they had to taxi for a take off. So help me, I even knew a mountain goat that ran around for a year with a piece of garden hose on his horns!

And that's not all. Plans were under way, the wildlife scientists told me, to start using telemetry, the system used by NASA doctors to keep tabs on the physiology of astronauts orbiting the globe. That way the zoologists and wildlife managers would know not only the location of a particular animal day and night but his temperature, rate of respiration, heart beat, and no doubt his politics.

All this I found depressing. Whoever expected wildlife managers to actually start managing the wildlife? I personally did not like scientists and the like fooling around with the fauna.

Then one day I said to myself, "You're a modern American male, aren't you? Yes. Therefore you are regimented, inoculated, tranquilized, numbered, recorded, transported, transplanted, poked, probed, polled, conditioned, and computerized, aren't you? Yes. Then," I said to myself, "why should a bunch of damn animals be better off than you are?"

After that I decided to get into the spirit of the thing. The time would come, I saw, when people would think that anyone showing a preference for naked animals must be some kind of pervert. Mothers would call their children off the streets whenever "Fruity Fred" walked by. Toughs would beat him up in bars, and he would have to move to a city where the police protected people like him. He would have to get his kicks by watching clandestine showings of old Disney nature films in motel rooms and maybe even by exchanging pictures of naked deer and bear with persons of similar inclinations. Maybe he would be forced to make his living by peddling picture postcards from an alley: "Wanta buy a dirty picture of a moose?"

None of that was for me. I got scared and started thinking of all the advantages this new scientific approach to game management would bring about. It took a while, but I finally thought of some.

For example, I wouldn't have to slog around in

the woods anymore hunting aimlessly for a deer. I would just stop by the local Electronic Game Control Center.

"What do you have in the way of a nice 125-pound whitetail buck at about 4:15 P.M. in the Haversteads' meadow" I would ask the technologist in charge.

"One moment, please." She would put the last touch to a phony eyelash and then program a card and run it through the computer. *Blink. Buzz. Hummm. Clink!* "You're in luck," she would say, looking at a piece of computer tape. "Buck Deer No. 5789-A will be crossing the Haversteads' meadow at exactly 4:32 P.M. He will be traveling due north at a speed of six miles per hour. His present weight is 135 pounds; pulse rate, 78; and temperature, 99.1. He has had all of his shots."

"Just what I'm looking for," I say, and rush out the door, heading for the Haversteads' meadow.

At precisely 4:32 P.M. Buck Deer No. 5789-A steps into the clearing, heading due north at a speed of six miles per hour. He is wearing a bright red vinyl jacket set off by blue ear streamers and a collar of blinking lights. I bust him with a .30-30 slug, which enters just slightly above his portable power pack and emerges to the left of his transistorized radio unit.

As I rush up to the fallen No. 5789-A, a feminine voice squawks from his radio pack, "Nice shot!" The voice belongs to the lady technologist at the Electronic Game Control Center.

"Thanks," I say.

"I will now put on a recording of the proper method for dressing a big-game animal," she says. Another female voice comes on:

"You have just shot what is known as your big-game animal. Here are the directions for dressing your big-game animal. First carefully remove from the big-game animal all electronic devices, its vinyl jacket and ribbons, and the collar of blinking lights. If this is not done immediately, the meat may have a strong flavor. Step Number Two . . ."

You can see the advantages.

The drawbacks, of course, would be minor. For one thing, we would have to add some new terminology. Hunting conversations then might go something like this:

"Heard you gotcher deer."

"Yeah, I busted old 5789-A."

"No kidding! How many transistors did the old boy have?"

"Four. And big! Why that devil was wearing a thirty-eight-inch collar, a size sixty-four jacket, and the biggest whip antenna I ever saw."

There might also be a few additional difficulties in the eating of game. Your wife might have to warn the children, "Be careful you don't crack your teeth on a piece of Daddy's buckshot and watch out for the little wires and electrodes; they might catch in your throat and choke you."

Nevertheless, any extra dental and doctor bills would be more than made up for by your savings on hunting clothes. Since all the animals will be wearing red, the hunters can wear any old thing they want—as long as it isn't red. Wearing red, in fact, might be disastrous. Hunters who mistake people for potential venison will plead, "I saw this flash of red and thought sure it was a deer. . . ."

Now I'm not one to swim upstream in the river of progress. The old days are gone. But I know that sooner or later I'll have a relapse and be carted off to a psychiatrist to be set right.

"What seems to be your problem?" the psychiatrist will ask.

"Well, Doc," I'll say, "I keep thinking about these naked animals."

"Yes," he'll say, "that is rather serious. Such tendencies are doubtlessly the manifestation of some childhood experience."

And you know, he'll be right.

The B'ar

RANCID CRABTREE was ranting and raving when he charged into our kitchen. "Thar's a gol-dang b'ar in maw brush pile," he said.

My grandmother's nose quivered. "Open the window, child," she said to me. Personally, I thought Rancid had a rather interesting smell, kind of tangy, like game hung a bit too long in warm weather.

"What's this about a bear?" Gram asked, shoving a couple of fresh-baked cinnamon rolls in front of Rancid and pouring him a cup of coffee.

"Thar's a b'ar in maw brush pile," Rancid repeated. "Ah thank the critter plans on passin' the winter thar."

"Well, what's that hurt?" Gram said.

Rancid looked at her in disgust. "You can't never tell when ah might need thet brush pile fer somethin'," he said. "What right's thet b'ar got movin' in like he owned the place? Any number of nice caves around but he's got to hole up in maw brush pile. Wall, ah ain't gonna stand fer it. B'sides, ah've been hungerin' fer some b'ar steak, anyway."

"Then just shoot him and be done with it," Gram said.

"That's what ah needs the boy fer."

"What?" Gram said.

"What?" I said.

"Ah needs him to stand on top the brush pile and poke a pole down into it and drive the b'ar out so ah kin get a shot. Won't be nothin' to it."

"There won't be nothin' to it, all right," Gram said, "because I ain't lettin' him do a fool dangerous thing like that."

Gram and I agreed on few things, but this happened to be one of them. Just to make it look good though, I threw out a half-hearted beg.

"Aw c'mon, Gram, let me do it," I said.

"Nope!"

"All right." There was no point in pushing her too hard.

"What's the matter?" Rancid said, giving me his mean look. "Yer begger broke?"

I could see he was disappointed.

"Hey," I said. "How about Ginger Ann? I bet she'd do it." Ginger Ann was a woman who lived alone back in the hills on a little ranch she had inherited from her father. I'd heard it said of her that she could out-work, out-fight, and out-swear any man in the county. Once I'd seen her ornery old cow horse throw her flat on her back, for no reason that I could see except he thought it might be a good joke. She was up in a flash, fists doubled and biceps knotted up to the size of grapefruit. She delivered the beast such a blow to the ribs he would have fallen over sideways except for a nearby tree. While he was still dazed she stepped back into the saddle and said to me, "Don't mind us, boy. We do this all the time."

That was one of the reasons I thought Ginger Ann might be just the person to drive a bear out of a brush pile.

"Gol-dang," Rancid said, "ah never thought of Ginger Ann. Ah bet she would do it."

"I wouldn't mind going along to watch," I said.

"Suit yerself," Rancid said.

"You just take care you don't get hurt," Gram warned.

"Shucks, thet b'ar ain't gonna hurt nobody," Rancid said.

"It ain't the bear I'm worried about," Gram said.

We got into Rancid's old truck and rattled over to Ginger Ann's place, an ancient log house slouched among a scattering of pine trees and the assorted remains of hay wagons, cars, trucks, tractors, and con-traptions that defied identification. She seemed de-lighted to see us.

"Ah was wonderin' if you would help me to shoot a b'ar," Rancid said to her.

"You bet," Ginger Ann said, taking her .30-30 off the wall. "Let's go."

"Hold on a minute," Rancid said. "You won't be needin' thet thang, because ah'm gonna do the shootin' mawsef. All ah needs you fer is to drive the b'ar out of maw brush pile."

Ginger Ann shoved a box of shells in her jacket pocket. "Why can't you drive the bear out and let me shoot it?"

"Ha!" Rancid said. " 'Cause yer jist a woman, thet's why. Ah never know'd a woman yet could shoot worth a dang."

Ginger Ann stepped out on the porch and pointed to an old car door leaning against a tree thirty yards away. "You see that itty-bitty patch of rust just to the left of the top hinge?" She jacked a shell into the chamber, put the rifle to her shoulder and fired. The door jumped. (There was some question later about whether the door actually jumped, but I saw it.) We walked over, and there was a single bullet hole in the door, drilled neatly through the rust patch.

"Wall anyway," Rancid said, "a car door ain't no b'ar, and ah git to do the shootin' and thet's all thar is to it."

"I'll arm wrestle you then," Ginger Ann said. "Winner shoots the bear."

Rancid sneaked a glance at her right arm. "Ah ain't arm wrastlin' no woman."

They argued and yelled at each other all the time we were driving back to Rancid's place, but finally Ginger gave in and said, yes, she'd drive the bear out of the brush pile.

"All this fightin' has set me on edge," Rancid said. "Let's go in maw cabin and ah'll bile us up a pot of coffee. Than we'll go git the b'ar."

Ginger Ann looked around the cabin while Rancid was blowing dust out of a couple of extra cups and putting the coffee on. "Why don't you ever clean this place up?" she said.

"Gol-dang, what are you talkin' about, woman!" Rancid said, his feelings obviously hurt. "Ah jist cleaned it up!"

"When?"

"Wall, let's see, what month is it now? Anyway, not too long ago."

While we were drinking our coffee Rancid laid out his plan for us. He drew a circle with his finger in the dust on the table. Inside the circle he put a dot. "This hyar's the brush pile," he said, indicating the circle.

"And this is the bear, I suppose," Ginger Ann said, pointing to the dot.

"Nope," Rancid said. "Thet's you, standing on top the brush pile. Directly underneath you is the b'ar."

"Oh," Ginger Ann said.

Rancid drew a little X six inches out from the circle. "This hyar is me." Then he made a dotted line from the dot in the circle halfway out to the X. "This is the b'ar comin' out of the brush pile. Ah'll shoot it right thar."

Ginger Ann reached forward with her finger and very quickly extended the dotted line out to the X and made a violent swirling motion that sent a little puff of dust into the air.

"What you go an' do thet fer?" Rancid said.

"That's what will happen if you miss the bear," Ginger Ann said with a laugh that rattled the stovepipe.

"Ha!" Rancid said. "Ah don't miss!" He looked down at the spot where the little X had been erased. "On t'other hand, ah can probably git a better shot if ah stand over hyar." And he drew another X some distance off to one side.

"Where's Pat going to stand?" Ginger Ann asked.

"There ain't enough room on the table to show that," I said.

When we had finished the coffee, Rancid put on his dirty red hunting shirt ("maw lucky shart"), picked up his ancient .30-30, and we headed out to the brush pile. Ginger Ann carried the pole over her shoulder. The brush pile was in the middle of a small clearing Rancid had cut in the woods when he was a young man and thinking of becoming a farmer. This evidence of ambition embarrassed him considerably, and he explained it away by saying, "Aw was insane at the time."

"Smell thet b'ar smell?" Rancid whispered when we got to the clearing.

"No," Ginger Ann whispered. "All I can smell is . . . When was the last time you took a bath, anyway, Rancid?"

"What y'ar is it now?" Rancid said.

The brush pile was about eight feet high and laced with small logs sticking out at every angle. On one side of it was what appeared to be an opening—the place where Rancid had indicated the bear would exit. After sizing up the situation and making a number of calculations based upon previous experiences I'd had with Rancid, I selected a moderately tall tamarack tree and climbed about halfway up it. My perch on a stout limb gave me a good view of the scene.

Rancid took up his position off to one side of what he had determined to be the bear's path of escape. He seemed a bit nervous. I could see him rummaging around in his pockets, looking for something. Then he took out a plug of tobacco and took a great chaw out of it. He limbered up his arms, and threw the rifle up onto his shoulder a couple of times for practice. All this time Ginger Ann stood leaning on the pole, watching him and shaking her head as if she couldn't believe it all. Finally, Rancid motioned her to climb up on top of the brush pile, and he went into a half crouch, rifle at the ready.

Ginger Ann made such a commotion climbing up the brush pile that I decided there wasn't a bear in there anyway, either that or he was dead or stone deaf. When she was at last on top of the brush pile, she poked several times down into it with the pole. Nothing happened. I could see that Rancid was getting exasperated.

"Gol-dang it, woman," he finally shouted, "jam thet pole down *hard!*"

"If you know so much about it, you knot-headed ignoramus, why don't you come do it yourself," Ginger Ann shouted back.

"Ah shoulda know'd better'n to brang a woman to do a boy's job," Rancid said. "Let me show you how to do it." He leaned his rifle against a tree and started for the brush pile.

By now Ginger Ann's face was red from rage. She lifted the pole above her head and drove it with all her might into the brush.

I didn't see all that happened next because I blinked. The bear didn't bother using the door to the brush pile but just crashed out through the side of it— the side toward Rancid. The brush pile seemed to explode, and Ginger Ann toppled over backwards, screaming, "Shoot, Rancid, shoot—before it's too late!"

Well, it was about the most exciting and interesting spectacle I've ever had the good fortune to witness for free. I saw Rancid turn and run, and I thought he was going for the rifle, but he went right past without even giving it a glance. Right then was when I blinked. When the blink was over, the bear was just a black streak twenty yards away. A few feet ahead of the black streak was a dirty red streak. Rancid's hat was still suspended in the air where he had been standing when the bear first came out of the brush pile. Ginger Ann finally hit the ground, still screaming,

"Shoot! Shoot!" Off in the distance I could see the black streak and the red streak going up a hill. About halfway up the hill, the black streak passed the red streak, but Rancid was apparently so intent on making a good showing, he didn't even notice. Or maybe he was running with his eyes shut. In any case, when they went over the hill, Rancid was still running hard and looked as if he might be gaining on the bear.

I slid down out of the tree, and Ginger Ann ran around the brush pile and grabbed Rancid's rifle.

"Are you going after them?" I asked.

"No," she said. "If they run by here again, maybe I'll shoot the bear for Rancid. Then again, maybe I won't."

After about twenty minutes, a bedraggled Rancid came shuffling back to the clearing. Without saying a word, he took his rifle out of Ginger Ann's hand and headed for the cabin. Ginger Ann and I trailed along behind.

"No point in feeling bad about it," Ginger Ann said after a bit. "It could have happened to anybody."

"Ah had maw mouth all set fer some b'ar steak," Rancid said, glumly. "Ah guess ah should have let you do the shootin'."

"Shucks," Ginger Ann said. "I couldn't even hit an old car door. You know that bullet hole in the rust spot? Why, that's been in there ever since my daddy shot it in there years ago."

"Ha!" Rancid said, brightening up. "Ah know'd thet."

"But . . ." I said.

"C'mon in the cabin," Rancid said to Ginger Ann, "and I'll bile us up another pot of coffee."

"Don't mind if I do," she said.

"But, Rancid . . ." I said.

"See you later," Ginger Ann said to me. She shoved Rancid into the cabin and shut the door before I could warn him.

I couldn't understand it. Here Ginger Ann had made one of the finest shots I had ever seen, and then she turned right around and lied about it. She had to be up to something, but I didn't know what, and it worried me. Before going home, I yelled at the top of my voice, "I saw the car door jump when she shot, Rancid! I saw it jump!"

He didn't seem to hear me.

The Rendezvous

EVERY HUNTER KNOWS what a rendezvous is. That's where one hunter says to another, "Al, you take that side of the draw and I'll take this one and we'll meet in twenty minutes at the top of the hill." The next time they see each other is at a PTA meeting five years later in Pocatello. That's a rendezvous.

It is simply against the basic nature of hunters to arrive at a designated point at a designated time. If one of my hunting pals said, "I'll meet you on the other side of this tree in ten seconds," one of us would be an hour late. And have the wrong tree besides.

We work out complicated whistling codes as a means of staying in touch. "One long and two shorts means I've found some fresh sign and for the other guy to come on over. Two shorts and one long mean . . ." etc. I go no more than fifteen feet and stumble onto the tracks of a herd of mule deer. They are so fresh the earth is still crumbling from the edges. I whistle the code, low and soft. No answer. I try again, louder. No answer. Then I cut loose with a real blast. Still no answer. By now I've forgotten all about the deer, and whistle so loud the crew at a sawmill three miles away go off shift an hour early. My upper lip has a charley horse and I think I have a slight hernia. The only way he could have gotten out of hearing so fast was if he had a motorcycle hidden behind a bush.

Some hunters have even resorted to two-way radios, but to little avail. "Charley One, this is Hank Four. Come in Charley One." Charley One doesn't come in. All you can get is some guy in Australia. He is saying, "Roger, I'm onto the bloody biggest tracks you ever saw. Roger? Where the 'ell are you, Roger?"

Why is it so difficult to keep a rendezvous? Usually it is because both hunters are not familiar with the terrain being hunted. But one thinks he is. He is the one who lays out the strategy.

A couple of years ago a friend and I were hunting near the Washington-Canadian border in country so rough it looks like it was whipped up in the lava stage by a giant egg beater and left to dry. The mountains do not have ranges like decent mountains: they have convulsions.

"You cut down over the side of the mountain," my friend said casually, "and I'll swing around with the car and pick you up on the road."

"You sure there's a road down there?" I asked.

"Of course," he said. "You'll come to a little stream and the road is just on the other side of it. There's no way in the world you can miss it."

True to the nature of rendezvous, there was at least one way in the world to miss it. Six hours later, after having scaled down cliffs that would have made a mockery of the precipices in alpine movies, I came to a stream. By my reckoning, it should have been running from my right to left; instead it was running from left to right. There was no sign of a road on the other side. I sat down calmly to take stock of the situation. When that proved too frightening, I leaped up, plunged into the stream, and started climbing the nearest mountain.

The thought that I might starve to death before getting out of that wilderness occurred to me, and I promptly shot the head off a grouse at about forty yards (a feat that prior to and after that moment has always eluded me), plucked it, dressed it, and stowed it away in the game pocket of my hunting jacket. Squads of deer, like characters out of some Disney film, gazed upon me from all sides, no doubt wondering what kind of strange creature this was crashing frantically through their forest primeval. They went ignored, except when I had to drive them out of my way with shrill and vulgar shouts.

Eventually I came to a road and flagged down a car by lying down in front of it. I was relieved to discover that the hunters in it spoke English and that I was still on American soil. An hour later I was seated at a roadhouse downing the first course of what I intended to be a ten-course meal, when my hunting partner burst through the door and started calling for volunteers for a search party.

"Who's lost?" I asked.

"You!" he cried. And then he uttered those words invariably uttered at the resolution of ill-fated rendezvous: "What the ——— happened to you? I waited . . ."

Such was the traumatic nature of my ordeal that I forgot all about the grouse I had shot. Late that night my wife was cleaning out my hunting jacket and thrust her hand into the game pocket to find out what that peculiar bulge was. The resulting scream sent half the people on our block into the street.

"What," my shaking spouse asked me as I came back in from the street, "is that bird doing in there?"

"That," I growled, "was provisions, in case I had to spend the winter in those ———— mountains."

One of the axioms of hunting is that more time is spent hunting for hunting companions than for deer. I always feel that a hunt is successful if just one rendezvous is completed. Whether or not we get any deer is incidental:

"How was your hunting trip?"

"Wonderful! We met where and when we were supposed to one out of nine times."

"Get any deer?"

"Didn't see a thing."

When I was a high school kid I used to hunt with an old man who had truly mastered the art of the rendezvous. He always directed the hunt, which may have been part of his secret.

"You cut down through that brush there, work your way around the side of the mountain, climb up to the ridge, and circle back to the truck. I'll do likewise on the other side, and we'll meet back here in an hour."

"That's impossible," I would say.

"Listen, if an old man like me can do it, you can."

Two hours later I would stagger in, scratched, bruised and torn, and there the Old Man would be, fresh as a daisy, sitting on the tailgate of the truck drinking coffee out of my thermos. More often than not he would have a deer.

"What took you so long?" he would say.

The uncanny thing about the Old Man was that

no matter when you got back to the truck, even if it was just fifteen minutes after leaving, he would somehow sense your return and with some superhuman effort manage to get back and be waiting for you. But he was always modest about his talent, this sixth sense for keeping a rendezvous.

"It's nothing, boy," he would say. "It's just a little somethin' that comes to you with old age."

Cigars, Logging Trucks, and Know-It-Alls

A WHILE BACK I was asked what I thought were the three greatest threats to a fisherman's well-being. Although this is not a question one hears every day, I have over the years given the subject much thought and was able to answer immediately: "Cigars, logging trucks, and know-it-alls."

My interrogator was somewhat taken aback by this reply, obviously having expected a listing of such standard dangers as bears, bulls, rattlesnakes, rapids, quicksand, dropoffs, etc. Although these are all very real dangers and may frequently threaten premature termination of one's existence, the whole bunch of them together does not equal the potential for destruction compressed into a single small cigar, let alone a logging truck or a know-it-all.

Twice in the past year alone I have been witness to two unwarranted and unprovoked attacks by a cigar upon innocent anglers. In the first instance the cigar, a small sporty El Puffo, nearly wiped out three fishermen, a dog, and a 1958 pickup truck. It happened like this:

My friends Herb and Retch and I and Herb's dog, Rupert, had spent the day fishing a high mountain lake and were headed home, the four of us crowded in the cab, by way of a road that traverses the edge of a one-thousand-foot-deep gorge named, appropriately, Deadman's. Herb usually smokes a pipe, but since he had run out of tobacco Retch had offered him a plastic-tipped cigar. Chewing nervously on the cigar, Herb pampered the pickup along the road, the outer wheels nudging rocks into thin air. The silence was broken only by the sound of dripping sweat, an occasional inhalation or exhalation, and the dog Rupert popping his knuckles. Then it happened. Forgetting he was smoking a cigar, Herb reached up in the manner of removing a pipe from his mouth and closed his hand over the glowing tip of the El Puffo.

"*Ahhhhaaaiiiigh!*" Herb said, grinding his foot down on the gas pedal.

"*Ahhhhaaaiiiigh!*" the rest of us said. In an instant six hands and two paws were clamped on the steering wheel. Retch claimed later that he jumped out twice but both times the pickup was so far out in space he had to jump back in. In any case there was about as much activity in that pickup cab as I have ever witnessed before in such cramped quarters. When it was all over and we were safe again, I was driving, Herb and Retch were crouched on the floor, and the dog was smoking the cigar.

Then there was the time down on the Grande Ronde River when Retch was so startled by a nine-pound steelhead hitting his lure that a lighted cigar stub popped out of his mouth and dropped inside the open top of his waders. Naturally a man doesn't turn loose of a nine-pound steelhead just because he has a lighted cigar roaming around inside his waders. He just makes every effort to keep the cigar in constant motion and, if possible, away from any areas particularly susceptible to fire-and-smoke damage.

Retch knew all this, of course, and managed to land the steelhead in record time. Although his injuries from the cigar were only minor I thought possibly some of the other fishermen nearby might bring charges against him. First, there was his use of vile language, but since it was screeched at such a high pitch as to be understood only by members of the canine family and lip-readers who had served at least one hitch in the Marine Corps, I thought it unlikely that much of a case could be made on that count. On the other hand, there was a good chance he might have been convicted of ob-scene dancing on a trout stream. And finally there was the felonious act of attempting to induce innocent bystanders to laugh themselves to death.

Cigars are dangerous enough, but logging trucks are a good deal worse. Some younger readers, par-ticularly those living in the plains states, may not be familiar with logging trucks, so here is a brief descrip-tion: the natural habitat of logging trucks is steep, winding, narrow roads situated between high mountain trout streams and the state highway. Where I live, in the Pacific Northwest, they are a protected species. They weigh several tons and are in the habit of hauling sec-tions of large trees around on their backs. No one knows why, unless they eat them. The term "logging trucks" is their scientific name; fishermen, however, commonly refer to them as blankety-blank-of-a-blank, as in "Great gosh-a-mighty, Harry, here comes a blankety-blank-of-a-blank!"

Logging trucks are almost always encountered

at the end of a steep, winding stretch of narrow road where the only turnouts are three miles behind your vehicle and ten feet behind the logging truck. To those inexperienced in such matters, the fair and reasonable course of action might seem to be that the logging truck would back up the ten feet to the turnout and let you pass, but that is not the way it works. The rules are that you must back up the three miles, usually at speeds in excess of 30 mph, while your passengers shout such words of encouragement as, "Watch that washout!" and "Faster! The blankety-blank-of-a-blank is gaining on us!"

Several years ago I made it to the turnout at the top of a mountain road just as a logging truck, its timing slightly off, was pulling up for its winding descent of the mountain road, no doubt intending to drive before it a car full of hapless, shouting, fist-shaking fishermen. The logging truck pulled abreast of my car, spat a chaw of tobacco out the window and said, "Shucks, that don't happen very often." I could see the logging truck was disappointed at not catching me ten feet short of the turnout but that was its tough luck.

Most of my friends and I have become excellent logging truck trackers over the years. You track a logging truck about the same way you track a deer. You get out and look for signs. The droppings from a logging truck consist of branches and twigs from its load of logs and occasionally the front bumper from a late model sedan. Any road with such signs scattered along it may be regarded as a game trail for logging trucks.

Occasionally there are other signs to be read. They say, DANGER—LOGGING TRUCKS. These signs are usually put up by other fishermen in the hope of keeping a good piece of fishing water to themselves. This is a despicable trick, since an angler can ignore such signs only at his peril. As with any other dedicated angler, I am not above putting fresh grizzly claw marks nine feet high on a pine tree alongside a trail to a good mountain lake. But I would never stoop to putting up a logging truck warning sign. That's going a little bit too far.

Know-it-alls are by far the greatest threat to the well-being of the angler. Your average run-of-the-mill know-it-all can reduce a fisherman to a quivering, babbling wreck with nothing more than a few well-chosen pieces of advice.

Know-it-alls are sometimes difficult to spot since they come in all sizes, shapes, and sexes. They are all equally dangerous. A trembling little old lady know-it-all can be as lethal as a three-hundred-pound madman with an ax in either hand. Their one distinguishing characteristic is a self-confidence as total as it is sublime.

Know-it-alls have probably gotten me in more trouble than all the other dangers put together. I recall one time a know-it-all and I were out fishing and decided to hunt for wild mushrooms. We drove up to a grassy meadow and I suggested that we leave the pickup on high ground and walk across the meadow because it looked wet to me.

"Naw, it ain't wet," the know-it-all said. "You can drive across."

So I steered the pickup down into the high grass of the meadow. After a bit the wheels started to slip in mud.

"Hey, it's getting wet," I said. "We better turn back."

"Naw. It's just a little damp here. You can make it across."

Then plumes of water started spraying out on both sides of the car.

"You better speed up a bit going through this puddle," the know-it-all said.

I speeded up. Pretty soon we were plowing up a sizable wake.

"Pour on the gas!" shouted the know-it-all. "We're nearly to the other side of the puddle."

By now I was in a cold sweat. The pickup was bouncing, sliding, and twisting through the high grass and waves of water were crashing across the windshield. Suddenly, the grass parted ahead of us and we shot out into a bright clear expanse of open water.

Later, dripping with mud and wrath, I paid off the tow truck man back at his gas station.

One of the hangers-on at the station finally put down his bottle of pop and asked, "How come y'all got so muddy?"

"Drove his pickup out into the middle of Grass Lake," the tow truck man said.

"Oh," the other man said.

Here are some statements that immediately identify the know-it-all:

"Hell, that ain't no bull, Charley, and anyway you could outrun it, even if your waders are half full of water."

"Quicksand? That ain't quicksand! You think I don't know my quicksand? Now git on in there and wade across."

"Course it feels hot. That's a sign they're beginning to dry. See how the steam is risin' off 'em? Now you just keep holding your feet over the fire like that till your boots are good and dry."

"Ain't no rattlesnakes in these parts."

"Ain't no logging trucks in these parts."

"You ever eat any of these little white berries? Taste just like wild hickory nuts."

"With thin ice what you have to do is just walk real fast so it don't have time to break under you. Now git on out there and let's see how fast you can walk. Faster! Faster! Dang it, didn't I tell you to walk fast?"

Because of such advice, the know-it-all is now listed as a threatened species. I myself have threatened a large number of them and, on occasion, have even endangered a few.

But Where's the Park, Papa?

ON ONE OF THE DOGGIER of last summer's dog days, my family and I simmered grimly in our own juices as we toiled along, a bit of the flotsam in a sluggish river of traffic. Our rate of speed was somewhere between a creep and an ooze. Heat waves pulsed in a blue sea of exhaust fumes. Blood boiled and nerves twitched. Red-faced, sweating policemen would occasionally appear and gesture angrily at the drivers to speed it up or slow it down. At least one of the drivers felt like gesturing back.

We were on one of those self-imposed exiles from the amenities of civilized life popularly referred to as vacations. I was in my usual vacation mood, which is something less than festive. My kids were diligently attempting to perfect the art of whining, while my mother expressed her growing concern and disbelief at the sparcity of restrooms along this particular stretch of highway. Whenever the speed of the traffic slowed to the ooze stage, my wife took the opportunity to spoon tranquilizers into my mouth from a cereal bowl, all the while urging me not to enlarge the children's vocabulary too far beyond their years. Mother, in her increasing anxiety, already had them up to about age forty-seven.

"Hey," one of the kids paused in mid-whine to complain. "You said you was gonna take us to a national park!"

"Clam up!" I counseled him, drawing upon my vast store of child psychology. "This *is* a national park!"

To keep the children amused until we found a park campsite, my wife invented one of those games which start with the idea of increasing the youngsters' awareness of their environment and end with them beating each other with tire irons in the back seat. As I recall, this particular game resulted in a final score of three, six, and eight points. Each kid got one point for every square foot of ground he spotted first that didn't have any litter on it.

I can recall a time when tourists visiting national parks appeared to be folks indulging themselves in a bit of wholesome outdoor enjoyment. Now they seem to have a sense of desperation about them, like people who have fled their homes nine minutes before the arrival of Genghis Khan. Most of them no longer have any hope of seeing unspoiled wilderness, but they have heard rumors that the parks are places where the ground is still unpaved. Of course, if they want to see this ground they have to ask the crowd of people standing on it to jump into the air in unison.

The individuals I really feel sorry for are the serious practitioners of littering. Some of these poor souls have hauled their litter a thousands miles or more under the impression they would have the opportunity of tossing it out into a pristine wilderness, only to discover that they have been preceded by a vast multitude of casual wrapper-droppers. (The Park Service does make a heroic effort to keep the litter cleared from along the highways but is handicapped because its rotary plows don't work well on paper and beverage bottles.)

Since there are many people who get the bends and have to be put into decompression chambers if they get more than thirty minutes from a shopping center, the parks, at least the one we were in, provide the usual cluster of supermarkets and variety stores. Here it was possible to buy plastic animals at a price that suggested they were driven on the hoof all the way from Hong Kong. I refused to buy my youngsters any of these souvenirs. I told them they should find something that was truly representative of the park, and they did. Each of them picked up and brought home a really nice piece of litter.

I find the rangers to be about the most enjoyable thing in national parks anymore. I always make a point to take my children by the ranger station to watch the rangers climb the walls. In recent years the rangers have been going on R and R in such places as New York and Los Angeles in order to get away from the crowds and noise and to get a breath of fresh air. By the end of the peak season they have facial twitches so bad they have to wear neck braces to guard against whiplash.

The park bears aren't what they used to be either. Most of the bears you see along the roads look as if they've spent the past five years squatted in a chair before a television set drinking beer and eating corn chips. Half of them should be in intensive care units. They have forgotten what it is that a bear is supposed to do. If panhandling along the roads were outlawed, they would probably hustle pool for a living. A dose of pure air would drop them like a shot through the heart from a .44 Magnum. Any bear that wanders more than a mile from the road has to carry a scuba tank on his back filled with carbon monoxide. As far as spectacle goes, the bears just don't have it anymore. I'd rather drive my kids across town to watch their uncle Harry nurse a hangover. Now there's a spectacle!

Camping in a national park is an invigorating experience. My seventy-year-old mother went off looking for a restroom among the sea of tents, cabins, and campers. After about an hour of unsuccessful searching, she was loping along looking for a path that led off into the wilderness and came upon a wild-eyed man loping in the opposite direction.

"Sir," she said as they passed, "could you tell me where I can find a restroom?"

"I don't know, lady," he shouted over his shoulder. "I've been here for three days and haven't found one yet!"

Some parks still have excellent fishing in them if you can find it, but on the easily accessible streams you would have better luck digging for clams in Montana. There are of course the tame fish planted by the park service, and these can be caught with a bent pin on the end of a clothesline with bubble gum for bait. The sight of a live insect or even a dry fly makes them nauseous. Catching one of them is almost as exciting as changing the water in the goldfish bowl. After being dumped into one of the park streams the fish quickly adjust to their new environment, however, and within a week or two are consuming vast quantities of soggy hot dog buns and cigarette butts. (Scientists estimate that eating one of these fish is equivalent to eating two loaves of bread and four packs of cigarettes.) If anti-littering eventually catches on, a lot of fish will be up alongside the highways with the bears. They'll be begging smokes from tourists.

Many people are under the mistaken impression that transistor radios come from Japan, but that is not the case. Transistor radios breed in national parks and from there move out to infest the rest of the country. Their mating cries at night are among the most hideous sounds on earth, approximately on the order of those of catamounts with arthritis. The offspring are prodigious in number. During the day you can see hundreds of youngsters carrying the baby transistor radios around the park. I proposed to a park ranger that a season be opened on the adults of the species with an eye to limiting the population growth. He said he himself was all for it but that park regulations forbid hunting of any kind.

The site on which we finally pitched our tent was in the middle of a vast caldron of writhing humanity. This made it easy to meet interesting people. Several times I chatted with the fellow next door about his hobby of pumping the exhaust from his car into our tent. The fellows on the other side of us were members of a rock band. For a long time I thought they were just pounding dents out of their bus, but it turned out they were practicing. Their rendition of "A Truck Full of Empty Milk Cans Crashing into a Burglar Alarm Factory" was kind of catchy, but the rest of their stuff was much too loud for my taste. People would also drop into our tent at all hours. They would look about for a second or two, a puzzled expression on their faces, then leave. Then we discovered that the trail to the restroom passed under our tent. This discovery made Mother noticeably happy and she vanished like a shot up the trail.

I decided that the best thing to do was to give up on tenting and try to get into one of the park tourist cabins. After mortgaging our home and indenturing two of the children for fourteen years, we managed to scrape together sufficient rent for two nights. The architecture of the cabin was about halfway between Neoshack and Neolithic. Frank Lloyd Wright would have loved it because it blended so naturally into its surroundings—a superb replica of a hobo jungle.

The only good thing about the cabin was that the roof didn't leak all the time we were there. Of course if it had rained, there's no telling what might have happened. It is doubtful that the seine net used for roofing would have kept us dry, but I figured we could always set up the tent inside the cabin.

Our days at the park were filled with the delights of viewing the marvelous phenomena. There was the spring hot enough to boil an egg in, and someone was running a scientific experiment to see if it would do the same thing for an old newspaper and a half-eaten hamburger. Reflection Lake was truly beautiful, with the scraggly spruce trees around its edges so sharply defined in the glass on the lake bottom that you could make out the hatchet marks on them. The Painted Rocks were interesting in their own way, especially where park employees had managed to remove some of the paint. The kids seemed to enjoy the ancient hieroglyphics to be found everywhere: "Fred & Edith Jones, Peanut Grove, Calif.—1968," etc. Then there were the antics of the wildlife. Once we were fortunate enough to observe two mature male Homo sapiens locking horns in a territorial dispute over a parking spot.

Just when I finally found a way to amuse myself in the park, my wife insisted that we leave. She was afraid I would get arrested for trying to poach transistor radios with rocks. Also, while attempting to photograph a bald woodpecker, she flushed a covey of young people deeply engrossed in their own particular study of nature. (If the truth were known, she was probably more flushed than they.) Anyway, she said the only vistas she wanted to see for some time to come were the insides of the four walls of our mortgaged house. We hit the road for home the next day.

Next summer I think I'll skip the national parks and take my family to a place I know up in the Rockies. It doesn't have all the conveniences and accommodations of a national park, of course. The bears aren't especially friendly (but if you do see one, he doesn't look as if he recently escaped from an iron lung). If you have the sudden urge to buy a plastic animal, you just have to grit your teeth and bear it. The scenery isn't all that spectacular, unless you get a little excited over invisible air. The place doesn't have even a geyser, but when I get there it will at least have an old geaser. Some people like to watch him sit on a log and smoke his pipe, in particular a certain middle-aged woman and four ignorant kids. If you need more spectacle than that, you can always go to a national park.

A Yup of a Different Color

ABOUT THREE WEEKS before the opening of the first deer season in which I had been guaranteed permission to be an active participant, our resident deer vanished. All that remained of them was some sign sprinkled arrogantly among the plundered rows of our garden. (Since I was only fourteen at the time and not much good at reading deer signs, I could only guess that the message was some complaint about the quality of our cabbage.)

Among the rules that had been laid down by my mother in allowing me to go in armed pursuit of that mythical creature, My First Deer, was one that stated in no uncertain terms that I would have to confine my hunting to our own farm. Somehow the deer had gotten word of this fine print in the contract and immediately (no doubt snickering among themselves) split for the next county.

When I reported this act of treachery to my friend and mentor Rancid Crabtree, the old mountain man offered scant sympathy.

"Why hell, boy, they wouldn't call it deer huntin' if you didn't have to hunt fer the critters," he said. "Shootin' a deer in yer own pea patch ain't huntin', it's revenge."

I explained to Rancid that if a grown, mature man of unsurpassed excellence in the art and science of hunting were to speak firmly to my mother about the importance of shooting one's first deer and to forthwith offer his services as a guide and overseer of such an endeavor, my mother probably would withdraw the stipulation that I hunt exclusively within the boundaries of the farm. Rancid replied that he had a bad headache, his old war wounds were acting up, and he thought he was going blind in one eye, but if he managed to live for a few days longer and just happened to run across such a man he would convey my message to him. We spent the better part of an afternoon sparring about like that until Rancid could stand it no more and finally broke down and invited me to go hunting with him and Mr. Hooker, a tall, stringy old woodsman who lived a mile up the road from our place.

"I don't know what ol' Hook is gonna think about this," Rancid said somewhat morosely. "Me and him ain't never took no kid with us before."

"Well for gosh sakes don't take one along this time," I told him severely. "Just you and me and Mr. Hooker."

"I reckon that'll be more'n enough," Rancid agreed.

I should mention that both my mother and grandmother were harshly critical of Rancid's lifestyle. One

time I asked Gram exactly what it was that Rancid
Crabtree did for a living.

"He's an idler," she said without hesitation.

I decided right then and there that I wanted to
be an idler too, because it gave you so much time off
from the job, and I intended at first opportunity to have
Rancid teach me the trade. It wasn't until I was thirty
years old that I realized he had succeeded at that task.

Although both Mom and Gram disapproved of
Rancid's artful striving for an uninterrupted state of
leisure, they were secretly fond of the man and even on
occasion spoke begrudgingly of his skills as an outdoorsman. As a result, Rancid's halfhearted suggestion that I
accompany him and Mr. Hooker on a hunting trip won
immediate approval from the family.

The great hunting expedition was set for the
middle of the season so I still had plenty of time to
sharpen my eye on pheasants, grouse, and ducks and to
put in an occasional appearance at school lest the teachers completely forget my name and face.

One of the interesting things about your first
deer is that it has a habit of showing up where least
expected, even in school. Toward the end of geometry
class my deer would occasionally drift in to browse on
the isosceles triangles and parallelograms, and once it
bounded right through the middle of sophomore
English, not only startling me but scaring hell out of
Julius Caesar and Brutus.

"Caesar, that deer almost ran you down!" cried
Brutus.

"Et tu, Brute?" exclaimed Caesar.

"Whatchername there in the back row," shouted
Miss Fitz, the English teacher. "Stop the dreaming and
get on with your work!"

It should not be assumed that my days at school
were devoid of serious scholarship. Indeed, every morn-

ing before classes started I and my cronies would gather in the gymnasium to exchange learned lectures on that aspect of alchemy devoted to turning a set of deer tracks into venison.

These morning gatherings presented an interesting study of the caste system prevalent among young deer hunters. One was either a Yup or a Nope, depending upon his answer to that age-old question, "Gotcher deer yet?" I, of course, was still a Nope.

Although Yups and Nopes looked pretty much alike they were as different as mallards from mongooses. For one thing, a Yup would preface all his lectures with the statement, "I recollect the time I shot my first deer." Now the reason he recollected this historic event so well was that it had probably occurred no further in the past than the previous weekend. The use of the word "first" of course implied that he had downed a good many deer since. Those little nuances in the use of language were the privileges of Yup rank, and none of us Nopes challenged or even begrudged them. We aspired to be Yups someday ourselves. In fact, I wanted to be a Yup so badly I could taste it. And the taste was very sweet indeed.

This caste system was an efficient and humane way of determining the proper social level of a new kid in school. While we were standing in the gym sizing him up on his first morning, somebody would ask, "Gotcher deer yet?"

Depending upon his answer, he would be accepted immediately as a mature, respected member into the community of Yups or relegated to the humble ranks of us unsuccessful Nopes.

If the new kid said "Yup" to the question, his tone would be so modest and matter-of-fact the uninitiated might assume that he was dismissing the topic as unworthy of further consideration. Nothing could be further from the truth. If he was a bona fide Yup, the entire defensive line of the Los Angeles Rams could not have dissuaded him from relating every last detail of that momentous occasion. He would start off with what he had for breakfast on the morning in question, whether he ate one slice of toast or two, whether the toast was burnt, on which side it was burnt, and the degree of the burns. It might be assumed that this toast would eventually play some crucial part in the shooting of the deer, but its only significance was that it was eaten on the morning of that great day. This known power of one's first deer to transform minor details into events of lasting historic significance was the chief test we used to determine the authenticity of Yups.

Announcing the news that you had just changed your status from Nope to Yup was a problem almost as great as getting the first deer. Obviously, you could not rush up to the guys shouting some fool thing like, "I got my first deer! I got my first deer!" The announcement had to be made with oblique casualness, in an offhand manner. The subtle maneuvers employed toward this end included the old standby of wrapping an empty rifle shell in a handkerchief. (Any old empty would do.) When the handkerchief was pulled out, the shell fell to the floor in front of the assembled Yups and Nopes. "Dang, I dropped my lucky shell," the new Yup would say. "Careful you don't step on my lucky shell there, I sure wouldn't want to lose my lucky shell." Only a person with uncommon restraint could keep from asking, "What's so lucky about that shell?" Most of us Nopes, it should be noted, were possessed of uncommon restraint.

Another trick was to wear deer hair on your

pants until someone noticed. Occasionally, you would pick a deer hair off and fling it to the floor, saying loudly, "Dang, I got deer hair all over my pants!" A skilled practitioner of this art could make a handful of hair last most of a week or until everyone within a ten-mile radius had been made aware of his new status as a Yup. Naturally, if during this period his parents or possibly school officials required that he change his pants there was the tedious job of transferring the deer hairs to the new pair.

My hunting trip with Rancid and Mr. Hooker approached with all the speed of a glacier, but I put the time to good use in making preparation. I studied every book and article on hunting in the local library. I even took notes, which I carefully recorded in a loose-leaf notebook. A typical note went something like this: "Deer Horns—Banging two deer horns together is a good way to get deer to come within shooting range. A hunter should always have a couple of deer horns handy."

The notebook contained about four thousand such tips, most of which I forgot immediately upon reading them. For a while I considered carrying this vast reservoir of knowledge along with me for quick reference just in case I should run into my deer up in the mountains and forget what to do.

At long last the great day arrived. Rancid picked me up in his old truck at four in the morning and then we rattled over to Mr. Hooker's place. Mr. Hooker was a fine, hard old gentleman with a temper slightly shorter than a snake's hind legs. I seemed to have a knack for setting off this temper. Mr. Hooker had no more than settled himself on the seat alongside me than he instantly shot up and banged his head on the roof. The string of oaths thus ignited sizzled, popped, and banged for upwards of five minutes.

"What in gosh almighty tarnation dingbat dang is that on the seat?" he roared at me. "It liked to stab me half to death!"

"Just my deer horns," I told him indignantly. "But they seem to be all right. I don't think you hurt them none."

Mr. Hooker said he was mighty relieved to hear that.

Going up into the mountains, everyone's mood improved considerably. Rancid and Mr. Hooker told all the old stories again, starting each one off with "I ever tell you the time . . . ?" And we drank scalding black coffee and ate the fat homemade doughnuts Gram had sent along, and the two men puffed their pipes and threw back their heads and roared with laughter at their own stories, and it was all a fine thing to be doing, going up into the dark, frozen mountains early in the morning with those two old hunters, and I knew that I wanted to do this very same thing forever.

I didn't get my first deer that day or even that first season, but that was all right. Up until then I thought the only reason people went deer hunting was to hunt deer. We were after bigger game than that, I found—game rarer than a four-point unicorn. And bouncing along in Rancid's old truck, squeezed in between those two rough, exotic-smelling, cantankerous old woodsmen, I became a Yup without ever having fired a shot, a kind of Yup that I hadn't even known existed. It never bothered me too much that nobody ever asked that particular question.

Besides, I'd had other kinds of hunting success, and when a new kid arrived in school and I wanted to size him up, I could always ask, "Gotcher duck yet?"

Mountain Goats Never Say "Cheese!"

SOMEWHERE UP AHEAD, beyond the green cleavage of a mountain pass, a Fish and Game helicopter was waiting for me on a wilderness landing strip. I was several hours late for the rendezvous, having been nearly swept into oblivion while fording the river. Then there had been the long climb up to where I now found myself, inching along a game trail that ran perilously close to the edge of the gorge. Far down below, through the lingering tatters of morning fog, I could see water churning among giant boulders. Every few feet I had to stop to catch my breath and wipe the perspiration from my eyes. It wouldn't have been so bad if I had been equipped with decent mountain-climbing gear—rope, ice ax, lug-soled boots—but I was driving my car.

Little would the casual observer of that strange scene have realized that here was a man at the apex of his career as a great outdoor photographer. I didn't realize it myself. Here I thought I was just getting started in the trade but already I was at my apex. Ahead lay defeat, humiliation, poverty. Sadly enough, that was also what lay behind. I have never ceased to marvel at how low some apexes can be.

One of my numerous ambitions as a youngster had been to become a great outdoor photographer. No sooner had a small box camera come into my possession than I was out taking pictures of the outdoors. I remember hauling my first roll of exposed film down to Farley's drugstore to get it developed. I supposed that Mr. Farley did the work himself in the backroom but he said, no, he "farmed it out" to a laboratory in a distant city. The film was gone so long I began to think the distant city must be Nome, the delivery service a lame sloth traveling by snowshoes.

I hounded Mr. Farley daily about the pictures. "Any word from Nome?" I would say. "Any sign of the lame sloth?"

"Patience, my boy, patience," he would reply. Still, I began to sense that he too was awaiting the photos with an expectancy only slightly less urgent than my own.

Finally, a little yellow-and-black envelope with my name on it arrived, and as I pried up the flap with trembling fingers, Mr. Farley leaned forward and peered breathlessly over my shoulder, which was a good way to have Mr. Farley peer over your shoulder; his breath could drive ticks off a badger. I pulled out a perforated string of glossy black-and-white prints and Mr. Farley let out a long sigh of appreciation, scarcely buckling my knees in the excitement of the moment.

"Wow! Look at this!" I said to him.

"Yes, indeed," Mr. Farley said. "Uh, what is it?"

"The outdoors," I told him, trying to conceal my contempt for his lack of perception. "That's what us outdoor photographers take pictures of—the outdoors."

"Oh, yes, I see that now. Some nice gray dirt and gray sky and some nice gray rocks and gray brush. Very nice, particularly if you like gray as much as I do."

We looked at another print.

"That's one of the finest shots of a flyspeck I've ever seen," Mr. Farley said.

I stared at him in disbelief. "That's a chicken hawk!"

"Of course it is. I was just joshin' ya. Over here is the chicken, right?"

"*That*," I said with controlled rage, "is a *flyspeck!*"

After Mr. Farley mistook four ants on a paper plate for a herd of deer in a snowstorm, I folded up my pictures and went home. Although outdoor photographers are noted for their patience, they can stand only so much.

From then on I spent endless hours out in the woods photographing wildlife. Most of the shots were just your routine beautiful wildlife pictures, but every so often I would get an exceptionally fine photograph which I would honor with a title. There was, for example, "Log Leaped Over by Startled Four-Point Buck One Half-Second Before Shutter Was Snapped." Many people told me the picture was so vivid they could almost see the buck. Another really great shot was "Tip of Tail Feather of Pheasant in Flight." My favorite was "Rings on Water After Trout Jumped."

I took these photographs and others into the editor of our weekly newspaper in the hope he would have the good sense to buy them. He told me he thought I had the instincts of a great outdoor photographer but possibly my reflexes were a bit slow.

The years slipped by almost without my noticing, and one morning I awoke to discover I had a wife and three kids. It was a surprise I can tell you. Nobody seemed to know where they had come from. I also had a job, which was an even bigger surprise. One day I said to the wife, "How will I ever fulfill my lifelong ambition of becoming a great outdoor photographer if I have to work at that job all the time to support you and our three kids?"

"Four kids," she said. "Last year it was three, this year it's four."

I could feel Old Man Time breathing down the back of my neck. At first I thought he was Mr. Farley, but then I discovered it was actually our kindly old landlord who was fond of giving me bits of advice—"Pay da rent, fella, or else. . . ."

It was at this juncture that I decided to quit my job and become a free-lance writer and photographer, specializing in the Great Outdoors.

"I feel so free," I shouted, after severing relations with my employer. "No more commuting, no more kowtowing to bosses, no more compromising my principles!"

"No more eating!" my wife shouted. A comical soul, she would do just about anything for a laugh, but I thought rending her garment while pouring ashes on her head was going a bit far.

The only things a great outdoor photographer needs to set up in business are some film and a good camera outfit. Film is about $1.50 a roll, and you can pick up a good camera and accessories for not much more than you would pay for an albino elephant that can tap dance and sing in three languages. Since I blew my life savings on the roll of film, I had to borrow the money for the camera and accessories. Fortunately, I had learned of a loan company run by about the nicest people you could ever expect to do business with, even though they had to operate out of the back seat of a car while their new building was under construction.

After we had shaken hands on the deal, I told the loan officer, Louie, that it was none of my business but I thought they could get a better return on their money than 10 percent a year.

"A year? What year?" Louie said. He quickly explained that the interest was by the week, compounded hourly and that the only collateral was a pound of my flesh to be selected at random fifteen seconds after I missed the first payment. I exaggerate, of course. It wasn't fifteen seconds but nearly a day after I missed the first payment that my wife reported to me that two bulky hominoids had stopped by to inquire of my whereabouts. "I think they were carrying arms," she said nervously.

"You must have been mistaken," I said. "Maybe a few fingers or toes but not arms!" What kind of monsters did she think I would borrow money from, anyway?

Such was the incentive instilled in me by this visit that within a month I had the loan paid off. Editors couldn't resist my photographs.

"Terrific!" one of them said to me. "This is a fantastic shot of a woman and children in rags, a real tear-jerker. What's she got on her head, anyhow?"

"Ashes," I said, "but that's a portrait of my family and not for sale. How about this great shot of the hind foot of a bear that's just walked behind a tree?"

"I'll take it, I'll take it!" the editor said.

As time went along both my photographic skills and my reflexes improved to the point where I was shooting pictures of whole animals. I still had trouble getting good shots of leaping fish, but I produced many a fine picture wherein my catch of trout dwarfed the creel and flyrod I used for props. The fish were only eight inches long, but the creel and flyrod belonged to a dwarf.

Steadily my career progressed upward until that moment I found myself steering my car down a game trail toward an appointment with a helicopter. When I at last came ploughing out of the forest and onto the landing strip, the helicopter was still there but the pilot was nowhere to be seen. The only person around was a grizzled old packer, sitting on a log and staring at the helicopter.

"Dang things weren't meant to fly," he said to me, nodding at the chopper. "Man has to be a crazy fool to fly around these mountains in one of them eggbeaters. Give me a good mule any day."

"Don't say things like that," I told him, "because I got to go fly in that eggbeater."

"So you're the feller," he said. "Well, let's git on with it then, 'cause I'm the pilot."

The pilot's name was Lefty, and he was a pleasant but rather serious chap. "Let me explain just what we're going to do," he said, after we had climbed into the cockpit. "If you understand what's happening, you won't worry so much about us crackin' up. I always like my passengers to just relax and enjoy the ride. Hell, there's no sense in both of us being terrified."

As we lifted off and made a quick clean sweeping turn up over a wall of pine trees, I concealed my modest anxiety under an expression of disinterest and a hint of boredom.

"Nervous?" Lefty shouted at me.

"Not at all," I shouted back.

"Good," he said. "Then maybe you'll let go of my leg. You're cutting off the circulation."

Once we were on our way, the pilot reached forward and patted a little statue of St. Christopher, the patron saint of travelers, mounted on the instrument panel.

"Catholic?" I asked.

"No," he said. "Cautious."

Lefty was a good tour guide. He pointed out miniature deer far below and a herd of elk galloping along like tall ants.

"There goes a bear!" he shouted. "Look at that rascal run! Must think we're a bear hawk!"

As we pounded up over a steep, thickly forested hillside, he indicated a tiny clearing. "Last year about this time I had to put the chopper down right there."

"Gosh," I said. "That clearing doesn't look big enough to land a helicopter in."

"Shoot," he replied, "until we landed, there wasn't a clearing there at all. We mowed down trees like tall grass. Flipped plumb upside down and spun like a top. Really held our attention for a few moments. Now there you go, cuttin' off the circulation in my leg again!"

"Sorry," I said. "I just became engrossed in your story."

A sheer rock cliff that seemed a mile high loomed directly in front of us, and Lefty showed every intention of flying us smack into it.

"I got to cut out the chatter now 'cause we're coming to the scary part," he said.

"The scary part?"

"Yup, we got to catch the elevator."

"Elevator?"

He quickly explained that because of the altitude and the limited power of the helicopter, he had to put the chopper right in close to the cliff so we could ride up on the strong updraft. "St. Christopher, don't fail me now!" he said.

The elevator ride was indeed an exhilarating experience. I broke the world's record for longest sustained inhale while the pilot kept mumbling something about a valley of death. In a second we came zooming up over the top of the cliff, where Lefty cut a sporty little figure eight and set us down on the mountain peak.

He wet his finger and marked up an invisible score in the air. "St. Christopher 685, Death 0."

What, you have probably asked, could have prompted me to risk life, limb, and my meager breakfast to soar up to this barren windblown pinnacle of rock? The answer is that I was there to photograph a mountain-goat-trapping expedition. The Idaho Fish and Game department was capturing goats, ferrying them off the mountain via helicopter, and transplanting them in a goatless area of the state. The action went like this: a goat would be lured into a net trap, then two Fish and Game men would jump on him, wrestle him to the ground, and give him a shot of tranquilizer to calm him down. The goat, for his part, would try to tap dance on the heads of his molesters while simultaneously trying to spindle them on his horns. There would be this ball of furious activity, consisting of legs, arms, eyes, hooves, horns, bleats, bellows, grunts and curses, until one of the F and G men would shout, "Quick, the tranquilizer!"

A hypodermic needle would flash amid the tangle of goat and men. "Got it! How's that?"

"Great," the other man would say. "Now let's see if you can get the next one in the goat."

It was all very amusing and provided me with some fine action shots. The one problem, as I saw it, was that the trappers tended to favor the smaller goats.

What I wanted was some photos of them tangling with a really big billy, right up on the edge of the cliff where it would be exciting, but they chose to ignore my suggestions, claiming that the small goats more than satisfied their thirst for excitement.

At last I persuaded Jack McNeel, a tall, lean conservation officer, to have a go at one of the big goats. I situated myself on an outcropping of rock close to the net at the edge of the cliff, camera at the ready. Presently, the King Kong of mountain goats came sauntering up the hill and strolled into the trap for a lick of the salt block used for bait. When the trap closed on him, that goat went absolutely bananas. Rock, hair, and pieces of goat trap flew in all directions. As Jack and another F and G man came racing toward the raging animal, I knew I was about to get the greatest action shots in the history of outdoor photography. But just as Jack was about to close in, the goat got a horn under the bottom edge of the trap and sent the contraption flying ten feet in the air. Caught up in the excitement of the chase and without thinking, McNeel made a lunge and grabbed the billy by a horn. What happened next was more than I had ever even dreamed of in my career as a wildlife photographer. I was absolutely awestruck by the sheer power of the spectacle. Perhaps you've never seen a mountain goat twirl a six-foot-four man over his head like a baton, but if you ever get the chance it's well worth the price of admission. That nifty little performance, however, was just the warm up for the grand finale. The grand finale was where the goat made a great running leap out over the edge of the cliff, Jack still clinging desperately to his horn.

I have not the slightest doubt that the conservation officer saved that goat's life, not to mention his own. As he hurtled out into space, McNeel reached down and grabbed a branch of a stunted little tree growing on the edge of the cliff. For an instant they dangled there, Jack clinging to the branch with one hand and to the goat with the other. Then he dropped the billy, who landed on an inch-wide ledge twenty feet below and galloped off. It was all absolutely stunning.

Jack crawled back up over the edge of the cliff and lay on the rock, panting. "I guess that must have made some picture, hunh?" he said.

"Picture?" I said. "What picture?" For the first time since the action started, I stared down at the camera clenched in my sweating hands.

I HAD FORGOTTEN TO TAKE THE PICTURE!

Like the great fish that got away and the great trophy buck that was missed, the great outdoor photograph that wasn't taken leaves no proof of its existence. But Jack McNeel of the Idaho Fish and Game department will swear to the absolute truth of what I have reported here. At least the last time I saw him, he was still swearing about it.

My spirit had been broken, and then and there on that windswept mile-high slab of granite I gave up my career as a great outdoor photographer. I packed my gear, shuffled up to the peak, and climbed aboard the waiting helicopter.

"Now comes the bad part," the pilot said. "Just sit back and relax."

Never Sniff a Gift Fish

Also by Patrick F. McManus

Kid Camping From Aaaaiii! to Zip
A Fine and Pleasant Misery
They Shoot Canoes, Don't They?
The Grasshopper Trap
Rubber Legs and White Tail-Hairs

NEVER
SNIFF
A
GIFT FISH

Patrick F. McManus

An Owl Book

Henry Holt and Company   •   **New York**

Published by Henry Holt and Company, Inc.,
115 West 18th Street, New York, New York 10011.
Published in Canada by Fitzhenry & Whiteside Limited,
195 Allstate Parkway, Markham, Ontario L3R 4T8.

Library of Congress Cataloging-in-Publication Data
McManus, Patrick F.
Never sniff a gift fish.
1. Hunting—Addresses, essays, lectures. 2. Fishing—
Addresses, essays, lectures. I. Title.
SK33.M43   1983   799'.02'07   83-147
ISBN 0-8050-0527-7
ISBN 0-8050-0031-3 (An Owl book: pbk.)

Henry Holt books are available at special discounts
for bulk purchases for sales promotions, premiums,
fund-raising, or educational use. Special editions
or book excerpts can also be created to specification.

For details contact:
Special Sales Director
Henry Holt and Company, Inc.
115 West 18th Street
New York, New York 10011

First published in hardcover by Holt, Rinehart and
Winston in 1983.

First Owl Book Edition—1984

Designer: Kate Nichols
Printed in the United States of America
20   19   18   17   16   15   14

All stories in this book originally appeared as follows: In *Field &
Stream:* "Blowing Smoke," "The Man Who Notices Things," "The
Short Happy Life of Francis Cucumber," "Well, Excuuuuse Me!,"
"The Mountain Car," "Never Sniff a Gift Fish," "Edgy Rider," "The
Fibricators," "The Family Camper's Dictionary," "The Big Match,"
and "The Elk Trappers"; in *Outdoor Life:* "Poof—No Eyebrows!," "I
Fish; Therefore, I Am," "Running on Empty," "The Cat and the Cat
Burglar," "The Christmas Hatchet," "The Kindest Cut of All,"
"Share and Share Alike," "Backseats I Have Known," "The
Hunters' Workout Guide," "Temporary Measures," and "The Bush
Pilots"; in *Audubon:* "Salami on Rye and Hold the Wild Gobo," and
"Two-Man-Tent Fever"(and *Reader's Digest*); in *Daiwa Fishing
Annual:* " 'Fish Poles,' and Other Useful Terminology"; in *Scotch
Game Call Annual:* "The Arkansas Prank Hound"; in *Spokane
Magazine:* "The Night Grandma Shot Shorty"; and in *Johnson
Outboards Boating 1980:* "Strange Scenes and Eerie Events."

To Patricia

Contents

Never Sniff a Gift Fish

Blowing Smoke

Many people think that my reputation as a great outdoorsman is a product of inherent athletic ability. Nothing could be further from the truth, which is that I have been cursed since birth with an extraordinary lack of coordination.

For years my fly-casting technique was compared, rather banally I might add, to an old lady fighting off a bee with a broom handle. My canoe paddling raised shouts of alarm among onlookers, who assumed I was trying to repel an assault by a North American cousin of the Loch Ness monster. My attempts to pitch the family tent terrorized entire campgrounds. As for marksmanship, any game I happened to bring into camp was routinely examined by my disbelieving companions for powder burns. ("The man has stealth," they would say. "Who else could place the muzzle of a rifle to the head of a sleeping mule-deer buck? Who else could still miss?")

1

For years I suffered the ridicule of my fellow sportsmen over what they perceived to be my ineptitude. Then one day I happened to recall a lovable old college administrator I had once served time under, Dr. Milburn Snodgrass. That casual recollection was to advance outdoor sports by a hundred years.

Doc Snodgrass had taken up pipe smoking as a young man and turned it into a highly successful career, eventually rising to the position of dean. Obviously, his success was not due merely to pipe smoking. No, he was also the master of two facial expressions: thoughtful and bemused. Those were the total ingredients of his success. The man was dumb. It is my considered opinion that if intelligence were crankcase oil, his would not have wet the tip of the dipstick let alone reached the add-one-quart mark. But he was an excellent dean.

No matter what problem was brought before Doc Snodgrass, his response was to sit back and puff on his pipe, alternating between thoughtful and bemused expressions. The effect suggested that Doc was bemused by a problem so ridiculously simple and was giving thought to firing the nincompoop who dared bother him with it. The problem-bearer would laugh feebly, to indicate it was all a little joke, and then rush off to find the solution himself. People thought Snodgrass was a genius and often wondered what great ideas he was mulling over as he puffed his pipe and looked thoughtful and bemused. Eventually, I would learn the truth: Doc Snodgrass was not smart enough to mull.

One example will serve to illustrate the effectiveness of the dean's approach to human relations.

During a campus uprising, the students demanded that the college administration do away with Poverty,

War, and Mashed Turnips in the Commissary, although not necessarily in that order. Doc Snodgrass appeared suddenly on the steps of the administration building, seemingly to confront the chanting mob but more likely because he had mistaken the exit for the door to the restroom. (His thoughtful expression was probably due at first to his wondering why so many students of both sexes were in the men's room.) As he fumbled about in his pockets looking for his tobacco pouch—the search for the source of the Nile took scarcely longer—the students fell silent, no doubt saving their breath for the purpose of shouting down the words of wisdom they expected to be forthcoming from the dean. (Youths are not called callow for nothing.) The pouch at last found, the dean began to fill his pipe, tamping and filling, tamping and filling, and all the while looking extremely thoughtful. Then he began probing his pockets for a match. Finally, an exasperated student in guerrilla attire lunged forward and thrust upon him a disposable lighter, little realizing that the dean was confounded by all such modern technology. His efforts to ignite the lighter by scratching it against a brick wall produced a good laugh from the students and a consensus among them that anyone with a sense of humor like that couldn't be such a bad guy after all. The mood of the crowd lightened. A game of Frisbee broke out. Someone threw a football. A coed burned her bra.

Having solved the riddle of the lighter, and tortured the tobacco into a state of combustion, Snodgrass began sucking away on his pipe as he looked increasingly thoughtful. He was, as I say, a master of the thoughtful expression. Even the hardliners among the students seemed unable to resist the impression that the dean was contemplating the eradication of Poverty, War, and Mashed Turnips. The crowd began to disperse, its members exchanging among themselves the opinion that the dean had not only a great sense of humor but a mind "like a steel trap." The truth was, he had a mind like flypaper, and not very good flypaper at that. His total intellectual arsenal consisted of his pipe and those two facial expressions.

The import of the dean's pipe did not strike me immediately, but when it did, I rushed out and bought myself a pipe and tobacco and began practicing my expressions. As a direct consequence of these efforts, I began rising through the professorial ranks as if by levitation. The ugly rumor that I had flunked three successive IQ tests (there were a lot of trick questions) was silenced once and for all. Faculty and students alike began referring to me as one who had a mind like a steel trap. And I continued to puff my pipe and look alternately bemused and thoughtful as promotion after promotion was thrust upon me. Still, not all was well. There was the problem of my ineptitude at outdoor sports.

Then one day I was struck by a marvelous idea. If my pipe and expressions had worked so well in advancing my career, why wouldn't they be equally effective in something worthwhile, such as hunting and fishing? The very next weekend, on a fishing trip with Retch Sweeney and Fenton Quagmire, I took along my pipe and tobacco and, of course, my ability to become bemused or thoughtful at the drop of a hat.

The fishing started out routinely, with Sweeney and Quagmire making snide remarks about my casting technique. For the most part, however, they confined their merriment to a few chortles, saving the belly laughs for the embarrassing predicament that my lack of coordination invariably lands me in.

Presently, I spotted a promising patch of water, but it was made almost inaccessible because of thick brush and high banks on one side and a monstrous logjam on the other. For that very reason I guessed that the deep hole beneath the logjam probably hadn't been prospected recently by other anglers. As I studied the situation, I noticed a slender log jutting out through the brush on the bank, and I quickly calculated that by sitting on the end of this log I could cast over the hole and still remain concealed from the fish. Five minutes later I was perched somewhat precariously on the end of the log and, in fact, had already extracted a couple of plump trout from beneath the logjam. Sweeney and Quagmire, both as yet without a single strike, glared enviously at me and cursed my ingenuity. Now it was my turn to chortle. But right in the middle of my chortle, a huge rainbow zoomed out of the depths like a Polaris missile and detonated on my Black Gnat. This was exactly what I had been anticipating, and with lightning reflexes, I fell off the log and dropped fifteen feet into a bed of assorted boulders, none smaller than a breadbox. Even though my impact on the rocks caused me to wonder momentarily whether pelvic transplants had yet been perfected, I immediately arose without so much as a whimper, whipped out my pipe, and began stuffing it with tobacco. Already I detected the sounds of Sweeney and Quagmire crashing through the brush, possibly to determine if I had suffered any serious injury but more likely racing each other for the fishing spot I had so recently abandoned. In any case, I knew that great booming laughs were already gestating in their bellies.

But I was ready. When their heads popped from the brush, I was calmly puffing on my pipe and looking thoughtfully up at the log.

"You hurt?" Sweeney asked, traces of a smile already playing in the corners of his mouth.

To such a question I normally would have snappishly replied, "No, you idiot, I've always been shaped like a potato chip!" Then would have come the wild howls of mirth, the ecstatic knee-slapping, and the attempts by Sweeney and Quagmire to re-create through mimicry some of my more extravagant moves during the course of the fall. But not this time.

Calmly, I blew a puff of smoke toward them and displayed my bemused look. I then returned my thoughtful gaze to the log.

I will not exaggerate the quality of my companions' mental processes by suggesting that they had flashes of insight. Nevertheless, I sensed some faint cognitive flickerings.

"Whatcha do that for?" asked Quagmire, referring to my fall.

"Yeah, you could've hurt yourself," Sweeney added, puzzled.

Without replying, I continued to study the log thoughtfully, occasionally tossing a bemused look in the direction of my audience of two.

Thoroughly befuddled, Quagmire and Sweeney at last wandered off to resume their fishing. They clearly were of the impression that I had deliberately planned and executed the fall from the log, possibly as a scientific experiment for a secret government agency. Success! Before shouting "Eureka!" however, I salved my injuries with emergency first aid, which consisted largely of defoliating all the flora within a five-foot radius by hissing a stream of colorful expressions, and hopping about like a rain dancer trying to terminate a five-year drought.

I could scarcely wait to test the pipe-and-two-expression ploy on wits quicker than those of Sweeney and Quagmire. The next weekend I was fishing alone on one of my favorite rivers and happened to run into a chap whose name turned out to be Shep. He obviously was an expert fly caster. His wrist would twitch and eighty feet of line would shoot toward the far bank, the tiny fly settling on the surface of the water as softly as a falling flake of dandruff. Even as I watched, he netted one of the finest trout I've ever seen taken from the river.

"I think I'll keep this one," he said to me. "Now the big ones, I always release them."

"Big ones?" I said, ogling his hefty catch. "Why, yes, I never take any of the big ones home myself. In fact, I often don't take home any small ones or middle-sized ones either."

"Now, that's what I call true sportsmanship!" Shep said, casually dropping a fly three inches from the far bank. "Say, there's plenty of room here. Why don't you try a few casts yourself?"

I had already dug out my pipe and lighted up. "Well, maybe, but first let me see you do that again, that, uh, cast of yours."

He obliged me with a repeat performance, this time placing the fly a mere inch from the bank. I puffed my pipe and gave him my bemused look.

"Something wrong?" he asked, a note of unease in his voice.

I puffed away, looking bemused, as he made another awesome cast. He was showing definite signs of discomfort.

"It's my elbow, isn't it?" he said. "I've never held my elbow the way you're supposed to. Maybe you can give me a couple of lessons."

I knocked the ashes out of my pipe, changed to the thoughtful expression, and unleashed a powerful twenty-foot cast, the splash from which lifted a flock of crows cawing into the air from a nearby cornfield.

Shep leaped back. "Are you okay? That was a nasty spasm you had just then."

I silenced him with my bemused look. Then I stoked up my pipe again, alternating between thoughtful and bemused expressions. That destroyed the last of Shep's confidence. Ten minutes later I had him totally under my power and was even giving him a few casting tips.

"There you go again," I scolded him, "casting over twenty-five feet. You have to learn control, man, learn control!"

"I know," Shep said, whimpering, "but I just can't seem to get the knack of it."

"Well, then, try this approach," I advised. "Just pretend you're a little old lady fighting off a bee with a broom handle."

Naturally, I was delighted to discover that this bit of business with the pipe and two expressions not only transcended my lack of coordination but conveyed the impression that I was actually an expert angler. Within six months, I had applied the technique to all the other outdoor sports and found that it worked equally well. Now when I missed an easy shot at a pheasant, say, I would no longer hang my head and look embarrassed. Instead, I'd stick the pipe in my mouth and look bemused. "You sure scared the heck out of that ol' ring-neck," my companion would say. "You've got to be darn good to miss a shot like that!"

To date, my greatest achievement with the pipe and two expressions occurred on a backpacking trip into a wilderness area of the Rocky Mountains. Sweeney, Quagmire, and I were hiking along a trail when we came across a bear track of approximately the dimensions of a doormat.

"*Bleep!*" hissed Sweeney. "Look at the size of that track!"

"It's fr-fresh, too," whispered Quagmire, swiveling his head about. "L-looks like grizzly. Can't be far away, either."

As I now do under all such circumstances, I dug out the pipe, calmly filled, tamped, and lighted it. Just then a grouse exploded from the brush at the edge of the trail and gave all three of us quite a start. Nevertheless, I puffed away on my pipe and looked bemused. Both Quagmire and Sweeney said later they were extremely impressed by my reaction. After all, it's no simple thing to puff a pipe and look bemused when you're running that fast.

Poof—No Eyebrows!

Just as I was assembling the ingredients for a small snack in the kitchen, the doorbell rang. My wife, Bun, went to answer it, and I heard her invite in Milt Slapshot, a neighbor who often seeks out my advice on matters pertaining to the sporting life.

"Is Pat home?" I heard Milt ask. "A fella told me he knows something about muzzleloading."

Realizing Bun could never resist a straight line like that, I jumped up and headed for the living room in the hope of stifling her.

"Does he ever!" she said, chortling. "Why, this very minute he's out in the kitchen loading his muzzle!"

A wife who chortles is an irritation, but one who also regards herself as a wit is a social nuisance. I grabbed Milt by the arm and guided him toward the den before Bun could embarrass the poor fellow further with another attempt at emulating Erma Bombeck.

"Stop the cackling, Milt," I told him. "It only encourages her."

Once his tasteless display of mirth had subsided, Milt explained that he was building a muzzleloader and needed some technical advice from me. A mutual acquaintance, one Retch Sweeney, had told him that I had once conducted extensive scientific research on primitive firearms. That was true. In fact, it would be difficult to find firearms more primitive than those utilized in my research.

"You've come to the right man," I said. "Yes, indeed. Now the first thing I need to know is, are you building it from a kit or from scratch?"

"A kit," Milt said.

"Good," I said. "Building muzzleloaders from scratch is a risky business, particularly when you work your way up to sewer pipe too soon. Now the first thing . . ."

"Sewer pipe?" Milt asked. "What do you mean, sewer pipe? Are you sure you know something about black powder?"

"Ha!" I replied. "Do you see my eyebrows?"

"No."

"Well, that should answer your question. All us experts on black powder have bald eyes."

Actually, I do have eyebrows, but they are pale, sickly fellows, never having recovered from the shock of instant immolation thirty years ago. Having my eyebrows catch fire ranks as one of the more interesting experiences of my life, although I must say I didn't enjoy it much at the time.

Indeed, my somewhat faulty eyesight may be a direct result of having my eyebrows go up in smoke. Either it was that or the splash of Orange Crush soda pop with which my sidekick Retch Sweeney, ever quick to compound a catastrophe, doused the flames.

As I explained to Milt, who had settled into a chair in the den and was attempting with some success to conceal his fascination, most of my early research into the mysteries of black powder took place during the year I was fourteen. Some of those experiments produced spectacular results, particularly the last one, which enabled Retch and me to attend the annual Halloween party as twin cinders.

The first experiment, in which my eyebrows were sacrificed to the cause of science, consisted of placing a small pile of black powder on a bicycle seat and touching a lighted match to it. I can no longer recall why a bicycle seat was employed as part of the apparatus, but I am sure my co-researcher and I had sound reasons for it at the time. In any case, we proved conclusively that a match flame serves as an excellent catalyst on gunpowder. I later concluded that the experiment might have been improved upon in only two ways: to have placed the powder on *Retch's* bicycle seat and to have let *him* hold the match. Instead, he chose to stand in awe of the experiment and about ten feet away, sucking absently on a bottle of Orange Crush. On the other hand, my sacrifice was not without its reward, since bald eyes and a hole burnt in my bicycle seat made great conversation openers with girls at school.

The success of the experiment had to be withheld from the rest of the scientific community for fear our parents would find out about it. Unfortunately, my mother inadvertently discovered the secret.

"Is anything the matter?" Mom asked during supper the evening after the bicycle-seat experiment.

"No," I replied casually. "Why do you ask?"

"Oh, nothing in particular," she said. "It just seems a little odd, your wearing sunglasses and a cap at the dinner table."

She then expressed her desire that I remove both glasses and cap instantly, sooner if possible. After some debate over the finer points of dinner-table propriety, I complied.

As expected, Mom responded with the classic question favored by the parents of young black powder experimenters everywhere: "WHAT HAPPENED TO YOUR EYEBROWS?"

Looking surprised and fingering the scorched area above my eyes, I tried to convey the impression that it was news to me that my eyebrows were missing, as if they might have dropped off unnoticed or been mislaid at school.

The truth was soon extracted from me with an efficiency that would have been the envy of medieval counterintelligence agents. This was followed by a bit of parental advice. But scarcely had this parental advice ceased reverberating among the rafters than I was already plotting my next experiments for unlocking the mysteries of black powder.

The discovery by Retch and me that we could purchase black powder in bulk from a local dealer was to have great impact on our lives, not to mention various parts of our anatomies. The dealer in question was the proprietor of Grogan's War Surplus, Hardware & Gun Emporium, none other than that old reprobate, Henry P. Grogan himself. We weren't at all sure Grogan would sell a couple of scruffy, goof-off kids something as potentially dangerous as black powder. Our first attempt at making a purchase was, therefore, cloaked in subtlety and subterfuge.

"Howdy, Mr. Grogan," we opened with, both of us so casual we were fit to burst.

"Howdy, boys. What can I do for you—assuming, of course, you got cash in your pockets and ain't just here to finger the merchandise?"

"Oh, we got cash," I said. "Uh, Retch, why don't you read Mr. Grogan our list?"

"Uh, okay, heh, heh. Yeah, well, here goes—one GI mess kit, one helmet liner, a parachute harness, a pound of black powder, and let's see, now, do you have any of those neat camouflage jackets left?"

To our chagrin, a look of concern came into Grogan's eyes. "Gosh, boys, I don't know if I should . . . It just don't seem right to sell you two young fellows . . . Oh, what the heck! Elmer Peabody wanted me to save those last two camouflage jackets for him, but I'll let you have 'em. Now, how much gunpowder was that you wanted—a pound?"

In all fairness to Grogan, I must admit that he did warn us that severe bodily harm could result from improper use of the black powder. His exact words, if I remember correctly, were, "You boys set off any of that stuff near my store and I'll peel your hides!"

The black powder we bought from Grogan had been compressed by the manufacturer into shiny black pellets, a form intended, I believe, to make it less volatile. Even before mashing them into powder, we found it was possible to touch off the pellets if they were first piled on a bicycle seat and a match held to them. The pellets did not ignite immediately even then, apparently for the purpose of tricking the person holding the match into taking a closer look at what was occurring on the bicycle seat. Then—*poof!*—no eyebrows.

Our first muzzleloaders were small and crude, but as our technological skill and knowledge increased, they gradually became large and crude. We never did develop a satisfactory triggering mechanism. On the average shot, you could eat a sandwich between the time the trigger was pulled and the gun discharged. A typical muzzleloader test would go something like this:

RETCH: Okay, I'm going to squeeze the trigger now. There!

MUZZLELOADER: *Snick! Pop! Ssssss . . .*

ME: Good. It looks like it's working. Better start aiming at the tin can.

MUZZLELOADER: *Ssss . . . fizt . . . ssss . . .*

RETCH: Say, give me a bit of that sandwich, will you?

ME: Sure.

MUZZLELOADER: *. . . sss . . . sput . . . ss . . . putt . . . ss . . .*

RETCH: What time is it?

ME: About time for me to—

MUZZLELOADER: *. . . ssst—POOT!*

RETCH (enveloped in cloud of smoke): How was my aim?

ME: I think it was pretty good, but the muzzle velocity leaves something to be desired. As soon as the smoke clears, reach over and pick up the ball and we'll load her up again.

Even as we increased the range of our muzzleloaders, the delay in the firing mechanism discouraged us from using them on game. If we had used one of them for rabbit hunting, say, we would have had to squeeze the trigger and then hope a rabbit would happen to be running by when the gun discharged. Squeezing the trigger before your game appears over the far horizon is the ultimate in leading a moving target.

Since we had up to three minutes of lead time on stationary targets, hunting with our muzzleloaders seemed somewhat impractical. There was also the probable embarrassment of having our shots bounce off the game. It didn't seem worth the risk. A hunter can stand only so much humiliation.

Our first muzzleloader was a small-caliber derringer, the ammunition for which consisted mostly of dried peas. This prompted Retch to remark derisively to a tin-can target, "All right, Ringo, drop your iron or I'll fill you full of dried peas."

"Okay, okay," I said, "I get your drift. We'll move up to the hard stuff—marbles, ball bearings, golf balls."

It was a mistake, though, and I knew it. Once you start escalating, there's no stopping until you achieve the ultimate weapon. Within a couple of months, we were turning out muzzleloaders in the .80-caliber range. Then we got into the large-caliber stuff. Finally, we decided the time had come to stop monkeying around with black powder pistols and rifles. We'd had some close calls. We had reached the point where there was some doubt in our minds whether we might be firing a muzzleloader or touching off a bomb. Thus it was with considerable relief that we abandoned our clandestine manufacture and testing of pistols and rifles. After all, a cannon would be much safer; you didn't have to hold it.

The cannon was constructed of sewer pipe, two-by-fours, baby-carriage wheels, rubber inner-tube bands, a clothespin, baling wire, and various other odds and ends, all of which, blending into a single, symmetrical unity, neared perfection on the scale of beauty. A croquet ball was commandeered from the Sweeney backyard for use as shot. In our enthusiasm of the moment, it was thought the croquet ball could be returned to the set after it was recovered from the firing range. Alas, it was not to be so.

Attired in our muskrat-skin hats, which we had sewn up ourselves, we mounted our bicycles and, with cannon in tow, set off for the local golf course, where a fairway would serve as a firing range, a putting green as a target.

As we had hoped, the golf course turned out to be deserted. We quickly wheeled the cannon into firing position and began the loading procedure.

"Think that's enough powder?" Retch asked.

"Better dump in some more," I advised. "That croquet ball is pretty heavy."

"And there's some for good measure," Retch said.

The croquet ball fit a little too tightly, but we managed to ram it down the barrel.

Then we both took up positions alongside the cannon to witness the rare and wonderful spectacle of a sewer pipe firing a croquet ball down a golf-course fairway.

"Ready, aim, fire!" I commanded.

Retch tripped the firing mechanism.

Eventually, the thunder was replaced by clanging bells inside our heads, the shattered pieces of earth and sky fell back into place, and the wobbly world righted itself. Retch and I limped over to the side of a utility shed and sat down to relax a bit and collect our senses. Presently, a deputy sheriff drove up. He stood for a moment gazing at the haze of smoke wafting gently over the golf course, the patch of smoldering turf ringed by fragments of sewer pipe, baby-carriage wheels, and pieces of two-by-four. Then, hoisting up his gun belt, he sauntered over to us.

"You boys know anything about an explosion out this way?" he asked.

"What kind of explosion?" Retch asked.

"A *big* explosion."

I was still so stunned I couldn't even think up a good lie. Anyway, I knew the deputy had us cold.

"Now, what I want to know," the deputy went on, "is why are you two boys sitting out here behind this shed smoking?"

"Shucks," I said, "if you'd been a little earlier, you'd have seen us while we were still on fire!"

I thought for sure he was going to haul us off to jail, but instead he just smiled, took one last look at the smoldering debris, and started to saunter back to his car. "Well, if you fellas turn up any information about the explosion," he said over his shoulder, "I'd appreciate it if you'd let me know. I don't reckon there'll be another one, do you?"

"Nope," Retch and I said in unison.

Then the deputy stopped and kicked gingerly at something on the ground in front of him. It was Retch's muskrat hat! The deputy turned and gave us a sympathetic look. "Too bad about your dog," he said.

The cannon pretty well quelled our enthusiasm for building our own muzzleloaders from scratch. Not only had it made a big impression on us; it had made numerous small impressions. Years later, while I was undergoing a physical examination, the doctor commented on some bumps under my skin.

"Pay them no mind, doc," I told him. "They're just pieces of sewer pipe."

At this juncture of my recitation, Milt Slapshot jumped up and headed for the door.

"Thanks," he said. "You've answered my question."

"Gee," I said. "I've even forgotten what the question was. But if you need any help putting your muzzleloader kit together, Milt, just give me a call."

He hasn't called yet. I suppose he's been tied up at the office a lot lately.

I Fish;
Therefore, I Am

Scholars have long known that fishing eventually turns men into philosophers. Unfortunately, it is almost impossible to buy decent tackle on a philosopher's salary. I have always thought it would be better if fishing turned men into Wall Street bankers, but that is not the case. It's philosophers or nothing.

I became a philosopher at age twelve, after a scant six years of fishing. One evening at supper I looked up from my plate and announced, "I fish; therefore, I am." Perhaps awed by this evidence of precocity in a young boy, my stepfather turned to my mother and asked, "Is there any more gravy?" Thus encouraged, I forgot about philosophy until I went off to college.

The intellectual experience of life in a college dorm proved to be enormously stimulating, and soon I was engaged in a variety of scientific experiments. My research paper, "Levitation: A Roommate's Response to a Garter Snake in His Bed," caught the fancy of a psychology professor who invited me to join him in research on abnormal behavior in lesser primates. Three months later, I made a remarkable discovery. If I pressed either the red or green buttons, nothing happened, but if I pressed the yellow, a bunch of bananas would drop out of a hole in the ceiling. Not caring much for bananas, I resigned my position and went in search of more serious, if not more fruitful, studies.

While trying to decide on a major in college, I picked up a minor in philosophy, one Maylene Whipple by name, who could have passed for twenty-five any day of the week. It came as a shock to me to learn that the precocious Maylene was only seventeen, particularly since we had already engaged in discourse on the Hegelian dialectic, which is a felony in most states even if committed by consenting adults. Maylene was amazed at my grasp of all the world's great philosophies, but less so at my grasp of her left knee, to which she responded with a karate chop that left my wrist bones in shambles.

"Where did you learn so much about philosophy?" Maylene asked, as I smiled suavely, clutching my throbbing wrist in an armpit.

"From fishing," I said. "I started fishing at age six, and by the time I was twelve, I was a full-fledged philosopher."

"Pooh!" she said. "Fishing can't turn you into a philosopher!"

"Oh yeah!" I said. "How about Francis Bacon? How about him?"

"What about Francis Bacon?"

"Why, Bacon was nothing but a humble tailor until he took up fishing. Five years later, he invented the scientific method and changed the course of history, despite never having landed a brown trout over fourteen inches."

"That's incredible!" Maylene gasped.

"Yes," I replied, "particularly when you consider there were plenty of really big brown trout around back then. The rule is, however, The worse the fisherman, the better the philosopher."

I went on to explain to Maylene that Aristotle was known among his associates merely as "one weird dude" until he met up with Plato. "Teach me to be a philosopher," Aristotle pleaded.

Plato was immediately intrigued by the young man. "All right," he said. "Let us begin with the basics: Truth, Justice, and How to Bait a Hook Properly."

Plato himself was so miserably inept at fishing that he eventually wrote *The Republic,* which is just about as bad as you can get when it comes to catching fish. Much to Plato's disappointment, *The Republic* was rejected by all the leading outdoor publications of the day.

"That sounds pretty fishy to me," Maylene said.

"Yes," I replied. "That is what I am trying to tell you. All philosophy is pretty fishy underneath."

"Underneath what?" Maylene asked.

"I don't know that yet," I said. "I'm only a sophomore."

And I was to remain a sophomore for several years, largely as a result of my study of philosophy at every lake and stream within a hundred miles of the university. The one great universal question I sought to answer was why the angler always should have been here last week.

After graduation, I studied with the great French existential philosopher Albert Camus, who told me that men must learn to live without hope.

"Why is that?" I asked, disentangling a backlash.

Taking advantage of the opportunity afforded by my backlash, Camus cast into the hole in which I had just had a nice strike. "Because that way, even if you don't catch any fish, you're never disappointed. You can always say you just enjoyed being out communing with nature on a nice day. Catching fish is not a matter of ultimate concern, unless, of course, we are talking about something over five pounds."

The other great French existential philosopher, Jean-Paul Sartre, once gave me an analogy to explain his concepts of Being and Nothingness. "This," he said, holding up a stick with one paltry eight-inch trout on it, "is Being. That," he said, pointing to my empty creel, "is Nothingness."

I have studied the philosophy of Karl Marx at considerable length, and although I understand it has gained a number of followers in certain parts of the world, I personally have never found it appealing, perhaps because I disagree with one of its basic tenets. Marx believed that anglers should put all their bait in the same can, from which each would take according to his need. I, on the other hand, believe that each fisherman should dig and fish his own worms, although I am not averse to going sharesies on the fly book of a really good tyer.

William James's philosophy of pragmatism was more to my liking. Pragmatism is the philosophy of doing that which works, no matter what your mother might have told you. James, who had pretensions of being a dry-fly purist, developed pragmatism from a simple experiment he performed one fishless day on a trout stream. He discovered that by making a slight modification in a No. 18 Caddis, he was suddenly catching monstrous brook trout. The James Ploy, as the experiment came to be called, is still popular with some fishermen, even though the technical difficulty of attaching a night crawler to a No. 18 Caddis has never been solved.

Ludwig Wittgenstein once explained logical positivism to me in a way that made it seem the answer to all the great philosophical questions, except what to do about spilled tackle boxes.

Morris Lippenstein, a friend of mine in college, developed the philosophy of transactional redundance. It was a lousy philosophy, but Morris, on the other hand, was a terrific fisherman. Even now his former professors still refer to him as "Morris the Sophomore."

The best philosopher I've ever known was a man by the name of Rancid Crabtree. Rancid lived in a little cabin in the woods behind our place when I was a boy, and since his time was free of all forms of gainful employment, he was able to devote himself to philosophy for up to twelve hours a day, not including cleaning and eating the catch. As a student of philosophy, I often sat at the feet of this great teacher, although I preferred a chair situated some distance upwind.

Rancid was at his philosophical best while on a trout stream.

"The water's a little murky for good fishing," I observed once.

Rancid took a chaw of tobacco and studied the water. "Ain't nothin' never just right to do what you wants to do when you wants to do it," he philosophized. "So you best just go ahead and do it anyways."

"Spinoza?" I asked.

"Naw, just a little tobaccy juice dribblin' down my chin."

Although Rancid's philosophy seemed to be centered on fishing, it shaped much of my attitude toward life. Here is a sampling of his philosophy:

"The two best times to fish is when it's rainin' and when it ain't."

"Smoked carp tastes just as good as smoked salmon when you ain't got no smoked salmon."

"There ain't no private property you cain't fish if you knows how to hunker a spell with the man what owns it."

"You cain't make fish bite just by wantin' 'em to."

"Any time a man ain't fishin' he's fritterin' away his life."

As I say, Rancid Crabtree's philosophy had an enormous influence on me. If it hadn't been for that, I might now be living a life adorned with the tawdry baubles of wealth, a life made sleazy and decadent by conspicuous consumption. I might even have turned out to be one of the jaded beautiful people of the jet set. Other than those drawbacks, Rancid's philosophy has served me pretty well.

Running on Empty

Some of the boys and I were sitting around Kelly's Bar & Grill the other evening, stretching and varnishing a few truths about our adventures in the Great Outdoors, when Kelly himself hauled a new round of iced schooners over to our table and sat down. He listened to the conversation for a few moments, shaking his head in a pretty good impression of annoyance and then muttered, "Fish, hunt, fish, hunt! Can't you guys ever talk about anything else?"

"You don't care much for outdoor sports, do you, Kelly?" Retch Sweeney asked.

"Oh, you guys are all right," Kelly said. "It's just that I can't understand what you see in hunting and fishing. Man, that stuff is boring!"

"Maybe to you it's boring," Al Finley put in, "but to us it's exciting."

"Ha!" Kelly said. "Exciting! Listen, I know, I fished once. It's boring!"

"Is not!" Al said.

"*Is!*" said Kelly. "Okay, wise guys, tell me, what's the most exciting thing about hunting and fishing?"

I thought for a moment. "Running out of gas."

The other guys all nodded in agreement.

"Running out of gas?" asked Kelly, astonished. "I would've thought something like being chased by a big bear."

"That's a good one, too," I said. "But for absolute, undiluted, marrow-chilling excitement, it's running out of gas."

"I can't believe I'm sitting here listening to this nonsense," Kelly snarled. With that, he got up and stomped back to the bar to spit-polish some glasses.

Like Kelly, most people unfamiliar with outdoor sports find it hard to believe that running out of gas is the most exciting part of hunting and fishing. That's because they know only about the typical, mundane experience of running out of gas on a well-traveled highway, such as happened to me just the other day.

On my way home from a business trip, I thought I could make it across a desert without being ripped off for a tankful at one of those seedy "Last Chance for Gas" places that loiter on the edge of deserts. A mere fifteen miles from the next gas station, my car choked, coughed a few times, and then chugged to a stop. Heat waves rippled up from the empty horizon and gusts of searing wind sandblasted my car. It was all I could do to keep from laughing. "You call this running out of gas?" I said to the fates that govern such things. "This is child's play!"

I then nonchalantly flagged down the eighty-seventh car to pass, a vehicle driven, as I judged, by a recent escapee from an institution for the criminally insane.

The man's conversation was diverting, based as it was on a considerable expertise in the use of poisons, stilettos, hatchets, and pipe bombs. Some twenty months later, we arrived at the gas station, where he dropped me off. When I thanked him for the ride and for sparing my life, he snapped his fingers as though reminded of some forgotten business, then drove off in a huff, apparently much disgusted with himself.

The gas station attendant, on the other hand, proved difficult. He said his station had a policy against providing any aid whatsoever to travelers in perilous distress, including the loaning out of tools, the restroom key, or containers in which to carry gas back to stranded vehicles. Without much coaxing, however, he agreed to sell me a rusty little gas can, a family heirloom, as he said, which his great-grandfather had had handcrafted of rare metals by a team of silversmiths imported from Switzerland. Snatching up my heirloom of gas, I hoofed it back to my car in a trice or, to be more specific, four hours and ten minutes. Although the trek was long and hot, the buzzards circling overhead afforded some shade, and I could not help but think how accustomed we are to zipping mindlessly along in our shiny tin capsules, totally oblivious to the ever-changing face of nature; and what a good thing it is, too.

For an outdoorsman, though, that sort of running out of gas doesn't even rank as a nuisance, let alone excitement. It requires no skill, no finesse. It is an accident, a result of faulty judgment, a miscalculation. The outdoorsman cannot leave such an important part of his avocation to mere chance. He must plan and practice his routine until he gets it perfect. Then, finally, when he has mastered the art, he can drive his vehicle to the far end of a wilderness canyon and, some fifty miles or so beyond the boundaries of the known world, with night closing in and storm clouds rising, turn to his companions and, with just the right degree of flair, announce, "G-great jumping gosh almighty, I think we're out of g-gas!"

Nothing so stirs the emotions and invigorates the vitals of an outdoorsman as that announcement, particularly when it is enhanced by a sappy, bug-eyed expression on the face of the announcer. Once the announcement has been made, the tradition is that the other persons in the car are supposed to respond in unison, "Ooooh *bleep!*" Sometimes, though, they merely sit there slack-jawed, staring at the gas gauge in disbelief. Also, on occasion, they will choose to unwind with a bit of horseplay, such as taking turns chasing the vehicle's driver and trying to hit him with a stick.

There are numerous ways of running out of gas in the wilderness. One of the best is to run over large, sharp rocks that puncture your gas tank. This method usually affords a much greater degree of surprise, since all the gas dribbles quietly out onto the ground while you are away from the car getting cold, hungry, and exhausted in the pursuit of fish or game. It is considered poor form, however, to clap your hands and emit happy yelps of surprise over the discovery that you ruptured the gas tank on some sharp rocks. The time is better employed getting a head start down the road while your companions are still selecting their sticks and testing them for tensile strength.

The problem with the punctured-gas-tank method is that you can't always depend on finding large, sharp rocks in the right places. Thus, running out of gas a sufficient distance out in the boonies to qualify you as a master of the art becomes largely a matter of chance. The punctured tank is fine, if the opportunity offers itself, but should not be counted upon.

The so-called short cut, on the other hand, is practically foolproof, and I highly recommend it. The "short cut" is usually recalled by one of the members of the party as a road he was told about in a bar by a fellow who discovered it while huckleberrying with his family at age six. The "short cut" sounds like a reasonable option to the driver, particularly if he hasn't filled his quota for running out of gas that year. "It will cut our driving time in half," he explains, and of course, it does. The rest of the time is spent walking, usually up an incline that appears to be leading to the Continental Divide.

Another good method involves the use of an auxiliary gas tank. When the vehicle stalls, the driver says to his nervous company, "Oh-oh, Fred, looks like we're out of gas." Allowing himself the enjoyment of seeing perspiration bead up nicely on the passenger's forehead, the driver then chuckles and says, "Only joshing, Fred. Now, I'll just switch over to the auxiliary tank." The trick here, of course, is to have neglected to check the auxiliary tank after your kid borrowed your vehicle to go out for a pizza and failed to mention that the pizza was on the other side of the state. Because your partner may not see the humor in the situation, you should be prepared to entertain him with some of your impersonations of famous personalities.

The next best thing to running out of gas is *almost* running out of gas. Fraught with suspense, these trips are often referred to as *white-knucklers*. The term is derived from the driver's tendency to increase the tightness of his grip on the steering wheel in direct ratio to the rate the gas is diminishing. One theory holds that as much as fifteen additional miles can be squeezed out of the steering wheel itself. Further mileage is gained by all the passengers rocking forward in unison and chanting "C'mon, baby, c'mon!" Chanting by itself is not good for more than two additional miles.

Because it may be difficult for the non-outdoorsman to understand the exhilaration we hunters and anglers get from running out of gas, I will give an example from my own personal experience. Al Finley, Retch Sweeney, and I had just returned to my car from a fishing trip into the Hoodoo Mountains and were heading back to the main highway when I noticed the needle on the gas gauge was hovering half an inch below the empty mark. Immediately, I took the recommended emergency measure, which consists of beating on the gas gauge with your fist in an effort to get the needle to rise up to the point where you have enough gas to get home. I then fell back on squeezing the steering wheel, while Retch and Al rocked and chanted. But it was all to no avail. The engine inhaled the last vapors from the carburetor and died.

We sat there for a few moments, coining some colorful phrases, and then Al asked the usual question: "Well, what are we going to do now?"

"Beats me," I said.

"I got an idea," Retch said. "How far back was that big old house we passed?"

"About five miles, I'd guess," said Al.

"You mean that big spooky old house with the porch caving in and the shingles falling off?" I asked, hoping to diffuse the hostility in the car with some casual conversation. "Boy, I wonder what kind of person lives in a place like that. Pretty darn weird, I'll bet. And those dogs! Did you see those two big wolfy dogs, standing under that sign that said 'Trespassers will be shot'? I wonder what they were gnawing on. Looked like it was wearing a hat! Hoo-boy, I would no more go into that place than—what? What do you mean, my fault? No. They probably wouldn't have any gas anyway and . . ."

A few hours later, I was back at the car with a can of gas. One of my pants legs was missing and the back had been ripped out of my shirt. Fortunately, I had finally been able to lose the dogs by circling through a swamp and wading up a creek before scaling the cliff. The sense of exhilaration was marvelous. For the first time since running out of gas on Bald Mountain, I felt fully and truly alive, except for the lower half of my body, which seemed pretty well shot.

"Any trouble?" Al asked.

"None to speak of," I said. "Just the usual."

"Fella lives in that house," said Retch, "pretty weird, was he?"

"Just the usual. He wouldn't take any pay for the gas, though."

"No kidding!"

"Yeah, but be careful of that gas can. It's a family heirloom."

The Cat and
the Cat Burglar

The sound of a vase crashing to the floor in the living room snapped my wife and me bolt upright in bed.

"It's the cat," Bun hissed. "You forgot to put the cat out again!"

"Oh, go back to sleep," I said. "It's probably only another burglar."

"You're trying to make excuses. I know it's the cat. You forgot to put it out!"

"Well, I'll prove it's a burglar," I growled, crawling out of bed and switching on the hall light. As I expected, a dark figure was wandering about the living room. "Hey you!"

The burglar pointed a questioning finger at his chest.

"Yes, you," I snapped. "You see anybody else in the living room? Now c'mere. I want to prove to my wife you're only a burglar and not the dang cat. Besides, there's no point in eyeing the TV—it blew a tube on California during the Miss America Pageant, which made two of us, heh, heh."

The burglar shuffled down the hall, a can of Blackjack Mugger's Spray trained on me. "Don't try no funny stuff."

"It was only a little joke."

"I know, but it was pretty bad, and I'm not up to it. I've had a hard night. How come your house is so empty?"

"We've had a lot of other burglaries," I explained. "For a while they were so frequent we thought about asking the burglars to each take a number so there wouldn't be so many here at one time."

"What did I say about da funny stuff?"

"Sorry. Say, I'd appreciate it if you would poke your head in the bedroom there so my wife will know you're only a burglar and not the cat."

The burglar peered cautiously around the door and looked at my wife.

"Oh, thank goodness you really are only a burglar," Bun said. "That cat makes such a terrible mess when it gets left in. My nice rug in the living room—"

"Can it, lady!" the burglar ordered. "I ain't got time to hear about no cat messes."

"Have it your way," Bun said. "But I really should tell you about Felix. He sometimes—"

"I said, *can it!*"

"Well, if you're going to be rude, I'll just go back to sleep. The last few burglars we had were at least civil!"

"Sheesh, do I ever pick 'em," the burglar moaned. Then he turned to me. "Say, you're da outdoor writer, ain't ya?"

"Well, sort of," I replied.

"Yeah, dat's what I was told. All you outdoor writers got big gun collections. Let's have a look at yours."

My gun collection! For years I had worried that some burglar would discover my secret gun room and clean it out. Now, under the threat of bodily harm, I was being forced to reveal my hoard of priceless firearms.

"Oh, all right, follow me," I told the burglar.

I led the way to the den, pressed a hidden button, and a wall panel slid silently back, revealing the secret gun room. The burglar whistled his approval at this bit of architectural ingenuity.

"And there's my fabulous collection," I said, pointing to the gun cabinet.

"Dat's it?" the burglar gasped, awestruck.

"Yes," I said, "that's it. A fence will pay you handsomely for these fine guns. Your fortune is made, I'm afraid."

Unlocking the doors to the gun cabinet, I decided to take one last desperate chance to save my collection. "Why don't you sit down and make yourself comfortable," I said to the burglar, "and I'll tell you about these guns. Should you decide to keep them for your own enjoyment, knowing their histories will increase the pleasure of owning them."

Apparently approving of this suggestion, the burglar flopped into an armchair, while I removed one of my favorite rifles from the gun cabinet.

"If you were a connoisseur of fine guns," I began, "I would first tie a bib around your neck so you wouldn't drool all over your clothes when I showed you this little .30/30. Notice, if you will, the grip of the stock."

"Yeah, what caused dat, termites? Or did your dog chew it?"

"To the contrary," I replied, "this is custom checking on the grip, which in all modesty I must admit I accomplished myself with a ball-peen hammer and a five-penny nail. True, the exquisiteness of the pattern is detracted from somewhat by the wrappings of baling wire and electrician's tape on the stock. You may also have noticed that the barrel is slightly bent to the left and downward, but I can assure you it's not more than an inch out of alignment. I won't go into how the stock got splintered and the barrel bent except to say that it saved me from a nasty fall. The gun is still remarkably accurate, however, provided you make the necessary adjustments in your aim. I assume you have studied calculus? No? Well, perhaps one of those pocket calculators would work just as well, although a bit bothersome on a running shot."

Feigning disgust, the burglar motioned for me to return the .30/30 to the rack. He pointed to another rifle. "What's dat, a .30/06?"

"Close," I said. "Actually, it's a .30/02, one of the predecessors of the .30/06. There was a little problem with the locking mechanism on the bolt, and the model was discontinued when it was discovered that the breech velocity sometimes exceeded the muzzle velocity. Otherwise, it's perfectly safe, as long as you don't forget to jerk your head away the instant you squeeze the trigger. My grandfather once killed a trophy elk with the bolt when the animal tried to slip past him forty yards to the rear. But that kind of shooting takes considerable practice and I don't recommend it for beginners."

A hint of gloom had settled upon the burglar's

features as he gestured irritably for me to return the .30/02 to the cabinet.

I next took down a wonderful old side-by-side 12-gauge shotgun I also had inherited from my grandfather—"Old One-Ear" they called him—on my fourteenth birthday. As I told the burglar, the shotgun had one interesting little eccentricity, which was that on about every third shot both barrels discharged simultaneously regardless of which trigger was squeezed. Since I weighed only 125 pounds at the time, most student pilots log less flight time than I did on an average hunt, and their landings are a good deal softer.

As for the effects of these double-barreled kicks on my anatomy, the high school football coach once observed me coming out of the showers and leaped to the conclusion that I had contracted a progressive disease in which one shoulder takes on the general shape and color of a Hubbard squash. There was also the problem that my nose from week to week seemed to drift about my face, sometimes anchoring under my left eye and at other times setting a course for the center of my forehead. This feature was nicely complemented by my right ear, which appeared to have been run through a pasta-shaping machine.

"I used this fine old gun for nearly twenty years," I told the burglar. "But people were always asking me about the 'accident,' and I got tired of telling them I had saved my commanding officer in Korea by throwing myself on a hand grenade."

The burglar stifled a yawn with his fist. "C'mon, guy, I ain't got all night, ya know. Let's speed it up on dese histories, huh?"

"Right," I said. "I think you'll like this next one."

I unracked the single-shot .22 rifle that had been given to me by my parents when I was eleven years old. Ah, never was a gun given more tender care than that one. I cleaned and oiled it three times a day whether it had been fired or not, and never allowed a speck of dust to settle on it for more than a minute.

"So how come it's all rusted and pitted?" the burglar asked, his voice fairly reeking with exasperation, perhaps because I was delaying my account of the .22 in an unsuccessful attempt to wrench the bolt back.

As I told the burglar, a couple of months after the .22 had come into my possession, I was out in the back pasture target-practicing on a tin can when who should show up but a neighbor by the name of Olga Bonemarrow. I didn't much care for girls at the time, and considered Olga in particular a great nuisance. Ignoring her, I continued to plink away at the can while she directed a torrent of prattle at the back of my head. Suddenly a single question leaped from the torrent like a sparkling cutthroat from the spring runoff.

"Do you want to come over to my house and play doctor?" Olga had asked.

By sheer coincidence, Olga had hit upon one of my great enthusiasms of the moment, namely the field of medicine. Such was my passion for the art and science of curing the sick that target practice and even my beloved .22 were immediately blotted from my consciousness. Attempting to comport myself in a dignified manner appropriate to a serious student of medicine, I raced panting after Olga to her house, where we slipped upstairs to her bedroom without detection by Mr. and Mrs. Bonemarrow.

While I grabbed a window curtain and dried my palms, which were sweating profusely from the previous exertion, Olga rummaged around under her bed, finally extracting a large flat box. The box for a moment consumed one hundred percent of my attention, for on its lid was printed the word "Doctor." Olga took off the lid, removed a board zigzagged with lines of squares, placed two tiny white wooden figures on the square bearing the title "Med School," and then began to shuffle little stacks of cards. Even as I sized up the situation, my interest in the field of medicine began to fall off sharply.

"I just remembered a previous engagement," I told Olga and headed for the door.

"Hold it, buster," Olga snapped, adding with ominous vagueness, "or I'll tell Pa!"

Pa, I should point out, was built like a nail keg and had a temper shorter than a gnat's hiccup. No matter what Olga might tell him, I deduced it wouldn't be good, and it was easy to imagine a hairy nail keg drop-kicking me through a second-story window. Still, I was not the sort of person to be intimidated by childish threats, as I immediately demonstrated to an astonished Olga. In fact, in only my first three throws of the dice, I got out of med school, interned at a major hospital, and was making big bucks performing cardiovascular surgery.

Not only was the game boring, but it lasted slightly longer than the last ice age. By the time it ended, my mental faculties felt as if they had been stir-fried in molasses. I staggered off home and dropped immediately into bed.

The next morning I awoke with a jolt, realizing that somewhere in the fiasco with Olga I had mislaid my rifle. I left the house so fast the screen door twanged for a week. But the .22 was not to be found. It was as if it had slipped from my sweating palms the day before and disappeared down a gopher hole. My grief was monumental and has lingered even into the present day, causing me still to hold the entire medical profession in general distrust and responsible for the loss of my .22.

The following spring I found the rifle on a stack of fence posts, where it had wintered over. As a boy, I often read many articles that warned of the ills of failing to clean and oil a gun after each use, but never did I read an article warning against leaving a gun on a stack of fence posts all winter. You would think some shooting editor might have mentioned that at least once.

"So that's how my .22 got rusted and pitted," I told the burglar, who seemed on the verge of suffering an infarction of some sort. "Now, moving right along, this rather peculiar-looking rifle here is actually a .270. I restocked it myself with the arm from an old rocking chair and—"

The burglar held up a hand for me to cease. "Listen, pal," he said, "maybe I'll just take da TV after all. You can keep da guns."

Clearly, the man had been touched by my show of affection for the guns, which was what I had hoped for. Out of appreciation for his change of heart, I led him back to the living room, loaded him up with the TV, and even tried to warn him when he started out the wrong door. When the ruckus in the yard finally died down, I went back to bed.

"Is the burglar finished?" my wife asked sleepily.

"I'm afraid so," I said. "If the poor devil had had enough sense to drop the TV, he probably could have made it over the back fence before Felix got him. You know, having an attack cat isn't such a bad idea; but if these burglaries ever let up, we're going to have to start buying cat food for him."

Salami on Rye
and Hold
the Wild Gobo

"Did you know that cattails are good to eat?" my wife asked me one evening, looking up from the book she was reading.

"Who says?"

"Euell Gibbons."

"Well, Gibbons may know something about the Roman Empire, but he doesn't know a damn thing about cattails," I responded authoritatively. "They are not good to eat!"

"That was Gibbon who knew about the Roman Empire. Gibbons is an expert on wild foods."

Well, it just so happens, as I pointed out to Bun, that I too am an expert on wild foods. I was taught about them as a boy by my grandmother.

Few things were more dreaded in our house during my youth than Gram's announcement, "I think I'll go out to the woods and pick us a mess of wild greens for supper. Don't that sound good?"

"Mmmmmmm," Dad would say, because he hated to hurt Gram's feelings.

"Aagghhh!" my sister and I would say, because we detested Gram's wild greens. Then Dad would get us off in a corner and make some threats. He always referred to these threats as "a piece of advice."

"Let me give you two a piece of advice," he would say. "You eat your grandmother's greens without a word, and if she asks you how you like them, you smile and go 'mmmmmmm.' *Or else!*"

We would try to get him to be more specific about the "or else" so we could weigh the punishment against eating the greens, but he would stand pat on the vague and ominous threat.

The truth was Dad hated the greens as much as we did. He told my mother once that he would rather see the wolf crouched at the door than Gram coming through it with a mess of her wild greens. But he would never for the world let Gram think that they weren't practically his favorite food.

At supper he would be solemnly munching his way through the generous portion of wild greens to which he had masochistically helped himself, when Gram would ask, "How do you like the greens, Frank?"

Dad would look up and smile and go "mmmmmmm," but his eyes would be all wild and terrible. Then he would shoot my sister and me his "or else" look, and we would attack our own portions, which would be about the size of postage stamps but more than ample.

"And how do you children like the greens?" Gram would ask. We would first check out our glowering father, then smile weakly and go "mmm-*gag*-mmmmm."

I vividly recall the time Dad drew among his portion of the greens a particularly noxious sprout, its presence in the mess no doubt due to Gram's failing eyesight. (It was generally suspected that if a thing was vaguely green and appeared not to be moving under its own power, Gram picked it.)

Dad bit into the renegade sprout just after he had smiled and gone "mmmmmmm" in response to one of Gram's inquiries about the greens. (When he was eating her wild greens she could have asked him if he'd had a hard day, and he would have smiled and gone "mmmmmmm.") Suddenly, he stiffened in his chair and his fork clattered to the floor. "What is it?" Mom asked, thinking he was having an attack of some kind, and I guess he was. He stomped his foot several times, shook his head, swallowed mightily, and then drained his water glass in a single gulp.

Wiping his nose and eyes discreetly on his sleeve, he glanced over at Gram and offered the opinion, "Some of these greens have a powerful flavor."

Gram, oblivious of the preceding activity, peered at him over her spectacles. "Don't they, though! Try 'em with a little cinnamon. They taste even better that way."

I don't know about the cinnamon, but I could have tried them with Dutch Cleanser and they wouldn't have tasted any worse.

Gram was also a great believer in natural remedies for illness. Once when my sister was sick, or claiming to be, possibly because we were scheduled to have a mess of wild greens for supper, Gram concocted one of her folk medicines. The only ingredient that I can recall with any certainty was sap from a balsam tree in our yard. There was some yellow stuff, too, either sulfur or mustard powder, and I believe some water and molasses.

She boiled the mixture down to concentrate it, and then took a tablespoonful in to my sister, the very picture of infirmity as she lay in bed.

"Here, dear, take this," Gram said, pinching Trudy's cheeks to open her mouth, and pouring in the yellowish-brown substance. "It will have you up and around in no time."

Well, Gram was right about that. Ol' Trudy was up and around in one second, gasping, gagging, choking, knocking over furniture, and kicking walls. It was a miraculously quick cure and worthy of being written up in medical journals. And not only did the remedy cure childhood illnesses instantly, but it had wonderful preventive powers. In fact, neither Trudy nor I was ever sick again in all the rest of the time Gram stayed with us.

When I grew up and married, I thought wild greens were behind me once and for all. Then Bun read *Stalking the Wild Asparagus* by Euell Gibbons. Soon she was insisting that we stalk not only the wild asparagus, but the wild cattail, the wild milkweed, the wild burdock, the wild pokeweed, and a dozen other wild foods. "You never know when a knowledge of wild foods might come in handy," she would say ominously.

It wouldn't have been so bad if we could have done our stalking in the woods and swamps, but we lived in a city. One day as we walked along the sidewalk past a weedy vacant lot strewn with the rusting carcasses of dead cars, Bun suddenly gasped, "Wild gobo!"

Well, I scarcely jumped more than a foot in the air, which says something for my self-control, for I fully expected some hulking menace to be charging in our direction. "Where? Where?"

"There," Bun said, pointing to some weeds. "Wild gobo, also known as great burdock, *Arctium lappa.*"

"*Arctium lappa* my clavicle," I snarled.

I hated stalking wild foods with Bun almost as much as I did eating them. (Bun, with tears welling: "You don't like my pokeweed ragout!" Me, smiling weakly: "Mmmmmmm!") The problem with stalking wild foods in the city was that they always grew on somebody else's property. There were two modes of operation open to us. We could sneak onto the lot, dig up or hack down some of the weeds, and then flee to the car for a fast getaway. Or we could ask permission of the property owner: "Sir, I wonder if you'd mind if I hacked off a bit of your wild gobo." It always seemed easier to me just to sneak onto the property without permission.

Through all of this I tried to explain to Bun how to interpret the terminology used in wild food books. For example, *edible* does not mean "good to eat." Edible means only that you won't flop over with your face in your plate when you take a bite of the stuff. *Choice* does not mean choice. It means only that if you feed the food to an unsuspecting dinner guest he won't chase you out of the house trying to plunge a table fork into your back.

"I don't believe it," Bun would say.

"It's true," I'd reply. "Listen, if the cattail was actually *good* to eat, they'd sell it in supermarkets for three dollars a pound. I rest my case."

I must admit that my experience with wild foods has not been all bad. Wild mushrooms are a case in point. I am a fungiphile of long standing, and devote countless hours searching for succulent morsels of the half-dozen varieties I know how to identify. Indeed, I owe it to the humble shaggymanes for once improving the general quality of my life, if not actually preserving my sanity.

Many years ago I had a friend named Stretch who worked nights at a warehouse. Apparently the job wasn't too difficult, because every night he found time to write half a dozen poems. After he got off work, in the morning, he would rush over to my house to read me his latest creations. While I ate breakfast, he would sit down at the table with me, refusing all offers of food and drink. Then he would say, "Oh, maybe I will have a cup of coffee, if it isn't too much bother." After a while he would add, "Say, that toast looks awfully good. Do you mind? Thanks. Please pass the jam." And a bit later: "Were you planning on eating both those strips of bacon?" And so on. Soon I would be at the stove frying him over-easy eggs and "a few hash browns, if you have some handy, and maybe three or four more strips of that bacon."

Now, Stretch was a fine fellow and good company, and I did not mind at all feeding him breakfast every morning. The problem was his poetry, which was of the Naturalistic school and leaned heavily on an *S* alliteration: "Sad, sorrow-sunk survivors of a sadistic society, saturated with strong, stiff stench of stifling strife . . ." In short, it was not poetry to eat breakfast by. Every morning I would go off to work in a somber, Naturalistic mood and throughout the day would find myself saying such things to my fellow workers as, "Sara, send Sally for six or so sheets of seven-cent stamps."

One day walking home from work I spotted a nice patch of shaggymane mushrooms growing on a lawn and, with the stealth known only to foragers of wild food in an urban setting, quickly filled my hat with them.

The next morning I cooked up the mess of mushrooms and was just sitting down to enjoy them when Stretch bounded through the door, the night's output of poems clutched in his hand.

"Breakfast, Stretch?" I asked as he sat down at the table and began arranging his works for the reading.

"No, nothing for me, thanks. This first poem I titled 'Slime.' I think you will like it. Oh, maybe I will have a cup of coffee, if it's not too much bother."

Then Stretch saw the dish of shaggymanes. "What's that?"

"Mushrooms."

"Mind if I try them?"

"Be my guest," I said, sliding the dish over and handing him a fork.

"Hey, these are delicious!" Stretch exclaimed and continued to fork in my shaggymanes between stanzas of "Slime." Upon completion of the reading, he asked, "How did you like it?"

"Great," I said. "How did you like the mushrooms?"

Stretch ran his finger around the dish and licked the juice off of it appreciatively. "Just the best thing I ever ate, that's all," he said. "What kind were they?"

"Beats me," I said.

"You don't *know*?" he said, staring at his licked finger as if it were a coral snake.

"I found them growing in the yard and thought they looked good enough to eat," I said.

Stretch looked around wildly. "But you're not supposed to do that!"

"Why not?" I said. "It's my yard, I can pick mushrooms in it if I want."

"No, that's not . . . I mean . . . look, I got to go!"

Since my eyes were in the middle of a blink at the time, I didn't see Stretch leave, but I noted that the swiftness of his departure had sent the poems floating about the kitchen like autumn leaves in a brisk wind. While conjecturing to myself about Stretch's intended destination, I gathered up the poems and placed them neatly on the shelf to return to him the next time he stopped by to give me readings at breakfast. The poems gathered dust there for many months, and now I'm not sure what happened to them. I suppose they weren't such bad poems either, particularly if you're unusually fond of the *S* sound.

Two-Man-Tent Fever

Fenton Quagmire was telling me recently about the weekend he had just suffered through at his lakeside retreat.

"Rained the whole time, and I didn't get outside once," he said. "By Sunday I had a case of the cabin fever like you wouldn't believe!"

Wouldn't believe? Why, I could barely keep from doubling over in a paroxysm of mirth!

I happen to know that Quagmire's "cabin" is a three-bedroom, shag-carpeted, TV-ed, and hot-tubbed villa overlooking a stretch of sandy beach that sells per linear foot at the same rate as strung pearls. Obviously, what Quagmire had experienced was nothing more than *villa fever,* which compares to cabin fever as the sniffles to double pneumonia.

True cabin fever requires a true cabin—four buckling walls, a leaky roof, a warped floor, a door, and a few windows. Furnishings consist of something less than the bare necessities. Wall decorations, while permitted, should not be such as to arouse any visual interest whatsoever. (The old Great Northern Railroad calendar with the mountain goat on it is about right.) A wood stove, preferably one made from a steel barrel, provides the heat, and also the only excitement, when its rusty tin pipe sets fire to the roof. That's your basic true cabin.

When I was six, we lived for a year in just such a cabin. My father speculated that it had been built by a man who didn't know his adz from his elbow, or words to that effect. The shake roof looked as if it had been dealt out by an inebriated poker player during a sneezing fit. Proper alignment of one log over another was so rare as to suggest coincidence, if not divine intervention. The man who rented the cabin to us, apparently a buff of local history, boasted that it had been built toward the end of the last century. "Which end?" Dad asked him.

Within a short while after we moved in, Dad had the cabin whipped into shape, a shape that might now be regarded as unfit for human habitation but which in those days would generally have been thought of as unfit for human habitation. After hammering in the last nail, Dad unscrewed the cap from a quart of his home brew, took a deep swig, and told my mother, "This is as good as it gets!" I have, of course, re-created the quote, but it captures the proper note of pessimism.

One might suppose that a family of four would be miserable living in a tiny, sagging log cabin in the middle of an Idaho wilderness, and one would be right. My mother and sister accepted our situation philosophically and cried only on alternate days. Dad arose early each morning and went off in search of "suitable work," by which he meant work that paid anything at all. I spent my time morosely digging away at the chinking between the logs, not realizing that the resulting cracks would let all the cold out.

One day in the middle of January, Mom looked up from her bowl of gruel at breakfast, as we jokingly referred to it, and announced, "Well, we've finally hit rock bottom. Things just can't get any worse." We soon discovered that Mom lacked the gift of prophecy.

Within hours, the mercury was rattling about like a dried pea in the bulb of the thermometer, and the wind came blasting out of the north. Strangely, Dad seemed delighted by the onset of a blizzard. Even now, four decades later, I can still see him bending over, rubbing a hole in the window frost with his fist and peering out at the billowing snow.

"Let her blow!" he shouted. "We've got plenty of firewood and enough grub to last until spring if we have to! By gosh, we'll just make some fudge, pop corn, and play Monopoly until she blows herself out! It'll be like a little adventure, like we're shipwrecked!"

The rest of the family was instantly perked up by his enthusiasm and defiance of the blizzard. Mom started making fudge and popping corn, while my sister and I rushed to set up the Monopoly game.

The blizzard lasted nearly two weeks, give or take a century. By the third day my sister and I were forbidden even to mention Monopoly, fudge, or popcorn. And Dad no longer regarded the blizzard as a little adventure.

"Why are you making that noise with your nose?" he would snarl at me.

"I'm just breathing."

"Well, stop it!"

"Whose idea was that calendar?" he'd snap at my mother.

"What's wrong with it, dear?"

"That stupid mountain goat watches every move I make, that's what! Look how its eyes follow me!"

A day or two later, as Dad himself admitted at the time, he became irritable.

Shortly after that, he came down with cabin fever.

Spending several days trapped in close quarters with a person who had cabin fever toughened me up a lot psychologically. A couple of years later, when I saw the movie *Frankenstein Meets the Wolf Man*, I thought it was a comedy. At the peak of his cabin fever, Dad could have played both leads in the film simultaneously and sent audiences screaming into the streets.

The only good thing about cabin fever is that it vanishes the instant the victim is released from enforced confinement. When the county snowplow finally opened the road and came rumbling into our yard, Dad strolled out to greet and thank the driver.

"Snowed in fer a spell, weren't ya?" the driver said. "Bet you got yerself a good case of the cabin fever."

"Naw," Dad said. "It wasn't bad. We just made fudge and popped corn and played a few games of Monop . . . Monop . . . played a few games."

"Well, you certainly seem normal enough," the driver said. Then he pointed to Mom, Sis, and me. "That your family?"

It seemed like an odd question, but I suppose the driver wondered why a normal man like my father would have a family consisting of three white-haired gnomes.

There are numerous kinds of fever brought on by

the boredom of enforced confinement over long periods. I myself have contracted some of the lesser strains—coldwater-flat fever, mobile-home fever, and split-level fever, to name but a few. I have never been able to afford the more exotic and expensive fevers, like those of my wealthy friend Quagmire. In addition to his villa fever, he will occasionally run a continent fever, one of the symptoms of which is the sensation that the Atlantic and Pacific coastlines are closing in on him. The treatment, as I understand it, is to take two aspirin and a Caribbean cruise.

Of all such fevers, by far the most deadly is two-man-tent fever, which, in its severity, surpasses even the cabin variety.

I had the opportunity of studying two-man-tent fever close-up a few years ago, when Parker Whitney and I spent nearly twenty hours in his tiny tent waiting for a storm to blow over. Parker is a calm, quiet chap normally, and it was terrible to see him go to pieces the way he did, after the fever overtook him.

For a while, during the first few hours of the storm, we were entertained by the prospect that we might momentarily be using the tent as a hang glider. After the wind died down to a modest gale, we were able to devote our whole attention to the rippling of the orange rip-stop nylon that enveloped us. Fascinating as this was, its power to distract was limited to a few hours. By then, I was formulating a geological theory that a major earth fault lay directly beneath, and crossed at right angles to, my half-inch Ensolite pad. While several of my more adventuresome vertebrae were testing this theory, I gradually became aware that Parker was beginning to exhibit certain signs of neurotic behavior.

"I hate to ask this, old chap," I said, kindly enough, "but would you mind not chewing that gum quite so loud?"

Parker replied with uncharacteristic snappishness. "For the fourteenth time, I'm not chewing gum!"

Mild hallucination is one of the early symptoms of two-man-tent fever. Not only did Parker fail to realize that he was chomping and popping his gum in a hideous manner, but he clearly was of the impression that I had mentioned the matter to him numerous times previously. Since hallucinations do not yield readily to logical argument, I thought that confronting him with the empirical evidence might work. Unfortunately, Parker was now in the grip of paranoia and responded to my effort by shouting out that I had "gone mad." I suppose he was referring to the manner in which I had grabbed him by the nose and chin and forced his mouth open, a maneuver that proved ineffective, since he had somehow managed to hide the gum from my vision and probing thumb, possibly by lodging it behind his tonsils. Such deception, I might add, is not at all unusual among victims of two-man-tent fever.

Parker remained quiet for some time, although I could tell from the look in his eyes that the paranoia was tightening its hold on him, and I began to wonder if my life might not be in danger. I warned him not to try anything.

"Why don't you get some sleep?" Parker replied. "Just try to get some sleep!"

"Ha!" I said, not without a trace of sarcasm. "Do you really think I'm going to fall for that old one?"

I twisted around in my bag and propped up on an elbow so I could watch Parker more closely. It was easy to see that the two-man-tent fever was taking its toll on him. He was pale and trembling, and stared back at me with wide, unblinking eyes. He looked pitiful, even though posing no less a threat to my life.

Then, as if our situation were not perilous enough already, I noticed that Parker had dandruff. Under normal circumstances, I can take dandruff or leave it alone, but not in a two-man tent. It wasn't the unsightly appearance of the dandruff that bothered me, but the little *plip plip plip* sounds it made falling on his sleeping bag. I soon deduced that Parker had contrived this irritation for the sole purpose of annoying me, a sort of Chinese dandruff torture, although I hadn't realized until then that Parker was Chinese. Informing him that I was on to his little game, I told Parker to get his dandruff under control or suffer the consequences. Not surprisingly, he denied any knowledge of his dandruff or its activities. I therefore retaliated by doing my impression of Richard Widmark's maniacal laugh every time I heard a *plip*. Parker countered by doing his impression of a man paralyzed by fear. It wasn't that good, as impressions go, but I withheld criticism of the poor devil's performance, since it seemed to take his mind off the fever.

At the first break in the storm, Parker shot out of the tent, stuffed his gear into his pack, and took off down the trail, leaving me with the chore of folding up the tent and policing camp. Before I was finished, a ranger came riding up the trail on a horse. We exchanged pleasantries, and I asked him if he had happened to pass my partner on the trail.

"I don't know," he said. "Is he a white-haired gnome?"

Fish Poles, and Other Useful Terminology

I have long held the opinion that a person should know the jargon of any activity in which he professes some expertise. A writer, for example, should not refer to quotation marks as "those itty-bitty ears." It is unsettling to hear the carpenter you have just hired refer to his hammer as "a pounder." A mechanic tinkering in the innards of your car arouses anxiety by speaking of a pair of pliers as his "squeezer." Similarly, it would be disconcerting to have a doctor tell you he had detected an irregularity in your "thingamajig." (If you're like me, you're composed almost entirely of thingamajigs, some of which you value a good deal more than others.) Ignorance of proper terminology often leads to confusion, alarm, and panic, especially when one talks about the sport of fishing.

I recently met a man and his son out bass fishing. The father was making superb casts with what was obviously a new rod.

"Is that a boron you've got there?" I asked.

The man turned and looked at his son. "Well, he ain't too bright, that's for sure," he said.

Here was a case where a man had mastered the art of fishing, but had failed to keep up on recent nomenclature. I could hardly blame him. I now spend so much time learning all the new fishing terms that I scarcely have time to fish.

Non-anglers think fishing is easy. Well, just let them spend a day poring over one of the new fishing catalogs and memorizing the terms. One 1982 catalog, for example, contains such terms and phrases as "fiberglass integrated with unidirectional graphite," "silicone carbide guides with diamond polished silicone carbide guide rings," "Uni bent butt," that sort of thing. I'm just lucky I didn't ask the man fishing with his son if he had a Uni bent butt. I might have come home with a Uni bent head.

Consider just a few of the terms you now must learn in order to go out and catch a few bass: *structure, isolated structure, sanctuary, stragglers, breakline, suspended fish, pattern, holding area, riprap, point, scatter point, contact point, cheater hook, buzz bait, Texas rig, crank bait, triggering, flippin', pH, jig and pig, spinnerbait, fly 'n' rind.* The aerospace industry requires less technical jargon than the average bass fisherman.

When I was a youngster, my friends and I could get by on fewer than a dozen fishing terms. No doubt we could have expanded our angling vocabulary by going to the county library and checking out a book on fishing techniques. The problem was that if one of the gang showed up at the library to check out a book, Miss Phelps, the librarian, might have suffered a heart attack on the spot. Enlarging our fishing vocabularies didn't seem worth the risk of taking a life. We chose to get by on the few fishing terms we knew.

Although our fishing terminology was limited, it was not without its own peculiar complexity. Take the word *keeper* for example. The first fish you caught was always a "keeper." This was not the result of outrageous coincidence, but of definition. The first fish was interpreted as a "keeper" merely by having a mouth big enough to stretch over the barb of a hook.

There were several advantages to this definition of *keeper* applying to the first fish. Suppose the first fish you caught during the day was also the only fish, and you had released it. That would mean you would have to go home *skunked,* an angling term every bit as significant then as it is today. Calling the first fish a "keeper" often prevented the emotional damage which resulted from going home "skunked."

Furthermore, if someone later asked you if you had caught any fish, you could reply, in reference to a fish no longer than a pocketknife, "Just one keeper." The phrase *just one keeper* implied, of course, that you had caught and released numerous *small* fish, thereby contributing to one's reputation as a "sportsman."

If the first fish was particularly small, it did not always remain a "keeper." A larger fish, when caught, became a "keeper" and the small first fish became a *badly hooked* one. You always explained, with a note of regret in your voice, that you had kept the "badly hooked" fish because it would have "died anyway." Proper fishing terminology even in the time of my youth was extremely important, both socially and psychologically.

Although some of our terms might seem simple by

today's standards, they were not without their subtle shades of meaning. Take the word *mess* for instance, which was the word used to denote your catch while telling someone about your day of fishing. *Mess* used without modifiers usually meant two fish—a "keeper" and a "badly hooked." A *small mess* referred to a single "keeper." A *nice mess* meant three fish, excluding any "badly hooked." Any number of fish over three was, naturally, a *big mess*. To ask for specific numbers was considered rude when someone told you he had caught a "big mess" of fish.

Today, the phrase *a mess of fish* is seldom heard, probably because anyone uttering it would instantly be identifying himself as a fish glutton. Quantity of the catch is now always referred to by specific numbers, although a certain element of deception is still retained. An angler who has spent twelve hours flailing a trout stream, and managed to land a total of three fish, responds to a question about the number of fish caught by saying "I only *kept* three." If asked exactly how many he caught and released, he will be overcome by a coughing fit and have to rush from the room. Now, as always, it is considered poor form to lie about the number of fish caught, unless, of course, the angler has not mastered the technique of the coughing fit.

It took me fifteen minutes the other day to memorize the name of my new casting rod, and I've already forgotten it. When I was younger, we didn't have to memorize the names of our rods because we didn't have any. We had what were called "fish poles." Even now, after nearly forty years, I will still occasionally refer to a three-hundred-dollar custom-built fly rod as a "fish pole."

"That's a nice fish pole you've got there," I'll say to the owner of the rod.

He will go white in the face, shudder, twitch, gurgle, clench his hands, and lurch toward me. "Wha-what d-did you s-say? F-fish pole? FISH POLE! Y-you called my three-hundred-dollar rod a FISH POLE?"

I will back away, hands raised to fend him off, and explain that I have never shaken a bad habit picked up in my childhood.

Fish pole, in the old days, was a generic term for any elongated instrument intended for the purpose of propelling hook, line, sinker, and worm in the general direction of fish-holding water, and then wrenching an unlucky fish to the bank with as little fuss as possible. Some fish poles were made from cedar trees that had been rejected as too short or too slender for use as telephone poles. A few fortunate kids owned metal telescoping fish poles. My first fish pole was a single-piece, stiff metal tube about six feet long. There was a wire that could be pulled out of the tip if you wanted "action." I never pulled the wire out. Action, in my fishing circles, was not considered a desirable characteristic in a fish pole. It merely complicated the process of wrenching the fish from the water, or *landing it.*

Landing, by the way, consisted of whipping the fish in a long, high arc over your head and into the branches of a tree, which you usually had to climb in order to disengage both line and fish. Sometimes the fish would come off the line right at the peak of the arc and whiz away toward the state line like a stone loosed from a sling. These fish were later referred to as "badly hooked."

Forked stick is a term seldom heard among anglers nowadays, which is too bad, because the forked stick once served to enrich both fishing and conversations about fishing.

"I prefer the forked stick to a creel for carrying fish," a kid would say. "The creel is too bulky and keeps catching on brush. It gets in your way when you're casting, too. Most creels are too small for a really big fish anyway. Give me a forked stick to a creel any time." This statement actually meant "Give me a forked stick any time until someone gives me a creel. Then I'll prefer a creel."

There was much discussion about the kind of tree or bush that produced the best forked sticks for carrying fish. In theory, the way you selected a forked stick was to seek out a good specimen from the preferred species of bush or tree, cut it off with your pocketknife, and neatly trim it to appropriate and aesthetically pleasing dimensions. Ideally, there would be a fork at both ends, one to keep the fish from sliding off and the other to be hooked under your belt, thus freeing both hands for the business of catching fish.

The theory of the forked stick didn't work out in practice, because the kid never even thought about cutting a forked stick until he had caught his first fish. To cut a forked stick prior to catching a fish would have been presumptuous and probably bad luck to boot. (Also, few things look more ridiculous than an angler walking around with an empty forked stick.) Once a fish had been caught, the youngster, in his excitement, would instantly forget the aesthetically pleasing proportions prescribed for the forked stick. He would twist off the nearest branch with a fork on it, gnaw away any obstructing foliage with his teeth, thread the fish onto it, and get back to his fishing. When you were catching fish, you didn't have time to mess with aesthetics.

The forked stick contributed much excitement to our fishing. Since a double-forked branch or willow was almost never available when needed, the forked stick could not be hooked under your belt but had to be laid down somewhere while you fished. Once or twice every hour, a panicky search would begin for a string of fish left on a log or rock "just around that last bend." Approximately thirty percent of your fishing time was spent trying to catch fish and seventy percent looking for fish you had already caught.

Thus, the term *forked stick* denoted not merely a device for carrying your catch, but a whole mode of fishing that the boy who grows up owning a creel can never come to know or appreciate. He should consider himself damn lucky for it, too.

There were a few other terms that filled out our fishing vocabulary. *Game warden* is one that comes to mind. I don't know if any state still has game wardens. Most have *Wildlife Conservation Officers* or persons of similar sterile title to enforce fishing regulations. Somehow it doesn't seem to me that "Wildlife Conservation Officer" has the same power to jolt a boy's nervous system as does "game warden." How well I remember a fishing pal once exclaiming, "Geez, here comes the *game warden!*" We jerked our lines from the creek, sprinted up the side of a steep, brush-covered hill, threw our fish poles and forked sticks under a log, and tore off across the countryside. And we hadn't even been violating any of the fishing regulations. The term *game warden* just had that sort of effect on you.

There is at least one indication that many terms and phrases closely associated with fishing may soon be made obsolete. A new reel on the market is reputed to virtually eliminate backlash, that wonderfully intricate snarl of line that has served to enrich the vocabularies of anglers ever since reels were invented. It seems likely the eradication of backlash could mean the end of such colorful expressions as *bleeping bleep of a bleep bleep*. Truly, the language of fishing will be the less for the absence of backlash.

And it's about time, if you ask me.

The Man Who
Notices Things

Fenton Quagmire has this irritating habit—
he notices things. Even when we were kids,
Fenton noticed things.

Our fourth-grade teacher, Mrs. Terwilliger, was
keen on noticing things herself. "All right, class," she'd
say, "who noticed anything different about our room
today? Pat?"

"There's a picture of George Washington on the
wall?" I'd try hopefully.

"That picture' has been there ever since they built
the school! Now, Eugene, do you notice anything different about the room?"

"Nope."

"Lester?"

"Unh-unh."

One by one, Mrs. Terwilliger would call out the
names of the boys in the class and ask if they noticed
anything different about the room. They would reply

with negative grunts, wild guesses, and looks of total befuddlement. (She never called on any of the girls, of course, since it is well known that girls notice things.) Finally, the teacher would get to Quagmire, who would have been waving his hand in the air and snapping his fingers for attention. "All right now, Fenton, I want you to tell these dunces what's different about the room today."

Quagmire would then point out some piddling detail, such as that the wall to the cloakroom had been removed, or all the seats were facing in a different direction, or Mrs. Terwilliger was dressed up like Woody Woodpecker. We dunces would emerge from our lethargy long enough to express our amazement that we had failed to notice the thing, whatever it was, and would whisper vows among ourselves to make life miserable for Quagmire at the next recess.

The casual observer might suppose that the rest of us boys enjoyed tormenting Quagmire, and we were frequently hauled into the principal's office to face such charges. The truth was, it was Quagmire who tormented the rest of us. I remember, for example, a championship softball game in which we were ahead by one run in the ninth inning, and the opposing team, with two outs, had the bases loaded. An easy fly ball was batted out to Quagmire in center field. The ball bounced alongside him and disappeared into a weed patch. He was on his hands and knees staring at the ground. Cries of rage and anguish went up from the rest of our team.

"Hey, guys," Quagmire shouted. "Guess what I just noticed out here—a four-leaf clover!" In his peculiar innocence, he assumed that the reason his teammates were converging on him so rapidly was to satisfy a life-long curiosity about four-leaf clovers.

I saw that it was up to me to save him. In the musical chairs of childhood relationships, Quagmire was from time to time my best friend, and this was one of those times. The code back then required that you do whatever you could to save your best friend, so I immediately took defensive action on his behalf. "Run, Quagmire, run!" I shouted. "But first, grab that four-leaf clover, because you're gonna need all the luck you can get!"

Sometimes I wasn't able to save Quagmire from the violence he called down upon himself. Once, he and I went fishing together on the opening day of trout season. I was still in the grip of first-cast-of-the-season jitters as we waded through some tall grass on the way to our favorite fishing hole. Suddenly, Quagmire pointed at my feet and shouted, "Look out!"

In response, I raised both knees up alongside my ears, then did some aerial gymnastics that would have shamed a Nadia Comaneci.

"What?" I yelled, still treading air. *"What is it?"*

"Why, didn't you notice these little globs of foam on the grass?" said Quagmire. "You nearly stepped on them. See, they look like spit, and there's a little bug inside each glob. I'll bet these little bugs make spit houses for themselves. If you'll notice, right here is a *glug arf ugh lo mawf froat!"*

Bug-spit houses! It was just lucky for Quagmire that my hands were too weak at age ten to effectively strangle a person. Nevertheless, it was some years before he again noticed anything in close proximity to my feet.

My friend and mentor, the old woodsman Rancid Crabtree, could not abide Quagmire. Once when Fenton and I were in high school, I suggested to Rancid that we take him hunting with us.

"No! No! No!" yelled Rancid. "He ain't goin' huntin' with us, an' thet's final! Ah cain't stand the way thet boy is all the time noticin' stuff what ain't even worth bein' noticed!"

"Oh, c'mon, Rancid," I urged. "Fenton doesn't have anybody else to hunt with."

"Waall, shoot!" Rancid said. "Mebby this one time. But you tell him we're goin' huntin' and not just out noticin' thangs. You got it?"

"Right."

I had a little talk with Quagmire, and he promised he would try not to notice anything on our hunting trip. He did try, too, I'm sure of that.

Driving up into the mountains on our hunt, Quagmire could scarcely contain himself. He would glance out the window and then swivel his head around. "Say, did you . . ." he'd start to say. I'd elbow him in the ribs and he'd shut up.

"What's thet?" Rancid would say, glaring. Quagmire's eyes would be wild with excitement over what he had just noticed.

"Nothing," he'd say.

Then Quagmire started studying the dashboard on Rancid's old truck as we bounced along. "Pardon me for mentioning this, Mr. Crabtree, but I noti—" I jammed my elbow into his ribs. "B-but . . . !" he sputtered. I shook my head at him. From then on, the drive was peaceful, and if Quagmire noticed anything else, he had the good sense not to mention it.

A couple of hours later we were trying to catch up with a herd of mule deer we had jumped earlier. Quagmire was making a sweep around the mountain above us, while Rancid and I, having about given up hope of ever catching sight of the mule deer again, rested at the foot of a high cliff. Rancid was stoking his lip with tobacco, when Quagmire appeared at the top of the cliff, frantically signaling to us.

"Gol-dang!" whispered Rancid. "The boy's seen the herd! Ah always said he warn't a bad feller! Ah guess the only thang we can do is climb the cliff."

"Gee," I whispered back. "It's awfully steep. I don't think we can climb clear to the top."

"Shore we can!" Rancid hissed.

Halfway up the cliff, Rancid spat his tobacco out into space. "Ah got some bad news fer ya," he said to me.

"What's that?" I asked.

"Ah don't thank we can make it all the way to the top," he grunted, his clawed fingers digging into a vertical slab of granite. "But thet ain't the bad news."

"Well," I gasped, "what's the bad news?"

"Ah don't thank we can climb back down nuther!"

I considered Rancid's assessment of our predicament much too optimistic. Fortunately, at that moment I discovered an inch-wide ledge that angled right up under the overhang that was covered with wet moss. "This way, Rancid," I said. "I see a way out." And sure enough, scraped, battered, and bruised, the two of us soon scrambled over the lip of the cliff.

"Dang," Rancid said, rubbing his knee as we looked around for Quagmire. "Ah shore wouldn't hev wore maw good pants iffen Ah'd know'd we was gonna climb thet cliff today."

"Tear 'em, did you?"

"No. Now, whar in tarnation is thet Quagmire?"

Presently, we saw him crouched behind some brush, signaling to us. Unslinging our rifles, we hustled over in a walking crouch, being careful not to make any sound that would spook the deer.

"Whar is they, Fenton?" Rancid whispered, peering around over the top of the brush.

"This is fantastic!" Quagmire said. "Look at these rocks here. I was just walking along when I noticed them. See how round they are? Why, they're river rocks! What are river rocks doing this far up on the side of a mountain? Do you know what this means?"

"Yup," growled Rancid. "It means, Quagmire, thet whan you pick up one of them rocks thar better be a herd of deer under it!"

The river rocks weren't even the worst part of our day. When we got back to Rancid's truck, it wouldn't start. "That's what I tried to tell you, Mr. Crabtree," Quagmire said. "I noticed on the way up here that your gas gauge was on empty."

Rancid leaned his head on the steering wheel. I didn't know whether he was crying or just counting to ten.

Middle age hasn't diminished Quagmire's obsession with noticing things. His hair is gray now, his face eroded by time and weather, but still the bright little eyes relentlessly ferret out things to notice. I dread having Quagmire come in the house when he picks me up to go fishing.

"I notice you got a new hairdo," he says to my wife. "Looks nice."

"Why, thank you," Bun says, adding, "I'm glad somebody noticed."

"My gosh, you did get a new hairdo," I exclaim. "When did you change from the bouffant?"

"Nineteen sixty-five."

"Oh."

Meanwhile, Quagmire has found something else to notice.

"What happened to your other goldfish?" he asks.

"It died last summer," Bun says.

"When did we get goldfish?" I inquire.

"I see you painted your living room blue," says Quagmire.

"You did?" I say to Bun. "Heck, I liked the brown."

"The brown was four colors ago," snarls Bun.

And so it goes. Needless to say, Quagmire is very popular with women, who seem to have a certain irrational regard for men who have a compulsion to notice trifling details. "Why can't you be more like Fenton?" Bun wails at me. "You never notice anything!"

Well, that's certainly not true, as I informed Bun in no uncertain terms. It's that I'm selective about what I notice. I don't just go around noticing indiscriminately, for pete's sake!

I recently spent three days hiking alone through the Cabinet Range of the Rocky Mountains, and Bun would have been amazed at all the things I noticed.

I noticed that the trails were a good deal steeper this year than last. This was no doubt the result of some foolishness on the part of the U.S. Forest Service. When I got back home, I fired off a letter to the USFS and told them to leave the trails alone—they're steep enough!

I noticed the nights are darker when you're alone in the mountains than when you have company. Scientists should investigate this phenomenon; it might be something the CIA could make use of.

I noticed, after a couple of hours of staring out into the abnormal darkness, that there was a hard, knobby object under my Ensolite pad, no doubt a seed dropped by a careless ant.

I noticed a mosquito, and marveled that a creature so small could be so enormously complex, and still could find nothing better to do with himself than walking around in my ear singing light opera.

I noticed an ant crawling up my leg, probably the same careless chap who had dropped the walnut that was under my Ensolite pad.

I noticed far off down in the valley the sound of a large, clawed foot pressing into moss.

I noticed that I didn't have a gun with me, and wondered if there was a tool on my Swiss Army knife with which to fend off a grizzly. Maybe the corkscrew. I imagined the headline in the newspaper: "Grizzly Corkscrewed by Lone Hiker."

I noticed that the ant had been joined by some friends and relatives. They were probably helping him look for his baseball.

I noticed the distant whistle of a train, and wished I was in the lounge car exchanging dry jokes and drier martinis with traveling salesmen.

I noticed that it was only a cold, slimy sleeping bag drawstring slithering across my neck, but not until I had killed it with a blow from my hiking boot. Should have waited until it was off my neck, though.

I noticed that the sound of the large, clawed foot was right next to me, and the beast was making an assault on my jerky bag! One usually doesn't find chipmunks with such large, clawed feet. He was a cheeky fellow, too. The sight of a man feinting wildly at him with a Swiss Army knife corkscrew scarcely fazed him.

I did enough noticing on that outing to give me my fill of it, and I haven't noticed anything since. A dog could ride past me on a unicycle smoking a cigar and doing an impression of Groucho Marx, and I wouldn't notice.

The first person I ran into on my return from the mountains was Quagmire. "That must have been quite a trip," he said. "I notice that you've lost fifteen pounds."

Ha! Quagmire isn't as perceptive as he likes to think. I hadn't lost an ounce over ten pounds!

The Elk Trappers

My wife and I were but a few years out of college and already surrounded by babies of our own making—a simple, inexpensive hobby that had somehow gotten out of hand. At the time, I was writing for all the big-name, high-paying national magazines. Unfortunately, they never bought anything I wrote. I did sell an occasional article to newspapers and regional magazines, but payment from these publications was small and slow in coming, often requiring that I go into the office to bend the editor's ear and sometimes his Adam's apple.

During my best year as a free-lance writer, our standard of living hovered constantly near the poverty level but was never quite high enough for us to qualify as poor. Bun's hopes and dreams had diminished in both number and magnitude since our marriage, and she now spoke wistfully of the day when we might move into a quaint little hovel of our very own. She was a marvelously inventive cook, however, and no matter how little food we might have, she was always able to come up with a delicious dish of some sort. One of my favorites was her Boston Baked Bean, which she served on holidays. I am probably the only person in the world who knows how to carve a bean properly. We used to tell the children it was a small turkey. "Who wants white meat?" I would ask.

After a while, our situation became so bad that even the surly henchmen from the collection agency stopped coming around, possibly because I kept bumming small loans off of them. Finally, I decided to commit the writer's ultimate act of despair, even though my own personal religion forbade such a drastic measure. Still, it seemed like the only way out of my predicament: I'd have to take a regular job.

In a disgustingly short time, I landed a position with a local television station as a reporter/photographer in the news department. It was dreadful. As I signed the W2 form, my whole life flashed before my eyes. Bun, however, was elated when I told her.

"Wonderful!" she cried. "We should celebrate! I'll go pop us a corn! What do you want to drink?"

"A schooner of tap," I said. "I've cultivated a taste for chlorine."

Right from the start, I did not get along with the news director at the station. He was a tough, burly individual, with a face like a fist and a temper shorter than a snake's inseam. His name was Pat Hooper. It was a simple enough name but for some reason I constantly messed up its pronunciation, particularly when we were doing a "live" show and I was supposed to say, "Now, back to Pat Hooper!"

"You idiot!" he would scream at me after the show. "You did it again!"

"Calm down, calm down," I'd say. "Now, just tell me nicely and quietly what it was I did wrong. After all, I'm still learning the business, Hat."

There were other problems. One time, rushing off to do an interview, I set one of the station's portable sound cameras on top of the news car while I loaded some other equipment. The next place I saw the camera was in my rearview mirror, bounding along behind my speeding car like a dog chasing after the family sedan.

Then there was the foggy night I called into the station from a pay phone on the outskirts of town. Hat himself answered.

"Boy, I never thought I'd be happy to hear your voice," he shouted over the phone. "The two-way radio in your news car must have conked out, huh? We've been trying to reach you for an hour. Anyway, we heard from the cops that some fool just drove his car into Mamford Lake! Drove right down the boat-launch ramp! And get this—*har, har!*—he told the cops he thought the lake was just a big puddle! Oh, *harharharheeeee!* Let me catch my breath! Okay, now here's what I want you to do. Get out to Mamford Lake as quick as you can and shoot some film and try to get an interview with the guy. It'll make a heck of a hilarious story for the late news!"

I waited until the news director's giggles had died down. "Listen, Hat, I'm already out at Mamford Lake, and I can tell you right now you're not going to find the story all that hilarious."

Probably the thing I hated most about being a television reporter was having to listen to a grown man sob so often.

Hat and I had got off to a bad start and our relationship had steadily deteriorated. After about a year, there was even some evidence that the news director had taken a personal dislike to me. Oh, there was nothing major, just little things I noticed, like the way he would slap at me if I passed too near his desk. I decided to confront him face to face and get the matter out in the open where we could deal with it like two mature adults.

During a quiet moment in the news room, I said, "Hat, there's something bothering you. I get the distinct impression that you are harboring some ill feelings toward me. Let's talk about it, what say, fella?"

"Get this maniac away from me!" Hat screamed to nobody in particular.

"Now right there is a good example of what I mean," I said. "Look, if I upset you so much, why don't you just go ahead and terminate me?"

"I might just do that," Hat replied. "Let's see, with time off for good behavior I'd be back on the streets in five years."

Then he sank back in his swivel chair and started doing his impression of a dog chewing hot pitch. Once he started acting silly like that, trying to converse with him in an intelligent manner was hopeless.

I was oddly upset over this little exchange with Hat. Indeed, it seemed likely that he was thinking of firing me. Never before had I worked at a job where I had even the slightest fear of being fired. (Usually, the news came as a total surprise.) What I needed, I knew, was a big story, something that would change Hat's opinion of me as a television reporter. I needed something with human interest, something with animals in it, big animals, wild animals, something with danger and courage and conflict, something with brave, dedicated men risking all to extend the horizons of human knowledge! And I knew of just such a story—The Elk Trappers!

A game biologist had recently told me about an elk-migration study being conducted in a wilderness area of a nearby state. Two men had been hired to trap—that's right, *trap*—elk. Once the elk were trapped, they were adorned with various paraphernalia for future tracking and identification on their travels about the mountains.

I could hardly wait to tell Hat about my story idea.

"What?" he said. "Elk trapping? Nonsense! What kind of stuff are you trying to pull on me now?"

"I'm not kidding, Hat," I said. "It'll make great film. Of course, I'll have to be away from the station for a whole week but. . . ."

"A whole week? You've got to stop reading my mind. I was just sitting here wondering when a good story on elk trapping might turn up!"

A few days later I was flailing my old sedan over a route that the U.S. Forest Service cartographer had designated with two parallel dotted lines. Only too late did I discover that the dots represented mountain goat tracks, the cartographer apparently having turned up some evidence that a mountain goat had managed to explore the region in rather aimless fashion sometime in the previous century. I could not help but agree that the goat's achievement had been heroic, but why the cartographer should choose to commemorate it with dots was beyond comprehension. A simple skull-and-crossbones with horns would have sufficed.

At long last I spotted the elk trappers' camp nestled

in a grove of cedars near the foot of a precipice, the upper rim of which my vehicle was momentarily teetering upon. Having come this far, I was not about to turn back simply because of a near-perpendicular descent of a few hundred feet. Shifting my weight, I tilted the car forward. Judges of free-fall events probably would have disqualified me on the technicality that my car's tires occasionally brushed protruding rocks on the drop. The wall of the precipice swooped outward in a curve similar to that of a playground slide, and I was able to regain control of the vehicle in sufficient time to bring it to a screeching stop a good six inches from the tent of the elk trappers. In fact for several moments after the stop, I continued to screech, as did the elk trappers, who had shot from the tent with a suddenness that caused me to wonder if the two of them might not have been sitting in some kind of spring-loaded catapult, awaiting my arrival.

Mort and Wally, as I'll call the trappers, turned out to be great guys, although not exactly the heroic types I had in mind for my television feature. Neither of them had had any previous experience at trapping elk, but, as the official who had hired them probably asked himself, who has? They were both college students, majoring in zoology, and had taken the elk-trapping job for the summer as a means of acquiring some experience in the field. Mostly what they had acquired was a deep and intense hatred for elk.

"We've seen all the elk we ever want to see," Mort told me.

"We've seen a whole lot more elk than that," Wally put in.

"I stand corrected," Mort said.

As we sat around the campfire that evening, Mort explained the trapping procedure to me. Basically, it consisted of luring an elk into a big corral with a salt bait rigged up in such a way that it dropped the corral gate behind the animal. The trappers would drive the elk into a confining chute, where a tag was attached to its ear and a bright orange collar fastened around its neck. Then it was released.

"I hate to say this, fellas," I said, "but it all sounds rather boring."

"Boring isn't the word for it," Wally said. "I've had more excitement planting potatoes!"

Egads, I thought. Here I had risked my life and practically destroyed my car in the hope of shooting some exciting footage of men and elk in hoof-to-hand combat, and now it turned out to be nothing more than a tedious routine! Even though I had been in the television business but a short while, I knew that, above all else, there were high standards of accuracy and truth and credibility to be maintained. One simply did not attempt to distort reality. So what that I had risked my life! So what that I had ruined my car! So what that I was about to lose my job! So what that we would have to fake it!

"How good are you fellows at feigning excitement?" I asked. "Let me see you do your bug-eyed-with-terror look."

I must say that I was rather surprised the next morning when, at the crack of dawn, Mort leaped from his sleeping bag and strode briskly out of the tent in the manner of a man eager to be about his business. Perhaps, I thought, these two elk trappers take their job more seriously than they let on. After all, their nearest boss was a good day of hard travel away. There was nothing to prevent them from sleeping in until ten or eleven if they wished.

Then Mort returned and climbed back into his sleeping bag.

"Get the fire going already?" I asked.

"What for?" Mort said. "We don't usually get up until ten or eleven. After all, our nearest boss is . . ."

"I know," I said.

Mort had exaggerated slightly. By ten, we were hoofing our way up a mountain so steep the trail was only eighteen inches away from my nose. At each gasp I stripped small pine trees bare of needles. I had charley horses that could have run in the Preakness. My tongue felt like a strip of smoked jerky. And most tiresome of all was that Mort and Wally strolled along, whistling and singing, and tossing a Frisbee back and forth.

We eventually arrived at the elk trap, which looked more like one of those stockades pioneers used for defense against the Indians. And it contained an elk! A huge cow was rushing back and forth, the whites of her eyes flashing with fear and rage.

"We caught one!" I shouted. "We caught an elk!"

Mort and Wally stared disgustedly, first at me and then at the elk.

"Listen, I don't want to disappoint you or anything," Wally said, "but this is going to be real boring. I wouldn't even bother setting up your camera if I were you."

He had disappointed me. "Well, since I've come this far I might as well shoot whatever I can."

While Mort and Wally ran around the trap, shouting and throwing small stones at the elk, trying to drive it into the confining chute at one end, I shot some rather dull film of the activity, then set my camera up next to the chute so I could get some good close-ups of the elk. Eventually, the cow, apparently thinking she saw an escape route, charged into the chute. Wally rammed a pole through the chute behind her to keep her from backing out and Mort slid another pole across the chute above her to keep her from jumping while the various paraphernalia were attached.

"Are you sure she can't get out of there?" I yelled at Mort, who was about to attach a bright orange collar to the elk.

"No way," Mort shouted back. "These poles are six inches thick. Take an elephant to break one of them. I told you this was going to be boring."

KerrAACK!

The elk had just snapped the pole that crossed the chute above her. Then, like a four-legged mountain climber, she went up the ten-foot-high wall of the chute, where she bashed another pole in two with her head, making an opening about the size of a basketball.

"She's getting out!" I yelled.

"No way," Mort said, calmly. "That hole is too small for her to get—"

Before he had finished the sentence, the elk had wriggled through the hole and was plummeting toward us! Even as the shadow of the descending elk expanded around us, I switched the camera to ON. This was my chance!

For ten seconds, chaos reigned. First, the elk was on Mort and Wally. Then Mort and Wally were on the elk and the elk was on me. Wally went by with the elk after him and Mort after the elk. I was going up a tree and the elk was coming down. There were shouts and bellows and grunts and groans; there were curses that must have stunted the growth of trees. Then the cow got her bearings and set a straight course for the Continental Divide, leaving me on my back in the dust, Wally perched on top of the elk trap, and Mort wearing the orange collar. And I had it all on film!

"Geez!" Hat said as we previewed my film back at the station. "What was that bit there?"

"That round thing that shot past? I think it was a close-up of a dust-coated eyeball. Now this blur here is where I jumped a log. That odd shape that flashed by was Mort with the elk on his shoulders! This is a great shot of some dust and blue sky. And here—"

I glanced at Hat, who was studying me thoughtfully, probably wondering how he could ever have so misjudged my talent as a television reporter.

"You know something?" he said.

"What's that?" I said.

"Five years isn't all that long. And besides, I could use the rest."

The Short
Happy Life of
Francis Cucumber

Almost every day the boy, Ace, would come over to the Jiffy Trading Post, and he and I would sit on the steps and talk. I remember one October morning in particular.

"What is it like to be a hunting guide?" Ace asked.

"It's very good to be a hunting guide," I said, "but the hard thing is to guide well and true and honorably."

"I wish you would stop talking like a Hemingway character," he said. "Nobody talks that way anymore."

"In the old days, everyone talked like a Hemingway character," I said.

"They don't anymore," Ace said.

"Yes," I said, "I know. It's sad."

"You're the only person left who still talks like a Hemingway character," he said. "You still talk that way. It makes me sick."

"I don't give a ————," I said. "I'll talk how I please."

"You don't have to use the dashes with me," he said. "I know that word."

"Do you know all the words?" I asked him.

"Yes," Ace said. "I know – – – – and – – – – and – – – – and – – – and – – – –."

"That's very good," I said. "How about – – – – – – – – – – – – –? Do you know that one?"

"I do now," he said. "That's a real dandy."

"Remember, you only use that word when you are being charged by a rhino and have missed with the second barrel of your .455 Rigby. It is a large-caliber word."

"I'll remember," Ace said. "Now, tell me again how it is to be a hunting guide."

I told him again how it was to be a hunting guide. Ace never tired of hearing about what it was like to be a hunting guide, possibly because he always fell asleep after the first five minutes.

In the old days, as I told Ace, the hunting-guide business was much more fun. When you met another hunting guide out in the bush and he wanted to know how you were getting along with your client, he would ask, "Are you still drinking his whiskey?" Now the question is, "Are you still drinking his mineral water?" Mineral water has taken a lot of the fun out of the hunting-guide business.

"How long has it been since you've had a client?" Ace asked.

"Eighty-two days," I said.

"That's a long time to go without a client," he said.

"Yes," I said. "My luck has been very bad. At least a dozen times now I have taken parties of five into the bush and come back with parties of only two or three. It may be an omen."

"It may be that you are a bad guide," Ace said.

I laughed and playfully snatched his motorcycle helmet and held it high overhead. He made some sounds of annoyance but finally managed to get the chin strap loose and dropped to the ground. He rubbed his neck.

"Why you old——!" he said. "Why did you do that?"

"I did it because you are a wise-elbow," I said. "You have always been a wise-elbow, ever since I have known you. That is why you are twenty-two years old and still in the fifth grade."

Ace pointed up the street. "Hey, would you look at that!" he said.

I turned cautiously, keeping one eye on him, because he likes to play tricks, sometimes hitting me on the ear with a big board when my back is turned. He was not tricking me this time.

A chauffeur-driven Rolls-Royce was coming down the street. It pulled up next to the Trading Post, and a middle-aged man and a much younger woman got out. I had great difficulty not staring at the see-through blouse; the skin-tight, shimmering, gold pants; the diamond necklace and earrings. The woman wore a simple print dress and no jewelry. She was blond and tan and slender with large blue eyes and a fine nose. She was very beautiful.

I can always tell Southern Californians when I see them. There is something different about them. I nudged Ace and whispered, "Check the license plate."

"Oklahoma," he said.

"Just as I figured," I said. "There is something different about Oklahomans."

There is something different about Texans too. I remember the Texan I guided up into the Hoodoo

Mountains. He had money written all over him. After that I could never stand to look at another tattoo. I sometimes wonder whether he ever found his way out of the mountains.

The man and woman started walking toward me and Ace. I pushed my hat back with my thumb, leaned against the porch post, stuck a wooden match in my mouth and chewed on it. Fortunately, I still have lightning reflexes and was able to smother the flames in my mustache before they took my eyebrows. Apparently, the man and woman had not seen lightning reflexes before.

"Are you all right?" the woman asked.

I squinted through the smoke of my smoldering lip stubble and grinned at her. "Mumpht bim scowp an maw mouph cot fahr, har, har," I said casually.

The man and woman glanced uneasily at each other.

"What can I do for you folks?"

"We're looking for Wilson, the hunting guide," the man said.

"At your service," I said.

"Oh?" the man said.

"Oh dear!" the woman said.

The man said his name was Francis Cucumber and the woman was his wife, Dill. He was after a trophy mountain goat. Friends had told him that Wilson was the best hunting guide in these parts. With all due modesty, I confirmed the truth of what his friends had told him.

"My services don't come cheap, though," I told Cucumber. "I get fifteen dollars a day plus expenses. Colorful expressions and ironic remarks are extra."

"We'll take the package." Cucumber said.

We made arrangements to pick up the Cucumbers at their hotel the following morning. I knew Ace would want to go along to help with the camp chores but was too proud to ask. Finally, when he couldn't stand it anymore, he blurted out, "C'mon, let me go!"

I chuckled good-naturedly and released him from the half nelson. "You remember to mind your manners around the clients," I told him. Since he had only two manners, I figured minding them was not too much to ask.

"One thing puzzles me," Ace said.

"What?" I said.

"How come you told them your name was Wilson?"

"Because Wilson already has more clients than he can handle."

That night I prepared for the safari into the mountains by rereading Hemingway's African short stories. If you are to guide well and true and honorably, it is very important to read Hem's African stories. Sometimes, if you have not read Hemingway in a long while, you cannot think of anything ironic to say to your clients. Clients become very upset with a guide who does not speak with irony, even when he doesn't get them lost in the mountains. Once, some clients and I were lost for three weeks and I ran out of ironic remarks and had to fall back on my knock-knock jokes. It is very dangerous to tell lost hunters knock-knock jokes, because sometimes they will charge you without warning and attempt to stuff used socks in your mouth. That is why you never go into the mountains without a good supply of ironic remarks.

The next morning we rode up into the Hoodoo Mountains and in the beginning everything went well and I thought we were going to have a fine hunt. Then Cucumber began to complain about his feet dragging on the ground.

"That is because your legs are long and the burro's are short," I explained.

"I know what the reason is," Cucumber snapped. "What I want to know is, why don't you let me ride the horse and you ride the burro?"

Clearly, the man was not without a sense of humor and I complimented him on his clever jest.

"It is a very good sign that you can make jokes even after the toes of your boots have worn off," I said. "You joke well."

"— — — — — — — — — — — !" Cucumber shouted.

I glanced swiftly around to see if we were being charged by a rhino, which is rare in Idaho. There was no sign of one. Already Cucumber was beginning to hallucinate. I had often observed this tendency in clients before, but never so early in the hunt.

That night we camped by a small mountain lake. While Ace and I prepared supper, Cucumber and Dill got into a furious argument. At one point I heard her scream, "How could you be such a fool as to get us into this mess! Anybody can see that that idiot doesn't know anything about guiding!"

That raised my dander. For one thing, this was only the fifth time I had brought Ace along on an expedition. You couldn't expect him to know anything about guiding with so little experience, even if he weren't an idiot. Ace didn't seem to mind what had been said about him, or so I judged from the fact that he burst into loud guffaws.

I fixed my famous Whatchamacallit stew for supper

and Cucumber and Dill even complained about that. Both of them said it upset their stomachs. If they had just tasted it, though, I'm sure they'd have found it not only hearty but delicious.

After supper we sat around the fire and talked and drank mineral water.

"Tomorrow we will be in goat country," I said. "The goats are very fine and white and beautiful this time of year and they are like patches of snow against the gray rock of the cliffs, and sometimes they are actually patches of snow, and then you know you are not yet in goat country at all, which is very discouraging after you have spent the day climbing a rock cliff."

"Huh?" Cucumber said.

"Egads!" Dill said.

"I have known hunters to shoot the patches of snow after they have climbed the cliffs," I said. "They do not laugh when they shoot the patches of snow either but are very serious about it and sometimes they even cry, which is bad for the morale of the other hunters."

"I'll bet," Dill said.

"The way you tell the goats from the patches of snow is that the patches of snow don't move or go 'baaa,' " I said.

"Go 'baaa'?" Cucumber said. "How far is it back to the road?"

"You don't understand," I said. "There are no goats between here and the road. Now, we'd better turn in. Tomorrow we must climb the cliffs and find the goats and we must hunt well and true and honorably."

"Your manner of speech reminds me of someone I've read somewhere," Dill said. "I think it's . . . it's . . ."

"Yes?" I said.

". . . Abigail Finley Dunlop!" she said.

"Well, enough of this silly prattle," I said sternly. "Let's hit the sack. We've got a gut-buster of a day ahead of us tomorrow."

"Ain'tcha gonna talk like a Hemingway character no more?" Ace asked. "I was startin' to like it."

"Shut up and douse the fire," I said ironically.

Shortly after sunup the next morning, Ace and I discovered that the Cucumbers had stolen my horse and vanished without a trace. Naturally, I was furious. What really made me mad, though, was not my clients' act of ingratitude and treachery and deceit but that my horse was the only one who knew the way home. Even worse, I couldn't get Ace to shut up: "It is not enough to guide well and true and honorably," he said. "You must also know which direction is the north and which direction is the south, and it is good, too, if you can tell east from west. Never ask for whom the bell tolls . . ."

The Arkansas
Prank Hound

My cousin Buck was three years older than I. When we were growing up he was the smartest person I knew or ever expected to know. Buck was a walking university. There wasn't anything he didn't know or couldn't figure out. He was amazing. Of course, that was back before his mind started to go bad. His mind started to go bad about the time I entered high school and began to detect certain flaws in the information he dispensed to me. When I pointed these flaws out to him, he said even he had noticed some deterioration of his intellect.

As the years went by, Buck's IQ continued to plummet, eventually leveling out at what he termed average but what I would judge to be a whole lot closer to the intelligence of asparagus than of genius. But no matter. The portion of Buck's intellectual history that we are concerned with here is the early period, when he still knew everything.

In those early days I followed Buck around constantly, listening to him discourse on such matters as sex, life, death, hunting, fishing, sex, outer space, cars, sex, motion pictures, horses, dogs, motorcycles, and sex. Even though Buck knew everything about everything, he did seem to favor certain subjects. Wildlife, for example, was a specialty of his. One time we saw a funny-looking little mouse hopping along through the grass.

"What kind of mouse is that?" I asked Buck. "See the way it hops!"

"That's called a hop mouse," Buck said without even a moment's pause.

The speed with which Buck could identify even the rarest and most obscure of species was something to marvel at, but no more than his knowledge of wildlife physiology.

"How come that mouse hops instead of runs like a normal mouse?" I would ask.

Without a second's hesitation, Buck would explain, "'Cause it's got a different kind of hinges on its hind legs."

"Hinges?"

"Yeah, hinges. If you ain't about the most ignorant kid I ever knowed! Hinges is what lets legs bend."

Buck knew all about feeding habits, too.

"What do hop mice eat, Buck?" I asked.

"Just your regular mouse food—grass, roots, bread, cheese."

Buck's real area of expertise was dogs, hunting dogs in particular. What Buck didn't know about hunting dogs you could fit in the eye of a needle and still poke a camel through. His own hunting dog was a rare and expensive breed, the Arkansas Prank Hound. Buck always had to laugh about the way he fooled the man who sold him the dog. The man was sitting in an old pickup truck when Buck happened by and stopped to admire the pup.

"I bet you never seen a pup like this un," the man said.

"No, sir, I ain't," Buck admitted. "What kind is it?"

The man cast an appreciative eye down at the pup and after a thoughtful pause said, "Why, this is what you calls your Arkansas Prank Hound. Bet you ain't never even heard of the breed before."

"Course I have," Buck said, because he knew all the dog breeds there are. "Pretty good dogs, are they?"

The man's eyebrows shot up. "Good? Why, they is the best!"

"I mean are they good hunters?" Buck said.

"You wouldn't believe how good they are," the man said. "My goodness, the Arkansas Prank Hound does everything for the hunter but load his shotgun, and he'd do that too if you showed him how. But the main thing about the Prank Hound is it knows how to talk. You take most bird dogs, about all they can do is point the bird, right? But the Prank Hound, he'll come right out and tell you, 'There's two ringnecks and a hen hidin' in that tall grass over there.' Their one fault is sometimes they'll argue with you about who's gonna retrieve the bird, you or them. They ain't above makin' a nasty remark either when you miss an easy shot."

"You don't mean they talk real human talk, do you?" Buck said.

"Well, no, it's not exactly human talk. It's dog talk. The thing is, it don't take you no time at all to learn it."

"I don't suppose you'd consider selling the pup?"

"I surely do hate to," the man said. "But I've fallen on hard times lately. My house burned down and I lost my job and my heart has been actin' up on me. I suppose if somebody came along and offered me five hundred dollars for the pup I'd have to sell him."

"Gee," Buck said, "all I got is three dollars."

"That's close enough," the man said, thrusting the pup into Buck's hands. "Of course, I'd have to hold out for the five hundred if his papers hadn't burnt up in the fire."

Buck had to laugh as he told me later. Here he had foxed the man out of a five-hundred-dollar dog for three dollars, and all the time he had another two dollars in his pocket. Besides knowing everything back in those days, Buck was *shrewd!*

Buck named the pup Gooch. We could scarcely wait for the dog to grow up and start talking. Every other day or so, I'd go over to Buck's house and ask him, "Has Gooch said anything yet?"

Buck would look down at his dog. "Nothin' worth mentioning."

Now there are a great many cynics in the world who might assume that Gooch's previous owner had lied to Buck about the dog's ability to talk. After about a year in which Gooch had not uttered even the most casual of remarks, I was starting to become one of those cynics. One day I said to Buck, "I don't think Gooch is ever gonna talk! I think that man lied to you! He pulled a fast one on you, that's what he did."

Buck, of course, was unaccustomed to having me speak to him in that way. Being three years older than I, he had no trouble pointing out the flaws in my reasoning.

"This here is an Arkansas Prank Hound, ain't it?"

"Yes," I had to admit.

"And all Arkansas Prank Hounds know how to talk, don't they?"

"Yes," I had to admit.

"So it stands to reason that Gooch is gonna start one of these days, don't it?"

"Yes," I had to admit. Only one question remained in my mind. Would I have had to admit all those things if Buck hadn't been twisting my arm?

Shortly after that incident, however, it turned out that Buck had been right all along about Gooch. The dog did know how to talk! It was about the most remarkable thing I ever witnessed.

I had stopped by Buck's house in my usual fashion to ask him if Gooch had said anything yet.

"Why, yes, he did," Buck replied. "It wasn't nothin' important. Just your usual dog talk."

"He *talked*?" I shouted.

"Sure," Buck said. "Actually, he's been talking for several months now. It was just that I didn't understand Arkansas Prank Hound. I was expectin' him to say somethin' in American, until it suddenly occurred to me that he don't speak American. Then I got busy and started studying the sounds he was makin' and right away I figured out a few words. Now I can understand just about anything he says."

I looked at Gooch in amazement. "What does he talk about?"

"Oh, just the neighborhood dog gossip," Buck said. "It was kind of boring, to tell you the truth, particularly if you don't care any more than I do about what nasty things the Whites' dog wrote on their gatepost."

"Well," I said, "pheasant season's open. Let's take him out hunting and then he'll have something interesting to talk about."

Buck said that sounded like a pretty good idea. He went in the house and got his single-shot 16-gauge and we headed for the stubble fields south of town. Gooch walked along behind us, not saying anything. As we passed an alley, the dog spotted a cat and took off after it barking for all he was worth, a sum I still believed to be at least five hundred dollars.

"What's he saying?" I asked Buck, who was yelling at the dog to come back.

"Huh?" Buck said. "Oh, you're too young to hear language like that. I don't know where Gooch picked up some of them words. I just hope there ain't any ladies in this neighborhood who understand Prank Hound."

When Gooch finally caught up with us, we were already out to the stubble fields. He rushed up to Buck whining and yapping.

"I don't care what that cat called you," Buck told him. "I want you to tend to business. And furthermore, cut out using them swear words! Now get out there and do some hunting."

Gooch made a woofing sound.

"Oh, all right, *please* then!" Buck said.

It wasn't long before Gooch flushed a pheasant. I might have been mistaken but I thought the dog had stepped on the bird with his hind foot. In any case, Gooch jumped around yelping in fright and snapping his jaws in the empty air. He flushed another three pheasants in approximately this same manner, never once first saying a word to either Buck or me about a bird being anywhere in the area. As we were trudging back home without Buck having had a chance to fire a single shot, Gooch trotted happily along ahead of us, possibly singing a Prank Hound folk tune. If so, I couldn't make out either the tune or the words.

"I'd sure hate to sell ol' Gooch," Buck said, "but I could probably let you have him for five hundred dollars. Ain't every kid owns a talking dog."

"All I've got is a quarter," I said.

"That's close enough," Buck said.

"It's my lucky quarter and I can't give it up," I told him.

Actually, it wasn't my lucky quarter at all. I just couldn't take advantage of one of my very own relatives, particularly one whose mind was starting to go bad.

Well, Excuuuuse Me!

It has come to my attention that some of you anglers are forgetting your manners. You offenders know who you are, so I won't mention any names, but I want this crude behavior to stop immediately.

Perhaps it is time to review the basics of fishing etiquette, for the benefit of those of you who have forgotten them and for the youngsters just getting started in the sport.

Let us begin with a typical situation. Your fishing partner has laid claim to the only hole on the stream that seems to be producing any fish. He has pulled three nice rainbows from the hole and is walking around on his knees, either because he doesn't want to spook the remaining fish with the sight of his profile or because he is praying the fish will keep biting.

You haven't had so much as a strike all day, and you know your partner will be giving you nonstop lectures for the next month on how to improve your fishing technique. What to do? Climbing up the cliff behind your partner and throwing a large rock in the hole is considered a breach of fishing etiquette. Furthermore, it will be difficult to convince the offended party that you threw the rock in the hole accidentally. The main reason it will be difficult is that a person can't think clearly while fleeing for his life.

According to proper fishing etiquette, you must accept your partner's good luck gracefully. Call out to him and offer encouragement and compliment him on his technique. "WONDERFUL CAST THERE, BOB!" you might yell. "I'LL BET YOU'RE GOING TO CATCH A REAL MONSTER OUT OF THAT HOLE!"

Since he may not be up on his fishing etiquette, Bob's response might be to grimace, shake his head furiously, and put his finger to his lips in the universal gesture of asking for silence. Or he may use some other universal gesture, depending upon his knowledge of fishing etiquette. In any case, don't fall into a sulk, because that is the worst of bad sportsmanship. Merely start crashing through the brush toward him, yelling, "WHAT, BOB? WHAT DID YOU SAY? GO AHEAD AND MAKE ANOTHER OF THOSE WONDERFUL CASTS OF YOURS! I'LL BET THERE'S A FIVE-POUNDER RIGHT OUT THERE WHERE THE TOP OF MY SHADOW IS FALLING ON THE WATER!"

You may be surprised to learn that such gentlemanly and polite conduct can be even more effective than the loutish behavior of throwing a big rock in the water.

Anglers often carry secrecy so far that it falls into the realm of unsportsmanlike conduct. Some fishermen I know laugh fiendishly and refuse to divulge the kind of fly they have hit upon that happens to be producing fish at the moment. Such behavior is disgraceful. There is absolutely no reason to laugh fiendishly when a simple, inscrutable smile will do. In the rare instances when I'm the one with the right fly, I like to explain to the other anglers, as I land another trout, that much of the pleasure of fishing is to solve for one's self the mystery of what the fish are taking. It would subtract from their pleasure if I solved the mystery for them, I say, smiling inscrutably.

Of course, this patient explanation doesn't work on all anglers. Take Retch Sweeney, for example. His approach to solving the mystery is to say, "Yeah, right, sure," as he wrestles me to the ground, hauls in my line, and takes a look at the fly. Retch cares nothing for mystery and even less for fishing etiquette.

When asked what fly you are using, the polite thing to do is to open your fly book and hand a fly to the person making the request. He will be so pleased by your openness and generosity that he will respond in kind when the time comes for you to ask him what kind of fly he is using. As he hands you the fly, don't stare at it in astonishment and exclaim, "A turkey feather lashed to a Number two hook?" Otherwise, he will respond by saying, "Yes, it works just as well as the horse-feather fly you gave me. Maybe even better."

Here is another situation that often comes up. You have forgotten your lunch and are starving when you get back to the car first after a long day of fishing. Your partner's lunch is sitting there in plain sight on the front seat as a deliberate temptation to you. He could have followed his usual practice of hiding it under the spare tire of his car or in the engine compartment, where you always found it anyway. But leaving it on the front seat is practically an invitation.

You open the lunch sack tentatively and peer in. There are two sandwiches, a piece of cake, and an orange. The question is, should you eat one of the sandwiches? The piece of cake goes without saying, and the orange you will leave for him, but should you eat one of the sandwiches? The answer is to eat one. If you eat both sandwiches, you have violated fishing etiquette, and even worse, you may have to walk home.

Should you help ladies in and out of boats? The new social standards permit women to open their own doors, and it follows that they should be allowed to get out of boats unassisted. I, however, tend to be chivalrous by nature and always reach out a hand to steady the woman I fish with as she climbs from boat to dock. It makes her feel more secure and less likely to drop the rods and tackle boxes.

Suppose you do inadvertently commit a fishing faux pas. Many anglers are totally at a loss in such a situation and blunder about saying, "Gee, I'm sorry! How clumsy of me!" Such abject apologies only cause embarrassment in most fishing circles. It is far better to treat the mishap in a jovial manner. Here are a few apt responses for a variety of circumstances.

"Great leap, George! If I hadn't bumped you off the rock, I'd have never known what a fine athlete you are. Need a little more practice on the landings, though. Heh heh."

"Three-hundred-dollar rod, huh? Didn't feel like much more than a dollar ninety-eight when I stepped on the tip. Ho ho. Seriously, though, I've heard it improves the action of expensive rods if you break about three inches off the tip like I did there. Now, you just dry your eyes and see if that ol' rod doesn't actually cast better."

"Oh, I don't know, I think you look rather rakish with a bass plug in your ear."

"George, you won't believe what I did! Prepare yourself for a laugh. I forgot I had your square-stern canoe on top of the car, and I started to back into the garage. What? Yeah, I know it wasn't square-stern, but it is now! Get it, George?"

In all of these instances, you will note that the mishap is dealt with in a bluff and hearty manner, which your fishing companions will appreciate much more than they would humble apologies. If they don't happen to be familiar with fishing etiquette, however, no harm is done, at least none that a good chiropractor won't be able to work out for you in half a dozen visits.

The Mountain Car

Budge Honeylip, proprietor of Honeylip's Auto Salvage and Junk Co., sold us the mountain car himself. As we said afterward, Budge was a man you could trust.

Retch Sweeney and I had bicycled out to Honeylip's prepared to deal with his head salesman and tow-truck driver, Slick Beasly.

"Sure as shooting, ol' Slick will try to pass off one of those junkers Honeylip intends to sell for scrap iron," I told Retch.

"Yeah," he said. "You got to watch a man like Slick Beasly."

"Here's what we'll do," I said. "As soon as Slick starts giving us the hard sell on some wreck, we'll just laugh cynically and start to walk away. Let me hear you laugh cynically, Retch. Okay, that's not bad."

Retch and I had worked in the hayfields for nearly the whole month of June in order to earn enough money to buy ourselves a mountain car. Our transportation situation had become critical when both our respective sets of parents had simultaneously refused to allow us to drive the family autos anywhere except on paved roads. They had ranted some nonsense about mud and rocks and tree branches and fenders and oil pans as their excuse. The problem was that our county didn't have all that many paved roads, and what there were didn't go anyplace interesting, such as to decent hunting and fishing areas.

The crisis forced us to indenture ourselves to a series of farmers, every one of whom was possessed of a maniacal obsession for extracting from his hired hands their last ounce of energy. If we so much as stopped for a drink of water and a bit of conversation, the farmers would yell at us to stop goofing off because they didn't want their hay to get snowed on before Retch and I got it in, which was ridiculous, since it was still only June.

Our suffering and exhaustion were almost too much to bear. Retch and I each contracted a blister, in fact. When we showed our injuries to the farmer of the day, all he did was to laugh cruelly and say that it was so rare and strange for blisters to rise up for no known reason he had a mind to send it in to *Ripley's Believe It or Not.* Farmers were an insensitive bunch.

Having come by our money through such hard labor, Retch and I were not about to be snookered out of it by some high-pressure salesman like Slick Beasly. By the time we had bicycled out Cemetery Hill Road to Honeylip's Auto Salvage and Junk Co., we had our plans laid. The main idea was to slip into the salvage yard and check out the cars before Slick even knew we were in the vicinity. That way we would be able to arrive at our independent judgments, without being confused by a barrage of sales talk.

Everything went well until we started examining the first car, opening and closing its doors, looking under the hood, kicking the tires, gazing in wonder at the miraculously low mileage recorded on the speedometer.

"Afternoon, gentlemen," a voice behind us said. "Anything I can help you with?" It was Slick, calmly leaning against a rusty Packard, pretending to clean his fingernails with a penknife.

"Oh, we're just looking," I said shrewdly.

"Too bad," said Slick. "I happen to have a nifty little number here that runs like a dream."

He slid into the car, started it, and gunned the engine into a banging roar. It sounded good.

Slick shook his head as he turned the key off. "A rich banker in town is supposed to stop out any time now and buy this vehicle for his spoilt brat of a kid. Oh, how I do hate to see them rich kids get everything! Shucks, I'd sell this car right now for half price just to prevent that from happening."

"How much?" I asked.

"Hunnert," Slick said.

Retch and I laughed cynically and started to walk away.

Then Budge Honeylip popped out of his office in the company's quonset hut. "Dang it all to heck, Slick," he yelled. "I got a good mind to give you the boot, trying to foist a car like that off on these boys for a hunnert dollars."

"But, boss . . . !" blurted Slick.

"Don't but me," yelled Budge. "You git on over to the shop and change the oil in the tow truck. Won't be nobody around there you can cheat out of their hard-earned money!"

Slick hung his head and slunk off toward the quonset hut. I felt sorry for him, but he had it coming.

Budge put his arms around Retch and me. "Now you boys just tell ol' Budge the kind of vehicle you're looking for."

"A mountain car."

"You mean like for hunting and fishing?"

"Yeah, you know, the kinda car that will go just about anywhere."

"Oh, you don't want something fancy then, something with fenders and all what might get caught in the brush."

"Naw," Retch said. "It don't need fenders."

Budge said in that case he had just the car for us. A lot of his customers were picky, he said, and wanted fenders and all the trimmings on their cars, but he could see we were practical, down-to-earth, no-frills men. In addition to all his other qualities, Budge could judge character pretty well.

The car he showed us had a bit fewer frills than we had expected. No seats, for example. A missing door. A glassless rear window. A lidless trunk. And, of course, no front fenders. There were, we would discover, other missing frills, but their absence was not immediately observable.

Budge set an apple box inside the car for a seat, climbed in, and started the motor for us. It sounded like a washing machine tumbling down a flight of stairs. Smoke billowed out from every crack and seam.

Budge stuck his head out of the cloud of smoke. "Course it needs a tune-up—*cough, cough*—but you two look like you might be pretty handy with tools. Seeing as how that ornery Slick tried to—*cough, cough*—pull a fast one on you, I could probably let you have this— *choke*—prime mountain car for, oh . . . forty dollars?"

We stared at him in disbelief. Forty dollars! For this car? He had to be out of his mind!

Budge apparently was reading our thoughts because he started to say, "On the other hand, now that I think about it, maybe I could—"

"We'll take it!" Retch blurted out.

"Yeah," I added quickly. "You said forty dollars. You can't change your mind now."

We could tell from the look of astonishment on Budge's face that he hadn't run into a couple of sharpies like us in a long while. Obviously, when he realized what a mistake he'd made, he had thought about raising the price, maybe doubling it. He even as much as admitted his blunder after we had completed the transaction: "I'll tell you something, boys. It ain't every day I sell a car like this one for forty dollars."

Scarcely believing our good fortune, Retch and I loaded the bikes into the back of the car and were driving off, when we saw Slick standing in the door of the quonset hut. His mouth gaped as he stared first at us, then back at Budge, then at us again.

We decided to give our mountain car a quick road test on Cemetery Hill. The hill was by no means as rugged as the terrain our mountain car was intended for, but it was sufficiently steep and winding, as may be judged from the fact that the hill did not have a cemetery on it. The name had been invented by loggers who had to drive trucks down the steep, twisting grade.

Our mountain car growled up the hill without difficulty, delighting us with its performance. At the top, Retch, who was driving, plowed the front of the car up a steep bank in order to get it turned around.

"Wow! Look at that! This thing is just like a tank!" he exclaimed happily. "Now let's see how it does going downhill."

One of the frills missing from the car turned out to be the brakes.

Immediately, I saw why there was no door on the passenger's side. Some passenger had undoubtedly kicked it off in his haste to abandon the car on a downgrade. Only two factors prevented me from leaping out: (1) a fierce determination not to abandon my friend, and (2) total paralysis. Sitting on the seatless floor of the car, I could look down through gaping holes and see the earth rushing past a few inches away. Even worse, on one turn, I could see sky rushing past. Somehow Retch managed to get down the hill without flipping us over. After we had coasted to a stop, we sat silent for a long while, savoring the sensation of breathing. Presently, a farmer drove up in a truck. He squealed to a stop and rushed over.

"You boys all right?"

"Yup," Retch said.

"You're lucky to be alive from the looks of it," the farmer said. "Your car's totally demolished!"

Retch and I smiled feebly but appreciatively. It isn't everyone who can joke like that and still keep a straight face.

Retch and I drove the rest of the way to his place in low gear. The trip was without further incident, except that while we were waiting for a train to go by on a crossing, Sheriff McGrady's head poked through the smoke on my side.

"I should've known," he said, recognizing me and Retch. "What in tarnation have you two gone and done now?"

"Just driving our mountain car home," I said.

"Car?" the sheriff said. "There's a car here? Why, for goodness sakes, so there is. What kind of fuel does it burn, wet leaves? Now, I don't wish to seem unkind, lads, but if I catch you driving this vehicle on the public roads again, *I'll skin the both of ya!*"

Sheriff McGrady had no great appreciation of mountain cars.

Retch's father was sitting on the front porch in his undershirt drinking a can of beer when we pulled into the Sweeney driveway.

"Well, what d'ya think of our new mountain car, Popper?" Retch shouted. "We practically stole it from ol' Budge Honeylip for a lousy forty dollars!"

Mr. Sweeney stared impassively.

"Pat and me, we're gonna get out your tools and tear it all down and put it back together, Popper. Course we'll need the garage, but I figure you can park your car out in the alley for a couple of days."

Mr. Sweeney continued to stare impassively.

I began to suspect that he had suffered a stroke. Then, slowly, his lips began to move. "Someday somebody will invent a pill," he said.

Weird! Retch and I attributed this muttered nonsense to a slight stroke or maybe temporary senility.

We worked on the mountain car for a week, dismantling it piece by piece and arranging the parts in neat order on the floor of the garage, and down the driveway, and around the lawn. Mr. Sweeney would come home in the evenings, park his car in the alley, stare balefully at us and dispersed parts of the mountain car, then go into the house muttering to himself about the invention of pills. The man was not well.

My fellow mechanic and I were not feeling all that great either. Bit by bit our confidence in being able to reassemble the mountain car eroded. Panic started to set in. We began to quarrel.

"The long gizmo with the holes in it bolts onto that big thing over there," Retch would say.

"You're crazy!" I'd yell. "The flat thingamajig with the do-hickies on it goes there!"

Nevertheless, the car was reassembled in a single weekend. All the gizmos and thingamajigs and do-hickies were bolted into their proper places with swift efficiency, if not actual frenzy. The work, however, was accompanied by a steady stream of creative cursing that turned the air of the neighborhood blue for weeks afterward.

Occasionally, Retch's mother would come out to the garage and complain about the vile invectives rolling up from the bowels of the mountain car. "Hush!" she'd cry. "The neighbors will hear!"

"I don't give a *bleep* if they do hear," Mr. Sweeney would reply. "Now hand me that box wrench, Retch, and be quick about it!"

"Sure thing, Popper. But are you certain that whatchamacallit goes there?"

"Shut up!"

Mr. Sweeney did a wonderful job of putting the mountain car back together, and it was almost as good as before. He even repaired the brakes.

To show our gratitude, we offered to take Mr. Sweeney along on our first fishing trip in the mountain car. His only response to the invitation was a long, quavering laugh that reinforced our doubts about his emotional stability.

The mountain car provided us with enormous pleasure, hauling us to the very ends of wilderness roads and, often as not, back again. We even gave the car a name, Mrs. Peabody, in honor of our favorite high school English teacher. Apparently, this caused no end of rumors about the teacher. For example, one day Retch and I were tossing back a couple of malts in Toby's Soda Fountain and discussing our favorite topic, the mountain car.

"I think Mrs. Peabody's rear end is about to go out," I said. Toby froze in mid-wipe on a glass he was drying.

"What makes you think so?" Retch asked. Toby cocked his head in our direction.

"Well, she was making these strange rumbling sounds when I had her out in the mountains the other day."

"You had Mrs. Peabody out in the mountains," Toby asked. "What for?"

"The usual thing," I said. "Retch and me take her out two or three times a week. Sometimes we stay out for days."

"For days?" Toby said. "You and Retch with Mrs. Peabody?"

"Sure," I said. "It's more fun that way. Gosh, Toby, maybe you'd like to come along sometime, too. You'd be more than welcome."

"I don't think my wife would like me going out with Mrs. Peabody."

"Oh," Retch said, obviously miffed. "You think you're too good for Mrs. Peabody. Just because she's old and shabby and got a few too many miles on her, you don't want to be seen out with us."

"Goodness no," cried Toby nervously. "And she's certainly not all that old. Thirty-five, I'd guess."

"Thirty-two," Retch said, his temper cooling. "Sure, I'll admit Mrs. Peabody needs some work done on her. In fact, my pop says he's going to grind her valves first chance he gets."

Toby's glass shattered on the floor. "Your father is going to grind her valves? I thought he was a bricklayer."

"Yeah, he's a bricklayer, all right, but he's gotten so he enjoys tinkering with Mrs. Peabody out in our garage. It's sort of a hobby with him."

Mumbling incoherently, Toby walked off to find a broom. It was obvious he didn't know much about mountain cars, so we never mentioned Mrs. Peabody to him again.

Our adventures with Mrs. Peabody in the two years we owned her are too numerous to mention here, so I will recount only the last.

Retch and I were grouse hunting with Mrs. Peabody up on Big Sandy Mountain. As we were driving along, a big blue grouse appeared at the edge of the road up ahead. Retch eased Mrs. Peabody to a stop on a turnout, and we grabbed our .22s and slipped out of the car. The grouse, in the meantime, had flown up into a spruce tree. Stealthily, we walked up the road, trying to pick out the dark shape of the grouse among the boughs. I inched around the far side of the tree, my rifle at the ready, but I still couldn't see the grouse. Retch was still standing on the road, impatient as always.

"Fire," he said.

"I can't even see it," I whispered. "Why should I fire?"

"FIRE!" Retch shouted.

"Fire yourself, you idiot, if you can see the grouse," I shouted back at him.

"Forget the dang grouse," he yelled, taking off down the road. "Mrs. Peabody is on fire!"

Indeed she was. Although Mrs. Peabody had always smoked, now there were tongues of flame licking the hood. We were too late to save her.

The loss saddened us, of course, but there were others who looked upon it as a blessing. Among these was the Forest Service whose lookout towers half a dozen times a summer would report Mrs. Peabody as a fire out of control. My mother, who referred to the mountain car as "a death trap," was much relieved to hear of its end. Retch's father could scarcely contain his joy. Budge Honeylip saw it as an opportunity to sell us another fine car. But perhaps the most relieved and delighted person of all was our high school English teacher.

The Christmas Hatchet

The best evidence I've been able to come up with that the human race is increasing in intelligence is that parents no longer give their kids hatchets for Christmas.

When I was a boy the hatchet was a Christmas gift commonly bestowed upon male children. In an attempt to cover up their lapse of sanity, parents would tell their offspring, "Now don't chop anything."

By the time this warning was out of the parents' mouths, the kid would have already whacked two branches off the Christmas tree and be adding a second set of notches to one of his new Lincoln logs.

It was not that the kid harbored a gene compelling him to be destructive. The problem was with the hatchet, which had a will of its own. As soon as the kid activated it by grasping the handle, the hatchet took charge of his mental processes and pretty much ran the whole show from then on.

Shortly after Christmas the kid would be making frequent trips to the woodshed with his father, and not to chop wood either.

"The hatchet did it!" the kid would yell as he was being dragged toward the woodshed by his shirt collar. "I was just walking through the gate and my hatchet leaped out and chopped the post!"

Some kids were gullible enough to try the old George Washington cherry tree ploy. "I did it with my own little hatchet," they would confess.

"I know," their father would say. "Now haul your rear end out to the woodshed!"

The moral most of my friends and I drew from the cherry tree story wasn't that George Washington was so honest but that his father was a bit slow. This showed that even a kid with a dumb father could grow up to be President.

The average length of time a kid was allowed to remain in possession of his hatchet was forty-eight hours. By then the hatchet would have produced approximately sixty bushels of wood chips, eight hundred hack marks, and a bad case of hysteria for the kid's mother. The youngster would be unceremoniously stripped of his hatchet, even as its blade fell hungrily on a clothesline post or utility pole, and be told that he could have it back when he was "older," by which was meant age twenty-seven.

Kids now probably wouldn't understand the appeal hatchets held for youngsters of my generation. If a kid today received a hatchet for Christmas, he would ask, "Where do you put the batteries?" He would have no inkling of the romance of the hatchet and what it symbolized to boys of an earlier time, presumably all the way back to George Washington.

In the time and place of my childhood, woodcraft still loomed large in the scheme of a man's life. A man sawed and split firewood for the home, of course, but more important, he could take care of himself in the woods. He could build log cabins and lean-tos and footbridges, chop up a log to feed a campfire, fell poles to pitch a tent on or to hoist up a deer or to make a stretcher to haul out of the woods the person who wasn't that good with his ax.

One of the best things you could say about a man back then was that he was a good woodsman. Being a good woodsman seemed to erase a lot of other character flaws.

"Shorty may have some faults," one man might say, "but I'll tell you this—he's a good woodsman!"

"Yep," someone else would observe. "Shorty is a fine woodsman, all right. If he made it to the mountains, I reckon it'll take the posse a month to root him out."

The ax was the primary tool of the woodsman. If he wished, a woodsman could go off into the woods with an ax and provide heat and shelter for himself and live a life of freedom and independence and dignity and not be at anyone's beck and call or have to comb his hair or take baths. Not that I recall anyone ever fleeing to the woods, not even Shorty, who was nabbed sitting on a barstool at Beaky's Tavern, still a long way from the mountains. But it was the *idea!* If you were good with an ax and a gun, of course, and a knife, you could always fall back to the mountains. What it was all about, underneath, was the potential for freedom, not the jived-up freedom of patriotic speeches but real freedom, one-to-one-ratio freedom, where man plucks his living directly from Nature. Of course, sometimes Nature plucks back, but that's not part of this dream, this vision, as symbolized by the Christmas hatchet.

I first realized I needed a hatchet when I was five years old and my mother read me stories about the pioneers chopping out little clearings in the great forests of the land. Ah, I thought, how satisfying it would be to chop out a clearing, to chop anything, for that matter. My campaign for a hatchet began immediately and achieved fruition on my eighth Christmas.

Although I wasn't allowed to touch any of the presents before Christmas Eve, I had spotted one package that bore the general shape of a hatchet. Still, I couldn't be sure, because my mother was a clever and deceptive woman, once wrapping a new pair of long johns to look like an electric train. Was she pulling a fast one on me this time or had she truly lost her senses and bought me a hatchet?

It turned out to be a hatchet, a little red job with a hefty handle and a cutting edge dull as a licorice stick. Even as I unwrapped it, I could feel all the thousands of little chops throbbing about inside, pleading to be turned loose on the world.

"Now don't chop anything," my mother said.

Within minutes, I had honed a razor edge onto the hatchet and was overcome with a terrible compulsion to chop. Forty-eight hours later, the hatchet was wrenched from my grasp and hidden away, presumably to be returned to me sometime after I had children of my own.

A few days after Christmas I learned that my friend Crazy Eddie Muldoon, who lived on the farm next to ours, had also received a Christmas hatchet.

"Where is it?" I asked. "Let's go chop something."

"Uh, I got it put away," Crazy Eddie said. "Let's use yours."

"Uh, I loaned mine to my cousin for a while," I replied. "He said, 'You don't have a hatchet I can borrow, do you?' and I said, 'Sure.' "

"Sure," said Crazy Eddie, who was only crazy part of the time.

As good luck would have it, an epidemic of permissiveness swept the county the following summer and both Eddie and I regained possession of our respective hatchets. There were still plenty of chops left in the hatchets and the two of us wandered off down to our woodlot in search of a suitable recipient.

A large tamarack soared up uselessly on the edge of the woodlot, and Crazy Eddie said maybe it would be a good idea if we built an empty space in the sky where it was standing. As it happened, I had long nourished a desire to yell "Timberrrrrr!" at the very moment I sent a mammoth of the forest crashing to the ground.

"Your folks can use it for firewood," Crazy Eddie said, in an attempt to explain his motive for felling the tamarack. But I knew he too yearned to hear the thunder of a great tree dashed to earth; he, as much as I, was into chopping for the pure aesthetics of the thing.

We spent all day chopping away at the tamarack, with Eddie on one side, me on the other, our hatchets sounding like slow but determined woodpeckers. At noon I went home for lunch.

"What are you boys up to?" my mother asked, with no great show of interest.

"Chopping down a big tree."

"That's nice," Mom said. "Don't fight."

After lunch, Crazy Eddie and I were back at the tree again, chipping out a huge U-shaped gouge all the way around its circumference. We were both exhausted, sweating, standing in chips up to our knees, but we could see now it was possible to accomplish the task we had set for ourselves. The tree began to moan and creak ominously as the hatchets bit into its heartwood. By late afternoon the huge tamarack stood precariously balanced on a gnawed core of wood slightly thicker than a hatchet handle.

Neither Crazy Eddie nor I had the slightest clue as to the direction in which the tree might fall, which heightened our anticipation with the added element of suspense. We took turns charging up to the tree, whacking out a quick chip, and then dashing back to relative safety.

Suddenly we heard it: the faint, soft sigh that signaled the tree's unconditional surrender to our Christmas hatchets. A silence fell upon the land. High above us the boughs of the tamarack rustled. Crazy Eddie and I shivered happily. We had accomplished something momentous!

Crrrrrraaa . . . went the tree, beginning a slow tilt. We were now able to determine the direction of its fall, which wasn't particularly good. Eddie's father, a short while before, had built a fence between our woodlot and theirs and now, even though I had not yet studied plane geometry, I was able to calculate with considerable accuracy that the tree would neatly intersect the fence at right angles.

"You better yell 'timber,' " Crazy Eddie said, his voice trembling.

"Timmmm . . . ," I started to cry. Then we heard another cry. It was that of Eddie's father, who had come down to the woodlot to call him to supper.

"Eddieeeee!" his father called. "Crazy Eddieee! It's time for supperrrrr!"

Cr-r-r-r-a-a-a-a-A-A-A-A-ACK! went the tree.

"Eddieee!" went Eddie's father. "EddieeEEEEEE!"

The monstrous tamarack smote the earth with a thunderous roar, rising above which was the twanging hum of barbwire. Fence posts shot into the air fifty yards away. Eddie's father shot into the air fifty feet away.

"Bleeping bleep of a bleep!" screamed Eddie's father, introducing me to that quaint expression for the first time.

There is an old saying that cutting firewood warms you twice: once when you chop it and once when you burn it. Well, chopping down that tamarack warmed Eddie and me *three* times, and one of those warmings was a good deal hotter than when the wood burned.

I learned a good many things from felling that tamarack with my Christmas hatchet, perhaps the most interesting of which is that a barbwire fence is regarded by its builder as merely a barbwire fence until a tree falls on it. Afterward it is looked back upon as a priceless work of art, surpassed in beauty and grandeur only by the Taj Mahal.

My Christmas hatchet disappeared immediately after the great tree-felling but surfaced again a few years later when I was old enough to conduct my own camping trips. Much to my surprise, I discovered the hatchet was almost useless for cutting wood. It was as if Excalibur had been reduced to a putty knife.

The very next Christmas, I gave my little cousin Delbert the hatchet as a present.

"Wow!" he said. "A real hatchet of my own! Thanks a lot!"

"You're welcome!" I shouted after him as he raced away, homing in on a stand of shrubs in his backyard. "But don't chop anything!"

The Night Grandma
Shot Shorty

When I was a boy, we kept a loaded pistol in the house with which to dispatch criminals who might come prowling around late at night. We never killed any criminals with the pistol, but there was one near-fatality. Unfortunately, the victim was not a criminal, at least so far as we knew.

The caliber of the pistol was very large, at least .45—maybe .50—and magnum to boot. The pistol could put a hole in you the size of a grapefruit, if you were a criminal trying to force your way into our house late at night. At least that's what I told the guys at school. What I didn't tell them was that the gun was a figment of my mother's imagination.

My father had died when I was six, leaving me the lone male in a family of women—my mother and grandmother and a sister, who was six years older than I. If I have never become too excited over women's liberation, it is because I grew up surrounded by liberated females, all tough, hard, and fearless. Any one of them could have taught a graduate course in assertiveness training. My sister held a black belt in aggravation.

Our farm was situated about a mile from a railroad, and it was not unusual for tramps to stop by and ask if they could chop some wood in exchange for a meal. My mother, bless her heart, never once turned away a tramp unfed, but boy did those suckers chop wood! There were no free handouts at the McManus farm.

Even with all the tramps drifting into our place (staggering away three hours later with a baloney sandwich clutched limply in hand), Mom never saw any need for a gun as a means of self-protection. After all, she viewed the tramps as harmless, easy-going fellows, who, if spoken to with a proper measure of firmness, were capable of chopping a good deal of wood.

Then one day Mom went into town and hired three local criminals to build an extension onto the chicken house. When they were about half done with the project, she saw they had no skill as carpenters, paid them off, and sent them packing.

"We'll get you for this!" one of the criminals, a mean little man called Shorty, yelled back over his shoulder.

"Ha!" Mom responded.

The threat, however, caused some concern among the rest of the family. What would we do if Shorty came sneaking back in the middle of the night, intent on murdering us all?

"Oh, all right!" Mom said. "Here's what we'll do." She explained that if we heard any strange noises outside at night or someone banged on the door, my sister would sing out loud and clear, "Do you want the gun, Ma? Do you want the gun?" To which my mother would loudly reply, "Oh, you'd better give it to me! But be careful—it's loaded!"

This system worked rather well. Not only did the imaginary pistol frighten off any criminals making strange noises outside our house, but it gave several innocent late-night visitors a bad case of the shakes.

In fact, the imaginary pistol turned out to be more deadly than any of us expected. One night my mother was sitting up alone playing a game of solitaire, when suddenly there was a banging on the door. Mom, who never thought the imaginary pistol was necessary in the first place, got up and answered the door without bothering to wait for my sister to sound the alarm.

The visitor turned out to be a diminutive young fellow by the name of Little Ernie and he had a terrible tale of woe to tell. He had joined the Civilian Conservation Corps that summer and had been working with a CCC crew back in the mountains eradicating blister rust. Somehow, Little Ernie had managed to antagonize the rest of the crew, and they had taken him down and shaved off all his curly blond hair. He had left the camp in a huff, his cowboy hat wobbling loosely atop his ears.

As he recited the story to Mom, his voice rose and fell, quavering with rage. He also refused to remove his hat to allow Mom to survey the damage. In that time and place, it was considered the ultimate rudeness for a man to wear his hat in the house. This was to be a contributing factor in the misunderstanding shortly to follow.

After one last outburst of rage, Little Ernie pounded the table with his fist. Mom was getting tired of hearing about the atrocity and she told Ernie he could spend the night in a spare upstairs bedroom. She then went off to bed herself, neglecting in all the excitement to mention to Ernie that another upstairs bedroom was occupied by my Aunt Gladys, who was visiting, and Gram.

When the banging on the front door had first sounded, Aunt Gladys and Gram had sat "bolt-upright" in bed. Soon they heard a loud male voice full of rage and incoherence.

"It's *Shorty!*" Gram hissed to Aunt Gladys, who had been told about the threat. Aunt Gladys went pale and her hair tightened in its curlers.

"We'd better go help Mabel," she whispered.

They listened a bit longer to the mad ravings rising from the living room. Then they heard the dull sounds of blows being delivered.

"My God, he's killed her!" Gram gasped.

After a period of silence broken only by the tinny rattle of hair curlers, they heard booted feet begin to ascend the stairs.

"Oh!" Aunt Gladys whispered. "Now he's coming for *us!*"

Through the open door of their bedroom, Gram and Aunt Gladys had an unobstructed view of the stairwell. *Thump . . . thump . . . thump . . .* came the booted steps. Given their emotional state, it was perhaps understandable that Gram and Aunt Gladys would mistake the slow plodding on the steps to be a result of stealth rather than weariness and nervous exhaustion.

Slowly, the crown of a cowboy hat rose above the edge of the stairwell, a sure sign the intruder was a killer. No one else would wear a hat in the house. Then the head and shoulders came into view. There was only one thing to do.

Gram drew the imaginary pistol.

Employing the tone of voice she reserved for breaking up dog fights and ordering the family hog out of her flower gardens, she let Little Ernie have it.

"Hold it right there, Shorty," she snarled, "or I'll blow your head off!"

Three days later, Little Ernie had recovered enough to be ready and willing to go back to the CCC camp. By then, if he held a cup in both hands, he could get it to his lips without sloshing coffee all over himself. Much of his color had returned too. Since the stubble of his hair had leaped up half an inch when he heard Gram's command, he now looked as if he had a crew cut, although it was somewhat lighter in shade than his original blond curls. We never saw Little Ernie again, so I don't know if he ever fully recovered. Perhaps he was still peeved at Gram, thinking that by calling him "Shorty" she had been referring to his modest stature.

Mom got rid of the pistol soon afterward. She said it was too dangerous to have lying around the house, where a young boy or an old lady might get hold of it and accidentally kill somebody.

The Kindest
Cut of All

Hal Figby, a newcomer to our little gatherings down at Kelly's Bar & Grill, doesn't care much for hunting or fishing. We don't hold that against him, of course, and even go out of our way to treat him just as if he were normal. He is soft-spoken, polite, does everything in moderation, and in general seems to be a perfect gentleman. Otherwise, he is a pretty decent sort of guy. He's even good for a laugh occasionally, such as the time we invited him down to Kelly's to watch the Saturday night fights. He said later he had thought we meant the fights would be on television! Broke us up. That's just the sort of person Figby is. Still, we couldn't have been more surprised when he committed the breach of etiquette.

Half a dozen of us had stopped by Kelly's after a hard day of fishing and were getting tuned up to spend the rest of the evening testing out some new lies on each other and maybe stretching a truth or two. Then Figby showed up. Scarcely had he sat down than he began staring across the table at Retch Sweeney.

"Something wrong, Figby?" Retch asked, in a tone that killed somebody's promising lie in midsentence.

"Uh," Figby said, "it's just that nasty scar on your face. I was wondering how you got it."

We were dumfounded. Of all the stupid things we might have expected Figby to say, this was absolutely the worst. Here we had just got a nice start on a pleasantly sociable evening, and Figby had to blurt out something like that. Even Figby should have known you never ask a man how he got a scar on his face. A couple of the guys got up in disgust and walked out right then. I later regretted I hadn't gone with them, because I didn't have much stomach for what happened next. And I must say, Retch was unmerciful. He talked steadily about that scar for upwards of two hours. It was dreadful.

There is nothing a man, particularly an outdoorsman, enjoys talking about more than his scars. Every scar has a story behind it. I have heard some scar stories approximately the length of Churchill's *A History of the English-Speaking Peoples,* but such brevity is rare. Once a question has been put to an outdoorsman about one of his scars, the man will go on a binge of scar stories. He cannot tell about one scar and let it go at that. As soon as he has exhausted all the scars on his face, he will move on to the scars on his hands and arms, and once he has recited the history of each of them, he descends to his lower extremities, finally rolling up his pant legs to search for old scars he might have forgotten about.

It is for that reason that no outdoorsman will ever ask another about a scar.

There are certain constants in the telling of any

scar story. One is that the recipient of the near-mortal wound from which the scar was derived never uttered a sound during the ordeal: "So, there I was, my arm laid open elbow to wrist, and me not making a sound. Several of the younger fellows fainted dead away at the sight of it, and I couldn't help but smile. Then ol' Pap Wiggens got out a saddle-stitching awl and sewed up my arm with a length of catgut leader, and I didn't so much as say 'ouch.' "

It may be nothing more than a coincidence, but I have yet to hear a scar story in which the injured party admitted to bellowing like a bull moose with bursitis.

Another characteristic of the scar story is that the scar always is much smaller than the original wound. In fact, each time the story is told, the difference between the size of the scar and the size of the wound becomes increasingly greater, until you begin to worry that if the story is told one more time the original injury might prove fatal. I've seen outdoorsmen express real astonishment that they somehow managed to survive a wound that left a quarter-inch scar on an index finger. Once during a physical examination, I asked the doctor the cause of this phenomenon, and he spent the rest of the afternoon telling me about a tiny scar on his elbow left over from the time he nearly severed his arm. I hadn't realized until then that he was an outdoorsman. Afterward he gave me a prescription for some drops to clear up my glazed eyes.

Another feature of the scar story is that the teller always remembers to make a dry, humorous comment to his companions as they gape in horror at his damaged hide. "It's just a scratch" seems to be the standard dry, humorous comment. Obviously, you can't expect great creativity from an injured person.

One interesting and amusing characteristic of the scar story is how easily an outdoorsman can be reminded of one.

"Have you seen John's boat?" someone might ask.

"No," replies the outdoorsman, "but that reminds me. I don't believe I've ever told you how I got this scar on my cheek."

Persons unknowledgeable about outdoorsmen might assume that a boat played at least some slight part in the acquisition of the scar. When the story is at last over, they will ask, "But what about the boat?"

"What boat?" replies the outdoorsman. "Say, that reminds me of the scar on my ankle."

Speaking of boats, there's quite a story behind this scar on my thumb.

The scar is merely a small, whitish crescent just behind the knuckle. I must explain, however, that the scar remained the same size but my thumb grew. When it received the original wound, my thumb was only seven years old. To fully appreciate the gash on my thumb, you must visualize the scar superimposed on a little seven-year-old thumb. Then you realize how truly ghastly the injury was.

The scar happened like this. Crazy Eddie and I were planning our first camping trip. We had both been sentenced to second grade and were due to start serving our time the following week. When you're seven years old, second grade lasts for life and a day. (When I was eight, second grade lasted only twenty years, which was a great improvement.) We wanted to have one last fling before the doors shut behind us, and a camping trip seemed like a good idea.

Finding enough grub for the camping trip was the big problem. We dug a few potatoes out of the garden, and Crazy Eddie sneaked half a loaf of bread from his house. But we needed some meat. Fortunately, Eddie's father had hauled a dead horse into their barnyard a few weeks before. He had cut up most of the carcass to feed to the foxes he raised for furs, but there were still some good parts left. Eddie borrowed his father's hunting knife while his parents were away, and we went out to the barnyard to cut off a few steaks to roast on willows over the fire we hoped to build by rubbing two sticks together because we weren't allowed to play with matches. Eddie sliced off a nice round steak for himself without incident or accident. Probably one reason he didn't cut himself was that he used one hand to cut with and the other to hold his nose. The hand that holds the knife doesn't usually get cut, so the trick is to keep the other hand out of the way and occupied with some useful task like holding your nose. Foolishly, I tried to brush the flies off the steak I was cutting. The knife slipped and laid open my thumb to the bone.

I didn't cry. That was the first time I had been hurt that badly and didn't cry. I remember thinking, "Odd, I just cut my finger to the bone and I'm not crying."

Eddie wasn't very supportive in that regard. "Geez," he said, "all your blood is leaking out!"

That made me want to cry, but I didn't. Maybe I somehow knew that years later I would have this wonderful scar and I wouldn't want to remember that I cried when I got it.

"Don't it hurt?" Crazy Eddie asked, apparently because he couldn't deal with the fact that I wasn't crying.

I decided to compound his amazement by making a dry, humorous comment about the cut, but I couldn't think of any. "Naw," I said finally, "it's just a scra . . . a scra . . . I got to go home." And I went.

Two weeks later I finally thought of a dry, humorous comment, but by then we were in second grade and Crazy Eddie was too miserable to appreciate it.

During the years of my childhood, I picked up dozens of tiny scars, but none worth showing to anybody. All my friends were constantly getting neat scars. One time Crazy Eddie and I were floating a log raft down the creek. Suddenly, up ahead, we saw a strand of barbwire stretched across the creek about six inches above the water. Crazy Eddie, who was on the front of the raft, lay down and pressed himself against the logs so that he would pass under the wire. He didn't press hard enough. The barbs raked him fore and aft, particularly his aft. (He wasn't known as "Crazy Eddie" for nothing.) When I came to the wire, I calmly stepped over it, averting my gaze from the bits of Eddie left on the barbs. Eddie picked up an interesting set of scars from the experience, and he liked to claim later that he never uttered a sound during the ordeal. Maybe so, but the workers at a nearby sawmill went home early that day because they thought they heard the shriek of the quitting whistle.

Crazy Eddie continued to add to his collection of scars with knives, hatchets, saws, arrows, fishhooks, tree branches, sharp rocks, just about anything that had any potential at all for lacerating his skin. By the time we were in sixth grade, Eddie looked like a walking display of hieroglyphics. He was the envy of every boy in school.

I, on the other hand, had only one good scar, the one on my thumb. The problem with a scar on a thumb is that it is not easily called attention to. Once I was lucky enough to fall facedown in a pile of rocks and get a deep gash on my chin. I had high hopes for that wound, but bit by bit the scar faded and within six months had vanished.

"Thank heavens," my mother said. "I thought you might be disfigured for life." Mothers just don't understand about scars.

I have an excellent scar on one of my feet, a gift from a double-bitted ax. But a foot is one of the worst places to have a scar. How do you explain taking off your shoe and sock and placing a smelly foot up on a table so the scar can be noticed? I have often been asked for such an explanation and, failing to come up with one, have on several occasions been forcibly ejected from Kelly's Bar & Grill. A scar on your foot is more of a nuisance than anything. It is, as Shakespeare put it, the unkindest cut of all.

One of life's worst misfortunes is to get a truly fabulous scar in a place where no one except maybe your spouse can notice it, and spouses, like mothers, are generally unappreciative of scars. A classic instance of such a scar occurred when my friends Retch and Birdy and I were about seventeen. We had been fishing in a place that required that we drive through a series of hayfields, opening and shutting half a dozen gates along the way. Retch was driving his old 1933 sedan, and, because he was furnishing the transportation, he insisted that Birdy and I open and shut the gates. Birdy complained that this was an unfair labor practice and violated constitutional rights as they apply to hayfield gates. A heated argument ensued, and certain vile names were exchanged. When we arrived at one of the gates, Birdy got out, swearing that this was absolutely the last gate he was going to open and close.

"*Ha!*" Retch said. "We'll see about that. Lock all the doors so he can't get back in. We'll make him walk all the way to the next gate and we won't let him back in the car until he opens and closes it. *Heh heh!*"

With that, he started driving slowly across the hayfield toward the next gate. What happened next came as quite a surprise to Retch and me, since neither of us had ever guessed that Birdy might possess ambitions to become a stuntman.

Once he perceived what we were up to, Birdy raced after the bouncing sedan, making no attempt to conceal his fury. He climbed on the back bumper, worked his way up over the trunk, across the roof of the car, and down onto the hood. Once he was on the hood, he sprawled across the windshield to block Retch's vision.

His plot foiled and his vision blocked, Retch became furious. "Well, I'll fix him!" he snarled, pressing down on the gas pedal until we were bouncing along at nearly twenty miles an hour. Birdy reacted by turning his back to us and, now astraddle the hood, grabbed hold of the rain gutters on each side of the windshield to steady himself. Retch hit the brakes.

Birdy shot off the front of the hood as if from a catapult. He made a nice eight-point landing, counting two points for each bounce. Retch and I expected that he would rest there on the ground for a spell and contemplate the error of his ways. Instead, he instantly leaped up and launched into a wild and wonderful dance to the accompaniment of his own whoops and hollers.

That was when we remembered the hood ornament, one of those little jobs with the wings raised in simulation of flight.

The little wings gave Birdy a spectacular matched set of scars. Unfortunately, they were in a place where they were not likely to be noticed in the typical social situation. In the thirty years since, Birdy has not once had occasion to tell the story behind those scars. It seems like such a waste.

Scars are often interpreted as evidence that a man has lived dangerously. I totally dismiss my wife's assertion that they are more likely proof that he has lived dumbly. She knows nothing about the masculine mystique.

My hope is that the cosmetic industry will soon come up with false scars for men, much as it did with false beauty marks for women. It would be only fair, not to mention a lot less painful. But it probably wouldn't work. After all, who would want to tell about getting a scar from the Avon lady?

The Bush Pilots

Mostly what I wanted to be when I grew up was a mountain man, but there was one brief period, during the summer of my eighth year, when I gave serious consideration to becoming a bush pilot.

It was Crazy Eddie who got me to thinking about the bush-pilot business. He came up with the idea immediately after our ill-fated venture into deep-sea diving, which, among other consequences, produced a rare form of hysteria in the Fergusons' herd of milk cows: not only couldn't they be made to drink; they refused even to be driven to water. A veterinarian was brought in to offer an opinion, but, because he had no experience with the effects of deep-sea diving on cows, he failed to come up with a diagnosis. Had the vet thought to ask Crazy Eddie and me, as people usually did when inexplicable phenomena occurred within the range of our travels, we could have told him what was wrong with the Ferguson cows. They had the bends.

Since the reader may have some difficulty grasping the deeper psychological implications of my bush-pilot phase, an examination of the deep-sea-diving venture may provide some insights, particularly in light of the fact that both experiences involved traumatized cows.

In my own defense, I must report that the entire deep-sea-diving experiment was Eddie's idea. I was recruited at the last minute, to help with the testing, after Eddie had designed and assembled the diving outfit himself. Although the technology of the outfit would be too difficult for the lay person to understand, I will mention that its component parts consisted of an old milk pail, a tire pump, a length of garden hose, and two bags of rocks. Eddie said he needed me to work the tire pump while he descended into the depths of Sand Creek, the test site being a deep hole in the creek behind the Ferguson place. The hole was next to the bank on one side of the creek. The creek bottom tapered up from there onto a gravel bar on the opposite side, where the Ferguson cows came to drink. Through oversight, Crazy Eddie hadn't factored the cows into the experiment.

As Eddie and I stood on the bank staring down into the swirling dark waters of the hole, my friend could scarcely contain his enthusiasm.

"Boy," he said, "I can't wait to get down there and start exploring. This hole is a perfect place for pirates to hide a chest of treasure. Probably some pearls down there too, and gold and—"

"C'mon, Eddie, let me go first!" I blurted.

"Okay."

While he was helping me on with the milk-pail helmet, Eddie said he was letting me go first only because I was his best friend and that he wouldn't even consider doing such a favor for anyone else. I said I appreciated it and, sliding down over the bank, asked Eddie if he was sure the diving outfit would work.

"Yeah," Eddie yelled, starting to work the pump furiously. "But if it doesn't, can I have your bike?"

Still contemplating Eddie's little joke, I plunged into the hole. I sank swiftly into the cool, swirling darkness, the bags of rocks tied to my belt working wonderfully well. There were, however, some bugs in the rest of the outfit. The helmet offered limited visibility, since the only way to see out of it was straight down. Mostly what I could see was the level of water rising in the inverted milk pail, despite the *hiss hiss* of the air hose. Of even more interest to me at the moment was the distinct tactile impression of long, slimy tentacles of octopus slithering around my body. Thus distracted, and with the water in the helmet now lapping about my eyes, I scarcely touched bottom before setting a course toward the incline of the gravel bank on the far side of the creek. Even though I maintained the calm demeanor I thought appropriate to a deep-sea diver, the vigor of my movements caused silt and gravel to boil up in such a fashion as to effect major changes in the creek channel, or so Eddie later remarked.

It so happened that at that very moment, the herd of Ferguson cows was moseying down to the creek for a drink, apparently mildly interested in the frantic activities of the boy on the far bank but with no expectation of a streaming, slime-covered creature with an inverted milk pail on its head to be emerging from their watering place. As Crazy Eddie later related the spectacle to me, for I was too preoccupied with gasping to notice such things, the entire herd rose straight up eight feet in the air, reversed direction, and to the accompaniment of a cowbell rendition of "The William Tell Overture," disappeared over a distant hill. Oddly, the route of the cows' departure was marked in later years by an unusually lush growth of grass. The wondrous vitality of the swath of grass became something of a local mystery, as did the refusal of the cows to go anywhere near the creek for two weeks afterward, despite the maniacal exhortations on the part of Mr. Ferguson to get them to do so and save him the chore of carrying water to them.

Naturally, Crazy Eddie was disappointed in the performance of his diving outfit.

"Maybe it was my fault," I said, untying the bags of rocks from my belt. "I probably did it wrong. Why don't you give it a try and let me stand on the bank and pump air?"

Eddie thought for a moment. "Gee, I would," he said, "but it's, ah, getting on toward suppertime. Besides, I've been thinking that maybe I'd rather be a bush pilot than a deep-sea diver."

As we walked home, dragging the deep-sea-diving outfit behind us, Crazy Eddie suggested that maybe I would want to go into the bush-pilot business with him. He explained how it would work. "We'll have this plane, see, and we'll fly hunters and fishermen back into the wilderness. We'll land on gravel bars in rivers and in little clearings in the forest, and the hunters and fishermen will be scared to death, but afterward they'll say, 'Boy, you sure know how to handle this plane!' and we'll just laugh like it was nothing. But we won't work all the time. Whenever we want, we'll go fishing and hunting ourselves. It'll be great!"

Already I could feel myself getting caught up in

Eddie's dream. "But where will we get the plane?" I asked. "We don't have any money."

"We'll have to build it. Of course, we'll start off with just a little plane, one we can use to practice our flying with and landing on gravel bars and small clearings in the forest. That can be tricky. Come on over to my place tomorrow and we'll start building the plane."

"Sounds good to me," I said, tilting my head to one side and batting some creek water out of my ear.

I did have some doubt that Crazy Eddie and I could actually build an airplane. As it turned out, though, Eddie was an aeronautical genius. When I showed up the next morning, he had already drawn up the plans on a sheet of Big Ben tablet paper. He said he had based the design on a plane in a comic book story about a bush pilot. It looked swell.

"Where will we get the motor?" I asked.

"My dad's got an old washing-machine motor out in his shop," he replied. "We can use that, and whittle a propeller out of a board." That sounded reasonable enough. I felt guilty about having doubted Eddie's engineering skills.

"We'll start off with a glider, though," Eddie continued. "After we've practiced landing the glider a few times, we can hook up the washing-machine motor to it, and work on our takeoffs."

"But we'll need some high place to launch the glider from," I said. "What can we use?"

"No problem," said Eddie. He pointed to the roof of the towering Muldoon barn. Why hadn't I thought of that? I supposed it was because I wasn't an aeronautical genius.

The finished plane bore only a slight resemblance

to Eddie's design, possibly because our escalating anticipation of the forthcoming flight caused us to rush construction. Then again, it may have been the limited supply
of materials available to us: two apple crates for the
cockpits, an empty dynamite box for the motor housing,
two long pieces of shiplap siding for the wings, a short
board on a rusty hinge for the tail, and the rear wheels
and axle from Eddie's wagon for the landing gear. All
things considered, the bush plane looked exceptionally
airworthy.

It had soon become obvious to us that the completed plane would be too heavy for the two of us to
carry up to the ridge of the barn roof, so we assembled
the parts up there. The roof had two angles to it, one
about 30 degrees, and the other, the lower one, a steep
45 degrees or so. A shed roof was attached to the bottom
edge of the barn roof. Near the eave of the shed roof,
Eddie and I built a ramp that, once our plane had picked
up sufficient speed in its descent, would loft us up into
the clouds, where we would spend the rest of the day
riding the wind. Toward evening we would find a gravel
bar or a small clearing in the woods on which to practice
our bush-pilot landing.

With the aid of a ladder, we managed to get all the
parts of the plane up to the ridge of the barn roof and
assembled. The bush plane, pointed nose-down, was held
in place by means of a rope attached to a weather vane,
the knot in the rope being tied in such a manner that
the pilot needed only to jerk an end of the rope to release
the craft for its descent.

The activities on the roof of the barn provoked
much interest among the resident population of spar-
rows, who kept darting about and offering advice and

encouragement, but because the construction had taken place on the side of the barn away from Crazy Eddie's house, his parents, both of whom seemed to suffer from severe nervous disorders, knew nothing of our activities.

Late in the afternoon, the plane, straining at its tether, was finished. Crazy Eddie, crouched beside me on the slope of the barn roof, could scarcely contain his excitement over the first flight.

"Boy, it'll be great," he said. "Just think about it. Soaring around up there in the clouds, looking down at the patchwork of fields, all the cars and animals and stuff real tiny like, and—"

"Yeah," I said. "You'll have to tell me all about it after you land."

Crazy Eddie looked at me. "The wind blowing in your hair, the plane sailing along like a hawk."

"Hmmm," I said. "Maybe we both should go. The plane's got two cockpits, after all."

"Well, okay," Crazy Eddie said, with what I took to be a slight ebbing of enthusiasm.

"Say, maybe your folks would like to see us test the plane," I suggested. "Why don't you go invite them to watch the takeoff?"

"Good idea!" Eddie scrambled down the barn roof and raced to the house, where he asked his mother and father if they would like to see us test a plane we had built out behind the barn. They said sure, they'd be right out. No doubt they were relieved to learn that Eddie was doing something sensible for a change, instead of getting involved in one of the crazy, dangerous schemes he was always coming up with.

When Eddie returned, I was already seated in the rear cockpit. "I thought you would like to be pilot on the first flight," I told him. I doubt that I had ever heard that the rear of an airplane is safer in the event of a crash, but my years of associating with Eddie had given me certain useful intuitions.

About then his parents, strolling arm-in-arm, appeared far down below in the barnyard. They stopped and looked around for the plane their son had built.

"Mom! Dad!" yelled Crazy Eddie. "Up here!"

Mr. and Mrs. Muldoon looked up. Both seemed momentarily paralyzed. Mr. Muldoon's jaw worked up and down, but no words seemed to come out. Mrs. Muldoon sagged against her husband. It was apparent that both of them were overcome with awe by the aeronautical feat accomplished by their only child and his friend.

"Contact!" I yelled.

"Roger!" Crazy Eddie yelled back, giving his parents a jaunty salute.

Mr. Muldoon yelled something, too, but we couldn't make it out, because Eddie had already jerked loose the knot and the wind was rushing in our ears. .

Our flight plan worked out just as we had intended. Oh, at first there was some shrill screeching from down below and I had the vague impression of cows leaping fences and trying to climb trees and terrified chickens and geese raising a terrible ruckus, but then the bush plane hit the ramp on the shed roof and we were lofted high into the air. The wind caught us and carried us even higher, and it was wonderful. Far down below we could see tiny houses and horses and cows in the patchwork fields and miniature farmers waving to us from miniature tractors, and there was Sand Creek, like an embroidered line of green and blue meandering through the countryside, and then we soared higher still and were in the clouds, white puffs of vapor floating up like cotton candy, and it was all very lovely and exciting, except I had this pain in my body, and my head ached.

When I opened my eyes, Mr. and Mrs. Muldoon were bent over me, both of them strangely white of face. They were blurred, too, but because their surroundings were in sharp focus, I determined it was because of their shaking.

"Are you all right?" Mrs. Muldoon asked, wringing a stream of perspiration from her hands.

"Yeah, I guess so," I said, propping myself up on an elbow. There was a manure pile nearby and on top of it a pile of kindling and two wagon wheels. Mr. Muldoon said the manure pile had probably saved our lives.

Not too bad, I thought. Any old bush pilot could land on a gravel bar or a little clearing in the forest, but I'd like to see one of them land on a manure pile and live to tell about it.

Both Crazy Eddie and I recovered quickly. In fact, the only lasting ill effect of the bush-plane flight was that the Muldoon cows walked around for weeks afterward with their heads turned to the sky, as if expecting some assault from outer space. Crazy Eddie and I used to chuckle at them while we were building the submarine.

Share and Share Alike

The sharing of a single big-game animal between two hunters is at once the most delicate and most complex problem encountered in hunting, with the possible exception of deciding whose vehicle to drive on the hunt. It may be useful to examine the problem in some detail.

Let us begin with a hypothetical situation. As is well known, an elk that is shot dead within fifteen feet of your hunting vehicle will still pull himself together enough to gallop to the very bottom of the steepest canyon within five miles. This is known as the elk's revenge. Assume you have just shot such an elk. You and your hunting partner, whom we'll call Bob, have tracked the elk to the bottom of the canyon. As you stand over the massive form of the felled but still magnificent animal, you become contemplative. One of the things you contemplate is how much bigger an elk is at the bottom of a canyon than it is fifteen feet from your vehicle. (Scientists have calculated that a wounded elk will add fifty pounds to its weight for every hundred yards it gallops down into a canyon.) You now ask yourself two questions: (1) How are you going to lug the elk back up to your vehicle? and (2) Why didn't you go golfing today instead of hunting?

With three round trips each, you and Bob manage to pack out the elk section by section. Neither of you experiences any extraordinary ill effects from the exertion, other than the seizing up of major portions of your cardiovascular systems. Bob lies wheezing by the side of the road, a haunch of elk still strapped to his back. You are walking around on your knees and mumbling about "getting in shape" and not caring if you "never see another *bleeping* elk." At this point you are willing to give the entire elk to Bob, provided that he lives. Your intimate association with elk meat over the preceding hours has diminished your appetite for the stuff and has resulted in a psychological malfunction known as excessive generosity. Wisely, you put off the decision of what share of the elk should go to Bob until you are rested and your mind has cleared.

The culinary aspects of elk meat improve in direct proportion to distance in time from the packing-out process. A week after the hunt, during which time the elk has been aging nicely in a cooler, the thought of all those steaks and roasts stashed away for the winter is intensely satisfying. There is still the problem of what portion of the elk should be Bob's share. You are now in the proper frame of mind to make this decision.

Your reasoning goes something like this: For openers, you consider giving Bob half the elk. Once you have enjoyed a few moments of mirth over this ridiculous notion, you get down to serious figuring. Using half an elk as base, you deduct from it five pounds for each day remaining in the elk season, days in which Bob might very well shoot his own elk. You make further deductions for the amount of whining Bob did while packing out your elk. Then there is the matter of that unseemly phrase Bob blurted out when he learned the elk you had shot was at the bottom of a three-thousand-foot canyon—more deductions, all of them choice cuts. You don't forget Bob's tripping over a log and cartwheeling down the slope with a hindquarter strapped to his pack-board. That bruised a lot of meat, some of which was elk. Further deductions. When you finally total the figures, you discover that Bob now owes you approximately one quarter of an elk. The charlatan hasn't even had the courtesy to mention the matter of this debt to you. And to think you trusted him enough to let him help pack your elk out of a three-thousand-foot canyon! Some gratitude!

In the end, your calculations are for naught. Your spouse demands that you give Bob a generous share of the elk. You acquiesce reluctantly but eventually conclude she was right—although this conclusion does not arrive until the middle of April, when even the thought of one more elk roast blights your day.

"What's for supper?" you ask your wife.

"Elk," she replies.

"*Aaaack!*" you say. "How about TV dinners? I'm sick of elk!"

"You shot it, you eat it!"

"I know, I'll call Bob. He would probably like some more elk."

"Are you kidding?" Bob responds. "I'm fed up to

my follicles with elk! I couldn't choke down another bite of elk if I lived to be five hundred!"

"Oh yes you can and you are! You didn't take your full share of the elk! You packed it out and you're going to eat it!"

In this way, the problem of sharing a single big-game animal between hunters usually resolves itself.

My first encounter with the problem of sharing a big-game animal occurred when I was sixteen. I was hunting with my cousin, Buck, who was several years older than I. At that time, Buck was at the height of his intellectual powers and knew all there was to know about hunting and most of everything else. Some people are stingy with their knowledge and try to hoard it, but not Buck. He handed his out freely and voluminously and endlessly, at all hours of the day or night, whether one was in the market for knowledge or not. Naturally, because of his towering intellect and absolute knowledge of all matters pertaining to hunting, Buck got to devise our field tactics.

Shortly after dawn, as Buck was bathing my semi-consciousness with a steady stream of his hunting knowledge, I glanced up the side of the mountain to clear the glaze from my eyes and spotted five specks. The specks were moving.

"Buck, there's a herd of mule deer up there!" I shouted.

Since part of Buck's knowledge consisted of the natural law that he was the only one who could spot deer first, he dismissed my report with a chuckle and the comment that the specks I saw were probably on my glasses.

Then he stopped the car and got out, casually, as

if to stretch and satisfy a need for a breath of fresh air. He got back in the car, shook a cigarette from a pack, lit it, blew out the match. "There's a herd of mule deer about halfway up the mountain," he said. "When you're driving out to hunt mule deer, it's a good idea to stop every once in a while and check the slopes. Now you take these deer here, we might have missed them if I hadn't stopped for a look around."

"Good, Buck, good. I'll try to remember that."

Buck then laid out the tactics. "Now here's what we're going to do. You work your way up the mountain toward the deer. I'll drive around to the top of the mountain and wait on the road just in case they try to cut back over the ridge."

"Why don't you climb the mountain and I drive around on the road?"

"Because it wouldn't work, that's why. Besides, if the deer cut back over the ridge, we want to have the best shot to be waiting there."

"Oh."

I got out to start working my way up the mountain, and Buck drove off, leisurely smoking his cigarette and fiddling with the radio dials. There was about a foot of new snow on the mountain, and the climb was cold, slippery, and exhausting. Occasionally a fir tree would unload a bough of snow down the back of my neck, and that didn't improve my mood, either. Nor did the thought of Buck sitting in the warm car at the top of the mountain, drinking hot coffee from the thermos and smoking and listening to the radio, while he gave the deer time to detect my presence and then retreat practically into his lap.

But it didn't work out that way. All at once I found

myself right in the middle of the herd of mule deer. A nice little buck stepped from behind a tree and stared at me, as if astonished to find a human being stupid enough to be climbing a snow-covered mountain that early in the morning. I downed him with a single shot. The rest of the herd raced off in all directions, except toward Buck. An hour later I was back down on the road with my deer. Buck, who had witnessed the "whole fiasco," as he called it, was waiting for me. He was hot, too.

"Boy, that was dumb!" he snarled. "Shooting that itty-bitty buck when there was one three times as big in the herd. I knew I shouldn't give you the best chance, but since you're just a kid and all, I thought I'd do you the favor. Boy, did you blow it!"

We rode in silence all the way home, Buck occupied with what I could easily guess were dire thoughts, and I, with gloating. When you're sixteen and wear glasses and aren't that good at sports and spend a good deal of time in the company of an intellectual giant, you don't get much opportunity for gloating. When you do, you savor it.

"You just remember," Buck said, after dropping me and my deer off home, "part of that deer is mine."

When I got around to cutting up the deer, I at first considered giving Buck a full half of it. On the other hand, I had my mother, grandmother, and sister to provide wild game for, and Buck lived by himself in an apartment. If he tried to eat half a deer all by himself, he would soon become sick of venison and wouldn't want to go deer hunting ever again. No, I told myself, it would be better if I gave him only a hindquarter. That would be about right for one person.

On the other hand, steaks cut from the hindquarter of a deer are awfully good eating. Buck might use a venison-steak dinner as bait to lure one of his girl friends into his apartment. That in all probability could lead to Buck and the girl committing a serious sin. Since my religion forbade even contributing to serious sin, I was not about to risk going to hell over a hindquarter of venison. No sir, Buck would have to make do with a front quarter.

But which front quarter? That presented no real difficulty. Because of Buck's interest in science, he would be intrigued by studying the effect of a .30/30 slug on the shoulder of a deer. There was still a lot of good meat on the shoulder, too.

Upon further consideration, I decided that Buck might prefer to forgo his scientific studies and have the shoulder ground up into venison burger. So I ground up the venison for him.

Well, that turned out to be an awful lot of venison burger for one person. I started dividing it up into neat little piles, until I found the exact amount that I thought would be suitable for Buck. I then left his share on the table while I went to deposit the rest of the venison in the cold storage locker.

A few days later I ran into Buck. "Hey, you little rat," he greeted me, "where's my share of our deer?"

I shook my head sadly. "You may have some trouble believing this, Buck, but while I was taking my share down to the locker, the cat got in the house and ate your share."

Buck did not take the news well.

Never Sniff
a Gift Fish

There is one thing about my neighbor Al Finley that irritates me. Well, actually, there are many things about Finley that irritate me, but one stands out from the others. It is his constant seeking after immortality.

I don't mean to say that Finley wants to live forever, although he probably has that in mind, too. And if the population of the world should one day increase to the point where people are standing on each other's shoulders, you can bet Finley won't be one of the guys on the bottom. No, he will be up on top, shouting orders to the fellow down below to step along faster and watch out for the bumps. That's the sort of person Finley is.

On the off chance he doesn't achieve immortality for his person, Finley at least wants it for his name. He is driven by this ambition.

For a while, he thought he might achieve lasting fame by writing poetry. When his masterwork, "Ode to a Liver Spot," brought him bad reviews and several threats against his life, he decided he might stand a better chance of achieving immortality in the sciences. His anti-gravitational device worked but once—when his wife stepped on it while cleaning the basement—and it worked then only because she thought it was something that had crawled out from behind the furnace.

After reading a book on Disraeli, Finley decided he was destined to become a great statesman. He won a seat on the city council and quickly became a master of political acrobatics. He now straddles fences, juggles books, and can change horses in midstream without rocking the boat. Nevertheless, it appears that he will not rise above the level of city councilman, which is a good sign that the system works.

Despite Finley's pitiful failures at achieving immortality, he continues to pursue his quarry, like an untrained pup let loose in the fields, to whom every grasshopper is a rabbit in disguise. His most recent quest for lasting fame took shape on a fishing trip with Retch Sweeney and me.

Retch and I honked Finley out of bed at four-thirty in the morning. He staggered out to the car, his gear in his arms, and muttered, "This is an ungodly hour to wake a man!"

"Early to bed, early to rise, makes a man healthy, wealthy, and wise," I replied.

"The early bird gets the worm," said Retch, chortling.

Finley's face brightened. "Who said that?"

"We did," said Retch. "You see anybody else in the car?"

"He means who said it first," I explained to Retch. "Those famous quotations are probably both from Ben

Franklin. Old Ben thought up about ninety-eight percent of all the famous quotations."

"I thought he invented kites," Retch said.

I could only shake my head in disgust. For a man with sixteen years of education, Retch was surprisingly ignorant. True, all sixteen years were spent in grade school, but he should have learned something.

Finley had turned thoughtful, as he does whenever he is contemplating his own immortality. "You know," he said, "Ben Franklin is probably remembered as much for his sayings as he is for his inventions. But have you ever noticed how few famous sayings have been derived from the outdoor sports?"

"Now that you mention it, I can only think of a couple," I replied. "There are the ones about a bird in hand being worth two in the bush and a miss being as good as a mile. That's all I can think of. Anyway, probably the reason there are so few famous quotations derived from the outdoor sports is that old Ben was primarily an indoor sport."

"You know," Finley mused aloud, "I bet that a person who thought up a lot of quotations related to the outdoor sports could practically achieve, uh, immortality."

I was instantly sorry the subject had ever come up and tried to change it by asking Retch if he had found another dry fly like the one he'd had such great luck with the previous weekend. He said he hadn't and was darn sorry to have lost the fly before having a chance to tie up some duplicates.

Finley, who had continued musing in the back seat, injected himself into the conversation. "For want of a fly, the fish is lost," he said.

Putting our lives at risk, for I was driving, I twisted

around in the seat to turn the full force of my glare on Finley. "That's horrible," I cried. "That is truly disgusting!"

"Curve! Curve!" Retch shouted.

"You stay out of this," I snapped. "This is between Finley and me."

"I thought it was pretty good," Finley said. "People probably didn't care much for Ben Franklin's 'early to rise' quote when they first heard it either."

"Truck! Truck!" cried Retch, obviously trying to distract me from giving Finley the tongue-lashing he deserved.

"You can't just think up famous sayings," I told Finley. "It doesn't work that way. Anybody knows that."

"Why not?" said Finley. "Somebody has to think them up."

"Train! Train!" yelled Retch.

I could tell I wasn't going to win any argument with Finley, particularly with Retch clowning around, so I calmed my nerves by concentrating totally on driving. I had seen men before who didn't know how to control their nerves. Retch Sweeney was one of them. Even while driving out for a little fishing and relaxation, he was all pale and twitchy and had even twisted his cap up into a knot. I think he drinks too much coffee.

"Never sniff a gift fish," said Finley.

I could see then that the situation was hopeless. We would just have to let Finley's malady run its course.

"Get it?" Finley continued. "That means you shouldn't be too critical of something that's given to you."

I told him I thought that bit of wisdom had been covered by gift horses.

"But how many gift horses have you received lately?"

Finley asked, smirking. "That's right, none. Now, a gift fish, that's a lot more common and people would identify with it."

"Well, I'd certainly sniff any fish you gave me, that's for sure," I told him.

Finley was quiet all the rest of the way to the river. I thought maybe I had hurt his feelings and discouraged him from thinking up more famous quotations. Unfortunately, that wasn't the case. The case was that thinking up famous quotations is more difficult than one might expect.

We set up camp and spent the rest of the day fishing, or, more accurately, practicing our fly casting. Toward evening we picked up a couple of smallish rainbows, which would have been enough for supper with a couple of gift fish thrown in. We drew straws for the trout, and Finley and I had to settle for a supper of canned hash. We set two plates of hash out on a log, ostensibly to cool but actually to let the darkness build up a bit. I knew a man once who tried to eat some canned hash in broad daylight, but his jaw froze up on him and had to be pried open with a spoon. Ever since then I have waited until dark to eat my hash. When the night was ripe enough, I dug in, giving a little shout before each bite to give any insect life a chance to escape. I explained to Finley that this was one of the lesser-known bits of woodlore I had picked up over the years.

"Yes," he said, "two bugs in the hash are worth one in the mouth."

"There's some truth to that one," I said, "but it's not particularly memorable."

"How about this one?" Retch put in. "When all the straws are the same length, the man that holds 'em gets to eat the fish! Har!"

Finley and I stared at him. "Now I've got one," I said. "The man who cheats his fishing partners had better learn to sleep lightly!"

"Listen, you guys, I was only kidding," Retch said, nervously. "I got the short straw! It wasn't *real* short, but it was short."

"The man who lies to his fishing partners may wake up with hash in his boots," said Finley.

"I like that one," I said. "It's the sort of famous quotation I can remember."

It was a mistake to offer Finley encouragement. As we lay in our sleeping bags, Retch and I trying to get to sleep, Finley ran off one freshly minted famous outdoor quotation after another:

"The pessimist complains that he just lost a lunker and the optimist brags he just had a great strike.

"What the tourist terms a plague of insects, the fisherman calls a fine hatch.

"No fisherman ever bragged that the huge fish he hooked turned out to be a log.

"What do you think of those?" he asked.

"Shut up and go to sleep is what I think of them," I growled. "Or to put it another way, how would you like a sock in the mouth?"

"All that's gruff isn't tough. Say, that's a pretty good *umph aggh muff—*"

It wasn't one of my clean socks, either.

The next day there was no holding Finley back. From way off down the stream, he shouted at Retch and me, "I got one! I got one!" Naturally, Retch and I rushed off toward him.

When we arrived, too late it appeared, Finley was standing there sorting through his fly box.

"Did you—*puff puff*—lose it?" I asked.

He looked up and smiled. "A man who fishes in sneakers never gets in over the top of his waders."

"Wha . . . ?"

"You've got to admit that's a pretty good one," he said.

"So, where's the fish?" Retch gasped, his mental agility having peaked at age six.

"There is no fish," I explained, plucking a section of devil's club from my armpit. "There is only another famous outdoor quotation."

Retch removed a small pine cone from his ear. "Listen, we could say he wandered off into the woods and disappeared. Nobody would know, nobody would care!"

Finley calmly tied on a fly and made a dismal cast that fell a good ten feet short of the pool he was aiming for. Inexplicably, a nice rainbow glommed the fly.

"A cast that reaches a fish is never too short," he said smugly. "I'd better write that one down."

Retch and I knew we were beaten and wandered off downstream. "Geez," Retch muttered. "If famous quotations were fish, he'd be over his limit by now."

"Don't you start!" I said.

"What?"

"Nothing."

On the drive back home, Finley was fairly spewing with famous outdoor quotations:

"The angler who doesn't look before he leaps will have his next cast made of plaster.

"There is no greater fan of fly fishing than the worm.

"I have never met a fish I didn't like.

"Who was that fish I seen you with the other night? That was no fish, that was my muddler.

"Even a fish stick once knew the glories of the deep."

And on and on.

Finally I screamed, "Enough, Finley, enough! You've invented enough famous outdoor quotations to compile your own *Bartlett's*. Henceforth, no angler will give an after-dinner speech without first perusing his *Finley's*. Now stop, before you flood the market."

"But so far I've only covered fishing," he replied. "There's still camping and hiking and boating and, of course, hunting."

"Please, Lord, deliver us!" cried out Retch, who had never before shown much inclination toward religion.

Finley cleared his throat:

"A goose may honk but will not wave.

"It is a foolish hunter who . . ."

Backseats
I Have Known

The backseat of my new compact sedan is so small and cramped we have to grease the children to get them in and out of it. That's what started me thinking recently about the decline of the backseat in American life, about all the wonderful adventures I've had in backseats, about all the backseats I've known and loved.

Among the older readers there are probably those who hold nostalgic recollections of the backseat mainly as the trysting place of young love. Indeed, I remember one such incident in my own steamy, R-rated adolescence.

At age sixteen I had already acquired a reputation as a suave and debonair ladies' man. My first real date, with the scintillating and sizzlingly beautiful Olga Bonemarrow, pretty much established my style as a worldly, dashing young-man-about-town, a person born to the fast lane of life. The only thing that crimped my style was parental reluctance to allow me to get my hands on our new car, a prospect Mom and Hank, my stepfather, equated with an imminent arrival of the apocalypse. Finally, I gave them an ultimatum.

Hank pondered the ultimatum a spell and then said to my mother, "As I understand it, either we let him have the car for a date with Olga Bonemarrow or he runs off and joins the French Foreign Legion and we never see him again. What's it going to be?"

"Don't rush me," Mom said. "I'm still weighing the options."

Eventually, they gave in and let me have the car. I cruised over to Olga's house and picked her up. "Neato!" she said. "What a neat car!"

To get Olga into the proper mood, I took her to a movie, a Randolph Scott western, and afterward blew nearly a whole buck on a double order of hamburgers, malts, and French fries. Then I drove her out to the gravel pit and parked. No dummy, Olga sensed right away that I was up to something.

"Whatcha stop here for?" she asked, giggling coyly.

"I dunno," I said, always quick with a quip. "Say, would you look at that pile of gravel!"

"Neato," Olga said.

We sat there without talking for a while, listening to the radio and staring out at the pile of gravel. Then, very cool and casual, I made a suggestion.

"Say, Olga," I said, "how'd you like to get into the backseat? It's real nice back there."

Olga giggled. "Neato," she said, her voice going low and husky, her lovely, thick eyelashes fluttering like a duet of moths. Nevertheless, there was something about her response that made me uneasy. Perhaps it was the way she took out her wad of bubble gum and stuck it on the gearshift knob before vaulting into the backseat.

So there we were, with Gene Autry crooning softly on the airwaves and the light of a full moon illuminating the sensuous curves of the highway department's gravel pile. I let the mood build, then asked suavely, "How do you like it back there? Lots of leg room, ain't there?"

"Yeah, neato," she said, icing up the windows. "Guess what, I just remembered, my folks were expecting me home a half hour ago."

Perhaps I was too wild and impetuous for Olga, or so I gathered from the fact that it was nearly six months before she again acknowledged my existence. In any case, I had learned a good lesson, namely that there are some women who just don't like to live life in the fast lane.

The Olga episode aside, my love affair with the backseat has nothing to do with romance or other such nonsense but with the great outdoors. Nowadays, when almost every outdoorsman owns a van, a camper, a trailer, or a motor home, only we old-timers recall that the predecessor of these conveyances was the backseat. The backseat of his car could provide an outdoorsman with emergency shelter, a bed for the night if need be; it was his gun and rod rack, his larder, tool chest, survival kit, closet; his sanctuary from mosquitoes, gnats, and strange sounds in the night; his garbage dump, woodshed, storage room, tackle box, and more. The test of an outdoorsman in the old days was his ability to find in his backseat whatever he needed to survive in the back-road wilds of America.

"We're done for now," his partner might say. "There's a big tree across the road."

The outdoorsman would shrug and reply: "Not for long. I got a chain saw, a peavey, two splitting wedges, a maul, and a double-bitted ax in the backseat."

In those days, a man needed only three things to survive for months in the outdoors: a gun, a good knife, and a properly outfitted backseat.

The backseat was not without its dangers. Retch Sweeney and I once ate for two days on a bag of jerky he found in a corner of his backseat. It wasn't great jerky or even good but still moderately edible, at least until Retch recalled that he had never put any jerky in his backseat.

"Well, if it isn't jerky, what is it?" I asked.

"I don't want to talk about it," Retch said greenly.

Another time, as Retch and I were rounding a curve on a steep mountain road, an avalanche swept down from out of my backseat and engulfed us. Somehow, I managed to bring the car to a stop and dig myself out. Then I went around to the other side of the car and probed the jumbled mass of camp gear with a stick until I found Retch, and just in the nick of time, too. Fortunately, his face was in a small pocket of air between a boot and a coffee pot, and he had been able to breathe. The air probably would have given out, though, if I had had to bring in specially trained search-and-rescue dogs to find him.

Another danger of backseats was that methane gas sometimes arose from decay in the bottom layers. For that reason, most experienced outdoorsmen never allowed an open flame inside the car, particularly after an outing lasting more than three days.

Retch's wife once accidentally opened a rear door of his camping car and later was found crouched in a corner of the garage, whimpering and sucking her thumb. The doctor sent her to bed under heavy sedation. He said he thought she was suffering from a psychosis of some kind. I think it was probably from a string of crappies mislaid in the backseat on a fishing trip the previous July.

I have long thought that a good horror movie could be made about the backseat of a hunter's car. These two hunters are driving along way back in the mountains on a dark and stormy night, see, and suddenly the backseat begins to pulsate. Slowly it begins to ooze forward, toward the necks of the unsuspecting hunters. At the end of the film a posse with a pack of dogs pursues the backseat into a swamp where it slips beneath the greenish ooze, burbling evilly. Retch scoffed at my idea.

I was miffed. "Listen," I told him, "I know for a fact a strange life form can originate in a backseat."

"Let's not get personal," he snapped.

There is a science to packing a backseat prior to a camping trip. Unfortunately, no one has ever discovered a suitable method for repacking it for the return trip. This is because camp gear during the course of the trip expands to half again its original volume and overflows into the front seat. On the way home from one camping trip, I was stopped by a traffic cop who claimed he thought the car was being driven by a water jug and a half-inflated air mattress.

Another reason that repacking the backseat poses problems is that the process always takes place during a thunderous rainstorm. The prescribed method of packing a backseat under that circumstance is to hurl the entire camp blindly and savagely through a rear door of the car. One time we came home from a Forest Service campground with a pine branch, several large rocks, a rest room sign, and a ranger who had stopped by to collect the fee.

One of the most efficient repackings of a backseat I've ever seen was accomplished by Retch's father when we were boys. Mr. Sweeney hated the outdoors and everything in it, but once, during a mellowness brought on by a quart of home brew, he promised to drive little Retch and me out for an overnighter. His wife held him to the promise. Grousing and grumbling, he drove Retch and me out to the first wide spot in the road, which happened to be a logging camp garbage dump. Retch and I set up the tent and stowed the gear in it while Mr. Sweeney sat in the car, frowning at his newspaper. Along about sundown, as Retch and I were frying supper, we looked up to see bears of all sizes, shapes, and colors streaming toward our camp. It was a startling sight, to which Mr. Sweeney responded with the quaint expression, "What the *bleep!*" He screamed at us to get in the car. Then he wrapped his arms around the umbrella tent, ripped it from its moorings, dragged it complete with contents to the car, and rammed, crammed, and stomped it into the backseat, all the while helping Retch and me expand our vocabularies. I was too shaken up to time him, but I doubt that more than eight seconds elapsed between our spotting the bears and our careening out of the dump at 60 m.p.h. It was a remarkable performance.

Sleeping in a backseat can be something of an art. As much gear as possible is moved to the front seat and the rest is thrown out on the ground to be repacked during a thunderous rainstorm the next day. Then you roll out your sleeping bag and climb into it. Because this step takes half the night, it should be begun early. Next, you tangle your hair, if any, in the door handle; this will prevent you from rolling onto the floor, which can be disastrous, particularly to the other parties who may be sleeping in the backseat with you. (Yes, it is entirely possible for more than one outdoorsman at a time to sleep in a backseat; however, check with your doctor, your minister, and the local health department before attempting to do so.)

I once spent a night sleeping in a backseat with two other guys, but never again. The next morning we got up, built a fire, cooked and ate breakfast, and hunted for two hours before we got completely untangled.

The backseat was, I suppose, as much a state of mind as anything. It was a symbol of freedom and adventure. It was the pioneer's Conestoga wagon shrunk down and upholstered; it was the prospector's burro with ashtrays and armrests. Then one day, I judge about the late fifties, some guy, a genius, probably an outdoorsman who had just spent the night sleeping in a backseat, came up with a fantastic idea: Suppose a vehicle could be built that was nothing more than a huge backseat equipped with engine and wheels! The motor home was born.

Edgy Rider

As a child I constantly begged my father to buy me a pony. One day I extracted from him the promise that if he saw an inexpensive steed at the auction he would buy it for me. He came home with a pig.

"Where's my pony?" I demanded.

He pointed to the pig. "You're lookin' at it."

I named the pig Trigger.

Naturally, I was enraged. Other farm kids had their own ponies to gallop about on while I had to ride a stupid pig! On the pig's behalf, I'll say that he cared as much for being ridden as I did for riding him.

"Whoa, Trigger!" I'd scream at the pig.

"Oink oink squeeeeeeeeee!" he'd reply, and race along a barbwire fence in an attempt to saw me into four equal sections.

The great humiliation, though, was when my pony-owning friends would come over to play cowboys. The only one who sat short in the saddle, I always had to be the villain. "Hey, Podner," one of the guys would say to his sidekick, "I think ol' Black Bart is trying to sneak up on us—I just heard his horse oink!" Then they'd laugh.

That fall I had little trouble containing my grief when Trigger was transformed into hams and salt pork. Seldom does one have the opportunity of eating an adversary without being subjected to criticism. Nevertheless, I was still without a suitable steed.

Crazy Eddie Muldoon, who lived on a nearby farm and was also horseless, came up with the theory that cows might be employed as satisfactory mounts. The theory seemed reasonable enough to me, as any wild scheme did in those days, and I agreed to help him test it.

"Since it's my idea, I'll do the hard part," explained Crazy Eddie. "That means you get to ride the cow first and have all the fun."

This seemed uncharacteristically generous of him, and I inquired as to the exact nature of the "hard part." He said it consisted of studying the results of the experiment and thinking up ways by which the ride might be improved upon. "And I have to keep a watch out for Pa, too," he concluded. "He's down working in the bottom pasture right now. But we don't want him showing up while you're riding the cow. Understand?"

I understood. Mr. Muldoon was a burly Irishman with a volcanic temper, and he strongly objected to scientific experiments being conducted on his livestock.

Getting on board a cow turned out to be more difficult than either of us had supposed. Crazy Eddie would try to boost me up, but the cow would give us an indignant look and walk away, with me clawing at her hide and Eddie running along grunting and gasping and trying to shove me topside. Finally, he said he had another idea, which was that I would climb up on a shed roof overhanging the barnyard and, when he drove a cow past, I would drop down on her back.

"And presto!" he exclaimed obscurely.

As soon as I was perched on the edge of the roof, Crazy Eddie cut out from the herd a huge Holstein, one approximately the size of a Sherman tank, and drove her unsuspectingly beneath my perch. According to plan, I dropped down on the cow's broad back, grabbing her bell collar as I landed. And presto! The Holstein emitted a terrified bellow, leaped straight up in the air, and executed a rolling figure eight with full twist. That was for openers, a little warmup exercise to get out the kinks and limber up her muscles. Then she stretched out like a greyhound after a mechanical rabbit and did four three-second laps around the barnyard, a maneuver apparently intended to build momentum for a straight shot down the narrow lane behind the barn.

With hands locked like sweating visegrips around the bell collar, and every toe gripping cowhide, I stuck to the back of the Holstein like a hungry, sixty-five-pound bobcat, which may have been exactly what the cow thought I was. During the first moments of my ride, I wondered vaguely if Mr. Muldoon's cows were equipped with burglar alarms, for there was a terrible din in my ears; only later did I attribute this fierce clanging to the cowbell.

About midway down the lane, I managed to unlatch my eyelids—a mistake, as I instantly realized, for the first thing I saw was a compounding of my troubles. There, plodding up the lane toward us, possibly with nothing more on his mind than the question of what his wife had fixed for lunch, was Mr. Muldoon. Now, unknown to me, the barnyard antics of the Holstein had terrorized the rest of the herd, which was stampeding along immediately behind us. It was this wild and violent spectacle that greeted Mr. Muldoon as he glanced up from his preoccupation with picking his way through patches of cow spoor laid down with the singular indiscrimination for which cows are noted. In retrospect, this preoccupation bore a certain similarity to concern about a few drops of rain just before one falls in a lake.

Overcoming the momentary paralysis that accompanied his first sight of us, Mr. Muldoon exploded into furious activity, which consisted largely of jumping up and down and waving his arms. The clanging of the burglar-alarm cowbell prevented me from hearing what he was shouting, which was probably just as well. Perceiving that his efforts to flag down the herd were not only ineffective but, if anything, were increasing the cows' RPMs, Mr. Muldoon turned and began to sprint ahead of us at a rate that under normal circumstances I'm sure I would have marveled at. As it was, we passed over him as if he were a tansy weed rooted in the ground.

My dismount from the Holstein was facilitated by a low-hanging limb on a tree at the end of the lane. I bounced several times, finally coming to rest in a posture similar to that associated with a lump of mush. Fortunately, I had landed beyond the exit of the lane, and the herd of cows that thundered close behind showed the good sportsmanship of fanning out on both sides of me. Mr. Muldoon had not been so lucky. When he came hobbling up to see if I was still alive, I noted that he appeared to have been pressed in a giant waffle iron, and one none too clean at that. I choked out the story of the experiment to him, and he showed considerable interest in it, mentioning in passing that he could scarcely wait to debrief Eddie in the woodshed. Crazy Eddie, I might add, was at that very moment in the house busting open his piggy bank to see if he had enough money for a bus ticket to another state. I was happy to learn that he came up short by several dollars.

My craving for a suitable mount, by which I mean one that did not go *oink* or *moo,* was never to be satisfied.

Years later, my own children began begging me for a horse. At the time, we lived in one of the humbler sections of suburbia, an area which, through some oversight of the planning commission, remained zoned for agriculture. This meant that it was legally possible for us to keep a horse on our two acres. I decided to broach the subject to my wife.

"I've been thinking," I broached, "every kid should have a horse. Caring for a horse gives a kid a sense of responsibility."

"What do you need a horse for?" Bun replied. "You already have a four-wheel-drive pickup with racing stripes and a chrome rollbar."

That woman can be incredibly dense at times. "Not for me! Ha! I can just see myself, dressed up like Clint Eastwood in *High Plains Drifter,* galloping off into the sunset!" Actually, I didn't look bad that way, not bad at all, but I wasn't about to give Bun the satisfaction of thinking she'd had one of her suspicions confirmed. "Yes, by gosh, I think we should buy the kids a horse."

"But we don't even have a barn!" Bun wailed.

"We can turn the garage into a barn," I explained. "Listen, all we need is a little imagination."

"All you need is a good psychiatrist," she muttered.

Later, when I was copping a plea of temporary insanity, I would remind her of that mutter.

Contrary to popular opinion, it is remarkably easy to buy a horse, but only if you know absolutely nothing about horses. I found an ad in the classified section of the newspaper that stated: "Good kids' horse, $150." It seemed like a steal. Surely, I thought, at this very moment hordes of eager horse buyers are converging upon the foolish soul who is offering such a fantastic bargain. I dialed the number, and the man who answered—he spoke in the soft, country drawl I had expected—confirmed that indeed he was all but overrun with potential buyers.

"I don't want to sell Pokey to just anyone, though," he told me. "Since you sound like a man who knows horses, I'd be happy to bring him by your place so you can take a look at him."

I said I'd be delighted if he would do that and gave him the address of my spread. Scarcely had I hung up the phone than an old pickup truck with a horse in the back came rattling down my driveway.

A lanky cowboy emerged from the cab of the pickup. Extending a hard-callused hand, he said, "Name's Bill. You the man what's lookin' for a good kids' horse?"

I replied that I was indeed that person. By this time, my brood of moppets were bouncing up and down around me, clapping their little hands together, and screaming, "Buy him! Buy him!"

"Hush," I scolded them. "I'm going to have to have a closer look at him first."

"Sure thing," Bill said. He dropped the tailgate of the pickup and ordered the horse, "Step out of there,

Pokey." Amazingly, the horse backed up and stepped down out of the pickup. Then the cowboy scooped up our little three-year-old and set her on Pokey's back. I'll swear that horse turned and smiled affectionately at Erin. He walked ever so carefully around the yard, stopping every time she teetered one way or the other until the little girl recovered her balance, and then he'd plod on.

My wife, who was witnessing the performance, also seemed impressed with the horse's gentleness, or so I judged from the fact that she had ceased pounding her chest in an apparent effort to get her heart started again.

"What'd I tell you," Bill said. "Pokey's a great kids' horse."

There was no doubt about it. While Bill was lifting Erin back down, I was writing out the check. Perhaps I wouldn't have been so hasty if I'd had the good sense to study the horse's face more carefully. When I finally did so, I had the distinct impression that it bore a combination of features that reminded me of W. C. Fields and, in a different mood, of Richard Widmark in one of his roles as a homicidal maniac. Probably just my imagination, though, I said to myself.

One little incident before Bill departed also caused me some wonder about my purchase. As Bill was wringing my hand as though I had just saved his life, Pokey plodded softly up behind him. I assumed the horse was going to give his former master an affectionate good-bye nudge. Instead, he clamped half a dozen yellow teeth onto the cowboy's shoulder. I recall the smirking look in the horse's eyes as Bill danced about, silently mouthing curses as he reached back and twisted one of Pokey's ears until the animal unlocked its jaws. Bill grinned sheepishly, if you can imagine the grin of a sheep that has just been gnawed on by a coyote. "A little game Pokey and I play," he said.

"Really?" I said. "I would have guessed that hurt like heck."

Bill casually flicked a tear off his cheek. "Naw! Heck no. Well, be seein' you."

Contrary to his last remark, I never saw Bill again. But I can say in all honesty, I really would have liked to, and preferably in some remote area where his shouts for help would have been to no avail.

Within a month, I could not look at Pokey without seeing "glue factory" written all over him. The only thing that saved him from taking up residence on the back side of postage stamps was that the children loved him. And, as far as I could determine, he loved the children. He lived with us for ten years, providing the children with almost as much pleasure as he did the tack-shop owner, the feedstore proprietor, the farrier, and the veterinarian. I viewed him largely as a malevolent machine for transforming five-dollar bills into fertilizer for my garden.

I must admit that I had some ulterior motives in acquiring a horse. My wife's charges that I intended to satisfy the cowboy fantasies of my childhood were, of course, too ridiculous to dignify even with denial. I did think, however, that the horse might come in handy for elk hunting, so I went out and purchased some of the essential gear for that purpose.

Bun knows nothing about elk hunting, but even so I thought her response to my acquisitions was uncouth, to say the least. Personally, I find it unladylike for a woman to stagger about holding her sides while squealing hysterically.

"Laugh all you want," I told her, "but if you weren't so ignorant of the subject you'd know that nine out of ten elk hunters wear cowboy hats. Cowboy boots are the only safe footwear for stirrups—anybody knows that. And the brush on the sides of trails will tear your legs to pieces if you don't have a good pair of chaps. The leather vest—well, you'd just be surprised at how handy a leather vest is when you're hunting elk!"

"B-but the spurs!" she gasped. "The sp-spurs!"

I didn't even try to explain the spurs. I mean, if a woman is so ignorant of elk hunting that she doesn't know about spurs, there's no point in trying to educate her.

It had been twenty years and more since I had ridden a horse, or a pig or cow for that matter, so before embarking on Pokey myself I considered it only prudent to study the horse's style while the children rode him about the two acres I now referred to in taverns as the "back forty." With the older children, he would gallop at a moderate gait around the fenced pasture, slowing for the corners and in general taking every precaution not to unseat the young riders. Several knowledgeable horsepersons who observed him thus in action told me I couldn't have found a better kids' horse. I would nod knowingly, chewing on a grass straw as I pushed my cowboy hat back with my thumb.

One day when the kids were off at school, I told Bun, "I think I'll take a little ride on Pokey, just to shape him up for elk season."

"I was wondering why you had your chaps on," she said. "Where are your—*hee! hee!*—spurs?"

"The spurs are for later," I said, ignoring her mirthful outburst. "Now, come on out to the back forty with me. I may need some assistance."

"Okay," she agreed, "but if you think I'm going elk hunting with you to help you get on and off your horse, you're crazy."

Perhaps it was fate that dictated I would have to suffer insults in my pursuit of horsemanship. The problem was, I had not yet been willing to mortgage the house in order to swing financing for a saddle. Since the children mounted the horse by using the board fence as a ladder, I figured I could do the same. This procedure, however, was made easier if someone held the horse's bridle while the mounting was taking place.

Maybe my imagination was acting up, but the expression on Pokey's face that day seemed more Richard Widmark than W. C. Fields. Nevertheless, I climbed the fence and, while Bun maneuvered the horse up close, I threw a leg over him. So far, so good. I took up the reins and told Bun to step back.

"Giddap," I said.

Nothing.

"Giddap!" I said, louder.

Still no response whatsoever. I looked at Bun. She shrugged her shoulders.

"GIDDAP, you miserable *bleep-of-a-bleep!*"

The *bleep-of-a-bleep* lowered his head, against which he had now flattened his ears, but refused to budge.

Once more I shouted "Giddap," but this time I dug my heels into his flanks. Before my hat hit the ground at the starting point, we were at the far end of the back forty. But it was not so simple as that.

The smooth, rhythmic lope with which Pokey carried the children about the pasture had been replaced by a gait closely simulating the motion of a jackhammer—a thousand-pound jackhammer. My eyeglasses flew off, the fillings in my teeth popped loose, my vertebrae rattled like castanets. With the instincts of a natural horseman, I hauled back on the reins. Unfortunately, the motion of the horse had bounced me so far forward, I had to stretch the reins far back behind me, and even then couldn't get the slack out of them. But this problem had ceased to concern me, since I now had another distraction.

For those unfamiliar with a horse's anatomy, there is a large bone at the point where the neck hooks on to the rest of him, technically speaking. I now found myself astraddle this bone, pounding against it at a rate of five times per second. On the scale of discomfort, this sensation rated somewhere between unbearable and unbelievable, thus motivating me to take defensive action. I flopped forward and wrapped both arms around the beast's neck, a move which had the purpose not only of enabling me to hold on but possibly to strangle the horse into submission. Alas, at that moment, Pokey cut sharply around a corner, so that I was swung beneath his neck. We arrived back at the starting point with me suspended from the horse's neck in the manner of a two-toed sloth from a limb. Pokey came to a reluctant halt, and I dropped to the ground. Calmly, I picked up my hat, beat the dust out of it on my chaps, and strolled over to Bun, who was sagged against the fence doing her impression of a limp noodle.

"Want to see any more trick riding?" I asked.

Despite my air of nonchalance, the ride had taken its toll on me. Suddenly, in fact, I detected what I thought was the symptom of a heart attack—an excruciating pain in my shoulder. Then, collecting my wits, I reached back, got hold of an ear, and twisted it until Pokey unclamped his jaws.

Pokey was truly a great kids' horse. But he hated adults.

Our next yard sale included a cowboy hat, cowboy boots, chaps, and a leather vest.

"Don't you want to sell the spurs?" Bun asked.

"No, I'm keeping them," I said, "just in case I ever run into Bill again!"

Strange Scenes
and Eerie Events

Every day weird things happen for which there are no rational explanations. Take, for example, the case of Retch Sweeney's watch.

Retch and I were trolling on a lake in Canada several years ago and, as he leaned over the side of the boat to net a nice rainbow trout I was bringing in, Retch's watch came loose from his wrist and fell into the lake. Not only was the watch expensive, but it held great sentimental value: Retch's wife had given it to him on their twentieth anniversary. It bore the inscription, "To Charley Bombi, for 40 years dedicated service to Acme Sand & Gravel Co." Retch's wife is a great one for sentiment.

Five years after Retch lost his watch in the Canadian lake, he and I went on a boat-camping trip on a lake in Montana. It is important to note that there is no waterway connecting the two lakes. After making camp, Retch and I went out to see if we couldn't hook into one of the monster rainbows reported in the vicinity. Sure enough, as we trolled past the mouth of a stream, Retch's rod whipped double and a few seconds later a beautiful rainbow was doing aerial gymnastics. We went back to camp and while I started preparing supper, Retch dressed out his fish. Suddenly he let out a great yell. I rushed over to see what had happened.

"Look what I found in this rainbow," he shouted, holding up a shiny object.

"I can scarcely believe my eyes," I said. "How could such a thing happen?"

"Beats me," Retch said. "I've never even heard of anybody finding a bottle cap in the stomach of a fish before."

"Me either," I said. "Now if it had been the watch you lost in the lake up in Canada, I could understand that. You read in the newspapers all the time about that sort of thing happening."

Some persons seem to possess almost supernatural powers. One of the ways Retch and I pass the time when the fishing slows down on a lake is to toss a floating ring well out from the boat and then hold casting contests to see who can hit the ring most often. Fred Dokes happened to be along with us one time and he couldn't miss the ring. Retch and I were impressed.

"All right, now I'll really show you something," Fred said. "Something that will amaze you." He took from his pocket a wad of stuff that looked like cookie dough and placed a plug of it over each eye. Next he tied a large bandana over the top of the dough. Finally, he took off his jacket and tied that around his head in such a way that it was absolutely impossible for him to see out, even if he hadn't had the dough over each eye.

"Hand me my rod," he said, standing up in the

boat. "Now what I want you to do is to spin me around five times. You don't need to worry about pointing me in the direction of the floating ring."

I spun him around five times. Naturally, the only thing I expected would happen was that Fred would stagger backwards and fall into the lake.

"Okay, just watch this," he said. Fred then took two steps backwards and fell into the lake.

Of all the people who seem to have supernatural powers, Fred proved that he wasn't one of them. When he offered to show us how he could shoot skeet blindfolded, we declined on the grounds that watching too many demonstrations of extrasensory perception can bring on a nervous condition.

Even weirder was what happened to Retch and me up in the Hoodoo Valley. We had spent the day fishing on a remote lake and had so much fun that it was practically dark before we knew it. Then the wind came up and big black clouds came rolling over the mountains, and the sky was cobwebbed with lightning. We got the boat loaded and headed off down the winding, two-lane highway. Even in the daylight, this highway is spooky but on a dark and stormy night it can really give you the creeps. Mist hangs in tattered shrouds over the swampy land; ancient, moss-draped trees line the road, their branches moaning in the wind, and from time to time dark, shaggy shapes scurry through the beams of the headlights.

Rain began to splatter the windshield before we had driven a mile. Then we saw him. Standing alongside the road up ahead was a slender, pale youth with long, streaming hair, his thumb beckoning us to stop.

"I've heard this one before," Retch said. "Don't stop for him!"

"We can't just let the poor devil stand out there in the rain. He'll drown," I said.

"The way the story goes," Retch said, "is that he has already . . ."

But before he could finish, I'd brought the car to a stop and the youth was crawling into the backseat. He appeared to be about eighteen, with pale eyes, pale lips, and pale hair.

We drove along in silence for some time, Retch tensely popping his knuckles and occasionally reaching back to pat down the hairs that persisted in rising on the back of his neck. Finally, I tried to strike up a bit of conversation with the lad.

"You from these parts?" I asked.

The boy said nothing.

"What were you doing out in a storm like this?"

My question was answered only by an eerie silence.

"Oh, my gosh!" Retch muttered under his breath. "I knew it. Next he's going to tell us that the bridge up ahead is washed out."

"Don't be silly," I whispered.

"The bridge up ahead is washed out," the boy said. "You'd better take the River Road to town."

I patted down a few unruly hairs on the back of my neck. "Right."

When we reached the intersection of the River Road, I stopped the car and climbed out to take a close look and make sure the road was passable. Retch scrambled out of the car with me.

"You were crazy to pick that kid up," he hissed at me. "I know he's the same one I heard about somewhere. I'm walking the rest of the way to town."

Just then a high wavering cry drifted out of the darkness up ahead.

"One thing's for sure," Retch said. "I'm not walking to town."

When we got back to the car, the pale youth was gone. We two pale, middle-aged men scrambled into the car, which spewed out twin rooster tails of mud over the boat and trailer as we shot off down the River Road.

We slid to a stop in front of the only bar in the town and bounded inside, both of us having the distinct impression that we were being trailed, possibly by a large bat. The barmaid and a scattering of patrons gave us curious stares.

"You look like you seen a ghost," the barmaid said.

"T-two double sh-shots of the st-strongest stuff you got," Retch ordered. "I don't know what he's having."

"The s-same," I said.

We then related our story to the folks in the bar. They listened with attentive solemnness, occasionally nodding as if to say, yes, yes, they knew what had happened. When we had finished, an old white-bearded fellow took off his rimless spectacles and wiped them. "I reckon you fellows have just become acquainted with the Jakes boy. He drove his car into the river a couple of years back."

"D-drove his car into the river?" Retch said.

"D-drowned?" I said.

"Drowned!" the old man said. "Heck no, he didn't drown! But driving his car into the river is apparently what give him the idea of thumbing rides on dark and stormy nights and scaring the bejeebers out of fishermen like you fellers!"

At that the regulars at the bar burst into hysterical laughter and slapped their knees black and blue and rolled around on the floor and generally gave the impression of being highly amused.

As Retch and I slunk for the door, the old man spoke again and the mirthful occupants of the room instantly suspended their hilarity. "There is one thing, though, that's a little strange about your experience. I'm kind of surprised you didn't notice it."

"What's that?" I said.

"There ain't no bridge on the highway up to the lake!"

Retch and I stomped out of the bar. If there's one thing I hate, it's a bunch of drunken yokels making a spectacle of themselves.

When we got to the car, I stared into the backseat where the Jakes boy had been sitting. "Wait a second," I said. "If that wasn't a ghost, why isn't the seat wet where he was sitting?"

Retch looked into the backseat. "You've got a point there," he said. "On the other hand, why would a ghost steal both our tackle boxes?"

The mystery was never solved, even though Retch and I spent a couple of dark and stormy nights driving up and down the highway hoping to give a lift to a lad with pale eyes, pale lips, pale hair, and two dark green tackle boxes that didn't belong to him.

The Hunters' Workout Guide

Since prehistoric times and even earlier, hunters have engaged in strenuous physical exercises to prepare themselves for the rigors of hunting. Strangely, most hunters are still out of shape by opening day of hunting season. Why? If one discounts the tendency of hunters to start their exercise program fifteen minutes before the season opens, then it must be concluded that standard exercises are ineffective in conditioning the human body for the postures, movements, and exertions peculiar to hunting. I have, therefore, devised an exercise program especially for the hunter.

The exercises are designed to be performed in the typical business office during interruptions in the work routine, such as coffee breaks or the boss being called out of the building. This is because, as my research shows, the average hunter doesn't have time to work out at a gym. Instead, he must slave away at two or three jobs in order to pay for all the expensive paraphernalia that makes serious hunting possible—jewelry, furs, fancy dresses, and the like. Otherwise, there's no way his spouse is going to let him spend all his spare time out hunting.

Some of the exercises are intended to condition the hunter psychologically for the ordeals often encountered in the field. It is a well-known fact that a hunter's mind usually surrenders to hardship before his body, which doesn't help the mind all that much since it can't go home alone and sit by the fire with a hot toddy until the body comes stumbling in. I, on the other hand, have had occasions when the body conked out first. That's a bad one, too. My mind would say, "C'mon, there's a deer right over this next rise!" But my body would reply, "Well, go get it then, but I'm sittin' right here on this log until you get back." The trick is to have the body and mind collapse simultaneously, which is the purpose of these exercises.

Be sure to get a checkup from your doctor before undertaking the exercise program. If the doctor bursts out laughing during the exam, don't believe him when he tells you he thought of a funny joke. Just forget about getting in shape for hunting this year and take up golf instead.

Here is a test you can perform in your own home to determine your level of physical fitness. Strip off all your clothes and lie down flat on the floor. Next, push yourself up into a headstand. If you have trouble maintaining your balance, you may wish to have someone hold your feet to steady you. My research shows, by the way, that only one person in ten thousand can keep a straight face while holding the feet of a naked man who is standing on his head. Simply ignore any unseemly displays of mirth by your helper. Also, a sharp word or two spoken with authority often serves to repress the natural human urge in this situation to tickle behind the knees. It is best if you learn to stand on your head unassisted.

Now note your physical responses. If the blood pounds in your ears and behind your eyeballs and you are overcome by nausea, there is nothing to worry about. These are merely symptoms of a minor malady common in persons of middle age, which is middle age. (If you are not yet middle-aged, of course, you should start worrying.) On the other hand, if everything suddenly goes dark and you have trouble breathing, you have a serious problem—your fat has slipped down and covered your head. Persons experiencing this condition should begin the exercise program immediately.

The field situations described below are for the purpose of comparison only. You may experience greater or lesser misery depending on how and where you hunt. Here, then, are the exercises.

The Ice-Breaker—For this exercise, you will need a pan of water and a large quantity of ice. Put the ice in the pan and let chill for an hour. Stick your hands in the ice water until they become totally numb. Now, jerk them out of the ice water and try to take your ballpoint pen apart and reassemble it in three seconds. This will give you the dexterity you need to reload for a quick shot during a freezing rain. Or it may give you frostbite, which is all right, too, since every hunter should be able to shoot with frostbite.

Spend your coffee breaks standing in the pan of ice water. Although your office-mates may at first think you a bit eccentric, they will soon avoid you during coffee breaks and at all other times if possible. Your concentration will thus be unbroken by idle chitchat. And it takes quite a bit of concentration to stand in a pan of ice water for fifteen minutes.

Every other day you should sit in the ice water instead of standing in it. If your supervisor asks you why you are sitting in a pan of ice water, tell him it keeps you mentally alert for the afternoon's work. Who knows, perhaps the whole office staff will be required to sit in pans of ice water during the coffee break.

To more accurately simulate the conditions of the hunt, arrange for one of your fellow workers to sneak up behind you from time to time and dump the pan of ice water down the back of your neck. The maximum conditioning will occur if, at the time, you are tired and miserable and feeling as if you can't survive for another minute.

Consistent practice of the various forms of the Ice-Breaker will prepare you for certain climatic conditions encountered on the hunt. Of course, there will be days when the weather turns bad, and nothing can prepare you for that.

The Candle—Hunters must learn to ignore pain if they are to fully enjoy their sport. A good way to condition yourself to pain is by holding your hand palm-down over a candle. Howling and dancing about during this procedure tends to detract from the desired effect of the exercise and should be avoided. Within a few weeks you should be able to hold your hand over the candle for up to five minutes without flinching. Some of your co-workers in the office may accuse you of showing off, of making a display of raw machismo. Others may openly ridicule you. Some sadist may even suggest that you use a lighted candle.

The Hindquarter Hustle—This exercise is intended to improve your upper body strength and your agility. From among your fellow workers, select one who weighs approximately one hundred pounds—about the weight of a hindquarter of an elk. Because of the size requirement, your subject will probably be a woman. Ask her if she will assist you in an exercise. Do not, I repeat, do not indicate that you have chosen her because she bears any resemblance whatsoever to the hindquarter of an elk. Then have her ride you piggyback while you step from floor to desk top, leap to a chair, step over the back of the chair and onto the floor, jump to the top of the table, down again, and finally climb up twenty-seven flights of stairs. Repeat. While this is going on, the woman should flop about and in every other way possible attempt to make you lose your balance. A word of warning: Since your employer may not be an elk hunter himself, and therefore may be incapable of comprehending the purpose of this exercise, you should perform it only when he is in a board meeting or similarly occupied.

The exercise, obviously, is intended to prepare you for the task of packing out a hindquarter of an elk you were stupid enough to shoot five miles from your vehicle in rough, steep terrain that didn't seem all that bad when you weren't packing out the hindquarter of an elk.

The Squat Walk—This exercise is sometimes referred to as the Moving Hunker. Lower yourself into the standard hunker position, with posterior no more than three or four inches above the floor. Now walk. That's all there is to it. You should try to work up to half a mile a day of the Squat Walk. Half a mile may seem rather far, but if you Squat Walk out to the water cooler or down the hall to deliver a report or out to lunch, you'll be surprised at how quickly you can do half a mile. Your fellow workers and passersby may give you odd looks and make snide remarks, but so what! Remember to keep moving, however. A stationary Squat Walk arouses suspicion, and may result in someone's calling the security people. It is very difficult to explain a stationary Squat Walk to security people.

The Squat Walk prepares you for hunting in open country where the only concealment from game is low brush. It is not unusual for hunters in this situation to Squat Walk four or five miles in a single day. Frequently, coyote hunters will Squat Run, a particularly difficult maneuver, in the direction of quavering howls wafting over the desert, only to discover the howls are coming from a Squat-Walking hunter trying to straighten up. Practicing the Squat Walk around the office will help you avoid such embarrassment.

The Five-Toe Grab—This exercise gives you the powerful toes so important to hunting. The basic technique consists of striding briskly across a room and suddenly freezing in midstride with the extended leg well forward and the foot approximately two inches above the floor. This is accomplished by gripping the floor with the toes of your other, or planted, foot. Sure it's difficult, particularly while wearing shoes, but far from impossible. Try to maintain a relaxed expression while performing this exercise, since uncontrolled grimaces have been known to rupture faces. At first, you may notice strange crackling sounds, but this is nothing more than fissures developing in your toe bones and should be ignored. After six weeks of practicing this exercise daily, you will be able to crack walnuts with your toes, though why you should want to is beyond me.

As most experienced hunters are aware, the situation for which the Five-Toe Grab prepares them is this: You are striding briskly back to your car after a day of deer hunting. The freshest tracks you have come across appear to have been made early in the last century. Deer are the furthest thing from your mind. Suddenly, as your fore boot descends toward a pile of dry twigs, you notice a nice buck standing on a knoll a mere thirty yards distant. The slightest sound will send him out of sight. You apply the Five-Toe Grab, halting the descent of your foot an inch from the twigs. While maintaining that posture, you put the crosshairs on the deer and get off your shot. This technique can be highly effective, but only on deer that are not startled by grunts that carry up to a mile on a still day.

The Desk Lift—With this exercise, you stand straddle-legged on the backs of two chairs, then bend over and pick up your office desk, after which you. . . .

But that's enough for today. I don't want you to overdo it before we get to the difficult exercises.

Temporary Measures

A full seventy-five percent of the sporting life consists of temporary measures—give or take sixty percent. Extreme cases on either end of the scale have been eliminated from the study. There was one angler, for example, who believed that if you can't do a thing right you shouldn't do it at all. A strict adherent to this philosophy, he hadn't been fishing once in the past thirty-seven years. I chastised the man for holding such a stupid belief—that there is a *right way* to fish—and told him I had a good mind to divest him of his title of angler. He told me he had a good mind to punch me in the nose. I replied that I'd like to see him try, but since I was three blocks away by then, he didn't hear me, and it's a darn good thing for him that he didn't.

Another extreme case, on the opposite end of the scale from the sorehead mentioned above, is myself. Approximately ninety-eight percent of my sporting life consists of temporary measures.

A line guide on one of my favorite fly rods is tied in place with little black mounds of sewing thread daubed with model airplane glue. As I tell anyone who notices, the mounds of thread are only a temporary measure. I intend to rewrap the rod properly as soon as I don't have something better to do. It is surprising, though, how many better things there are to do than rewrapping a rod properly. Even more surprising is that sewing thread and model airplane glue will hold a guide in place for upwards of ten years.

Someday I intend to build a decent duck blind. It will be supported by stout posts, chemically treated against rot. There will be a built-in bench inside, with a drawer underneath to hold boxes of shotgun shells. A small table will fold out from the side for lunch. I've even thought of attaching a camouflaged canvas roof that slips back automatically when I stand to shoot. For a temporary measure, though, I'll continue to stand hip-deep out in the marsh with a bunch of cattails tied around me.

As soon as I don't have something better to do, I'm going to patch that leak in the tent. Of course, rewrapping a line guide on my fly rod would be something better to do than patching a leak in a tent, so it may take a while. For a temporary measure, I sleep on the side of the tent that doesn't leak. If I have a companion along, I simply say, "Why don't you sleep on that side of the tent? It has a nice view of the stars." It also has running water, but I let him discover that for himself.

I really do want to organize my tackle box. Several years ago, I fished with a man who actually had his tackle box organized. He expressed some disapproval of my technique of hauling out a cluster of lures and spinning it around until I found the spoon that I wanted. Naturally, I was embarrassed and realized I had to do something to correct the situation. For a temporary measure, I didn't go fishing with the man anymore.

Pretty soon, when all the kids are through college, I'm going to buy myself a decent four-wheel-drive hunting rig. It will be so high off the ground I'll need a ladder to climb into it. That hunting rig will go anywhere. And there will be a nice little camper on the back, with a propane heater, comfortable beds, a refrigerator and cookstove, and a table on which my buddies and I can play cards after a hard day of fishing or hunting. Best of all, there will be a special rack up on top for hauling back the deer and elk and moose that I bag. But until I can afford the new rig, I can certainly make do with the family sedan, that's for sure. What do I care if some of the wealthier hunters get a chuckle out of my hunting rig? You'd think they had never seen a man driving home with his deer seat-belted beside him on the passenger seat.

As soon as the mortgage is paid off, I think I'll get me one of those new compound bows, the ones with all the little pulleys that enable you to hold at full stretch without trembling or without your eyeballs getting tangled in the cord. For right now, I'll have to settle for my old recurve, with its pull ranging from fifty-five to three hundred pounds, depending on how late in the day it is. As I tell my bowhunting companions, the recurve is just a temporary measure, until I get my new compound. Besides, my eyeballs need the exercise.

One of the things that has always bothered me about three-week fishing expeditions for record-busting black marlin in the South Pacific is the design of the fighting chair. After thirty minutes of fighting even a medium-sized black marlin, you can get a terrible pain in your lower back if the chair isn't just right. I want to get a custom-made fighting chair for my deep-water cruiser. For now, though, I'll get by with a boat cushion. A custom-made fighting chair would look out of place in a twelve-foot aluminum cartopper. Besides, I don't get much pain in my lower back from fighting even the big two-pound rainbows up at Trout Lake. But Trout Lake, too, is only a temporary measure, until I get enough money together for the deep-water cruiser and the three-week expeditions after black marlin in the South Pacific.

Someday I want to be able to tie size-22 flies perfectly, but until then I will have to put up with some defects. The biggest defect is that Clipper John's Fly Shop clips me $1.50 each for them. Of course, if my recurve bow continues to exercise my eyeballs, I may soon be able to see well enough to tie my own size 22s.

I've always wanted to have a good fishing companion, a man of learning and culture and good taste, a man who appreciates classical music and literature, good Scotch and fine foods, a man who knows the Latin names of flora and fauna, a man who enjoys the opportunity to commune with nature whether or not any fish are caught. Instead, my fishing companion is Retch Sweeney, who says things like, "Not one lousy fish! Don't that beat all! I wish those *bleeping* birds would shut up—they're getting on my nerves! This cheap beer ain't too bad, but it has an awful aftertaste when you belch it." Strange as it may seem, even after forty years of fishing with him, I still like to think of Retch as a temporary measure.

A friend of mind recently got himself an insulated survival suit that keeps him cozy-warm when we're out icefishing. "You ought to get one of these," he says, as the north wind comes strafing across the ice. "They keep you cozy-warm."

"Yeah, I know, that's what you keep saying," I reply. "Actually, the cold makes me feel *alive*. Say, would you mind checking my pulse to see if I still am?"

Freezing out on the ice is only a temporary measure. I fully intend to get one of those insulated suits, but I wouldn't want to give up icefishing until I do.

My sleeping bag is one of those September models. You know the kind—too hot for summer and too cold for winter, but just right for September. In fact, it's just right only for the second week of September. Unfortunately, I always have to work that week, and have never yet had the opportunity to experience the bag when it is just right. Pretty soon I'm going to buy a bag for summer and another one for winter. It seems like the only sensible thing to do. But for now, the September bag is all right, even though it's nearly July and I have to sleep with it unzipped. After all, somebody has to take care of feeding the carnivorous insects.

My wife points out that if I didn't spend so much time out hunting and fishing and "cavorting about in the wilds," I would have time to earn more money and then I could buy all the stuff I need to do things properly, and I wouldn't have to put up with so many temporary measures. But I have an even better solution. If you just leave temporary measures alone long enough, they eventually become permanent measures. Then you don't have to take any time away from your hunting and fishing and cavorting about in the wilds to earn a bunch of money. I've been aging some of my temporary measures for over thirty years now and, if my guess is right, several of them are just about ready to turn permanent.

The Fibricators

Young Elwood Fitch stopped by the house the other day to tell me he had caught a five-pound cutthroat under the bridge on Sand Creek. He said he had taken the fish on a No. 16 Black Gnat he had tied himself. Elwood is only twelve, but even so I couldn't help but be disappointed in him.

"Elwood," I said, "you don't expect me to believe a fish story like that, do you?"

Embarrassed, the lad hung his head and scuffed some shag off my carpet with the toe of his boot. "I sorta hoped you would."

"Not a chance," I said. "Now, tell me the truth."

Elwood confessed that actually the fish was a perch that weighed considerably less than half a pound and he had caught it in Bott's Lake on a night crawler his little brother had sold to him for a nickel.

I shook my head. "Elwood, don't you know that

when you tell fishing lies the way you just did you tarnish the credibility of all the rest of us anglers?"

"I'm sorry," he said.

"All right, everybody makes mistakes," I said. "But I want you to promise me one thing."

"What's that?"

"That you'll learn how to tell fishing lies properly. No self-respecting angler would believe a fish story the way you told that one. Pull up a chair and I'll give you a few pointers."

As I told Elwood, I have been a student of fibrication most of my life. In fact, I remember the very first story I ever fibricated.

I was about six years old and had stopped by the cabin of an old couple who lived back in the woods near our farm. Homer and Emma seemed delighted by my visit and invited me in for a glass of lemonade. After we were seated comfortably around their table, the old man leaned over and asked me, "Well, young man, what's the news?"

News? There was no news that I was aware of, but my hosts were looking at me with expressions of such eager anticipation that I didn't feel I should disappoint them.

"Just the bus wreck," I said.

The two old people snapped upright. "What'd he say, Emma?" the old man shouted.

"He said there was a bus wreck!" Emma shouted back.

I hadn't expected my small contribution to the conversation to arouse such excitement, but was pleased to have interrupted the day's tedium for the old folks with a bit of "news." I thought they would be satisfied with just the headline, but they weren't. They pressed me for details.

"When did it happen?" Emma asked me. "We haven't heard anything about a bus wreck."

"About a half hour ago," I said, for no particular reason other than a vague notion that news should be as fresh as possible.

"Good lord!" cried Homer. "Where?"

"Why, down at the big bend in the highway near our place."

Never before had my efforts at small talk aroused such interest and enthusiasm in adults. Homer and Emma bounded to their feet, danced around the table, knocked over chairs, stepped on assorted dogs and cats, and shouted questions at me so fast my head began to heat up from the strain of concocting new and frightful details.

"Anybody killed?" cried Homer.

I took a long drag on the lemonade and wiped my mouth on my sleeve. "Fifteen people," I said.

Not having any great experience with numbers, I had selected fifteen more or less at random. From the way Homer's and Emma's jaws sagged, I knew I had picked a good number, one the old couple held in high esteem.

"Most of them women and children," I added, shaking my head for dramatic effect and to give emphasis to the sheer awfulness of the disaster.

While I was pondering the possibility of having an airplane crash into the bus, the old couple scooped up towels, sheets, and blankets, and before I knew what was happening, they had loped off in the direction of the accident, apparently with the idea of offering aid and comfort to the survivors, if any.

Amid an uproar of dogs and cats, I sat alone at the table, nervously sipping my lemonade, happy to have brought a note of excitement into the lives of Homer and Emma, but fighting off the ominous feeling that I was not yet finished with The Great Bus Wreck, as it was to be henceforth known. After hiding out in the woods for most of the day, I was finally driven home by threat of darkness. My sister, The Troll, was waiting for me on the back porch. She turned and called out happily to my mother, "Hey, Ma, Walter Winchell finally got home! Do you want me to bring the stick?" Even in those days the news business was filled with stress.

Technically, The Great Bus Wreck fib doesn't qualify as a fish story, because a fish wasn't included among the ingredients. It does, however, contain the essentials of proper form: an attitude of casual disinterest on the part of the fibricator, a gradual compounding of the magnitude of the event being fibricated, and the insertion of a variety of specific details. I was a natural fibricator. Still, at the age of six, I lacked the necessary craft and polish to "take in" experienced anglers with one of my fish stories.

A few years later, much to my good fortune, I became acquainted with Rancid Crabtree, who had devoted his whole life to mastery of the art of fibrication. Rancid was the Picasso of the fib. He could do little white fibs, big blue fibs, realistic fibs, impressionistic fibs, expressionistic fibs, abstract fibs, surrealistic fibs, nonobjective fibs, and even pop fibs. As with any genius, Rancid extended the limits of the art far beyond anything that had been known before. Fibrication was an all-consuming activity to him. In the years I knew him, I don't think I caught him in more than half a dozen truths, and each of those so minuscule as to be unnoteworthy except for its rarity, like, say, a one-legged woodpecker.

Rancid tended to be a purist, and most of his fibs were created primarily as fibs for fibs' sake. On the other hand, he never hesitated to manufacture a functional fib whenever an occasion arose.

One time Rancid and I were just returning to the road from one of our secret fishing spots when we ran into three characters whom Rancid regarded as unsavory, which is to say that they were known to engage in activities the old woodsman despised—regular jobs. The trio consisted of the town barber, dentist, and undertaker, and two guys who worked at the sawmill. They gawked at our string of plump trout and then took some sightings along the corridor we had just carved through the thick brush that concealed a lovely set of beaver dams a quarter mile distant. Scarcely taking time to grunt greetings at us, the men extracted their fly rods from an automobile and began to assemble them.

"What'd you take them fish on?" one of the men asked.

"Got any pickled sow's yars with ya?" Rancid asked. "Thet's the only thang these fish'll bite on."

"Yars?" the man said.

"Pickled sow's ears," I translated.

"No, we ain't got any of them," one of the other fellows put in, "but we got some mighty fine flies."

"Wall, good luck to ya," Rancid said, starting to walk away. Then he stopped and turned and said, "Say, iffin you fellers see maw big black dog, Wuff, would you mind haulin' him back to town? He can find his way home from thar."

"Oh, I reckon," a man said without any great show of enthusiasm.

"I'd be beholdin' to ya," Rancid said. "Course, if

Wuff be all tore up when ya find him, jist put him out of his misery."

"Tore up?" another man said.

"Yep. I 'spect thet big cat might of kilt him outright, but mebby not."

"Big cat?"

"Jist an ol' mountin' lion. But don't worry none, cause they almost never attacks a hoomin bean lessen they's hurt an' starvin'."

The three men faltered in the assembly of their rods.

"Come to thank of it," Rancid continued in a musing manner, "thet ol' cat did seem a bit on the thin side, didn't you thank so, boy?"

"You could count his ribs," I said.

Rancid raised an eyebrow at me in an expression that said, "That ain't bad." By now the men were taking down their rods, so Rancid and I ambled off up the road.

"Hope you find your dog," one of the men called after us, apparently thankful we had saved him from being torn to bits.

"Oh yeah, me too," Rancid said. "Ol' Rex, he was a purty good ol' dog."

"Wuff," I corrected, but the three men were too distracted to pay attention to minor discrepancies.

"Shucks," Rancid said later. "Ah didn't even git to use the part about the quicksand."

"Or the poisonous ticks," I said.

"Yeah," Rancid said. "The pisonous ticks. Ain't nobody yet gone up agin the pisonous ticks!"

That's your basic functional fib. But Rancid used the functional fib only in emergencies. His preference, as I said, was for the pure fib, the fib for fib's sake. I

think the motive behind Rancid's fibrication was his belief that ordinary life was insufficient and required en-
hancement. I'd spend a wet, cold, dull day out in the
woods with Rancid and my general impression of the
experience was that it had been wet and cold and dull.
But later, upon hearing Rancid tell someone about the
day, I would discover that it had been full of wild adventures and startling occurrences and rare spectacles.
Afterward, I always remembered Rancid's version of the
day rather than my own impression of it, because Rancid's was so much more interesting and entertaining and
even magical. Reality always played second fiddle to
Rancid's imagination.

At the close of my lecture, I could see that young
Elwood was fairly bursting with a question. It is a wonderful thing to see intellectual curiosity suddenly take
flower in youth.

"Yes, Elwood, what is it?"

"You got any good junk food in the house?"

"No, you little toad, I don't believe in junk food!
You can have some celery or carrot sticks if you like."

"Naw. Well, I'd better be going. See ya."

After he left, I worried about how Elwood would
survive modern life with no more understanding of fibrication than he has. Indeed, such was my anxiety over
poor Elwood that I wandered out to the kitchen and
absent-mindedly consumed a whole package of Yummy
Yum-Yums, half a leftover pizza, and two cans of cream
soda.

The Family
Camper's Dictionary

Every year thousands of Americans are introduced to the sport of camping. (Many of them are wives and mothers who don't want the meeting to occur in the first place, but no matter.) To ease their transition from the comforts of home to life in the wilds, I have compiled the following dictionary of terms, phrases, yelps, howls, and miscellaneous weird sounds.

Camping itself is a rather vague term. For example, the infliction of the average family camping trip on prisoners of war would be considered a violation of the Geneva Convention. On the other hand, it is considered perfectly all right, and even *fun,* for a father and mother and their young children to subject themselves to the same experience. When it comes to camping, cruel and unusual punishment is in the eye of the beholder, along with smoke from the campfire.

This is not to say that family camping trips are free of protest. Generally, the protest occurs in the middle of a stormy night while the family bobs about on air mattresses in the flooded tent. One of the common forms of protest is: "You just try to pull something like this again, George, and I'm consulting a divorce lawyer!"

There are many kinds of camping. *Car camping,* for example, is where the camp is within twenty feet of the car, and a portion of each night is actually spent in the car, either because the tent collapsed or somebody thought he "heard a bear."

Backpacking is where the camp is located more than twenty feet from the car, and no portion of the night is spent actually in the car, except in the case of dire emergencies, such as when somebody thinks he "saw a bear."

Solitary camping is where a lone camper lies awake all night wondering how he could have been so stupid as not to have brought somebody along to camp with him. You know you are involved in solitary camping when you ask "Did you hear that funny sound just then?" and nobody answers. Of course it may be that the reason you are suddenly involved in solitary camping is that the person you were with heard that funny sound just then and is now engaged in car camping.

Group camping may consist of as many as forty individuals, none of whom thought to bring a can opener. A Cub Scout outing is typical of group camping, and it often ends with the adult leader spending the night pressed inside a pup tent with fourteen Cub Scouts because somebody had the bright idea of telling scary stories around the campfire.

Roughing-it camping is where the camp is so basic as to be devoid of even hot showers.

There are many other forms of camping, but they are mostly combinations or variations of the above or with no relation to them at all. Let us, therefore, proceed to the Family Camper's Dictionary:

Corn flakes—A common camp food. Often eaten dry with salt and pepper since no one thought to bring milk.

Hominy—Whenever there is a camping disaster, the only food saved.

"Looks like we may be stranded here for a week," a camper says. "Did we save any of the food?"

"Just the fifteen cans of hominy," he is told, which scarcely seems worth the trouble of surviving.

Oddly enough, the only food saved is never the canned beef stew. Cans of beets, parsnips, or squash may turn up as substitutes for the hominy. The mysterious thing is that nobody can ever remember seeing any of these foods in the grub box prior to the disaster.

The aroma of frying bacon—What campers love to wake up to.

As my wife and I climbed into our sleeping bags one evening a while back, I told her, "You know what I love to wake up to on camping trips, Bun? The aroma of frying bacon."

"Oh, yeah?" she said. "Well, I'll have to see if I can find it in a spray can next time I'm in the store."

If you're unlucky enough to have an insensitive and stubborn spouse, you may go through many years of camping without waking up to the aroma of frying bacon.

"Something hairy just ran across my neck!"—An announcement made by a young child immediately after the lantern has been shut off in the tent. Once the screaming from the other children has died down, the parents explain to the kid that it was just his imagination. Then for the rest of the night the parents experience the sensation of hairy things running across their necks

Cloudburst—A natural phenomenon that, when it occurs in the middle of the night, reminds a young child that he forgot to go to the bathroom before turning in after being told to do so nine times.

A big black stump—What the young child thinks is a bear while he is going to the bathroom in the middle of the night during a cloudburst, and which his father, peering through the rain and urging the child to act with expediency, also thinks is a bear.

A bear—What is thought to produce any night sound within a mile radius of the campsite. Also, what is standing on your picnic table munching your camp cooler when you stroll out of the tent, saying to the children, "See, Daddy isn't afraid. He knows it is just a little chip—!"

Yip-yip-yip-Owoooooo!—The haunting, melodic call of coyotes singing to each other in the hills. Also, the spine-tingling cry of a camper trying to pound in a tent peg with a rock.

Camping manuals—Books filled with ingenious camping tips which are forgotten the instant the camper sets foot in the field. "I read about a way to cook a chicken with a camera lens and a wire clothes hanger, but I can't remember how," he says. "Better just fry it."

Wire clothes hangers—The most useful camping tools ever invented. May be used for roasting meat over a fire, holding cooking pots, lashing tent poles together, and many other services. Once, I even saw a camper hang his clothes on one.

S'Mores—Child's standard camping dessert, consisting of chocolate bars and toasted marshmallows sandwiched between graham crackers. Have been known to cause child to become semipermanently attached to his clothes, sleeping bag, pine needles, and anything else he comes in contact with. Although a child may consume half a dozen S'Mores, two are considered a lethal dose for adults.

Unimproved Forest Service Campground—A designation on Forest Service maps to indicate a small swamp used for experimental breeding of killer mosquitoes.

New binoculars—What one of your children vaguely remembers having last seen when he set them on a log during a rest stop earlier in the day. *New camera* may be substituted for *new binoculars*.

"What do you mean, get up? It's still dark out!"—What your youngest child says upon awakening upside down in his sleeping bag.

Pants pockets—Containers to which young campers eventually transfer the entire contents of their packs.

Suspenders—What the young camper needs to hold up his pants pockets. Not unusual for a kid's suspenders to shoot him out of camp when he dumps his pockets.

"When hell freezes over"—An expression used by wives and mothers to indicate the next time you'll get them to go on another camping trip.

"A nice hot bath"—An odd phrase that wives and mothers insert into every other sentence after the second day of a camping trip.

A toasted marshmallow—What a kid calls the flaming projectile he lobs at your lap from the end of a sharpened willow.

Call of the wild—Sound made by parents as they search the woods for a kid who is asleep in the back of the station wagon.

Downwind—Whichever side of the campfire you happen to be on.

Bicycle campers—Hearty individuals who walk about camp with a pained expression on their bodies.

Cowboy coffee—A beverage made by throwing a handful of coffee in boiling water, and which causes your legs to bow when you take a sip of it.

"Come and get it!"—Plea telephoned to tow truck company by camper who was dumb enough to back his car into an Unimproved Forest Service Campground.

A roasted wiener—What your wife says you look like after you have spent a July day hiking shirtless in shorts.

Squirrel—Guy in neighboring campsite who plays transistor radio at full volume most of the night.

Gorp—A mix of fruits and nuts. Also, a derogatory term applied to the rowdy group in the next campsite.

Eye-opener—Early-morning shot of cowboy coffee. Also, loud snuffling sound just outside the tent.

Woodcraft—Sneaky tactic used to fool your spouse into getting up and building the morning fire.

Last beer—The one you forgot you drank *before* you took the kids on a hike to the top of the mountain.

National Park Campground—What all the campers came here to get away from.

Bug bite—What the camper tries to avoid taking while he is eating outside in an Unimproved Forest Service Campground.

Grill—The questioning of a child who vaguely remembers having set your new binoculars on a log a few rest stops back.

Granny knot—What you feel like after spending a night sleeping with your spouse and three children in a pup tent.

"I'll hold my breath"—Childish threat made to keep from eating the special stew you've prepared for supper. Tell her if she doesn't eat it she'll be setting a bad example for the children.

Camp dump—The back seat of your car on the way home.

"Don't tell me it's over already"—Sarcasm used by wives and mothers at the termination of camping trips.

"Who's going to help me wash all this stuff and put it away?"—An indication that it's not over already.

The Big Match

The long-distance phone call from my nephew and fishing manager, Dr. Mike Gass, was typical of him—warm, witty, and with the charges reversed.

"Hey, Unc, I got a great match arranged for you," Mike shouted over the phone. "This guy is a top contender."

"Sounds good," I said. "Who is it?"

"Tuck Harry."

"Not *the* Tuck Harry," I gasped. "Listen, Mike, maybe you'd better call the match off. I've been slowing down a lot lately, and my reflexes aren't what they used to be. Tuck Harry may just be too good for me."

"Come on, Unc, don't try to kid me," Mike said jovially. "You haven't been beaten yet, have you?"

That was true. I had defended my title dozens of times against some of the top contenders in the sport and always emerged victorious. You see, I am the World

Champion of not-catching fish and not-shooting game. Oh, for recreation and relaxation, I will occasionally catch a fish or shoot a grouse or pheasant. Indeed, as a youngster I was never without a fishing rod or shotgun in hand, which was awkward at church and while taking baths, but otherwise a great way of life. My skill at hunting and fishing was surpassed only by an abundance of luck, and I had no trouble keeping the family table well supplied with fish and game.

Alas, tragedy brought to an abrupt end my carefree and happy life. At the tender age of twenty-five, I was struck down by the necessity of having to take a regular job. As a result of this catastrophe, my hunting and fishing were limited to weekends and sick leave, the latter so frequent that my boss would have fired me if he hadn't thought I was terminally ill and would be leaving soon anyway.

As the amount of time I could spend in the outdoors diminished, so did my skills and luck. My hunting and fishing friends began to feel sorry for me and took to arranging special little outings to their secret places.

"Listen," one of them would say, "I guarantee you will catch fish where I'm taking you." We'd go there and I wouldn't catch any fish. "All right," the fellow would say. "Now I mean business. I'm taking you to a spot I've never even told anybody else about. You must swear never to tell where you caught the fish." We'd go there and I wouldn't get a strike.

Hunting was no different. A pitying friend would tell me, "This time you're going to get your deer for certain. I've got this secret place staked out, with a deer practically tied to a tree for you. You won't be able to miss." And I wouldn't miss. I wouldn't even get to shoot.

At best, we'd find some stale tracks in the secret place, indicating that a deer had passed earlier in the century.

I concealed my disappointment over these failures by the ruse of gnashing my teeth and kicking trees. Reflecting upon the phenomenon, however, it occurred to me that not only didn't I catch fish or shoot game on the outings, neither did anyone in my party. I began to think that perhaps I had some peculiar psychic power that nullified the rhythms of the natural world. It was as though a magnetic field radiated out from me and affected even my companions. Unfortunately, my companions came to a similar conclusion. Soon I couldn't suggest a hunting or fishing trip to them without it conflicting with one of their "previous engagements" on that date, which was odd, since most of these guys usually didn't even know the months of the year. All they knew were the seasons—trout season, grouse season, deer season, etc.

It is the nature of the true sportsman, however, to seek out a challenge. If the taking of fish or game becomes too easy, he soon tires of it, and begins looking for ways to make the sport more difficult for himself and to improve the odds for the quarry. The angler, for example, will go from hooks baited with worms to wet flies to dry flies so tiny that they look as if they've been tied under an electronic microscope. His fly rods will become increasingly lighter until they are all but invisible. I've seen fly fishers using rods so light I didn't know if they were casting or trying to catch gnats in the air with their bare hand. My friend Orvis Fenwick once made half a dozen casts before he realized he hadn't picked up his rod.

Thus it was that the master hunters and anglers in

our area began to look upon me as the ultimate challenge. "Catching any fish lately?" one of these master sportsmen would be asked. "No, I haven't had a strike all summer," would come the answer. "But I fish exclusively with McManus, you know." An expression of awe would come over the questioner's face. "Gee," he would say admiringly. "I would like to work up to that some day."

Eventually, word spread about my prowess at not-catching fish and not-shooting game, and fishing and hunting guides from around the country began sending me invitations to go a few rounds with them. They knew that if they could induce me to catch fish or shoot game, their reputations would be made. I skunked them all. Some of them even gave up halfway through the bout, complaining of stomach cramps.

So many invitations were arriving, I finally asked my nephew Mike to become my manager, and to take over the business of arranging matches.

"I've got a great idea," he told me. "How about this? You start out by catching a few fish, see, and then we make a bet with the guide that you won't catch any more fish. We'll clean up!"

"Sounds good to me," I said. "But how do I catch the first few fish?"

"Yeah, I suppose that might be a problem, given your past record."

We decided to scrap the idea of my becoming a not-catching-fish hustler.

Even so, I have been banned from several states. When I went hunting in Montana a few years ago, no one in the state got so much as a shot the ten days I was there. It was an outstanding display of power on my part, but now the only way I can get into Montana during the hunting season is by wearing my Truman Capote disguise. This explains why several Montanans have reported seeing Capote gnash his teeth and kick trees because he missed an elk—missed it by at least three weeks, if the condition of the tracks was any sort of indication.

Members of outdoor clubs in Idaho take turns patrolling the borders in an effort to keep me out of the state, but I can usually manage to elude them. To punish them, I frequently extend my stay in the state well after I've become bored with not-catching fish and not-shooting game.

Steelheaders in Oregon, I understand, have put a bounty on me, and will pay it to anyone who brings in my license and steelhead card. This seems a bit extreme, since I shut off the fishing in Oregon only a dozen or so times a year. Furthermore, I have it on reliable testimony that the instant I leave the state, the steelheading becomes fantastic and remains so for some weeks afterward.

But now I was worried about the match that Mike had arranged for me with Tuck Harry. Tuck is a young fishing guide who works the rivers of western Washington state. He has built up a formidable reputation for helping his clients connect with steelhead. He would be tough to beat. Still, I had left some of the best and toughest fishing guides in the country sobbing into their bait buckets.

The reason I was worried is that, fishing alone the previous week, I had caught three nice trout. Naturally, I hadn't told anyone about the catch, except my wife, whom I revived by rubbing an ice cube on her forehead. Then there was the close call last summer, when I was stream fishing. A monstrous trout had made a pass at my Renegade, and I saved the day only by snapping the fly away from its jaws and integrating thirty feet of line with a thorn apple immediately to my rear. It had been close. I was haunted by the thought that maybe my luck was about to go good.

In the grim light of a cold and foggy dawn, Mike and I met Tuck Harry on the bank of a river, the name and location of which I was sworn not to divulge. The local steelheaders are more secretive than the Mafia. It is rumored that if one of the members reveals the fantastic fishing in the river to an outsider, one of the other steelheaders will grab him and kiss him on both cheeks. Strangely, this does not often prove fatal, although the victim will have recurring fits of nausea for the next five years.

I quickly sized up Tuck, as Mike and I watched him wrestle the drift boat from the trailer and, grunting and gasping, drag it to the river. We would have helped him, but long experience has taught me that this kind of exertion takes a lot out of a guide, particularly with Mike and me in the boat. Nevertheless, the young man retained an air of confidence and seemed in complete control of the situation. I found this disconcerting and began to wonder if I was not in over my head. As it turned out, I was in only up to my armpits, having inadvertently stepped backward out of the boat.

"Thatta way to go," Mike whispered to me as I changed into dry clothes. "That staggered Tuck, and it's only the first round!"

Tuck recovered quickly, however, and no sooner had we shoved off than he retaliated by drifting the boat through a wild stretch of whitewater. Cleverly, Mike and

I concealed our anxiety from the guide by reciting the Twenty-third Psalm in unison.

Tuck pulled up across from one of his secret holes and rigged me an outfit. "Keep your thumb lightly on the spool of the reel when you cast," he explained, since I had told him most of my experience in recent years had been with spinning rather than with bait-casting reels.

"That's it, you've nearly got it," Tuck said encouragingly, after my first attempted cast. "Now, let me get my knife and I'll have your thumb freed from that backlash in no time."

"Actually," I replied casually, "I'd just as soon you freed my elbow and left foot first, if you don't mind."

I soon mastered the bait-casting reel with a few practice casts. Then Tuck instructed me to cast up to the head of the hole, take up the slack quickly, and allow the sinker to bounce along the bottom of the river. "They're in there," he said of the steelhead. "You should get a strike."

His confidence in my hooking a steelhead was unnerving. I countered immediately by fastening hook, line, and sinker irretrievably to some rocks on the riverbed, a technique that proved so effective I repeated it a dozen times during the next hour. Then I switched to snagging limbs, logs, and curious livestock that watched us drift by. By noon, Tuck was on the ropes.

The fear that my luck might be turning good proved unfounded. In two days of drifting down the river from dawn to dark, I got not a single strike. Furthermore, neither did Mike nor Tuck. Nor did the hundred or so other steelheaders on the river. Some of the latter, recognizing me and knowing of my reputation, shook their fists and yelled at Tuck, "Get him out of here!" It was, if I do say so myself, one of my most inspired performances.

I felt sorry for Tuck, of course, since he had put up a fine scrap and shown good sportsmanship and didn't gnash his teeth and kick trees, as do some guides. That's why I was so happy to hear that, the day after I left, everyone in Tuck's boat took limits of steelhead, and the other steelheaders reported that it was the best day of fishing they had ever seen on the river. It's hard for me to control my elation over news like that.

**They Shoot Canoes,
Don't They?**

Also by Patrick F. McManus

Kid Camping from Aaaaiii! to Zip
A Fine and Pleasant Misery
Never Sniff a Gift Fish
The Grasshopper Trap
Rubber Legs and White Tail-Hairs

Patrick F. McManus

THEY SHOOT CANOES, DON'T THEY?

An Owl Book

NEW YORK

HENRY HOLT AND COMPANY

Published by Henry Holt and Company, Inc.,
115 West 18th Street, New York, New York 10011.
Published in Canada by Fitzhenry & Whiteside Limited,
195 Allstate Parkway, Markham, Ontario L3R 4T8.

Library of Congress Cataloging-in-Publication Data
McManus, Patrick F.
They shoot canoes, don't they?
1. Outdoor recreation — Anecdotes, facetiae,
satire, etc. 2. Camping — Anecdotes, facetiae,
satire, etc. 3. Fishing — Anecdotes, facetiae,
satire, etc. 4. Hunting — Anecdotes, facetiae,
satire, etc. I. Title.
GV191.6.M33   796.5'0207   80-24131
ISBN 0-8050-0165-4
ISBN 0-8050-0030-5 (An Owl book: pbk.)

Henry Holt books are available at special discounts
for bulk purchases for sales promotions, premiums,
fund-raising, or educational use. Special editions
or book excerpts can also be created to specification.

For details contact:
Special Sales Director
Henry Holt and Company, Inc.
115 West 18th Street
New York, New York 10011

First published in hardcover by Holt, Rinehart and Winston
in 1981.

First Owl Book Edition — 1982

Designer: Joy Chu
Printed in the United States of America
20 19

All stories in this book originally appeared in Field &
Stream *or its allied publications,* Field & Stream Deer
Hunting Annual *and* Field & Stream Fishing Annual,
with the exception of "Meanwhile Back at the B Western,"
which first appeared in Colt American Handgunning
Annual 1979, *Aqua-Field Publications, Inc.*

TO DARLENE

CONTENTS

They Shoot Canoes, Don't They?

All You Ever Wanted to Know About Live Bait but Were Afraid to Ask

☞ ☞ ☞Surprisingly, many anglers are ashamed to admit that they fish with live bait. You'll run into one of these so-called purists on a trout stream and ask him what he's using. He'll say, "A Number thirty-two Royal Coachman on a three-ounce leader." Then he'll get a bite, snap his line out of the water, and there will be a worm on his hook. "That's the problem with these tiny flies," he'll say. "You keep catching worms with them."

The truth is that live-bait fishing has a long and noble history. Live bait was totally unknown to the early cavemen, who had to make do with a rather limited assortment of dry flies, nymphs, and a few streamers. One day, whether out of exasperation or simple impatience, a caveman made a backcast with a gray hackle he had not bothered to remove from a sage hen. Instantly, it was taken by a brontosaurus. The caveman was elated by his discovery, even though it was several centuries before anyone learned how to take a brontosaurus off the hook.

The caveman reasoned that if you can catch a

1

brontosaurus with live bait, you can surely catch fish with it, and he immediately began conducting experiments. He tried live chickens, ducks, and geese, but he soon found these very undependable, particularly on casts that passed directly overhead.

When he was about to give up and go back to dry flies, the caveman decided to bait his hook with a worm. He cast out into a deep, dark pool and immediately received the surprise of his life. A five-hundred-pound wild boar charged out of the brush and chased him for eighteen miles, and he never did learn whether worms were good bait.

Thus the discovery of worms as fishing bait was left to a humble cook in the army of Genghis Khan. After a busy day of conquering the Civilized World, the Khan decided he would like fish for supper and dropped a casual hint to one of his lieutenants. The lieutenant, who had had considerable experience with the Khan's casual hints, nearly trampled three foot soldiers getting the news into the kitchen. Dismounting, he said to the cooks, "Guess what? Old G.K. wants fish for supper." Since fishing had been extremely poor and no one had had so much as a nibble in days, the kitchen staff immediately bought tickets and caught the first stage out of town, the single exception being a little hors d'oeuvre specialist, Leroy Swartz, who knew absolutely nothing about fishing. Leroy had never developed the knack for plundering and pillaging—though he wasn't bad at razing—and as a result his total loot for the campaign was a spade with a broken handle. For a reason known only to Leroy, he started digging up the ground with the spade. The lieutenant, assuming he was digging a grave, said, "If we can't get G.K. any fish for his supper, you might as well make that big enough for two." Then Leroy started picking up worms and stuffing them into his pocket, tomato cans not yet having been invented. He grabbed a fishing pole and went off to the nearest river, from whence he shortly returned with his limit, in those days as many as you could carry plus one fish. Everyone danced and shouted over Leroy's discovery that worms were excellent fishing bait. Even the Khan was beside himself with joy, a condition that caused Mrs. Khan considerable annoyance since they slept in the same bed. Leroy Swartz was henceforth known as the Father of Worms, a title he did not much care for, but it beat employment as a battering ram on the next fortress to be attacked.

Toward the latter part of the eighteenth century, grasshoppers were discovered to be exceptional live bait. Up until then they were thought to be good only for devouring grain crops and causing widespread famine. One day an angler was walking along a country road in search of a good place to dig a supply of worms. He happened to glance out into a field fairly alive with grasshoppers and noticed a man leaping about on all fours and slapping the ground with his hat. The angler thought the fellow must be crazy to behave in such a strange manner and walked over to see what he was up to. It turned out the man *was* crazy, but the angler didn't discover this until he had helped him catch a dozen grasshoppers. Since by then it was too late to dig any worms, the angler decided to bait his hook with grasshoppers—and the rest is history.

Up until the Industrial Revolution and the invention of tomato cans and the flat tobacco can, there were no suitable containers for live bait, and anglers had to carry their bait around in their hands, pockets, and hats. In the case of grasshoppers, wealthy fishermen would sometimes hire a boy to drive a herd of them along the bank. In later years worms were carried in pokes similar to those used for gold coins. There is at least one recorded instance in which a card-playing fisherman narrowly escaped lynching when he attempted to bluff with a poke of nightcrawlers.

So much for the history of live bait. We will now examine some of the various kinds of live bait, where to find it, how to preserve it, and assorted techniques for using it.

First off, there are only two kinds of bait: live bait and dead bait. Worms, grubs, grasshoppers, minnows, and the like are live bait, unless left unattended in a hot car too long, in which case they become dead bait. I have on occasion forgotten to remove a can of worms from my car on a blistering July day, a mistake that has led to attempts to bait hooks with little balls of worm paste, not to mention the necessity of driving with all the car's windows open until approximately the middle of February. On the other hand, I've carried around salmon eggs and pickled pork rind until they were showing definite signs of life.

My favorite method of preserving live bait is to store it in the refrigerator until it is ready for use. There are two schools of thought on the proper execution of this procedure. Some hold it is better to tell your wife first, and the others claim it is better to let her make the discovery for herself. I'm a member of the latter group and have been ever since my wife came across a jar of my hellgrammites while she was sorting through the refrigerator in search of some mayonnaise. The incident would probably have passed without any lingering ill effects had she not at the time been entertaining her church bridge club. It is difficult to describe the resulting commotion with any accuracy, but I learned later that cards from our bridge deck were found as far away as three blocks and one of the olive-and-avocado sandwiches served at the party turned up in a ladies' restroom halfway across town. Our dog was asleep on the front sidewalk when the ladies left, and it was weeks before we could get all the dents out of him left by their heels.

I have on occasion attempted to lay in a supply of worms during the spring months while they are still near the surface and one doesn't have to dig down to the aquifer to find them. I'll stash a couple of hundred of them in a washtub filled with dirt and feed them coffee grounds. The reason I feed them coffee grounds is that numerous people have told me that that is what worms like to eat. Whether they do or not, I'm not sure. In any case, I've yet to find a single worm when I dump out the tub later in the summer. I'm beginning to suspect that worms can't stand coffee grounds (or maybe coffee grounds like worms). When you stop to think about it, where would your average worm develop a taste for coffee anyway?

The beginning angler is often of the impression that there are only three kinds of worms: small, medium, and large. Actually, the size of the worm makes little difference. Temperament and character are everything. These two characteristics seem to be determined primarily by environment. For example, I've never found a worm raised in a manure pile who could earn his keep as fishing bait. Manure-pile worms are soft and pale and accustomed to easy living. To a worm, a manure pile is a suite in the Ritz, a villa on the Riviera. He never has to worry about where his next meal is coming from. (If he knew, he would probably worry, but he doesn't know.) Manure-pile worms don't have any street savvy. Now, you dig up a worm out of a garden, an individual who has been through a couple of rototillings, and that worm has been around. He's going to go out and put up a good fight. Nothing builds character in a worm like a good rototilling.

Some time ago a sporting-goods company sent me a package of freeze-dried worms. Honest. At first I thought it was some kind of veiled threat, but then I found a note saying that if I soaked the worms in water they would reconstitute into fishing bait. I stuck the package in my backpack with my other freeze-drieds and a couple of nights later at a mountain lake took it out and soaked the contents in some water. It turned out to be macaroni and cheese sauce. "That's funny," my friend Retch Sweeney said. "I thought we ate the macaroni and cheese sauce last night." The freeze-dried worms never did turn up.

The most troublesome of all live bait is the grasshopper. By the time you've caught enough of them you're usually too tired to go fishing. Furthermore, grasshoppers are not content simply to sit around in a bottle waiting to be fed to some fish. Once a worm is in the can, he pretty well knows his fate is sealed and will lie back and take it easy until his number comes up. Not so with grasshoppers. They are no sooner in the bottle than they're plotting their escape. Every time the lid is lifted to insert a new inmate, half a dozen of the others will try to make a break for it. While I was still a young boy, I learned that the only way to foil their escapes was to shake the bottle vigorously and then slip the new grasshopper in while the others were still dazed. What apparently happens is that the grasshoppers get high from the shaking and like it so much that after a while you can hardly chase them out of the bottle with a stick. They just lie on their backs, smiling. Of course this is confusing to the new grasshopper, who thinks he has been incarcerated with a bunch of degenerate insects who keep calling out, "C'mon, man, give us another shake!"

To my mind, the best live bait is the hellgrammite, an

insect that resides on streambeds and builds little cocoons for itself out of pebbles. Fish cannot resist them, in their shells or out. They are the salted peanuts of baits. Not long ago I was fishing a stream in Idaho and hadn't had a nibble all day. Then I discovered a nice patch of hellgrammites and within a half an hour had nearly filled my limit with plump cutthroat. There were a dozen or so other anglers on the stream, and they were so astonished at my success that they could not help expressing their awe by jovially threatening to slash my waders the next time I was in deep water. Finally, after I had creeled my final catch, a couple of them came over and demanded to know what I was using.

"These," I said.

"Jeez, those are ugly-looking things!" one of them said. "I almost hate to touch them."

"Trout love 'em," I said. "Here, take a couple of mine just to try them out." I thought it was the very least I could do.

As I was climbing into my car, I heard one of the other fishermen yell, "What was he using?"

"These nasty-looking things," the first fellow yelled back. "Big, red, white, and blue flies!"

I felt a little bad about the deception. On the other hand, you can never tell. There *could* be such a thing as patriotic fish.

The Green Box

☞ ☞ ☞ **T**he other day I came home and found my wife cleaning out the garage. She was covered from one end to the other with dirt and cobwebs. Beads of sweat were dripping off the tip of her nose as she came staggering out of the garage carrying a huge green box in the general direction of the garbage cans.

"You shouldn't be doing that," I scolded.

"I shouldn't?" she said, putting the box down and massaging the small of her back with both hands.

"No, you shouldn't," I said. "I'm saving the stuff in that box. Now you carry it right back to where you found it."

I could tell I had hurt her feelings, partly because her eyes got all teary and her mouth formed into this cute little pout, but mostly because of the way she sprang forward and tried to crush my instep with her sneakers. After she had calmed down a bit, I explained to her that the box she was attempting to commit to oblivion was filled with priceless relics of my sporting youth.

"You must be thinking of some other box," she said. "I checked, and this one is just filled with a bunch of old junk."

"Ha!" I exclaimed, thrusting my hand into the box and withdrawing an artifact at random. "And just what do you call this?"

"Junk," she said.

"Well, it just so happens that this little metal band is a 1950 deer tag. This is the tag of my very first deer."

"You shot your first deer in 1950?"

"No, my very first deer got away that year, but this was its tag."

The deer tag tripped the hair trigger of my reminiscence mechanism, and suddenly the last hour of daylight was flitting away on the last day of deer season, 1950. I was crouched behind a log at the edge of an abandoned apple orchard on the side of a mountain. A quarter of a mile away, my very first deer and several others were meandering down a brushy slope in the general direction of the orchard. My hope was that they would step out into the orchard while there was still light enough to shoot. The only sounds were those of my own nervous breathing and Olga Bonemarrow's impatient popping of gum in my ear.

"Jeez, I'm freezing," Olga said in a nasty tone. "I don't know why I ever let you talk me into this."

"Shhhh!" I said. I slipped out of my mackinaw and told her to put it on over her own coat, which she did. I myself was wondering why I had talked Olga into coming along. As a matter of fact, I hadn't had to talk that much. Olga had stopped by my place just as I was getting ready to go hunting. All I had said to her was, "Hey, Olga, how'd you like to take a little ride up into the mountains with me?"

She had given me a long look. "What for?"

I smiled mischievously, an expression I had been attempting to perfect in front of my bedroom mirror for the past few days. "You'll find out," I said. "It's something you ain't never done before."

"I wouldn't bet on it," Olga said. "But okay."

It turned out that this was indeed Olga's first experience with hunting. She tried her best to conceal her surprise under a veneer of rage. Despite my best efforts to keep her quiet as we waited for my first deer to step into the orchard, she continued to growl and complain and whine, her hands thrust deep into the pockets of my mackinaw. In the thicket on the far side of the orchard, my straining eyes picked up a movement. Then a buck stepped halfway out of the brush and ran an inventory on the orchard. This was it. Tensely, I slipped the safety off my Marlin .32 Special.

"Hey," Olga said suddenly. "How do you unlock this dumb cheap bracelet?"

I looked at her in horror. Snapped shut around her wrist was my deer tag!

I stood up, slipped the rifle safety back on, and jacked out the shells. My first deer vanished in a single bound.

"How come your eyes are watering?" Olga said.

" 'Cause I'm cold," I said. "Give me back my mackinaw."

The sound of my wife's voice snapped me back to the present. "I don't know what's so great about an old deer tag," she said. "Look, it's even been snipped in two. Why would you lock it and then snip it in two if you never used it?"

There are certain things the female mind is incapable of fathoming, so I ignored the question. Rummaging around in the box, I found the first dry fly I ever tied and held it up for my wife to view. She screeched and jumped back.

"It's just a dry fly," I told her.

"Thank heavens!" she said. "I thought the cat had killed another bird."

"So, you're interested in birds, are you?" I said, pulling from the box one of my most prized treasures. "This is the first grouse I ever shot. I mounted it myself."

"Why, that's just some feathers glued on a board."

"Actually," I explained, "I was a little close to the grouse when I shot. That's all that was left. Anyway, I *think* that's all that was left."

It happened like this. I had pursued the grouse into a swamp near my home and had just stepped over a deep drainage ditch, my old double-barreled 12-gauge at the ready, when I spotted the grouse on a limb a scant twenty feet away. He spotted me too, revved his engine, and took off. I pointed the shotgun and fired, thereby learning once and for all the valuable lesson of having the butt of the stock pressed firmly against one's shoulder, not six inches away from it, at the moment one squeezes the trigger. Even so, I probably would have survived the impact a good deal better had not both barrels fired simultaneously. Upon regaining my senses, I immediately assumed I would spend the rest of my life with my right shoulder wrapped around my back in approximately the shape of a taco shell. What really scared me though was that I was cold all over, my vision was blurred, and I couldn't breathe. Then I realized that I was a five-foot-eight person standing in a six-foot-deep drainage ditch filled with green slime. I scrambled out of the drain ditch with the alacrity of a person who has a profound dread of green slime, and went in immediate pursuit of the grouse. A few feathers were still drifting in the air, but there was no other sign of the grouse. "I couldn't have missed at that range?" I mumbled, scarcely able to bring myself to accept the obvious. It was almost too sad even to think about. *I had vaporized my first grouse.* Glumly, I picked up as many feathers as I could find, took them home, and glued them on a board, printing neatly underneath them with lead pencil the words MY FIRST GROUSE, 1948.

"Maybe you just plain outright missed the grouse," my wife said. "Did you ever consider that possibility?"

"No, I would never consider that possibility," I informed her. "Anyhow, if I missed, it wouldn't have been my first grouse, would it? How do you explain that?"

While she was still struggling with this flawless bit of logic I extracted another relic from the green box. "Now this lovely piece of material is what remains of what once was one of my finest fishing hats. I called it my lucky hat."

"Looks like an old grease rag to me," my wife said.

"That's just because you don't have any true sense of aesthetics and . . . uh . . . say, this *is* a grease rag! How'd it get mixed in with these valuables? I bet I had you fooled when I let on like it was my lucky hat. Heh, heh."

"Heh, heh," she said without enthusiasm.

The next item extracted from the green box evoked a memory of high school. It was a moldy plug of tobacco, with one sizable chaw taken from a single corner.

In the days of my youth I spent a great deal of time in the company of an old woodsman by the name of Rancid Crabtree. He was my idol. More than anything I wanted to be like Rancid, a man who owned himself, who spent his life roaming the woods, hunting and fishing and trapping, almost always enjoying himself. I tried to emulate him in every way, and even went so far one time as to try a chaw of tobacco.

On that memorable occasion, some of the guys and I

were discussing deer-hunting tactics in the back of the classroom while we waited for the teacher, Mrs. Axelrod, to come in and start haranguing us about the French Revolution, as if it had been our fault. I casually hauled out my plug of tobacco, took a good healthy chaw, then stuffed the plug back in my pocket. Not one of the guys so much as blinked, but I could tell they were impressed. At that moment Mrs. Axelrod sailed into the room and ordered us to our seats. Since she didn't even allow gum chewing in class, I decided I had better get rid of the tobacco fast. So I swallowed it.

A few minutes later, it became apparent to me that one does not actually get rid of a chaw of tobacco by swallowing it. The chaw, in fact, was traveling up and down my esophagus like a yo-yo on a short string, and was giving every indication that it was about to reenter society at any moment.

"Now, who can tell us the underlying causes of the French Revolution?" Mrs. Axelrod asked. She looked at me. "Pat."

I pointed a questioning finger to my chest, hoping to delay answering until the chaw was on the downstroke.

"Yes, you, the green person with the bloated cheeks!" Mrs. Axelrod snapped.

One second later I departed the room in a manner I hoped was not totally without dignity but which was later described to me by Peewee Thompson as a "sort of greenish blur."

Peering into the green box, I could scarcely refrain from emitting a shout of joy. There, nestled among such collector's items as gopher traps, a single warped bear-paw snowshoe, a rusty machete, a jungle hammock, a collection of spent cartridges, a collection of dried toads, a perforated canteen, a casting reel encased in a permanent backlash, a dog harness made out of nylon stockings, and other rare and priceless mementos of my sporting youth, was without doubt what had to be the world's most powerful hand-held slingshot. I had thought the slingshot lost to posterity.

The slingshot had been designed and built by me at about age ten. I describe it as hand-held because later I also had built a more powerful slingshot, one that consisted of two live trees and a series of bicycle inner tubes. That slingshot almost earned the distinction of putting the first human into orbit, a kid by the name of Henry, who, when a gang of us stretched the inner tubes back to the limit of our combined strength, failed to hear the order "Fire!" Henry reported later that the lift-off actually had been a lot of fun, but he had run into difficulty at the termination of reentry.

The fork of the world's most powerful hand-held slingshot consisted of a Y-shaped section of trunk from a birch tree that I hacked down with my machete. The bands were made of strips cut from a tractor inner tube. These strips were then woven together in such a manner as to greatly increase their firing power. The pouch consisted of a tongue cut from a leather boot. Whomper, as I called the slingshot, was a magnificent and awesome instrument. Originally, my intention in building Whomper had been to hunt elk with it. I was disappointed to discover upon its completion, however, that, strain as I might, I could no more stretch the bands than if they had been made of cast iron. I considered this only a minor defect, however, and took to carrying Whomper about with me in a special holster attached to the back of my belt. I also carried a regular slingshot for utilitarian and sporting purposes. It was this combination of elastic armaments that resulted in one of my more satisfying experiences as a youngster.

My old woodsman friend Rancid Crabtree had taken me to the Loggers Picnic, an annual event in which the loggers competed in eating, drinking, and feats of strength. Rancid said he figured he could hold his own in two of the categories but that he was too old and feeble for feats of strength.

"Ah'll leave the feats of strangth to you," Rancid told me.

Actually, I figured I might do quite well in some of the events, but I was immediately sent to humiliating defeat in arm wrestling by the strapping offspring of a logger.

Rancid tried to console me. "Don't fret about it," he said. "Some of them girls is a lot stronger than they look. You'd a probly won iffin she'd been a boy."

No doubt my defeat by Mary Jane Railbender would have gone unnoticed by most of the picnickers had it not been for the presence of a large, loud, loathsome fellow by the name of Whitey. Whitey, though ten years older than myself, was one of my most despised enemies and passed up no opportunity to torment me.

"Har, har, har!" he roared. "Got beat by a little snip of a girl, did you? Har, har, har!" He then rushed to spread the news among the loggers and their kin, who, while they didn't exactly find the news of my downfall sidesplitting, seemed at least mildly amused. To me, that constituted excessive mirth at my expense, and I stalked off beyond the reach of their har, har's.

While I was drowning my sorrow in a bottle of orange crush, I happened to notice a flock of crows flying over. As was my practice in those days, I sprang to my feet, drew my regular slingshot to its full capacity, and let fly at them with a rock. I missed the crows by a quarter of a mile, but suddenly somebody yelled out, "Holy cow! Who threw that rock? That's one heck of a throw!"

"That was just Pat," somebody else said. "But he done it with a slingshot."

"A slingshot!" shouted out Whitey. "Pat's got a slingshot? Must be made out of wishbone and a rubberband if he can shoot it, anybody who lets himself get beat by a little girl in arm wrastlin'." Whitey took the little sounds of amusement from the other picnickers for encouragement. "Here, Shrimpy, toss me yore peashooter. I'll show you how a man does with a slingshot."

From deep inside me I could feel this great, evil, hysterical laugh welling up, but I fought it back down. Calmly, with just the right touch of nonchalance, I reached behind me and drew Whomper from its holster. The big slingshot landed with a solid *chunk* at Whitey's feet. He stared down at it: the massive fork, the woven rubber bands thick as a man's wrist, the boot-tongue pouch, all of it bound together with wrappings of baling wire. Even from where I stood I could tell he was impressed.

"C'mon, Whitey," shouted Rancid from the crowd of spectators. "Show us how a man does with a slangshot!"

"All right, I will," said Whitey, and he scooped up the slingshot, fitted a stone the size of a walnut in the pouch, and hauled back. Well, it was a terrible spectacle to have to witness, and I've always felt a little remorseful that I enjoyed it so much. Up to the part where the buttons started popping off the front of Whitey's shirt and flying about like shrapnel, I thought Whitey might actually stretch the sling an inch or two. But by the time the women and little children were sent away because of the horrible sounds he was making, I knew there wasn't a chance.

At last, quivering with rage and exhaustion, Whitey threw the slingshot to the ground. "Ain't nobody can pull that thing," he gasped. For a second, I thought I detected a wave of sympathy, even admiration, flowing from the spectators toward Whitey.

Then Rancid stepped forward. "Shucks," he said. "Let a feeble old man give thet thang a try." He grabbed up Whomper, hauled back until the woven tractor-tube bands hummed like guitar strings. He then shot the rock out of sight. His face split in a big grin, Rancid handed Whomper back to me. The loggers laughed and applauded and slapped both me and Rancid on the back. I never again had any trouble from Whitey.

When we were driving home, Rancid still had the big grin on his face.

"What's so funny?" I asked him.

"Ain't nuthin' funny," he said through his teeth.

"How come you're grinning like that then?"

"Ah ain't grinnin'," he said. "Ah thank Ah ruptured maw face pullin' thet dang slangshot!"

My wife kicked the green box with one of her sneakers. "All right, all right, I won't throw this junk out if it means so much to you that you have to reminisce for twenty minutes over every piece of it."

"What?" I said. "No, of course you're not going to throw it out. I won't let you. Say, look at this! Look at the stuff in this jar. It's some of my old bear grease!"

"Oh, good heavens," she said. "Now I suppose you're going to tell me how you used to grease bears."

That really burned me up. Who would have thought she would guess the punch line of one of my best stories?

Skunk Dog

☞ ☞ ☞ **W**hen I was a kid, I used to beg my mother to get me a dog.

"You've got a dog," she would say.

"No, I mean a real dog," I'd reply.

"Why, you've got Strange, and he's a real dog, more or less."

Strange was mostly less. He had stopped by to cadge a free meal off of us one day and found the pickings so easy he decided to stay on. He lived with us for ten years, although, as my grandmother used to say, it seemed like centuries. In all those years, he displayed not a single socially redeeming quality. If dogs were films, he'd have been X-rated.

I recall one Sunday when my mother had invited the new parish priest to dinner. Our dining room table was situated in front of a large window overlooking the front yard. During the first course, Strange passed by the window not once but twice, walking on his front legs but dragging his rear over the grass. His mouth was split in an ear-to-ear grin of sublime relief, and possibly of pride, in his discovery of a new treatment for embarrassing itch.

"Well, Father," Mom said in a hasty effort at distraction, "and how do you like our little town by now?"

"Hunh?" the pastor said, a fork full of salad frozen in mid-stroke as he gaped out the window at the disgusting spectacle. "Pardon me, what were you saying?"

During the next course, Strange appeared outside the window with the remains of some creature that had met its end sometime prior to the previous winter, no doubt something he had saved for just such a formal occasion. As he licked his chops in pretense of preparing to consume the loathsome object, Mom shot me a look that said, *"Kill that dog!"* I stepped to the door fully intending to carry out the order, but Strange ran off, snickering under his breath.

"More chicken, Father?" Mom asked.

"Thank you, I think not," the priest said, running a finger around the inside of his Roman collar, as if experiencing some welling of the throat.

Fortunately, the dinner was only four courses in length, ending before Strange could stage his grand finale. A female collie, three dead rats, and the entrails of a sheep were left waiting in the wings.

Mom said later she didn't know whether Strange was just being more disgusting than usual that day or had something against organized religion. In any case, it was a long while before the priest came to dinner again, our invitations invariably conflicting with funerals, baptisms, or his self-imposed days of fasting.

Strange was the only dog I've ever known who could belch at will. It was his idea of high comedy. If my mother had some of her friends over for a game of pinochle, Strange would slip into the house and slouch over to the ladies. Then he would emit a loud belch. Apparently, he mistook shudders of revulsion for a form of applause, because he would sit there on his haunches, grinning modestly up at the group and preparing an encore. "Stop, stop!" he would snarl, as I dragged him back outdoors. "They love me! They'll die laughing at my other routine! It'll have them on the floor!" I will not speak here of his other routine.

In general appearance, Strange could easily have been mistaken for your average brown-and-white mongrel with floppy ears and a shaggy tail, except that depravity was written all over him. He looked as if he sold dirty postcards to support an opium habit. His eyes spoke of having known the depths of degeneracy, and approving of them.

Tramps were his favorite people. If a tramp stopped by for a free meal at our picnic table and to case the place, Strange would greet him warmly, exchange bits of news about underworld connections, and leak inside information about the household: "They ain't got any decent jewelry, but the silver's not bad and there's a good radio in the living room." The tramp would reach down and scratch the dog behind the ears as a gesture of appreciation, and Strange would belch for him. Face wrinkled in disgust, the tramp would then hoist his bedroll and depart the premises, no doubt concerned about the reliability of food given him by a family that kept such a dog.

My friends at school often debated the attributes of various breeds of dogs. "I tend to favor black labs," I'd say, going on to recite the various characteristics I had recently excerpted from a *Field & Stream* dog column. Somehow my classmates got the impression that I actually owned a black lab and had personally observed these characteristics. While I was aware of the mistaken impression, I didn't feel it was my business to go around refuting all the rumors that happened to get started.

Sooner or later, however, one of these friends would visit me at home. Strange would come out of his house and satisfy himself that the visitor wasn't a tramp in need of his counsel. That done, he would yawn, belch, gag, and return to his den of iniquity.

"That your uh dog?" the kid would ask.

"I guess so," I'd reply, embarrassed.

"Too bad," the kid would say. "I always thought you had a black lab."

"Naw, just him. But I'm planning on buying me a black lab pup first chance I get."

"I sure would," the kid would say, shaking his head.

As a hunting dog, Strange was a good deal worse than no dog. Nevertheless, he clearly thought of himself as a great hunting guide. "Fresh spoor," he would say, indicating a pine cone. "We can't be far behind him. And for gosh sakes shoot straight, because I judge from the sign he'll be in a bad mood!"

Chances of shooting any game at all with Strange along were nil. He had no concept of stealth. His standard hunting practice was to go through the woods shouting directions and advice to me and speculating loudly about the absence of game. I would have had more luck hunting with a rock band.

Strange did not believe in violence, except possibly in regard to chickens. He couldn't stand chickens. If a chicken walked by his house, Strange would rush out in a rage and tell the bird off and maybe even cuff it around a bit in the manner of early Bogart or Cagney. "You stupid chicken, don't ever let me catch you in dis neighborhood again, you hear?"

Some of our neighbors kept half-starved timber wolves for watchdogs. Occasionally one of these beasts would come loping warily through our yard and encounter Strange. Since Strange considered the whole world as his territory, he felt no particular obligation to defend this small portion of it. He would sit there, figuratively picking his teeth with a match, and stare insolently at the wolf, who was four times his size, its lip curled over glistening fangs, hackles raised, growls rumbling up from its belly. After a bit, the wolf would circle Strange, back away, and then lope on, occasionally casting a nervous glance back over its shoulder. "Punk!" Strange would mutter. Probably the reason none of these wolves ever attacked Strange was that they figured he was carrying a switchblade and maybe a blackjack.

Despite the peculiar passive side to his character, Strange did commit a single act of violence that was so terrible my mother actually considered selling the farm and moving us all to town. At the very least, she said, she was getting rid of Strange.

The episode began one warm spring evening when my grandmother sighted a skunk scurrying under our woodshed.

"He's probably the one that's been killing our chickens," Gram said. "I wouldn't be surprised but that he has his missus under there and they're planning a family. We'll be overrun with skunks!"

"Well, we'll just have to get him out from under the woodshed," Mom said. "Land sakes, a person can scarcely get a breath of fresh air in the backyard without smelling skunk. Maybe we should get Rancid Crabtree to come over and see what he can do about it."

"He'd certainly overpower the skunk smell," Gram said, "but I don't see that's any gain."

"What I mean is," Mom said, "maybe Rancid could trap the skunk or at least get it to leave. It's worth a try."

"I don't know," Gram said. "It just doesn't seem like a fair contest to me."

"Because Rancid uses guns and traps?" I asked.

"No, because the skunk has a brain!"

Gram and Rancid were not fond of each other.

The next day I was sent to tell Rancid we needed his expertise in extracting a skunk from under our woodshed. His face brightened at this news.

"Ha!" he said. "Thet ol' woman couldn't figure out how to git a skonk out from under yore shed, so fust thang she does is start yelling fer ol' Crabtree! If thet don't beat all!"

"Actually, it was Mom who told me to come get you," I said.

"Oh. Wall, in thet case, Ah'll come. Jist keep the ol' woman outta ma ha'r."

When we arrived, Gram was standing out by the woodshed banging on a pot with a steel spoon and whooping and hollering. The old woodsman nudged me in the ribs and winked. I could tell he was going to get off one of his "good ones."

"Would you mind practicin' your drummin' and singin' somewhar else?" Rancid said to her. "Me and the boy got to git a skonk out from under thet shed."

If Gram could have given the skunk the same look she fired at Rancid, the creature would have been stunned if not killed outright. The glare had no effect on Rancid, however, since he was bent over laughing and slapping his knee in appreciation of his good one. It was, in fact, one of the best good ones I'd ever heard him get off, but I didn't dare laugh.

"All right, Bob Hope," Gram snapped. "Let's see how you get the skunk out from under there. Maybe if you stood upwind of it, that would do the trick!"

"Don't rile me, ol' woman, don't rile me," Rancid said. "Now, boy, go fetch me some newspapers. Ah'm gonna smoke thet critter outta thar."

"And burn down the shed most likely," Gram said.

"Ha!" Rancid said. "You thank Ah don't know how to smoke a skonk out from under a shed?"

Fortunately, the well and a bucket were close at hand and we were able to douse the fire before it did any more damage than blackening one corner of the building.

During these proceedings, Strange had emerged from his house and sat looking on with an air of bemusement. There was nothing he loved better than a ruckus.

"Maybe we should just let the skunk be," Mom said.

"Land sakes, yes!" Gram shouted at Rancid. "Before you destroy the whole dang farm!"

Rancid snorted. "No skonk's ever bested me yet, and this ain't gonna be the fust!"

After each failed attempt to drive out the skunk, Rancid seemed to become angrier and more frenzied. Furiously, he dug a hole on one side of the shed. Then he jammed a long pole in through the hole and flailed wildly about with it. No luck. He went inside the shed and jumped up and down on the floor with his heavy boots. Still no skunk emerged. At one point, he tried to crawl under the shed, apparently with the idea of entering into hand-to-gland combat with the skunk, but the shed floor was too low to the ground. Then he grabbed up the pole and flailed it wildly under the floor again. Next he dropped the pole and yelled at me, "Go git another batch of newspapers!"

"No, no, no!" screamed Mom.

"Leave the poor skunk alone," Gram yelled. "I'm startin' to become fond of the little critter!"

Rancid stood there panting and mopping sweat from his forehead with his arm. "Ah know what Ah'll do, Ah'll set a trap fer him! Should of did thet in the fust place. No skonk is gonna . . ."

At that moment, the skunk, no doubt taking advantage of the calm, or perhaps frightened by it, ran out from under the shed and made for the nearby brush.

"Ah figured thet little trick would work," Rancid said, although no one else was quite sure which trick he was speaking of. "And this way, there ain't no big stank, which is how Ah planned it."

Then Strange tore into the skunk.

The battle was short but fierce, with the skunk expending its whole arsenal as Strange dragged it about the yard, up the porch and down, into the woodshed and out, and through the group of frantically dispersing spectators. At last, coming to his senses, the dog dropped the skunk and allowed it to stagger off into the bushes.

Strange seemed embarrassed by his first and only display of heroism. "I don't know what came over me," he said, shaking. "I've got nothing against skunks!" Still, I couldn't help but be proud of him.

The skunk was gone, but its essence lingered on. The air was stiff with the smell of skunk for weeks afterwards.

"That dog has got to go," Mom said. But, of course, Strange refused to go, and that was that.

It was years before Strange was entirely free of the skunk odor. Every time he got wet, the smell came back in potent force.

"Phew!" a new friend of mine would say. "That your dog?"

"Yeah," I'd say, proudly, "he's a skunk dog."

Cold Fish

☞ ☞ ☞ Show me a man who fishes in winter, and I'll show you a fanatic. Actually, I'll get the better of the deal, because for sheer spectacle a fanatic doesn't hold a candle to a man who fishes in winter.

I have often thought that if you could capture a half-dozen winter fishermen and put them in a circus sideshow you could make a fortune on them: "Step right this way ladies and gentlemen—no children please, we don't want to warp any young minds—and see the men who actually fish during the winter! They are amazing, they are absolutely astounding! Their skin is blue, their hair is blue, ladies and gentlemen, even their *language* is blue!"

Much as it pains me, I must confess that I too am a winter fisherman. It has been said that the first step toward recovering from this affliction is to admit that you are one, but I have been admitting it for years without noticeable effect. Actually, I take a certain pride in being a member of this select but compulsive group of hearty anglers. We even have a number of sayings: "No man is an icicle unto himself, but each a piece of the whole cube." And: "If one ice fisherman is defrosted, another will freeze to take his place." This goes to show that you can't expect memorable sayings from a bunch of demented fishermen.

Frequently I am asked why a man of my age and character persists in fishing right on through the most bitter months of winter. If I recall correctly, the exact wording of the question is: "Why does an old fool like you persist in going fishing in sub-zero weather?"

My answer is succinct and to the point. "Shut up and help me off with these *bleeping* boots. And be careful with my socks! I don't want my toes falling out and rolling under the chesterfield!"

There is a thin streak of sadism that runs through the directors of state fish and game departments. I have long suspected the requirements for fish and game directors include the following: "Must be outstanding citizens of their communities; must have demonstrated deep interest in outdoor sports and recreation; must have not less than three years experience as fiends."

How else explain their declaring certain waters open during the winter months? Indeed, I have no difficulty imagining the directors roaring with maniacal laughter as they debate the subject of which waters to open for winter fishing.

"Hey, fellows," says Milt Thumbscrew, "how about opening Lake Chill Factor during February?" He giggles wildly.

The other directors stomp their feet and pound on the table as they try to withdraw from fits of hysterical laughter.

"Oh dear, that's absolutely great!" says Adolf Wrinklebunn. "Can't you just see those poor devils up to their armpits in snow and ice, fighting their way to the lake!" He slides from his chair, shrieking.

"And they aren't even out of their cars yet!" screams the chairman. "Oh, stop, stop, you're killing me! Quick, somebody call for the vote!"

Now, even though I know that is basically how and why certain water is open for winter fishing, I find the enticement almost impossible to resist. Consider, if you will, a telephone conversation I had with my friend Retch Sweeney a while back.

"Speak up," I said. "The wind is howling so bad outside I can't hear you."

"I said," Retch shouted, "I tried to get through to you earlier, but the lines were down. I guess the ice got so heavy on them they broke. Anyway, I got this terrible urge to go fishing."

"Well, that's easily cured," I said. "Just go out in your backyard and stand in a bucket of ice water while your wife shovels snow down the back of your neck."

"I already tried that, but I still got the urge," Retch said.

"Have you talked to a psychiatrist?"

"As a matter of fact I did. I ran into Doc Portnoy over at the hospital. He was the one who told me about catching a five-pound rainbow up on the Frigid River. It's open in February, ya know."

"A five-pounder! Did he say what he caught it on?"

"Salmon eggs. That was all I could get out of him before the nurses rushed him into the furnace room in a last-ditch effort to thaw him out."

"I'll get my gear together and pick you up in half an hour," I said. Actually, it took me a bit longer than I had anticipated. I hadn't figured in the time it would take to stand in a bucket of ice water in the backyard while my wife shoveled snow down the back of my neck.

When I was a kid still in my single-digit years, I got my start in winter fishing under the tutelage of old Rancid Crabtree. Rancid was a man who believed in teaching a kid the basics.

"You know how to check fer thin ice, boy?" he would ask me. "Wall, what you do is stick one foot way out ahead of you and stomp the ice real hard and listen fer it to make a crackin' sound. Thar now, did you hear how the ice cracked whan Ah stomped it? Thet means it's too thin to hold a man's weight. Now pull me up out of hyar and we'll run back to shore and see if we kin built a fahr b'fore Ah freezes to death!"

Our usual practice was simply to hike out on the frozen surface of the lake or river, chop a hole in the ice, and try to catch some fish before either the hole or we froze over. One year, however, we built ourselves a luxurious fishing shack. It was made of scrap lumber, rusty tin, tarpaper, and other equally attractive materials. We put a tiny airtight heater inside with the stovepipe running out through the roof at a rakish angle. I always expected the stovepipe to set fire to the roof and was not often disappointed. Having the roof catch fire became so much a part of our fishing routine that Rancid would say to me, "Go put the fahr on the roof out, will ya? Ah thank Ah jist had a bite."

The truth is I was always glad for an excuse to step outside of the shack for a breath of fresh air. Rancid was a man who bathed only on leap years, and the previous leap year had escaped his notice. He smelled bad enough dry; wet, he could drive a lame badger out of its hole at forty yards. Sometimes in the warmth of the tiny shack he would actually begin to steam, and that was the worst. I'd sit there hoping the roof would catch fire so I'd have an excuse to step outside.

Sometimes when I knew I'd be cooped up in the

fishing shack with Rancid for several hours on the following day, I'd try to induce in him the desire to take a bath.

"You know what I like to do after a nasty chore like this," I'd tell him as we worked together at his place. "I like to climb into a nice hot tub of soapy water and soak and scrub and soak and scrub and soak and scrub. Doesn't that sound good?"

"Nope, it don't. Now watch what yore doin' thar! How many times I got to show you how to skin a skonk?"

Despite Rancid's aversion to bathing, the days we spent fishing together in the fish shack were among the best I've ever known. From the darkness of the shack you could peer through the hole in the ice clear down to the bottom of the lake and watch the fish move in to take the bait. And Rancid would tell me all the old stories over again, changing them just enough each time so that they always seemed fresh and new. He gave me little fishing tips, too. He said one good way to warm up bait maggots was to stick a pinch of them under your lower lip. I said I'd have to try that sometime when the need arose. After thirty years and more, the need has not yet arisen, but it's a good thing to know anyhow.

Another interesting thing he told me was about the time he went fishing in winter and it was so cold his line froze right in the middle of a cast. He said it was downright comical the way his line just stuck out in the air stiff as a wire from the end of his pole. He had to stand his line up against a tall snag and build a little fire near it. As the end close to the fire thawed out, the line just slid down the snag and formed itself into a nice little coil. Rancid knew all kinds of neat fishing lore like that.

The one problem with the fishing shack was that dragging it about the lake from one fishing site to another bore a striking resemblance to hard work.

Rancid said that he didn't have anything against hard work in principle and that if other folks wanted to indulge themselves in it that was all right with him and he certainly wouldn't hold it against them. He said that some folks were born with that flaw in their character and just couldn't help themselves. All a decent man could do, he said, was pretend that such folks were just as normal as anybody else and that they should never be looked down upon or ridiculed or in any way be made to feel inferior.

Rancid told me that what a normal man did when confronted with a task that bore a striking resemblance to hard work was to sit down and try to come up with an idea for avoiding it. That is exactly what Rancid did in regard to the fishing shack.

"Ah got a great idea," he said. "What we is gonna do is rig up a sail fer the fish shack! We'll let the wind blow the fish shack along the ice and we'll jist foller along behind and steer it whar ever we wants it to go."

In practically no time at all, Rancid had a tall, slender cedar pole bolted to the front end of the fish shack for a mast. A massive canvas tarp was converted swiftly into a sail. A confusion of booms, lines, and pulleys allowed the sail to be hauled up the mast, in which position its general appearance was not unlike some of the sails on the boats pictured in my geography book.

"Say, it looks just like a Chinese junk," I told Rancid, realizing at once that I had hurt his feelings.

"Ah don't care iffin it looks like a whole gol-durn Chinese dump," he snapped, "jist so it works."

Looking back through the corrective lens of time, I now realize that Rancid was one of those men who just can't let a good idea be but have to keep improving on it right up to the point where it turns into a catastrophe. I didn't know that back then, of course, and just assumed that what happened was one of those unavoidable mishaps that occurred with surprising regularity while I was in the company of Rancid.

Much to my surprise, the sail worked like a charm. The gentle breeze on the lake filled the billowing tarp and moved the little fish shack steadily if somewhat jerkily across the wind-burnished surface of the ice. We walked behind or alongside the shack, guiding the little vessel this way and that by pulling on various lines, much as one guides horses with a set of reins. Then Rancid came up with his improvement on the basic idea.

"Say," he said, "Ah got me a good notion to get inside the shack and jist ride along. Ah bet Ah kin steer it jist by pushing a stick along the ice through the hole in the floor. Iffin the critter gits to movin' too fast, Ah'll jist drag maw feet to slow it down."

The breeze had fallen off for the moment, so we made fast all the lines and Rancid climbed into the shack and made himself comfortable. Later Rancid was to accuse me of having dropped the spike through the latch on the outside of the door, thereby locking him inside; but if that was the case, the action was merely an absentminded reflex on my part and bore not the slightest hint of mischief. Besides, how was I to know that anytime he wanted out I wouldn't be there to pull the spike out of the latch?

I stood around outside the shack stomping my feet and rubbing my hands together, waiting for a breeze to come up and get us under way again. Every so often, Rancid would shout at me from inside the shack. "Any sign of wind out thar yet?"

"Nope," I'd reply. "It's pretty quiet." If I'd been more attuned to the weather, I would have known that the particular quiet we were experiencing was the kind known as "ominous."

I heard a distant rustling behind me. Turning, I observed a rather startling phenomenon. Clouds of snow were billowing up off the far side of the lake and moving in our direction.

"HOLY COW, RANCID, THE WIND . . . !"

"The wind's comin' up is she? Hot dang! Now yore gonna see . . ."

He never finished his sentence.

As soon as I got to my feet after being knocked down by the first blast of wind, I tried to track the fish shack as best I could. I felt I owed it to Rancid, since by then I had remembered dropping the spike through the latch. Rancid wasn't a person you wanted to have mad at you.

For a long ways, I could see the skid marks Rancid had made with his boots on the ice. After that I saw some scratches that looked like they had been made by two sets of fingernails. Then there were only the ski marks made by the sled and an occasional board or piece of tin from the fish shack. Over several long stretches, where the shack had become airborne, there were no signs at all.

After a while I came across two ice fishermen fighting against the wind on their way home. I asked them if they had seen Rancid go by in the fish shack. They said they had.

"I don't know what that durn fool will think of next," one of the men said, "but he was reachin' out a little winder with a hatchet, and it looked like he was tryin' to chop down the pole holdin' up that hay tarp. He went by so fast we couldn't rightly see what he was up to."

"Did you hear him say anything?" I asked.

"Nothin' I'd repeat to a boy your age," the man said.

A half-mile farther on, I ran into another fisherman. Before I could ask him anything, he said, "Land sakes, boy, you shouldn't be out alone in a blizzard like this! Why, I just saw some farmer's hay tarp fly by here.

Somehow it got hooked onto his outhouse and was draggin' it along too. Just tearin' that privy all to pieces. Strangest dang thing I ever seen! Anyway, come along with me and I'll give you a ride home."

I was about to refuse, when I glanced off across the lake and saw the figure of a tall, lean man striding purposefully in our direction through the clouds of driven snow. Even though he was downwind from me, I could tell it was Rancid. I could also tell he was carrying what looked like a piece of broken ski in one hand.

"I'll ride home with you on one condition," I told the fisherman. "And that is that you leave right now."

The Rifle

☞ ☞ ☞At least once a week from the fifth grade on, I made it a practice to stop by Clyde Fitch's Sport Shop after school. Clyde was always glad to see me, and we would josh each other.

"Hi, Clyde," I'd say as I came through the door.

"Don't handle the guns," Clyde would say.

"Yeah, there is a chill in the air," I'd respond. "Folks say it's gonna be an early winter."

"You got peanut butter on one of the twelve-gauges last time," he would retort. "I wish you'd find someplace else to eat your after-school snack."

I would nod appreciatively at Clyde's sharp wit and mark up a score for him in the air. Then, as he turned to wait on a customer, I would hear a soft sweet song beckoning me to the gun racks. It would be the rifles and shotguns singing to me:

"You drive me to distraction
When you work my lever action," sang a .30-30.

"When you give my stock a nuzzle,
You send chills down to my muzzle," trilled a .270.

"I lie awake nights

After you peer down my sights," moaned a .30-06.

I'll admit they weren't great lyricists, but they had nice voices and the melody was pleasant. Before I knew what was happening, a .30-06 would have leaped into my hands and I would be checking its action.

"DON'T TOUCH THE GUNS!" Clyde Fitch would yell, doing a fair impression of an enraged businessman.

"Good, Clyde, good," I would say as I set the rifle back in the rack and peered down at a sleek, inviting .300. Apparently displeased by my lack of enthusiasm for his performance, Clyde would rush over, grab me by the back of my coat collar and belt, and rush me out the door of his establishment. We kidded around with each other like that for about four years, occasionally working in new bits of dialogue but with Clyde always opening with his favorite line, "Don't touch the guns!" I suppose the reason he liked it so much was that it always got a laugh.

Just a few days short of eternity, my fourteenth birthday finally arrived. I had expected it to come bearing as a gift one .30-30 rifle, about which I had dropped approximately 30,000 hints to my family. No rifle! I could tell from the shapes of the packages. They were all shaped like school clothes. "Something seems to be missing here," I said, nervously ripping open a package of Jockey shorts. "You sure you didn't forget and leave one of my presents in the closet?"

"No," my mother said. "That's the whole kit and kaboodle of them right there."

"I was, uh, sort of expecting a, uh, thirty-thirty rifle."

"Oh," Mom said. "Well, if you want a rifle, you'll just have to get yourself a job and earn enough money to buy one."

It was not unusual in those days for parents to say brutal things like that to their children. There were no laws back then to prevent parents from saying no and, worse yet, meaning no. Life was hard for a kid. Still, I couldn't believe that my mother was actually suggesting that her only son go out and find a job.

"Surely you are jesting," I said to her.

"No," she replied.

Naturally, I had heard about work. My family was always talking about it within range of my hearing, and, as far as I could tell, seemed generally to be in favor of it. I didn't know why. Nothing I ever heard about work made it seem very appealing. My old friend Rancid Crabtree had told me that he had tried work once as a young man. He said that he was supposed to cut down trees for the man who had hired him, but when he picked up the ax and started to chop, his whole life passed before him. He gave up work then and there. He said that he knew some folks loved to work, and that was fine, but that he himself couldn't stand even to be near it. Of the two opinions about work, I favored Rancid's.

Still, if I wanted to hunt deer that coming fall, I would need a rifle. On the other hand, if I got a job, that would ruin my summer and leave me only mornings and evenings and weekends to fish. At best, I might be able to get in some more fishing on days I was too sick to work. I weighed my need for the rifle against a ruined summer and, after much long and painful thought, arrived at a distasteful decision: I would have to borrow a rifle.

Then, as now, people did not stand in line to loan out their rifles to beginning hunters, or to anyone else for that matter. Rancid Crabtree seemed to me to be the best prospect for the loan of a rifle.

"By the way, Rancid," I said to him casually one day, "how about loaning me your thirty-thirty for deer season this year."

Rancid's face erupted into that beautiful snaggletoothed grin of his. "Thet's a good-un," he said. "Make it up yersef or somebody tell it to you?"

"It's no joke," I said. "I need a deer rifle, and I don't see why you can't loan me your thirty-thirty."

"Wall, Ah would loan it to you except fer one thang," Rancid said. "An' thet is, Ah don't want to."

Rancid had only two defects to his character: He had never learned the art of mincing words, and you could never talk him into doing something he didn't want to do.

I shook my head in despair. "You're the only person I can think of, Rancid, who might loan me a rifle. I guess the only thing left for me to do is to get a job and earn some money."

"Now don't go talkin' like thet," Rancid said, as soon as he had recovered from the shock. "A young fella like you, got everthang to live fer, talkin' about gettin' a j-j-jo—throwin' away his life. No sar, Ah won't stand fer it! Now, hyar's what you do. You go ask the Inyun if you kin borry one of his rifles."

"Pinto Jack?"

"Why shore, ol' Pinto'd give you the hide offen his scrawny carcass iffin it had a zipper on it."

I found Pinto Jack puffing a pipe on the front porch of his cabin, and put my request straight to him.

Pinto Jack smiled only on rare occasions, and this was not one of them. "You want to borrow my rifle?" he said, studying me thoughtfully through a cloud of pipe smoke. "If I loaned you my rifle, what would I use when I raided the ranchers and burned their buildings and drove off their livestock, and like that?"

"Couldn't you use a bow and arrow for a few raids?" I said.

"You tell me, how am I going to drive my old truck and shoot a bow and arrow at the same time? No, I got to have my rifle for raiding the ranchers."

I looked crestfallen, having many years before learned that this was one of the best looks to use on Pinto Jack.

"Tell you what," he said after a moment. "I could maybe let you use the old rifle my father brought back from the Great War."

"First World?"

"Little Big Horn. It's a single-shot and kicks a bit, but you're welcome to it."

I rushed home lugging the monstrous firearm, pinned a target to a fence post backed by a sandbank, paced off a hundred yards, drew a bead on the target, and gently squeezed the trigger. Later I heard that all the livestock within a mile radius sprang two feet into the air and went darting about in all directions at that altitude. Apples rained down out of the trees in the orchards. Three lumberjacks swore off drink, and two atheists were converted to religion. My own interpretation of the event was that I had just been struck by lightning, a meteorite, or a bomb. When my vision cleared, I knew I was in trouble. Not only would my folks be upset about my shooting one of their fence posts in half, but the neighbors would be mad at me for destroying their sandbank. Nevertheless, I decided to try one more shot, this one left-handed. The second shot went off a little better, since by now I knew what to expect. It was easier for me to keep my nose out of the way, too, because the first shot had moved it up into the vacant area above my right eyebrow where it would be safe. By the time I had finished sighting in the rifle, I figured I'd be the only kid in the school talent show who could applaud behind his back with his shoulder blades.

My first deer managed to elude me that year. Even though I had opportunities for several good shots, by the time I had grimaced enough to pull the trigger, the deer was always gone. At the end of the season, I returned the rifle to Pinto Jack.

"Any luck?" he asked.

"Nope."

"Well, don't feel so bad about it," he said. "Come on in and have yourself an orange pop, and I'll show you how I can applaud with my shoulder blades. Bet you don't know anybody who can do that."

By the time the next summer rolled around, it had become apparent to me that the only way I was ever going to get a deer rifle was to earn the money for it. There was a dairy farmer by the name of Brown who lived nearby and whose reputation in the community was that of a kindly, if somewhat frugal, gentleman. Out of desperation for a deer rifle, I broke down and indentured myself to him at the rate of fifty cents an hour manufacturing postholes. Mr. Brown gave me the job after asking if I thought I could do a man's work. My ingenious reply was: "It depends on the man." The farmer said later that he supposed the particular man I had been referring to was an Egyptian mummy. For all his other drawbacks, Mr. Brown did not lack a sense of humor.

About his other drawbacks. It was only after going to work for him that I discovered that he wasn't a kindly gentleman at all but the former commandant of a slave-labor camp. Our mutual misfortune was that he had somehow missed the last boat to Brazil and had been forced to escape to Idaho, where he took up dairy farming as a cover.

"Vork, vork!" he would scream at me, slapping the leg of his bib overalls with a swagger stick. "Make die postholes, make die postholes, fahster, fahster!"

And I would streak about the landscape, trailing fresh-dug postholes. Sometimes, after glancing nervously around, I would step behind a tree to catch my breath. The farmer would drop out of the branches and screech at me: "Vot you do-ink? I not pay-ink you fifty zents an hour to breathe! Vork! Vork!"

At day's end, my mother would drive over to the farm to give me a ride home. She and the farmer would chat about my capacity for hard labor.

"I'm surprised you can get any work out of him at all," Mom would say.

The old farmer would laugh in his kindly way. "Actually, I have found him to be a bit slow, but he is doing better. Just today, while he was digging a posthole, I thought I detected some motion in one of his arms." Then he would give me a pat on my sagging, quivering back. "Off you go now, lad. See you bright and early in the morning!"

Odd, I thought. He seems to have lost his accent.

Bright and early the next morning the farmer would tell me: "Vork, vork, lazy Dummkopf! Make die postholes, fahster, fahster!"

At the end of the very hour in which I earned the last fifty cents I needed to buy the rifle, I resigned my position. When I told the farmer I was quitting, he tried to conceal his disappointment by leaping in the air and clicking his heels. There are few things, by the way, more disgusting than a dairy farmer clicking his heels in the air.

"I'll say this for you," he told me. "You have dug what I regard to be the most expensive postholes in the whole history of agriculture. If it was possible, I would gather them all up and put them in a bank vault rather than leave them scattered randomly about my property. Nevertheless, lad, should you ever find yourself in need of a job to buy yourself, say, a shotgun, why you just come to me. I'll be happy to recommend you as a worker to my neighbor, Fergussen, who, though I may say a harsh word about him now and again, is not a bad sort at all, particularly for a man who is stupid and greedy and probably a thief."

Naturally, I was flattered by this little farewell speech. I even changed my mind about his being a former commandant of a slave-labor camp. "Thanks," I told him, "but now that I've tried work and found it to be about what I expected, I think I'll avoid it in the future."

Mr. Brown said he thought that would be a good idea and that, as far as he had observed, I had consider-able talent for that line of endeavor and was practically assured of success.

The very next day, with the money for the rifle wadded up in a pocket of my jeans, I sauntered into Clyde Fitch's Sport Shop.

"Hi, Clyde," I said.

"Don't touch the guns!" Clyde shouted.

I took out my wad of money and began to unfold it.

"Seriously though, my boy," Clyde said, "I was just asking myself why ol' Pat hadn't been in lately to fondle the guns. Yes indeed. Now, good buddy, I'd be much obliged if you would try out the action on this new thirty-thirty and give me your expert opinion of it."

They Shoot Canoes, Don't They?

☞ ☞ ☞**A** while back my friend Retch Sweeney and I were hiking through a wilderness area and happened to come across these three guys who were pretending to cling to the side of a mountain as if their lives depended on it. They were dressed in funny little costumes and all tied together on a long rope. Their leader was pounding what looked like a big spike into a crack in the rock. We guessed right off what they were up to. They were obviously being initiated into a college fraternity, and this was part of the hazing. Not wishing to embarrass them any more than was absolutely necessary, Retch and I just let on as if everything was normal and that scarcely a day went by that we didn't see people in funny costumes hammering nails into rock.

"We seem to have taken a wrong turn back there a ways," I said to them. "Could you give us some idea where we are?"

The three pledgies seemed both angered and astonished at seeing us. "Why, this is the North Face of Mount

Terrible," the leader said. "We're making an assault on it. You shouldn't be up here!"

"You're telling me!" I said. "We're supposed to be on our way to Wild Rose Lake."

"Say, it's none of my business," Retch put in, "but this thing you're makin', don't you think you would get it built a lot faster if you found some level ground? It's pretty steep up here."

That didn't seem to set too well with them, or at least so I interpreted from their flared nostrils and narrowed eyes.

"Say, don't let a couple of flabby, middle-aged men disturb you," I said. "We'll just mosey on past you and climb up to the top of this hill and get out of your way. Maybe we can get a bearing on Wild Rose Lake from up there."

Well, I was glad they were all roped together and the rope was fastened to one of the spikes they had hammered into the rock. Otherwise, I think they would have taken off after us, and that slope was so steep you could just barely walk on it, let alone run. They would have caught us for sure.

"Those guys certainly weren't too friendly, were they?" Retch said later.

"No, they weren't," I said. "The very least they could have done was offer to give us a hand with the canoe."

Upon later reflection, I came to the conclusion that it was probably the canoe itself that had disturbed the pledgies. There are people who can't get within fifteen feet of a canoe without turning psychotic or, as my psychiatrist puts it, "going bananas."

I've been around canoes most of my life and have high regard for them. They're versatile and efficient and serve the angler and hunter well. But I have no truck with the sentimental nonsense often associated with them. Some years back I wrecked an old canoe of mine that I had spent hundreds of happy hours in. When I saw there was no way to salvage it, I tossed it on top of the car rack and hauled it out to the city dump. That was it. There was no sentimental nonsense involved. Just to show you some of the strange things that can happen, though, a few days later my wife went out to clean the garage and found the canoe back in its old place.

I had to laugh. "Well, I'll be darned," I said. "The old thing must have followed me home from the dump! Well, if it cares that much about me, I guess we'll let it stay."

After babbling sentimentality, the next most prevalent form of irrational behavior evoked by canoes is raw terror (occasionally there is boiled terror or even fried terror, but usually it's raw). Take my neighbor Al Finley, the city councilperson, for example. I figured that anyone so adept at floating bond issues as Finley certainly wouldn't have any trouble floating a canoe—a duck to water, so to speak. I've taught him most of the paddle strokes and he is quite proficient at them, but he has never gotten over his fear of canoes.

"Careful!" he screams. "It's tipping! It's tipping! Watch that rock! Careful!"

The way he acts is absolutely pathetic. I don't know what he'd do if we ever put the canoe in the water.

Some canoe-induced behavior is so odd you can't even put a name to it. Take the time I was canoeing up in Canada with Dork Simp, a chap who had been a staunch atheist for as long as I could remember. When we saw that we had made a mistake and had to shoot the Good God Almighty Rapids (named by the first trapper to take a raft of furs down the river), Dork yelled out that he had recently had some serious doubts about the intellectual validity of atheism.

"Forget philosophy, for pete's sake!" I screamed at him. "It's getting rough! Get off that seat and kneel down in the canoe!"

"Amen to that," he yelled back. "You say the words first and I'll try to follow along!"

We smacked into a rock and broke several ribs, two of which, incidentally, seemed to be mine. As we slid sideways off the rock, Dork shouted out that he had just found religion.

A few seconds later, as we were paddling up out of the vortex of a whirlpool, he swore off smoking, drinking, and profanity, the last of which cut his vocabulary by approximately half. When we were at last forcibly ejected from the lower end of the rapids, Dork said that he had decided to enter the ministry.

"It's been a lifelong ambition of mine," he added.

"What!" I said. "Why, not more than fifteen minutes ago you were an atheist."

"Was it only fifteen minutes?" he said. "I could have sworn it was a lifetime!"

The weirdest reaction to canoes that I've ever observed took place in Kelly's Bar & Grill. I had just walked in and mounted a barstool next to Doc Moos, owner and operator of Doc's Boat Works, where I had Zelda, my old wood-and-canvas canoe, in for repairs. Doc was chatting with a new bartender Kelly had hired, a great dull slab of a man but pleasant enough, or so he seemed at first.

"How's my Zelda doing, Doc?" I asked.

"I got bad news for you," Doc said. "I couldn't save her."

"Oh no!" I moaned. "I can't get along without her."

The bartender gave me a sympathetic look. "Gee, I'm sorry fella," he said. "Here, have a drink on Kelly."

I thanked him brusquely, not wanting him to mistake my concern about Zelda for maudlin sentimentality.

"What went wrong?" I asked Doc.

"Well, first of all, as you know, she was cracked and peeling all over, but that was no real problem since we could have put a new fiberglass skin on her. But . . ."

"You can do that now, can you, Doc, put on a fiberglass skin?" the bartender asked.

"Sure," Doc told him. "It's quite a bit of work and expensive, but it wears forever."

"I bet it does," the bartender said. "But how does it look?"

"Just like new," Doc said. "Paint it a nice glossy red or green and it'll knock your eye out."

The bartender looked astounded. "I would've thought pink," he said.

"Pink!" Doc and I both shuddered. The man was totally without taste.

"Anyway," Doc went on, doing his best to ignore the bartender, "some of her ribs were busted up pretty bad. I was going to work up some new ones out of some oak boards I got in the shop . . ."

"What won't they think of next!" the bartender said. "Wood ribs!"

"But as I was saying," Doc continued, shaking his head, "that was when we found the dry rot."

"Oh no, not dry rot!" I moaned.

"Gee, dry rot," the bartender said. "I think my brother got that once from not washin' between his toes."

"Well, it was fatal for Zelda," Doc said.

"Here, have another drink on Kelly," the bartender said.

Up to this time the bartender had seemed like a decent enough fellow, if only slightly smarter than a

grapefruit. Now he started to act a bit weird, particularly
after I had said something about how much I enjoyed
paddling Zelda, even when she was loaded down with all
my camping gear. Then Doc asked me what I wanted to
do with Zelda's remains. As I say, I'm not much on
sentimentality so I told him just to keep them around the
shop and use them for parts.

"It's about time I got myself a new one anyway," I
said.

"So much for grief, hunh, fella?" the bartender
snarled. "Beat the old thing, make her carry all your
campin' junk, and then forget her, just like that!" He
snapped his fingers so close to my face I jumped.

"What's with you?" I said. "All along I thought you
were a canoeist."

That was when he tossed Doc and me out of the bar.

"Call me a canoeist, will you!" he shouted from the
doorway. "Listen, fella, I may not be too smart, but I'm a
lot more normal than you!"

I suppose these strange attitudes toward canoes are
to be expected of persons who don't establish a meaningful relationship with them early in life. My own association with canoes began at age ten. That was when I built
my first one. Even if I do say so myself, it was one of the
most beautiful canoes I've ever seen.

I built it in a vacant upstairs bedroom out of some
old lumber I found in the hog pen. The lumber was dirty
and heavy, and I had great difficulty dragging it through
the house and up to the bedroom. Most of the difficulty
was caused by my mother and grandmother, who kept
making nasty remarks about my character and trying to
strike me with blunt objects.

It took me about three weeks to build the canoe. If
you've never built a canoe, you probably don't realize
that the hardest part is shaping the bow and stern just

right. I came up with an ingenious solution to this problem that, if it had caught on, would have revolutionized canoe design. I put square ends on it. There were a couple of other minor modifications that also simplified construction—the bottom and sides were flat! I painted it with some red barn paint as a final touch, and the end result was a sharp-looking canoe. Everyone else in my family thought so, too, except Gram. She said it looked like a coffin for someone's pet boa constrictor. Gram, of course, knew next to nothing about boat design.

The canoe's one drawback was that it weighed just slightly less than a Buick, and since I was the only man in the family, we had to ask the old woodsman Rancid Crabtree to come over and help us carry it out of the house.

As Rancid was walking up the stairs, he sniffed the air and asked, "You been keepin' hogs up here? Smells like . . ."

"Never mind what it smells like," Gram snapped. "Just help us carry that contraption out of the house."

Mom, Gram, and I got at one end of the canoe and Rancid at the other, and with a great deal of shouting and groaning managed to lift it until it was resting on our shoulders. We carried it out of the bedroom to the head of the stairs, at which point Rancid gasped that he couldn't hold up his end a second longer. While he was looking around frantically for something to rest the canoe on, he accidentally stepped down backwards onto the stairs. We at the rear end of the canoe naturally assumed from this gesture that he had changed his mind about resting, so we charged forward. It was just one of those innocent misunderstandings. As it turned out, no one was seriously injured, but some of the language would have made the hair of a wart hog stand on end. The only ill effect I suffered was psychological. As we all galloped around the sharp turn at the landing, I caught a glimpse of the expression on Rancid's face, and it just wasn't the sort of thing a ten-year-old boy should be allowed to see. For years afterwards, it would cause me to wake up whimpering in the night.

When Rancid came into the kitchen for coffee after the ordeal was over, he complained that he felt two feet shorter. Gram pointed out to him that he was walking on his knees. Rancid was always doing comical things like that.

Beautiful as it was, my first canoe was never launched but sat for years in the yard at the place where it was dropped. My mother later filled it with dirt and planted flowers in it. Strangers sometimes got the mistaken impression from it that we were holding a funeral for a tall, thin gangster.

The first store-bought canoe with which I had a meaningful relationship was hidden in some brush on the banks of a creek near where I lived. During the spring of the year, the creek was deep and fast with some nice rapids in it, but I had enough sense to realize that it would be dangerous for me to attempt to paddle the canoe down it. The main reason it would have been dangerous was that the big kid who owned the canoe had threatened to put me in a sack and toss the sack in the creek if he caught me messing around with it.

The big kid's name was Buster, and he divided his time among eating, sleeping, and beating up people, although not necessarily in that order. Sometimes he would catch me down by the creek and practice his beating-up techniques on me. Although these sessions were more monotonous than painful, they were sufficiently instructive to make me realize that I didn't want Buster performing real beating-up on me.

Nevertheless, I could not force myself to stay entirely

away from the canoe, a lovely little fifteen-footer, mostly green but with a patch of white on the side where Buster had attempted to paint over the words PROPERTY OF SUNSET RESORT. Once, I even slipped the canoe into the water just to see how it floated. It floated fine. After giving considerable thought to the questions (1) how much fun would it be to paddle the canoe around a bit, and (2) how difficult would it be to swim while confined in a sack, I slipped the canoe back into its hiding place and wiped off my fingerprints.

About a mile from my home, the creek wound through a swamp that was full of dead trees, rotting stumps, quicksand, mud flats, snakes, frogs, slime—all the usual neat swamp stuff. Brook trout the size of alligators were said to inhabit the deeper waters of the swamp, and I would occasionally pole my log raft into the dark interior in search of them. It was on one of these excursions that I happened to come upon Buster's canoe, bobbing gently among the cattails that surrounded a small, brush-covered island. My heart leaped up.

"Well, I'll be darned!" I said to myself. "Ol' Buster's canoe has somehow slid itself into the crick and drifted into the swamp. Won't he be tickled pink when I bring it back to him—in a day or two or the week after next at the latest?"

My elation, however, was diluted by a sense of foreboding, even though there wasn't a sign of human life in any direction. I eased myself silently into the canoe and set the raft adrift, just in case someone might get the notion of using it as a means of pursuing me.

That the canoe had somehow drifted upstream and tied itself to a branch with a length of clothesline and a square knot were matters of no little curiosity to me, and I remember making a mental note to ask my arithmetic teacher what the odds of such an occurrence might be.

As I was untying the square knot, I happened to glance out from among the cattails. What I saw momentarily freeze-dried my corpuscles. Strolling right toward me, arm-in-arm from out of the brush in the middle of the island, were Buster and a girl by the name of Alvira Holstein. Even as it was locked in the grip of terror, my fertile mind groped with the question of what the two of them could be doing on the island, Buster never having struck me as much of a picnicker On the other hand, the occasion didn't seem appropriate for casual conversation. I did take some comfort in the fact that Buster did not appear to have a sack with him.

Upon seeing me crouched in his canoe, Buster let out a roar that is best described as approximating that of a grizzly bear having a bicuspid extracted without benefit of anesthetic. I had never paddled a canoe before, but at that instant, such was the inspiration of seeing Buster charging toward me, I instantly discovered that I had a talent for it bordering on genius. Within seconds I had the canoe moving at sufficient momentum to plane easily over half-submerged logs, mud flats, and flocks of waterfowl caught unawares. I looked back once, and Buster was still in hot pursuit, even though he was up to his armpits in swamp slime. He was screeching almost incoherently, something to the effect that he would make sweeping but imaginative alterations on my anatomy once he laid hands on it. Alvira Holstein was jumping up and down on the island, crying and screaming, and yelling out, "Don't kill him, Buster, don't kill him!" Even to this day it sets my nerves on edge to hear a woman yell something like that.

I paddled the canoe halfway to my house, which was remarkable only in that the water ended some distance short of that. My grandmother was in the kitchen when I burst through the door.

"Land sakes, what's after you?" she said.

"Never mind that now," I said. "Just tell me this. Is there really quicksand in the swamp?"

"There certainly is," she said. "And you just stay out of that swamp if you don't want to get swallowed up by it!"

I crossed my fingers. "Come on, *quicksand!*" I said.

Actually, it was Gram who finally saved me from the sack or, at best, going through life as a very odd-looking person. When she found out Buster was after me, she just scoffed.

"Buster ain't going to hurt you," she said, neglecting to mention why I should be an exception to the rule. "If he does, you just tell the sheriff on him. The sheriff's a tough man, and he don't stand for no nonsense."

"Yeah, he's tough all right," I said, pulling back the window curtain an inch to peer out. "But he don't bother about kids' fightin'. He says it's just natural."

"Oh, I don't know," Gram said. "Sheriff Holstein's a pretty sensible man, and I think if you just told him . . ."

"Holstein?" I said. "That's right, it *is* Sheriff Holstein, isn't it?" I walked away from the window, cut myself a slab of fresh-baked bread, and smeared on a layer of raspberry jam.

"Well, forget about Buster, Gram," I told her. "I got to go paddle my canoe."

My First Deer,
and Welcome to It

☞ ☞ ☞ **F**or a first deer, there is no habitat so lush and fine as a hunter's memory. Three decades and more of observation have convinced me that a first deer not only lives on in the memory of a hunter but thrives there, increasing in points and pounds with each passing year until at last it reaches full maturity, which is to say, big enough to shade a team of Belgian draft horses in its shadow at high noon. It is a remarkable phenomenon and worthy of study.

Consider the case of my friend Retch Sweeney and his first deer. I was with him when he shot the deer, and though my first impression was that Retch had killed a large jackrabbit, closer examination revealed it to be a little spike buck. We were both only fourteen at the time and quivering with excitement over Retch's good fortune in getting his first deer. Still, there was no question in either of our minds that what he had bagged was a spike buck, one slightly larger than a bread box.

You can imagine my surprise when, scarcely a month later, I overheard Retch telling some friends that his first deer was a nice four-point buck. I mentioned to Retch afterwards that I was amazed at how fast his deer was growing. He said he was a little surprised himself but was pleased it was doing so well. He admitted that he had known all along that the deer was going to get bigger eventually although he hadn't expected it to happen so quickly. Staring off into the middle distance, a dreamy expression on his face, he told me, "You know, I wouldn't be surprised if someday my first deer becomes a world's-record trophy."

"I wouldn't either," I said. "In fact, I'd be willing to bet on it."

Not long ago, Retch and I were chatting with some of the boys down at Kelly's Bar & Grill and the talk turned to first deer. It was disgusting. I can stand maudlin sentimentality as well as the next fellow, but I have my limits. Some of those first deer had a mastery of escape routines that would have put Houdini to shame. Most of them were so smart there was some question in my mind as to whether the hunter had bagged a deer or a Rhodes Scholar. I wanted to ask them if they had tagged their buck or awarded it a Phi Beta Kappa key. And big! There wasn't a deer there who couldn't have cradled a baby grand piano in its rack. Finally it was Retch's turn, and between waves of nausea I wondered whether that little spike buck had developed enough over the years to meet this kind of competition. I needn't have wondered.

Retch's deer no longer walked in typical deer fashion; it "ghosted" about through the trees like an apparition. When it galloped, though, the sound was "like thunder rolling through the hills." And so help me, "fire flickered in its eyes." Its tracks "looked like they'd been excavated with a backhoe, they were that big." Smart? That deer could have taught field tactics at West Point. Retch's little spike buck had come a long way, baby.

At last Retch reached the climax of his story. "I don't expect you boys to believe this," he said, his voice hushed with reverence, "but when I dropped that deer, the mountain *trembled!*"

The boys all nodded, believing. Why, hadn't the mountain trembled for them too when they shot their first deer? Of course it had. All first deer are like that.

Except mine.

I banged the table for attention. "Now," I said, "I'm going to tell you about a *real* first deer, not a figment of my senility, not some fossilized hope of my gangling adolescence, but a *real* first deer."

Now I could tell from looking at their stunned faces that the boys were upset. There is nothing that angers the participants of a bull session more than someone who refuses to engage in the mutual exchange of illusions, someone who tells the simple truth, unstretched, unvarnished, unembellished, and whole.

"Even though it violates the code of the true sportsperson," I began, "I must confess that I still harbor unkind thoughts for my first deer. True to his form and unlike almost all other first deer, he has steadfastly refused to grow in either my memory or imagination; he simply stands there in original size and puny rack, peering over the lip of my consciousness, an insolent smirk decorating his pointy face. Here I offered that thankless creature escape from the anonymity of becoming someone else's second or seventh or seventeenth deer or, at the very least, from an old age presided over by coyotes. And how did he repay me? With humiliation!"

The boys at Kelly's shrank back in horror at this heresy. Retch Sweeney tried to slip away, but I riveted him to his chair with a maniacal laugh. His eyes pleaded with me. *"No, don't tell us!"* they said. *"Don't destroy the myth of the first deer!*" (which is a pretty long speech for a couple of beady, bloodshot eyes).

Unrelenting and with only an occasional pause for a bitter, sardonic cackle to escape my foam-flecked lips, I plunged on with the tale, stripping away layer after layer of myth until at last the truth about one man's first deer had been disrobed and lay before them in all its grim and naked majesty, shivering and covered with goose bumps.

I began by pointing out what I considered to be one of the great bureaucratic absurdities of all time: that a boy at age fourteen was allowed to purchase his first hunting license and deer tag but was prevented from obtaining a driver's license until he was sixteen. This was like telling a kid he could go swimming but to stay away from the water. Did the bureaucrats think that trophy mule deer came down from the hills in the evening to drink out of your garden hose? The predicament left you no recourse but to beg the adult hunters you knew to take you hunting with them on weekends. My problem was that all the adult hunters I knew bagged their deer in the first couple of weeks of the season, and from then on I had to furnish my own transportation. This meant that in order to get up to the top of the mountain where the trophy mule deer hung out, I had to start out at four in the morning if I wanted to be there by noon. I remember one time when I was steering around some big boulders in the road about three-quarters of the way up the Dawson Grade and a Jeep with two hunters in it came plowing up behind me. I pulled over so they could pass. The hunters grinned at me as they went by. You'd think they'd never before seen anyone pedaling a bike twenty miles up the side of a mountain to go deer hunting.

I had rigged up my bike especially for deer hunting. There were straps to hold my rifle snugly across the handlebars, and saddlebags draped over the back fender to carry my gear. The back fender had been reinforced to support a sturdy platform, my reason for this being that I didn't believe the original fender was stout enough to support a buck when I got one. My one oversight was failing to put a guard over the top of the bike chain, in which I had to worry constantly about getting my tongue caught. Deer hunting on a bike was no picnic.

A mile farther on and a couple of hours later I came to where the fellows in the Jeep were busy setting up camp with some other hunters. Apparently, someone told a fantastic joke just as I went pumping by because they all collapsed in a fit of laughter and were doubled over and rolling on the ground and pounding trees with their fists. They seemed like a bunch of lunatics to me, and I hoped they didn't plan on hunting in the same area I was headed for. I couldn't wait to see their faces when I came coasting easily back down the mountain with a trophy buck draped over the back of my bike.

One of the main problems with biking your way out to hunt deer was that, if you left at four in the morning, by the time you got to the hunting place there were only a couple of hours of daylight left in which to do your hunting. Then you had to spend some time resting, at least until the pounding of your heart eased up enough not to frighten the deer.

As luck would have it, just as I was unstrapping my rifle from the handlebars, a buck mule deer came dancing out of the brush not twenty yards away from me. Now right then I should have known he was up to no good. He had doubtless been lying on a ledge and watching me for hours as I pumped my way up the mountain. He had probably even snickered to himself as he plotted ways to embarrass me.

All the time I was easing the rifle loose from the handlebars, digging a shell out of my pocket, and thumbing it into the rifle, the deer danced and clowned and cut up all around me, smirking the whole while. The instant I jacked the shell into the chamber, however, he stepped behind a tree. I darted to one side, rifle at the ready. He moved to the other side of the tree and stuck his head out just enough so I could see him feigning a yawn. As I moved up close to the tree, he did a rapid tiptoe to another tree. I heard him snort with laughter. For a whole hour he toyed with me in this manner, enjoying himself immensely. Then I fooled him, or at least so I thought at the time. I turned and started walking in a dejected manner back toward my bike, still watching his hiding place out of the corner of my eye. He stuck his head out to see what I was up to. I stepped behind a small bush and knelt as if to tie my shoe. Then, swiftly I turned, drew a bead on his head, and fired. Down he went.

I was still congratulating myself on a fine shot when I rushed up to his crumpled form. Strangely, I could not detect a bullet hole in his head, but one of his antlers was chipped and I figured the slug had struck there with sufficient force to do him in. "No matter," I said to myself, "I have at last got my first deer," and I pictured in my mind the joyous welcome I would receive when I came home hauling in a hundred or so pounds of venison. Then I discovered my knife had fallen out of its sheath during my frantic pursuit of the deer. Instant anguish! The question that nagged my waking moments for years afterwards was: Did the deer know that I had dropped my knife? Had I only interpreted it correctly, the answer to that question was written all over the buck's face—he was still wearing that stupid smirk.

"Well," I told myself, "what I'll do is just load him on my bike, haul him down to the lunatic hunters' camp, and borrow a knife from them to dress him out with." I thought this plan particularly good in that it would offer me the opportunity to give those smart alecks a few tips on deer hunting.

Loading the buck on the bike was much more of a problem than I had expected. When I draped him crosswise over the platform on the rear fender, his head and front quarters dragged on one side and his rear quarters on the other. Several times as I lifted and pulled and hauled, I thought I heard a giggle, but when I looked around nobody was there. It was during one of these pauses that a brilliant idea occurred to me. With herculean effort, I managed to arrange the deer so that he was sitting astraddle of the platform, his four legs splayed out forward and his head drooping down. I lashed his front feet to the handlebars, one on each side. Then I slid up onto the seat ahead of him, draped his head over my right shoulder, and pushed off.

I must admit that riding a bike with a deer on behind was a good deal more difficult than I had anticipated. Even though I pressed down on the brake for all I was worth, our wobbling descent was much faster than I would have liked. The road was narrow, twisting, and filled with ruts and large rocks, with breathtaking drop-offs on the outer edge. When we came hurtling around a sharp, high bend above the hunters' camp, I glanced down. Even from that distance I could see their eyes pop and their jaws sag as they caught sight of us.

What worried me most was the hill that led down to the camp. As we arrived at the crest of it, my heart, liver, and kidneys all jumped in unison. The hill was much steeper than I had remembered. It was at that point that the buck gave a loud, startled snort.

My first deer had either just regained consciousness or been shocked out of his pretense of death at the sight of the plummeting grade before us. We both tried to leap free of the bike, but he was tied on and I was locked in the embrace of his front legs.

When we shot past the hunters' camp, I was too occupied at the moment to get a good look at their faces. I heard afterwards that a game warden found them several hours later, frozen in various postures and still staring at the road in front of their camp. The report was probably exaggerated, however, game wardens being little better than hunters at sticking to the simple truth.

I probably would have been able to get the bike stopped sooner and with fewer injuries to myself if I had had enough sense to tie down the deer's hind legs. As it was, he started flailing wildly about with them and somehow managed to get his hooves on the pedals. By the time we reached the bottom of the mountain he not only had the hang of pedaling but was showing considerable talent for it. He also seemed to be enjoying himself immensely. We zoomed up and down over the rolling foothills and into the bottomlands, with the deer pedaling wildly and me shouting and cursing and trying to wrest control of the bike from him. At last he piled us up in the middle of a farmer's pumpkin patch. He tore himself loose from the bike and bounded into the woods, all the while making obscene gestures at me with his tail. I threw the rifle to my shoulder and got off one quick shot. It might have hit him too, if the bike hadn't been still strapped to the rifle.

"Now that," I said to the boys at Kelly's, "is how to tell about a first deer—a straightforward factual report unadorned by a lot of lies and sentimentality."

Unrepentant, they muttered angrily. To soothe their injured feelings, I told them about my second deer. It was so big it could cradle a baby grand piano in its rack and shade a team of Belgian draft horses in its shadow at high noon. Honest! I wouldn't lie about a thing like that.

The Crouch Hop
and Other Useful
Outdoor Steps

☞ ☞ ☞ While going through my mail at breakfast the other morning, I noticed a picture on a magazine cover of what was purported to be a group of backpackers. The individuals portrayed were all neat, clean, and beaming with happy smiles as they came striding up over a grassy knoll.

"Those aren't backpackers, they're fashion models," I told my wife.

Always keen to assimilate my wisdom on such matters, she fixed me with an intense look. "Did you eat my piece of bacon? That last piece of bacon was *mine!*"

"Well, first of all," I explained patiently, "they're all neat, clean, and beaming with happy smiles, whereas backpackers are generally messy, grubby, and grunting. Second, they're climbing a grassy knoll instead of a forty-five-degree, rock-strewn snake path the Forest Service laughingly calls a trail. What really gives them away, though, is that they're *striding*. No self-respecting backpacker would be caught dead striding."

"You even ate my English muffin!" my wife shouted.

This enlightening exchange got me to thinking that there are probably many people like my wife who have waited in vain for someone to erase their ignorance concerning the various foot movements, or steps, as they are sometimes called, employed in the practice of outdoor sports. I herewith offer as a public service the following compendium of the basic forms of outdoor pedestrianism.

THE PACKER'S PLOD—Backpackers, being generally optimistic souls, will start off on an excursion at a brisk pace, which they maintain for approximately nine steps. They then shift into the standard packer's plod. One foot is raised and placed forward three inches on the trail. The backpacker then breathes deeply, checks his hip strap, wipes the perspiration off his face, takes a swig from his canteen, eats a piece of beef jerky, snaps a photograph of a Stellar's jay, and consults his map. Then he repeats the process. A good backpacker, if he had a table handy, could play a hand of solitaire between steps. His forward motion defies detection by the human eye. Nevertheless, his progress is steady and unrelenting, and during the course of a day he can eat up a surprising number of miles, not to mention several pounds of jerky.

It always amuses experienced backpackers to see neophytes of the sport go racing past them on the trail. The tale of the tortoise and the hare leaps instantly to mind. Last summer my old backpacking partner Vern Schulze and I took his two boys, Wayne and Jim, on their first overnight hike. Our destination was a lake high up in the mountains of Idaho. Vern and I set off at the standard packer's plod, while the boys tore off up the trail ahead of us, soon disappearing from view. After about an hour they came racing back down the trail.

"What happened?" they shouted. "When you didn't show up at the lake, we thought maybe you had fallen and hurt yourselves."

Vern and I just winked at each other. "Don't worry about us. You fellows just go on ahead. We'll catch up."

After the boys had charged back up the trail, I said to Vern, "You know, when Wayne and Jim are exhausted and we pass them up, it would be better if we didn't tease them too much. It's a bad thing to break a boy's spirit."

"Right," Vern said, munching a handful of beef jerky while he snapped a picture of a Stellar's jay.

A couple of hours later the boys came jogging back down the trail.

"Look," I whispered to Vern. "They're already starting to slow down."

"Hey, Dad!" Wayne shouted. "The fish are really biting great! We've already caught enough for supper!"

It was all we could do to suppress our mirth. Both youngsters were showing definite signs of burning themselves out.

"You guys better speed it up a bit," Jim said.

"We can take care of ourselves," Vern replied, giving me a nudge with his elbow that almost toppled me off the trail. "Say, if you guys want to sit down and take a rest, go right ahead. It's nothing to be ashamed of. Just because Pat and I never stop doesn't mean you shouldn't."

"I thought you were stopped right now," Jim said.

"No," Vern said, "as a matter of fact we have just quickened our pace."

"We'd better be going," Wayne said. "We've got the tent pitched and a rock fireplace made and want to finish gathering wood for the fire."

They made three or four more trips back to check on us, each time moving a little slower. Along about evening we came upon them sitting alongside the trail eating huckleberries, and they both looked plumb tuckered out. Vern and I passed them up without so much as a single unkind remark. When we had dumped our packs in camp, though, I couldn't help offering a bit of advice to Wayne, who was hunkered at my feet.

"Easy does it," I told him. "If you pull a man's boots off too fast it hurts his ankles."

A boy is never too young to start learning the basics of backpacking, I always say.

THE SIDEWINDER—Skilled anglers the world over are masters of this rather peculiar outdoor step. Essentially, it consists of sauntering sideways. While looking straight ahead as if wearing blinders, you attempt to give the impression that you are oblivious to what is taking place on either side of you. The situation in which it is used is this: Your partner has laid claim to a nice piece of fishing water twenty yards or so downstream from you. Suddenly he gets a strike and flicks his fly into the uppermost branches of a thorn apple. You know the fish was a big one because of the way your friend suddenly crouches down and scurries about like a hyperactive crab as he tries to untangle his line and stay out of sight of the fish at the same time. There is a great temptation on such occasions to be overwhelmed by your partner's desperate maneuvers and to laugh yourself senseless. A master angler, however, will maintain an expression that is not only sober but that conveys the impression he is totally unaware of anything but his own rhythmic casting. While maintaining this expression, he then performs the sidewinder, which carries him sideways along the bank to that portion of water where the monster trout has signaled its presence. Upon arriving at this position, the master angler must make a pretense of being in a trance of sufficient depth that it cannot be penetrated by the vile epithets screamed at him by his former friend. The former friend will at this point give up all caution and throw himself into all-out combat with the thorn apple in order to free the offending line. Catching and landing a fish under such trying circumstances is what qualifies one as a master angler, sometimes referred to by fishing partners as a "no-good *bleep* of a *bleep*." Good sportsmanship requires that one refrain from maniacal laughter after performing a successful sidewinder.

THE MOSEY—This is a walk that belongs almost exclusively to game wardens, and they reserve it for occasions when they are moving in to make a pinch. If you see a man moseying toward you while you are fishing or hunting, you had better make a quick study of your game regulations because you may be in trouble. If game wardens in your area are prone to being sneaky, a stump or a bush moseying toward you also may mean trouble. I myself have on occasion put the mosey to good use. Indeed, it is rather amusing to see how quickly other anglers can be cleared from a stream by the simple expedient of moseying toward them.

THE HEEL-AND-TOE—This is essentially the same step employed in the track event of the same name. It is characterized by quick, tiny steps, an exaggeratedly straight vertical posture, and a facial expression combined of equal parts of indignation and suffering. It is not unusual to see a whole party of elk hunters going about camp in this fashion after a twenty-mile horseback ride into the mountains.

THE CROUCH HOP—This is usually performed midway through the process of driving in a tent peg with a large flat rock. The individual will suddenly leap up, clamp one of his hands between his thighs, and, making strange grunting sounds, begin to hop madly about the camp. I have performed this exercise many times, and it does wonders for relieving the pain resulting from a finger caught between a rock and a tent peg. It is equally important to recognize the crouch hop for what it is when you see it being performed. Once in Yellowstone Park, blinded by tears, I accidentally crouch-hopped into the adjoining camp space where an hysterical lady tried to run me through with her wiener stick. Luckily for me, she didn't have sufficient foresight to remove the wiener and I escaped with a single bruise no larger than the business end of a Ball Park frank.

THE SAUNTER—The saunter is applicable almost exclusively to bird hunting. I can remember the very first time I used it. I was fourteen and grouse hunting with my friend Retch Sweeney. We were moving stealthily through a thick stand of evergreens where we knew a grouse to be hiding. Suddenly the bird exploded off a limb almost directly above us and roared away through the trees. Startled, I whirled, pointed my old double-barrel at a patch of sky as big around as a bread box, and fired. Out of sheer coincidence, the shot and the grouse arrived at that patch of sky simultaneously, and the bird landed with a dead thump ten yards away. All my instincts told me to race over, grab up the grouse, and clamp it to my throbbing chest, all the while exclaiming, "Holy cow! Did you see that shot? Holy cow! What a shot!" For the first time in my life, however, I defied my instincts. I s-a-u-n-t-e-r-e-d over, picked up the grouse, and nonchalantly deposited it in my game pocket. "That one sort of surprised me," I said to Retch, whose tongue still dangled limply from his gaping mouth.

Now, had I gone bounding and bawling after that grouse like a hound pup after a squirrel, Retch would have known the shot was an accident. Instead, my saunter filled the great empty spaces of his mind with the impression that I was a fantastic wing shot. He frequently commented afterwards that he didn't understand how anyone who was such a great shot could miss so often. I have found, in fact, that a properly executed saunter after downed game will sustain one's reputation as a great shot through an unbroken string of twenty-five misses.

If one hunts with a dog, by the way, the same effect can be achieved by teaching it to retrieve game in a manner that suggests unrelieved boredom. Personally, I haven't had much success in this area with my own dog, since I've never been able to break him of the habit of doing a histrionic double take every time I hit something. You just can't compensate for bad breeding, so there is nothing for me to do but saunter to make up for a stupid dog who aspires to be a stand-up comic.

THE TRUDGE—Used primarily for returning to one's car after a cold, wet, windy day of hunting and you missed three easy shots and it's the last day of the season and you can't remember where you left your car.

THE LOPE—Basically a fast saunter, in that it implies casualness. Say you're out fishing a remote mountain stream with your boy and along toward dusk the hair on the back of your neck, for no reason at all, rises. You have the distinct impression that you are being *watched*. You halt a cast in mid-air and reel in.

"What you doin'?" the boy says. "I just had a good bite."

"It's getting late," you say. "We'd better head home." You then take off at a lope.

"Well, shoot!" the boy says.

THE SHAMBLE—What the boy does in the above situation.

THE BOLT—What the lope is changed into if the feeling of being watched is followed by a low, rumbling growl and a crashing in the brush. Actually, a low, rumbling growl or a crashing in the brush are sufficient reasons in themselves to engage in a bolt.

THE TRAMPLE—What the boy does to you when he hears the low, rumbling growl and crashing in the brush.

There are literally dozens of other interesting and enjoyable outdoor steps, but those given above are basic. It might be well to practice them at home until you feel both comfortable and confident with them. As a matter of fact, my wife just crouch-hopped past the door of my study. I wonder what she was doing driving a tent peg with a flat rock when she was supposed to be hanging a picture.

Meanwhile, Back at the B Western

☞ ☞ ☞**F**ew people appreciate the great contribution the handgun has made to television and motion pictures. What would police shows, for example, be without .38 Specials and .357 Magnums? Imagine police detectives standing around the squad room in shirtsleeves, rifles dangling from under their armpits. Ridiculous!

The shows that would really suffer from an absence of handguns, though, would be the westerns. Without the pistol, there would be no fast draw, and without the fast draw, westerns would be a whole lot different. Consider, if you will, and if you have the stomach for it, a quick-draw scene with rifles. Matt Dillon clumps out into the street from the Long Branch Saloon to issue a warning to one of the quaintly named villains so characteristic of "Gunsmoke."

"Chester and I caught you red-handed stealin' buffalo humps up on the flat, Ick Crud," he says. "You be outta town by sundown if you know what's good fer ya. Folks here 'bouts don't take kindly to buffalo-humpers."

Ick Crud sneers. "Reach fer yer iron, Marshal!"

The camera zooms in for a close-up of Matt's low-slung Winchester, the tie-downs knotted around his ankle. Quicker than Dean Martin can sing "Old Man River," Matt draws . . . and draws . . . and draws. Ick Crud uses a frantic hand-over-hand draw on his Sharps-Borchardt. During the draw, Chester, Doc, and Miss Kitty go back into the Long Branch for a drink to steady their nerves.

"Three whiskeys and be quick about it," Miss Kitty snaps to the bartender. "Matt's drawin' out there in the street, and we ain't got much time before the shootin' starts."

"I don't know why Matt don't git outta the marshaling business," Doc grumbles. "I keep tellin' him, 'Matt, sooner or later a gunfighter's gonna shade your draw by just a minute or two, and that'll be it fer ya.' "

"We better git back out there," Chester whines. "They should be just about finished drawin', and I don't want to miss the shootin'."

No doubt about it, the handgun and the fast draw are essential to the true western, and any movie fan worth his hot-buttered popcorn not only expects them to be in the western but knows the ritual by heart. The ritual usually begins with the "call out." The villain stands in the street and calls out the hero—"C'mon out, Ringo, you yellow-bellied, chicken-livered, varicose-veined, spastic-coloned wimp!"

Upon hearing himself being called out, the hero immediately begins his preparations. He tosses down his shot of whiskey and grinds out his cigar on the greasy nose of the belligerent bartender. He slips his pistol out of its holster and checks the cylinder to make sure he reloaded after his last shoot-out. (There is nothing more disappointing than to beat the other fellow to the draw and then discover that you forgot to reload.) He then reholsters his gun and slips it out and in a few times to make sure it isn't sticking. (A stuck gun is just about as bad as an unloaded one.) Next he unstraps his spurs, his motive here apparently being that, should he change his mind about the fight, it is a lot easier to run when you're not wearing spurs. He pulls his hat low over his eyes, limbers up the fingers of his gun hand, and tucks his jacket back behind the butt of his revolver. One purpose of all this preparation may be the hope that the villain will get tired of waiting and go home. The villain never does, of course, although sometimes he gets a cramp in his lip from holding a sneer so long.

Back in the olden days when I was a kid, we had what were called the B westerns. The B stood for "best." These were movies starring Roy Rogers, Gene Autry, and Hopalong Cassidy. They weren't anything like the westerns nowadays starring Clint Eastwood, the ones where you have to buy a program to tell the good guys from the bad guys. In the B westerns, you always knew the good guys. They were neatly dressed, clean-shaven, and didn't cuss, smoke, drink, kiss, or do anything else that was bad for health or morals. Even the bad guys didn't do most of these things, but you could tell them anyway. For one thing, they all used the interrupted curse:

"What the . . . !"
"Well, I'll be . . . !"
"Why you . . . !"

They had real action in the B's too, not like the "modern" western where you spend half the movie watching Eastwood squint his eyes and ripple his jaw muscles. Clint holsters his gun like he was setting a carton of milk back in a refrigerator. Why, Roy, Gene, and Hoppy wouldn't even think of putting their guns back into their holsters without giving them a twirl or two first.

I don't recall seeing Roy, Gene, or Hoppy ever shoot anybody, but they probably did. Usually, they just shot the gun out of the villain's hand and let it go at that. Sometimes they would rope the bad guys, often getting a single loop of their lasso around the whole gang. Heroes knew their business in the B westerns.

One nice bit of business Roy, Gene, and Hoppy perfected was to leapfrog over the rumps of their horses and land smack in the saddle. They never landed on the saddle horn either, although once I think I heard the Lone Ranger cry out in a shrill voice, "Hii *owwww* Silver away!"

My cousin Buck, who was several years older than I and knew everything, told me he was an expert at getting on horses like that and that there really wasn't anything to it. I said I couldn't believe that. He said if I had a horse handy he would show me. I said I didn't have a horse but I had a cow. Would a cow work? He said sure. We went out to the pasture and found a cow engaged in licking a salt block. Buck said that one would do just fine. I suggested that we warn the cow of what to expect, but Buck said that wouldn't be necessary. As it turned out, Buck was wrong about that and the rest as well. I still think the cow probably would have cooperated and even entered into the spirit of the thing had we just let her know what to expect. As it was, Buck got back twenty yards or so and made a dash for her. At the exact instant he got his hands on the cow's rump and his legs had crossed over his arms in mid-vault, the cow let out a frightened bellow and bolted forward. As the cow disappeared over a nearby hill, Buck was still perched on her tail bones in a strange variation of the lotus position and screaming, "Whoa, you stupid cow, whoa!"

"Well, I'll be . . . !" I said.

The B western heroes were big on tricks. Say the

villain got the drop on Roy in a little cabin out in the middle of the desert. Just as the baddy was about to plug him, Roy would shout "Watch out!" and point over the other man's shoulder. The villain would spin around, and Roy would jump him and thump his head to a fare-thee-well. These villains were *dumb!* Otherwise, why would they expect the guy they were about to gun down to warn them of a surprise attack? They were slow to learn. Roy, Gene, and Hoppy would catch them with this little trick movie after movie. Maybe the reason they were so dumb was from getting their heads thumped so often.

Eventually, however, they did start catching on to the trick. "You ain't foolin' me with that old trick, Rogers," the bad guy would say, as if he had seen some of these movies before himself. But this time Gabby Hayes would actually be sneaking up behind him and would thump his head a good one. Again, one might wonder why Roy thought it necessary to warn the villain when his comical sidekick was in fact sneaking up behind the man. The reason, of course, was to complicate matters for the villain when this particular situation arose in future movies. Roy, Gene, and Hoppy all worked half a dozen different ploys of this same routine, always with success. After a while the villain could scarcely get the drop on one of them without instantly becoming a nervous wreck from wondering whether or not he was about to be jumped.

The B western villain was a sucker for pebbles, too. Anytime the hero wanted to draw the baddy's attention away from himself, he would toss a pebble. The villain would whirl around and empty his six-gun into the pebble. Then he would see that it was only a pebble and would get this worried, expectant look in his eyes, which said, *"Head, get ready for a thumping!"*

Counting shots was a favorite tactic of B western

heroes. They would wave a hat around on a stick or perform some other trick to draw fire, all the time counting shots. Then, suddenly, they would walk right out in the open and announce, "Six! That was your last bullet, Slade!" Villains liked to try this trick too, but having the IQ's of celery, they could never get it straight. There was scarcely a villain in B westerns who could count to six without making a mistake. "Six," the bad guy would say, walking out from behind his rock. "That was your last bullet, Autry!"

BANG!

If the movie patron wondered what it was the villain was muttering as he lay sprawled in the dust, it was probably, "Let's see now, two shots ricocheted off the rock, two went through my hat on the stick, that makes five . . ."

Even among the B western audiences there were those who counted shots. They counted the number of shots the hero fired without reloading. I hated these wise guys. Right in the tense part of the movie, they would guffaw: "That's nine shots without reloading! Roy must be using a nine-shooter!"

"Why you . . . !" I would say under my breath. If there was anyone who couldn't appreciate a B western, it was a nitpicker.

The last B western I ever saw in a theater was in a small college town in Idaho. It starred Randolph Scott, and in the big scene the baddies had ganged up on Randolph in the saloon. When they started blazing away at him, Randolph jumped behind a cast-iron stove and, if I recall correctly, used the stove lid as a sort of shield while he returned their fire. The theater was filled with college kids and, as is the nature of college kids, they began whooping and jeering and laughing at Randolph's plight. Seated just behind me were an old farmer and his wife who had paid their hard-earned $1.50 for an evening of serious entertainment. As the slugs were spanging off the stove like lead hail and the college kids were whooping it up, I heard the old woman whisper nervously to her husband. The farmer, in a gruff but gentle voice, reassured her. "Don't worry, Mother," he said, "Ol' Randolph, he'll figure a way to git hisself out of this mess."

You bet! The farmer and his wife were my kind of people.

Looking back, I now realize it was a good thing Hollywood stopped turning out B westerns when it did. I was grown up and had a job by then, and folks were beginning to ask, "What's that big fellow doing down there, sitting in the front row with the kids?"

The Education
of a Sportsman

☞ ☞ ☞The letter came in the spring of my eighteenth year, telling me when to report in, and later that summer I packed my few belongings in my rucksack and an old battered suitcase and prepared to depart my home in the mountains of Idaho. Little did I know what lay in store for me during the months ahead, but my mother and grandmother offered plenty of warnings.

"Don't try to be a hero," Gram said.

"You don't have to worry about that," I consoled her.

"I know," Gram said, "but in the off chance the urge com s over you, don't try to be one."

"Right," I said.

"Those people are savages, many of them," Mom said. "They're not like us. I remember the atrocities your father used to tell about when he was in . . ." Her voice trailed off.

"I can't believe it's that bad," I said. "Lonny Henderson went, didn't he, and he came back okay."

Mom shook her head. "No, there's something wrong

with Lonny. Folks say he talks strange now. I don't want that to happen to you."

"Look, don't worry," I said. "I'm going to come back all right. After all, it's not as if I'm going off to war. College is different than that."

Mom and Gram helped me with my packing, and there was considerable discussion over what a young college man should take or leave behind.

"Let's see now," Mom said, surveying my assembled belongings. "You have your fishing rods, your tackle box, your twenty-two, your thirty-thirty, your shotgun, your hunting knife, your hunting boots and wool socks, your lucky hunting hat, your good pair of pants, and your good shirt. Since you're going to be gone for almost a whole year, do you think you might need a change of underwear?"

"Wouldn't hurt," I said. "Why don't you throw in a set?"

"How about the dictionary?" Gram asked.

"Naw," I said. "It'd take up the space of at least four boxes of shells. I know most words, anyway."

"Of course you couldn't think about leaving behind these hides you tanned and the deer head you mounted yourself," Mom added.

"Yeah, I thought my dorm room might need a little decoration, something to make me feel at home." I did wonder a bit about the head, since it had turned out with this stupid grin on its face.

Gram pointed to the big tangle of rusty traps. "You think you might actually have time to run a trap line between classes and studying?"

"There's lots of streams and wild country near the college," I said. "And muskrat hides are probably going to get up to near three dollars this winter."

"Why didn't I think of that?" Gram said.

As it turned out, college was not nearly so dangerous as Gram and Mom had led me to believe. The campus was located in the middle of a vast farming region bordered on one side by a fairly decent range of mountains. The surrounding countryside was dotted with lakes and laced with streams ranging from rivers to creeks to cricks with an occasional swamp thrown in for good luck. From my dorm window, pheasants could be seen strutting the wheat fields and deer were abundant in the mountains. It was my kind of place.

Originally an agricultural school, the college now enjoyed a reputation for research and scholarship in dozens of different academic areas. The chairman of my major department was himself a scholar of international reputation, to which was added the honor of having me as one of his advisees. Later in my college career, after I knew him better, Dr. Osgood revealed to me the peculiar circumstance under which he became my faculty adviser, once and for all clearing up the mystery of how great universities arrive at decisions that will forever influence the future life of a student. "I drew the short straw," he said.

Even now I remember our first meeting. A secretary showed me into an office, where Dr. Osgood, his great mop of white hair seemingly suspended in mid-explosion, sat staring intently at a file folder on his desk. He looked up, smiling.

"From a brief study of your academic record, young man, I see a great future ahead of you as a scholar."

"Gosh," I replied, hanging my head and digging at the carpet with my toe. "I don't know about that."

"Now now now," Dr. Osgood said. "You have amassed a wonderful academic record and are obviously a brilliant student. There's no need for false modesty, Heinzburger."

"*McManus,*" I corrected.

"Oh, *McManus?*" Dr. Osgood picked up another file folder and perused it, occasionally allowing himself a slight shudder. "*Harumph!* Well, now, perhaps I spoke too soon, McManus. It appears from your record that you have every reason for legitimate modesty."

I laughed, not wishing to embarrass him, even though I didn't find his little joke particularly funny.

"By the way, McManus, what happened to the top of your head there, an auto accident?"

"That's my lucky hunting hat, sir."

"Oh. Is it removable or permanently attached?"

"I almost always take it off when I go to bed," I said. "Unless I happen to forget."

"That's most admirable," he said. "One must always strive to cultivate the little niceties." As far as I know, that was the first and only compliment I ever received from Dr. Osgood.

Then we got down to a serious discussion of my academic career, during which Dr. Osgood at times raved incoherently and at other times appeared on the verge of physical violence. Finally, he sat up very straight in his chair and began to perform what I later learned were deep-breathing exercises. Afterwards, for a while, he seemed calmer.

"Let's take a different tack," he said, forcing a small smile that trembled at the corners. "Let's concentrate for a moment on your future, presuming you have one. Now think about this very carefully. All other things aside, what is your ultimate goal in life? When you're as old as I, what single achievement would you like to look back upon, the one great shining accomplishment?"

I could see that we had now got down to serious business, and I sorted through all my vague hopes and desires and finally selected one that stood out among all others, the impossible dream.

"I have it," I said.

"Yes? Yes?" Dr. Osgood implored.

"I'd like to shoot a world's-record trophy moose!"

Dr. Osgood appeared at that moment to have suffered an infarction of some sort. He rose slowly from his chair, his face twisted in anguish, leaned forward across the desk, and croaked, "Moose? Moose? What do you mean, MOOSE!"

I must admit that my first meeting with Dr. Osgood made me a bit uneasy, but in our later sessions over the years I was able to relax and banter with him about my grades and various other trifles. Often I would leave his office in a state of high good humor, slinging one last witty retort over my shoulder, while Dr. Osgood would put on a show of weeping uncontrollably, at which he was very good. The man could have made his fortune as an actor.

Life in the dorm was not nearly so bad as Mom and Gram had predicted. Oh, sure, occasionally some of the guys would commit a minor atrocity, but nothing out of the ordinary as atrocities go. There were the usual panty raids, water fights, short-sheeting of beds, and dropping of stink bombs into the ventilation system, that sort of innocent fun.

During the first semester of my freshman year I had extremely bad luck with roommates. My first roommate, Wilson Fawfush, flipped out after a few weeks and finally insisted upon being moved to another dorm. The dorm director told me confidentially that Wilson had been suffering from hallucinations, even to the extent of claiming he saw snakes crawling all over the floor of our room.

"Poor Wilson," I said.

"Yes, it's too bad," the director said. "Sometimes the human mind can play strange tricks on us."

"No question about it," I said.

The next roommate assigned me was a real dilly. His name was Lester T. Lillybridge III. It immediately became apparent that Lester had been spoiled rotten as a kid, one result of which was that he had just been expelled from a classy private college back East. His lips seemed to be curled in a permanent sneer of superiority. Scarcely had he dropped his leather-trimmed luggage on the linoleum of our room than we had our first exchange of hostility.

"What are all the guns doing in here?" he asked.

"I'm a hunter," I said.

"Figures," he said. "My parents have arranged this as a punishment for me. What's that ugly thing on the wall?"

His words momentarily crippled my ego. No sooner had I learned I possessed an ego than some fool had to come along and cripple it. "That," I said indignantly, "is a deer head. I mounted it myself."

"Why does it have that stupid grin on its face?"

"That question just goes to show you know nothing about deer," I snapped. "In their natural state, all deer wear stupid grins like that."

Lillybridge laughed evilly. He walked over and kicked a crate I had built in the corner of the room. "What's in there?"

"Snakes," I said.

"Don't be a wise-elbow," Lillybridge said, opening the lid on top and peering in. He slammed down the lid and jumped back. "There *are* snakes in there!"

"Yes."

"Can they get out?"

"Well, they did one night a few weeks ago. That's why I built the crate for them. They can't get out now."

"Geez!" Lillybridge said. "My parents have really done it to me this time!"

Lillybridge found some of the other guys in the dorm more to his liking and spent most of his free time with them, planning and executing various atrocities. When not in class, I spent most of my time in the museum of natural history, where I had a part-time job assisting the curator in various chores. I was thinking of becoming a naturalist. The work was so much fun I would sometimes take it home with me.

"Where's that last batch of snakes we caught?" the curator would ask me.

"I took them home to study," I'd say.

"Well, bring them back!"

Occasionally, the curator would let me try my hand at taxidermy, but the results were never up to his standards. "You didn't do too badly on that ground squirrel," he'd say, "but why does it have that stupid grin on its face?"

During the day, when there were people milling about, the museum was quite pleasant. But at night, when I was there late sweeping the floors or cleaning up a mess of some kind, not always of my own making, the place was downright creepy. The live rattlesnakes in their glass cages, for example, would strike at me, popping the glass with their noses as I walked by. I knew that the snakes couldn't strike through the glass, but my adrenal glands, being ignorant of that fact, would pump a quart or so of adrenaline into my system every time a rattler struck at me. Pretty soon my nerves would be jangling, and shadows would seem to dart and dance among the displays. The huge, mounted timber wolf would blink his eyes as I scurried by with my dust cloth. The mounted cougar would lash its tail. The bobcat would twitch its whiskers.

There was one particularly loathsome room that I had to venture into in order to empty the various waste receptacles, some of which occasionally held startling surprises. This was the dissection room, where dead animals were prepared for whatever purpose the curator had in mind for them. One large glass case contained a kind of carnivorous beetle, thousands of them, used for cleaning the flesh off bones, leaving them shiny clean. I would imagine I could hear the beetles at their work, performing a grim symphony with their infinitesimal *chomp-chomp-chomps*. Between the rattlesnakes and the beetles, my late night chores in the museum would often leave me in a state of barely controlled terror.

The dissection room contained a dingy gray freezer about the size and shape of a coffin, only somewhat deeper. I often wondered what it might hold. One night when I was there alone, my curiosity overpowered my terror sufficiently for me to peek in. Ever so carefully I raised the lid, feeling the beat of my heart in every single goose bump on my body. Bit by bit, with cold sweat flooding off of me, I raised one eyelid. Nothing! The freezer was empty.

At that moment I thought of an atrocity to commit.

I had happened to mention to Lester, as we lay in our bunks one night, that my nerves were a bit frazzled from my work at the museum. He had laughed in his nasty, evil way and expressed the opinion that I was "just chicken." Confiding my fear to a person like Lilly-bridge had been nothing less than a lapse of sanity on my part. He had soon told all the other guys on our floor, most of whom up to that moment had regarded me with a certain amount of trepidation. Now they began to feel that I was a safe subject upon which to perform their practical jokes. This was a theory in need of puncturing.

I set my trap for Lillybridge with great care. First I wrote on a sheet of paper the message, "Dr. Smith, please finish with the dissection of this cadaver as soon as possible. It's beginning to spoil."

Then I waited until late one night when Lillybridge and I were in our bunks exchanging a few nasty barbs with each other before going to sleep.

"Let's be serious for a moment, Lester," I said.

"I am being serious, worm wit," he replied.

"Naw, come on, I mean it. I've got to tell somebody about this. It's really getting to me. I may even have to quit my job in the museum because of it."

"So, what is it, mussel mouth? You can tell your old Uncle Lester anything in complete confidence. Har! Har! Har!"

"Well, you see, there's this freezer in the dissection room at the museum. It's about the size and shape of a coffin. And I'm dying to look into it. I just have this uncontrollable compulsion to see what's inside. But I'm scared of what I'll find. I'm torn between my fear and my curiosity. I just can't stand it any more!"

"Har har har har har har har har!" Lester said. "Har har har."

"And what I was wondering, Lester, is if maybe you and I could sneak out to the museum right now and open that freezer. I've got a key."

"Sure!" he said. "Sounds like fun!"

"No kidding, Lester? You promise you won't chicken out? That no matter what, you'll open the freezer? I'd hate to have to tell the guys that you were afraid to open the freezer!"

"Let's go," Lester said, bounding out of his bunk.

After checking to make sure the campus security police were nowhere in sight, I unlocked the door to the museum and we slipped inside. I told Lester we couldn't turn on any lights because that would alert campus security to our presence. We'd just have to make do with the lights from the display cases, which cast an eerie glow about the room.

"You're not getting nervous are you, Lester?" I asked, as we worked our way through the museum.

"Har! Har! Har!" Lester laughed.

I led him up alongside the rattlesnake case. Lester stared dully at the snakes. Then, *buzzzzz-buzzzzz pop! pop! pop!* The snakes hit the glass a few inches from his face.

As soon as he had stopped dancing up and down, Lester said, "You should have told me they were alive! How was I to know they would strike at me!" I could see the level of adrenaline rising through his eyes.

We moved on a ways. "What's that behind you?" I asked suddenly. Lester spun around to stare the timber wolf in the fangs. Even in the soft glow of the display lights, I thought I could see outward signs of Lester's heart ricocheting around his rib cage. "Oh, just an ol' timber wolf," I said. "Nothing to be afraid of." By now, I calculated that Lester's circulation system was pumping about 80 percent adrenaline. And I hadn't even shown him the carnivorous beetles yet.

When we reached the door of the windowless dissection room, I told Lester to wait outside until I had gone in and turned on the light. He didn't argue. I slipped in and placed my note on top of the freezer, then flipped the wall switch. The lights came on in a blinding glare. Then I opened the door and motioned Lester in.

"Here's something you might find interesting, Lester," I said, in the manner of a tour guide. "These beetles are used to clean all the flesh off skeletons. Gee, I wonder what they are working on now."

Lester stared at the quivering black mass of beetles, his eyes widening in horror.

"Hear their tiny little *chomp-chomps?*" I asked.

"Yeh," Lester said weakly.

I turned and pulled Lester stumbling along behind me. "Now over here we have the freezer. Looks sorta like a coffin, doesn't it? Maybe now you can see why it gives me the creeps. Can't tell what might be in there, but I've got this terrible compulsion to find out! How about you, Lester?"

"Hunh?"

"Boy am I glad you came along to open up the freezer for me, Lester. But what have we here? Seems to be a note. Dang! I forgot my spectacles! Read it for me, will you, Lester?"

Lester's eyes fastened on the note like a matched set of vises. "*Good jumpin' gosh almighty,*" he hissed through his teeth, something that's not that easy to do even in the best of times.

"Well, forget the note, we're wasting time," I said. "Go ahead and pop her open, and let's see what's inside."

"N-no!" Lester said.

"C'mon!" I said. "Quit kidding around! Flip up the ol' lid there!"

"Un-unh," Lester said, shaking his head.

"You mean you're too chicken to open the freezer?" I asked.

"Un-hunh," Lester said, nodding affirmatively.

"Har! Har! Har!" I replied. "Too chicken to open a measly old freezer! Wait till the guys hear about this! I guess I'll just have to open it myself!"

I grabbed the lid and flipped it up, watching Lester's face all the while in order to record every detail of his reaction so I'd be able to provide the guys in the dorm with an accurate report. There was, for instance, this little popping motion of his eyeballs as he stared into the open freezer. Then there was the way his jaw sagged and a bit of drool rolled over his lower lip. Overall, there was the general response of someone accidentally sticking a finger in an empty light socket. The effect was even better than I had hoped for.

"Har! Har! Har!" I laughed. "There, you see, it's empty!" I turned to point into the freezer. "Har! Har! HAAAAAAARRRRRR!"

Ol' Lester may have been a spoiled brat, but he sure knew how to run. I counted at least three times that he passed me on our way back to the dorm.

Later, I learned that, unbeknownst to me, the curator had stored a dead black bear in the freezer, its skin partially peeled off.

Lester and I went on to become good friends, and that winter I even taught him how to trap muskrat, just in case he ever ran short of money. He changed into as nice a guy as you would ever want to meet. It seemed as if the scare at the museum had purged all the meanness and smugness and arrogance out of Lester. Heck, I was even a little purged myself.

The Gift

☞ ☞ ☞Christmas is an uneasy time for me. Maybe it's because my father was a practical joker. When I was small he would tell me that if I didn't behave myself Santa would fill my stocking with kindling sticks and rotten potatoes. I would try to behave myself but could never seem to get the hang of it. Christmas thus became a matter of great apprehension to me, because even though I couldn't behave I wasn't stupid, and I figured Santa Claus had to have my name on some kindling and rotten potatoes. Sure enough, come Christmas morning I would creep out of bed, peek around the corner at my stocking, and there would be some kindling sticks protruding from it, along with a few sprouts from rotten potatoes.

"AAIIIGHHHHHH!" I would exclaim.

"Ho, ho, ho!" my father would laugh.

Then, of course, he would show me that under the kindling sticks and rotten potatoes were a ball, a top, some dominoes, a tin soldier, and maybe some candy orange slices. I would punish him by playing all day with kindling and potatoes. We didn't have psychology in those days; otherwise, I might have been emotionally scarred for life by my father's little trick. As it is, I become uneasy at Christmastime.

One of the reasons I become uneasy is the cost of things I put in my own kids' stockings: digital watches, rock-concert tickets, skiing lessons, and the like. Fortunately, the kindling sticks and rotten potatoes don't cost much and never fail to give me a good laugh. There's nothing funnier than teenagers dumping out their stockings and exclaiming, "AAIIIGHHHHHHHH!" They exclaim that when they discover the stocking doesn't contain a set of keys to a new car.

Probably the main reason for my unease, however, is the gifts I receive for Christmas. Whenever the kids ask my wife what to get Ol' Whosis for Christmas, she tells them, "You know how he loves outdoor sports. Why don't you get him something outdoorsie?"

"Good idea," they cry in unison. "How much can he afford for us to get him?"

Let me state here that there should be a law prohibiting any person who uses the term "outdoorsie" from dispensing advice about what kinds of presents to buy an outdoorsman. A few years ago, after my spouse advised her I would like something outdoorsie, one of my wealthy aunts gave me something called the Ultimate Fishing Machine. As near as I could make out from the operational manual, you stayed at home and watched TV while the UFM went out and caught the fish, cleaned them, cooked them, and ate them. When it got back home, you asked the UFM what kind of luck it had and it told you lies.

The manufacturer claimed in his literature that the Ultimate Fishing Machine had been made possible through the miracle of miniaturization. I would have preferred a miracle that assembled the machine before passing it on to me. At the very least, the company could have miniaturized an engineer and enclosed him in the package to help put the UFM together.

I never even attempted to assemble the Ultimate Fishing Machine and so cannot report on its competence at fishing. Bothersome as it may be, I'd just as soon go to the trouble of catching, cleaning, cooking, and eating my own fish. If I work at it, I can probably even learn to tell fishing lies.

Nothing gladdens the heart of a sporting-goods store proprietor more than to be approached by a lady who says something like, "My husband is the outdoorsie type. I wonder if you might suggest a suitable Christmas gift for him."

The proprietor grins evilly and rumples his hair so as to conceal the horns protruding just above his temples. Here is his chance to revenge himself on one of the arrogant sportsmen who have snorted derisively and even guffawed openly at certain items of the proprietor's stock.

"Here's something fishermen are absolutely crazy about," he says. "The musical fishing creel! Every time a fish is inserted, it plays Beethoven's Fifth Symphony. If they go over their limit, Elvis Presley sings 'I Ain't Nothin' but a Hound Dog.'"

"Marvelous!" the wife exclaims. "I'll take it! Any other suggestions?"

"Now here's a nifty item—a pair of sleeping-bag warmers for backpackers."

"They look like bricks."

"That's what they are—but not just your ordinary bricks. No ma'am. These are special high-density bricks —just feel how heavy they are. The way they work, the backpacker heats them in the campfire and then inserts them in his sleeping bag. Keep him toasty warm all night."

"What a nice idea," the wife says. "I'll take a set."

"How about a gag gift for the fellow who likes to go out exploring by himself in the wilds—a trick compass. See, every time you look at it, North shifts to a different direction. Ha! Ha! It comes with maps that instantly dissolve when they come in contact with cold sweat. The compass and maps together are sold as The $8.95 Do-It-Yourself Divorce Kit."

"It's tempting," the wife says, "but I'd better not."

"Here's a nice gift for the man who has nothing," the proprietor tells her. "A tiny inflatable vest for grasshoppers. Keeps them afloat, and with this little harness to fasten them to the hook, they can be used over and over until a fish takes them or they die of old age."

"That is absolutely *darling!*" the wife exclaims. "I'll take two."

"Did I show you the grasshopper water skis . . . ?"

There are other reasons for my unease at Christmas.

After my father died, Christmas was a rather bleak occasion at our house for a number of years. I got a foreshadowing of just how bleak one Christmas was going to be when my mother warned me, "If you don't behave, all Santa is going to put in your stocking is kindling sticks."

"What about the rotten potatoes?" I asked.

"He can't afford them this year," she said.

Santa always seemed to come through with something though, even if it was pre-owned, as they say. I would get some used clothes, used books, used toys, used candy. It was my sister, the Troll, who gave me the used candy.

"This Snickers bar has teeth marks on it," I said.

"I know," the Troll said. "I forgot, I don't like caramel."

"You didn't lick it all over, did you?" I asked, examining the bar carefully for lick marks.

"No," she said. "What kind of a person do you think I am?"

Thinking that she was the kind of a person who would lick a Christmas present, I worried for weeks after eating the candy bar that I would come down with some terrible disease carried by sisters.

Even back when I was nine or ten I was known as an outdoorsie type among the relatives. Rich Aunt Maude wrote my mother and asked what kind of outdoorsie present I would like for Christmas. My mother wrote back that I would "just love something related to fishing." We speculated for weeks whether Maude would send me a fine fishing rod or a fine reel or a tackle box filled with tackle. I thought possibly she might even come through with a boat, motor, and trailer. When the gift arrived though, the boat, motor, and trailer were instantly ruled out because of the package's minuscule dimensions, so minuscule in fact that they also ruled out the fine fishing rod, reel, and tackle box. I figured all it could be was a fly book filled up with expensive flies. Christmas morning we all got up and rushed down to the Christmas bush, and the family waited with bated breath—mouthwash being unknown to us in those days—as I tore open the package from rich Aunt Maude. Even to this day I can recall my response upon unveiling the present:

"AAIIIGHHHHHHHH!"

There, lying in state before me in a monogrammed box with glittering foil wrapping and soft crinkly tissue paper were . . . *two silk neckties . . . with pictures of fish on them!*

"Don't be so upset," my mother pleaded, pulling me down off the wall. "You can wear them with your new suit—whenever you get a new suit."

"And whenever you get a neck," the Troll added. "Now open my present!"

"What is it?" I said, my bitterness ebbing.

The Troll smiled sweetly. "Gum."

I must say it was pretty good gum, too. There was still a lot of flavor left in it.

My mother always used to say that we should be grateful for whatever we received. "Just think," she would admonish us, "there are millions of people all over the country living in poverty, who can't even afford popcorn to decorate their Christmas bush with."

I tried not to think of the poor people as I decorated the bush. "How does this look?" I would ask as I stepped back to study my placement of the popcorn.

"Why not put it right up on the tip?" the Troll would suggest. "That way it'll look like a little tiny white star."

The only poor person I knew at that time was Rancid Crabtree, the old woodsman who lived at the foot of the mountain about a mile from our place. I spent a large part of my early life following Rancid around and studying him and learning all sorts of interesting things. But Rancid was poor. He didn't seem to know that he was poor, however, and I never had the heart to tell him, because he was the happiest person I'd ever met. If he had known he was poor, of course, then he would have been sad and miserable all the time. As it was, Rancid was able to live out his whole life in blissful ignorance of the fact that he was poor.

A few days before Christmas one year, I wandered over to Rancid's cabin to see what he was up to. He was carrying an armload of firewood into the cabin and invited me in. I looked around, expecting to see a Christmas bush with some presents under it. There was nothing but the rumpled bed, the old barrel stove, a table and some broken chairs, rusty traps, a shotgun and some rifles on wall pegs, and a few other odds and ends.

"Where's your Christmas bush?" I asked him.

"If Ah was to have anythang, it 'ud be a Crimmas *tree*. But Ah don't see why Ah got to brang a tree into the house when all Ah's got to do is look out the winder and see all of 'ems Ah want."

"But what do you put all your presents under?" I persisted.

Rancid stared at me for a long moment, then snorted. "Ah use to git all kinds of presents. They'd be piled up n'ar to the ceilin' and Ah be kickin' an' stumblin' over 'em all the time. So finally Ah just up an' tells folks to shet off givin' me all them presents. Ya know, Ah ain't missed 'em one bit. A man jist outgrows presents, Ah guess."

I hoped I'd never outgrow presents, and while I was thinking about that, a great wave of sorrow crashed down upon me and poured right down into the insides of my feet and filled up my toes and then came welling back up again into my throat.

"What's wrong with you, boy?" Rancid said.

"Your stove is smoking," I choked. "I better get some fresh air," and I bolted out the door.

Rancid came out on the porch and watched me as I gasped cold air into my lungs.

That was when the great idea occurred to me.

"Say, Rancid," I said, "why don't you come have Christmas dinner with us at our house?"

"Naw, Ah couldn't do thet. You know yer ol' granny an' me don't git along."

"Why, it was her who told me to invite you," I lied. "She said to me, 'Now you go give Rancid Crabtree an invite to Christmas dinner!' "

"Wall, dad-gum maw hide! Shore! You tell her Ah'd be happy as a hawg at a hangin' to shar' yer Crimmas vittles with y'alls."

When I told Mom that I had invited Rancid to Christmas dinner, she said she didn't know if we could afford the extra expense.

"Heck, he won't eat that much," I said.

"The expense I'm talking about is repairing the hole in the roof when your grandmother goes through it."

Gram didn't go through the roof when she heard the news about Rancid. She took it rather well as a matter of fact, as soon as she got done hopping up and down in the middle of the kitchen and saying "AAIIIGHHHH!"

"Good gosh almighty, boy, do you know what you've done? That Rancid Crabtree ain't took a bath since he fell in the crick in '27. Folks pay him just to walk by their farms so the smell will drive the ticks off their critters. And you invite him to Christmas dinner! Well, all we can do is put the extra leaves in the table and set you and him down at the far end!"

"Hoooray!" I shouted. "I'll even help get things ready. How many extra leaves we got for the table, Gram?"

Gram shook her head. "Not nearly enough, boy, not nearly enough!"

Personally, I didn't think that Rancid smelled all that bad, but there was a story told that his approach from an upwind direction had once raised an alarm that the stockyards had caught on fire. In any case, there was a great deal of moaning and groaning among the women-folk that Rancid's presence at Christmas dinner would be a lingering one. The Troll practiced eating with her nose pinched together, and Gram and Mom debated whether we should eat with all the windows open and hope a blizzard would come up and provide a strong cross draft.

All of this carrying on began to worry me, because I didn't want to ruin Christmas dinner for the rest of the family. So, the day before Christmas I hastened through the snow to Rancid's cabin with the notion of persuading him that coming to dinner might not be such a good idea after all. Upon approaching the cabin, however, I noticed great white clouds rising from the doors and windows and cracks in the roof. I thought the place was on fire, and ran yelling for Rancid to get out of the cabin.

Rancid stuck his head out of a steam cloud. "What in tarnation is all the ruckus about?"

I peeked past him into the cabin. There was a great tub on top of the barrel stove, which was belching out smoke and flames on all sides, and the clouds of steam were boiling up from the tub.

"Whatcha got in the tub?" I asked.

Rancid shuddered. "Water. Ah'm gonna do somethin' Ah ain't did since '27. It's a torture to me, but Ah'm gonna do it jist fer you. Ah hope you appreciate it. An' don't never ast me to do it ag'in, 'cause Ah ain't!"

"Oh, I won't, I won't never ask you to do it again, Rancid." I turned to sprint happily back to my house. "See you at Christmas dinner tomorrow!"

When I burst into the kitchen, Gram was just removing from the oven a batch of cinnamon rolls.

"You don't have to worry about eating with the windows open at Christmas dinner tomorrow," I told her.

"Oh? Rancid ain't comin'?"

"He's coming all right, but this very moment he's fixing us up a nice surprise."

"A gift! Land sakes alive, we didn't think to get that dirty ol' rascal anything!"

"Well, it's not exactly . . ."

Gram slapped a hot cinnamon roll out of my hand. "Don't tell me exactly. I'll just wrap up these cinnamon rolls for him. Ain't nobody gives us a present we don't give him a present back!"

"But . . ."

"No but's!"

Christmas day, as we waited for Rancid to show up for dinner, Mom said, "I'd feel better about this if we already had all the windows open when he came. That way we wouldn't be so likely to hurt his feelings."

"That's the way I feel about it, too," Gram said. "And we should of put the extra leaves in the table."

Suddenly, the Troll, who had been looking out the window, shouted, "Here he comes! And wow! You're not going to believe this!"

There was a knock on the door, and Mom called out, "Come right on in, Rancid!"

In burst Rancid with a big snaggletoothed grin. "Surprise!" he shouted.

And were we surprised? Why, you could have knocked every last one of us over with a feather!

As soon as Mom had recovered from her astonishment enough to speak, she said, "Rancid, why don't you throw open a few of those windows over there and let in some fresh air while we put the extra leaves in the table. Then I want to get a better look at those skis."

"Steamed the curve into the tips mawsef," Rancid said proudly. "Put a couple birch boards in a tub of water on top of maw stove and them ol' tips bent up jist as purty as you please. Ain't made a pa'r of skis since '27."

"A mite wider on that window, if you please,

Rancid," Gram said. "My, don't that blizzard feel good!
Now let me feast my eyes on them skis."

"Thar fer the boy," Rancid said. "But Ah made them
big nuff y'all can use 'em if ya wants."

That was one of the finest Christmas gifts and one of
the finest Christmas dinners I have ever known. As Mom
said as we sat shivering happily around the table, "It's a
chill wind that blows no warmth."

The Sensuous Angler

☞ ☞ ☞ There would be a lot less divorce in this country if more husbands and wives fished together. Spouses that fish together stay together.

My wife, Bun, for example, used to absolutely detest fishing. Whenever I dragged her out on the lake, she would sit there in the boat with her eyes fixed on me in an unblinking stare that I often imagined to be almost murderous. From time to time I'd even speak a few kind words to her in an effort to break the spell: "Row a bit faster along here, will you, Bun? I don't want my lure to get snagged in the weeds." Of course, there are some people who just don't respond to kind words, and Bun seemed to be one of them.

Besides my compulsive interest in fishing, what complicated our marital situation even more was that women find me extraordinarily attractive. "Irresistible" would not be too strong a word. I sometimes have to laugh to myself at the great show they put on to make me think they're totally unaware of my existence. Just recently I was sitting next to a beautiful woman on the uptown bus. I could tell she was flustered by the way she rummaged around in her purse, finally dug out a compact, and started fixing her face. It was absolutely hilarious, particularly when she wiped off some excess eye shadow with the tip of my tie. I mean, there are no lengths to which women will not go in their pretense of ignoring me!

Bun, quite forgivably, used to be terribly jealous. I'd try to kid her out of it. When we would come home from grocery shopping, I'd say, "Did you see how that cute blonde at the store was pretending to ignore me? I nearly laughed out loud!"

"There's only one can of tuna here," Bun would say. "I could have sworn I bought two cans of tuna."

That's how bad it was. Mad, uncontrollable jealousy was practically destroying our marriage.

The combination of my obsession with fishing and my irresistible appeal to women took a more extreme turn for the worse one day when Bun discovered a reddish smudge on the collar of one of my white dress shirts.

"Aha, I've got you now, you rascal," she snarled. "What's this red smudge on your shirt collar?"

How had I ever managed to overlook that smudge? My mind raced, feverishly searching for a plausible lie.

"It's probably just a lipstick smudge from one of the girls at the office," I tried.

"Ha!" Bun snapped. "I wasn't born yesterday, you know! This is salmon-egg juice! Here I think you're down at the office working, and actually you're sneaking off to go fishing. You've probably rented a secret apartment where you keep an extra set of fishing gear!"

"But there's this other woman . . ." That's as far as I

got. If there's one thing I can't stand about Bun, it's the way she expresses her jealousy by laughing uncontrollably.

Actually, there *was* another woman. Her name was Jennifer, and she worked in the same advertising agency I did. There was something about her that made it almost impossible for me to keep my eyes off of her. As with most women, she made a great show of ignoring my existence. There was that time, for instance, when I was standing by the coat rack and she tried to hang her coat on me. Of course she had laughed in an embarrassed way, but not until she had made repeated efforts to keep her coat from slipping off my shoulders.

My job at the agency was to invent benevolent lies about a client's product. So distracted was I by Jennifer that one day I allowed a truth to slip into my copy and was nearly fired. Naturally, I was upset by the mishap, and as soon as the boss had gone down to the shop to resharpen his reamer, I whipped out my portable fly-tying outfit and began to tie a few Royal Henchmen to soothe my nerves. Suddenly I felt a pair of eyes on me. At first I thought it was Charley Fife, playing another one of his grotesque practical jokes. Then I realized it was Jennifer watching me. She came over to my desk.

"Hello," she said, holding out a hand. "I'm Jennifer. You must be new here."

"Oh, I've been here awhile," I replied suavely.

"How long?"

"Four years."

"Strange that I've never noticed you before. Our desks are only twenty feet apart."

"Yes, well *I've* noticed you, Jennifer."

"You have? Anything in particular."

"Is there ever!" I breathed. "For one thing, there's the way you read *Field & Stream* so avidly at lunch while the other girls are gawking at *Glamour*. Then I saw the way you took that casting reel apart and put it back together when you were supposed to be typing the annual report."

"Oh dear!" she cried, tittering. "You caught me in the act, did you? I was just cleaning my Protron Ninety Double-Widget Power-Glide Pro-Caster."

"You're telling me!" I said. "You have about the prettiest little Pro-Caster I've ever laid eyes on."

A flush of embarrassment filled Jennifer's cheeks, reminding me of the red-bellies I used to catch in the creek behind our house when I was a kid. As she bent over to whisper in my ear, I detected the faint, lingering fragrance of OFF! "Did you notice anything else?" Her voice was husky.

"You mean . . the way you rewrapped the split bamboo rod during your coffee breaks last February? Of course I noticed! It nearly drove me wild!"

She smiled. "You're really a very attract . . . You're not that bad look . . . I like large ears a lot, I really do."

I chuckled. The poor girl was practically tongue-tied.

"What attracted me to you most, though," she continued, "was your little portable fly-tying outfit. It's lovely! Say, I've got an idea. Why don't you stop by my place tonight and we'll . . . well, you know?"

"I know!" I said. "I know!"

After I had slipped into Jennifer's apartment that evening, she poured us each a glass of wine and turned on the stereo. Then we got right down to business. I was amazed, I must tell you, at what that woman knew. In fifteen minutes she taught me more about how to cure fresh steelhead eggs for bait than all the grizzled old anglers I've ever known. Such was our mad frenzy of curing steelhead eggs that some of the juice apparently splashed on my collar. That was the spot my wife detected.

"No one must ever find out about us," I told Jennifer as we shook hands at the door of her apartment as I was leaving.

"Oh, I know, I know," she said. "But next time, next time . . ."

"What?" I gasped. "Tell me what, Jennifer!"

"Next time . . . I'll show you how to filet perch!"

I was puzzled. "But, Jennifer, I know how to filet perch."

She gave me a lascivious smile. "Not the way *I* do it."

My imagination did a wild dance, raising goose bumps on my flesh the size of bongo drums. "When can we do it?" I asked. "When can we filet perch together?"

"Maybe next Tuesday night. Call me after eight. But if a man's voice answers, hang up."

"A man's voice?"

"Yes, my husband's. He is very big, with a short temper. And he hates fishing and fish. It would be most unfortunate for you if he caught us—you know—fileting together."

I shuddered at the image conjured up by her warning.

It was a long week. Every time I looked up, I saw Jennifer typing reports a few yards away. I could scarcely tear my eyes away from her flying fingers, those very fingers which, but a few days before, I had watched . . . had watched knead alum into a sinewy mess of steelhead eggs. Once a man, an angler, has experienced that with a woman, there is no turning back. And she had this lovely way of tossing her head. It reminded me of the way a fly fisher, hands filled with rod and line, will toss his head in order to shake a deer fly off his nose. It was beautiful.

At home during supper, I found myself staring absently at my plate. All I could think about was fileting with Jennifer.

"What's wrong with Pop?" one of the kids asked one evening. "How come he doesn't tell us those stupid stories about his childhood any more?"

"Don't complain," their mother said. "Your father has important things on his mind."

"We ain't complaining!" the kids said in unison. "We ain't complaining!"

"Have some respect!" I shouted at them. "I never once talked to one of my parents like that! Why, one time when I was only eight years old and had just walked the fifteen miles home from school in knee-deep snow . . ."

"Forget I mentioned it," the first kid said.

After supper Bun followed me into my den, also jestingly referred to as "the hole under the stairs." She put her hands on my shoulders and said, "Something's wrong. I know something's wrong. You get upset over the smallest things. I saw the way your eyes became all teary when you couldn't stab that last pea with your fork at supper. You can tell me! What's wrong?"

"Nothing's wrong," I said. What made me feel so bad about my affair with Jennifer is that Bun's a great wife. Sure, she has her faults. There was that time she screamed as if she had found Jack the Ripper in our refrigerator instead of merely a mayonnaise jar containing live hellgrammites. Heck, Jennifer would never have screamed at the sight of a few crummy live hellgrammites.

The truth was that Jennifer didn't really stand a chance of coming between my wife and me. Ol' Bun and I had just been through too many things together. She had stuck with me through thin and thin. The only thing to do, I told myself, was to try to forget Jennifer. But I couldn't.

When Tuesday night rolled around, I slipped out to a pay phone and called Jennifer's number. Jennifer answered.

"Is it all right?" I asked.

"Yes," she said, breathlessly. "Hammer is flying out of town on a business trip tonight and won't be back until tomorrow."

"Great!" I said. "I'll sneak right over."

I told Bun I was going to spend the evening with the boys down at Kelly's Bar & Grill and not to expect me home too early. She said fine, that she would leave the key under the cushion on the porch swing. I was halfway over to Jennifer's before it occurred to me that there isn't a cushion on the porch swing. We don't even have a porch swing. We scarcely have a porch. I wondered if Bun suspected anything.

A sudden thought jolted me: *Hammer? Her husband's name is Hammer?*

When Jennifer met me at the door, I was disappointed to find her dressed in a low-cut, filmy negligee.

"You're early," she said. "Mix yourself a drink while I slip into something a little more comfortable." Presently she returned from the bedroom dressed in baggy, patched fishing pants and a plaid wool shirt sprinkled with fish scales.

"Hey hey hey!" I said. "Now that's more like it!" I thrust a package into her hands. "By the way, here's a little something for you."

Her hands tore eagerly at the wrappings. Nervously, I wondered if maybe I had made a mistake, giving her such a personal gift so soon in our relationship.

"Oh!" she cried, clapping her hands together in

delight. "They're beautiful! You shouldn't have! They must have cost you a small fortune!"

"Nope," I said, smiling modestly. "I caught them myself. Off the old Grand Street fishing pier. Do you really like them?"

Jennifer wiped her joy-streaked cheeks on her shirt sleeve. "Oh, I love them! They are absolutely gorgeous perch! All Hammer ever gives me are long-stemmed red roses and dumb furs."

It was obvious her husband was either a thoughtless clod or totally insensitive. Some men just don't know how to treat a woman!

Overcome by the excitement of the moment, Jennifer and I rushed into the kitchen and began to filet madly. Never have I known a woman who could filet like Jennifer! Perch after perch fell under her flashing knife. I became mesmerized by her very motions, the way she whacked off the heads, stripped away the skins, and sliced off the filets. Time ceased to exist for me, and all space seemed confined to Jennifer's laminated maple chopping block.

Then the earth moved.

"Did the earth move for you, Jennifer?" I asked.

"Yes yes yes yes yes!" she cried. "And do you know what made it move?"

"What?"

"Hammer! He always trips on that last step at the top of the stairs!"

"HAMMER?" I yelled. "I thought you said he was away on business!"

"Maybe he missed his flight! Maybe he suspects something! But that is Hammer coming down the hall!"

Now I could feel the earth move with every step Hammer took down the hallway. The steps sounded angry.

"What'll we do?" I hissed at Jennifer.

"What do you mean 'we,' you burglar you!" she snapped.

Somehow I felt that Jennifer had chosen that moment to break off our relationship. Very soon I expected her husband to break off more than that.

"Look at the evidence!" I hissed, as Hammer rattled his key in the lock. "He'll know we've been fileting together. No matter what you tell him, he'll know a burglar didn't break into the apartment and force you to filet!"

Jennifer scooped up all the evidence and flung it into the freezing compartment of the refrigerator.

"Jen?" called out Hammer, his voice rumbling into the kitchen like a slow freight.

A second before Hammer's shadow fell upon us, Jennifer lunged across the kitchen, threw her arms around me, and planted a big, wet, utterly disgusting kiss on my mustache. And then Hammer filled the doorway.

"Who dis?" he demanded, pointing at me with a finger the size of a zucchini.

"Oh," said Jennifer, "this is just one of my professors from night school who heard you were going to be out of town tonight and thought he'd sneak by."

"You 'spect me to buy a cock'n'bull story like dat? It smells fishy in here! You two been up to somethin' wid fish, ain'tcha? Filetin'! I'll bet the two of you have been filetin' behind my back. Or maybe even, even—I can't stand the thought of it—curin' steelhead eggs for bait! As soon as I leave town to do a little job for the Godfather . . ."

"No, no, Hammy, it wasn't anything like that," Jennifer cried. "Please don't kill him!"

"Repeat that last part, would you, Jennifer?" I whispered to her. "I don't think Hammy heard it."

At that moment Hammer blinked, giving me the opportunity to leap out the kitchen window and sprint to safety down the alley. When I finally stopped to catch my breath, I made up my mind right then and there that never again was I going to filet with another man's wife, particularly one whose apartment was higher than the ground floor. For one thing, it's so darn hard to sprint to safety with your legs protruding from your armpits.

I had learned my lesson about other women and decided that the thing to do was to give my own wife more instruction in the art of fileting. That way she might even learn to enjoy the sport. And the very next weekend I started her lessons.

"All right, Bun," I instructed, "just remember that balance is everything. There, you've nearly got it. Raise your right arm a bit more. Good. Now you've got the idea! Heck, you could carry the canoe all day like that if you had to. Get started toward the lake now, and I'll grab my fly rod and be right along behind."

Bun still isn't too enthusiastic about fishing yet. As a matter of fact, just the other day when we were out on the river she said if I would forget about the idea of making her my fishing pal, she wouldn't complain about another woman or two.

Not a chance! "Listen, Bun," I said, "you're the only woman for me, and I'm going to make you love fishing if it's the last thing you do."

I could have sworn that she was so touched by this remark that a single tear trickled down her cheek. It was hard to tell for sure, though, because of the cloud of mosquitoes around her.

And Now
Stay Tuned for
"The Camp Chef"

☞ ☞ ☞**A** friend of mine, Fred Flim, is a television producer, and at lunch a while back I suggested to him that what the tube needs now is a show about camp cookery. Scarcely able to conceal his enthusiasm for such a show, Fred pretended to be totally absorbed in an effort to suck the pimento out of a martini olive.

"Great concept, hunh?" I said.

"Fantastic," Fred said. "Hey, man, can you believe those Yankees! What a team! After those first two games, I would have . . ."

"You really like the idea that much?" I said, almost overcome by excitement. "You're not just putting me on? Wow! I hope you're not just saying this because we're such good friends."

Fred turned serious, his gravity only slightly lessened by his having clenched a large, pitless green olive grotesquely in his eye. "May I have this dance, Miss?" he asked me, hunching his neck down into his shoulders and reaching out with two bread sticks protruding from his sleeves. People who are not friends of Fred's often have difficulty telling when he's being serious.

I chuckled appreciatively at his little performance and told him that it reminded me of the time his wife thought he was on a three-day fishing trip with me but wasn't and what a kick she'd get out of the story.

Fred plucked the olive from his eye and put the bread sticks back in their basket. "What are you thinking of calling this show of yours?" he asked.

" 'The Camp Chef,' " I replied. "It will be kind of an outdoorsie 'The French Chef' but with me as the star instead of Julia Child."

"Fantastic," he said. "Really fantastic. It sort of gets a person right here."

"How come there?"

"Well, I was never very knowledgeable about anatomy. Tell you what, you work up a script and get the necessary props together and be down at the studio at ten sharp Monday morning and we'll shoot a pilot of 'The Camp Chef.' "

"Fantastic!" I said, just to show Fred I was already picking up on the technical jargon.

"By the way," he said, "you don't happen to know any reliable hit men, do you?"

"No, I don't," I replied. "Anyway, the hit-man concept has been worked to death on television. I'd scrap that idea if I were you."

Fred smiled thinly and drummed his fingers on the table. I could tell he was already calculating the Nielsen ratings on "The Camp Chef."

I was a little late getting to the studio on Monday. For some unknown reason, my brakes failed just as I was approaching the steep, winding stretch of highway between my home and the television studio. The mechanic at the garage said it looked as if my brake line had been sabotaged, but I told him that was ridiculous. Then, while I was hoofing back to the house to get my camper truck, some idiot in a big black sedan nearly ran over me—twice!—which was odd, since I was walking across a cow pasture at the time.

Anyway, I was late getting to the studio, and I guess Fred had just about given up on me, because he seemed more than a little astonished when I showed up carrying all my props.

"Boy," I told him by way of explanation, "you just can't hire competent help anymore."

"You're telling *me!*" Fred interrupted.

"Yeah," I went on, "I had this guy do some repair work on my car last week, and the incompetent fool accidentally filed my brake line nearly in half. Lucky I wasn't killed."

"Hmmmmmm," Fred said. "What's all that junk you got in the gunnysack there, anyway?"

"These are the props for my show, 'The Camp Chef.'"

Fred shook his head. "Gee, I'm really sorry, but I forgot that we were going to do a pilot of your show today. All the studios are being used."

"That's all right, Fred, ol' buddy," I said. "Think nothing of it. Danged if it doesn't remind me of that time you were supposed to be on a three-day fishing trip with me but . . ."

Fred picked up a phone. "Clear Studio Five," he snarled. "We need it for a show on camp cookery. . . . That's right—*camp cookery!* Are you deaf or something!"

Just as we were stepping into the studio, a concrete block dropped from the darkness above us and crashed at my feet. It was a close call, and I must say I've never seen Fred more upset. Glaring up into the shadows, he screamed, "Not *here*, you meathead, not *here!*" I could tell this wasn't one of Fred's better days either.

Knowing that time is money in the television business, I immediately dragged my sack of props out to a lighted platform in front of the cameras and started to get everything arranged. I had studied Julia Child's technique for many years and consequently was quite familiar with the format, as they say, of cooking shows.

I quickly organized my cooking ingredients, utensils, and props, using as a table a piece of television equipment that didn't seem to be in use at the moment. My friend Retch Sweeney showed up about then, dragging several dried-up Christmas trees and a red-faced receptionist.

"You can't haul that junk in here," the receptionist whined.

"Where do ya want these trees, Pat?" Retch asked.

"Arrange them around the set," I said. "It's all right, Miss," I told the receptionist. "He's with me."

"Who are you?" she asked.

"I'm with Fred," I explained.

"Gee, I dunno," she said. "I better call the guard."

"Ha! Ha!" I laughed. "That reminds me of a funny story. One time Fred was supposed to be on a three-day fishing trip with me . . ."

"Oh, no!" she responded. "I remember you now! Yeah, come to think of it, Fred did tell me about your idea for a show."

"I bet he said to take good care of me, too, didn't he?"

"Gosh, I dunno. I thought he said he had arranged for somebody else to take care of you."

"Good ol' Fred," I said. "It would be hard to find a more considerate guy."

Even though dried out, Retch's trees gave a nice woodsy effect to the set.

Two cameramen came into the studio, yawning and scratching themselves, and started pushing the television cameras into position. I could see Fred in the director's booth arguing with a couple of technicians who kept shaking their heads. Finally Fred's voice came over a speaker: "You ready?"

"Yes," I said. "But there are only two cameramen here. I thought we'd use at least three cameras."

"Julia Child uses only two cameras," Fred said.

"In that case," I said, "I'm ready."

"Is your friend going to be on the set with you?" Fred asked. "We wouldn't want viewers confusing your show with 'The Incredible Hulk.'"

"Yeah, I'll need his assistance," I said.

"What'd he say?" Retch said.

"Nothing," I said.

"Okay, you're on!" Fred said.

I had no sooner gone into my introductory remarks than I detected a technical difficulty. The red light that indicates a television camera is on wasn't functioning on either camera. As soon as I had called Fred's attention to the problem, he corrected it, and I got my show under way again.

Looking back, I wish I hadn't tried quite so many complicated dishes on my first show. Otherwise, I don't think matters would have gotten out of hand.

I opened with my Whatcha-Got Hunters' Stew. As I explained, this stew derives its name from the situation of a group of hungry hunters meeting at night at the end of a mountain road and deciding to cook up a hearty meal before undertaking the long drive home.

"What we gonna cook?" one hunter will ask.

"How about a stew?" another hunter will say.

"What we gonna put in the stew?" still another hunter will inquire.

Then the hunter who suggested the stew will say, "Well, whatcha got?"

At that point the hunters will start rummaging around in their lunch sacks and food boxes and game pockets and trunks of their cars, tossing whatever they find into the stew pot. No one knows exactly what the ingredients of Whatcha-Got Hunters' Stew are because there is a firm rule against anyone shining a light onto it. I am told that once a hunter broke this rule and as a result had to be placed under a doctor's care for treatment of hypergagging.

Of course, I couldn't concoct an authentic Whatcha-Got Hunters' Stew in the television studio, but I came fairly close, or so I judged from the fact that when one of the cameramen zoomed in for a close-up shot of it he dropped to the floor, curled up in the prenatal position, and jammed a thumb in his mouth.

"One thing about camp cooking," my commentary went, "you can't be too picky about a few gnats, mosquitoes, ants, or even an occasional deerfly that happens to land in your stew. Since there are no live insects flying about the studio, ha, ha, I have to make do with some dried ones my kids gathered up for me in the garage. They are by no means as good as fresh insects but . . ."

At this point I was distracted by the sound of running footsteps headed for a restroom at the far end of the studio. I wondered in passing if television cameras can be operated by remote control, since cameramen seem to be such a temperamental lot. Still, there was nothing to do but continue with the show.

My Chipped Beef on a Shingle was a real smasheroo, judging from its impact on the individuals in the control booth.

My one moment of embarrassment came when I started to prepare Creek Mussels in Marshmallow Sauce and discovered that the piece of equipment on which I had placed the ingredients had heated up and the marshmallows had melted and dribbled down inside the thing. I was shocked, of course. You know how much marshmallows cost these days?

I had counted on Retch's assistance in the show, but early on a rather distinguished-looking lunatic in a pinstripe suit tried to rush onto the set. The guy probably would have ruined the whole show if Retch hadn't been able to get a half-nelson on him and wrestle him to the floor. There are some people who will do just about anything for a chance to clown around in front of a TV camera.

My most spectacular dish was the Flaming Bacon. It also provided me with the opportunity to demonstrate the proper procedure for extinguishing a small forest fire. I explained to the viewing audience that a shovel should always be carried for the purpose of smothering forest fires since one can't always expect to find the jacket of a pinstripe suit out in the woods.

Just as I was finishing up "The Camp Chef," my closing comments were practically drowned out by the sounds of sirens. As I told Retch while we were slipping out a back exit, you'd think television executives would wise up. Viewers are tired of all the violence on crime shows.

Several days later I happened to stumble across Fred as he was crawling under the front of my car with a hacksaw.

"Any idea when 'The Camp Chef' might be aired?" I asked him.

"Hoo hooo heeee haa hooo," he replied.

I could tell ol' Fred had been under a lot of strain

lately. That television business can really take it out of a person.

"Listen," I told him, "what you need is a good three-day fishing trip with me. Some of my camp cooking will straighten you out in nothing flat."

Oh, I tell you, the look of gratitude Fred gave me would have wrenched your heart!

The Heartbreak
of Astigmatism

☞ ☞ ☞When I was about fourteen the world turned fuzzy. I wasn't particularly concerned with the phenomenon at first, attributing it to the lateness of spring that year or possibly the Communists. It was a history teacher, Mrs. Axelrod, who finally diagnosed my affliction. She asked me to step to the front of the room and, with a long wooden pointer, indicate on the wall map the region occupied by Gaul. Not knowing Gaul from my left elbow, I decided to take a random stab at it anyway, since I figured the whole world, including the map, had become so blurred that no one would know the difference anyway. Also, my walk to the front of the classroom would give me an opportunity to display the attitude of debonair nonchalance I had been attempting to perfect. Arriving at the front of the room, I directed the pointer to a likely little fuzzy blotch. This drew a good laugh from the other kids, which I immediately capitalized on by doing a Gene Kelly soft-shoe routine on the way back to my desk.

"All right, Fred Astaire!" the teacher snarled. "I

want to see you dance yourself right back into this classroom immediately after school tonight!"

I was miffed. How could anyone mistake my Gene Kelly for a Fred Astaire? On the other hand, ever since the world had turned fuzzy, I myself was having trouble distinguishing the two of them even when they were forty feet high on the showhouse screen. Perhaps, I told myself, her *faux pas* was excusable.

I was hoping that by the time school was out, Mrs. Axelrod's rage would have withered a bit, but I found it still in full bloom. There was a rumor going around that the history teacher could kill flies in mid-air with her sarcasm, but I doubted there was any truth to it. Sure, a few flies may have been stunned but certainly not killed.

"Ah!" Mrs. Axelrod exclaimed as I entered the classroom. "The master of comic impersonations arrives!"

"Uh, I'm really sorry about that little dance," I apologized. "It was Gene Kelly, by the way."

"Oh, I should have known!" she replied. "I do hope you will forgive me!"

I flicked a stunned fly off my shoulder. "No problem," I said. "Anybody can make a mistake."

"Has anyone ever told you how obtuse you are?" she asked.

"No," I said, blushing, "but thank you very much. You're not so bad yourself, no matter what the kids say."

"Indeed!" she said, attempting to conceal her pleasure under a veil of wrath. "Well, now that the exchange of compliments is over, we are still left with the problem of Gaul."

"Actually," I confessed, "I didn't have the foggiest notion of where Gaul was, so I just took a flying guess. What country did I get?"

"Oh, you didn't get a country," she said with what I

thought I detected as a softening of tone. "You are apparently unaware that I also teach hygiene in this classroom. What you got was the bladder on an anatomical diagram of the human body!"

"Gee," I said, stunned. "It's a good thing you didn't ask me to point out Rome. We all would have been embarrassed."

"No doubt," she replied. "Are you by any chance having some trouble seeing clearly?"

"Not at all," I replied, gallantly scooping her folded coat up off her desk and helping her on with it. "Why do you ask?"

"Just a woman's intuition," she replied. "And little observations, such as the way you just now helped me on with the American flag."

"I did?" I said. "Well, to tell the truth, you look pretty good in stripes. Besides, it's so blurred that nobody would even guess it's a flag. Surely, you've noticed how fuzzy the world has become lately. I think it's the Communists doing it."

"My dear young man," she said. "I have some news for you. The world has not become fuzzy. Only *you* have become fuzzy. *You need glasses!*"

I was stunned. People had said a lot of bad things to me in my day, but this was the worst. I hadn't expected even Mrs. Axelrod to stoop this low, mean as she was. Didn't she know that I was famous for my vision, that my friends all called me Hawkeye. My gosh! Glasses! Spectacles! What was she saying? My mind reeled; my body beaded with sweat. If what Mrs. Axelrod said was true, that the world was not blurred, then my whole career was finished. No professional big-game guide could wear glasses! Jeez, could you imagine what one of my clients would think if I told him, "All right, we know the rhino's wounded and is going to charge as soon as we go in after him. But don't worry, I'm backing you up with my double-barreled elephant rifle. Before we start in, though, let me wipe the dust off my spectacles because I want to be able to see him real good."

And my squint! All the years I'd been practicing my squint, and now it was down the drain. A squint just doesn't look right behind a pair of glasses.

I tried to swear Mrs. Axelrod to secrecy, but she would have none of it. You probably have never met a person as mean as Mrs. Axelrod, so you may find it hard to believe the next thing she did. She called my parents and told them I needed glasses.

My folks wasted no time in hauling me down to an eye doctor to get me outfitted with spectacles. I did not go easily. My rage was such that it even worried the doctor. At one point he said to my mother, "Would you check his ropes again please? I think he's starting to work them loose."

Well, as I always said, you can buy a kid spectacles, but you can't make him wear them. I wore them only when my folks were around, and the rest of the time I carried them stuffed in my pocket where they stood a good chance of being broken. Then one day I was out in our pasture target practicing with my .22 rifle. After I had put ten successive shots right in the bull's-eye, the thought occurred to me that maybe if I wore my glasses I could hit a smaller bull's-eye, one less than three feet across. First, I made sure that no one was in the vicinity, a precaution I accomplished by shouting out "Hello! Anybody around!" Then I slipped the glasses out of my pocket and put them on.

The world snapped into focus. I could see mountains, trees, barns! I could see flowers and blades of grass and even ants crawling on the blades of grass. I hadn't seen ants in a year. I thought they had become extinct. It was . . . fantastic!

So after that whenever I went out into the great outdoors I wore my glasses, but only when alone. The real problem came when I was with the other guys. When we would go fishing, for example, I always had to pretend that I was clowning around.

"Hey, look at ol' Pat, he keeps casting his fly across the crick onto the sandbar! Ho, ho! That ol' Pat, he'll do anything for a laugh!" So then I'd have to go along with the gag and put on my hyena grin and wear my hat upside down. It was a real pain.

One day when my friend Peewee Thompson and I were sitting in my bedroom, I decided to sound him out on what he thought about people who wore glasses.

"Say, Peewee," I said. "You know that kid in the school band, Marvin Phelps, the one with the glasses, what do you think about the way he looks? He's a pretty good-looking kid, don't you think?"

Peewee gave me a nervous, sidelong glance. "I got to go home," he said.

"No, you idiot, what I mean is, do you think wearing glasses makes him look, uh, kinda funny?"

"Heck no. He's always worn glasses. He would look funny if he didn't wear them. He wouldn't even look like Four-Eyes Phelps if he didn't wear glasses. Why do you ask?"

"No reason," I said. "Just forget it."

"I'll tell you though," Peewee went on. "I sure wouldn't want ol' Four-Eyes Phelps backin' me up if I was goin' into the bush after a wounded rhino."

"I SAID FORGET IT!"

My greatest dread was that Rancid Crabtree would find out about my spectacles. If there was one thing

Rancid respected in another outdoorsman, it was keen vision. His own eyesight was superb. He was always the first to spot deer on a hunting trip. Pointing to a line of dots moving through the snow on the side of a mountain, he would say simply, "Deer." Then, while the rest of the hunters were straining to make out the dots, Rancid would say, "Mulies." The other hunters would stare at each other in disbelief. "Looks like they's all does, though. No, by gosh, one of 'em's a little spike buck!"

Rancid was the last person in the world I wanted to find out that I wore glasses. He wouldn't have any use for me after that.

One day we were in Rancid's old pickup truck on our way out to do some fishing, and, in his usual fashion, the old woodsman was pointing out distant sights to me. "Look up thar on thet side hill! Huncklebarries! Two or three of the little buggers are startin' to tarn color. Won't be long till they's ripe!"

I stared morosely off in the general direction he was pointing and tried to penetrate the green blur. "Yup. They sure do look like they're ripening up."

"Say, look at the size of them deer tracks crossin' the road. The deer thet made them was a biggun. Come fall, you 'n' me, we's gonna come up hyar an' look fer him, Ah kin tell you thet!"

"Yup," I said.

"What's wrong with you?" Rancid said. "You sound about as happy as a badger in a bees' nest."

"Nothin'," I said.

It was shortly after we got started fishing that Rancid began acting peculiar. Right at first he suggested that I fish upstream and he fish downstream.

"That's no fun," I told him. "We always fish together."

"Yeh," he said sheepishly. "Oh, all right, c'mon!"

The only good thing about my impaired vision was

that I could see perfectly up to a range of two feet. I therefore had no difficulty tying on the tiniest flies in my book, which I instantly deduced were the only flies likely to take trout in that particular time and place.

In the next twenty minutes or so I caught half a dozen fish. Rancid didn't get a single bite. "How come you don't change over to one of these little white flies?" I kept asking him. "That's what they're taking."

"Shoot," Rancid said. "Ah got this big ol' Grasshopper already tied on. Ah'll fish it."

Now this was totally unlike Rancid. I knew he didn't care all that much for work, but changing a fly didn't require any great effort. Usually he would have tried a dozen different flies by the time we got our feet wet. Then a whooper cutthroat (one that causes you to whoop, as distinguished from a mere whopper) smashed into my white fly. It took me a couple of minutes to land the fish.

"Wow, it's a beaut!" I whooped, thrashing my way across the creek to show Rancid the fish. When I was close enough, within two feet of him, I could see that his little eyes were bugged out in their comical fashion, as was their habit whenever he got excited.

"Gol-dang, thet's a purty fish!" he said, almost trembling. Instantly, he became stern. "You got any more of them itty-bitty white flies? All I brung with me was these big ones."

"Sure," I said, and handed him a couple.

Then Rancid did a remarkable thing. He reached into his pants pocket and hauled out a pair of spectacles, the kind you buy off the counter in a variety store. He put the glasses on, snipped the big fly off his tippet, and tied on the tiny one. Then he leveled a fierce glare at me.

"Wipe thet smirk off yer face," he snarled. "If you so much as open yer yap, I'll . . ."

I stepped back and thrust my hand into my pants pocket, took out my own glasses, and put them on. The stubby whiskers on Rancid's face snapped into focus. They quivered for a moment, then rippled out into the great crescent-shaped waves of his grin.

Neither one of us in all the years after that moment ever said a word about glasses. There was no need.

If a man like Rancid could wear glasses, I figured there couldn't be any shame in my wearing them. So the very next time I went out fishing with the guys, I showed up with my glasses on. The guys were all lifelong friends of mine, fellows I'd suffered with on a hundred camping trips. We had shared each other's triumphs and defeats, happiness and sorrows, the sweet and the bitter. When they saw me for the first time wearing my glasses, I learned once and for all the true meaning of friendship. It is that you don't thrash your friends within an inch of their lives if they laugh themselves silly when you show up wearing spectacles.

"What the heck," Peewee said later, after he had stopped pounding his thighs and had wiped away the tears of his mirth. "We ain't likely to run into a wounded rhino in this part of the country anyway."

Sneed

☞ ☞ ☞**B**ack in the shadows of time when I was a youngster, a man by the name of Darcy Sneed lived in our county. I don't think I ever heard anyone say a kind word for Sneed, and I'm sure nobody ever heard me say one. He was always showing up without notice when and where he wasn't wanted and causing folks grief. Several times he scared the daylights out of me, catching me alone out in the woods, but except for one time I always managed to escape. As far as I know, Sneed never smiled nor cracked a joke. He was cold and hard and tight-lipped and generally unlikable. Besides that, he was the game warden.

Now, the truth is I seldom broke the game laws, not because I had any love for rules and regulations but because it seemed unsporting. Once, though, my friend Retch and I did sneak down to the creek early one morning three days before the opening of fishing season. We hid in some deep brush along the bank and at the first hint of dawn cast our salmon eggs out toward a logjam, where we knew some cutthroat had to be waiting. But I was so filled with dread and guilt that I couldn't enjoy fishing, and I knew that if I caught anything it would just compound the existing dread and guilt. Retch, on the other hand, didn't seem burdened by any doubts and was intently working his line so the eggs would drift under the logs. Somehow, I had to impress upon him that what we were doing was wrong. I searched for the right words, the kind of words that would convey to him the deep moral and ethical implications of our action. Then I thought of them.

"Sneed's comin'!" I hissed at him.

Retch instantly grasped the deep moral and ethical implications and reeled in his line so fast only its being wet saved it from instant combustion. We stashed our rods under a log and beat it out of there, hurrying down the creek trail. Retch was in front. As he rounded a bend, he turned his head slightly and said out of the corner of his mouth, "Good thing you seen him comin'."

"Who?" I said, already having forgotten the lie.

"Sneed," he said.

And there was Sneed, striding purposefully toward us down the trail.

"Howdy, Mr. Sneed," we said politely.

Sneed didn't say anything for a moment. He just let his glare rove over our quaking carcasses. The seconds passed, ticked off by the sound of our dripping sweat.

"What you boys doin' here?" he demanded finally.

We answered simultaneously: "Lookin' for a cow." "Pullin' up thistles."

Sneed didn't smile at these contradictory explanations. He was not a fun-loving man.

"I'm going to ask you boys one more time, what you *doin'* here?"

By now I had forgotten who had told him what, so I nudged Retch to go ahead and answer, he being the more experienced and polished liar. But Sneed's glare had penetrated Retch's brain and tangled his speech mechanism.

"We was just pullin' up cows," he said.

Sneed replied with another long silence. Then he said, "Let me see if I've got this straight. You two were down here on the crick at five in the morning pullin' up cows, is that correct?"

Right then I figured Sneed was going to throw us in jail, and for what? Not being able to think of a decent lie when we had to.

Sneed reached out and thumped a bony finger on Retch's chest. "I know and you know that you boys were down here fishin', gettin' a jump on the season. I'd arrest you both, but I didn't catch you at it. Next time I will."

Sneed knew how to put fear into a person. If he didn't manage to keep people from breaking the game laws, he at least kept them from enjoying it. He never forgot me after that morning on the creek, having filed me away in his memory bank as a person who took the game laws lightly and who bore watching.

Sneed was not one of those game wardens who come semi-attached to the seat of a pickup truck; he knew how to walk and was infamous for suddenly materializing in remote and roadless places. There was a friend of our family who was widely regarded as the best trapper in our part of the state. During the winter he would snowshoe far back into the high country to work his trap line. "It's real nice to be up there alone in the winter," he told me once. "There's just you and the silence and the snow and Sneed."

Numerous theories were set forth regarding the game warden. One was that there were actually three Sneeds. This was based on multiple sightings of Sneed in different parts of the county at the same time. Men would shake their heads and say, "There's something unnatural about Sneed."

One time I was sitting in the kitchen of a chronic poacher, and he told me how he had outsmarted Sneed once.

"I strapped my heels down on my snowshoes and walked backwards with the deer over my shoulder. Funniest thing you ever seen. I hid in some trees at the top of a rise to watch, and pretty soon Sneed hits my trail. He looks one way and t'other, and then he takes off followin' my tracks toward where I been." The poacher nearly split his sides laughing at the memory of his little trick.

His wife glared at him. "Now, Otis, you tell the boy the rest of the story, you hear?"

Otis sobered up and reluctantly finished the tale. "Well, when I got the deer back to my truck and started scrapin' the frost off the winders, there's ol' Sneed sittin' inside, smokin' a cigarette calm as you please."

"Cost us a hunnert dollars!" the wife snarled. "Ain't no deer worth no hunnert dollars!"

"Durn that Sneed," the poacher muttered, glowering into the coffee grounds at the bottom of his cup.

Another time, three men poached a deer close to the bottom of a rocky gorge and waited until after dark to sneak it up to their car parked on a road a half-mile up the mountain. The going was rough, and as they fought their way upwards over logs and rocks and through brush, one of the poachers plopped down on the ground for a rest and gasped, "Man, this is hard! It's a good thing there's four of us to drag this here deer, 'cause otherwise I don't think we'd make it."

One of the other poachers looked around, counting heads in the darkness. "Ain't *s'posed* to be but three of us draggin' this deer," he said nervously.

"Ain't s'posed to be nobody draggin' it!" Sneed said.

Over the years, I heard dozens of such tales about Sneed, some true, some imaginary, but their net effect was to leave me with the impression that the game warden was possessed of powers not generally found among the psychic accessories of ordinary human beings. I never went afield with rod or gun that I didn't feel Sneed's presence. One of my great fears was that I would sometime lose count and catch one fish over my limit, and Sneed would nab me. Then I'd be fined a hundred dollars and since neither my family nor I had ever seen a hundred dollars altogether at the same time, I would have to go to jail. Well, I wouldn't be able to stand being in jail, so I'd have to break out and steal a car and escape in a hail of gunfire. After that I'd probably kill a bank guard and be fatally wounded myself. And while I was sprawled on a sidewalk breathing my last, a reporter would come up to me and ask, "What made you do it, son?" And I'd tell him: "I caught one fish over my limit." It was easy to see how it all would work out, so anytime I got anywhere near my limit I practically wore my fish out counting them. It was a heavy burden for a kid, especially for one who didn't have any better grasp of mathematics than I did.

In the light of this background, it will be clear that my decision to fish the forbidden waters of the creek that fed the town reservoir was not arrived at casually. Despite all my fears and misgivings, I was simply over-powered by the logic that led me to the conclusion that that creek had to be crammed full of giant eastern brook. I should mention here that water pollution as such was unknown at the time. It was simply referred to then as "dumpin' stuff in the cricks." A few enlightened and farsighted individuals would occasionally speak out in the cause of pure water. "I wish folks would stop dumpin' stuff in the cricks," they would say, thereby branding themselves forever after as wild-eyed eccentrics. The only creek that was sacrosanct was that of the town reservoir, the townspeople being in unanimous agreement that they didn't want anyone dumping stuff in their drinking water. My reasoning, however, was this: (1) a dry fly wouldn't dirty the water; (2) I would be providing a civic service by removing trout that certainly had to be dirtying it; and finally (3) my family got its water out of a well. There was only one flaw in this logic: Sneed.

My plan of attack seemed foolproof, however. I would sneak into the reservoir under cover of predawn darkness, follow the creek up into the dense woods that would provide me cover through the day, then do my fishing and return after nightfall. I would carry a few carefully selected flies, a length of leader, and some line, and cut myself a willow pole when I reached the spot where I wanted to start fishing. The night before I launched my assault on Reservoir Creek, I went to bed early, chuckling evilly over the boldness of the plan, beautiful even in its very simplicity. Ol' Sneed, as I told myself, had finally met his match.

Thus it was that I found myself returning home late the following evening with a fine catch of brook trout. The fishing had been just as fantastic as I had known it would be. Nevertheless, I was filled with fear and remorse and a dark sense of foreboding about what the future held for me. Part of the reason for these feelings was that I knew I had deliberately and maliciously broken the law, discovering too late that I possessed neither the temperament nor the taste for crime. The rest of the reason was that I was sitting alongside of Sneed in the front seat of his dusty old Dodge sedan.

As I had come sneaking up over the edge of a logging road on my way out of the reservoir basin, there was Sneed, sitting in his car with the lights off. True to his fashion, he didn't say a word. He just leaned over, pushed open the door on the passenger side, and motioned for me to get in. For an instant I thought of running, but then decided against it. You just can't move all that fast when you're paralyzed.

While Sneed drove along in his usual silence, I tried to appeal to his sympathy, even though from all the reports I'd heard no one had ever detected a smidgen of it in him.

"Look, Mr. Sneed," I said, "maybe it don't matter none to you, sending a kid to jail, but don't you care nothin' about that poor bank guard? What's his little children gonna do without him?"

"What bank guard?" Sneed said.

Before I could explain, a voice from the back seat said, "Ain't no use pleadin' with him, boy. When he was born, they heated him white hot and tempered him in oil, and he's been hard ever since."

This dismal report had issued from a tall, lean young man sprawled across the back seat and chewing on a match. He was covered with dirt and bits of grass and brush, apparently acquired in an attempt to escape from Sneed.

"What did he get you for?" I asked my fellow criminal, feeling an instant kinship with him.

"Nothin' a-tall. I was just up there on the mountain tryin' out my new jacklight. It must have riled up this ol' buck deer, 'cause first thing I know he come chargin' at me out of the brush. I had to shoot him to save my life!"

"Shut up, LeRoy," Sneed said. "You can tell it all to the judge."

About that time we drove up in front of my house. Sneed stopped the car and motioned for me to get out.

"You mean you ain't arresting me?" I said.

"What for?" Sneed said. "It ain't my responsibility to keep folks from fishin' that reservoir; it's the Water Department's. They own the water, and they own the fish in it. Besides, I get my drinkin' water from a well."

The game warden went on to tell me, in his tone of cold certainty, that he would turn me over to the Water Department for appropriate punishment if he ever caught me within a mile of the reservoir again. I nodded solemnly, even though inside I was chuckling silently to myself. Ol' Sneed did have a soft spot after all, and I, with my boyish charm, had touched it. No doubt I had reminded him of his own son or perhaps even of himself as a boy. Even before the sound of Sneed's old Dodge had faded off in the distance, my resolve to retire from a life of crime had vanished and I was already plotting my next raid on the reservoir. Even if he did catch me, I knew the game warden wouldn't have the heart to turn me in to the Water Department.

What changed my mind was an item my grandmother read in the newspaper the following week.

"I see by the paper where a fellow by the name of LeRoy Sneed was fined a hundred dollars for poaching deer," she said. "When are folks ever gonna learn to obey the law?"

One folk learned right then, and I'm happy to report that I've never intentionally violated so much as a single game regulation since. Oh, I've been tempted several times, but even though Sneed has been dead for fifteen years now, you just never can tell about a man like that.

The Hunter's Dictionary

☞ ☞ ☞**M**any persons who have just started hunting mistakenly assume that they understand the specialized terminology and jargon of the sport. As a result, they spend years in a state of befuddlement, wondering at the perversity of fate and cursing the contrariness of experienced hunters.

The problem is that they simply don't grasp the true meaning of the terms, phrases, and casual utterances as used by the hunting fraternity. I have therefore compiled *The Hunter's Dictionary,* published below in its entirety. It will do nothing to improve the beginning hunter's skills but should go a long way toward preserving his mental health.

It has long seemed to me to be an affectation of the overeducated to insist that dictionaries be printed in alphabetical order. If during my years spent in first grade I had succeeded in learning the alphabet, I might now feel more kindly toward it. In fact, I am rather fond of that portion of it that runs up to the letter *G*; beyond that point my feeling is largely one of hostility. So much for the explanation of why this dictionary is presented in a random and, to my mind, more meaningful order.

One further note: For the purpose of conciseness, "beginning hunter" and "experienced hunter" are abbreviated "BH" and "EH," respectively.

Without further display of my mastery of lexicography, I herewith present *The Hunter's Dictionary.*

FIVE MINUTES—This refers to a period of time ranging from five minutes to eight hours, generally speaking, but has been known to run as long as five days. It is used in this way: "Wait here. I'll be back in five minutes." What happens is that the EH who makes the statement will step off into the brush to check for tracks or possibly for some other business. While there, he will catch sight of a deer fifty yards or so up the slope, but the deer's head will be behind a tree. The hunter crouches down and sneaks up to a little rise off to one side to get a better look and determine the sex of the deer. It turns out to be a nice buck, which is just stepping over the ridge of the hill. The hunter, still in his crouch, scurries silently up the hill, expecting an easy shot. Cresting the hill, he catches a glimpse of its tail as the deer rounds the bend of an old logging road. The hunter will be occupied with this pursuit for the next few hours. His companion, if he too is an EH, will wait no longer than it takes to consume half a sandwich and a cup of coffee. By then he knows that the "five minutes" is a period to be measured in hours, and he will immediately proceed with his own hunting. A BH, on the other hand, assuming that "five minutes" means five minutes, will remain rooted loyally to the waiting place until lichens begin to form on him. When the EH finally returns, the lichen-covered hunter will yell at him, "I thought you said you'd be back in five minutes!"

The EH, somewhat puzzled by this display of wrath, will glance at his watch and say, "Well, here I am, ain't I? I left at ten-thirty, and now it's only five-fifteen! If I was going to be gone longer than five minutes, I would've told you!"

HUNTING VEHICLE—The BH assumes that what is meant by this phrase is any vehicle used to transport persons on a hunting trip, preferably a four-wheel drive of some sort. What the EH means by a "hunting vehicle" is *any* vehicle so long as it isn't his. If a BH is along on the trip, it means the BH's vehicle specifically. It matters not that the EH owns an outfit capable of swimming rivers and climbing trees or that the BH owns a sports car. The EH will merely glance at the sports car and observe: "Nice little hunting rig you have here."

FUNNY NOISE—A sound the EH reports the engine of his vehicle to be making any time the subject arises as to whose rig should be used for the hunting trip.

IMPASSABLE ROAD—Any road that gives indications it might mar the paint job or muddy the hub caps, provided the vehicle under consideration belongs to the EH.

PRACTICALLY A FOUR-LANE HIGHWAY—Any terrain slightly less hazardous than a streambed at flood stage, provided the vehicle under consideration does not belong to the EH.

BUILT TO TAKE IT—Describes any hunting vehicle not the EH's.

OOOOOOOOEEEEE-AH-AH-AH!—If there's one thing I hate, it's putting on cold, wet pants in the morning!

PNEUMONIA—What the EH claims to have whenever it's his turn to climb out of a warm sleeping bag and build the morning fire. Between spasms of hideous coughing, the EH may also request that someone say some kind words over his remains if he drops dead while returning from starting the fire.

MIRACULOUS RECOVERY—What the EH experiences as soon as he hears the morning fire crackling cheerily and smells coffee perking and bacon frying.

CAMP COOK—The guy who draws the short straw.

OVERDONE—Used by camp cooks to mean "burnt to a crisp."

BURNED—At some point the meal was totally engulfed by flames. The meal is still regarded as edible provided the hunting trip has been under way for at least three days.

RARE—The wood was too wet to start a cooking fire.

HASH—What all hunting-trip breakfasts appear to be. There is yellow hash, brown hash, gray hash, black hash, and green hash. Only a fool eats green hash.

STEW—Basically the same as green hash.

BLEEPING BLEEP-OF-A-BLEEP!—Phrase used by EH to announce he has just stepped out of a boat three feet short of the duck blind in the darkness of a cold December morning.

IMPOSSIBLE SHOT—What the EH has made anytime he downs game farther away than fifty feet.

FAIR SHOT—Any impossible shot made by someone other than the EH.

DID YOU FEEL THAT EARTH TREMOR JUST NOW?—Question asked by EH immediately after missing an easy shot.

A BIT—A lot.

SOME—All. As in, "I ate some of those little cheese-flavored crackers you had hidden in the bottom of your pack."

LEG CRAMP—What the EH insists is killing him and which requires that he get out of the hunting vehicle and "walk it out" on any occasion that a treacherous stretch of road appears up ahead.

TO MAKE A LONG STORY SHORT—The EH is about to

relate a story approximately the length of the history of mankind since the Creation.

I'M ABSOLUTELY CERTAIN THIS IS THE RIGHT TURN— There's one chance in ten this is the right turn.

IT AIN'T GONNA RAIN—Pitch tent on high ground and begin work immediately on a log raft.

AAAIIII!—The hash has become too hot for the camp cook's stirring finger.

BAFF MAST PIME IG BEAD FEAS MID MIFF PIFE!—That's the last time I try to eat peas in the dark with my hunting knife!

WHAT'S THAT? DID YOU HEAR SOMETHING PROWLING AROUND OUTSIDE THE TENT JUST NOW?—Questions hissed to arouse snoring tent partner and keep him awake for the rest of the night, listening.

DEER STAND—What the BH is placed on to keep him out of the way of the EH.

JAMMED RIFLE, DAMAGED GUNSIGHT, BLINDING HEADACHE, BAD KNEE, FOGGED SPECTACLES, ACUTE IRREGULARITY, SPONTANEOUS REGULARITY, and GREEN HASH—Any one or all of these are given as reasons the BH got a deer and the EH didn't.

CONSUMMATE SKILL—Why the EH got a deer and the BH didn't.

MEETING PLACE—An imaginary point in space that hunters are supposed to converge upon at a particular time. It is sometimes referred to as The Big Snag, The Old Apple Orchard, The Car, and Camp. The EH knows that such a place is merely a figment of the imagination and that the proposed meeting will never occur. It is hard for an EH to keep a straight face whenever a meeting place is spoken of.

A TRUE STORY—A collection of the most outrageous, preposterous, and unmitigated lies ever assembled.

DRESSED OUT AT 140 POUNDS—Dressed out at eighty pounds.

A RUNNING SHOT AT OVER 200 YARDS—I don't know how those powder burns got on its hide.

FLAT TRAJECTORY—Describes the movement of a hunter leaving his sleeping bag one hour after having eaten green hash for supper.

DID ANYONE THINK TO BRING—I left it sitting on my kitchen table.

MY CARDIOLOGIST—A mythical person casually referred to by the EH whenever it is suggested that he help haul a dead elk up the side of a steep mountain.

A HUNTING TIP—What the EH pays his hunting guide to keep his mouth shut and not to regale the boys back at the camp with an amusing account of what happened.

LEAVE THE LANTERN ON; IT'LL ATTRACT THE INSECTS AND KEEP THEM OFF OF US—I have trouble getting to sleep without a night light.

I SCOUTED OUT A LOT OF REAL NICE COUNTRY ON THE OTHER SIDE OF THE MOUNTAIN—The EH was lost for most of the day.

DON'T WORRY—Worry.

WIND, SNOW, COLD; THIS IS THE MOST MISERABLE DAY I'VE SPENT IN MY LIFE—Had a great time.

NEXT TIME, KID, TRY NOT TO MAKE SO MUCH RACKET, TROMPING THROUGH THE BRUSH THE WAY YOU DO. BOY, I'VE NEVER SEEN SUCH A CASE OF BUCK FEVER AS THAT ONE OF YOURS! ALSO, YOU'VE GOT TO LEARN NOT TO SHOUT, "THERE'S A BUCK!" JUST AS I'M SETTIN' THE CROSS HAIRS ON HIM. HA! AND THOSE TRACKS YOU THOUGHT WERE FRESH? WHY, YOU COULD HAVE GATHERED THEM UP AND SOLD THEM TO A MUSEUM AS FOSSILS! GEEZ!—You did all right, kid.

Tenner
Shoes

☞ ☞ ☞ "**W**hy don't you throw out some of these shoes?" my wife shouted from inside the closet.

"Are you crazy, woman?" I replied. "I *need* all those shoes—my bowling shoes, my jogging shoes, my hiking shoes, my canoeing shoes, my sailing shoes, my black dress shoes, my brown dress shoes, my brown casual shoes, my black casual shoes, my white casual shoes, my moccasins, my hip boots, my waders, my canvas wading shoes, my hunting boots, my mountain-climbing boots, my down booties, my camp shoes, my sandals, my . . ."

"Stop! Stop!" my wife screamed. "I give up! You can keep them! What I wish, though, is that somebody would invent a pair of shoes that could be used for everything."

Well, as a matter of fact, somebody once did. I wore them every summer when I was a kid. The shoe's inventor, I believe, was a Mr. Tenner. At least that's what we called them—Tenner shoes.

Once a rich kid moved to our town and tried to tell us that the shoes we were wearing were not called Tenner shoes at all but tennis shoes. We'd never seen anyone as ignorant as that kid. He didn't even wear Tenner shoes, so we wondered why he thought he knew so much about them.

"You tryin' to tell us these shoes weren't invented by a Mr. Tenner?" Retch Sweeney said to the kid. "How come everybody calls them Tenner shoes, then?"

"Only illiterates call them Tenner shoes," the kid shot back. Naturally, that got us all riled up, and we started yelling at him and pushing him and trying to get him to fight one of us.

"Listen," Peewee Thompson said. "We're all just as normal as you are, except for maybe Birdy—he's a little weird."

"No, no!" the rich kid shouted. " 'Illiterate' means you don't know how to read and write." Well, as soon as we found out that we hadn't been insulted, everybody cooled down and started patting the kid on the back and telling him he was all right after all, and we hoped he wouldn't harbor any hard feelings against us because of a little misunderstanding.

"Just the same," Retch said, "I ain't never heard of anybody by the name of Tennis."

"I did once," I said. "I think his son was one of them English poets, but I doubt either one of them knew anything about shoes."

Tenner shoes were made out of black canvas and had rubber soles and little round patches over the part that covered your anklebones. They were ugly. Tenner designed them that way on purpose so girls wouldn't want to wear them.

You got your pair of Tenner shoes each spring about the time the snow began to recede from the lowlands. There was an interesting little ritual that went with the purchase of each year's Tenner shoes. My mother would take me down to Hobbs's dry goods store, where Mr. Hobbs himself waited on the shoe customers.

"Howdy," Mr. Hobbs would say. "By golly, I bet you brought that young colt in to get him shod." Mr. Hobbs and my mother would cackle at monotonous length over this witticism. Interestingly enough, when I was very young and first heard the little joke, I thought Hobbs had said, "to get him shot." My fright was such that I behaved myself for the better part of the day and wondered long afterwards in what manner my sentence had been commuted.

Hobbs's arsenal of wit seemed to consist of the single joke, and as soon as he had spent that round on his customers he seemed to revert immediately into his natural self, perhaps best described as peevish.

"Siddown and take off your shoes," he would order. The shoes he referred to were generally some kind of clodhopper boots well along into the first stage of oblivion, heels and tongue missing, soles flopping loose, seams gaping, the laces a Chinese puzzle of knots and frayed ends. As I peeled off the boots, Mr. Hobbs and my mother would both leap back and gasp.

"I thought I told you to wash your feet!" my mother would screech, more for Mr. Hobbs's benefit than my own. "I've never seen the likes of it."

Mr. Hobbs would mutter under his breath about having seen the likes of it, something about hygiene films in Navy boot camp.

"How's that?" my mother would say.

"Nothing," Mr. Hobbs would snort. "Nothing."

He would then lock one of my feet in a measuring device, all the while doing his impression of a person removing a long-dead rat from a trap. The measurement taken, Hobbs would get up and return shortly with a box of Tenner shoes, which he would drop in my lap and order me to try on.

Even to this day I recall with ecstasy the pure sensual delight of slipping my feet into a brand-new pair of Tenner shoes, my ol' toes up in the forward part wiggling around, checking out their new quarters, the ankles swelling boastfully under the protective cushions of the rubber patches as the fat clean laces snugged tight the embrace of canvas and rubber. After a winter of wearing the clodhopper boots, I felt like I was strapping on a pair of wings.

"I better go try them out," I would say.

"Stay in the store!" Mr. Hobbs would shout. "Don't take them out of the store!"

But it would be too late. I would be out on the sidewalk, and the Tenner shoes would be carrying me in free soaring flight around the block. The test completed, I would brake to a screeching stop and reenter the store.

"Maybe just a half-size larger," I would tell Mr. Hobbs. "Gosh, I don't know why anyone would let their dog run loose on the sidewalk, but I washed these Tenner shoes off good as new in a mud puddle and as soon as they dry . . ."

"Dog?" Mr. Hobbs would say. *"Dog!* Nothing doing! Those are your size! That'll be ninety-eight cents, Missus."

"Ninety-eight cents!" my mother would say. "My land, I don't know what folks are going to do if prices keep going up the way they are."

"Terrible," Mr. Hobbs would mutter. "Don't know these young whelps are worth it anyways." He always sounded as if he meant it, too.

To my mind, the Tenner was the ultimate shoe. You could use it for running and hiking and jumping, for playing football and basketball, hunting and fishing, mountain climbing, rafting, spelunking, swimming, bicycling, horseback riding, cowback riding, pigback riding. Whatever the activity, the Tenner shoe adapted itself to the task in noble and admirable fashion.

The one area in which the Tenner shoe may have fallen a bit short was as a dress-up shoe. Suppose, for example, that you had to go to some social event where all the youngsters were dressed up in their best clothes. You showed up wearing your good pair of pants, your good shirt, your good socks, and your Tenner shoes, which by now may have been showing the strain of hunting, fishing, pigback riding, etc. Now, as soon as you got within hearing distance of some of the other mothers at the affair, your mother would look down at your feet, conjure up an expression of absolute horror, and say, "I thought I told you to wear *your brown oxfords!* My land, you'll mortify me to death! Just look at those filthy old Tenner shoes."

Now of course all of the other mothers would look at your mother and smile and shake their heads in an understanding way as if to say, "What can you expect of little boys?" What was truly shrewd about this charade was your mother's use of the phrase "your brown oxfords." This not only implied that you *had* brown oxfords but also black ones and possibly white ones. Maybe one of the reasons the ruse worked so well was that most of the other guys had protruding from the cuffs of their good pairs of pants the unmistakable rubber noses of Tenner shoes. If there was a poor kid present at one of these social functions, by the way, his mother would look down at his feet and say, "Land sakes, Henry, didn't I tell you to wear shoes!" Of course, all of us guys knew that Henry didn't have any shoes. Otherwise, why would he paint his feet to look as if he were wearing Tenners? It made you kind of sad if you thought about it.

The great thing about Tenners was their almost unlimited versatility. They were great for wearing inside a sleeping bag, for example. Nowadays, of course, there are little down booties especially designed for wearing inside of sleeping bags. The one problem with these booties is that they really aren't designed for outside wear, and if you have to get up in the night for any reason, they're not much good for wandering around over rough ground in the dark. Of course, when you're camping out as a kid, there is only one thing that can make you get up in the middle of the night, and that is the necessity of running for your life. And if ever there was a shoe designed for running for your life, it was the Tenner. Many was the dark night that a troop of us young campers made our way home, trailing in our wake the distinct odor of smoldering Tenners.

Tenners made great fishing waders. Mr. Tenner, who must have been an absolute genius, had designed them without any insulation so that when you waded out into an icy spring stream it took only a few minutes for your feet to turn numb. From then on you could fish in complete comfort. The numbness also prevented you from feeling any pain when your Tenners slithered into narrow and odd-shaped openings between slippery rocks. You could continue fishing in blissful comfort up above while down below the rocks committed various acts of depravity on your feet, rearranging the bones in imaginative ways, doing trick shuffles with your toes, and playing football with your ankles. We would often return from a fishing trip with an affliction known technically as cauliflower feet. Fortunately, we had the good sense never to remove our Tenners until they had dried, thereby preserving our feet in the shape, if not exactly of feet, at least of Tenners. Indeed, I was often afraid to remove my Tenners after a fishing trip for fear of what I might find inside them. I have always had a weak stomach.

There was considerable controversy among us about how often Tenners should be taken off. The conservatives argued for once a week, the liberals for three or four times a summer, and the radicals for never, preferring to allow decay and disintegration to take their natural course. Although I was one of the conservatives, I shared the radicals' curiosity over whether, when their Tenners finally self-destructed, there would be any feet left inside.

I frequently shared space in small tents with Tenner radicals, and the idea occurred to me more than once to take a caged canary in with me so that its sudden demise could warn me when the gas escaping from the radicals' Tenners had reached a lethal level. To my knowledge, there were never any human fatalities from this cause, although large numbers of flying and crawling insects in the tent died mysteriously.

There were many other theories concerning the proper use of Tenner shoes. These theories were passed on from the older fellows to the younger ones and were usually taken at face value. One of these theories was passed on to me by my cousin Buck, several years my senior, who told me that little slits should be cut in the canvas of new Tenner shoes so that in an emergency you could thrust some of your toes out through the slits and get better traction. This seemed to me to be a good idea, even though I could never bring myself to cut a brand-new pair of Tenners. It was just as well. In fact, I'll never forget the day I saw this theory put to the test.

Buck had taken me on a little hiking trip in the

mountains for the purpose of instructing me in wood-craft. He was one of those people who loved to teach but can never be bothered learning anything. What Buck taught me was any odd thought that happened to pop into his head, and some of the thoughts were pretty odd. He taught me, for example, that woodpeckers were tapping out code on the trunks of dead trees, warning other woodpeckers of our approach. He even let me in on the secret that he had cracked this code and knew what they were saying. Sometimes, he said, the wood-peckers even made jokes in code, and Buck had to laugh when he heard them.

"What did that one say?" I would ask Buck when he laughed.

"Oh, you're too little for me to repeat a joke like that to," he would say. "But I can tell you this—them woodpeckers is pretty funny birds!"

It turned out that Buck's theory about slitting Tenners to stick your toes out of was on a par with his knowledge of ornithology. After what happened that day on the mountain, I never again had any use for Buck's teachings. What happened was this: We were walking along single file, with Buck, of course, in the lead, reciting all sorts of incredible nature lore to me. The weather was chilly and the earth on the mountain frozen hard, with patches of snow still lingering here and there. As we were making our way down the unexplored back side of the mountain, we came to a huge slab of rock approximately fifty feet square and slanting down to a drop-off. The surface of the rock was smooth and covered with frost. Buck started walking straight across the rock. I stopped.

"Whatcha stop for?" Buck asked, turning around about halfway across the slab. "Tenner shoes don't slide on rock. The little suction cups on the soles, they grab right onto the . . ."

Buck was sliding.

"Well, this frost makes it a little slick," he said. "I better . . ."

By now Buck was *really* sliding. He gave up all efforts at further conversation and devoted his full attention to scrambling back up the rock. The problem was that no matter how fast and furious Buck's scramble was, his downward rate of slide seemed to be greater by about an inch per second. I had no idea how much of a drop awaited him at the brink of the slab—a hundred feet, half a mile? I remembered all the mountain-climbing movies I'd ever seen where a climber loses his grip and plummets downward until he is just a tiny, noisy speck hurtling toward the patchwork farmlands below. From the look on his face, I knew Buck was remembering the same movies. Then I noticed that Buck had forgotten to stick his toes out through the slits in his Tenners.

"Stick out your toes, Buck," I screamed at him. "Stick out your toes!"

Buck's toes suddenly emerged from the slits like little pink landing gear, and I have to admit that he did some marvelous things with his toes—in fact, just about everything it is possible to do with toes and not get arrested. But nothing worked.

Buck shot backward right off over the edge of the cliff. His drop was accompanied by a long, horrible, slowly diminishing scream.

I was a bit puzzled by the scream, since Buck was standing there on a wide ledge just three feet down from the brink of the slab, his whole top half still in full view of me. Later, he tried to tell me he was just doing his imitation of Tarzan's ape call. Well, I'd heard his imitation of Tarzan's ape call numerous times, and it had never before made my hair stand on end. Buck was finished as a mentor. I was just happy that I hadn't followed his advice and violated a perfectly good pair of Tenners by cutting slits in them for an emergency.

As with all good things, Tenners did not last forever. Spring eased into summer and summer wore on, and the Tenners would begin to fade, the dark rich black of the canvas turning to pale dirty gray. Then the seams where the rubber was glued to the canvas would start to peel loose. The eyelets for the laces would begin popping out. The laces themselves would break and have to be knotted; their ends would fray out into tiny pompoms. The round rubber ankle patches would fall off. The canvas at the balls of the feet would wear through. Then a tear would move back along the instep. By September the Tenners would be done for.

On the first day of school, your new clodhopper boots felt good. Their weight gave you a sense of security, of substance, of manhood, and the will to face another year of school. But there would be a note of sadness, too, because Henry, the poor kid, would be there, his feet painted to look like new boots. You tried not to think about it.

My wife's muffled voice came from inside the closet. "How about this pair of shoes? Can I at least give these to the Salvation Army?"

"Those old tennis shoes? Sure, go ahead," I said. "Hell, I never play tennis, anyway."

Reading Sign

☞ ☞ ☞ **B**ack when I was a kid, the mark of a true woodsman was his ability to read sign. Knowing this, many persons trying to pass themselves off as woodsmen would make a great show of staring at sign for a few minutes and then offering up profound remarks about it:

"I'd judge from this broken twig that we're about ten minutes behind a herd of mule deer, most of them yearlings or does, but there's one big fella I'd guess to be a trophy buck. You'll know him when you see him 'cause he favors his left front leg when he's running flat out and . . ."

The only way to deal with a person like that was to walk over, look down, and say, "For heaven's sake, so that's where I dropped my lucky twig! The amazing thing is, I broke it three months ago and it still works!" You then picked up the twig, put it in your pocket, and strolled away.

My cousin Buck was one of these impostors. Even though I was several years younger than Buck, sign was serious business to me and I spent long hours reading about it and studying it first-hand and trying to find out what it meant and whether it was sign at all or maybe just an accident. Buck, on the other hand, couldn't concentrate on any subject longer than fifteen seconds unless it wore a dress and smelled of perfume, which sign seldom if ever did. Still, ever so often I had to endure his hauling me out to the woods to instruct me on how to read sign.

"Hey, looky here," he would hiss at me. "Elk sign!"

Now, any fool could see that the sign was not that of an elk but the handiwork of a mule who stood nearby with a smile on his face and a snicker in his voice. If I hadn't been smarter than I looked, I would have pointed that fact out to Buck. But not wishing to have my head thumped, I said, "Yes! Elk! Elk! I can see now they were elk!"

Thumping your head was Buck's way of proving to you that he could read sign.

If I, on the other hand, happened to discover some fresh deer sign, Buck would always dismiss my find with a shrug of his shoulders and the profound bit of wisdom: "You can't eat sign."

He lived to regurgitate those words.

One frosty November morn Buck had dragged me out deer hunting with him. I wasn't old enough yet to carry a rifle, but Buck needed someone along to brag to about how he could read sign. We were cruising down a back road in Buck's old car, listening to Gene Autry on the radio and looking for deer. (Buck believed the way to hunt deer was to drive up and down roads; that's the sort of woodsman he was.) For breakfast I had brought along some chocolate-covered peanuts in my jacket pocket, and ever so often I'd sneak one into my mouth so Buck wouldn't see it and demand a share. There was some fool notion in those days that if someone saw you with something good to eat, all he had to do was yell "divvies" at you and then you had to share with him. If you didn't share with somebody when he yelled "divvies" at you, he got to beat you up and take it all—but only if he was bigger than you were. If he was smaller, he could yell "divvies" till the sun went down and you didn't have to share with him. In that way, I suppose, it was an equitable system. But I digress.

So anyway, there we were driving down the back road, and all at once Buck hit the brakes and yelled out, "Deer tracks!" Sure enough, even from where I now sat, wedged up under the dashboard, I could see that sometime during the past six months a deer had come sliding and bounding through the soft dirt of a high bank above the road. As soon as the car had slid to a stop, we jumped out, Buck breathlessly thumbing cartridges into his rifle, and rushed over to examine the tracks. All the while, Buck was making sure he got full credit for spotting the tracks.

"I told you they was deer tracks, and you didn't believe me, did you?" he whispered, his voice shrill with excitement.

"I believed you, Buck."

"Hell, we musta been drivin' past fifty miles an hour and I looks out and I says to you, 'There's some deer tracks!' Now didn't I say that?"

"That's what you said, Buck."

We looked at the tracks. Buck got down on his knees and felt the edges of the tracks, apparently to see if they were still warm. Then he bent over and sniffed them! It was almost too much to bear for a serious student of deer tracks. Any fool could see those tracks were so old they could have been classified as fossils. The deer who made them no doubt had since known a long and happy life and finally expired at a ripe old age.

"They fresh, Buck?" I asked.

Buck stood up and tugged at his wispy beard as he studied the tracks. "I'd say he went through here, oh, about a half-hour before daylight."

"Gee," I said, stifling a yawn. "We just missed him, hunh? Dang. If we had just been a few minutes earlier, hunh, Buck?"

"Yep," Buck said. "Well, win some, lose some."

While I was racking my brain trying to think of some that Buck had won, a terrible idea occurred to me. And the instant the idea occurred, I implemented it. Even after thirty years and more I am still ashamed of pulling it on Buck. That I am still convulsed with laughter upon recalling the expression on his face is even more despicable. Only the desire to ease my conscience compels me to confess the deed. What I did—oh, I shudder still to think of it—was to take a handful of the chocolate-covered peanuts and sprinkle them on the ground by my feet.

"Hey, Buck," I said, pointing. "Sign. Looks fresh, too."

Buck looked at me in disgust and shook his shaggy head. "How many times I got to tell ya: Ya can't eat sign!"

At that, I reached down, picked up a chocolate-covered peanut, snapped it into the air, and caught it in my mouth.

Buck's jaw dropped halfway to his belt buckle.

For years afterwards, Buck couldn't stand the sight of chocolate-covered peanuts. Offer him one and his upper lip would flutter like a broken window shade. Sure, when ol' Buck figured out the trick I'd played on him, he thumped my head until both of us were worn out, but that didn't change the obvious truth: He just wasn't a proper woodsman.

Much of my early knowledge about sign was gained

from reading books and magazine articles. These usually included drawings of the tracks of various wild animals, and all you had to do was memorize the shape and the number of toes and so on to be able to identify the track out in the wilds. I spent endless hours at this sort of study, but it was well worth the effort. For one thing, it taught me about true friendship. If you were out with one of your friends in the woods, you could point to a set of tracks and say, "Look, lynx tracks."

"Gee," the friend would say in a properly appreciative tone. If he didn't say that or an equivalent expression, he wasn't your friend.

Now, if you followed the lynx tracks and at the other end of them found a skunk waddling along, you would say to your friend, studying him closely, "Sometimes skunks make lynx tracks, did you know that?"

"No, I didn't," he might reply. "That's really interesting." Such a reply could mean only two things: This guy was impossibly stupid, or he was a *really* good friend.

Strangely enough, many of the magazine articles on sign were written by a lady. Her underlying principle was that wild animals were actors on the stage of the great outdoors. If you could read the scripts, namely their tracks in the snow, you could decipher the plot. A typical plot would go like this: Rabbit tracks are crossing the snow from one direction and coyote tracks from another. The two sets of tracks intersect at the base of a tree. Only the coyote tracks continue on from the tree. Hmmmmmmmmmmmm. How did the the rabbit get away from the tree without making any tracks? Did he climb the tree? The mystery was almost mind-boggling. The author of these articles could take an hour's walk through the snow and encounter a dozen fascinating little dramas, none of which, I might add, were ever comedies.

I hate to admit it, but at a certain age I was intrigued by these articles and was forever searching the snowy countryside for evidence of little wildlife dramas. Unfortunately, most of the dramas I encountered went about like this: Rabbit tracks emerge from thicket, go under barbwire fence, mess around in a patch of blackberry brambles, cross a creek over thin ice, go under another barbwire fence, mosey back across the thin ice, meander through the blackberry brambles again, pass under another barbwire fence, and go back into the thicket. That would be it. Although the drama itself might be deadly dull, following the "script" around the countryside could be fraught with pain, danger, and excitement. Several times I nearly froze to death in my wet clothes while rushing home to bandage my scratches and cuts and to dig out the stickers.

Where I really learned to read sign was from the old woodsman Rancid Crabtree. Rancid didn't care a hoot about reading little woodland dramas. To him, sign was not a form of entertainment but an essential element in a complex scheme that he had devised to make working for a living unnecessary. About the only things Rancid needed money for were a few clothes, rifle and shotgun shells, salt and pepper, some gas for his old truck, chewin' tobacco, and his medicine, which a local pharmacist, a Colt .45 stuffed in the waistband of his pants, delivered at night in quart-sized Mason jars. These commodities required cash, particularly the medicine. Rancid acquired his cash by running a little trap line each winter. And successful trapping required a rather extensive knowledge of sign. The intensity and seriousness with which Rancid studied sign can be fully appreciated only by realizing that to him it was virtually the same thing as tobacco and medicine. To Rancid, sign was a matter of ultimate concern.

A stroll with Rancid through the woods was a course in post-graduate study in reading sign. "B'ar," he would say, pointing to the ground as we walked along. "Porky-pine . . . bobcat . . . skonk . . ." And so on. One day we were going along in this fashion and he pointed down and said, "Snake."

"Snake?" I said to myself, glancing down. "This is a new . . . SNAKE!" My bare foot was descending toward the fat, frantic reptile. Despite my precarious posture, I managed to execute a successful lift-off before coming into actual contact with the creature. While involved in this effort, I left my vocal cords unattended and they took advantage of their moment of freedom to get off a loud and startling shriek. Upon hearing this, Rancid leaped to the conclusion that he had misjudged the snake as being a member of a benevolent sect and immediately began to curse and hop about and flail the earth with his walking stick. It was all pretty exciting, and Rancid was more than a little annoyed when he found out the snake hadn't taken a bite out of me after all.

"Gol-dang," he said, "don't never scream like thet ag'in fer no reason. Let the thang at least git a taste of you 'fer you starts hollerin' like you's bein' et. Now tarn loose maw ha'r and neck and git down offen maw shoulders!"

Over the years, my wife has become quite an expert on reading sign, ferreting out clues here and there and matching up odd bits of trivial information from which to deduce an ingenious conclusion that couldn't make the slightest difference to anyone. I like to call her the Sherlock Holmes of sign. Just recently she came in and reported that the reason the grass in an orchard up on the hill was matted down was that a herd of elk had been sleeping there.

"Ha!" I said. "Probably just cows. What makes you think it's elk?"

"Alimentary, my dear Watson," she said. "Alimentary."

There are, of course, worse things than a smart-aleck woman. A fellow even told me what they were once, but I can never remember.

Campgrounds are my wife's favorite places for sleuthing. As soon as we arrive at a campsite, she's out of the car in a flash, reading the sign. "Party of four camped here last. Spent at least three days, I'd say from the amount of ash in the fireplace. At least one of them was a slob."

"How do you know that?"

"Threw the pull-tabs from his beer cans all over the place—boy, that's really disgusting. You'd think he'd care what kind of example he was setting for his kids."

"His kids?"

"Yeah, there are three wiener sticks leaning against the tree over there. You can see the remains of toasted-coconut-covered marshmallows on two of the sticks. Only kids can eat burnt toasted-coconut-covered marshmallows and live. Boy, if I were married to that lazy slob!" she said, holding up the third wiener stick. "Look, the wife's stick has a fork on the end of it. That's so she could cook a wiener for the old man while she was doing her own! Well, I never!"

"The guy sounds like a real slob, no doubt about it," I said. "Hey, don't throw that forked wiener stick away. You never know when something like that might come in handy."

One good thing about forked wiener sticks: It's difficult to run a person through with them.

I myself don't have much opportunity to read sign

anymore. To tell the truth, my reading tastes have changed a good deal over the years and I'd just as soon curl up with a good book or magazine. Also, books and magazines are nicer to keep around the house and you're much less likely to get dirty looks if you read them in public waiting rooms.

Tying
My Own

☞ ☞ ☞ **S**omeday there will be a how-to-tie-flies book written for people like me. It will read something like this: "While holding the tying thread between two thumbs of your left hand, take a hackle feather between the big and little thumbs of your right hand . . ."

I am a person who is just naturally thumby. My eyesight isn't all that good either. When I read in a fly-tying book that I should "wrap each successive turn of tinsel next to the preceding one, edge to edge without overlapping," I can only shriek with delight and hope the author can sustain this level of humor through the rest of the book. I am seldom disappointed. Here's a line that really split my sides: "Wind the two hairs around the hook, keeping the darker one to the left." *Keeping the darker one to the left!* Oh what I wouldn't give to be able to come up with gems like that!

Contrary to the rumor spread by some of my alleged friends, I started fishing with artificial flies several years *after* the invention of the real ones, not *before*. Back when I was a kid, you could buy a good fly for fifteen cents.

And I mean a *good* fly. One Black Gnat would last you a whole season, providing you were willing to retrieve it from such receptacles as stumps submerged in rapids, thorn bushes on the sides of cliffs, and rotting logs balanced over the edges of precipices. I was always willing to retrieve it. After all, fifteen-cent flies didn't grow on trees (although a casual observer of my casting technique might assume they did). Sure, by the end of the season there would be some signs of wear and tear: the body would be on the verge of coming apart; the head, lumpy and gouged; and the general appearance, one of having been mauled and chewed on. The fly, on the other hand, would still look pretty good.

My friends and I kept count of the fish taken on each fly. Truly great flies were given names like Killer or Ol' Griz, unless, of course, they failed to attract fish on a given day, at which time they might be called simply Harold or Walter. It was not unusual for us to become quite attached to a fly. Equally common was for a fly to become attached to us. Since none of us enjoyed the prospect of having a fly surgically removed from whatever part of our anatomy it had become attached, we would occasionally pretend we were starting a new fad: wearing a fly on an ear, a shoulder blade, or an elbow. Lest the reader think we were sissies, let me hasten to add that the "surgeon" who excised the wayward fly was more often than not a burly miner (thus the expression "miner surgery"), who would haul out his pocketknife, run the flame of a kitchen match up and down the big blade a few times, order the women and children from the arena, and then say something like, "All right, you men grab hold of him and I'll have that fly out of his hide in a jiffy!"

When you found yourself in this predicament, the better part of valor if not of wisdom was simply to grab the embedded fly and remove it with a quick jerk and a muffled cry of pain, the latter sometimes causing all the cows in the vicinity to "go dry" for a month. This tactic not only saved you from "miner" surgery but for a brief period also enabled you to bait fish and fly fish simultaneously with a single hook.

The fifteen-centers were the expensive flies. The cheap flies cost about thirty-five cents a dozen and came in a little cellophane packet labeled "World's Greatest Fishing Bargain" or something like that. Neither fish nor entomologists have ever seen an insect bearing the slightest resemblance to any members of the world's greatest fishing bargain. Nevertheless, these eccentric flies served an important function: They filled up the empty space in our fly books. This function was important because the first thing you did when you and your fishing companions arrived at a fishing spot was to scoop a dead insect from the surface of the water—any bug would do—and studiously compare it with the contents of your fly book. After a couple minutes of such careful scrutiny, you would say, "By golly, I think what we have here is a hatch of black gnats." You would then take out your venerable fifteen-cent Black Gnat and tie it on. All the other guys would usually go along with this assessment unless, of course, the fifteen-center belonging to one of them happened to be a Silver Doctor or a Royal Coachman, in which case this individual would take exception to the verdict and argue heatedly that the hatch consisted of silver doctors or royal coachmen.

I must confess that if there were still good fifteen-cent flies on the market I'd hop naked on a pogo stick through a feminist picnic before I'd tie my own. But flies have gone up in price. Last summer I heard about a new pattern that was supposed to be good. My plan was to buy one, dissect it, and from the anatomical knowledge thus obtained, counterfeit a few copies. When the clerk told me the price of the fly, I was not only shocked but embarrassed. Unable to bring myself to ask if I could purchase the fly on an installment plan, I said, "Maybe I should have a look at some of your other flies."

"Oh, you mean the expensive ones," he said. "I'm sorry, but our new order hasn't come in yet."

As near as I could make out, either Lloyd's of London had refused to insure the shipment or the armored car service was late in making the delivery. It was all I could do to keep from sticking my hand in my jacket pocket, thrusting it toward the clerk, and saying, "This is a stickup! Give me all your dries, nymphs, and streamers, nothing larger than a six. And no funny stuff—this finger is loaded!"

A number of years ago—about the time investors started buying up fishing flies as a hedge against inflation —I decided that once and for all I'd better learn how to tie my own. After all, I'd been giving out advice on fly-tying for years, so I reasoned that it shouldn't be that difficult to learn how to construct the little buggers. Since I was a fly fisher of consummate skill, word spread that I knew absolutely everything there was to know about flies, including how to tie them. It beats me how a rumor like that got started, but no matter. Pretty soon, fishermen from all over came seeking my advice, and, not wishing to appear rude and secretive, I dispensed it to them freely. Although innocent of such fundamentals as how one got all those feathers and stuff to stay on a hook, I felt competent to offer consultation on the finer aspects of the art.

"I want to make some of my nymphs sink faster," a fellow said to me once. "Got any suggestions?"

"That's simple," I replied. "All you have to do is make them heavier."

"Gee, I wonder why I never thought of that," he said, and walked away shaking his head, no doubt at his own stupidity.

When the time came for me to learn how to tie my own flies, I couldn't very well ask the same people I'd been advising what tools and materials I would need to get started. If nothing else, I might have shaken their confidence in all the tips I had given them over the years. I decided the best approach would be to seek out an establishment specializing in fly-tying paraphernalia and located in an area of town where I was not likely to be recognized. I soon found just such a shop, the proprietor of which turned out to be an attractive lady of approximately my own youthful age.

"Say, don't I know you from somewhere?" she asked, scarcely before the bells on the shop's front door had ceased jangling the news of my arrival.

I smiled modestly. "Possibly you're confusing me with the actor Robert Redford, for whom I'm often mistaken despite his being of somewhat slighter build and a smidgen younger."

"No, no," she said, studying me curiously. "Now I've got it! There used to be this fellow who went fishing with my husband—Farley Quartze? I think his name was Pat or Mac or something like that, a roly-poly guy with thinning gray hair."

I was instantly overcome by pity for the frumpy wretch. Not only was the poor soul suffering from seriously impaired eyesight, she was married to a notoriously loud-mouthed know-it-all whose presence I had in fact endured on a fishing trip or two. Unless, of course, there were two Farley Quartzes, which seemed unlikely. In any case, it would not do for word to get back to *the* Farley Quartze that I had shown up at his wife's shop to buy a beginner's fly-tying outfit. There was nothing to do but pull the dubbing over the lady's lovely but afflicted eyes.

"Well, so much for chit-chat," I said, kindly. "Here's what I need. My fly-tying outfit has become such a mess, after twenty years or so of turning out thousands and thousands of flies, that I've decided to replace the whole shebang with a totally new outfit, something of professional caliber, of course. Why don't you just go ahead and whip me up one, all the usual feathers and stuff, you know?"

"Wow!" she said, staring at me in a way that I could only attribute to a momentary return of visual acuity. "That's really something! First, let me show you a really nifty little vise."

"Perhaps some other time," I replied. "Right now I think we should confine ourselves to matters related to fly-tying." The poor dear was struck speechless with disappointment by my rejection of her overture, and I couldn't help but feel sorry for her, particularly considering that she was married to an insensitive lout like Farley Quartze. Noting that she had absentmindedly extracted from a display case a tool I instantly recognized as an instrument of fly-tying, I tried to change the subject by calling her attention to it. "I see you have a hook-clamper there in your hand. I'm going to need one of those for sure, and that certainly looks like a good one."

After a moment she asked, "How long have you been tying flies?"

"You wouldn't believe me if I told you."

"Probably not," she said, and immediately began removing materials from boxes, bins, jars, and cases and stuffing them into clear plastic bags for me. I was happy to note that she was attaching to each bag a label that identified the contents, few of which I could otherwise have told from the plumage of a yellow-crested cuckold, ornithology not being one of my strong points. Having depleted the inventory of the store to her apparent satisfaction, Mrs. Quartze began computing my bill on an electronic calculator, her fingers dancing happily over its buttons. For some reason, this simple exercise in digital dexterity seemed to improve her mood just short of total delight, and I thought the moment an appropriate one to impress upon her that I was not only an experienced, nay, an expert, tier of flies but also one possessed of certain ethical standards.

"By the way," I said, surveying the mountain of packages stuffed with furs and feathers. "I hope none of these materials are derived from threatened or endangered species."

"Like what?" she said.

"Well," I said, picking up a package and reading the label, "like these chenilles."

Not only was Mrs. Quartze afflicted with poor vision, but she also had the rather distasteful mannerism of allowing her mouth to gape open every time a question was addressed to her. "Why, no," she said presently, regaining control of her jaw muscles, "there are plenty of chenilles left. They reproduce faster than lemmings."

"Good to hear it," I replied. "They're such colorful little beggars, it would be a shame if they became a threatened species."

"Yes," she said smiling. "You'll probably be happy to learn that the flosses are doing fine too. And the tinsels . . ."

Well, that conversation took place many years ago. I have since learned a good deal about the fundamentals of fly-tying, not that I ever really believed there were such creatures as chenilles and flosses and tinsels. That was just a little joke for the benefit of Mrs. Quartze. I don't think she got it, though, because a few days after our transaction somebody sent me a book in the mail —*Fly-tying Made Easy Even for Imbeciles*. Talk about your nerve! On the other hand, it turned out to be a pretty good book, once I got past the hard parts.

Psychic Powers
for Outdoorsmen

☞ ☞ ☞Even as a child I possessed psychic powers. For example, I once was fighting with my sister, the
Troll, and, as she sat on my chest braiding my fingers into
a potholder, I suddenly had this vision of a snake
slithering happily about in the dresser drawer where the
Troll stored her fresh underwear. Naturally, I immediately dismissed the vision as preposterous. How could a
simpleminded snake manage to climb the sheer side of
the dresser, open a drawer, crawl inside, and finally pull
the drawer shut behind? Why would a snake even want to
do this? What could its motive be? The very next day,
however, the Troll announced the discovery of a snake in
her underwear drawer. Her announcement was made
simultaneously with the discovery and had a certain
operatic quality to it, beginning with a rather elaborate
inhalation, which was followed by a series of staccato
sounds similar to aborted sneezes, then culminated in a
long, quavering, sirenlike screech, the whole performance lasting not more than twenty seconds and concluding with several loud thumps, these last caused by the

Troll's rebounding off the wall in an effort to get a clear shot at the bedroom door. As pure entertainment it left something to be desired, but I found the routine not to be without a certain psychological interest. As with most psychic phenomena, the mystery of the snake in the drawer and my precognition of its being there never yielded to logical inquiry, although for years afterwards the Troll insisted upon advancing a pet theory of her own as to the unknown cause of the event. No one, of course, pays much attention to the theories of a person who goes through life forking her underwear out of a drawer with a long stick.

Quite often in those days our house would be invaded by strange odors. "Smells like something died," my grandmother would say, giving me a look heavy with accusation. I would then perform an age-old rite of exorcism, which consisted of removing from a secret storage place and burying outside by the light of the moon a bait can of deteriorating worms, a collection of more-or-less drying sunfish, or possibly a box of ripening freshwater mussels. Shortly after I had performed the rite, the mysterious odor would begin to diminish in power and soon be gone altogether. My family should have been grateful that they had me around to exorcise odors, but they were generally unappreciative.

I have managed to achieve true levitation only twice. In the first instance, I not only raised the person several feet off the ground in a prone position but propelled him over a fence, across the countryside, and into his own house, where his abrupt entrance through a locked screen door caused his mother to spill a cup of hot cocoa on the cat and his father to blurt out a word that nobody supposed he even knew—or so the subject of my feat of levitation reported to me upon returning to his senses several days later.

What happened was this: A kid by the name of Lester was spending the night with me, and we were sleeping on an old mattress out in my backyard. I had complained of an earache the previous night, and my grandmother suggested that I wear something around my head to keep the cold night air from my ear. Although I possessed half a dozen stocking caps, a search of the premises unearthed not a single one of them. Finally, my grandmother said she would find me something of hers to wear. She went to a trunk in the attic and fished out one of her old bonnets, a thing made out of bearskin and which she claimed once to have worn on hayrides. At some point prior to the bonnet's being stored in the trunk for reasons of sentiment, a dog had apparently attacked it, either out of anger or fright, and had managed to tear loose several large hanks of hair, leaving in their place grotesque patches of naked skin. It fastened under the chin with two cords. Naturally, I didn't want Lester to see me wearing such a monstrosity, since he might spread rumors about me around the schoolyard, a place where rumors about me were already rampant.

I concealed the hairy bonnet inside my shirt until Lester had dozed off, rather fitfully it seemed to me, even though I had entertained him for several hours with true accounts of the numerous grisly murders that had taken place in our neighborhood and which remained unsolved. I then whipped out the bonnet, put it on, knotted the cords under my chin, and slid down under the blankets, being careful not to disturb Lester and hoping that I would be the first to awaken in the morning in order to remove the headpiece before my bedmate saw it.

Sometime during the night, as luck would have it, the bearskin bonnet became twisted around my head in such a manner that it was leaking cold air to my faulty ear and shutting it off altogether from my nose and mouth. I awoke in a panic of suffocation and tore at the knots under my chin, but to no avail. There was only one thing to do. I lunged for Lester, hoping the moon was bright enough that he could see to untie the knots. *"MOW WAAAA OOOD AAAAAAHHH!"* I shouted at him. Through a ripped seam in the bearskin, I glimpsed one of Lester's eyelids lift tentatively. Then both eyes popped open. Without further ado, Lester levitated.

After Lester's departure, I groped my way into the house to my mother's bedroom and shook Mom awake to have her untie the cords of the hairy bonnet. That's when the second levitation occurred. It was less spectacular than Lester's but every bit as good as what one might see performed on stage by the average professional magician, although, on the whole, considerably less dignified.

I also possess considerable talent for rainmaking, although only in collaboration with my friend Vern Schulze. When we were still kids, Vern and I discovered that we could produce rain any time we wished simply by going on a camping trip together. Our sleeping out in the backyard would produce a steady drizzle for most of the night. A camping trip away from home for a couple of days would call forth a series of cloudbursts that would awaken new interest in arks and set people to arguing about the meaning of "cubits." Once when we were about sixteen, we even managed to work up a major blizzard in the middle of June by going camping in the mountains for a week. We learned from that experience that the severity of the weather is in direct but inverse proportion to the warmth of the clothes we wear camping. Our light attire, appropriate to the normal weather of late June, had in that instance brought on a blizzard. If we had gone naked, we probably would have launched a new ice age.

This past summer we had not a drop of rain for nearly two months in the region where I live, and forest fires were erupting all over the place. I called up Vern.

"Vern," I said, "this drought has gone on too long. The whole country may burn up if we don't do something about it. Get your gear ready. Any questions?"

"Yeah," he replied. "Who is this?"

"You know who it is! Don't try to pull that wrong-number routine on me, Vern!"

"You must have the wrong number," he said. "There's no Vern here."

"I told you not to try that routine on me," I snapped. "Do you want to be responsible for letting the whole country go up in flames?"

"I suppose not. What's your plan?"

"Well, I figure a week-long backpacking trip into the Hoodoo Mountains would do the job."

Vern gasped. "Are you crazy? Think of the floods, man! No, three days would be more than enough! A few roads may wash out, but a three-day backpacking trip shouldn't cause any more damage than that. And it will certainly produce enough rain to put out all the forest fires."

As soon as the word got out that Vern and I were going backpacking, the local television weatherpersons began qualifying their announcements: "The official forecast is for continued hot, dry weather; however, Pat McManus and Vern Schulze are going backpacking for three days, and rains ranging from severe to torrential should be expected." Farmers, whose crops had been dying on the vine, hoisted their children to their shoulders to catch a glimpse of Vern and me as we drove by on our way to the mountains. Their wives, cheeks wet with tears of joy, waved handkerchiefs in the still air and blew us kisses. Upon being notified that our backpacking trip was under way, forest service officials began pulling in their firefighting crews. Long lines of weary, smoke-blackened firefighters cheered our two-man relief team as we passed, and fire-retardant bombers flew low over us and dipped their wings in salute. We drove on, our jaws set in grim determination.

"I sure wish they'd discover a less extreme way of making rain," Vern said. "I'm getting too old for this sort of thing."

"Me too," I said. "It wouldn't be quite so bad if they paid us to go backpacking, but when we do it for nothing, that's a lot to ask."

"Yeah," Vern said. "Say, the bridge over that dry streambed we just crossed looked a little low to me. On the way back, watch out that it's not washed away."

"Right," I said.

By the time we had hiked the first mile up the trail, we could already hear the thunder.

Materialization is one of the more difficult of the psychic arts. To perform this, I need to hike fifteen miles up a canyon to fish a stretch of water generally supposed to be barren of fish and which hasn't been visited by *Homo sapiens* since the beginning of the last century. I'll climb over giant logs, battle brush, slog through swamp, and tunnel through clouds of mosquitoes and gnats. At last I'll arrive at a long, beautiful pool at the base of a waterfall, tie on a fly, and cast out into the pool. Crazed cutthroat slightly larger than French bread boxes will rush for the fly. I'll try to set the hook too soon, and my line will whip back over my head and become one with a fifteen-foot-high bush embellished with thorns the size of ice picks. The fly will dangle down in front of my face. At that instant, three other anglers will materialize out of thin air, gather around my dangling fly, and say, "Too bad, fella. Look Fred, what he got that strike on is one of them with hackle from unhatched pterodactyl, wings of gossamer, and body wrapping from the hair of the tooth fairy. Lucky we happen to have plenty of them along."

I'm also good at dematerialization. Once, using only a map and a compass for props, I made myself and two companions vanish for three days in a Montana wilderness area. I have attempted to repeat this feat several times since and have succeeded.

Generally, however, I like to practice my dematerialization in a really wild place—Kelly's Bar & Grill. I simply say aloud the magic words, "Speaking of big fish, that reminds me of the time . . ." At that point, half of Kelly's customers will disappear with a suddenness that leaves half-filled schooners of beer suspended in mid-air.

I'm not bad at hypnosis, either. All I need to do is finish expounding on my recollection and the rest of Kelly's customers will fall into a trance or, as Kelly puts it, "stupor." (Well, one man's trance is another man's stupor.)

Even Kelly, ignorant of the psychic arts as he is, can't help but admire my powers. Quite often he will point me out to a new customer and warn, "Stay away from that guy. He's a great psycho!"

"Psychic!" I correct him. "A *psychic!"*

Kelly will just chortle. If there's one thing I hate more about Kelly than his abuse of words, it's his asinine chortling.

The Fishing Lesson

☞ ☞ ☞**O**ver the years, I've introduced several dozen people to the pleasures of outdoor sports. So what that some of them didn't want to be introduced! They might otherwise have ended up as criminals or drug addicts or golfers. I like to think I've had some small part in saving them from such dismal fates.

My neighbor Al Finley, the city councilperson, is a good example of what can be accomplished if you put your mind to it. Up until a few years ago, Finley had never been fishing in his life. One day he happened to mention that fact to me, and I couldn't help but feel sorry for him.

"Al," I said to him, "nobody's perfect. All of us have our faults. Want to talk about it?"

"Talk about what?" he said.

"Your degeneracy," I said.

Then he called me one of those nasty anatomical names so popular with guys who like to pretend they're tough.

"Listen, you dirty no-good elbow," he said, "just because I don't fish doesn't mean I'm a degenerate!"

"Somebody call me?" said Retch Sweeney, who had just walked in.

I explained to Retch that Finley had never been fishing. Retch, as a way of expressing amazement, has the irritating quirk of repeating the same rhetorical question over and over.

"You never been fishing, Al?" he asked.

"No," Finley said, irritably.

"I'll be darned, you never been fishing, hunh?"

"No!"

"That's really something! You never been fishing?"

Finley's eyes looked as if they were going to pop out of his head.

"NO!NO!NO!NO!NO!" he screamed. "I HAVE NEVER BEEN FISHING, NOT ONCE IN MY WHOLE BLINKETY-BLANK LIFE, YOU FRACTURED KNEE-CAP!"

"Well, that's probably what makes you so irritable," Retch said.

After I had helped pry Finley's thumbs off of Retch's windpipe and they had both calmed down, I suggested that the three of us take a little fishing trip together. Neither one of them was too happy with the idea at first, but I eventually brought them around.

"Hell, Finley," I said, "take a few days off from City Hall. The taxpayers can use the rest. Besides, learning to fish will open up a whole new way of life to you."

Once he sets his mind to do something, Finley goes all the way. He rushed out and bought himself rods, reels, lines, leaders, hooks, creel, waders, fishing vest, etc. He practically cleaned out the local sporting-goods stores. What made me mad wasn't that he put together a better fishing outfit than mine but that the city's rate for garbage collection went up in direct proportion to what he spent. If I had suggested an African safari to him, we wouldn't have been able to afford garbage anymore.

The night before we were to leave on the fishing trip, Retch and I went over to Finley's place to make sure he was properly outfitted and to make last-minute arrangements. Finley was flitting about getting his stuff ready, and it was enough to make a petrified toad smile.

He had everything arranged in neat little piles according to function, size, color, etc. His tackle box alone was so neat and orderly it was pathetic.

Retch looked at it and grinned. "This will never do, Finley."

"Why not?" Finley growled.

"It just don't look right," Retch said. "It ain't got any character. What you need is a good snarl of leader in there with sinkers and hooks and maybe a dried worm still attached. And it ain't very efficient either. With my lures, I just keep them all dumped together down in the bottom of the box. Then all I got to do is grab one of them and they all come out in a big clump. I just turn the big clump around till I find something that looks good and pluck it off. You gonna waste a lotta time pokin' around through all them compartments."

Finley was obviously embarrassed by his own ineptness in organizing a tackle box. Still, that was no reason for him to refer to Retch as an "ingrown toenail." Retch may not be smart, but he has feelings just like anyone else.

Retch and I did everything we could to help Finley get his stuff into some kind of respectable condition so we all wouldn't be embarrassed if we ran into other anglers on the river. But Finley said he liked for his stuff to look neat and clean and brand new. He wouldn't even let me smear some salmon-egg clusters on his fishing vest or leak some dry-fly dressing on his shirt.

Finally, Retch could stand it no longer. He grabbed Finley's hat, threw it on the floor, and jumped up and down on it.

"Now, that looks more like a fishing hat," he said, holding it up for approval.

"I can see that, you shinbone," Finley said. "Too bad it isn't my *fishing* hat!" Turned out it was his politicking hat.

Retch and I had a good chuckle over the little misunderstanding, and even Finley was mildly amused by it, although not until several years later.

To make amends, Retch offered to let Finley stomp on *his* fishing hat. Finley said all right but only if Retch would agree to leave his head in it.

I could see that Finley was becoming irritated, since he had acquired a rather severe twitch in his left eye and was pacing back and forth popping his knuckles. It was apparent that all those years without fishing had taken their toll on his nervous system. I tried to be as gentle as I could in giving him the last few bits of essential information about our fishing trip.

"I've got some bad news and some good news for you, Al," I said.

"What? Tell me. I can hardly wait."

"First, the bad news. The road into the Big Muddy, which is where we're going to fish, is pretty treacherous—steep, winding, narrow, washouts, logging trucks, that sort of thing."

"The good news?"

"We're taking your car, and you get to drive."

"What's so good about that?"

"Well, there are several high old wood bridges where Retch and I have to get out and walk across just to make sure they're safe for you to drive over. Then there's the stretch of road along the top of Bottomless Canyon, where we have to get out again and guide you along just to make sure your outside tires don't hang so far out in space they might slip off. Hell, all that walking would sap your energy, and we want you to save it for fishing."

"I see, I see," Finley said, twitching and popping.

The plan we worked out was for Finley to pick us up at three in the morning. Finley, not knowing anything about fishing, expressed some amazement at the early hour for getting started. We explained that it was necessary if we were to catch the first feed on the Big Muddy.

"And don't be late," Retch said. "The one sin I can't forgive is for a guy to be late for a fishing trip."

The resulting foul-up was probably my fault. I should have taken into account the fact that Finley knew absolutely nothing about fishing and its practitioners, and I should have explained the nuances more thoroughly to him. Right in the middle of the night, I was awakened from a deep sleep by a horn blaring in my driveway. I got up and staggered over to a window to look out.

"What is it?" my wife mumbled.

"I don't know," I said. "Some maniac is down in our driveway honking his fool horn off. What kind of a person honks his horn in front of your house at three A.M.?"

It was Finley, of course. As I stuffed my gear into the back of his station wagon, I tried to be as kind as possible.

"Al," I said, "when a fisherman says he is leaving on a fishing trip at exactly, absolutely and positively, three A.M., he means five-thirty at the earliest. If he's leaving at three, he says midnight."

After we had honked Retch out of bed, he staggered to the car looking like something put together by an inept taxidermist.

"Wha-what is it?" he said. "The dam bust? We gonna be flooded?"

By four we were on the road, pumping hot coffee into our veins from the thermos Finley had had the good sense to bring along. In a little while, we felt good. There is nothing better than to be headed into the mountains on a clean fresh day with the sun rising through the trees and good company and good talk and the sense of ease that comes from the knowledge that you are in somebody else's car and it is not your transmission that is going to get torn out on a big rock. Even Finley seemed to be enjoying himself. Then we came to the road that leads up to the headwaters of the Big Muddy.

"Hang a left there," I told Finley.

"A left where? All I see is that rock slide coming down off the mountain."

"That's it, buddy," I said. "By the way, Al, how do you feel about transmissions? You don't strike me as the sort of man who would develop an attachment to them."

I am happy to report that Finley is a superb driver and negotiated the Big Muddy road without the slightest damage to his car. In fact, the only incident worth reporting was when the car started to teeter on the edge of a washout and Finley became confused and jumped out of the car at the same time Retch and I did. When we explained to him that we had merely had a sudden urge to check the huckleberry crop along the road, he climbed back in and drove around the washout, by which time Retch and I had pretty well exhausted our interest in the huckleberry crop and were able to rejoin him.

"Why is it that every time we come to a bad stretch of

road, you two are overpowered by an urge to leap out and study the local flora?" Finley asked, mopping the sweat off his brow so it wouldn't drip into his twitching eye.

"Must be just a coincidence," I said. "Say, isn't that a beautiful specimen of Birdwell's lichen on those rocks up ahead there?"

"You mean up there where the road seems to be cracking off from the side of the cliff?"

"That's it, buddy," I said, opening the door. "Remind me sometime to show you my extensive collection of lichen."

As I say, we arrived at the Big Muddy without incident, and aside from the fact that Finley went about for some time afterwards with his hands shaped as though they were still gripping a steering wheel, we were all in fine fettle and high spirits. Finley even commented that he didn't know how he had managed to get through forty-three years of life without fishing, he was having so much fun.

"You ain't seen nothing yet," Retch told him. "Just wait till you actually start fishing."

"I can hardly contain myself," Finley said.

Retch and I helped Finley rig up his tackle, and then we all cut down through the brush toward the Big Muddy. It was rough going, and the mosquitoes came at us like mess call at a fat farm. I led the way and did the best I could to point out the obstacles to the other two, but apparently I stepped right over one beaver hole without noticing it. Suddenly I heard a strange sound and turned around to see what it was. I was shocked. There was Finley's head resting on the ground, its eyes still blinking in disbelief! It was about as horrible a thing as I've ever seen. Then the head spoke to me.

"You *gluteus maximus*," it said. "Why didn't you tell me about this hole?"

"I didn't see it, head," I replied. "It looks pretty deep though—we better warn Retch about it."

"Ha!" Finley said. "Whose shoulders do you think I'm standing on?"

That was about the only real catastrophe to befall us. The rest of the day was pretty much your routine fishing trip. Oh, Finley did lose his sack lunch and made quite a fuss about that, but it was nothing really. As far as we could figure out, the lunch apparently washed out of the pocket in the back of his fishing vest. There was a pretty strong current at the place where he was trying to swim to the north bank of the Big Muddy, and that was probably when his lunch washed away. Actually, I had thought there were good odds that Finley would make it all the way across that high log over the river, even if he was running. But before Retch and I could shake hands on our bet, he ran right off into space and dropped like a shot into the river. Of course, I hadn't taken into account the fact that he was holding up his pants with one hand and had all those yellow jackets swarming around him. I had told Finley that yellow jackets sometimes hole up in old brush piles and don't like to be disturbed, but he didn't listen. I won't go into how he was disturbing them or why he was holding up his pants with one hand, because it isn't especially interesting. Anyway, to hear Finley tell it, you would think he was the only fisherman to have such an experience. You would think Retch and I had personally put those yellow jackets under that brush pile.

"Look, Finley," I told him, "it's no big deal. Fishermen lose their lunches all the time."

I dug a sandwich out of my own fishing vest and gave

it to him and patted him on the shoulder. He stared down at the sandwich. "Looks like peanut butter and jelly," he said.

I didn't have the heart to tell him it was supposed to be just peanut butter, even though I could have put those salmon eggs to good use. He didn't seem to notice, anyway.

One of the most difficult things about introducing a guy to the sport of fishing is determining whether it has taken hold on him. Finley had done so much complaining all day, I couldn't be sure. As we were driving back into town, I decided to ask him.

"I'm of two minds about it," he replied. "One bad and one good."

"What's the bad?"

"I won't be able to get out of bed for a week."

"What's the good?"

"Next time we're taking *his* car."

"Whose car?" Retch said.

"Yours, armpit, that's whose," he said.

I could see Finley was hooked. Already he had picked up one of the most important techniques.

The Hunting
Camp

☞ ☞ ☞ The guys and I were practicing our lies down at Kelly's Bar & Grill the other night, and before I knew it Fred Smits had got started on a long and boring tale about one of his hunting trips. Something of an expert on long and boring tales, I can usually spot one and snuff it out while it is still in the larval stage. On this occasion, however, Mavis, Kelly's barmaid, had just leaned over my shoulder to replenish the beverages at our table. At that instant I noticed something flutter into my drink. At first glance it appeared to be an emaciated centipede. Since Kelly's is not exactly a showcase of the County Health Department, it was only natural for me to assume that the creature had lost its grip while being pursued across the ceiling by a pack of cockroaches. I shrank back in disgust from the loathsome creature and began to stab at it with a pepperoni stick in the hope of either flipping it out of my glass or drowning it before it drank too much.

Without warning, Mavis grabbed the pepperoni stick

and, trying to wrench it away from me, hissed in my ear, "It's mine, you idiot! Give it back!"

Mavis not seeming the type to own a starving centipede, I quite logically leaped to the conclusion that she was referring to my pepperoni stick. "It is not yours," I snapped. "It's mine, I bought it, and I'm going to eat the darn thing!"

This simple assertion seemed to touch off a burst of maniacal strength in Mavis, and, gasping with rage, she twisted my wrist back in such a manner that she was able to remove from the tip of the pepperoni stick the sodden centipede. She then stalked off, sniffling something about my trying to eat her eyelash!

Her eyelash, for pity's sake! It should be easy for anyone to understand how a man of my sensitivity would be upset by such a bizarre assault on his person and character, not to mention his pepperoni. I relate this dreadful experience only by way of indicating the magnitude of event necessary to distract me sufficiently that someone is allowed to get a long and boring tale under way without having it instantly snuffed. By the time I tuned in, Fred had covered the first couple hours preceding the hunt, leaving no detail unturned, no matter how lacking in relevance or consequence. The other guys at the table had already been poleaxed by trivia and were staring catatonically at Fred as he droned on: "So a couple of minutes after Ralph knocked the ash off his cigar, we pulled off the road and made camp, and then me and Ralph starts up the trail to look for deer sign and I steps on a twig but it don't make no noise 'cause it's wet—did I say it rained the night before? Anyway . . ."

"Hold it right there, Fred," I said, noticing how barren of detail was the reference to making camp. "Did you say 'made camp'?"

"Yeh. Now where was I? Did I tell you the part about the wet twig?"

"C'mon, Fred, don't try to weasel out of it," I said. "Admit that all you did was turn off the ignition on your camper truck and set the hand brake. That doesn't constitute making camp."

"We had to let down the camper jacks, too," he said sheepishly, looking about the circle of faces, which had suddenly filled with accusation.

I shook my head. "You know the rules, Fred. It's all right to lie about unimportant things as long as it's entertaining. Add a few points to your buck, a few inches to your trout, a few miles to a trail—but don't ever say you *made camp* when you didn't."

"I'm sorry, I'm sorry!" he cried. "I don't know what came over me. It just slipped out."

"All right," I said, patting his hand. "We'll forgive you this time. Just don't ever let it happen again." Snuffing out a long and boring tale can sometimes be cruel, but it has to be done.

Then Fred made his second blunder of the evening. He looked at me and, in a penitent tone, asked, "Say, Pat, just what does constitute making camp on a hunting trip?"

Well, if that didn't create an uproar! Everyone started jumping up and down and shouting threats at Fred, and the situation looked as if it might turn ugly. Then Kelly got out his baseball bat from behind the bar and charged over. By the time the fellows had got him calmed down and made him promise not to try to hit Fred with the bat, I had managed to scribble out an outline and a few rough notes on a napkin.

"I'm glad you asked that question," I said. "I can certainly tell you what constitutes making a hunting camp, but it may take a while, so you fellows might just as well sit down and relax."

They sank into their chairs, muttering.

"I'll have to ask you mutterers to be quiet," I said.

"Watch da language," Kelly said. "Dis is a nice bar."

Since he was still fingering the bat in a psychotic manner, I resisted the impulse to retort and got my lecture started. It went something like this.

The first hunting camps were invented by prehistoric man, who divided his time equally between hunting for wild meat and having wild meat hunt for him. Interestingly, if a man made a hunting camp when he should have made a hunted camp, he was thereafter referred to as "et." (As in: "How come I never see Iggy around anymore?" "Got et.")

The hunting camp consisted of nothing more than a few branches thrown on the ground for a bed, whereas the hunted camp utilized but a single branch, one attached to the upper part of a tall tree, where the hunted would spend the night standing on it. Occasionally, a fun-loving catamount would climb the tree and send the men fleeing wildly among the branches. From this activity arose the expression "tearing limb from limb." Usually, however, the hunted camp provided adequate security, not to mention a cure for sleepwalking.

These prehistoric hunters were the first to come up with tha boon to camping, the shelter. The first shelters, simple affairs made of rock, eventually came to be called caves, after the cavemen who lived in them. Unlike the hunted camp, the caves provided protection from wind and rain as well as from wild beasts, but they made for a heavy pack on a long trip.

Since matches and camp stoves had not yet been invented, primitive man was forced to carry his campfire right along with him from place to place. Archeologists believe this may explain why hunting camps in those days were located only ten yards apart. These early firebearers are thought to have contributed to mankind the ten-yard dash and also the expressions "Ow!" "Ouch!" "Yipe!" and *"Bleeping bleep-of-a-bleep!"*

Harsh as these early camps may have been, they probably had a great many similarities to the hunting camps of today. Indeed, it is not hard to imagine the following conversation occurring around one of their prehistoric campfires.

"All right, who forgot to bring the salt? If there's one thing I hate it's pterodactyl wing without salt!"

"Squatty was supposed to bring it."

"The heck I was. I carry the cave, remember? It's Pudd's job to bring the salt."

"Ow! Ouch! Yipe! No sir! I carried the *bleeping bleep-of-a-bleep* fire!"

There is some evidence that early man very nearly invented the interior-frame umbrella tent. Apparently, a hunter one day got the idea of stretching dried skins over a framework of poles he had lashed together. The contraption aroused a great deal of curiosity among his fellow hunters, who up to that time had thought the man an imbecile.

"What is it?" they asked him.

"A brontosaurus trap," he replied.

His fellow hunters concluded that the man was indeed an imbecile. Because of his quick-witted reply, however, the anonymous inventor saved countless generations from the agony of pitching interior-frame umbrella tents, and he thus came to be regarded as one of the great benefactors of mankind.

Before the invention of sleeping bags, the hides of hairy mammoths and saber-toothed tigers provided cozy warmth through the long nights of the approaching ice age, but, unfortunately, only for hairy mammoths and saber-toothed tigers. Early cave paintings, however, indicate that one group of prehistoric hunters devised a clever substitute for a sleeping bag. They would lure a saber-toothed tiger into their cave, where one of the hunters would knock it out with a club. Then the hunters would all lie down in a row and tug the tiger up over them for warmth and try to get a few hours of sleep before the beast regained consciousness. The little band of hunters is thought to have vanished suddenly and mysteriously. The only theory for their disappearance that archeologists can offer is that one night the man in charge of the club forgot to put the cat out.

At this point in my lecture, Kelly began to shout incoherently and had to be wrestled back into his chair and disarmed of the baseball bat.

"All right," I said. "So much for the history of hunting camps. I will now move right along to my analysis of the phenomenon known as the modern hunting camp." And I did.

First off, as I told the boys at Kelly's, I don't consider anything that's comfortable a camp. I know one guy who goes hunting in a $50,000 motor home that has everything but a front lawn and a basement. Driving a hunting camp fifty-five miles an hour down a freeway goes against everything I believe in, and I simply won't stand for it. A hunting camp, after all, is not so much a thing as a state of mind.

Mention the phrase "hunting camp" to any hunter worth his fluorescent-orange vest and the picture that immediately leaps into his mind is this: A classic cabin-style tent, suspended from a framework of slender, unpeeled saplings that have been lashed together by the hunters, is situated on a flat, stoneless, grassy piece of ground with a backdrop of evergreens, tastefully splotched here and there with patches of autumn color. The pipe of a wood-burning stove pokes up through the roof of the tent. A small, pure, ice-cold mountain stream tumbles among boulders off to one side. From a stout tree limb dangles the standard fourteen-point buck. One of the hunters is splitting the evening's firewood from blocks that are miraculously dry, straight of grain, and the right length. The other hunter is pouring himself a steaming cup of hot coffee from the pot hung over the near-smokeless campfire. There are no insects in the picture, and the only snow glistens on a distant peak, made rosy by the sun setting gloriously in the west.

This picture, of course, represents the ideal of the hunting camp, which is seldom if ever achieved. The average hunting camp, infinite in its variety, falls somewhat short of the ideal. Here are but a few versions of it:

THE NO-FRILLS CAMP—This is the camp that is resorted to upon arriving at the hunting site very late on a cold and rainy night. One of the hunters will suggest something like this: "Hell, why don't we just sleep in the car. It's only five or six hours until dawn." A curious aftermath of the no-frills camp is that the hunter who suggested it is not spoken to again by any of the other hunters for approximately six months. The no-frills camp may be injurious to your health, but only if you should greet one of the occupants of it too cheerfully on the following morning.

THE FLAT CAMP—This is the camp that is resorted to after someone asks, "Okay, where are the tent poles? Who put them in the car?" And nobody answers.

THE SLANT CAMP—The commonest of all camps used in the mountains, the slant camp is the source of several interesting phenomena, one of which is that anytime something is dropped, it falls horizontally. Several times I myself have seen men encased in sleeping bags shoot out through the side of a slant camp tent like a burial at sea. One of the drawbacks of the slant camp is that by the middle of the night all the sleeping hunters are stacked on one another at the low side of the tent. And the guy on the bottom is always the one who drank a beer before turning in.

THE HANG-GLIDER CAMP—This camp results from the suggestion, "Let's pitch the tent right on top of the peak. That way the wind will blow the insects away from us."

THE HORSE CAMP—Where everyone except the packer eats standing up.

THE DOUBLE-BARREL CAMP—Where . . .

At this point, my lecture was interrupted by Mavis, who had returned sullenly to replenish our beverages. As luck would have it, her eyelash plopped into my drink again. I fished it out with a toothpick and handed it to her. You've never heard such screaming. I told Kelly afterwards, "Either fatten up these centipedes or make Mavis get rid of the false eyelashes. Otherwise, I'm not going to give any more lectures in this establishment."

So far, he has failed to heed my warning.

If You Don't Mind, I'll Do It Myself!

☞ ☞ ☞ **A**ll together, I was off the stuff for nearly six weeks. Did it cold turkey, too. Then I couldn't stand it any longer and sneaked down to the basement for a quicky, just a little something to steady my nerves. But one of the girls caught me at it and rushed upstairs to tell her mother. I could hear her in the kitchen, sobbing out the news of my relapse.

'I just found Dad hiding in the coalbin, and he's at it again."

"Oh dear! I was afraid of this!" my wife exclaimed. "I thought I had gotten rid of them all, but he probably had one stashed away under the coal."

Another kid wandered into the kitchen. "What's all the ruckus?"

"Your father's hitting the kits again."

"Figures. What is it this time?"

"Looks like another muzzleloader," the informer said.

My wife moaned. "I tried to get him to take the cure."

"Actually, there's no cure for do-it-yourselfism," Big

Mouth said. "Our school brought in a do-it-yourself addict to tell us kids how he got hooked on the habit. He said a friend of his got him tying his own fishing flies. Then he started refinishing his own split-bamboo rods. Before he knew it, he was into the hard stuff—making his own surf-casting rods, mountain tents, muzzle-loaders . . ."

"Oh, don't I know!" my wife said.

"The really terrible thing," the kid went on, "was that while this guy was talking to us, he rewired the teacher's reading lamp, overhauled the pencil sharpener, and was starting to sand the desk tops when his attendants dragged him off."

Well, everybody's got to have a hobby of some kind, I always say. And the next time I go on the wagon, I'm going to make it myself. I've never built a wagon before.

There's a lot of prejudice against us do-it-yourselfers. Most of it derives from jealousy. Take my neighbor, Al Finley, for instance. He had to give up headaches because he couldn't figure out how to get the tops off the new child-proof aspirin bottles. But do you think he would admit his incompetence? Not a chance.

"I prefer to buy my stuff ready-made," he told me a couple years ago. "If I wanted to waste my time doing it myself, I certainly could. I'm pretty good with tools, even though I just keep the basic ones around the house—a pounder, a screwturner, and one of those cutters with the sharp little points . . ."

"A saw?"

Finley sniffed. "You do-it-yourselfers just love to toss that technical jargon up at a fellow, don't you?"

"Not especially," I replied. "But now that you mention it, I'd appreciate your returning the squeezer you borrowed from me. You're never going to get the top off that aspirin bottle anyway."

Usually, I can just shrug off the nasty cracks hurled at us do-it-yourselfers, but once in a while they get to me. When I built my kids a sleek little soap-box racer, Finley leaned over the fence and asked me why I was putting wheels on a packing crate. That was bad enough, but when I built my dog a new house, employing some of the most advanced designs and technology of modern architecture, Finley called up on the phone and hissed into my ear·

"Don't make a sound! Some kind of huge, squat, brown, ugly creature has landed in your backyard! And that's not the worst!"

"What's the worst, Finley?"

"The worst is, I just saw it eat your dog! Har, har, har!"

Three questions instantly crossed my mind: Is it possible to cement a man's mouth shut while he is sleeping? Would it be considered a crime or, in Finley's case, a public service? And finally, would he be awakened by the sound of a pre-mix truck backing up to his bedroom window?

I must admit that do-it-yourselfism may be getting a bit out of hand in this country. There are do-it-yourself baby deliveries, do-it-yourself marriages, do-it-yourself divorces, and do-it-yourself funerals. If there were a kit and a set of instructions, there are probably people who would undertake do-it-yourself brain surgery. In fact, I once gave myself a haircut that was commonly mistaken for brain surgery.

Although I will tackle just about any do-it-yourself project, my specialty is outdoor gear. Nowadays I prefer to work with store-bought kits, but back when I was a youngster and just getting started on do-it-yourselfism, there weren't any kits on the market. You had to make your own kits.

The way you made a kit was to wander around gathering up the necessary parts as you found them. You then threw the parts into a large, handy container, often referred to as your bedroom. This procedure usually presented no problem if you were putting together a simple kit, like for a slingshot. On the other hand, if you were putting together a more complex kit, like for a four-wheel-drive ATV, family relations could become strained. I recall one particularly ugly scene with my mother, grandmother, and sister. To have heard them rave and carry on you would have thought there was something abnormal about a kid's bedroom leaking crankcase oil.

I have since read in child psychology books that parents are supposed to give their children "positive reinforcement" as a means of stimulating their creative urges. My family never gave *me* any positive reinforcement. The following account is an example of their narrow-minded and negative attitudes.

The peaceful quiet of a warm fall afternoon was suddenly shattered by a shrill scream from my sister. "There's something decaying in his bedroom! I know there is!"

"Nonsense!" I exclaimed. It was a pretty good word for a ten-year-old, and I exclaimed it every chance I got.

My mother and grandmother appeared at the bottom of the stairs. They conferred a moment and then, without warning, charged. I tried to bar the door but was too late. Gram got her foot in the crack, and they started forcing their way in.

"Most likely he caged some poor animal in there and let it starve to death," Gram said, reaching around the door and trying to swat me out of the way.

I ducked. "I wouldn't do anything like that."

"How about the worms, young man?" Mom snarled. "You remember the can of worms you left under the stairs last July?"

Then they burst in upon me, their fierce feminist eyes sweeping over the various kits in progress.

"There it is," Gram shouted. "Land sakes, what did I tell you? Just look what he's done to that poor creature!"

Horrified, my mother sucked in her breath. Even I could have told her that it's unwise to suck in one's breath in close proximity to a deer hide being tanned by a ten-year-old boy in a closed bedroom during an unseasonably warm fall. Her reaction was impressive and well worth observing from a scientific viewpoint. Nevertheless, I'm almost certain that there have been longer and more sustained fits of gagging, and for her to claim a record was sheer nonsense, as was her charge that she had suffered permanent damage to her olfactory system. I proved on several later occasions that her sense of smell was fully intact.

My reason for tanning the deer hide, a donation from a hunter I knew, was to put together a kit for making myself a suit of buckskins. I had used an old Indian recipe for my tanning solution, but I should have known that the old Indian was pulling a fast one on me because of the way he kept wiping smiles off his face. Some of the ingredients seemed pretty ridiculous to me at the time, but lots of things seem ridiculous to a ten-year-old, so I couldn't go by that. Probably it would have served Pinto Jack right if I had told Mom that he was the hunter who had given me the deer hide in the first place.

"You ever get your hide tanned?" Pinto Jack asked me some time later.

"Darned near did," I said. "But it's hard for a woman

to run and gag at the same time, particularly when she's carrying a rake handle."

Over the years I put together kits for bows and arrows, dogsleds, snowshoes, packframes, tents, caves, log cabins, canoes, a forty-foot sportfisher, and dozens of other neat things I can no longer recall. The kits eventually flowed out of my bedroom, through the house, into the yard, filled up the outbuildings, and started spreading over the fields. The neighbors considered me an unnatural disaster and worried that their own lands would soon be inundated by my kits. One old neighbor lady complained to my mother that she and her husband lived with their bags packed and in fear that my kits would break loose without warning and flow over them in the middle of the night before they could flee. Another neighbor accused me of stunting his potato crop, which was absurd. A forty-foot sportfisher just doesn't shade that much ground, except possibly in the late afternoon. Nevertheless, tiring of the constant stream of complaints and periodic attempts on my life, I finally curtailed my output of kits and construction projects in general and took up with girls as a means of filling in my spare time. Girls eventually turned out to be almost as interesting as kits, and they didn't take up so much space.

Over the years, I have learned a good deal about putting together do-it-yourself kits, and I herewith pass on to the reader a few helpful hints.

Never buy a beginner's kit. It is much more interesting to jump in at an advanced stage and strike out from there. After you have mastered a particular skill, you can always go back and pick up the basics. Nothing stimulates a high level of interest like a good dose of desperation.

After you have put together a firearm of any kind,

be sure to take the following safety precautions when you test fire it. First, it is absolutely essential to carry a pair of sunglasses with you when you drive out to the firing range. Never test fire a homemade firearm when you are alone; always take a friend along. Then, load the firearm in strict accordance to the standard procedures. Finally, hand the firearm to your friend and say, "Here, why don't you fire off a few rounds? I forgot my sunglasses in the car and have to go back and get them."

Over the years, I've learned that it never pays to publicly put a name to the results of one of my do-it-yourself projects. For example, when I made myself a really superb goose-down hunting jacket, other hunters I happened to meet in the woods would ask me why I was wearing a red sleeping bag. Actually, it isn't at all difficult to come up with a good many sound reasons for wearing a red sleeping bag, particularly if you give the subject a little thought.

Another good strategy is just to make up an appropriate name. Say, you've just put together a mountain-tent kit, but it didn't turn out quite right. Now if your friends happen by and ask what it is, you're going to be subjected to a lot of ridicule, or worse yet, sympathy, if you identify the object as a mountain tent. So what you do is call it a flamph.

"A flamph?" they will say.

"Yeah, a portable flamph."

"What's it for?"

"For sleeping in up in the mountains."

"Hey, man, that's pretty neat, kind of like a mountain tent, hunh?"

The final precaution is this: Never encourage do-it-yourselfism among your immediate neighbors. I know this because Finley finally caught the do-it-yourself bug from me. One day I saw him out in the backyard working away feverishly with his pounder and cutter and my squeezer.

"What are you doing?" I asked, forgetting to restrain a contemptuous laugh.

"Building a boat," he replied matter-of-factly.

"A toy boat?"

"No, a real boat."

I must say his antics provided me with a good deal of amusement. When he finally had it finished, I couldn't resist one final little jab at him.

"Tell me this, Finley, what kind of boat is that?"

"A flumph," he said.

Well, he had me there. There's just no way you can say a flumph doesn't look like a flumph. The one thing that I can say about the damn thing is that it has stunted the growth of my potatoes. A forty-foot flumph shades a lot more ground than you might think.

Useful
Outdoor Comments

☞ ☞ ☞ Every year thousands of sportspersons suffer unnecessary ridicule because they don't know the proper comments to make in particular outdoor situations. Merely extracting one's self from a predicament is insufficient; one must do so with grace and style. The proper comment not only enables one to prevail over embarrassment but, in many instances, even to survive.

Consider the following case: When my nephew Shaun and his friend Eddie were about twelve, they considered themselves to be master woodsmen. They demanded to be hauled out to a remote campsite and left to survive for four days with nothing but a handful of matches, their sheath knives, sleeping bags, a small tent, and forty pounds of food. I drove them to the campsite and dropped them off, giving each a firm handshake and a manly look in the eye to let them know how much I respected their courage and that I never expected to see either of them again.

On the second day of their adventure, Shaun's

mother, my sister, had to be repeatedly and forcibly detached from the walls she insisted upon climbing. That day, too, one of the worst rainstorms in the history of our county struck and continued on through the night. The next morning my sister argued persuasively that the time had come for me to retrieve the boys, which I set about doing the very instant I pried her thumbs off my Adam's apple.

As I arrived at the campsite, an ominous feeling settled over me. The rain had scarcely subsided to a downpour, and the clouds of mist hung in the trees. There was no sign of the boys, except for the soggy remains of a campfire and the pitiful little tent. They had pitched the tent in a low area, and the waves of a shallow lake now lapped its walls. I waded into the lake, pulled back the entrance flap, and peered hesitantly inside. Shaun and Eddie, encased in their sleeping bags and awash in a foot of water, peered back. Both looked embarrassed. Several seconds passed before Shaun spoke.

"Well, so much for woodcraft," he said.

Right then I knew that Shaun was a master woodsman and that there was nothing more I could teach him—except possibly the feasibility of pitching one's tent on high ground. He had said the perfect thing for the situation and, in so doing, had triumphed over it. Even his posture and facial expression were exactly right: body prone, limp, waterlogged; eyes telling mutely about the other side of despair; pale lips moving just enough to deliver the appropriate comment in a matter-of-fact tone: "Well, so much for woodcraft." Perfect!

Since then I have found countless opportunities in which to use a paraphrase of his comment:

"Well, so much for mountain climbing."

"Well, so much for scuba diving."

"Well, so much for flying lessons."
"Well, so much for seven-X leaders."
"Well, so much for sex."
"Well, so much for shooting rapids."
"Well, so much for sex while shooting rapids."

As a service to my readers, I have put together a compendium of situations and appropriate responses. It is my hope that these recommendations will be studied carefully and will enable you to comport yourself properly in the outdoors and in a manner worthy of a sportsman.

SITUATION—You have climbed into your mummy-style sleeping bag, wiggled around to sort the rocks under your Ensolit pad according to size and shape, and finally are about to drift into peaceful sleep. Then you detect what appears at first to be a minor problem—the wool sock on your left foot has become partially pulled off.

A partially pulled-off sock does not pose a threat to one's continued existence. On the other hand, it is not the sort of thing that can be totally ignored. It gives one the feeling that all is not right with the world, that everything is not in its proper place, performing its designated function in the prescribed and traditional manner. A partially pulled-off sock is an irritation, perhaps not one of the magnitude of, say, a mosquito walking around inside one's ear or nostril, but an irritation nevertheless.

After twisting and turning in your sleeping bag for some time, telling yourself that the sock is of no consequence, you at last arrive at the conclusion that it will drive you absolutely mad if you allow it to continue its insubordination for another minute. The simplest way in which to settle the matter is to unzip your sleeping bag, sit up, and pull the sock back on with a firm and reprimanding jerk. The problem is that unzipping the bag will invite in a blast of cold air, which will then require turning your metabolism back on to get everything warmed up again, and that in turn will result in your staying awake until you are once more nice and cozy. Another problem is that your previous twisting and turning have relocated the sleeping bag zipper between your shoulder blades at the top and your *peroneus longus* at the bottom. You therefore decide to try pulling up the sock without unzipping the bag.

Your first thought is that you can simply raise your leg high enough so that you can reach the sock. But no, your leg wedges against the sides of the bag, keeping the sock just a few inches out of reach of your clawing fingers. This effort has caused you to become turned at right angles to your Ensolite pad, but no matter; the contest with the sock has now engaged your honor. Since there is more room in the top of the bag, you now reason that by tilting your head forward onto your chest, you should be able to double over enough to get a grip on the sock. As you execute this maneuver, the nylon bag squeaks from the strain and squeezes your shoulders in against your ears. You are now locked into a semi-prenatal position inside the bag, presenting a spectacle that an outside observer could not help but compare to a defective German sausage in need of recall. But at last you have the offending wool in hand and pull it back on your foot with a pained but satisfying grunt. All that remains to be done now is to extract yourself from your compressed posture. Alas, the gentle slope you selected for a bedsite begins to take an active and aggressive role in compounding your plight. You topple over onto your side. With herculean effort and gasped curses that would provoke envy in a Marine drill sergeant, you manage to roll onto your knees. This is immediately determined to be a mistake, since it leads to a series of flopping somersaults down the incline, which becomes increasingly steeper. You come to rest jammed under a fallen tree fifty feet or so away from your starting point.

In the morning your companions get up, stare with some puzzlement at your vacated Ensolite pad, shrug, and begin preparing breakfast. Eventually you are discovered under the tree and extricated. At this moment you can either suffer ridicule or you can make the appropriate comment and earn your companions' everlasting respect and esteem. ("Everlasting" nowadays means approximately two weeks.)

What, then, is the proper response in this situation? Whining and inane jabber about a partially pulled-off sock simply won't cut it, particularly if you insist upon hobbling about in the posture of a chimpanzee with lumbago. Here's what you do: Smile, yawn, stretch luxuriously, and, as soon as your vertebrae cease their popping and pinging, say with a slightly lascivious chuckle, "Boy, I didn't think they made dreams like that anymore!"

SITUATION—The bush pilot returns to pick up you and your companion after a week of fishing on a wilderness lake. "Now you fellas are about to enjoy some real sporty flying," he says. "Did you notice how on my takeoff from here last week I had to flip this old crate over on her side when I went between those two tall pine trees and then how I stood her right up on her tail to get over that ridge?" He now doubles over with laughter and pounds his knee as you and your partner exchange glances. "Well," the pilot continues, "with the two of you and your canoe and all your gear on board, the takeoff is gonna be a little tricky this time. What I was wonderin' is if maybe I could get each of you fellas to straddle a pontoon, and if we come up a little short on the ridge there, maybe you could just sort of walk us right on over the top. How does that strike you?"

Naturally, it will be difficult for you and your partner to contain your joy at the prospect of being allowed in this way to assist in the takeoff. Since it is considered bad form to jump up and down and clap your hands in glee, you must restrict yourself to a few lip tremors and an eye twitch or two.

The important thing to keep in mind in selecting just the right response in this situation is that the pilot is probably joshing you. Therefore, you just shrug and say, "Which pontoon do you want me on?" If he isn't joshing, remember to walk really fast as you go over the ridge.

SITUATION—Back when I was about fifteen, my stepfather, Hank, and I drove out to the neighboring county to fish a stream that meandered through a series of dilapidated farms, none of which showed any visible means of support. After the day's fishing, we returned to our car to find that someone had stolen our battery. My stepfather was a gentle man of great kindness and understanding, and he said that the person who had taken our battery probably did so only because he was too poor to buy one. Therefore, Hank said, he would not place a curse on the thief that would strike him instantly dead but merely one that would make all his skin fall off. Suddenly. All at once. While he was square dancing Saturday night. And just as he was winking at the prettiest girl at the dance. As we trudged along the dusty road, Hank kept adding to and improving upon the curse until it seemed to me that the kinder thing would be to have the thief struck instantly dead.

Presently a car came by headed in the direction of town, and we waved it down. The driver was an elderly lady with a little flowered hat on her head. She asked if we would like a ride, and we said yes, but there seemed to be a problem. The lady had two large dogs in the car with her, and they were carrying on as if we were the first decent meal they had seen in months. Hank suggested that maybe he and I could just stand on the running boards, one of us on each side, and that way, "heh, heh," we wouldn't disturb her dogs. The lady said that would be just fine. "Hold on good and tight," she warned.

We immediately discovered that she had not offered this bit of advice frivolously. She took off so fast our fishing lines came loose and cracked like whips in the air behind us. We were a quarter-mile down the road before our hats hit the ground back at the starting point, not that either Hank or I were concerned with such minor details at the moment.

The lady seemed to think she needed to explain the sudden start. She rolled down her window and shouted out, "Bad clutch!"

Hank arched what he called his "vitals" back from the snapping jaws of a dog. "All right!" he yelled. "Perfectly all right!"

As the lady rolled the window back up, Hank and I dug our fingernails deeper into the rain gutters on the roof of the car and clutched our fishing rods with our armpits. By then we were traveling sufficiently fast that grasshoppers were splattering on our clothes. And still the car seemed to pick up speed. Again the driver rolled down her window and the dogs competed with each other to see which would be first to get a bite of Hank's belly.

"Bad gas pedal!" she shouted out, by way of explaining the speed with which we were hurtling down the road.

"All right! All right!" Hank cried.

She rolled the window back up.

A grasshopper exploded on the left lens of my spectacles. The air was being sucked from my lungs. My fingers were paralyzed, and I wasn't sure how much longer I could hang on. Then the situation took a sharp turn for the worse. A deputy sheriff's car sped by in the opposite direction. Upon seeing us about to break the world's record for fastest ride on running boards, the deputy whipped a bootlegger's turn in the road and came roaring up behind us with red light flashing and siren going. Hank released one hand and pounded on the glass to get the little old lady's attention. When she looked at him, he pointed back at the deputy sheriff. She smiled and nodded and pushed the faulty accelerator pedal to the floor. The deputy stayed right on our rear bumper. Every so often he would try to pass, but the old lady would cut over in front of him and force him to drop back. Then the driver rolled down her window again and grinned up at Hank. "What'd you think of that? Pretty fancy bit of driving for an old lady, huh?"

"All right! All right!" Hank said, as one of the dogs clipped a button off the front of his pants.

"Wait till you see the way I handle my rod!" she yelled, cackling wildly as she rolled the window up.

"What'd she say?" I yelled at Hank.

"She said, 'Wait till you see the way I handle my rod!'" Hank screamed back at me over the roof of the car.

"That's what I thought she said. What do you make of it?"

"I think she's going to shoot it out with the *bleeping* deputy," Hank screeched.

"I thought that's what you'd make of it," I yelled back. "She must be some kind of criminal!"

"Yeah, the crazy kind!"

At that instant the old lady whipped the car over to

the edge of the road and braked to a stop in a cloud of dust. Hank and I dropped from the running boards, coughing and gasping, and wiped our eyes with our deformed fingers. The deputy slid to a stop on the opposite side of the road, and both he and the old lady jumped out of their cars and went into gunfighter crouches, the deputy's hand hovering over the butt of his revolver.

"Oh my gosh!" Hank moaned.

Then the dogs went for the deputy. Both of them leaped simultaneously for what I thought would be the jugular, but he caught them both in his arms and staggered backwards as they licked his face and wagged their tails.

"Heeeee heeeee!" the deputy laughed.

"Heeeee heeeee!" echoed the old lady. Then she pointed at the deputy and said, "That there's my son, Rod! Ain't he somethin'? I can still handle the big bugger, though!"

"Caught you again, Ma!" the deputy squealed.

"Only 'cause I had to be careful these fellas didn't fall off the running boards, that's the only reason!" Ma shouted back.

"Somebody stole my battery," Hank said to the deputy.

"You don't say," the deputy said. "Well, I got to be going. Lots of crime in these here parts. Y'all be careful now, ya hear?" And he took off in pursuit of crime.

The old lady ordered the dogs back into the car, and they obeyed instantly, scarcely bothering to take a snap or two at Hank.

"Well, hop back on the running boards and hold on good and tight," she said to us, "and I'll haul you fellas on into town."

"Thanks anyway," Hank said, "but we can walk from

here. Can't be much more than five miles to the nearest town."

"Fifteen," the old lady said.

"Shucks, is that all?" Hank said. "Why that's even better than I figured. Thanks again for the lift."

That's the sort of comment that not only saves the outdoorsman embarrassment but enables him to survive.

Journal of
An Expedition

☞ ☞ ☞ **R**ummaging through my files some time ago, I happened across the journal I kept as leader of the expedition to Tuttle Lake during the winter of '75. I was immediately struck by the similarity the record of that momentous and heroic struggle bore to the journals of earlier explorers of the North American continent, and, lest it be lost to posterity, I immediately began editing the material for publication.

The other members of the expeditionary force consisted of my next-door neighbor, Al Finley, and my lifelong friend, Retch Sweeney. Neither man was particularly enthusiastic when I first broached the idea of a mid-winter excursion to Tuttle Lake.

"You must be crazy!" Finley said. "Why would we want to do a stupid thing like that?"

"Well, certainly not for fame or fortune," I said. "We'd do it for the simple reason that Tuttle Lake is there."

"Hunh?" Retch said. "Ain't it there in the summer?"

"Of course it's there in the summer," I told him

irritably. "What I mean is that it would be challenge for the sake of challenge."

Finley pointed out that there were two feet of snow on the ground.

"We'll use snowshoes," I told him. "We'll start early Saturday morning, snowshoe into Tuttle Lake, spend the night in my mountain tent, and snowshoe back out Sunday. It'll be a blast."

"Gee, I don't know," Finley said. "I've never been on snowshoes before. I better not go."

"That's a wise decision, Finley," Retch said. "A man your age shouldn't take any more chances than he has to."

"What kind of snowshoes should I buy?" Finley said.

Thus it was that the three of us found ourselves at trail's head, preparing for the assault on Tuttle Lake. The journal of the expedition begins at that point.

History of the Tuttle Lake Expedition
Under the Command of Patrick F. McManus

JANUARY 18, 1975—9:22 A.M. The weather being fair and pleasant, the men are in high spirits as they unload our provisions and baggage from the wagon for the trek into the mountains. The drivers of the wagon, a Mrs. Finley and a Mrs. Sweeney, offered to wager two of the men that they would "freeze off" various parts of their anatomy. I warned the men against gambling, particularly with wagon drivers, who are a singularly rough and untrustworthy lot. The throttle-skinners hurled a few parting jibes in our direction and drove away, leaving behind a billowing cloud of snow. This cloud apparently concealed from their view the man Retch Sweeney, who raced down the road after the departing wagon, shouting "Stop, Ethel, stop! I left the fifth of Old Thumbsucker under the front seat!" It was truly a heartrending spectacle.

9:45 A.M. I have assumed command of the expeditionary force. The men informed me that this is a false assumption, but I will not tolerate insubordination, particularly at such an early stage in the journey. I threatened both of them with suspension of rations from my hip flask. They immediately acquiesced to the old military principle that he who has remembered his hip flask gets to command.

11:00 A.M. The expedition has suffered an unexpected delay. I had directed two of the men to take turns carrying the Snappy-Up mountain tent, but it made them top-heavy and kept toppling them into the snow. We have now solved the difficulty by obtaining an old toboggan from a friendly native, who seemed delighted over the handful of trifles he requested for it. On future expeditions I must remember to bring more of those little green papers engraved with the portrait of President Jackson, for the natives seem fond of them.

All of our provisions and baggage are lashed to the toboggan, and I have directed the men to take turns pulling it. I myself remain burdened with the heavy weight of command. Rations from the hip flask cheered the men much and, for the time being, have defused their impulse to mutiny.

12:05 P.M. We have been on the trail for an hour. Our slow progress is a cause of some concern, since by now I had expected to be out of sight of our staging area. Part of the delay is due to Mr. Finley, who is voicing a complaint common to those who travel for the first time on snowshoes. He says he is experiencing shooting pains at the points where his legs hook on to the rest of him. To use his phrase, he feels like "the wishbone of a turkey on the day after Thanksgiving." I counseled him to keep tramping along and that eventually the pains would fade away. For the sake of his morale, I did not elaborate on my use of the term "eventually," by which I meant "in approximately three weeks."

1:10 P.M. We have stopped for lunch. Tempers are growing short. After kindling the propane camp stove, I had to settle a dispute between the men about who got to roast a wiener first. I narrowly was able to avert a brawl when Mr. Sweeney bumped a tree and dumped snow from a branch into Mr. Finley's Cup-a-Soup. Mr. Sweeney claims the mishap was unintentional, but his manner of bursting out in loud giggles gives me some cause for doubt. I have had to quick-draw the hip flask several times in order to preserve order.

I sent one of the men ahead to scout for a sign to Tuttle Lake. He returned shortly to the main party, very much excited, and reported a large number of fresh tracks. I went out with him to examine the tracks and to determine whether they were those of hostiles. Upon close study of the imprint of treads in the tracks, I concluded that a band of Sno-Putts had passed through earlier in the day. Upon our return to camp, the band of Sno-Putts appeared in the distance, and, sighting our party, came near and gunned their engines at us. After the exchange of a few friendly taunts, they went on their way.

For the last half-mile, Mr. Finley has been snowshoeing in a manner that suggests he is straddling an invisible barrel. We attempt to distract him from his discomfort with copious ridicule.

We are now about to begin the last leg of our journey—a two-mile ascent of Tuttle Mountain. The weather has turned raw and bitter.

5:05 P.M. After a lengthy and difficult climb, we have at last arrived at our destination—Tuttle Lake. During our ascent of the mountain, I found it prudent to order frequent rest stops, since I feared the excessive wheezing of the men might bring avalanches down upon us. Indeed, such was the extreme state of my own weariness that I at first did not grasp the obvious fact that we had arrived at Tuttle Lake. Mr. Finley was the first to make the discovery.

"This is Tuttle Lake," he gasped.

"I don't see no lake," Mr. Sweeney said.

"This is Tuttle Lake!" Mr. Finley shouted. "We make camp here!"

It took but a moment for me to perceive that Mr. Finley was correct in his assessment of the situation; the lake is frozen over and blanketed with a good three feet of snow. We are no doubt standing above its very surface. I am filled with wonderment, not only that we have finally triumphed in achieving the noble purpose of the expedition, but that Tuttle Lake should cling at an angle of forty-five degrees to the side of a mountain.

Snow is now falling with an intensity that beggars the imagination; either that, or we are caught in an avalanche. We are unable to see more than a yard before our faces. It is imperative that we get the Snappy-Up tent erected immediately.

7:15 P.M. The [obscenity deleted] Snappy-Up tent is not yet up. We are taking a rest break, whilst Mr. Sweeney, employing a cigarette lighter, attempts to thaw his handlebar mustache, which he fears might snap off if bumped. Mr. Finley went behind the tent to bury a snow anchor, whereupon he discovered a precipice. The drop was not great, or so we judged from the brief duration of his scream. The rest of the party were about to divide his share from the hip flask when they detected sounds of someone or something ascending the slope. We assumed it to be Mr. Finley, since few men and even fewer wild beasts possess the ability to curse in three languages. We celebrated his return with double rations from the hip flask.

9:30 P.M. We are now ensconced in our sleeping bags in the tent, after devouring a hearty stew, which I myself prepared. Darkness and the considerable violence of the snowstorm prevented me from reading the labels on the packages of dried food, which I emptied into the cooking pot. I then supplemented these basic victuals with a can of pork 'n' beans, several handfuls of spaghetti, four boiled eggs, six onions, half a head of cabbage, six wieners, a package of sliced salami, one wool mitten (recovered from the pot after dinner), and a sprig of parsley. The men were full of compliments about the tasty meal, although not until after I served dessert —each a cupful from the hip flask.

Strangely, I have been unable to find my package of pipe tobacco, which I had stashed in the provisions sack for safekeeping. It seems to have been replaced by a package of freeze-dried shrimp curry. Since smoking shrimp curry may be injurious to one's health, I have denied myself the pleasure of an after-dinner pipe. The disappearance of the tobacco is a matter of no little curiosity to me.

Upon preparing to enter his sleeping bag, which is of the style known as "mummy," Mr. Finley discovered that the snowshoeing had bowed his legs to such an exaggerated degree that he was unable to thrust them into the bag. The alternative of freezing to death or allowing Mr. Sweeney and me to straighten his legs was put to Mr. Finley. He pondered the alternative for some time and finally decided upon the latter course. I administered to him from the hip flask a portion commonly referred to as a "stiff belt," and, whilst Mr. Finley clamped his teeth on a rolled-up pair of spare socks, Mr. Sweeney and I bent his legs back into a rough approximation of their original attitude and inserted Mr. Finley into his bag, he now being capable only of drunken babbling. Now, to sleep.

JANUARY 19, 1975—1:30 A.M. Have just been startled awake by a ghastly growling seeming to originate from just outside the tent. After failing to frighten off the creature by the subterfuge of breathing rapidly, I regrouped my senses and immediately determined that the growling was gastronomical in nature and was emanating from the expeditionary force itself. I was suffering from a monumental case of indigestion, an affliction that comes upon me every time I succumb to eating parsley. My men, who seemingly possessed no greater immunity to that treacherous herb than I, moaned dreadfully in their sleep. In the knowledge that the growling is caused by something we've eaten rather than something we might be eaten by, I shall once again retreat into deep but fitful slumber.

6:15 A.M. The day dawned clear and cold. The men arose early, kindled the propane camp stove, and huddled around it for warmth. I have no notion of the temperature but have deduced from the fact that frost keeps forming on the flames that it is considerably below the freezing mark. The men complain bitterly over the loss to the cold of various parts of their anatomy, and I could not help but remind them of my advice pertaining to betting the wagon drivers against that possibility. They failed to express any gratitude, choosing instead to make threats on my life.

It is becoming increasingly clear to me that the hardships encountered on this expedition have taken a great toll on the men. They both say they have no appetite for breakfast and claim to have a strong taste of tobacco in their mouths, even though neither has been smoking. This sort of delusion is common among members of expeditions, and it is only with a great act of will that I force myself to the realization that the bits of pipe tobacco stuck in my teeth are only imaginary. When I try to encourage the men to down a few bites of frozen shrimp curry, they can only shudder and make strange gagging sounds that are scarcely audible over the chattering of their teeth. I realize now that time is of the essence, and that we must prepare for the return journey with the greatest expedience. The men realize this also, and without waiting for the command, rip the Snappy-Up tent from its icy moorings, wrap it around the baggage and leftover provisions, and heave the whole of it onto the toboggan.

I dispense to each man a generous ration from the hip flask. The retreat from Tuttle Lake begins.

7:35 A.M. We have descended the mountain much sooner than expected and, indeed, much faster than the main body of the party deemed either possible or agreeable. In the event that I fail to survive this expedition and so that the offending party may be suitably disciplined, I offer this account of the affair: Upon realizing that my hip flask was either empty or contained not more than a single shot which would not be wasted on him, Mr. Finley mutinied. He refused to take his turn at pulling the toboggan. He sat down in the snow alongside the craft and displayed a countenance that can only be described as pouting. After arguing with him briefly, Mr. Sweeney and I went off down the mountain without him. It was our mutual judgment that Mr. Finley would pursue and catch up with us, as soon as he came to his senses. We had progressed scarcely two hundred yards down from the campsite when we heard a fiendish shout ring out from above us. Upon turning, we could hardly believe what we saw, and it was a fraction of a second before we realized the full import of the mutinous madman's folly. He was perched atop the mound of baggage on the toboggan and hurtling down the slope toward us at a frightful speed. Before we could external-ize the oaths forming on our tongues, he had descended close enough for us to make out quite clearly that he was grinning maniacally. "How do you steer one of these things?" he shouted at us. Dispensing with any attempt at reply, the main party broke into a spirited sprint that would have been considered respectable for Olympic athletes even if it had not been executed on snowshoes. All was for naught. The flying toboggan caught us in mid-stride, flipped us in the air, and added us to its already sizable load. We descended to the foot of the mountain in this unsightly fashion, clipping off saplings, blasting through snowdrifts, and touching down only on the high places. The ride, in retrospect, was quite exhilarating, but I was unable to overcome my apprehen-sion for what awaited us at its termination. This appre-hension turned out to be entirely justified. Indeed, some of the finer fragments of the toboggan are still floating down out of the air like so much confetti. Immediately upon regaining consciousness, Mr. Sweeney and I took up clubs and pursued the unremorseful villain across the icy wastes, but the spectacle of Mr. Finley plunging frantically through the snow, even as he laughed insane-ly, struck us as so pathetic that we were unable to administer to him the punishment he so justly deserved.

12:30 P.M. The wagon drivers rendezvoused with us at the appointed time, and we are now luxuriating in the warmth of the wagon's heater. The mutineer Finley has been pardoned, perhaps too soon, since he has taken to bragging monotonously of his exploits on the expedition to Tuttle Lake.

"I wouldn't mind doing that again," he said. "How about you fellows?"

"Perhaps," I replied, "but only for fame and fortune. I've had enough of just-because-it's-there."

"I'll tell you one thing," Mr. Sweeney said to me. "The next time I go on one of these winter expeditions, I'm going to get me a hip flask just like yours. Where do you buy that two-quart size, anyway?"

Before I entrust him with that information, I shall have to assure myself he is fit for command.

Rubber Legs
and White Tail-Hairs

Also by Patrick F. McManus

Rubber Legs and White Tail-Hairs

Patrick F. McManus

An Owl Book

Henry Holt and Company • New York

Copyright © 1987 by Patrick F. McManus
Published by Henry Holt and Company, Inc.,
115 West 18th Street, New York, New York 10011.
Published in Canada by Fitzhenry & Whiteside Limited,
195 Allstate Parkway, Markham, Ontario L3R 4T8.

Library of Congress Cataloging-in-Publication Data
McManus, Patrick F.
Rubber legs and white tail-hairs.
I. Title.
PN6162.M35 1987   814'.54   87-8494
ISBN: 0-8050-0544-7
ISBN: 0-8050-0912-4 (An Owl book: pbk.)

Henry Holt books are available at special discounts for bulk purchases for sales
promotions, premiums, fund raising, or educational use. Special editions or book
excerpts can also be created to specification.

For details contact:

Special Sales Director
Henry Holt and Company, Inc.
115 West 18th Street
New York, New York 10011

First published in hardcover by Henry Holt and Company, Inc., in 1987.
First Owl Book Edition—1988

Designed by Jeffrey L. Ward
Printed in the United States of America
10 9 8 7 6 5 4 3

All stories in this book appeared previously as follows: In *Outdoor Life*: "Shooter";
"The Belcher" (originally titled "The Sharps"); "To Filet or Not to Filet"; "A
Really Nice Blizzard"; "The Last Flight of Homer Pidgin"; "What's in a Name,
Moonbeam?"; "The Big Fix"; "A Boy and His (Ugh!) Dog"; "Throwing Stuff";
"Muldoon in Love" (originally titled "Show and Gawk"); "Letter to Santa" (origi-
nally titled "Dear Santa"); "Nude, with Other Wildlife" (originally titled
"Gummy"); "Claw of the Sea-Puss" (originally titled "Mutiny on the Sea-Puss");
"The MFFFF"; "The Mountain"; "Pigs"; "Not Long for This Whirl"; "Cry
Wolf" (originally titled "The Bridge"); "Outdoor Burnout"; "Advanced Duck-
Hunting Techniques" (originally titled "The No-Fail School of Duck Hunting"). In
Outdoor Life Hunting Guns, 1985-86: "Gun-Trading" (originally titled "A Trader in
Our Midst"). In *Reader's Digest*: "Muldoon in Love." In *Field & Stream*: "Angler's
Dictionary"; "Rubber Legs and White Tail-Hairs" (originally titled "Getting
Hooked on Fly-Tying"); "The Cabin at Spooky Lake" (originally titled "A Strange
Occurrence at Nowhere Lake"). In *Field & Stream Hunting Annual 1981*: "The Fine
Art of Delay" (originally titled "Art of Delay"). In the Spokane (Wash.) *Spokesman-
Review*: "Summer Reading" (originally titled "Books for the Beach"). In *Chrysler-
Plymouth Spectator*: "Loud Screeching and Other Tips on Getting Lost."

To my mother,
  Mabel McManus DeMers

Contents

Rubber Legs
and White Tail-Hairs

Muldoon in Love

Afterwards, I felt bad for a while about Miss Deets, but Mom told me to stop fretting about it. She said the problem was Miss Deets had just been too delicate to teach third grade in our part of the country.

Besides being delicate, Miss Deets must have also been rich. I don't recall ever seeing her wear the same dress two days in a row. To mention the other extreme, Mr. Craw, one of the seventh-grade teachers at Delmore Blight Grade School, wore the same suit every day for thirty years. Once, when Mr. Craw was sick, the suit came to school by itself and taught his classes, but only Skip Moseby noticed that Mr. Craw wasn't inside the suit. Skip said the suit did a fair job of explaining dangling participles, which turned out to be a kind of South American lizard. I would have liked to hear the suit's lecture, because at the time I was particularly interested in lizards. But I digress from Miss Deets.

No one could understand why a rich and genteel lady like Miss Deets would want to teach third grade at Delmore Blight, but on the first day of school, there she was, smelling of perfume and money, her auburn hair piled on top of her head, her spectacles hanging by a cord around her long, slender, delicate neck. We stood there gawking at her, scarcely believing our good fortune in getting this beautiful lady as our very own third-grade teacher.

We boys all fell instantly in love with Miss Deets, but none more than my best friend, Crazy Eddie Muldoon. I loved her quite a bit myself at first, but Eddie would volunteer to skip recess so he could clean the blackboard erasers, whether they needed cleaning or not. For the first month of school, the third grade must have had the cleanest blackboard erasers in the entire history of Delmore Blight Grade School. For me, love was one thing, recess another. God had not intended the two to interfere with each other. But Crazy Eddie now skipped almost every recess in order to help Miss Deets with little chores around the classroom. She was depriving me of my best friend's company, and bit by bit I began to hate her. I wished Miss Deets would go away and never come back.

Worse yet, in his continuing efforts to prove his love for Miss Deets, Eddie started studying. He soon became the champion of our weekly spelling bees. "Wonderful, Edward!" Miss Deets would exclaim, when Eddie correctly spelled some stupid word nobody in the entire class would ever have reason to use. Then she would pin a ridiculous little paper star on the front of his shirt, the reward for being the last person standing in the spelling bee. It disgusted me to think Eddie would do all that work, learning how to spell all those words, for nothing more than having Miss Deets pin a ridiculous little paper star on his shirt.

Then one day Miss Deets made her fateful error. "Now, pupils," she announced, "I think it important for all young ladies and gentlemen to be able to speak in front of groups. So for the next few weeks we are going to have Show and Tell. Each day, one of you will bring one of your more interesting possessions to school, show it to the class, and then tell us all about it. Doesn't that sound like fun?''

Three-fourths of the class, including myself, cringed in horror. We didn't own *any* possessions, let alone interesting ones! Miss Deets looked at me and smiled. ''Patrick, would you like to be first?''

I put on my thoughtful expression, as though mentally sorting through all my fascinating possessions to select just the one with which to enthrall the class. My insides, though, churned in terror and embarrassment. What could I possibly bring to Show and Tell? The only thing that came to mind was the family post-hole digger. I imagined myself standing up in front of the class and saying, ''This is my post-hole digger. I dig post holes with it.'' No, Miss Deets probably had a longer speech in mind. I glanced around the room. Several hands of the rich kids from town were waving frantically for attention.

''Uh, I need more time,'' I told Miss Deets. Like about fifteen years, I thought, but I didn't tell her that.

''All right, then, Lester?'' Miss Deets said to one of the rich kids. ''You may be first.''

The next day Lester brought his stamp collection to Show and Tell, and held forth on it for about an hour. An enterprising person could have cut the tedium into blocks and sold it for ice. But Miss Deets didn't seem to notice. ''That's wonderful, Lester!'' she cried. ''Oh, I do think stamp collecting is such a rewarding hobby! Thank you very much, Lester, for such a fine and educational presentation. Would you like to clean the blackboard erasers during recess?''

I glanced at Crazy Eddie. He was yawning. Eddie had a habit of yawning to conceal his occasional moments of maniacal rage. Good, I thought.

At recess, Eddie refused to play. He stood with his hands jammed in his pockets, watching Lester on the third-grade fire escape, smugly pounding the blackboard erasers together. "Did you ever see anything more boring than that stupid stamp collection of Lester's?" he said to me.

"I think I did once," I said. "But it was so boring I forget what it was."

"I've got to come up with something for Show and Tell, something really good," Eddie said. "What do you think about a post-hole digger?"

Lester's stamp collection, however, was merely the beginning of a competition that was to escalate daily as each succeeding rich kid tried to top the one before. There were coin collections, doll collections, baseball-card collections, model airplanes powered by their own little engines, electric trains that could chew your heart out just looking at them, and on and on until we had exhausted the supply of rich kids in class. We were now down to us country kids, among whom there were no volunteers for Show and Tell. Miss Deets thought we were merely shy. She didn't realize we had nothing to show and tell about.

Rudy Griddle, ordered by Miss Deets to be the first of us to make a presentation, shuffled to the front of the class, his violent shaking surrounding him with a mist of cold sweat. He opened a battered cigar box and tilted it up so we could see the contents. "This here's my collection of cigarette butts," he said. "I pick 'em up along the road. You'll notice there ain't any shorter than an inch. If they's an inch or longer they's keepers. Some folks pick up cigarette butts to

smoke, but I don't. I just collect them for educational purposes. Thank you." He returned to his desk and sat down.

The class turned to look at Miss Deets. Her mouth was
twisted in revulsion. Suddenly, someone started clapping!
Crazy Eddie Muldoon was applauding! And somebody else
called out, "Yay, good job, Rudy!" The rest of us country
kids joined in the applause and cheering and gave Rudy a
standing ovation. He deserved it. After all, he had shown
us the way. From now on, Show and Tell would *really* be
interesting.

Farley Karp brought in the skunk hide he had tanned
himself and gave a very interesting talk on the process, even
admitting that he had made a few mistakes, but after all, it
was the first skunk hide he had ever tanned. He said he
figured from what he had learned on the first one, the next
skunk hide he tanned he probably could cut the smell by a
good 50 percent, which would be considerable.

Bill Stanton brought in his collection of dried wildlife
droppings, which he had glued to a pine board in a tasteful
display and varnished. It was a fine collection, with each
item labeled as to its source.

Manny Fogg, who had been unable to think of a single
thing to bring to Show and Tell, was fortunate enough to
cut his foot with a double-bitted ax three days before his
presentation and was able to come in and unwrap the ban-
dages and show us the wound, which his mother had sewed
shut with gut leader. It was totally ghastly but also very
interesting, and educational too, particularly if you chopped
firewood with a double-bitted ax, as most of us did.

Show and Tell had begun to tell on Miss Deets. Her face
took on a wan and haunted look, and she became cross and
jumpy. Once I think she went into the cloakroom and cried,

because when she returned, her eyes were all red and glassy. That was the time Laura Ann Struddel brought in the chicken that all the other Struddel chickens had pecked half the feathers off of. Laura Ann had set the chicken on Miss Deets's desk and was using a pointer to explain the phenomenon. The chicken, looking pleased to be on leave from the other chickens, but also a little excited at being the subject of Show and Tell, committed a small indiscretion right there on Miss Deets's desk.

"Oh, my gahhh . . ." Miss Deets gasped, her face going as red as dewberry wine, while we third-graders had a good laugh. This, after all, was the first humor introduced into Show and Tell. From then on, those of us who still had to do Show and Tell tried to work a little comedy into our presentations, but nobody topped the chicken.

So many great things had been brought to Show and Tell by the other country kids that I had become desperate to find something of equal interest. Finally, I went with my road-killed toad, explaining how it had been flattened by a truck and afterwards had dried on the pavement, until I came along and peeled it up to save for posterity. The toad went over fairly well, and I even got a couple of laughs out of it, which is about all you can expect from a toad. Even so, Miss Deets chose not to compliment me on my performance. She just sat there slumped in her chair, fanning herself with a sheaf of arithmetic papers. I thought she looked a tad green, but that could have been my imagination.

Now only Margaret Fisher and Crazy Eddie were left to do their Show and Tells. I knew Eddie was planning to use several pig organs from a recent butchering, provided they hadn't spoiled too much by the time he got to use them. But Margaret changed his plans.

She brought in a cardboard box and proudly carried it to the front of the room. Miss Deets backed off to a far corner, her hands fluttering nervously about her mouth, as Margaret pried up the lid of the box. A mother cat and four cute baby kittens stuck out their heads. Everyone *ooh*ed and *aah*ed. Miss Deets went over and picked up one of the kittens and told Margaret what a wonderful idea she had had, to bring in the kittens, and would Margaret like to clean the blackboard erasers at recess?

At recess, Eddie was frantic. "I can't use the pig stuff now," he said. "I got to come up with something live that has cute babies."

"How about using Henry?" I suggested.

"Yeah, Henry's cute, all right, but he don't have no babies."

"Hey, I've got an idea!" I said. "I know some things we can use and just *say* they're his babies. But you'd better call Henry a girl's name. Heck, Miss Deets won't know the difference."

Eddie smiled. I knew he was thinking he would soon have back his old job of cleaning the blackboard erasers for Miss Deets.

Everyone in third grade counted on Crazy Eddie Muldoon to come up with a spectacular grand finale for Show and Tell. An air of great expectation filled the room as Eddie, carrying a lard pail, marched up to make his presentation. Even Miss Deets seemed to be looking forward to the event, possibly because it was the last of Show and Tell, but no doubt also because she expected one of her favorite pupils to come up with something memorable.

With the flair of the natural showman, Eddie deftly flipped off the lid of the lard pail, in which he had punched air holes. "And now, ladies and gentlemen," he announced, "here is Henrietta Muldoon . . . my pet garter snake." He held up the writhing Henry.

Miss Deets sucked in her breath with such force she stirred papers on desks clear across the room.

"And that's not all," Crazy Eddie continued, although it was plain from the look on Miss Deets's face that Henry all by himself was excessive. Beaming, Eddie thrust his other hand into the pail.

"Here, ladies and gentlemen, are her babies!"

He held up the squirming mass of nightcrawlers we had collected the evening before.

At first I thought the sound was the distant wail of a fire siren, a defective one, with a somewhat higher pitch than normal. It rose slowly and steadily in volume, quavering, piercing, until it vibrated the glass in the windows and set every hair of every third-grader straining at its follicle. We were stunned to learn that human vocal cords could produce such an unearthly sound, and those of a third-grade teacher at that.

Mr. Cobb, the principal, came and led Miss Deets away, and we never saw her again. We heard later that she had gone back to teach school in the city, where all the kids were rich and she could lead a peaceful and productive life.

As the door closed behind her, I turned to Eddie and said, "I think you've cleaned your last blackboard eraser for Miss Deets."

"Yeah, I suspect you're right," he said sadly. Then he brightened. "But you got to admit that was one whale of a Show and Tell!"

Cry Wolf

Sometimes it seems I can scarcely turn around nowadays without being entertained. I am surrounded by TV sets, radios, videocassette recorders, video games, stereos, and assorted other electronic home entertainment. Then there are movies, plays, concerts, and the symphony. (True, I only attend the symphony when my wife can rent the straitjacket that looks like a tuxedo, which, too, is considered by many people an entertainment.) Spectator sports exist in such copious variety and number that I can scarcely find time for matters of more consequence, such as my hunting and fishing. In short, I live in a veritable sea of entertainment. But it was not always so.

During the years I was six and seven, my mother taught all eight grades in a little log schoolhouse tucked back into a remote valley of the Rocky Mountains. There was no electricity, no running water. Our stove had been constructed out of an old steel barrel by a local madman. Countless fires had burned little holes through the metal of the stove. Sparks popped through these holes to provide our only home

entertainment, which consisted of stomping out the fires
they started. The closest newspaper route ended forty miles
away. Our mailbox was sixty miles away, which was all
right, because we didn't have any magazine subscriptions
or anyone to write to us. We didn't have a radio. Our only
source of news was the Ouija board, and it wasn't reliable,
always trumping up phony illnesses in healthy but distant
members of the family or giving accounts of those who had
passed on. The departed generally seemed to be having a
better time than we were.

I did what I could to create my own entertainment. Once
I affixed a pry pole to the girls' privy and hid in the brush
until my victim entered, a foxy eight-year-old by the name
of Opal. Then I leaped out and pushed up and down on the
pole, causing the privy to rock precariously to and fro. (This
was one of my earliest experiments in physics, and, I believe, quite a successful one.) The rocking produced immensely satisfying screeches from inside the privy, thus
proving my hypothesis as to that effect. Little did I realize
that this innocent prank would typify my future relationships with women, all of whom would regard me with suspicion, even when I wasn't carrying a pry pole.

Winter bored me most, with the roads to town blocked for
months by snowdrifts, and the privies frozen solidly to the
ground. Aside from stomping out stove-spark fires, our family's only other entertainment during the winter occurred on
Tuesday evenings. Although we had no radio, our nearest
neighbors did. Their cabin could be reached only by hiking
three-quarters of a mile on a narrow trail cut through thick
second-growth forest. The trail began with a long, winding,
decaying bridge once used by a logging operation to cross
several meanders of a creek and a swampy area. The bridge
consisted largely of gaping holes suspended high in the air

and roughly defined by rotting timbers. A cautious person would think twice before crossing it in daytime and summer. Only desperate fools would consider the possibility of crossing the icy structure in the dark of a winter night.

"Watch where you step," my mother said one wintry Tuesday night. "This log is really slick."

She carried a torch made of a length of broomstick and a cloth dipped in kerosene. Huge shadows of ourselves leaped and played among the trees as the Troll and I, in single file, followed Mom inch by inch along the log.

"Hurry," the Troll said. "We don't want to be late."

"There's plenty of time," my mother said. "Careful! Lord save us! I nearly slipped off the bridge! Here, Trudy, grab my hand and pull me back up, so I can hook my other leg over the log. Ah, thank you, dear. Whew!"

"C'mon, Ma," I said. "Stop foolin' around. Now you've gone and dropped the torch in the crick. We're gonna be late for sure."

"Would you stop your eternal whining! Reach back and whack him one, would you, Trudy dear? Thank you. All right, now just another four hundred feet and we'll be off the bridge."

Exactly what was this entertainment for which we risked crossing the bridge? Why, nothing less than the "Henry Aldrich" radio program, a joyous half hour of unrelieved laughter and entertainment. I remember that the show opened with the teenager's mother calling out, "Henreeeeeeee! Henry Aldrich!" Even now, the recollection of that parental cry gives me a warm feeling of joyous anticipation. I have a soft spot in my heart for dumb ol' squeaky-voiced Henry Aldrich, for without him to look forward to each Tuesday night I surely would have died of boredom at age six in a remote valley of the Idaho Rockies.

The rich people who owned the radio, the Burfords, were a family of woodcutters: a stringy little father, a plump mother, and four sons the size and intelligence of pickup trucks. We would all gather around the radio and listen to the hilarious predicaments Henry was all the time getting himself into, and we would laugh until our sides ached, which was what everybody said every Tuesday evening, "I laughed till my sides ached!" After the program was over, someone would repeat something Henry had said, and we would all be off again, laughing until our sides ached even more than they had before.

"I don't know how one boy can git hisself into so much trouble," Mr. Burford would say, wiping his eyes. "A week don't go by but what that Henry pulls some fool stunt."

As soon as the Henry Aldrich show was over, Mrs. Burford would clean off the kitchen table and my mother, Mr. and Mrs. Burford, and the smartest of the Burford boys would play a few rounds of pinochle. The Troll and the—it goes without saying—dumbest of the Burford boys would sit in a corner and giggle. I would curl up with the dogs by the stove and try to get a bit of sleep, if for no other reason than to take my mind off the fact that we still had the bridge to cross on our way home.

The pinochle game served not merely to milk more entertainment out of a Tuesday evening, but had a practical purpose as well. A wolfpack roamed the valley in those days, and the playing of pinochle gave us the opportunity to get a reading on the whereabouts of the wolves. The point of this was to improve the odds that the paths of the wolves and the McManuses would not intersect on our way home. Every so often, Mr. Burford would say to one of the boys, "Cleetus, go check on the wolves."

Cleetus would step outside the cabin and stand there in

the frosty air until he heard the wolves. Then he would step back inside and report, "They's movin' along the ridge above Wampus Crick, Pa!"

"Still too close," Mr. Burford would say. "Whose bid is it?"

When Cleetus finally reported the wolves a sufficient distance away, the McManus family would spring into action. Coats would be thrown on, hasty good-byes shouted, and we would charge out the door of the Burford cabin and race for home.

On the Tuesday night in question, the wolves failed to raise their usual ruckus, possibly because there was no moon and the night was black as pitch. Cleetus stood outside until he frosted over, without hearing a single wolfish yip. "Cain't hear 'em, Pa," he reported. "They could be anywheres."

"Maybe you all should spend the night," Mrs. Burford suggested.

"Thank you, no," Mom said. "We'll go home."

"Wha . . . ?" I said. "We don't know where the wolves are! You gotta be kidding! Wild horses couldn't budge me out that door!"

Five minutes later we were scurrying along the trail toward home, walls of darkness towering above us on both sides. The wolves, gaunt and hungry, their black lips curling over their sharp white fangs, could be lying in wait for us anywhere, watching for any telltale signs of weakness in this panicky herd of hurrying humans. Crouched beside the trail, the leader of the pack points to the small human lagging farther and farther behind the two larger ones. "That's the best bet," he says.

"Wait for me," I hissed through frozen breath, as the long legs of my mother and the Troll churned up clouds of powdery snow in the distance.

I caught up with them at the bridge, where they stood panting and gathering their wits for crossing this last but major obstacle to safety. I stared glumly at the lacework of logs, whitened by snow and ice, outlining the dark and gaping holes.

"Remember," Mom said, her voice shaky with barely restrained terror, "just one step at a time. Keep your balance and take it nice and slow. I'll go first and—"

At that instant, from the darkness of the trees right above us, came the loud hoot of a wolf!

"Wolf! Wolf!" I screamed. "They got us!"

As a mist of snow settled around my small, defenseless body, I vaguely made out the darting, hurtling, leaping, bounding figures of Mom and the Troll midway across the bridge. They sailed over an open expanse of darkness, scarcely touched down on an icy log, then took off again, zagging and zigging in midair, picking out occasional footholds as if by radar, and elbowing each other for position on the turns.

The wolf hooted again above me.

"Wolves don't hoot," I said to myself, smiling with satisfaction over the proof of another of my hypotheses about human motivation. "Owls hoot." Everybody knew that, but Mom and the Troll had momentarily forgotten it when subjected to the proper stimulus. Interesting. I felt a little guilty, conducting experiments on live humans, but still, a small boy snowbound in a remote valley of the Rockies had to invent his own entertainment as best he could.

Pigs

Retch Sweeney, Al Finley, and I were returning from a fishing trip in Finley's new station wagon, when we saw the crudely lettered sign nailed to the gatepost of a ramshackle farm: PIGS $7.

"Holy mackerel!" Retch said. "Did you see that? Pigs for only seven dollars!"

"Just keep driving," Finley mumbled peevishly. Exhausted, irritable, and still shivering from a little tumble he had taken into the river, he had ordered me to drive us home, while he sprawled pouting on the rear seat. He claimed Retch had bumped him off the log on purpose.

Still, the drop into the river couldn't have been more than fifteen feet at most, although from Finley's long, quavering screech you might have supposed he had fallen off the Matterhorn. Also, if he had just relaxed and collected his senses, he would have realized that there was no point in trying to swim upstream in rapids, thus saving himself a lot of wasted effort. The waterfall he went over was nothing to brag about either, but, typically, Finley had to create practically a major drama before he was swept over the brink. I think what irritated him the most, though, was Retch's yelling, "Stop thrashing about, Finley, you're scaring all the fish!" That, of course, was inconsiderate of Retch and even untrue, because I caught a nice rainbow just a few seconds after Finley washed by me.

"Pigs for seven dollars apiece!" Retch cried. "Stop the car! Listen to me! I got an idea!"

"Will miracles never cease," Finley grumbled.

"Here's what we'll do," Retch went on. "You guys buy two pigs for each of us, that's two times three times seven which comes to . . . uh . . ."

"Forty-two dollars," I said, since I didn't want to grow old waiting for Retch to work out the arithmetic.

"That's right," Retch said. "So here's what we'll do. You guys buy the pigs and I'll raise 'em. Then, come fall, we'll have them turned into smoked hams and bacon and sausage. Don't that sound good?"

"That's the dumbest thing I ever heard of," I said.

"Wait a second," Finley said, using his shrewd tone. "You mean next fall I end up with two full-grown hogs for a total price of twenty-one dollars? You'll do all the work and pay all the cost of raising them, Sweeney?"

"Yeah," Retch said. "I'll just gather up all the spoiled food the supermarkets throw away. Won't cost me nothin', except maybe for some grain."

"Sounds good to me," Finley said. "But we can't haul six pigs in my station wagon. You'll have to come back and get them with a truck or a trailer."

"That's over two hundred miles round trip," Retch said. "No, we got to take them now. What we'll do, see, is fold down the backseat. They'll just be little pigs, so we can tie 'em up in gunnysacks. No problem."

"Well, okay," Finley said, ever alert for a bargain. "I just don't want pigs messing up my car."

My own reluctance remained intact. Unlike Retch and Finley, I'd had actual experience with pigs. I was but seven years old when my friend Crazy Eddie Muldoon asked me if I wanted to ride one of his family's pigs. "Why not?" I said, never one to spend much time contemplating consequences. We walked out to the pigpen and Eddie pointed to three huge hogs snoozing in the odorous mire.

"That one's Champ, next to him is Trigger, and the biggest one, that's Silver. Ol' Silver, he'll give you the best ride, 'cause I ain't broke him yet. Just climb up on the fence there and plop down on Silver's back and grab him by the ears. You can be the Lone Ranger and I'll be Tonto."

"Which one is Tonto going to ride?" I asked.

"Tonto ain't gonna ride. He's gonna sit here on the fence and keep a lookout for my pa."

Caught up in my anticipation of trotting about on Silver, I had forgotten about that standard precaution. Ninety percent of the things Eddie and I did required keeping a lookout for his pa.

I climbed the fence and plopped down on Silver's back, grabbing him by the ears in a single smooth movement, and started my Lone Ranger yell: "Hi . . . !" In one second flat, two hundred pounds of furious pork sizzled around the pen like a piece of ice on a hot griddle. Champ and Trigger joined in the general ruckus, but without anywhere near the enthusiasm of Silver. I quickly tired of the ride and began looking for a way to dismount, finally deciding that the next time Silver tried to scrape me off on the fence, I would make a jump for it. Intelligent beings that pigs are, however, Silver made a few quick calculations in elementary physics, arriving at the conclusion that if he was to stop suddenly, whatever was on his back would continue on at the same momentum until the pull of gravity counteracted the original force. He instantly put this theory to the test, and with great success. The hog's sudden stop launched me like a torpedo off his back and sent me streaking headfirst through six-inch-deep residue of pig.

I got up and shook off as much muck as I could, carefully wiping a couple of eyeholes so I could see. Tonto sat unperturbed on the fence, nibbling a straw as he studied the situation. Without speaking to him, I climbed out of the pen and headed for the creek. I knew what Tonto wanted to say, that it was building up in him, demanding to be said, because an opportunity like this might never arise again in his lifetime. When I was a safe distance away, but not so far that I couldn't make out the words uttered in a small, pleased voice, he said it:

"Who was that masked man, anyway?"

From that moment on, I never had any use for pigs. They had left a bad taste in my mouth.

"I don't want to have anything to do with pigs," I told Retch and Finley. "They're nothing but trouble."

"No trouble for you and me, though," Finley said. "We won't even see them again until they're hams and bacon."

He had a point there. I swung the car around and we drove back to the farm. A grizzled little man came out of the house picking his teeth and rubbing his rounded belly as though he had just finished a large dinner.

"Let me handle this," Finley said out of the corner of his mouth. "This guy looks like a sharpie. That seven-dollars sign was probably just a come-on. Guy probably thinks he's lured some dumb city slickers into his snare. Ha!"

I was glad we had a shrewd person like Finley along to handle the deal.

"Howdy," the farmer said. " 'Spect you fellas want to buy some pigs."

"Might be," Finley said. "If the price is right."

The farmer appeared a little puzzled, and I could see that Finley had got in a deft stroke.

"If you seen the sign, you seen the price," the farmer said. "Seven dollars."

"Uh-huh," Finley said shrewdly. "Now, we're not talking about the runts of the litter, are we? We're talking good, healthy pigs?"

"Yep," the farmer said. He pointed to a large, fenced area where about fifty little pigs ambled about. "There they are. You can take your pick."

"Well, that seems fair enough," Finley said. "You got a deal. We'll take six pigs."

"Good. That'll be forty-two dollars. I'll throw in some gunnysacks for free to haul 'em in."

Finley handed him the money. The farmer counted it and tucked it into the bib pocket of his overalls. "They're your pigs now," he said. "Go catch the ones you want."

"We have to catch them ourselves?" Finley asked. "How do we do that?"

"Don't know," the farmer said, turning to walk back to his house. "Ain't none of 'em been caught yet. But you fellers might be faster than most folks."

"Uh, I don't suppose you would be interested in buying the pigs back?" Finley said, now more nervous than shrewd.

"Nope. I already got a surplus of pigs."

Our first tactic consisted of each of us selecting a pig and trying to run him until he tired out. But all the pigs looked pretty much alike. So when one of the chased pigs got tired, he would charge into a crowd of other pigs, and a fresh pig would race out the other side, so that we were competing individually against what amounted to a pig relay. Another problem was, the pigs stood only about a foot high on all fours. When we closed in on one, we had to run stooped over in order to grab at it, the posture not unlike that of a person doing a toe-touching exercise while sprinting. After an hour of this fruitless—or pigless—effort, we met for a consultation.

"I think we should all three of us concentrate on one pig at a time," I said. "That way we can run it into a corner, grab the bleep-of-a-bleep, and dump it into a gunnysack."

"Good idea," Retch said. "Now, can any of us straighten up enough to hold the sack?"

"I can raise my hands to my knees," Finley said.

"Close enough," I said. "You hold the sack."

Only a few minutes after midnight, we cornered the sixth of our pigs and sacked him. We folded down the backseat of Finley's station wagon, spread out a couple of plastic rain slickers, dumped our sacks of little porkers on them, and headed for home.

"I still say it's cheap hams and bacon," Retch said, his body still curled in the shape of a question mark. "What say, Finley?"

"I say, 'Owww owww ooooooh ah oh my aching back,' that's what I say! And I better never lay eyes on these pigs again until they are hams and bacon!"

"You got nothing to fear," Retch said, thereby proving his inadequacy as a prognosticator.

The pigs, apparently content in their gunnysacks, occasionally emitted a quizzical grunt but otherwise caused no commotion. Retch and Finley dozed off. I hung on the steering wheel, sucking an occasional drag from a vacuum bottle of cold coffee to keep my eyelids from sneaking shut.

After half an hour or so, we hit the freeway and had a straight shot home. Tired and aching, I paid little attention to a scuffling noise behind me. Suddenly, on the back of my neck, I felt a moist snout, bristly little whiskers, and a hot panting breath. I must have been dreaming with my eyes open, because for a second I thought it was my old high school girlfriend, Olga Bonemarrow. I quickly realized, however, that the cause of these sensations wasn't chewing bubble gum, which ruled out Olga.

"A pig's loose!" I yelled.

"Ye gads!" Finley said. "He's off the rain slickers too! Don't scare him! If he does anything on the carpeting, I'll kill him now with my bare hands!"

Alas! The shrill tone of Finley's voice prompted the pig to commit an act of hygienic indiscretion right on the station wagon's new carpeting, even as the culprit stood blinking his little pig eyes at his would-be assassin. The resulting wail from the carpeting's owner sent the pig tearing about the rear of the station wagon in a frenzy almost equal to that of Finley. This alerted the other prisoners to the festivities, and in a matter of seconds they had torn loose from their sacks and joined in the bedlam. The hysterical squealing was deafening.

"Would you please stop squealing, Finley?" I said. "You're giving me a headache."

"Stop the car!" Finley ordered. "We've got to get the pigs back in their sacks!"

"Shucks," Retch said sleepily. "They won't hurt nothin', Finley. You can hose out the back of the station wagon tomorrow and it'll be good as new. Let the little porkers have their fun."

"I said stop the car!"

"I can't stop," I said. "You can only stop on the freeway

if you have an emergency. You know that, Finley. Now calm down.''

"Then someone's got to climb back there and stuff the pigs back in their sacks!''

"Be my guest," Retch said.

"Oh, good heavens, I should know better than to hang out with you nitwits," Finley said, climbing into the back and grabbing at a pig.

The station wagon rocked and swayed as Finley thrashed about, stuffing pigs into sacks, only to have them escape when he lunged after another one. I turned up the radio in an effort to drown out the hideous sounds. Distracted as I was, and possibly because of strong motivation to end the drive as quickly as possible, I pressed down on the accelerator pedal a bit too hard. At that moment a pig leaped over my shoulder and into my lap, only to be pursued by a sweating, snarling Finley, who dragged the squalling beast over my face and into the back. The car swerved. No sooner had I got it back under control than a pulsing blue light filled the interior of the vehicle, followed by the wail of a state patrolman's siren rising ever so slightly above the din of Finley and the pigs.

"Cripes," Retch said. "Now you gone and done it, Finley."

A fragrant hush fell over our little group as I pulled the station wagon to the edge of the road and stopped. The patrolman walked cautiously up to my lowered window, his right hand resting on the unbuttoned flap of his holster. The man knew a wild bunch when he saw one.

"I can explain, officer," I said, handing him my driver's license.

"I bet," he said, not at all friendly. "Had a bit too much to drink, right, sir?"

"Haven't had a drop," I replied. "I'm waiting until I get home to have too much to drink."

"Oh, yeah? Well let me just take a whiff of the inside of your vehicle, sir. Whewwweeeeee! *Choke! Gag!"* He staggered back, barely catching his balance and almost falling into the ditch.

"As I tried to explain, officer," I said, "we have a man in back here trying to stuff pigs in sacks and—"

"That's enough of that, pal. I don't put up with wise—" The patrolman flicked the beam of his flashlight into the back of the station wagon. Six pigs and Finley returned his stare. Smiling weakly, Finley held up a gunnysack, apparently as proof that he was engaged in a legitimate activity.

"You see," I continued, "what happened was—"

"Okay, okay, stop explaining," the patrolman said. "I'll let you off this time. But don't ever let me catch you guys driving while stuffing pigs in sacks again!"

"Rest assured, officer," I said. "You never will." Seldom have I been so confident in one of my predictions.

The MFFFF

No matter what you may have heard, hunting is a competitive sport. The competition, of course, comes not from seeing who can shoot the most or biggest game, but from the display of one's physical fitness. How often have you been taunted by your hunting companions when you've suggested taking a rest after a steep climb to the top of a hill? I myself once regularly underwent such humiliations, even when the climb up the hill wasn't made in a vehicle.

Finally, I said to myself, "You must do something about your rotten physical condition. You must get in shape once and for all." As it happened, I wasn't listening to myself at the time, and thus I was saved endless hours of boring exercise.

Most of my exercise has come from strenuously avoiding all forms of physical fitness, although I do find it amusing to run the Jane Fonda workout cassette at fast speed on the VCR. But, you ask, how do you avoid being taunted by your hunting companions for being out of shape? I'm glad you asked that, because otherwise this article would end right here. The answer is the McManus Formula for Fitness Fakery. By carefully following the MFFFF, you too can be a winner in the Great Outdoors.

First, you must instill in your hunting partners the belief that you have hidden reserves of supernatural strength that can be called up at any moment. Here's one ruse that works very well. Conceal your lunch somewhere on your person, such as in the game pocket of your jacket. Then, when you are a couple miles downhill from your hunting vehicle and in need of extensive rest, you say, "Oh-oh, I forgot my lunch. I'll just run back to the car and get it. You fellas wait here."

Naturally, this announcement is going to be greeted by hoots and hollers and a few threats of bodily harm from your companions, but you must persist. Charge off into the brush. As soon as you are out of sight of your companions, slow to a walk—this goes without saying—for the next fifty yards or so. Make sure you are far enough away so you can't hear their comments about you, because that would depress you unnecessarily. Sit down on a log and rest for fifteen or twenty minutes. Then return to your companions, bursting out of the brush at a speed sufficient to impress them but not enough to make you breathe hard.

"You back already?" one of them will say. "Ha! You didn't go back to the car for your lunch after all!"

"I did so," you say. "But the car was locked and you forgot to give me the keys, Harold!"

Now repeat the entire performance, this time with the car keys, and return with your lunch. Works like a charm. Your friends will be so impressed by your superhuman feat that they will not want to risk humiliation by challenging you to a race up a mountain with a hindquarter of elk on your back, or some similar form of suicide. You will become a legend in your own time, or at least someone might mention your feat in a bar sometime during the following week, but, of course, don't hold your breath.

Next we have the Nature Lover ploy. Recently I was on a three-state turkey hunt that outfitter Ron Dube (pronounced "Doobee") conducts out of Buffalo, Wyoming. Ron runs the spring hunt up where the corners of Montana, Wyoming, and South Dakota meet. Thus, during a typical week-long hunt, you can shoot a turkey in each of three states, provided you're not as selective about turkeys as I am. (I select only slow, dumb, nearsighted gobblers, in my dedicated effort to improve the gene pool of the North American wild turkey. But what thanks do I get?)

After I had followed Dube around the hills for a couple of hours, I became more than a little impressed at the speed with which he moves up vertical ground.

"How many states *wheeeeeeze* have we covered so far?" I asked him.

"Jeepers criminy," Ron said, using his most serious cussword. "We're still in South Dakota. Why, you getting tired?"

"Me? Are you *wheeeeeeze* kidding? Heck no."

"Good," Ron said, pointing to a mountain that must have been an offspring of the Grand Tetons. "Because there's a big gobbler hangs out on the other side of this rise."

"My lunch *wheeeeeeze!*" I cried. "I forgot my *wheeeeeeze* lunch! Back at the *wheeeeeeze* car."

"Don't worry about your lunch," Ron said. "I always carry plenty of food in my pack."

Always expect any single ploy in the McManus Formula for Fitness Fakery to be countered by a companion, espe-

cially an experienced outfitter like Dube. Now, note carefully how I moved smoothly from the Lunch gambit to the
Nature Lover ploy.

Ron and I started up the Teton, his legs gobbling up a
yard of altitude at every stride while mine nibbled on inches.

"Hey, hold up a second, Ron," I called. "What's this
little *wheeeeeeze* flower here?"

Dube came back down the mountain, ready as always to
impart some bit of exotic nature lore to an interested client.
He stared at the little flower.

"Why, that's a buttercup," he said. "Jeepers criminy,
haven't you ever seen a buttercup before?"

"I guess not this close," I said, since my face hovered
mere inches above the ground, watering the little yellow
flower with dribbles of sweat.

A few yards more up the mountain, I ran out of breath
again. "Hey, Ron, what's this *gasp* flower?"

Dube loped back down the mountain. "Still a buttercup," he said.

"Oh," I said. "It's a little different shade of *gasp* yellow.
What *gasp* makes it a different shade of yellow?"

Thus cleverly did I slow our ascent of the hill, engaging
Dube in a discussion of each species of flora on the moun-
tainside, including everything from lichen to ponderosa
pine, some of them three and four times. Never once did
Ron catch on to my clever tactic, even when I led him into
the realm of geology.

"What's this *choke gasp* odd protrusion?" I asked, pointing
at the object with my tongue.

"A rock."

"Well, *gasp* I'll be darned. A rock."

Clare Conley, the editor of *Outdoor Life* magazine, also
hunts with Ron Dube, usually for elk. He refers to a trek

with Ron as a "Dube death march." He claims that since
Dube always carries a backpack, the best method for slowing him down is to sneak a bunch of rocks into his pack
when he isn't looking. I consider such conduct unsportsmanlike, mean, and contemptible, and besides, as far as I
could tell, Dube didn't even notice the rocks. As I told Conley, if you are going to use an unsportsmanlike, mean, and
contemptible method of slowing down your hunting partner,
use one that's guaranteed to work.

Such is the Picture-Taking ploy. This is a truly wonderful
gimmick. When the point of exhaustion is arrived at where
your feet are no longer taking orders from your brain and
each is just wandering around on its own, then you call out
to your partner, who may be but a speck on the horizon
ahead of you, "Hey, Harold! Come back here! This will
make a great shot!"

"So shoot it!" the speck on the horizon calls back.

"No!" you yell. "I want you in the picture!"

The speck on the horizon then scuttles back toward you
until finally it becomes Harold. It is a well-known truth that
no outdoorsman can resist having his picture taken against
a wild and rugged backdrop.

Naturally, when Harold arrives he immediately realizes
that the scenery here is absolutely identical to all the other
scenery within a fifty-mile radius.

"What's so great about this shot?" he asks.

"Good gosh, don't you see it?" you say, putting Harold
on the defensive, because he has always been insecure in the
area of art appreciation. (It helps to have a companion who
had trouble coloring inside the lines back in elementary
school. In fact, I make this one of my main criteria in selecting a hunting companion.)

"Man," you continue, "look at the rare quality of light

on the snow (water, grass, sand, dirt, mud) here. Stand over
there so I can get this light on your face. Take off your hat.
No, put the hat back on. Take off your jacket. Hold your
rifle in your left hand. No, right. Good, hold that pose while
I put a roll of film in the camera." And so on. With any
skill at all, you can stretch the Picture-Taking ploy into a
good thirty-minute rest.

Warning! Merely feigning to take a picture under these
circumstances may cause your partner to break off your
friendship, not to mention various parts of your anatomy,
because he will insist on seeing and having copies of each of
the two dozen shots you took of him on the trip. ("And
here's the one of you standing in a field of gray snow. Oh,
this is a good one of you standing in a field of gray snow.
Look at this one of you in the field of gray snow. And this
one . . .")

Finally, we come to the Sock-Changing ploy. Most of
your companions won't catch on to the fact that you're
sneaking a rest if you sit down to change your socks every
so often, particularly if you comment, "Blisters can inca-
pacitate an outdoorsman faster than anything. The best precaution against blisters is to change your socks frequently."
The one problem consists of having to leave most of your
gear behind in order to have enough room in your pack for
socks. But a night or two in the wilds without a sleeping bag
can be an invigorating and memorable experience, particularly if you have the right attitude and aren't exhausted
from charging up and down mountains all day without sufficient rest stops. I have tested this ploy thoroughly and have
found that you can get away with one sock-change per mile
of terrain covered, if you have sensible and considerate companions. But how often does that happen? Right. I have
some hunting partners who change their own socks only

once a month on the average, so with them I go directly to the Picture-Taking or Lunch ploy. The Nature Lover ploy doesn't work well with them, either, because if you ask one of them to identify a plant for you, he's likely to say, "That's just your regular old weed. Now quit foolin' around and get a move on."

One further cautionary note on the Sock-Changing ploy. It should be carried out expeditiously. For example, I have found that if you try to extend the rest period by playing "this little piggy went to market" on your toes, some hunters will become irritated and attempt to throw you off a cliff.

Well, those are all the tips I have for sneaking a rest on hunting trips without suffering ridicule from your macho friends. If you don't like the tips, however, you can always go to an extreme and start getting in shape. Just don't ask me to hunt with you.

Summer Reading

Of all the classifications of literature, the only one distinguished by season is "summer reading." Why is that? Do you really care? I thought not. Nevertheless, I have put a good deal of work into this essay and you had better darn well pay attention.

The phrase "summer reading" seemingly reeks of literary permissiveness. Many readers interpret this to mean they can read anything they please between May and September. Not so. A set of rules governs summer reading, and the consequences of ignoring them can be serious. For example, a man was arrested recently for reading Proust's *Remembrance of Things Past* on a public beach while naked. If you have any sense, you'll leave Proust in the library where he belongs.

Now for the rules. First of all, books containing any of the following disqualify themselves as summer reading.

Ideas—Nothing so provokes disgust in a summer reader as suddenly coming upon ideas in a seemingly innocent book. This is why my own books are often recommended for summer reading. An idea occasionally will creep into something I write, but usually I catch it before the book goes to press. An editor once found a small idea in one of my stories and nearly suffered an infarction. "Listen, McManus," he snarled, "we pay you to write, not think." Thinking and summer reading are incompatible. If the book has caused either you or the author any thought, then it is probably regular reading and not fit for summer consumption.

Socially Redeeming Qualities—I'm reading a book right now in which medieval monks are being murdered by someone or something. At first I thought this in itself might be a socially redeeming quality, but apparently it isn't. Although this book does contain some ideas, the author had the decency to introduce them with Latin phrases, so they can be easily recognized and thus skipped over. Several times I've caught myself almost thinking while reading the book, so I doubt I would recommend it for summer reading.

Self-Improvement—Summer is the time of degeneration, if not degeneracy. We readers of summer have no interest in improving our minds, bodies, sex, children, pets, lawns, manners, mileage, etc. We are loath to read anything that might improve us in any way. Generally, we prefer summer books that leave us a little bit worse for having read them.

Dust-Jacket Blurbs—The perfect summer book lacks even one dust-jacket blurb. This means that reviewers could not find a single favorable thing to say about the book. Also, any book containing blurbs with the words *sensitive, intelligent,* or *brilliant* should instantly be rejected. Blurbs containing the words "gross," "disgusting," "insipid," and "truly rotten" suggest the books might make good summer reading, but they are hard to find.

Any summer-reading book should contain one or more of the following.

Sharks—If a shark doesn't show up someplace in a book, it's probably not worth summer reading. I just finished a police action novel in which the villain gets eaten by a shark in the final chapter. I thought it was great. My wife tried to read the book but said she thought it would have been better if the author had been eaten by a shark in the first chapter. She lacks the necessary credentials of a summer reader, however, and her judgment can't be trusted in these matters.

Illicit Sex—Combine sharks and illicit sex and you have a darn good summer read. The sex scenes should not be too graphic, of course. Otherwise, they are offensive or, worse yet, fall into the category of self-improvement.

Murder—A murder or two should occur early in the book, unless a shark is present, in which case a minor character can be eaten. By early, I mean no later than the first half of the second page. *Gorky Park* opens with three murders on the first page, which is about the maximum number you can expect in that limited space. The murders should be tastefully done, preferably in the manner of the early British mystery writers. They should also be fairly tidy and conventional. Summer readers don't like their victims turning up as pot roasts or that sort of thing.

Cardboard Characters—Nothing ruins a good summer-reading book faster than well-rounded, complex characters. They slow the action. The plot sits there idling while the hero ponders some moral dilemma. There should be no moral dilemmas in summer fiction. If the hero must ponder, he should ponder sharks, illicit sex, or the villain. Ideally, he will ponder nothing and get on with his pursuit of one of the above.

That pretty well sums up summer reading. Now hop to it. Summer doesn't last forever, and before you know it we'll be back reading the heavy thinkers—Fyodor Dostoyevski, Herman Melville, Sigmund Freud, Shirley MacLaine. . . .

Angler's Dictionary

Note from the lexicographer: In my continuing effort to compile a dictionary of uncommon angling terms for use by newcomers to the sport of fishing, I have recently defined the following words and phrases as they are commonly understood by experienced fishers. You will note that the dictionary is not in alphabetical order. This is a labor-saving device. I have never been very good at the alphabet anyway, and have come to regard it as a frightful nuisance, useful only for soup. If some critics see this as a shortcoming in a lexicographer, I have only this to say to them: Picky, picky.

Here, then, is the "Angler's Dictionary."

Wicker creel—This is a lively folk dance often performed by a fisherman on the occasion of slipping the point of a No. 4 hook under a fingernail. While the dancer performs the wicker creel, his companions typically will clap rhythmically and encourage him with shouts of "Go, man, go!"

Kitchen table—Of all the dangers that confront an angler, the one seldom mentioned to beginners is the kitchen table. It is a repository of various essential fishing tackle that

35

never makes it out to the fishing site. As a personal example, I laid a brand-new, ninety-dollar, 6-weight flyrod on our kitchen table one day last summer, and it was never seen again. This is an extreme case, of course. Usually the item can be found still on the kitchen table upon the angler's return, although it often has been buttered and drenched with maple syrup.

Car roof—This is a deadly variation of the kitchen table. Car roofs are to fishing what black holes are to outer space. Whatever is placed on them even for a few seconds gets sucked into another dimension. "Where's my fly book?" one angler will say to another. His companion will reply, "I saw you place it on the car roof at our last stop!" The two anglers look at the car roof. It glares back at them with smug emptiness. I have had cameras, fly reels, sack lunches, and numerous other items sucked into the void by car roofs. Never place any fishing gear on a car roof, and, even more important, never sit on one yourself.

Spinning reel—This is a form of comical walk performed by anglers who have spent an evening around the campfire exchanging stories and sipping 150-proof rum. The spinning reel is usually attributed to excessive consumption of night air, although a doctor friend of mine claims that theory is nonsense. He speculates that the true cause is altitude. "We're only three hundred feet above sea level," I told him once. "Well, that's altitude, isn't it?" he replied. "In every instance of the spinning reel that I've ever witnessed, there has been altitude present." I for one am certainly not going to argue with scientific evidence.

Cast—There are almost as many kinds of casts as there are kinds of anglers. There's the foot cast, the leg cast, the arm cast, the full-body cast, and many more. One of the common methods of achieving a full-body cast is by following the advice of a fellow fisherman who yells, "Take a running jump, Stan! You can make it!"

Sinker—An angler who steps off a dock with a ten-horse outboard motor in his arms is referred to as a *sinker*. Some athletic anglers claim they have actually swum fifty or sixty feet to shore while dragging a ten-horse motor, but it is generally believed that they simply walked along the bottom until they reached shallow water. Since the other anglers present continued to concentrate on putting their tackle together, no eyewitness accounts exist as to what actually may have been the case.

Split-shot sinker—An angler who suddenly drops into the water while standing with one foot on the dock and the other in a drifting boat and holding a ten-horse motor in his arms is known as a *split-shot sinker*. First he splits, then he sinks like a shot. The split is usually accompanied by a hideous screech, so horrible in fact that other anglers present have been known to look up briefly from sorting their tackle boxes.

Purist—An angler who doesn't catch any fish, because he uses only dry flies the size of dandruff, often conceitedly refers to himself as a *purist*. Other anglers refer to him as a *loon*.

Fresh air— This is what the purist claims he enjoys getting out in, even though he doesn't catch any fish.

Fishing journal—An imaginative work of sub-literature in which the angler records the weight, length, and species of fish he didn't catch.

Rock—This is a tool used in the field to make delicate repairs on expensive fishing reels, because the tool kit was sucked into the void by the car roof.

Pink nighty—Dry-fly purists enjoy coming up with colorful names for the various bits of fluff they employ not to catch fish. However, when they see a lunker brook trout that they really want, they will often tie on a No. 10 Pink Nighty, which usually does the job. Also known as a *ten-inch nightcrawler*.

New car—An expensive dehydration chamber that ten-year-old boys use to dry out strings of perch on hot July days.

Blue upright—Although primarily the name of a dry fly, it also denotes ice fishermen in Wisconsin.

Blue darter—Refers to a Wisconsin ice fisherman who has just stepped through a hole in the ice.

Best fishing time—Yesterday or last week.

Worst fishing time—Now.

Gaff—What old gaffers do when they have a young fisherman trapped in a boat with them. Fatal only if the young angler leaps out of the boat and attempts to swim three miles to shore while carrying his tackle box.

Fishing tackle—This is an extreme but useful maneuver for preventing a fellow angler from reaching the best fishing hole before you do.

Carp—This is a form of immature behavior displayed by fishing partners, often consisting of whining, after you have clipped off the tips of their flyrods by inadvertently pressing the switch on your car's automatic windows.

Forked stick—Stylish fishermen often use forked sticks to carry their catch, after a sixty-dollar creel has been claimed by the kitchen table.

Who wants raw egg in their beer?—A little joke that charter-boat fishing captains wish they had never called out to their clients after the boat has been tossing about in rough seas for six hours.

Fair-to-middlin'—This is the standard reply used by

fishing resort owners to describe the worst fishing in fifteen years.

Good—Fishing resort owners use this word to describe fishing that's fair-to-middlin'.

Awesome—A favorite word of resort owners to describe fishing, it is based on the fact that they heard of some kid who caught two small perch the previous week.

Let's tell Mommy I caught some of the fish—This is a pathetic plea that comes up anytime a father takes his little son or daughter fishing for the first time. The situation is delicate and should be handled with utmost care. One way is to promise the youngsters ice cream or candy. Then there's a good chance they'll let you get away with the ruse.

The Mountain

"April," the poet wrote, "is the cruelest month." Boy, no kidding! If I had read that poem while in third grade at Delmore Blight Grade School, I might very well have said, "How true! How true!" Although it's more likely I would have said, "Do I really have to read this stupid poem?"

Outside the grimy windows of third grade, April was dissolving the last lingering stains of winter. Inside, however, Miss Goosehart was stretching us pupils on the rack of the multiplication table, a fiendish device once used to torture young children. April was slipping from our grasp. Flowers were bursting into bloom, trees were leafing out, and the sap was rising, namely one Milton Clinker, to give the answer to four times seven. Who cared about four times seven, anyway? Only a sap like Clinker would want to multiply while all outdoors filled up with April.

Miss Goosehart cranked up the rack another notch. "Pat, would you take one of your wild guesses at three times six?"

I scratched my head in a show of concentration. Crazy Eddie Muldoon, who sat behind me, leaned forward and whispered something. I thought maybe it was the answer. But it was, "Saturday, let's climb the mountain."

Eddie was so far gone with April he didn't even realize it was my turn on the rack. He wasn't called Crazy Eddie for nothing.

"Give me a hint," I said to Miss Goosehart. "How many letters does it have?"

Had Eddie really said, "Let's climb the mountain"? What a terrific idea! My heart did a handspring at the very thought. "Okay," I whispered back. Eddie groaned. Miss Goosehart now had him on the rack, trying to wrench out the answer to seven times seven. It was ghastly.

The mountain Eddie and I intended to climb reared up abruptly from the valley about a mile from our farm. At night, in the glow of the moon, the mountain took on the shape of a sleeping dragon, the high, ragged peak forming the hump of its back; a long, descending ridge was its neck, and another knob of mountain was its head. The head of the dragon rested on the valley floor not far from Delmore Blight Grade School. It was easy to imagine the dragon awakening one night, stretching out its neck, and gobbling up the school in a single bite. In the morning the only evidence of what had happened would be a gaping hole in the ground and the smile on my face.

The dragon lived only at night. Daylight revealed a solid, no-nonsense mountain, with a craggy granite peak, sheer cliffs, a crosshatching of crevices and ledges, and, lower down, thick forest.

The mountain talked to me. I don't mean to imply that we held long philosophical conversations, but even as a small boy, sitting on the back steps of my house, I could hear it calling: "Pat! Pat! Come climb me! It will be fun! And I won't try to kill you, as I do some folks!"

On an April Saturday at the age of eight, I learned that mountains don't always tell the truth.

Before setting out for the mountain, Crazy Eddie and I told our mothers that we were going for a hike. It seemed like the only decent thing to do.

"Don't you go barefooted," my mother ordered. "It's too early in the year, and you'll catch your death. Stay away from the crick, because it's too high and you might fall in and drown. Don't tease the Guttenbergs' bull, because he might gore you to death. Don't cut yourself with your jack-knife because you might bleed to death. Don't wander around in the woods, because you might get lost and starve to death." She stopped to catch her breath and search her memory. "Oh yes, don't climb any tall trees because you might fall to your death."

Mothers can be depressing. Mom couldn't recall any disasters with me and a mountain, and I saw no reason to give her further cause for worry by going into a lot of unnecessary detail about the hike. My mother was downright permissive compared with Eddie's parents. On Saturday mornings at his house, the family had to get up an hour early to run through the list of don'ts for Eddie and still have time enough to get the milking done by eight.

Eddie, as I expected, was late getting to my house. He looked good, swaggering into the yard, his eyes bright with the anticipation of great adventure. His broken arm had healed nicely. I envied the scar at his hairline, the result of his not having ducked quite low enough as we threw ourselves under the Guttenbergs' fence, and just in time, too. (There's nothing quite so disgusting as getting bull slobber

sprayed all over you.) I thought maybe Eddie was concealing his limp from me, but apparently the fall from the cottonwood tree hadn't done any lasting damage. He seemed
fit, which was more than I could say for his parents, the two
most nervous people I'd ever known. As Eddie said, they
probably drank too much coffee.

"Your folks skipped 'Don't mountain climb,' didn't
they?" I said, grinning.

"Yep," Eddie said. "Never even occurred to them. They
hit everything else, except dirt-clod throwing. The lump on
your head go away?"

"More or less," I said. "It was my fault. I would have
ducked faster if I'd known you were gonna charge my fox-
hole. You ready?"

"Sure," Eddie said. "Let's go!"

An hour later we were working our way up the lower
slope of the mountain. Here and there the April sun had
slipped in among the trees and incited a riot of buttercups.
We each picked a handful of the little yellow flowers and
put them in our shirt pockets to take home to our mothers.
For some reason, mothers seemed thrilled by these little
squished balls of withered flowers. So what the heck. The
effort more than paid for itself with the PR spinoff. Say
you were found guilty of getting home five hours late and
had been sentenced to some whacks, the number to be determined by how long it took the parent's arm to feel as
though it were about to fall off; the idea was to haul out
the pitiful little bouquet and present it to your mother just
before the penalty was to be executed. Nine times out of
ten the bouquet got you a stay of execution. Wilted bou-
quets of wildflowers were not only good PR but excellent
insurance.

"You got enough buttercups?" I asked.

"Yeah," Eddie said. "These should do the trick. Anyway, we probably won't get home that late."

We climbed the mountain for an hour, expecting always to reach the top at the next rise. But there was always another rise and another after that and still another. Finally we broke free of the sloping forests and could survey the valley down below. The familiar fields and pastures had taken on a new look, shaping themselves into intricate rectangular patterns of spring browns and greens. Mouse-size cars scurried up and down the roads.

The climbing had now become more difficult. Eddie, a born leader (the worst kind), took charge of planning our ascent. It seemed to me his motive was not to find the easiest route but to test our character. When we came to a rocky knob we could just as well have walked around, he insisted that we make a frontal assault on it, finding little cracks and protuberances with which to pull ourselves upward. When I complained, he said, "This is the way mountain climbing is done. Any sissy could walk around."

Now we were high up on the mountain. The cars below had shrunk to the size of ladybugs; cows and horses appeared no larger than ants.

"It's getting steeper," Eddie said, panting.

"And colder," I said, shivering.

"That means we're nearly to the top," Eddie said.

"I don't know," I said. "We've been 'nearly to the top' fifteen times already. Maybe we should turn back."

"Only a sissy would turn back," Eddie said.

"I'm not turning back," I said.

"Okay," Eddie said.

Among the patchwork of fields below, I could see my own little tiny warm house. It called to me in the same way the mountain had. "Turn back," it called. "Turn back."

"I'm not turning back," I muttered.

"Okay, okay," Eddie said. "I didn't say you were."

Eddie no longer had to seek out difficult routes. *Every* route had become difficult. Once we had to drop into a deep ravine, losing altitude we had already paid for, only to have to buy it again, inch by inch, foot by foot. On the shaded side of a ridge we encountered deep drifts of snow, streams of ice water gushing from beneath them. The April sun had rotted the drifts, and at every step we sank in almost to our waists, the gritty snow stinging our legs raw.

Once, as we stopped to rest against a gnarled, stunted tree, my pants freezing to my legs, my lungs aching, I stared out over the empty space to where Delmore Blight Grade School snuggled up against the edge of town. Old Delmore Blight Grade School, I thought. Well, this is a heck of a lot better than being *there*. The thought gave me strength to go on.

Late in the afternoon, finally, the jagged peak of the mountain came into view. There was no mistaking it. A few hundred yards more and we would reach the ridge that led up to the peak. After that, the summit would be as good as ours!

But our ascent now appeared to be blocked. A twenty-foot cliff rose directly above us. To get around it we would have to drop far back down the mountain and climb up again by another route. I knew now that we would have to turn back. Only a crazy person would try to scale the cliff.

"Boy, this looks dangerous," Eddie said. "Great! I bet a lot of guys would chicken out right now. Here, let me give you a boost."

I hauled myself over the lip of the cliff only to discover a great expanse of rock sloping steeply toward me. Water bright with sunlight trickled in tiny streams down the face of the rock. There was no going back now. I began to crawl on my belly up the slippery slab of granite—five feet, twenty feet, fifty feet. I thought: *Just about got it made. Then I can watch ol' Eddie climb up here. Ha! Bet he'll be sacred. Just a bit more and I can reach for the upper edge of the slab. Only ten inches to go! Six inches! Three inches! Oh-oh, I slipped back an inch. Better get a foot in a crack or something. Still slipping. Still slipping! Dig my fingernails into the rock! No! Wait! What's happening? I can't stop sliding! I'm going too faaaaaaaaaaaaaaast!*

Buttons flew off my jacket and shirt like shrapnel. The knees ripped out of my pants. I felt as though I were leaving a streak of hide all the way down the rock. I whipped over on my back to see where I was going. Then I saw where! I tried to whip back on my stomach so I wouldn't have to see. But it was too late. I shot off over the edge of the cliff.

WHUFFF!—I saw green. I had flown spread-eagle right into a scrawny but merciful fir tree. It bent over and deposited me with a plop on a patch of snow.

I lay on my back, eyes closed, letting life drain back into me. Except for a few miscellaneous patches of missing clothing and hide, I seemed all right. Presently I heard a scrabbling in the rocks off to one side. I knew it must be Eddie. So I played dead to teach him a good lesson. He didn't say anything, but I could sense him looking down at me. I held my breath so he couldn't see me breathe. I could feel him studying me intently, wondering how he could explain the fatal accident. ("I tried to talk Pat out of it, but he wouldn't listen. Can I go play now?") Peeking from beneath my eyelids, I saw him bend over me. What was he doing? Checking to see if I might still be alive? Eddie set a large rock on my chest. He put another rock next to it, and then another. He was burying me.

"Stop!" I yelled. "I'm alive!"

"I knew you were still in there," Eddie said. "I saw you peeking out from under your eyelids. I just wanted to practice burying a person, in case I ever have to. Did you know you're bleeding through your shirt?"

"Just a scratch," I said. I had always wanted to say that.

"Good," Eddie said. "But next time you get up near the top of that slab of rock, grab hold of a branch or something. Otherwise, you'll just slide off again. C'mon, I'll give you a boost to get you started."

I stared hard at Eddie. "Forget it," I said. "I'm not climbing back up there."

"But we're so near the top!" Eddie cried. "You can't quit now. Look, you can even see the peak."

Against my better judgment, I looked at the peak, that ragged, twisted point of granite gleaming against the dark blue of the April sky, so beautiful and majestic that the mere sight of it could make a person dizzy with awe. Suddenly I knew what I had to do, and I did it.

"Cripes!" Eddie wailed. "Not on my shoes!"

I wiped my mouth on my torn, bloody sleeve. "Sorry about your shoes, Eddie, but I'm going back down the mountain. You can climb to the top by yourself if you want."

"I will, too!" Eddie said.

I limped back the way we had come. Then I heard Eddie running after me. "But I'll climb it some other time," he said. "Now I'd better help you."

"To do what?" I asked.

"To pick buttercups," Eddie said. "When your mom sees those clothes, you're going to need a whole lot more buttercups than you've got."

Not Long
for This Whirl

As at the beginning of every spring in our part of the country, water invaded the world and ruled over it with a cold and merciless hand. It drizzled out of the murky sky, oozed up from the saturated ground, and roared in torrents from the melting snow in the mountains, filling the creek and river channels to overflowing, washing out bridges, pump houses, and any other structure within its grasp. Water that could find nothing more enterprising to do with itself turned the dirt roads of the country into sloughs of mud the color and consistency of butterscotch pudding.

It was not a fun time for a teenage outdoorsman. More or less trapped in the close confines of our farmhouse with my mother, grandmother, and sister (the Troll), I grew increasingly frustrated and irritable that my weekend had been washed out by the water. Seeing her chance, my grandmother rushed to aggravate my sorry state of mind.

"Your grandpap wouldn't let a little water keep him all wrapped up in the house like a festering sore, I can tell you that!" Gram said smugly, barely containing her glee. "He'd be out there right now, cutting down trees and skidding 'em to the mill. I can't even get you to go cut a pile of kindlin' wood. Nope, your grandpap shore wouldn't let a little water keep him in the house."

"Yeah, I can see why," I said meanly, trying to cut right to the quick. But Gram had tough, quick, thick skin, and a stirring spoon with which she bonked me on top of the head.

"You're practically as worthless as that old reprobate Rancid Crabtree," she probed. "I ain't seen hide nor hair of him since the melt came, which is one good thing. You and him are both pantywaists, lettin' a little dampness make you hole up by the fire like a couple of sick pups."

"Arrrrh!" I yelled, bringing a burst of delight to Gram's face. "I am not a pantywaist, whatever that is. And besides, Rance is sick. He says he's dying."

Gram activated her scoff to full power. "You believe that? Well, let me tell you, Crabtree is too mean and ornery and dirty and smelly to die. And he's so lazy, nobody could tell if he did. What ails him is probably somebody offered him a job and scared the old windbag so bad he took to his bed."

I yawned to show her how bored I was with the debate, but I hoped Gram was right. My heart had welled with grief ever since the old woodsman told me, "Ah ain't long fer this whirl." I assumed he meant "world," but on the other hand he loved a good whirl as much as any man I've ever known, so I couldn't be sure. Rancid had taught me everything I knew about woodcraft, hunting and fishing and trapping and numerous other manly arts. Now my mentor in all things I valued most seemed to be dying. I had hesitated for several days even to visit him, for fear I might find him dead. Gram's subtle attempt to cheer me up had helped a little. I began to accumulate enough gumption—one of Gram's favorite words—to make a watery trek to the Crabtree shack, just to see if Rancid still lingered among the living.

"Why don't you heat up some of that chicken noodle soup we had for supper?" I said to Gram. "Maybe I'll take some over to Rancid. It can't make him any sicker than he already is."

"You think I'm going to waste good soup on old Crabtree, you must be tetched in the head!" Rancid was not one of Gram's favorite *Homo sapiens,* or even, for that matter, vertebrates. She stomped off to the kitchen, muttering to herself.

Turning back to the window, I practiced my melancholy stare, getting it perfected for the time I became a writer. All writers have melancholy stares, because they have seen so much misery. I couldn't wait to leave home so that I could start seeing misery.

Through the sheets of rain, I noticed a cloud of smoke moving down the mud road toward our house. It was accompanied by a series of explosions, like a tiny war advancing across the country in search of a truce. I recognized the phenomenon immediately—Mrs. Peabody. Mrs. Peabody was a mountain car that my friend Retch Sweeney and I had built ourselves and named after our favorite high school teacher.

Retch sloshed up the walk to our door. "You ain't gonna believe this," he said. "But I got Mrs. Peabody with me."

"I know that," I said. "I'm not blind and deaf, you know."

"I mean the first Mrs. Peabody, our teacher!"

I wouldn't have believed it, either, except for the beaming of Retch's big ugly face with the rain dribbling off the wispy chin-whiskers. As Retch hurriedly explained, Mrs. Peabody had telephoned the Sweeney house and asked Retch if he could drive her out to a friend's house in the country, where she had been invited for the weekend. With the roads so bad, she said, she thought it would be safer if she had a man drive her. I guessed that she hadn't been able to find a man, so she called Retch. Although Retch probably could have borrowed the family sedan for such an important mission, he thought this would be a good opportunity to show off the mountain car to Mrs. Peabody.

"Want to go along?" Retch asked me. "Mrs. Peabody's friend lives up past the Market Road junction. Shouldn't take more than an hour both ways."

"Hey, Gram," I yelled. "I'm going out with Retch. I'll have him drop me off at Rancid's to see how he's doing. You don't mind, do you, Retch?"

"Naw. That road up to Crabtree's will really show Mrs. Peabody what the mountain car can do."

"Well, you just hold your horses," Gram yelled, "till I get this hot soup poured in a jug."

Gram poured the soup in a little crockery whiskey jug we kept in the kitchen for decoration. I thought Rancid would probably appreciate the appropriateness of the container, since he had several just like it that he didn't use for decoration.

Mrs. Peabody sat hunched over in her namesake, a bit of wet hair plastered to her forehead. "How do you like our mountain car, Mrs. Peabody?" I asked, climbing in beside her.

"Oh, it's fine, fine," she said. "Quite lovely."

"I thought you'd like it," I said. "Retch and I built it ourselves."

"Really? I never would have guessed."

"Yep, what we did was, we left off everything that wasn't essential, like fenders and the exhaust pipe and muffler."

"And seats," she said, smiling tightly.

"Yeah, well, actually we couldn't find any seats. I hope that apple box isn't uncomfortable."

"Good heavens, no! Shall we go now, boys? The fumes in here are beginning to corrode my nasal passages."

"Wasn't me," Retch blurted.

"The exhaust fumes," I said. "That's one of the reasons we didn't put any windows on the car. The fumes dissipate to the outside. How'd you like the way I tossed in that vocabulary word, Mrs. Peabody—'dissipate'?"

"Very nice," she said, wiping a drop of water from the tip of her nose. "Very nice."

"Did you know we named the car after you?"

"Yes, I know," she said. "It's a rare honor."

I noticed a distinct lack of enthusiasm on the part of Mrs. Peabody when I asked Retch to swing by Rancid's shack so I could drop off the jug of soup. Her lack of enthusiasm became even more pronounced as we started slipping and sliding down the mud road that led to the Sand Creek bridge.

"Stop! Stop!" she shrieked. "There's no bridge! No ——— bridge!"

Later, Retch and I vaguely recalled that Mrs. Peabody had inserted into her shriek a bad word, but decided that couldn't possibly have been the case, she being a teacher.

Retch and I laughed. "Sure, there's a bridge," Retch said. "You just can't see it because it's about a foot underwater. Now I got to stop talking, so I can concentrate on exactly where the bridge is supposed to be, 'cause I sure wouldn't want to miss it. Har dee har!''

The mountain car crept slowly across the flooded bridge, the current trying to get a hold on the vehicle and hurl it and us into the maelstrom. Mrs. Peabody snatched a cigarette out of her purse and lit it with a trembling hand.

"I didn't know you smoked," I said, smoking not being common among the ladies I knew at that time.

"Only on occasion," she said. "This happens to be one of the occasions.''

Having safely traversed the bridge, we ran out of luck on the steep slope of mud leading up the hill to Rancid's shack. Its tires spinning wildly, the mountain car suddenly lurched sideways into a ditch of rushing water, where it stuck fast.

Mrs. Peabody heaved a sigh that could have knocked a bird off a fence post, if the bird had been stupid enough to be out in the driving rain. "What'll we do now?'' she asked, her voice quavering only slightly.

"No problem," I said. "I'll go get my friend Rancid Crabtree and have him tow us out with his truck. I just hope he's not dead yet, because then we'll be in a real fix.''

"Dead?'' Mrs. Peabody said, digging frantically in her purse for another cigarette. "What do you mean, dead?''

I didn't waste any time explaining, because the car seemed to be sinking deeper into the ditch by the second.

Splattered with mud halfway to my neck, I bounded through Rancid's door.

"Knock! Knock!'' he croaked, his hand reaching for a shotgun beside his bed. "How many times Ah got to tell you?''

He didn't look well, wrapped up with a blanket all the way to his stubbly chin. His energy seemed drained out of him by the long winter, the watery spring, and, of course, his fatal illness.

"Good," I said. "You're not dead yet."

"Not yet," he growled feebly. "Ah'm gettin' thar, though."

I held up the whiskey jug of chicken noodle soup. "Look here! I brought you a little something."

Rancid's face broke into his big, snaggletoothed grin. "My, my! Ah knew thar was some reason Ah let you hang out with me all these y'ars. Mighty thoughtful of you. Now hand me thet jug. Iffen Ah got to die, Ah might jist as well die happy."

"Don't you want a bowl and spoon?" I asked. "It's chick—"

Rancid tilted the jug back and took a big swig. His eyes popped wide in horror. A huge shudder convulsed his body, and he spat the chicken noodle soup from one side of the shack to the other. "Gol-dang a-mighty!" he cried. "It's spiled! It's got dead worms in it!"

"No, it's not spoiled," I said. "It's not whiskey, for gosh sakes. It's chicken noodle soup. Gram sent it."

"Ah shoulda known!" he said. "Why, thet ornery old she-critter. I wasn't dyin' fast enough to suit her, so she put thet soup in a whiskey jug to disappoint me to death."

I quickly explained about the stuck mountain car to Rancid and suggested that he tow us out with his truck. "I hate to bother you while you're dying, but we've got to get the car out."

"Cain't," Rancid said, taking a tentative sip of the soup. "Ah'm too sick. Jist leave her be till the ground dries out. Thet's what Ah'd do."

"I know. But we got our teacher, Mrs. Peabody, in the car," I pleaded. "She can't wade through mud all the way back to our house."

A thoughtful expression came over Rancid's face. "This Mrs. Peabody, what's she look like?" Even fatally ill, Rancid still had a strong interest in good-looking women, a promising sign.

"She's beautiful," I said, without lying much.

"Whar's Mr. Peabody?"

"I don't think there is one. I never ever heard him mentioned."

"Hmmmmmm," Rancid said. "Mebbe Ah could tow you out. This hyar soup seems to be bringin' some of maw strangth back."

He whipped off the blankets and climbed out of bed, fully clothed right down to his boots.

"You don't take your clothes off when you go to bed sick?" I asked.

"What fer?" he said. "If Ah got well, Ah'd jist have to put 'em back on again."

It made sense to me.

After much fussing around, finding chains and ropes and Rancid's cranking his old truck to life, we arrived back at the scene of the accident. He parked the truck at the top of the hill, since he didn't want to get it stuck, too. If he didn't die right away, he said, he might need the truck again before the mud dried out. Rancid slogged down the hill and peered in at the huddled forms of Retch and Mrs. Peabody—particularly Mrs. Peabody, I was sure, because he had told me many times he had seen all he ever wanted to see of Retch.

"Howdy, ma'am," he said. "What seems to be the trouble here?"

It was a dumb thing to say, since any fool could see what the trouble was. I knew Rancid was just making conversation, even if Mrs. Peabody didn't. From the look on her face, I suspected she doubted the solution to the problem had just arrived.

"We're stuck," Mrs. Peabody said.

"Yep, and pretty good, Ah'd say. Ah'll tell you what we's got to do hyar. You and the animal has got to git out of the car, 'cause maw truck won't pull it out with you in it."

I poked Rancid in the back. "You don't expect Mrs. Peabody to wade in mud all the way up to her knees, do you?"

"Nope. Ah'll carry her up the hill and put her in maw truck."

"Uh, you think that's wise, you dying and all?"

"Sheddep and mind your own bidness."

At that moment, I realized that Rancid possessed the soul of a romantic, and that right here, on a mud-choked, rain-splattered mountain road in a remote corner of Idaho, chivalry was about to be resuscitated by a grizzled old woodsman. I was embarrassed.

As soon as the plan was explained to Mrs. Peabody, Rancid scooped her up in his arms and, ignoring her embarrassed protests, began tromping heavily up the slope to his truck. I soon ascertained that Mrs. Peabody was a bit plumper, the distance to the truck greater, and the mud deeper than the old woodsman had judged.

To conceal the strain on him, Rancid began to hum: "Hmmmm mmmmm mmmmm." Presently, however, the hum turned into more of a rhythmic and sustained grunt: "Mmmmm mm mmunh uuunh UNNNNNGH UNNGH UNGH!" And slowly his shoulders began to cave in and his back to bend, with Mrs. Peabody swaying precariously above and ever closer to the mud that sought to claim her.

"You're dropping meeee!" Mrs. Peabody wailed.

With a herculean effort and a hideous groan, Rancid wrenched the lady back up and plodded on, his boots making great long sucking sounds with every slow step he took in the mud. My teacher looked as if she was on the verge of hysteria, and I began to wonder how this might affect my grade in sophomore English. I also wondered if what I was witnessing might qualify as a misery, just in case I ever wanted to write about it.

At last Rancid reached the truck, and plopped Mrs. Peabody on the seat. He collapsed on the running board, alternating between wheezing and sucking in great gasps of air.

"Well, thank goodness," Mrs. Peabody said. "I certainly never thought we would make it. I did get some mud splattered on my coat, but it will probably brush right off when it dries. Now maybe you should hurry and get the car out of the ditch, Mr. Crabapple."

"Wheeeeze GASP Wheeeeze GASP," Rancid replied.

Presently, he pushed himself up and started dragging the heavy logging chain back down the hill to the mountain car. After a good deal of work, we finally got the chain hooked up and the car pulled out of the ditch, turned around, and headed back in the direction of the invisible bridge.

Rancid and I unhooked the tow chain and tossed it in back of the truck.

"Well, all that's left to do now is carry Mrs. Peabody back down to the car," I said. "Maybe you should just let her walk, you dying and all. I think my grade in English is already shot anyway, so it wouldn't hurt much."

"Nope," Rancid said. "Ah wouldn't feel right, lettin' her

walk through this slop. What a man's gotta do, a man's gotta do, even if he is dyin'.''

"I'm ready for another ride," Mrs. Peabody called. "But please do try to be more careful this time."

"Yes, ma'am," Rancid said. Suddenly he turned and staggered backwards up to the door of the truck, where Mrs. Peabody stood on the running board. He bent over and put his hands on his knees. He seemed to be suffering some kind of attack. The exertions of carrying Mrs. Peabody and towing the car out of the ditch had taken their toll on him, and now seemed to be hastening his departure from this whirl even sooner than he'd expected. I was almost paralyzed with shock and grief.

"Good heavens!" cried Mrs. Peabody. "Are you all right, Mr. Crabapple?"

"Ah ain't exactly feelin' chipper, if thet's what you mean," Rancid said. "So Ah'd 'preciate it if you'd climb aboard before Ah sink any deeper in the mud."

It was astonishing. In one afternoon I had seen chivalry suddenly reborn and just as suddenly snuffed out again. And chivalry was not the only thing snuffed out. Watching Rancid carry my English teacher piggyback down the hill to the mountain car, where the genetic accident known as Retch Sweeney howled in delight, I knew for certain that my slight hope of ever passing sophomore English had also just expired.

Tagging along behind Rancid and his human backpack, I could not help but feel sorry for Mrs. Peabody. All she had wanted was to be driven out to her friend's home in the country, where the two dignified ladies would spend the day sipping tea and discussing great literature. Now here she was, suffering the humiliation of being carried piggyback through the mud and rain by a smelly old mountain man.

Rancid turned and backed up so that Mrs. Peabody could dismount into the open doorway of the car. I braced myself for the lash of sarcasm for which Mrs. Peabody was famous.

But to my astonishment, she was laughing. She held out her hand to the dumbfounded mountain man. "Rancid, you dear man," she said. "That was wonderful! I haven't ridden piggyback since I was a little girl! How can I thank you for all you've done?"

Rancid made some strange sound as he tried to untie his tongue.

"Oh, I'll tell you what," Mrs. Peabody went on. "I'll have you over to my house for tea. I'll bet you're a wonderful conversationalist."

"Yup," Rancid said.

Retch cranked up the mountain car's engine. Mrs. Peabody, coughing only slightly, stuck her head out of a cloud of exhaust smoke. "Remember the tea, Rancid. I'll give you a call."

The rain had stopped. Rancid and I waved at the departing mountain car, he thinking he was waving good-bye to a new lady friend and I knowing I was waving good-bye to a passing grade in sophomore English.

All at once, the sun broke through and set all the water and even the mud to gleaming as far as the eye could see. The new buds in the birch trees sparkled like emeralds, the mountains emerged from mists, and somewhere off in a meadow, a lark warbled.

"Shucks, Ah feels pretty good," Rancid said, grinning his snaggletoothed grin. "Ah reckon Ah won't die after all." His grin vanished. "Dang it! That Miz Peabody didn't ask for maw number!"

"Even if she had asked for your number, Rancid, it wouldn't do any good. You don't have a phone."

"Ah knows that, but she don't. Probably when she tries to call me and Ah don't answer, she'll write me a letter." His grin revived.

"Yeah," I said. "She'll probably write you a letter."

I chose not to remind Rancid that he didn't have an address, either.

Claw of the Sea-Puss

One day some years ago, I awoke to find myself washed up on a beach in Hawaii. I made a mental note never again to partake of happy hour at a waterfront bar in Seattle.

Then it all came back to me. In atonement for some minor indiscretion, I had agreed to accompany my wife thousands of miles over the Pacific Ocean for the purpose of lying on sand, which is a popular pastime in Hawaii. Considerate husband that I am, I tried to conceal from Bun that I rank lying on sand well up on the list of the World's Ten Greatest Tediums.

"Boy, this sure is fun," I said. "Feel that sand, Bun? It's made out of pulverized diamonds. That's why the hotels have to charge the rates they do. Maybe later we can tour the diamond-pulverizing plant, what say? Wow, have you tried pouring the sand through the cracks between your toes? Fantastic! When I tell the boys back at Kelly's Bar & Grill about this, they'll be amazed. 'Tell us again, Pat, about pouring the sand between your toes,' they'll beg, but I won't tell them right away. I'll just tantalize them with . . ."

Bun propped herself up on an elbow and shot me a glance that missed by a hair and knocked an innocent seagull head-over-tailfeathers into the surf.

"I've got an idea," she said. "There was a dark little alley we passed yesterday. I saw a sign down there for a deep-sea charter office. I don't know why I didn't mention it then. Anyway, why don't you go see if you can charter a fishing trip for yourself?"

"What!" I said. "And give up lying on sand with you? A man would have to be an inconsiderate lout to do something like that!"

The sand was still spraying out of my thongs as I scurried down the alley in search of the charter office. A crudely lettered sign identified the establishment as Scroom & Scram Deep Sea Fishing Charters.

A sporty-looking chap extended his hand. "Welcome to Scroom & Scram! What can I help you with, pal?"

"Marlin," I said, shaking the hand.

"Biff. Good to meet you, Marlin."

"My name's not Marlin."

"I understand. My name's not Biff, either."

"What I mean is, I want to fish for marlin."

"Hey, no problem, pal. I can fix you right up."

The one-day charter cost me scarcely more than a two-week cruise on the Love Boat, but Biff said he was able to give me a discount because I would be sharing the boat with three strangers, provided they all made bail, ha ha. "Have a good time, Marlin."

Early the next morning I drove my rental car down to the lagoon where the fishing fleet moored, and began looking for the *Sea-Puss,* the boat I had chartered. It occurred to me that the owner of the boat must be of literary bent, for I recalled that the author James Thurber had somewhere written about a *Sea-Puss*. I think the line went, "The claw of the Sea Puss will get us all in the end." Although I hadn't known him personally, Thurber did not seem the fishing type, and I doubted that he had ever chartered the actual *Sea-Puss*. Still, one never knows. In any case, I was to recall the Thurber quote several times during the day.

At last I spotted the *Sea-Puss,* and was relieved to see that it was a large and nifty craft. There had been something about Biff that gave me the uneasy feeling my charter boat might turn out to be a nautical hybrid achieved by crossing the communal bathtub of a skid-row hotel with a sieve. This excursion might turn out all right after all, I thought. Since the captain and crew had not yet arrived, I sat down on the dock to wait. "No doubt," I muttered to myself, "the catch here is that my three charter partners will turn out to be mobsters, homicidal maniacs, or life insurance salesmen."

Presently, a taxi pulled up and three mild-looking individuals got out. They appeared legitimate and sane enough, and none carried a briefcase. They came over, shook hands, and introduced themselves as Ron, Bill, and Ed, a dentist, a college professor, and a minister. Much to my surprise, they were not old friends but had met only the day before on the *Sea-Puss*.

I said, "You fellows must have had a pretty good time yesterday, since you're going out on the *Sea-Puss* again today."

They smiled inscrutably, although none appeared to be an Oriental. When a non-Oriental fisherman smiles inscrutably, it means only one thing—he knows where to catch fish and he's not telling anyone. "Hoo-boy," I said to myself. "Today's my lucky day."

Soon afterwards the captain showed up, followed by a clothed primate of indeterminate species. The captain had a narrow, pinched face, with mean little eyes. The primate was the crew. Its name was Igor. The captain's name was Bly.

"So, back for some more," Bly greeted my three companions, who nodded meekly. The captain laughed evilly. Igor made guttural sounds of amusement.

"You!" Bly yelled, pointing at me.

"Wha-what?"

"Clean off those shoes. You think I want you tramping dirt all over my deck?"

"Uh, no, sir. I mean, yes, I'll clean them."

"One more thing. I hope you're not one of those posies who get seasick, although you certainly look the type. If you are, don't use the head."

"Don't use the head?"

"No—over the side. And another thing. NO BA-NANAS!"

"No b-bananas?"

"Right. Bringing bananas aboard a fishing boat is bad luck. Boats have been known to go for years without catching a fish after someone ate a banana on board. I catch you eating a banana on board, I'll keelhaul you! Now clean those shoes and go aboard."

Igor made threatening noises as I wiped off the soles of my sneakers with my handkerchief. Bly then ordered us aboard. My fellow charter partners scurried up the ladder to the deck ahead of me. I could tell from their frightened demeanor that they were intimidated by the captain and Igor. They were also insane. Otherwise, why return to a boat like this?

I had previously encountered rude charter captains, but

only rarely. This fellow and his crew took the prize as the worst I'd ever run afoul of—real nasties, if you get my drift. How, I wondered, could a boat like this stay in business, given its customer relations? Then I caught a whiff of a familiar odor. It was the sweetish smell of a tax shelter. Bly's only interest in clients was to snooker enough of them aboard to qualify the boat as a business and thus make it tax-deductible! The captain may have been rude and surly, but he wasn't dumb.

Still, why had my companions returned for a second outing? Perhaps the boat really did catch fish.

"How'd you do yesterday?" I asked Bill.

He glanced around to see if the Bly or Igor might overhear him. "Terrible," he whispered. "Didn't get a single strike. Captain spent half the day letting the boat drift to save fuel. It was horrible, worst day of fishing I've ever had."

"Oh."

Before putting out to sea, the captain lined us all up and gave us orders. "Don't touch any of the tackle! Don't ask a lot of fool questions! Don't get in the way of the crew, because Igor will run you over and squish you on the deck! Anyone thus squished on the deck must clean it immediately. Don't . . ."

I wondered vaguely where I might find a secondhand mast from which to hang the sporty Biff of Scroom & Scram Deep Sea Charters. I even thought about the size of the splash the scrawny captain would make if someone inadvertently threw him overboard. The sight of the hulking Igor quickly erased the thought from my mind.

The four of us charter clients cowered in the cabin as the boat put out to sea. I did not much care to be in such close quarters with three lunatics, even though they were nice enough. Besides lunacy, they all seemed to have in common a peculiar meekness.

After four hours of alternately trolling and drifting, we were overtaken by a dense cloud, which I thought at first was fog but which turned out to be boredom. The boredom sat on me like a foggy elephant. Two things I can't stand are work and boredom. I drifted off into merciful sleep.

Suddenly—POW!—one of the lines snapped from its outrigger. The reel screamed. Bly had assigned each of us a fifteen-minute section of the hour in which a fish hooked on any line would be that of the person assigned that time slot. The marlin had chosen my time slot in which to strike.

I ran toward the fighting chair, only to be squished by Igor, who was rushing to tangle the lines. I immediately leaped up, wiped all signs of the squishing from the deck, bounded into the fighting chair, strapped on the fighting harness, and waited for Igor to hand me the rod with my marlin on it. And waited. And waited. The primate was still busy tangling the lines.

"Lines tangled," Igor informed the captain, who quickly came down from the bridge to help tangle the lines even more.

"Oh-oh, he got off," the captain said, shrugging.

"No, he's still on," Igor said, giving Bly a wink.

"Oh yeah, right, I see that now," the captain replied. "Why did I ever think he got off while the lines were tangled?"

Bly thrust the rod at me. "Reel fast! Reel fast! Take up the slack!"

I cranked the reel furiously. But the whole line was slack.

"You lost him!" the captain shouted. "You lost him! Didn't I tell you to reel fast?"

I climbed out of the fighting chair. As I slunk back into

the cabin to join my companions, I noticed a change in them. Tension crackled in the air.

"Ask him if he's going to throw in with us," Ed whispered, indicating me. "After all, they did lose his marlin. That should be reason enough."

"We're going to scuttle Bly, Igor, and the whole damn boat," Ron whispered to me. "We've had enough of these louts. This is our revenge for the way we were treated yesterday. We sat up all night in a bar making plans. Are you with us?"

"You guys really are crazy!" I hissed. "Igor will kill you! Even if he doesn't, this is mutiny on the high seas—a hanging offense!"

"They'll never catch us," Bill whispered. "Are you in?"

I thought of the only marlin I had ever had a chance for in my entire life. Igor and the captain had lost it and then blamed me. I watched Ron open a satchel and begin taking out the blunt instruments. I didn't know if I was up to this kind of violence.

"You want one?" Ron asked.

"Yeah," I said. "Give me that eight-incher."

"Know how to use it?" Bill asked.

"Sure." I wiped my sweaty palms on my pants.

"Okay, let's do it!" Bill cried. "Now!"

Savagely, we ate the bananas. Bly and Igor never knew what hit them.

A Really Nice Blizzard

Henry P. Grogan, proprietor of Grogan's War Surplus, glanced up from his cash register as Crazy Eddie Muldoon and I bolted through the front door of his establishment.

"Quick, Mr. Grogan," Crazy Eddie shouted, "we need to buy a parachute!"

"A parachute? What you boys need a parachute for? And why ain't you in school? You fellas playin' hooky?"

"No, we're not playing hooky," I said. "They let us out early when the blizzard got too dangerous for us kids to stay at school. We've got to hurry because the school bus leaves to take us home in fifteen minutes."

"I don't know about sellin' a parachute to two fool kids," Grogan said. "You probably got some notion about jumpin' off a barn roof with it, ain'tcha? Gitcher selves killed or worse doin' something like that. No, I wouldn't feel right about it."

"We got over seven dollars between us," Crazy Eddie said, looking the proprietor right in the eye.

"But I've been wrong before," Grogan said. "Lemme see your money."

That was one of the things I liked about Crazy Eddie and Mr. Grogan. They both knew how to do a deal.

As Eddie and I hurried toward the door with our parachute, Grogan called after us. "Just out of idle curiosity, boys, what *are* you gonna do with that parachute?"

"Oh," I said, "because we got out of school on account of the blizzard, Eddie and I thought we could rig a sail with the parachute on a sled and sail across a field. This is the only good blizzard we might get this year, and we don't want to waste it."

"Sounds reasonable to me," Grogan said. "I always did like a good blizzard myself."

When we got home and tried to hook up the sail to my sled, we discovered that rigging a mast with an old two-by-four and a broom handle wasn't easy. We struggled with the contraption until we were both half frozen. Finally I said, "We'd better go get Rancid to help us. He'll know how to hook up a sail. Rancid knows just about everything."

Crazy Eddie and I tramped through the blizzard to Rancid's shack and, covered with a snow veneer, burst in without bothering to knock. The old woodsman was standing by his barrel stove, stirring something in a frying pan with a hunting knife. He leaped back with the knife raised in a stabbing position, and yelled, "Aiiigh! Aiiigh!" (Later he told us that yelling "Aiiigh! Aiiigh!" in a shrill voice is a good way to confuse evil forest spirits until you can think of a good way to deal with them.)

"Gol-dang an' tarnation, ain't you fellas ever heard about knockin'? Why, in another second Ah mighta had both of you chopped up into itty-bitty pieces! Ah got light-nin' relaxes.''

Eddie and I shook off our coating of snow onto Rancid's floor and rushed over to warm our hands by his stove.

"Why cain't the two of you shake off thet snow outdoors? Now it'll just melt and turn to mud. Ah'll be slippin and slidin' on it all day. You raised in a barn?''

"Sorry,'' I said. "We were just about frozen. Anyway, what we want is to have you help us build something we can use to sail on the snow. We've got a parachute for the sail. It'll work great in this blizzard.''

"Hmmmm,'' Rancid said. "Let me thank about it a spell. You boys want somethin' to eat? Ah got plenty to go around.''

"I don't think . . .'' I said.

"Sure,'' Crazy Eddie said. "I'm starved.'' He had never yet had the experience of eating with Rancid.

Rancid blew the dust off a couple of tin plates he kept for guests and scraped out a glob for each of us from the skillet. He ate his share out of the skillet with the hunting knife.

"This is pretty good, Mr. Crabtree,'' Eddie said. "What is it?''

"As best Ah can recall, it's some chopped up b'ar meat, b'iled taters, beans, a chunk of hog fat, and, uh, let's see, oh, some dried wild mushrooms and a couple of squirrels. Why, you thank your momma might want the recipe?''

"She might,'' Eddie said. "She wouldn't use the wild mushrooms, though, because she can't tell the difference between the good ones and the poison ones.'' He chuckled, presumably at his mother's ignorance of wild mushrooms.

Rancid joined him in the chuckle. "Thet's okay, Ah cain't tell them apart neither."

"You *can't?*" Eddie croaked, staring down at the few little bites left on his plate.

"Nope, Ah cain't. But don't you worry none. Ah always tests wild mushrooms out on maw dog, Sport. If he likes 'em and don't drop daid, Ah eats 'em mawsef. Fed him a batch of these mushrooms a couple hours ago. Here, Sport, come show Eddie here you ain't daid. Sport! Here, Sport! Sport! Where is thet dang dog? He always comes when Ah calls him."

Eddie rose slowly from his chair, wild-eyed and suddenly pale. I stared uneasily at him as he selected a finger to put down his throat.

"Don't do it, Eddie," I said. "I'm still eating. Besides, Rancid doesn't have a dog."

After we'd all had a good laugh over the mushrooms and Rancid's mythical dog, Eddie and I presented our idea about the sailing parachute to the old woodsman.

"If thar's one thang Ah knows about, it's parachutes," he said authoritatively. "Ah done a lot of parachutin' in the Great War. General used to have me dropped behind enemy lines to do spyin' work. Ah ever tell you about the time—"

"Yeah," I said. "But what about using the parachute as a sail in the blizzard?"

"A sled won't work," Rancid said. "The sled will cut through the snow crust and you'll be stuck tighter'n a fly on a stirrin' spoon. You needs somethin' flat on the bottom, somethin' like a big pan."

"Shoot!" Eddie said. "There ain't no pan that big. Right now we've got this great blizzard and no way to use it!"

"Hold on a sec," Rancid said, putting on his thoughtful expression. "Hot dang, Ah thank Ah got just the thang!"

He stomped outside and soon returned with a large, curved metal object. He banged the snow off it onto the floor, in his enthusiasm apparently having forgotten about turning the floor to mud.

"What is it?" I asked.

"A fender off an old wrecked truck. Been keepin' it out in the yard. Figured some use would turn up fer it, and one has."

Eddie and I shouted with joy and relief. We would be able to put the blizzard to good use after all.

Rancid was a person who could never take a good idea and leave it alone. He had to improve on it. Eddie's plan had been for us to sail across the open fields on the icy crust burnished to a high polish by the wind and driven snow. Rancid, however, said the best idea would be to hike over to the Old Market Road. "It's just one long strip of shiny ice," he said. "It's so slick thar won't be nobody drivin' on it, thet's fer shore. We can have it all to ourselves."

"But what about a mast?" Eddie said.

"Won't need a mast," Rancid said. "Ah'll show you how it's done."

We cut through the woods to the Old Market Road, and sure enough, there was not a vehicle on it as far as we could see through the driven snow. Off in the distance, an undisturbed snowdrift slanted across the road. We had to lean into the wind in order to stand, and even then our feet skittered along on the snow-polished ice. It was slick.

Rancid threw the fender down with a metallic *ker-whump*. "Which one of you boys wants to go fust?"

"Let me try it," Crazy Eddie said.

Getting no argument from me, he climbed into the cavity of the upside-down fender and lay down on his belly.

"Thet ain't no way to do it," Rancid said. "Git up out of thar and let me show you how."

Rancid got in the fender, sitting upright. "Now hand me the parachute harness." For an old experienced parachuter, he didn't seem to know much about putting on the harness, but I suppose so much time had passed since the Great War that he had forgotten. Finally, he simply tied various straps of the harness around his waist and let it go at that. Then he grabbed a cluster of shroud lines in each hand like so many reins.

"Now here's the idear," he said. "Eddie, you take the bundle of parachute out in front. When Ah gives the signal, you throw the chute open so the wind can catch it. Pat, you push on the back of the fender to get me goin' so's the chute can pull me along. Ah'll show you how it's done. Then you fellas can give it a try."

Crazy Eddie and I, slipping and sliding on the icy roadway and fighting against the fierce wind, took up our assigned positions.

"Okay, ready?"

"Yeah!" Eddie and I yelled against the pounding wind.

"On the count of three!" Rancid yelled. "One! Two! ThreeEEEEEEEEEEEEEE . . . !"

Eddie and I skated along the road, driven by the wind at our backs. There was no sign of Rancid, except an occasional blasted-out snowdrift marked by a spray of tobacco juice and claw marks that looked as if they might have been made by human hands.

After a while we stopped at a farmhouse and knocked.

A skinny old man in bib overalls and a flannel shirt opened the door and stared down at us.

"What in tarnation you boys doin' out in a storm like this? You look half froze. Come in by the fire and thaw out."

"Thanks," I said. "But we were lookin' for our friend, Rancid Crabtree. He went by here on the road about half an hour ago."

The farmer scratched his jaw. "Nope, can't say I seen anybody go by. You're lookin' for Crabtree, you say. What was he drivin'?"

"An upside-down truck fender," Crazy Eddie said.

"Yes," I said. "And he was wearing a parachute and—"

"Oh, Mavis," the farmer called out to his wife. "Better put some hot chocolate on for these boys. I think the cold's about got 'em. How do you fellas feel, anyway?"

"I don't feel so good," Eddie said. "But I think it may have been some poison mushrooms I ate for lunch."

"I see," said the farmer. "Poison mushrooms. Hurry up with that hot chocolate, Mavis."

After the hot chocolate, and not knowing anything else to do, Eddie and I returned to Rancid's shack. Much to our relief, the old woodsman came in a short while later, looking like a tattered icicle in more or less human form. The cut ends of the parachute harness dangled from his snow-caked waist.

"You don't look too good, Mr. Crabtree," Crazy Eddie said with rare understatement.

Rancid sank down on a chair and dug some snow out of his whitened ears with a blue finger. "Oh yeah?" he snarled. "Wal, you wouldn't neither if you'd been blowed halfway 'cross the gol-dang county in a truck fender. Ah'd still be goin' iffen Ah hadn't had the good fortune to get snared by a barbwire fence and torn dang near to shreds and . . ."

As he ranted on, I heard a sad sound from outside. With one last thrust at tearing the shakes from the roof, the wind dropped away with a rattling moan. The blizzard was dying. It had been a fine blizzard, and I was sorry to see it pass away.

Rubber Legs
and White Tail-Hairs

Caught up in the media craze of placing one-hundred-dollar bills end-to-end to see if they reach to the moon and back, as a way of making the national debt more understandable and poignant to the taxpayer, I recently laid all my fly-tying books end-to-end to see how far they reached. They reached from my writing desk to the cat box in the utility room. How far is that? Not nearly far enough, believe me.

"Look," I said to my wife, Bun. "I laid all my fly-tying books end-to-end to see how far they would reach. What do you think?"

So who cares what she thinks? The point I wished to illuminate with this comparison is simply that an unfathomable copiosity of fly-tying books exists, and I possess most of the copiosity. I have been studying fly-tying books for forty years and have yet to succeed in tying a single fly that resembles anything more than a hair ball.

The fault lies with the books and not with me, despite my childhood nickname of "Thumbs." Here is the problem.

Fly-tying books all contain a powerful spring in the binding. Whenever I reach Step 15 in the tying of a fly, with both hands fully engaged in maintaining a cat's cradle of thread in the vicinity of a wad of feathers and fur clinging precariously to a hook, the powerful spring is activated and snaps shut like a bear trap. I lean over and open the book with my ear. Using my tongue, I flip pages back to the instructions for the fly. Holding the book open with my chin, I read Step 15 with my nose while telescoping my eyes around to watch what my hands are doing. When the fly is finally finished, I remove it from the vise and place it in my fly box. You never can tell when the fish might go for a hair ball.

The other problem with fly-tying books is that the author has deliberately designed each fly so that it will contain one material that the fly-tyer doesn't have on hand. This requires the tyer to drive forty miles around town looking for a shop that hasn't sold the last of the material to some guy who came in fifteen minutes before the tyer arrived. Recently I was tying a fly that called for rubber legs. I rushed down to the nearest sporting goods store, hoping to get there before the guy who always arrives fifteen minutes ahead of me. The lady clerk stared at me wearily, as she always does, her fat elbows propped on the counter.

"You got rubber legs?" I asked.

"No, just tired," she snarled. "So whatta ya want?"

"I mean rubber legs for fly-tying. You know, the little—"

"Guy come in here just fifteen minutes ago and—"

"Yeah, I know him," I said. "Thanks anyway."

Boy, I just hope that guy is fifteen minutes late someday, and I'll show him a thing or two.

When I reached Step 18 of my latest fly, I could hardly

believe my nose. "Next take a pinch of white tail-hairs of calf . . ." it began. I repeated these words aloud, causing our cat to rise screeching like a banshee from the cat box. "White tail-hairs!" I repeated in a more moderate tone. "Who's got white tail-hairs of calf?"

Just then my finicky neighbor Alphonse Finley barged into my den and demanded to borrow his lawn mower.

"Oh, all right," I said irritably. "Just remember to return it."

"You sound irritable," he said. "What's the matter?"

"It's just this stupid fly-tying book," I said. "The instructions for this fly I'm tying call for white tail-hairs of calf. Now, where am I going to find white tail-hairs of calf?"

Finley studied the makings of the fly in my vise. "Odd," he said. "Why would a No. 16 hair ball need white tail-hairs? However, I may be able to help you out. I was driving in the country a few miles from here and noticed some calves in a barnyard. If I recall correctly, and I do, they had white tail-hairs, or fairly white, calves being what they are."

"Great," I said. "Let's drive out right now and you can show me where they are. I'll ask the farmer if we can clip a few tail-hairs from his calves."

"I assure you, my good man, that I have much better things to do than to assist you in clipping hairs from the tail of a calf."

As I say, Finley is a finicky character. Even so, I was surprised he would dress in a pinstriped suit to mow his grass, as I deduced from the fact that he was thus attired when he came begging to borrow his lawn mower. I called this perversion to his attention.

"Dear boy," he said, "I have no intention of mowing

my lawn in a suit and tie or any other way. I'm going to hire young Raymond down the block to handle the chore for me. I'm wearing a suit and tie because I'm speaking at a luncheon this noon."

"You're going to pay Raymond real money to mow your lawn? What will the other bankers think? They might drum you out of the union. Listen, you go out and show me where the white-tailed calves are, and I'll mow your lawn for free. Actually, I'll have Raymond do it, since I've already advanced him the money for approximately twelve hundred lawn mowings."

"Really? And I don't have to do anything else but show you where they are? I just wait in the car?"

"Yep."

"Gosh, I don't know. Every time I get involved in one of your escapades, I end up in some humiliating predicament."

"What could happen to you, Finley? All you have to do is wait in the car."

Twenty minutes later we drove into the farmer's yard. Sure enough, Finley had been right. Half a dozen calves with white tails were moseying about in the goo of the barnyard. They were quite a bit larger than I had expected, more the size of adolescent cows than calves, but they did have white tails. How would fish know where the white hairs came from? Would they care? They probably would, at least if they had ever seen a calf mucking around in a barnyard, paying little or no attention to proper hygiene, but that wasn't my problem. My problem was how to ask the farmer if I could clip some tail-hairs off one of his calves.

I decided on a direct approach: "Sir, this may seem like an unusual request, but I could use a few of your white tail-

hairs to tie flies with. You have plenty of them and I doubt
if they're of any use to you. I'd even be glad to pay, and
I'll clip them myself.''

Unfortunately, the farmer failed to respond to my knock
on his door, and I assumed that he must have gone to town
to buy feed or barbwire, or whatever it is farmers do away
from the farm. It seemed unlikely to me that the farmer
would miss a few tail-hairs or that he would care one way
or the other about the loss. I scribbled out a hasty note
informing the farmer of my intended acquisition and inserted three one-dollar bills as payment. Having no idea
what tail-hairs go for these days, I guessed that three dollars
would be more than adequate. Perhaps, I told myself, the
note and the money would alert the farmer to a whole new
market, the tail-hair market, which in the long run might
prove more profitable than the calves themselves. Not a little
pleased with myself over this contribution to the economics
of agriculture, I headed for the barnyard.

I climbed through the barnyard fence and extracted from
a pocket my folding fly-tying scissors, looking around for a
promising candidate. Much to my somewhat nervous surprise, for I had expected the calves to be suspicious of strangers, the herd of a half-dozen or so converged upon me and
began nuzzling my clothes with their slimy muzzles. I attempted to shove away the friendliest of my assailants, but
they were a stout and aggressive lot. Apparently disappointed that I didn't conceal a feedbag somewhere on my
person, they began to bump me about in a rather rude fashion. Trying my best to ignore their brazenness, I selected
one of the nasty beasts and began to work my way down his
back in the direction of his tail, but the calf, suspecting that
I was up to something not in his best interest, quickly swung
his rear end away from me. He had repeated this maneuver

several times, when I heard a supercilious chuckle from Finley. He was standing there, one foot propped on a fence board, thoroughly enjoying my lack of success.

"C'mon, Finley, be a good sport," I said. "Give me a hand here."

"You must be mad," Finley replied. "Do you think I want to get calf slime or worse all over my new suit?"

At that instant, the other calves lost interest in me and wandered off to other parts of the barnyard, while the one in my embrace amused himself by trying to suck the buttons off my shirt.

"It'll only take a second, Finley," I said. "Just come over here and hold the calf, while I clip off some tail-hairs. Then I'll drive you back to town for your luncheon."

"Oh, all right." Finley tiptoed through the barnyard ooze, complaining about its effects on his shiny black oxfords. "What shall I grab on to, the ears?" he asked in a whiny tone scarcely conducive to arousing confidence in his skill as a calf-wrangler.

"No, I'll hold him by the ears until you can get a good grip on his tail. Leave the white hairs hanging down, so I can slip back and cut some off."

A grimace puckered Finley's face as he gingerly took hold of the calf's tail.

"Got a good grip?" I asked. "Okay, I'm letting go of the ears."

"Just hurry, that's all I—!"

The calf had lunged forward. Finley's feet spun in the muck. Flailing his legs wildly in an attempt to regain his balance, he pulled the tail straight back from the point where it was hooked onto the calf, thus saving himself from a disgusting fall. The calf, deciding it had had enough of Finley's uncouth intimacy, charged across the barnyard.

Finley sailed after it in the angled posture characteristic of water skiing, a sport at which luckily he is proficient, for the calf's tail made an extremely short tow rope.

I rushed after the two of them, hoping to get my white tail-hairs while Finley still had the calf in hand. Upon glimpsing me in hot pursuit, the calf, alas, broke into a frenzied gallop, with the result that Finley's shoes now sent up two curling and overlapping wakes of barnyard muck. The other calves, caught up in the excitement, stampeded ahead of Finley and his calf, all of them bellowing and bawling and in general creating an uproar typical of the bovine species. I must say the whole hullabaloo was beginning to get on my nerves, particularly the bellowing, not the least of which came from Finley.

I wondered briefly if perhaps Finley might be enjoying himself, since as a child I had often played grab-the-cow-tail in our own barnyard. As the calf rounded the corner of the barn, however, and as Finley cut a wide arc and jumped the curl of his own wake in the classic manner of the expert water skier, I was disabused of the notion that the man was having fun. His spectacles were askew on his nose, his eyes protruded like soft-boiled eggs from egg cups, and his pin-striped suit had acquired a splattered effect not unlike that of a Jackson Pollock painting, only in a bland monotone lacking aesthetic appeal.

It was upon rounding the corner of the barn myself that I discovered that the farmer was home after all. In a nearby field, two men, one of them presumably a hired hand, were tinkering with the innards of a tractor. They straightened and turned to determine the cause of the commotion, namely Finley's skiing, rather stylishly I must admit, behind one of the farmer's calves. Naturally I can't say for sure, but judging from the expressions on their faces, I would venture to guess this was the first time the farmer and his hired hand had witnessed an event of this sort.

Approaching the far end of the barnyard, the calf gunned itself into a right-angle turn, at which moment Finley let go of its tail and skied gracefully into the fence, to which he clung in an attitude that suggested extreme agitation. The farmer and his hired hand moved somewhat cautiously in Finley's direction, each carrying a large wrench, and neither perhaps entirely dismissing the possibility that, instead of a mere prankster in a business suit, they might be confronting a lunatic.

At this point I decided that Finley, after all, was an articulate person and fully capable of explaining the situation as well as I. Just in case that wasn't well enough, I returned to the car and revved up the engine, pausing only briefly to remove from the farmer's door my note and the three dollars. As I told Finley when next I saw him, I certainly wasn't going to pay for white tail-hairs I didn't get.

Nude,
with Other Wildlife

In my youth, there were two things I wanted to be when I grew up: either a mountain man or an artist. Deep down, I had a strong preference for mountain man, but even at a young age I realized that course in life was closed to me because of a severe handicap—acute fear of the dark. I had given much thought to inventing a portable night-light suitable for mountain darkness, but its bulk would have been impractical. It was too easy to imagine a band of hostile Indians closing fast on me as I galloped uphill, towing my night-light. So I opted for artist.

From age seven to ten, I worked very hard at becoming a wildlife artist. My first efforts revealed enormous talent, recognized only by my mother. I would show her one of my drawings, and she would say, "Very nice maybe you'll be an artist when you grow up have you seen my car keys?" Without such encouragement, I surely would have given up, if for no other reason than the ridicule directed at my art by my sister, the Troll. Once I had the bad judgment to show her a picture I had drawn of a mallard duck in flight.

She turned the drawing this way and that, studying it intently.

"I've got it!" she exclaimed, as if I had asked her to solve a puzzle. "It's a dead chicken run over by a car and flattened out on the road, right?"

"Right," I said.

"But why did you put that dog collar around its neck? Chickens don't wear collars."

"It's a pet chicken," I said.

"What's the dead chicken got in its mouth? Looks like a piece of toast."

She was referring, of course, to the duck's bill. I was still in my straight-line phase, and I suppose it was possible for a person ignorant of art to mistake a duck's bill for a rectangular piece of toast. Later I would experiment with curved lines.

Although I worked exclusively on wildlife art, I also wanted to paint nude women. I never mentioned this to my mother, and certainly not to the Troll, since our family was devoutly religious and probably would have been upset by a ten-year-old boy bringing home nude models to paint. With the exception of my dog, Strange, I was the only deviate in the family.

Ideally, when I was grown up and had my own studio, I would be able to combine my two great interests—nudes and wildlife—in paintings titled *Nude with Grazing Elk* or *Nude Hunting Ducks.*

Lacking any instruction in art, I had to make my way as best I could through trial and error. The problem was, I couldn't tell which was the trial and which was the error. Furthermore, I had no idea what a nude woman looked like, never having seen one. I asked my friend Crazy Eddie Muldoon if he had ever seen a nude woman, and he claimed he

had. Eddie tried to describe her to me while I drew, but just
as I was finishing up the details, my mother walked by and
glanced at the picture. Both Eddie and I were scared, but
she said only, "Oh what a nice duck maybe you'll be an
artist when you grow up have you seen my car keys?" It
was a close call but also made me suspect that Eddie had
never seen a nude woman either.

The only artist I knew in our area was a logger who whittled interlocking chain links out of boards. Whittled chains
are nice, but once you've seen one, you've pretty much seen
them all. Besides, I didn't have the patience to whittle even
one link, which is scarcely enough to impress anyone, let
alone an art critic. Then one day Eddie and I discovered a
real, honest-to-goodness artist, an old man by the name of
Gummy Johanson.

Gummy Johanson got his nickname not because he lacked
teeth—he had a fine set—but because he constantly chewed
gum. Gummy looked after a ranch for the banker who
owned it but who lived in town. Crazy Eddie and I occasionally passed by Gummy's little white house on our way
to fish a stream that wound through a meadow on the ranch.
One day Gummy was sitting out on his porch, and we exchanged a few pleasantries with him. To anyone who didn't
know him, Gummy might have appeared a bit weird and
even a little scary. His eyes bulged, giving him a look of
extreme intensity, and his white-stubbled jaws worked ferociously at the ever-present wad of gum, which he snapped,
crackled, and popped in a frenzied manner. Ranch hands
claimed they would rather be beaten with a stick than have
to work beside Gummy and listen to his gum-chewing. But
Crazy Eddie and I didn't mind it, particularly since
Gummy usually offered us sticks of gum, and we would
stand around and chew ferociously with him.

On this particular day, Gummy said to us, "If you got a
minute, boys, c'mere. I wanna show you something." We
followed him into the house, which was usually neat and
clean but now was a total mess. Dirty clothes and piles of
rubbish covered the scant furnishings, the dishpan and stove
were heaped with unwashed dishes, and strewn about the
floor like silvery leaves were hundreds of empty gum wrap-
pers. A whole case of chewing gum rested on the kitchen
table. Eddie and I had never seen so much gum, and we
thought that was what Gummy wanted to show us. But he
walked into the bedroom. "In here, boys," he said. We
followed him.

While I wondered what possibly could have happened to
the tidy old man I had previously known, Gummy led us
over to his grungy, blanket-tangled bed. The metal bedposts
were painted a dull blue, except for one, which was covered
from top to bottom with a strange, grayish glob, something
that looked as if it might have been deposited by insects.

"This is it," Gummy said, pointing at the glob.

Crazy Eddie and I backed away. "What is it?" I asked.

Gummy beamed. "My sculpture."

He turned on a bedside light and tilted the shade so that
the light threw the glob into relief. We gasped in astonishment and delight. The glob had been transformed into a
cluster of tiny deer, elk, bears, ducks, and various other
fauna and even flora. It was magnificent!

"Holy smokes!" I said.

"Wow!" Crazy Eddie said. "It's beautiful! It's all made
out of—"

"Yep," said Gummy, his bulgy little eyes twinkling with
pride. "Chewing gum!"

Gummy explained how the sculpture had come about.
Every night just before he went to sleep, he said, he took

out his wad of gum and stuck it on the bedpost. Over the years, the gum had accumulated until it became the glob. The oldest layers of gum had turned almost black with age, with each successive layer lighter than the one before, the gradation from dark to light producing the illusion of depth sought by all the great classic artists, in whose company Gummy Johanson must certainly have belonged.

One morning, Gummy went on, he had awakened early and was lying in bed thinking about nothing in particular, when he glanced at the glob, backlighted as it was by the rising sun in the window. He imagined he saw the shape of a deer's head in the glob, much as Michelangelo saw the figure of David in a block of marble. He got a kitchen match and began to poke and mold with it, until the deer head emerged in relief from the glob.

Gummy was so excited by his newly discovered talent that every moment he had free from ranch chores he spent sitting by the bed chewing gum as fast as he could and molding it with the match into all the wonderful creatures that had so awed Crazy Eddie and me with their exquisite and delicate beauty.

"Where did you learn to do this?" I asked.

"Never had an art lesson in my life," Gummy said, giving his suspenders a pleased snap with his thumbs. "I'm self-taught."

"Gosh, you're the best artist I've ever seen," Eddie said.

"Thank you," Gummy said modestly. "Say, how would you boys like to watch me do some sculpture work? You can help me chew up a batch of fresh gum."

"We'd love to," I said. At long last, I had found someone who could teach me fine art. I imagined apprenticing myself to Gummy Johanson, first serving as a chewer for him, then maybe doing some of the detail work on the flowers and animals, and finally, after years of study, being given the opportunity to create my own chewing-gum sculptures. Maybe someday I too would have my own glob of gum on a bedpost, and people would come from miles around to look at it. It was not too difficult to imagine my bedpost displayed in an art museum. I shivered with excitement at the awesome opportunity suddenly opened up to me.

Eddie and I hauled some chairs into the bedroom and began to chew sticks of gum for Gummy as he worked on his sculpture of a Canada goose in full flight. Every so often he would lean back and hold the kitchen match up and sight along it at the sculpture. Apparently this helped him get the right proportions for the goose, and I could tell it was a very professional thing to do. In practically no time at all the goose was finished, and it was one of the finest geese I'd ever seen. Eddie and I shouted and applauded, and Gummy looked as if he would burst from excessive pleasure, he was so pleased.

"Well, boys," he said, "I got time for just one more before I have to get back to chores. What would you like to see next?"

The room filled with silence. I could practically hear Crazy Eddie's brain cells clicking together as he thought about what he wanted to see next, and I knew it was the same thing I wanted.

"Oh," I said casually, "how about a nude woman?"

"I was thinkin' the same thing," Eddie said.

Gummy looked startled. "Well, I don't know. I ain't never done a woman before, nude or not. All I ever done is other kinds of wild critters."

Our shoulders sagged. Well, what the heck, it was worth a try.

"Shoot!" Gummy said, apparently noticing our disappointment. "If I can do a nude goose, I should be able to do a nude woman."

Finally—I said to myself—I get to see what a nude woman looks like!

Crazy Eddie and I began to chew gum like mad, cramming stick after stick into our mouths, until our jaws ached. Gummy hunched over his sculpture, working furiously with the matchstick, molding and carving, poking and smoothing, as Eddie and I tried to peer around him. We chewed and chewed and chewed.

"More gum! More gum!" the artist cried feverishly, and we boys feverishly passed him our wads of chewed gum and crammed more sticks into our mouths. Beads of sweat formed on the back of Gummy's neck, and his long gray hair stood out at all angles. "More gum! More gum!" he croaked.

Slowly the sculpture began to take shape. Aha, I thought, a nude woman looks a lot like a moose. Then the artist wiped out his creation and started over. Oh, I thought presently, I see now, a nude woman looks like a bunch of grapes. Once I even thought that a nude woman was going to look like one of my own drawings of a duck. I began to suspect that Gummy didn't know any more about what a nude woman looked like than Crazy Eddie did.

Gummy suddenly stopped working. He slumped down in his chair and held his face in his hands. Eddie and I glanced at each other.

"What's wrong?" Eddie asked.

The artist didn't answer. He got up slowly and walked to the window, where he stood for a long while, looking out over the meadow.

"I guess I can't do nudes," he said after a bit. "I just can't seem to do them!"

Eddie said, "You do good geese."

"Thanks," Gummy said sadly. He seemed enormously disappointed by the discovery of this major void in his talent, although, I must say, scarcely more than Eddie and I.

We got our fishing poles and walked out across the meadow toward the creek, rubbing our aching jaws. There was still enough light left for us to catch a few fish.

"What do you suppose was wrong with Gummy?" I asked.

"He was just tormented," Crazy Eddie said. "All artists are tormented. Didn't you know that? If you want to be an artist, you got to learn how to be tormented."

"I don't want to be tormented," I said. "Maybe I'll be a mountain man after all."

I knew mountain men weren't tormented, at least not if they had night-lights. The next day I started inventing a very large portable night-light.

The Belcher

While I was making a minor adjustment on my muzzle-loader one day last fall, several parts fell off. I thought maybe I hadn't tightened the doohickey enough or maybe had allowed too much play in the thingumajig. In any case, while I was banging the barrel on the concrete floor in the garage, all these parts fell off. So much for amateur gunsmithing.

Fortunately, I have a friend who is a certified gun nut, one Gary Roedl by name. (Rhymes with *yodel.*) For a living, Roedl teaches metal shop in a high school, as is evident from his wild, darting eyes and facial twitch. To calm his psyche after school, he goes home and tinkers with his guns. He even writes about guns. His gun articles are so technical they don't have any words in them, but only numbers, abbreviations, and a smattering of punctuation. The average gun nut probably finds them interesting, but to me they're deadly. I read his ''Origins of the Cleaning Patch'' aloud in the garden to bore insects to death. It makes a wonderful pesticide.

I threw the parts of my muzzle-loader in a box and rushed them over to Gary's house. "Can you fix it?" I asked him.

Roedl looked at the gun and almost burst into tears. "What did you do to it?" he cried. "Beat it on a concrete floor?"

The man's intuition is eerie.

At first he said he thought the gun had been damaged beyond repair and probably should be put to sleep. I begged him to save it. He agreed to try, and finally got all the parts reassembled.

"Looks good as new," I said.

"Not quite," Roedl said. "When you shoot it in the future, I recommend you trip the trigger a little differently."

"How's that?"

"With a long string."

"But that will ruin my accuracy."

"Not all that much," Roedl said. "Not all that much. Say, did I tell you, I bought that Belcher I've been looking for."

"You've already got a dog," I said. "What do you want with another one?"

"It's not a dog, it's a gun. Belonged to a famous old buffalo hunter. I'm writing a book about him and the gun."

"No kidding. Going to use words in this one, or just go with the abbreviations and numbers?"

Ignoring my protests and skidding feet, Roedl dragged me into his gun vault, which is fashioned after the gold bullion room at Fort Knox. He held up the Belcher. "Now there is a gun!"

Why he told me this, I don't know. Even I, non–gun

nut, could identify it as a gun at a hundred paces with one eye blindfolded.

"Right," I said. "Well, I've got to be running along. Thanks for fixing my muzzle-loader."

Before I could move, Roedl deftly kicked shut the door of the vault and set the time lock for two hours. If there's one thing gun nuts love to do more than tinker with guns, it's talk about them. "Now here's something you'll find interesting," he began. "This .50-70 M-1874 Belcher blaw blaw 12 lbs. blaw blaw .50 cal. 2½-in. straight case blaw blaw 70 grn F or FFG & 370 gr. PP. . . . "

I immediately took off on an out-of-body experience, my consciousness floating gently up to the ceiling. Looking down, I could see my own body seated in a chair listening to Gary, the head nodding and saying, "Yeah, uh-huh, right, fascinating." I saw two bugs race across the floor, trying to get out of hearing range, but they were overcome with boredom before they could escape. They rolled over on their backs, kicked a few times, and were still. What a rough way to go, I thought, even for an insect. I vowed never again to read Gary's "Origins of the Cleaning Patch" aloud in the garden. A bug bomb would be more humane.

Finally, I heard Roedl say, "And that's about it for the .50-70 M-1847 Belcher. Pretty fascinating, what?"

Instantly, I was sucked back into my body.

"Kept me on the edge of my chair the whole time. Can I go now?"

"One more thing. When we go hunting in Montana next week, I'm—are you ready for this?—going to hunt with the Belcher! What do you think about that!"

My jaw hinges cramped up from stifling a yawn. "Wow.

I can hardly wait. But please don't tell me any more. I'm already hyperventilating from excitement.''

Thus it was that on the following week I found myself trapped in the cab of a pickup truck on a five-hundred-mile journey into the wilds of Montana with not one but two gun nuts, the second being the outdoor writer Keith Jackson. Jackson, by the way, is a wonderful fisherman, possessing the rare ability to make fish materialize out of thin air. On several fishing trips I've taken with Jackson, I have been under the misapprehension that we both had got skunked, only later to read his accounts of the expeditions and learn that Jackson had done very well indeed, landing numerous monstrous fish on No. 28 dry flies, whereas I, failing to follow his advice, had landed only a single fingerling with a bait consisting of a nightcrawler, a kernel of corn, and a pink marshmallow.

As might be expected, Keith and Gary droned on endlessly about calibers and grains and muzzle velocities and trajectories and other boring gun stuff. I tried to ignore them by leaning back in the seat and catnapping, but they wouldn't allow it, often resorting to screaming and calling me vile names. I told them if they didn't like my catnapping, they could just stop talking about gun stuff. Otherwise, one of them could drive.

True to his word, Roedl hunted with the ancient Belcher. On the first day of the hunt, a mule deer buck strolled out of some brush about fifty yards ahead of us. This was Gary's first opportunity to try out his prized possession in an actual hunting situation. From what I had been told about the power and accuracy of the Belcher, I expected the first shot instantly to transform the buck into a pile of venison steaks and chops ready for the freezer.

Roedl raised the Belcher and fired. A rather longish *BOOOOOM!* and a plume of smoke issued from the muzzle. The deer was stopped in his tracks. Apparently the ruckus raised by the Belcher had aroused his curiosity, because after stopping in his tracks he stared intently at us for a few moments. Then he noticed the slug traveling in his direction. He watched the slug for some time and then, becoming bored with it, nibbled some grass, occasionally glancing up to check on the progress of the slug. When the slug was nearly to him, he stepped aside and let it plop onto the ground at his feet.

Roedl was demolished. I tried to comfort him, but without much success, possibly because I was squealing with mirth. Upon recovering, I advised Roedl that on his next shot he should lead the deer by about twenty yards.

"He's not even moving," Roedl snarled.

"Yeah, I know," I said. "If he starts moving, you'd better lead him by at least eighty yards! Har har!"

"Here's the problem," Roedl said. "I loaded that shell at sea level. This higher altitude is affecting the ballistics. Fortunately, I brought along some shells with a little more oomph to them."

"Sea level!" I cried. "Oh, my aching sides! Har har heee!"

"Okay, wise guy," Roedl said. "You get the honor of taking the next shot with the Belcher."

"Har . . . what? No, I don't wanna."

"Hush! This is not a request. You will take the next shot."

I always hate it when Gary uses his teacher voice. It's so intimidating. I get the feeling that if I don't obey, I'll be sent to The Office.

"Oh, all right," I said, "If it will make you feel any better. Hand me the Belcher."

Instantly, my hand sagged to the ground from the weight of the rifle. I now knew why it was called a .50-70 Belcher. It was .50 caliber and weighed 70 pounds. I wondered if the famous old buffalo hunter had killed the buffalo by shooting them or by dropping the Belcher on them. It should have been equipped with wheels—and a team of draft horses to pull it.

In the meantime, the buck, grinning and shaking his head in disbelief, had retreated to a little grove of pine trees. Roedl claimed it was still within easy range of the rifle, and handed me one of his handloads. The shell was about the size and shape of a wiener—a .50-caliber wiener. I slipped it into the breech and snapped the gun shut. Staggering about under the weight of the Belcher, I tried to set the sights on the deer. My finger brushed the hair trigger.

When my vision cleared, the deer was gone, possibly vaporized but more probably merely escaped. A mature ponderosa pine had been shot in two near where the buck had stood. Beyond it, a smoldering gravel pit had been gouged out of the hill. Aftershocks rolled under my feet. Echoes of the deafening blast boomed up and down the valley.

"Dib I miss hib?" I asked, feeling about my face in search of my nose.

"Eh?" Roedl said.

"Eh?" Jackson said.

"I think you loaded that shell a might heavy with the FF or the PP," I said. "Probably it was the PP. Well, no harm done. I suppose Bozeman has a doctor who can surgically remove the stock of a Belcher from a person's shoulder. By the way, anyone seen my shoulder around?"

On the ride back home, Roedl continued to insist that his Belcher didn't kick. "It was the way you were holding it," he explained. "Technically speaking, there's going to be 14 psf of recoil, but with a .50-70 straight-case Belcher shell with 85 XYZ cubed to 400 PF blaw blaw MV 40,000 FPS blaw blaw 52 IRAs blaw blaw 87 BBDs. . . . Are you listening to what I'm telling you, McManus?"

"Eh?"

Shooter

Retch Sweeney and I fished the little creek up on the old Bone place one day last summer for the first time in thirty years. Weeds had grown up shoulder-high in the meadow, and a ragtag army of volunteer pine trees had invaded the pasture. On the hill above us, a weary privy stood sentry amid an orange explosion of honeysuckle. A short distance away, a brick chimney poked up from a pile of blackened rubble that had once been the Bone house.

"I can scarcely believe it," Retch said, unhitching his creel and flopping down on the bank to rest. "The fishing here hasn't changed one bit since we were kids!"

"You're right," I said. "I remember it was lousy back then, too. That's probably why we haven't fished here for thirty years."

"Yeah," Retch said. "Thirty years. The last time was before that house burned down. The folks who lived there, what was their name?"

"Bone," I said. "Mr. and Mrs. Bone, and they had a

boy our age. His name was, uh, uh, oh yeah, Henry. You remember Henry Bone.''

''No, can't say as I do.''

''Sure you do. He went to school with us in the sixth grade.''

''Couldn't have! I'd remember him. Oh, wait a minute . . . was he kind of . . . of . . . well, uh . . . ? No, I can't place him. You certain he went to school with us?''

''He was the Shooter.''

''The Shooter! Henry Bone was the Shooter? Good gosh almighty!''

I could easily understand why Retch might have trouble remembering Henry Bone, even though he had gone to school with us for a whole year. Henry Bone was one of those people so totally average that they're almost invisible. He was neither smart nor dumb, rich nor poor, ugly nor handsome, polite nor rude, dirty nor clean, just average everything. Shy and unobtrusive, Henry blended so perfectly into his surroundings that he scarcely seemed to occupy space.

If Henry had played sports, of course, he would have been noticed. A person could be terrible in sports, as I was, and still have a public identity, such as being the person always chosen last for a team. Everyone in school knew that I had laid claim to that particular athletic distinction. In softball, the advice given to a batter on the opposing team was always, ''Try to hit to McManus.'' In football it was, ''Okay, we'll run the next series of plays over McManus.'' Being the worst athlete wasn't much of an identity, but it was at least an identity—something Henry Bone lacked. For one brief moment, though, Henry was to emerge from obscurity and achieve the fleeting fame of the grade-school playground. He was to become the Shooter.

During much of the school year, Delmore Blight Grade School was held in the icy fist of North Idaho winter. The ball fields and the basketball court lay under two feet of gray, gritty snow packed hard as concrete. Then, in late March, the sun warmed the brick walls of the school and the snow began to recede, leaving an irregular margin of bare dirt along the south side of the building. Bare dirt! No field of wildflowers ever looked so beautiful to us as that naked piece of earth. Marble season began.

I was a fair marble shot and could hold my own against most of the other guys. There were three top nibslingers, though, with Retch Sweeney being about the best of the three. The other two were Elwood Scopes and Lonnie Custer. By the end of the marble season, these three would have won all the marbles in the school. They kept their winnings in quart jars on shelves in their rooms. I remember that Retch had seven or eight jars of marbles in his bedroom, arranged on a shelf like trophies. The rest of us would supply marbles by buying little netting bags of them for ten cents apiece. After school each day, a big marble tournament would be held in which Retch, Lonnie, and Elwood would win all the marbles. The next morning all of us losers would go out and buy more bags. I think there must be a lesson in economics here, but I've never understood what it is.

One March afternoon, we regulars had all anted up for the first marble game when a shy voice said, "Can I play?" We looked at the owner of the voice. He was vaguely familiar, but none of us could place him right off. After a bit, Scopes said, "Hey, ain't I seen you someplace before?"

"I sit across from you in the back row in sixth grade," the boy said.

"Oh," Scopes said. "I knew I'd seen you someplace."

"Is it all right if I play?"

"Sure, kid," Retch said. "The more the merrier, heh heh."

The kid took some marbles from his pocket and anted up. The "pot," drawn on the soft dirt with a stick, was a good six feet in diameter and contained at least a hundred marbles. We lagged with our laggers, marbles about the size of ping-pong balls, toward a line some distance from the playing circle. The stranger's lagger stopped right on the line, giving him first shot. Next in the shooting order were Elwood, Retch, and Lonnie. Well, at least the kid would get a shot, which was more than the rest of us could expect.

While the top nibslingers stood around warming and limbering up their trigger fingers, the kid took out his handkerchief and began to unfold it, revealing a beautiful agate shooter.

Scopes eyed the kid's aggie. "Shooters are up for grabs, too," he said.

"Okay," the kid said.

I didn't know much about him except that he had to be really dumb to risk that beautiful aggie in a game with these marble sharks.

"No way," I said. "Shooters are safe."

"Forget that," Scopes said, making a threatening move in my direction.

I smiled and stepped over next to my good friend and protector, Retch Sweeney. "Tell him shooters are safe, Retch."

"Forget that!" Retch said.

"It's all right," the kid said. "I don't mind."

He knelt down and studied the arrangement of marbles in the pot. Apparently satisfied, he made a little tripod with the fingers of his left hand, placed his right hand atop the tripod, loaded the beautiful agate shooter between the tip of his forefinger and his thumb knuckle. Snack! We all jumped at the sound of the kid's first shot. Three marbles had flown out of the pot like shrapnel, with the aggie stopping dead still at the point of impact on the target marble. Dumbfounded, we all leaned forward to watch the kid's next move. Snack! Snick! Pop! Snap! Crack! Marbles began flying out of the circle in all directions. Within a few minutes the pot was bare.

New pots were anted up. The kid cleaned them, one after another, until darkness fell. Then he pulled a long brown cotton sock out of his pocket and placed his winnings in it. The sock looked like a lumpy sausage hanging over his shoulder as he walked off into the darkness.

"Hey, kid!" Scopes yelled after him. "What's your name?"

"Henry Bone," came the reply.

"Tomorrow I'll take him," Scopes said.

"If I don't," Retch said.

"Or me," said Custer.

"You've got to get a shot first," I said.

"Shut up," Scopes said irritably.

I looked at my protector.

"Yeah," Retch said. "Shut up for once."

In the days that followed, the marble competition quickly narrowed down to Retch, Scopes, Custer, and Henry Bone. The stakes were too high for the rest of us. And day after day, Henry went home with his sock bulging with winnings.

Nearly every kid in school and even some of the teachers had become spectators at the marble shoots. Henry would make his way through the crowd, trailed by little first- and second-graders trying to touch him. "Yay!" the kids would yell. "Here comes the Shooter! Yay!" And every time Hen-

ry's beautiful agate would go sizzling into the pot to deci-
mate the antes of Retch, Scopes, and Custer, a great roar
would go up from the crowd.

One day toward the end of March, Retch took me aside.
"Tell me something," he said. "Where do you buy them
little bags of marbles?"

I was stunned. Retch Sweeney, forced to buy marbles!
He could scarcely conceal his humiliation. The Shooter had
won his whole stash, his whole hoard of marble winnings
from the eternity of years we had spent in grade school!

I helped Retch sneak down to the five-and-dime to buy
some marbles. We met Scopes and Custer coming out.
They said they had come to buy candy.

Retch handed the money to the clerk for two bags of marbles. "They're for my kid brother," he explained. Later he
said, "How embarrassing! I actually paid money for marbles! I ain't ever, as long as I live, gonna forgive the Shooter
for this!"

Although it seemed much longer at the time, I believe the
marble season lasted only about three weeks at most. In that
brief span of time, Henry Bone achieved fame and glory,
and even riches of a sort, in the form of colorful little glass
spheres. A fifth-grader who had visited the Bone home, or
so he claimed, reported that Henry "the Shooter" Bone had
lined one whole wall of his bedroom with gallon milk jars
full of marbles. Nobody believed the report. Fifth-graders
as a group were suspect in general and considered totally
unreliable.

Everyone wanted to be Henry's friend, with the obvious
exceptions of Retch, Scopes, and Custer. Kids casually
dropped his name: "I was talking to Shooter today and he
told me . . ." "I ate lunch with Bone today and . . ."
"Look at the marble Henry gave me. . . ." The Shooter

wore his new popularity well. He was still quiet and even shy, but we noticed a confidence in him that we had missed before. That was natural, I suppose, because we had never even noticed Henry himself before.

At the very peak of his fame, Henry was struck by one of those disasters that seem to stalk us all at one time or another: the last of the snow melted off the softball diamond. Marbles were instantly forgotten. Henry Bone was forgotten. Within a matter of hours he faded back into the same obscurity from which he had emerged but a short time before. What he thought of the fickle nature of fame, I don't know. I never asked him. In fact, I never even really noticed him again. I was too busy dealing with my own fame as the worst softball player in the history of Delmore Blight Grade School.

Shortly thereafter, the Bone house burned down and Henry and his family moved away. He was not missed.

Those events of thirty years ago flashed through my mind in seconds as I stared up the hill at the ruins of the old Bone place. "Hey," I said to Retch. "Let's go up and poke around in the rubble. Might find something interesting."

"Even if we don't, it'll beat the fishing," Retch said.

We kicked through the ashes for a while and were about to leave when I noticed a strange lump. I picked it up, a heavy glob of something, and brushed it off. For a moment I was puzzled. Then I held it up against the rays of the dying sun and saw that it was composed of melted glass shot through with a thousand colors.

"Wow!" I said. "You know what this is? It's a gallon jug of Henry Bone's marbles melted by the heat of the fire!"

"By gosh, it is!" Retch said. "Well, I'll be!"

We started digging through the rubble and found a half-dozen more of the melted blobs. We polished them off and

set them up in a row on the stone foundation so that the
sunlight played through them and sent the colors dancing
across the ruins. So, I thought, this is what the brief fame
and glory of the Shooter came to—a bunch of melted glass,
and colors dancing on old ashes.

"It's kind of sad, isn't it?" I said to Retch.

"What?"

"All those marbles Henry won, all those hours of shooting, all that excitement, all of it reduced to globs of colored
glass. It's sad."

Retch stared at the colors dancing on the ashes, a slight
smile on his face.

"Oh, I don't know about that," he said.

The Last Flight
of Homer Pidgin

Back during the Paleozoic era, when I was just
getting started with camping, any kid who fled
home from a camping trip about the time it started to get
dark was known as a "homer," a term possibly derived
from "homing pigeon." It so happened that the boy most
endowed with this characteristic had the last name of
Pidgin. Thus it was even more appropriate that he acquired
the nickname of "Homer."

I should mention here something about the use of nicknames in that distant time and place of my youth. The idea,
as I understood it, was to give a kid a nickname appropriate
to his appearance or eccentricity of behavior, the crueler the
better. A kid with warts, for example, might be known as
"Toad" or "Frog" or maybe simply "Warty." In the
course of time, the warts might vanish, but the nickname
would remain, continuing its work of warping the kid's
personality and kicking holes in his psyche. Nicknames
were fun.

Often the nickname would come to dominate the kid's

whole identity, and even teachers and parents would know him by it. Coaches in particular were quick to adopt the nicknames of their charges: "Okay, here's the batting or- der—Toad, Pig, Goat, Larry, and Lizard." In the case of Homer, his parents soon started calling him by the nick- name his friends had conferred upon him, although it's unlikely they knew that the name derived from cowardice in the face of darkness. Little did they realize that every time they said something as simple as "Homer, eat your peas," they were calling attention to a major defect in his character.

The only thing worse than being known by a monstrous nickname—say, Slug, Snake, or Wormy—was to have no nickname at all. I myself had the good fortune to be honored with a nickname by my friends and associates. Alas, time and Freudian slippage have erased it from my memory. Too bad. Let's just say that it was "Rocky."

Oddly, although I can no longer recall my own nickname or how it came about, I have a vivid recollection of the event by which Ralph Pidgin became known as Homer Pidgin. Ralph loved to plan things, particularly camping trips. To him, an hour's excursion into the wilds of the Fergussons' woodlot required all the planning and preparation of an ex- pedition to the South Pole. An overnight camp-out on one of the creeks in the nearby mountains posed complications comparable to those of a voyage into the outer realms of the universe.

Ralph was a maker of lists. For his first overnighter with us, he called a meeting of the expedition party. "All right, guys," he told us. "First, I've made up this list of provisions we'll need. Salt, pepper, butter, lard—the butter and lard should be in leakproof containers, ditto the jam and syrup. To continue: two loaves of bread, one pound pancake flour, three cans pork 'n' beans . . .'' He had a list for each of us, with the shares of the provision evenly divided. After he had distributed the individual lists, the other members of the party made paper airplanes out of them and sailed them back at him.

"Look," Retch Sweeney said, "why doesn't each of us just bring what grub he can lay hands on at home, and when we get to our campsite we'll dump it all out in a pile and see what we got. How does that sound to you, Rocky?"

"Sounds good to me," I said.

"Me too," said Birdy Thompson.

"I'll take my .22 along and shoot us some fat squirrels for meat," Retch said.

"Maybe somebody should bring wieners," Birdy said. "Last time you shot only one squirrel, and the drumstick I got looked like a burnt match. Tasted like it, too." Retch held a fist up in his face. "Good, though."

Ralph shook his head. "This trip requires planning. You guys can do what you want, but I'm going to make sure my own gear and provisions are in order."

He did, too. On the morning of the camping trip, he had all of his stuff spread out on the lawn, food items in one section, gear in another, fishing tackle in another, and extra clothes in another. He went from section to section, checking items off his lists. Not a little annoyed, we gave him a few hints that we wished to be off on the adventure without wasting any more time.

"Step on it, Ralph, or we'll leave you behind!" Retch hinted.

"Get a move on," Birdy said. "We don't have all day, Pidgin."

"Yeah," I said kindly. "Throw your junk in the pack and let's go!"

". . . extra handkerchief, check," Ralph said. "Extra socks, check. Okay, that's it. Now as soon as I arrange everything neatly in my pack, we can depart."

"ARRRGGHHHHH!" his friends said.

The hike to our camp took less than two hours. In contrast to Pidgin's tidy, compact pack, ours weighed upwards of eighty pounds each. Our reasoning was that too much time would be wasted selecting only the equipment appropriate to an overnighter. So we took all the camping gear we owned, mostly war-surplus stuff, dumping it expeditiously into our packsacks. The size of our packs also helped in selecting our campsites. The first guy to collapse from exhaustion automatically dropped onto our campsite, whether it was in the middle of a swamp or on a steep mountain slope. Even today I marvel that such an efficient process for finding a campsite should have been discovered by a bunch of fourteen-year-old boys of average intelligence, excluding Retch Sweeney, of course.

As soon as we had made camp, which consisted largely of dumping our packs on the ground, we set out to catch some fish for supper. Even at that age, we had developed a sportsmanlike attitude toward angling. The first rule was never to catch more fish than we could eat. I don't recall that we even once broke this rule, our restraint continuing to be a source of some pride to me. We were also careful to throw back "the little ones." As we set off to fish, Retch shouted, "Remember, don't keep no little ones!" This was understood to mean no fish under four inches.

Toward evening, we met back at the camp and discussed our luck at catching fish.

"I told you we should bring wieners," Birdy said.

"I'd shoot us some squirrels, but there don't seem to be

none around here," Retch said. "I wonder how chipmunk tastes."

As the first shadows of evening crept across our camp, we chopped firewood, smoothed out the ground for our sleeping bags, and generally prepared for the night. It was then that a strange look came over Ralph's face. He swiveled his head about, peering into the recesses of the forest, as though surprised by the deepening darkness. Somehow, despite all his meticulous planning, he had apparently overlooked the possibility that sooner or later darkness might occur on an overnight camping trip.

Without a word of explanation, Ralph began stuffing his gear into his pack, paying little attention to neatness. He whipped his pack on, pulled his hat down over his ears, and tore out for home, leaving behind nothing of his presence but a few wisps of smoke from the soles of his tennis shoes.

We stared after him in dumbfounded silence. Presently, Birdy said, "Cripes! What happened to Ralph?"

Retch stuck a match in his teeth and pondered the mystery. "Well," he said, "it looks like Ralph is a homer."

"A homer?" I said.

"Yeah," Retch said. "You know, a kid that runs home every time it starts to get dark."

"Ha!" I said. "Homer Pidgin!"

And that was how Homer acquired his nickname. I should mention that we did not hold his flight home against him, or even consider it extraordinary for human behavior, based on the humans we were familiar with. It never occurred to us to exclude Homer from future camping trips. He always came along. Apparently his pleasure in camping at that stage of his life consisted of planning the camping trip in infinitesimal detail, preparing his pack, hiking into the campsite, and joining in the futility of trying to catch enough fish for our supper. At that point he had acquired the maximum pleasure from camping of which he was capable. He then had the good sense to terminate the excursion before it was ruined by darkness.

We soon became accustomed to Homer's style of camping. As darkness approached and the strange look came over his face, we would matter-of-factly bid him farewell:

"So long, Homer."

"See you, Homer."

"Have a good trip."

Retch, Birdy, and I naturally assumed that Homer had no intention of camping through the night with us, but we were apparently mistaken. As we later deduced, Homer never even considered that he would flee home, until the very moment the urge to take flight came upon him.

What led us to this deduction was a trip we took twenty miles up Pack River, one of our grumbling parents driving us to our destination in the wild upper regions of the river. We were to camp out there for four days or until one of our parents remembered to retrieve us. Of course, we assumed that Homer would refuse to come, since the distance from his home was approximately thirty miles. But as soon as the proposed trip was announced, Homer immediately set about planning and making up his lists. We were puzzled by his intentions, still believing that he included the flight home in any of his camping plans.

We were dumped off at our campsite about seven in the morning, with the parent immediately roaring back toward town in an effort to get to his job on time. I could tell that Homer's intentions were much on Retch's mind.

"Uh, say, Homer," he said casually. "You know, if a

fella happened to decide he wanted to run home from here before dark, it—uh—it might be a good idea to start right about now."

"Are you kidding me?" Homer said. "Who would be dumb enough to run home from here? It's almost thirty miles."

Retch shrugged. "Just thought I'd mention it."

We went through our usual camping routine of building a ring of rocks for our fire, chopping up three cords of firewood, fishing for our supper, and then, suddenly, without warning, the sun slipped behind the mountain. Birdy started preparing our supper of fried wieners, fried potatoes, and fried pork 'n' beans. We were all joshing each other and messing around, when I glanced up and saw Homer standing still and silent, with the familiar strange look creeping across his face.

"Don't try it, Homer," I said. "It's too far."

Birdy looked up from his frying. "You can't, Homer."

Retch threw his arm around Homer's shoulders. "Listen, Home, it's gonna be all right. You'll see. We're gonna have a lotta fun tonight, burn a few marshmallows, tell some jokes, poke at the fire."

Homer didn't take off for home, but he didn't relax either, and the strange look remained. It seemed as if a huge invisible rubber band stretched between Homer and his house, growing ever tighter, and at any second would snap him in the direction of home.

About ten o'clock we climbed into our sleeping bags under the lean-to we had built as a precaution against rain. Homer hadn't said a word all evening, but at least he was now in his sleeping bag. The rest of us began to relax a bit, assuming that Homer's urge to flee home had given in to reason. We were about to drift off when all at once we heard the frantic scrabbling of Homer stuffing gear into his pack. Without further notice, he rushed off into the night.

We lay there silently for a while, thinking about Homer scurrying the thirty miles home. As we were mulling over the odds of his making it, lightning flashed and thunder boomed. Then rain began to pound down on our lean-to and, of course, on Homer, out there all alone in the night, racing madly down the road.

"Poor old Homer," I said. "Think he'll make it?"

"Yeah," Retch said. "Probably by about next Tuesday."

"We should have tried to stop him," Birdy said. "We had a responsibility to—"

"Shut up, Birdy," Retch said.

Suddenly it happened. A long, loud, quavering screech came down off the mountain above us. We had never heard anything like it before, the kind of sound that spikes your hair and raises goosebumps the size of peas.

"Cr-cripes," Birdy whispered. "Wh-what was that?"

"I d-d-d-d-don't know," I explained.

"It was s-s-somethin' b-big, though," Retch whispered. "Wh-where's my .22?"

"Y-you didn't bring it," Birdy said. "We brought w-w-wieners instead."

Then the screech came again, louder and closer this time.

"J-j-jeeeez," Retch said. "I think it's coming for us."

"M-maybe it's just s-some weird bird," I said.

"You really think it's only a b-b-bird?" Homer said.

"Y-yeah," Retch said. "Probably only a b-b-bird. A b-big b-b-bird, though."

"G-good," Homer said.

"Homer?" I said. "You're back?"

"Homer's back!" yelled Birdy.

"Hey, Homer!" Retch said. "What brought you back, Homer?"

"I don't know," Homer said. "I just thought, what the heck, I might as well spend the night with you guys."

We never did find out what made the horrible screech in the night, and we never heard it again. It did, however, make the night memorable, almost as much as did the last flight of Homer Pidgin.

A Boy and His (Ugh!) Dog

Retch Sweeney's dog, Smarts, has distinguished himself over the years as the least aptly named animal with which I've ever been associated. Retch, of course, thinks Smarts is the Einstein of hunting dogs. For example, as Retch and I were driving his old sedan out for a little bird hunting the other day, Smarts interrupted his pastime of slobbering down the backs of our necks long enough to emit an excited yelp, causing my eardrums to vibrate like bongo skins during a Jamaican festival.

Retch chuckled. "Ol' Smarts said he can't wait to get out there and start rounding up pheasants for us."

"No, he didn't," I said irritably.

"He didn't?" Retch said. "What did he say then?"

"He didn't say anything. Dogs don't talk."

"Well, *excuuuuuuse* me!"

"Don't get your tail in a knot," I said. "It's just that I can't stand all the anthropomorphizing going around nowadays."

"Me neither," Retch said, turning thoughtful. "I think

it gets spread by toilet seats in public restrooms. But what's that got to do with dogs talking?''

"Anthropomorphizing," I explained patiently, "means the attribution of human characteristics to animals or even inanimate objects."

"Holy cow!" Retch said. "It's even worse than I thought. I can tell you one thing, I ain't using public restrooms no more!''

"Let's forget it," I said. "All I meant was, I don't like people pretending their dogs talk, that's all."

"Oh yeah? I just so happen to recall you letting on that your miserable old dog Strange used to talk. How about that?''

"That's different," I said. "Strange did talk. He could say more with one raised eyebrow than Smarts could yelping night and day for a week. But I'll admit I didn't care much for what he had to say."

"Ha!" Retch said, as if he had just won an argument. "I don't remember you was very proud of Strange, neither."

"No, I wasn't," I said. "I tried to be, but it was impossible, particularly after we learned he was an incorrigible lecher."

"I didn't know that. I thought he was mostly mutt with a little spaniel mixed in. How come you to keep a worthless, disgusting dog like Strange anyhow?''

"We didn't *keep* him, exactly. He just sort of hung around—for about twelve years."

As I explained to Retch, when Strange first started hanging out around our place, I didn't pay much attention to him. I thought he was just passing through our farm on his way home. I fed him a few scraps from the dinner table, thinking he would be gone in a day or two. Weeks later he was still loitering around the house, hitting me up for a handout at every opportunity. When it became apparent that he was intent on establishing a permanent relationship with us, I decided I had better think up a name for him.

Since I was doing a stint in the Cub Scouts at the time, I thought at first that I might name him Scout. It soon became apparent, however, that he was untrustworthy, disloyal, unhelpful, unfriendly, discourteous, mean, disobedient, uncheerful, unthrifty, cowardly, dirty, and irreverent. I decided it wouldn't be right to name such a dog Scout.

My mother suggested Stranger, still hoping the dog might be passing through. For a few weeks, we called him Stranger, but this was soon shortened to Strange. The name fit. In the years to come, we would learn only how well.

Strange lived in a dog shack in our backyard. It was a doghouse, of course, but the rest of the family cruelly referred to it as the dog shack, because I had built it with my own two ten-year-old hands. Driven by powerful but vague ambition in those years, I had intended the doghouse to be a replica of a medieval castle, complete with towers and battlements. The project turned out to be much more complicated than I had first imagined, and I finally gave up on it, after completing only one tower (often mistaken for a chimney—but why would anyone think a dog needed a chimney?), a half-dozen battlements, and the drawbridge. Visitors sometimes expressed curiosity about the shallow ditch around the dog shack. It's surprising how many people don't recognize a moat when they see one.

The dog shack matched nicely Strange's shabby pretensions of nobility, and he seemed not to mind it particularly, although he chose to ignore my instruction on how to raise the drawbridge.

During the early part of his excessively long life with us, I still hoped Strange would exhibit some talent or characteristic to make me proud of him. None became evident. He would slouch around making rude comments, swearing, belching, burping, gagging, and in general engaging in any disgusting activity that occurred to him, and many did. Visitors would recoil at his approach, perhaps expecting not so much that he would bite but that he might try to mooch some change for a bottle of cheap wine or sell them some dirty pictures.

More than anything else at that stage of my life, I wanted to be able to brag to the kids at school about some neat trick my dog could perform. I tried to teach Strange to fetch sticks, but he would only shrug and say, "You threw it, stupid, you go get it." He refused to roll over on command, stand on his hind legs, play dead, heel, sit, or even acknowledge that he had been spoken to. Then one day a marvelous thing happened. Returning home from school, I glanced at the roof of our house, and sitting up there like a degenerate prince surveying his domain was Strange!

My dog climbed houses. Now that was something to brag about. *Why* he climbed the house, I could not even speculate. *How* was fairly easy to determine. He obviously had climbed a stack of firewood, jumped from it to the back porch roof, and from there made his way to the roof of the main house.

There was no way for me to know, of course, that my dog's learning to climb houses was not an isolated incident, but was instead a line of fate that would converge with other lines of fate upon a single point in time and space and produce what is commonly thought of as a coincidence. In this case the coincidence would also be a near-catastrophe. Somewhere it is written that any coincidence traced back far enough will prove to have been inevitable, and I'm sure that must have been the case here.

These were the converging lines of fate:

(1) The long history of genetic malfunctions that eventually combined to create Strange; his aimless meanderings that brought him to our farm; and finally his learning to climb to the roof of our house.

(2) All the genetic and societal forces that combined to shape the particular rebellious nature of my stepfather, Hank; his deciding to grow a beard; and most important, his fractious relationship with my mother's cousin Winnie.

(3) The continuum of factors that led to the creation of Winnie's haughty personality, her fractious relationship with Hank, and her peculiar compulsion to visit us for a week or two every year.

Beards were not popular in that era, and that, as much as anything else, was probably why Hank decided to grow one. He was a man who enjoyed going against the grain of society, or at least what little society existed locally. Winnie, who harbored no great fondness for Hank in the first place, associated beards with comic-strip anarchists who went around carrying bombs that looked like bowling balls with fuses. The stubbly growth of beard seemed to prove her suspicions about my stepfather.

Hank, for his part in the relationship, regarded Winnie as a "mindless twit." Her arrival for the annual visit produced considerable unease for the family, an unease that was well founded, even though Mom had browbeaten Hank to be on his best behavior on this particular occasion. Since even Hank's best behavior left something to be desired as far as Mom was concerned, the tension in our house during Winnie's visit could have been "cut with a knife," to use my mother's phrase.

"Good heavens!" Winnie greeted Hank immediately upon her arrival. "What is that horrible hairy growth on your face?"

"A beard," Hank mumbled, picking up Winnie's suitcase to lug to the upstairs guest room.

"Uh, I think the beard's kind of . . . of . . . dashing," Mom blurted out with a faint laugh, hoping to extinguish the fuse smoldering in Hank's eyes.

"Really?" Winnie said. "Reminds me more of tree moss. I suppose various flying insects might find it irresistible, though. Hee hee."

Hank scurried upstairs with the suitcase, clearly straining to be on his best behavior. Throughout the next few days, Winnie never missed an opportunity to poke fun at Hank's beard. It seemed to have become an obsession with her. Oddly, Hank never responded with any of the biting and usually off-color wit for which he was locally famous. My guess is that he took considerable pleasure in Winnie's loathing of his beard, and the more she pecked away at him about it, the keener was his enjoyment.

And then the fates converged.

After breakfast one morning, Winnie announced that she was going to take a long, leisurely bath, and departed upstairs. Hank shook his head in disbelief. "Another bath," he chuckled. "Why that's the second bath she's took in less than a week. What a twit!"

"Now, now," Mom said soothingly.

Hank and I then went out to clean the rain gutters on the roof. I held the ladder while Hank climbed it to dig away at the muck in the gutter. Strange, already perched on the roof, wandered over to breathe his road-kill breath at Hank.

Hank gasped and choked. "Git out of my face!" he snarled, taking a swipe at Strange.

Strange showed Hank his teeth, made a couple of rude remarks, and then wandered off to another area of the roof, the one containing the dormer window to the bathroom where Winnie was taking her leisurely bath.

As we learned later, Winnie, naked as a noodle, had just emerged from her bath and was drying her hair with a towel prior to putting on her spectacles, without which she was considerably nearsighted. At that very moment, Strange decided to prop his paws on the sill and peer in through the window. Winnie was staring vacantly in the direction of the window. Slowly her eyes came into focus, or as much focus as they were capable of without her glasses. There, on the other side of the glass, was a hairy, leering face—peeping at her.

As Mom said later, Winnie's shriek could have wilted the flowers on the wallpaper. It started at a high, marrow-chilling pitch and went up from there, quavering off into a range beyond human hearing. Among the members of the family, all of whom suffered temporary nerve damage, Hank was the closest to the source of the screech. Following his natural instincts, he took off running at the first high warble. He said later that he noticed right off that he was having trouble getting traction. Then he remembered he had been standing on top of a ladder. Fortunately, he had not traveled any great distance when he remembered the ladder and was able to reach back and get a hand and finally one foot on it. He said the exertion of getting back to the ladder took so much out of him that it might have been better just to take the fall and be done with it. But he said he thought Winnie was being murdered, and if he happened to get knocked unconscious in the fall, he would have missed out on it.

By the time Hank had got himself safely back to the ladder and sucked in a couple of deep breaths, and Winnie had collected her wits, her bathrobe, and her spectacles, Strange had vanished from sight. I suppose it was only natural that upon seeing a hairy, leering face at her bathroom window, Winnie would leap to the conclusion that it must belong to Hank, particularly given her opinion of his character defects. In any case, she jerked up the window, stuck her head out, and shot fierce glances around the roof. And there, to confirm her worst suspicion, was Hank's grizzled face poking up from the edge of the roof.

"You hairy pervert!" Winnie screeched. "I saw you, you . . . you . . . you peeper!"

Hank, of course, had not the slightest notion of what she was talking about, and cared even less, as he was still regrouping his senses after his recent acrobatics. Even after Winnie's head had disappeared back in the window, he clung silently to the top of the ladder.

"You gonna come down or what, Hank?" I asked.

"Yeah," he said. "Pretty quick. As soon as I can make my hands let go of the ladder."

"What was Winnie screeching about?"

"I don't know. Probably tryin' to scare me to death, the crazy twit!"

I could tell from his tone that Hank had abandoned his best behavior.

We soon got the whole mess straightened out, and Winnie had a good laugh over the misunderstanding. Hank, however, seemed depressed. He disappeared into the bathroom for a while and then returned, clean-shaven.

"You shaved off your beard!" Winnie yelped. "Why, you know, I think I liked you better with it. Covered up your weak chin."

Hank responded with a comment that indicated he was off his good behavior. Winnie laughed. Hank was back to normal, and the tension began to melt away. He and Winnie matched insult for insult, and if I'm not mistaken, both of them thoroughly enjoyed the rest of her visit.

But every so often, I would catch Hank staring moodily off into the distance, and it wasn't too hard to guess what troubled him. I'm sure he didn't care one way or the other about being mistaken for a Peeping Tom, but it bothered him no end to be mistaken for Strange.

As usual, the dog escaped unscathed and unrepentant, but he kept a wary eye out for Hank the next few days, and for good reason. Shortly after we had determined the identity of the true culprit in the troublesome affair, Hank made a strangling motion with his hands and snarled, "Where is that miserable mutt?"

"I don't know," I said. "Probably at the dog shack, trying to figure out how to raise the drawbridge."

Strange never again climbed the house, and it was a long, long wait before he did anything else of which I could be proud.

To Filet
or Not to Filet

During the years I was a college sophomore, I became interested in philosophy and signed up for several courses, hoping the intellectual discipline would improve my mind, or, failing that, help me get girls.

Even to this day, I still read philosophy on occasion. I have just been perusing Mortimer J. Adler's *Ten Philosophical Mistakes*. Surprisingly, Mr. Adler forgot the most important philosophical mistake: enrolling in philosophy courses as a sophomore. In his chapter "Consciousness and Its Objects," he cuts right to the heart of the problem: "If two persons are talking about an object that is an object of memory for both of them, or an object of imagination for both, or an object of memory for one and an object of imagination for the other, the question about whether that common object is an entity which also really exists, which also once existed, or which also may exist in the future, cannot be so easily answered."

Right! In fact, I found such problems absolutely impossible to answer. I never even knew they were problems, no one in my family ever having mentioned them.

But I have no regrets about studying philosophy. For one thing, it comes in handy for fileting bluegills. Just the other night, my friend Keith Jackson and I went out on the lake and caught a nice mess of bluegills. As is well known among pan fishermen, there is no such thing as catching too many bluegills while you are catching them. It is only when you must start fileting them that you realize that any number of bluegills is too many to catch.

Upon returning home late at night, Jackson and I were both overcome with the traditional generosity of successful bluegill fishermen the world over. "You take all of them," I told Keith. "Then when we go walleye fishing, you can pay me back."

Jackson said he would stand for nothing of the sort. "I took all the bluegills last time," he said. "No, it's your turn. You take 'em. Be my guest!" This last exclamation being expressed in the intimidating tone of Clint Eastwood's "Make my day!" and given the fact that Eastwood is but a puny shrimp compared to Jackson's six-foot-five, two hundred fifty pounds, I reluctantly acquiesced and hauled the whole mess of bluegills into my house.

My wife, Bun, was stretched out on the couch, wineglass in hand, watching the late news. "Catch anything?"

"A couple thousand bluegills," I said. "I'll just stow them in the refrigerator for tonight and get up first thing in the morning and filet . . ."

Bun's eyes narrowed instantly to the slits that thirty years of marriage have taught me mean trouble and, even worse, work. No doubt she recalled the last time I had stowed a plastic sack full of crappies in the refrigerator. Her friend Lulu had been spending the night. I had told Lulu a dozen times that a lady of her intelligence and sophistication should not watch movies like *Son of Killer Piranha,* in which a vicious fish comes ashore and eats tourists.

Futhermore, I told her, piranha are seldom if ever found lurking in the fitting rooms of chic dress shops, although that's not a bad idea. Even less are they likely to be found crouched in suburban refrigerators. All right, I will admit that a crappie does look something like a piranha. So what happened was, Lulu can't sleep and gets up in the middle of the night and goes down to the refrigerator for a glass of milk. She opens the refrigerator door, reaches for the milk carton, and a half-expired crappie flops out of the plastic bag in front of her. There is no way that it could have gone for her throat, as she hysterically claimed. I, on the other hand, would have been happy to go for her throat, a voluminous organ that no doubt instantly raised all the neighbors a good three feet straight up out of bed. I personally was raised to within a few inches of the ceiling. Hovering there, exuding cold sweat, I calmly tried to deduce the reason for the psyche-shredding screech emanating from my kitchen. The only thing I could come up with was that a burglar had broken in and was feeding Lulu through the pasta-making machine. Later, when I learned that a mere crappie had set off Lulu's alarm, I gladly would have paid a burglar to perform that service.

Rising menacingly from the couch, Bun pointed to the back porch and my fish-cleaning table. I slouched out, the bulging bag of bluegills sagging from my weary casting arm. It is at times like this that my years of delving into the quirky, quicksand depths of philosophy pay off.

I spread newspapers on the porch, then dumped the spiny, slimy pile of bluegills on them. Immediately, as I stared down at the pile, the philosophical question of guilt came to mind. Would there be any reality to the guilt I would feel if, instead of fileting the bluegills, I used them in their entirety as fertilizer for Bun's roses? Would my guilt amount to anything in the endlessly expanding universe with its trillions of stars, some of which were probably orbited by worlds containing intelligent life, one being of which was probably at that very moment staring down at the equivalent of a slimy, spiny pile of bluegills, wondering how he could get out of fileting them? That would certainly be one test of his intelligence. As to the question of guilt, I could only answer, "Yeah, probably." I had killed them. So I would filet and eat them. I picked up a bluegill and had at it with the fileting knife.

An exhausted and shivering person fileting ten thousand bluegills at midnight could easily slip into insanity and scarcely notice it. Thus, the need to invent ever more difficult philosophical questions to keep the mind firmly astride the track of rational thought. Here is one of the tougher problems I came up with: "If a wife has never expressed an interest in hunting in the past or the present and shows no inclination of doing so in the future, and if she has shown no discernible enthusiasm for guns, and indeed mildly distrusts them, would it be a relevant and significant act to give her a really nice .257 Roberts for her birthday?" In the existential sense, the answer is, of course, yes. Still, the risk must be weighed. As the great philosopher Immanuel Kant pointed out, under such circumstances one must be alert to every slight deviation in one's normal existence, such as having your oatmeal taste funny three days in a row.

Perhaps the single most difficult question that has stumped philosophers since the time of Aristotle is, "Why do men fish and call it sport?" Clearly, the act of sport fishing is absurd, lying as it does outside the realm of reason. No sport fisherman can deny the absurdity of his activity, particularly at one o'clock in the morning as he stares down at a pile of twenty thousand bluegills that he must filet. Nevertheless, one must learn not only to accept the absurdity of one's acts but to triumph over it. In one of the Greek myths, a character by the name of Sisyphus is caught by the gods in some misdemeanors involving wine, women, and song while he is supposed to be boringly dead. For his punishment, the gods force Sisyphus to push a huge stone uphill for eternity. As soon as Sisyphus gets the stone to the top of the hill, the stone rolls back to the bottom, and Sisyphus must walk back down and start pushing it up again. One version of the myth has it that Sisyphus triumphs over his fate and the gods, because, on his way back down the hill, he *laughs!* Okay, so it's not that big a triumph. Nevertheless, it appeals to me, because that is often the only triumph we have over our fates—to laugh.

Bun jerked open the back door. "Would you stop that silly cackling!" she hissed. "You'll wake the neighbors! You've got every dog in the block barking his head off!"

So much for Greek myths.

At 2:00 A.M., with the eyes of fifty thousand unfileted bluegills staring gleefully up at me, I turned to the philosophical question of identity. Say, for instance, you have wooden boat A. You remove a piece from it and use it to start building wooden boat B. You transfer each piece of boat A to boat B. Eventually, you have transferred all the pieces. Now what is the identity of the boat—is it A or B? That's a tough question to answer, unless, of course, I am doing the work, in which case boat B leaks like a sieve.

Finally, with 200,000 bluegills glutting the porch at three o'clock in the morning, I came to the ultimate philosophical question. Is it possible for lifeless matter, such as rock and ice swirling in space, which the world once was, to evolve eventually into intelligent life, or approximately one-sixty-fourth of the human population on the planet today? I mean, go out and look at a rock and ask yourself how long it would take that rock to become a divorced public-relations man who is three months behind in his child support. Quite a while, right? In fact, just about the same length of time it takes to filet half a million bluegills.

What's in a Name, Moonbeam?

One of my daughters and her husband were recently going through the mystical ritual of naming a new baby, which, upon its arrival, they claimed, would be either my grandson or granddaughter. They had failed to take into consideration that I am much too young to be a grandfather. As I told my wife, Bun, I'll be danged if I'll have some little whippersnapper going about referring to me as "Gramps."

"Don't be so crotchety," she said.

"Crochety!" I bellowed. "Do you realize what you said, woman?"

"I must have been out of my mind," she said. "I meant to say 'irascible.' "

"That's not any better."

"Miffed?"

"Okay. Now, do you know the name they're thinking of giving this new baby, if it's a boy? *Treat!*"

"I think Treat's a nice name for a boy."

"Nice! Why you couldn't even call the kid without sounding like a damn bird."

"So what kind of name do you think is appropriate?"

"Well, certainly not any of these nature names you hear all the time nowadays: Rain, Breeze, Sky, Snowflake, Moonbeam. What's wrong with the good, solid-sounding names we used to have? They could call him Horace, for instance. Now there's a name with character built into it."

"Horace! I wouldn't feel right about calling a little baby Horace."

"He's only a baby for a little while. He and you can put up with it for a little while. But he's going to be a man practically forever, and Horace is a man's name. I sure as heck can't imagine myself saying, 'Watch closely, Treat. I'm gonna show you how to gut an elk.' "

"That's so disgusting!" Bun said.

"Right," I said. "Why would anyone name a kid Treat? I can tell you this, I won't call one of my grannnnn . . . grannnnn . . . one of my small relatives Treat. I'll give him a name of my own, probably Horace."

At this, I drifted into one of my dream sequences. My small relative was now ten years old, and he and I were on our way out to fish the beaver ponds on the Conckle place. Only the lad had shown any signs of aging. I looked the same as I always have for the past thirty-seven years, since the age of sixteen. The fishing trip was but another of the many lessons in the extensive outdoor education I would provide the youngster.

When we got out of my pickup truck, I locked it up tight and then put the keys on top of the right front tire.

"Pay attention to this, Horace," I said. "All outdoorsmen always hide their keys on top of the right front tire. No one would ever think to look there if he wanted to steal your vehicle.''

''That's a wonderful bit of outdoor knowledge, sir,'' Horace replied, his eyes shiny-bright with appreciation.

As we were climbing through the barbwire fence onto the Conckle property, Horace caught his back on a barb, tore his shirt, and cut a bloody scratch across his back. ''Ha, ha,'' he laughed. ''I just cut a very painful bloody scratch across my back, sir.''

''You handled that very well, Horace,'' I said. ''As I have taught you many times, a person cannot enjoy the outdoors unless he is willing to laugh off a few cuts and bruises. No outdoorsman ever screeches or whines over a bit of pain. Let me hear you do the laugh again.''

''Ha ha, sir.''

''Good. You don't want to overdo it.''

We then waded into the swamp that surrounds the beaver ponds, sinking into the slimy, smelly muck almost up to our knees. Actually, since my knees were higher than Horace's, he sank in almost to his hips. Clouds of mosquitoes descended, and queued up in dozens of lines so each would get its fair turn at us. Deerflies soon arrived and tried to crowd in line. Threats were exchanged. Fights broke out.

''This is bad,'' I said. ''Still, it is much better than some other things you could be doing. What are some of those things, Horace?''

''Lying around the house watching TV,'' Horace said. ''And hanging out in shopping malls. Those are two of the worst things, sir.''

''Right.''

We soon emerged from the swamp and passed through a

grove of aspen. In the branches above us, a bird went "Tweet."

"What, sir?" Horace said.

"I didn't call you, Horace. I never call you by that name."

As we strolled along the stream bank, I suddenly did a one-legger down a beaver hole. After a bit, I smiled grimly.

"It's all right, then," Horace asked, "to screech when you do a one-legger down a beaver hole?"

"Only if you think the beaver has hold of your leg," I replied, "and has mistaken it for a cottonwood limb. That was what I surmised in this instance. By screeching the way I just did, you can often frighten the beaver into letting go."

"That is a useful bit of information, sir. Are the other words used to frighten the beaver, also?"

"Yes. However, they also frighten mothers, so I advise you not to use them around your mother or Granny. Use them only when you do one-leggers and after you are twenty-one or older. Now, if you will excuse me for a moment, I would like to say this: OWWW! OOUCH! OOOOOH! AHHHHHHHH!"

"When are you going to do the laugh, sir?"

"In about six months, Horace, in about six months."

We finally arrived at the beaver ponds, and I showed Horace how to hold large boulders over the water in the slight chance that a beaver might stick his head out. I then made several deliberately bad casts in order to show the boy how to remove a $1.50 fly from the top of a fir tree. I further demonstrated to him how to make a No. 14 dry fly splash like a diving osprey, which is a good way to excite fish from midday doldrums and get them to strike. A good outdoorsman, as I told Horace, must be a keen observer of the psychology of wildlife. Later, when he was older, I would teach him what Freud had to say about the subconscious of fish, and why Jung was ridiculed by Freud for his interpretations of perch dreams.

I did not neglect his instruction in aquatic insect life, explaining the various stages of development: egg, baby bug, child bug, adolescent bug, and finally, of course, adult bug.

"I'm sorry, sir," Horace said, "but all this is too technical for me. I'm only ten."

One of the worst things you can do while educating a youngster about the outdoors is to push him along too fast. I decided to instruct him in more practical matters, such as how to build a campfire to cook a couple of our trout. I cleared a spot on the ground with my boot, carefully arranged a handful of tinder on it, built a tiny pyramid of sticks around the tinder, and touched a match to it.

"See," I said, "if you touch a match directly to the tinder, Horace, nothing happens. First you must strike the match on something. Here is a good way to strike a match. Place the underside of your thumbnail on the head of the match. Then snap it down and back like this and . . ."

"It's all right then, sir," said Horace presently, "to say those words when you have fire shooting out from under your thumbnail?"

"Yes," I said. "Also, I hope you noticed how I grasped my thumb with my crotch and leaped about in a circle. That is an excellent way to extinguish the flames shooting out from under a thumbnail. So, anyway, that is how you build a fire. Remember, don't practice it in your bedroom. Now I will show you how to take the fish home and trick Granny into cleaning and frying them."

"That is something I would really like to learn, sir," Horace said. "It is wonderful to be your small relative."

"Thank you, Horace," I said. "You are a very fine small relative, and someday you will be a great outdoorsman."

At that moment, my dream sequence was interrupted by the ringing of the telephone. Bun answered it. She came back a few minutes later, beaming.

"Guess what. You have a new baby relative—a girl."

"Great!" I said. "Just think, in ten years I can start teaching her all I know about the outdoors. She will make a fine woodsperson. By the way, what did they name her, 'Moonbeam'? 'Snowflake'?"

"Clementine."

"All right! Now that's a name I can live with."

Loud Screeching and
Other Tips on Getting Lost

Summer is that time of year when thousands of otherwise normal citizens are overcome with the urge to rush out to the great forests and mountains of America and get themselves lost. Most of them, however, have not the slightest notion of how to get properly lost, and if they do somehow manage to achieve that exhilarating state, it is by mere accident. Since getting lost in the woods is almost always the highlight of any outdoors vacation, it should not be left to chance.

Getting lost requires planning. Otherwise, you will discover your vacation almost at an end without your having been lost even once. Then you will have to rush to get it done, and in the process you will probably botch the whole thing.

If, for example, you have a week for your wilderness vacation beginning on Saturday, set aside the following Wednesday for getting lost. That will give you Thursday, Friday, and the next Saturday to recover, to let the shakes die down and the goosebumps recede, and to sit around camp savoring the experience of, first, getting lost, and second, getting found. Some people claim that getting found is even more satisfying than getting lost, but my research shows that people tend to treasure the memory of being lost much more than of being found.

Another thing about getting lost on Wednesday is that it gives the Search and Rescue people Thursday and Friday to find you, and therefore doesn't use up their weekend. My own forty years of experience at getting lost in the woods has proven to me that it is much better not to get lost at all than to be found by Search and Rescue people who have spent their whole weekend looking for you. They are often tired and irritable and may have a tendency to regard you as a nuisance rather than as a pathetic but nonetheless heroic lost person. Actually, Search and Rescue people will regard you as a nuisance under any conditions, but more so on weekends. So plan your getting lost for midweek.

Keep in mind, also, that you will need several days to polish the account of your harrowing adventure for the folks back at work. Imagine yourself telling the people at the office, "Yeah, I got lost in the woods and sat down on a log and an hour later a park ranger came by with a nature-study group and found me." That simply won't do. To return to work without a polished and suspenseful story about getting lost deprives you of much of the enjoyment of the experience.

Now, how should you go about getting lost? Naturally, you don't want to tell the other members of the party, "Well, now that it's Wednesday, I think I'll wander off in the woods and get lost." You must appear to have some other objective in mind. Efficiency is a good one. If you are camped in a public campground, simply say that you are going to take a shortcut to the communal spigot to fill the water bucket. Since you have absolutely nothing else to do in a public campground but go for water, someone may inquire as to the need for a shortcut. You could take three hours to fill the water bucket and nobody would care or even notice. Therefore, simply ignore any inquiries about the need for a shortcut.

Shortcuts rank number one among ways to get lost quickly and thoroughly. The typical shortcut requires triple the time to traverse as the long way around. Some shortcuts to destinations no farther away than the campground restroom stretch into days and weeks, which many lost persons find excessive and even tedious.

Before starting your shortcut, take careful note of the position of the sun. This will give the impression that you know what you're doing but otherwise is absolutely useless, because the next time you try to take a bearing on the sun, it will have moved. The North Star is much more reliable, but you can only see it after dark, when you have other things on your mind, such as the strange loud snuffling noises at the foot of the tree you've climbed. Under such circumstances, I've never found that the North Star had the power to hold my attention for any length of time and was best ignored.

Always study on which side of the trees the moss is growing. Guides and other experienced woodsmen are fond of giving this advice, because looking at moss helps even them to get lost. The moss would help you get unlost if it always grew on the side of the tree facing camp or the nearest population center or some other meaningful direction. The sad truth is that moss—rather perversely, I might add—grows on any side of a tree it takes a mind to. That is why it is such an invaluable aid in getting lost.

If you have been out in the woods for an hour and still

aren't lost, you must resort to drastic measures. Start picking wild berries, for example. When I was a child, my father
and mother always used huckleberry or dewberry picking
for getting us lost in the woods in a quick and efficient manner. We would start out with our empty lard buckets roped
to our waists, the individual berries making pleasant little
plunking sounds as we dropped them on the tin bottom.
The standard joke shouted back and forth, as we worked
our way from bush to bush, was, "Is your bottom covered
yet? Ho! Ho!" It was always good for a laugh.

"Over here," my father would call. "These bushes are
loaded."

"Oh, my goodness," Mom would say. "Look up there!
The berries are as big as grapefruit!"

We would charge from one berry patch to another, and
in practically no time at all we would be lost. I always knew
when we were lost because my parents would suddenly get
into a loud and complex argument about the direction back
to the car. "I know the way!" Dad would shout. "The sun
was off to our right and the moss was growing on the other
side of the trees, and—"

"It certainly was not!" Mom would yell. "I remember,
I climbed over a big log and there was a little creek . . . !"

Both of them would have wild, desperate looks in their
eyes, and I could see that it was time to introduce a little
levity into the situation.

"Is your bottom covered?" I would ask, thereby learning
that lost persons are the toughest audience in the world to
get a laugh out of.

What should you do once you know you are actually lost
and not merely standing behind some brush next to a shopping center? Well, the first thing you do is panic. Get the
panic out of your system immediately, so that you can start

thinking straight. Inexperienced lost persons often try to hold the panic in until it explodes and sends them ricocheting off rocks and trees, or propels them over entire mountain ranges. Years ago, I invented the Modified Stationary Panic, which consists of madly running in place and screeching. (You may wish to substitute an inspirational song for the screeching, but you would be the exception.) The MSP has the advantage over uncontrolled panics in that when you are finished you are still in the same place and in one piece, thus making yourself easier and neater for Search and Rescue to find.

Once the MSP has been performed to your satisfaction, sit down and calmly carve a notch on a piece of wood. All lost persons carve notches on pieces of wood, each notch indicating another day they've been lost. Carving notches is part of the tradition. Actually, it's a good idea to carve several notches right away, just in case you get found within the next fifteen minutes. The people back at work might laugh if you showed up with only one notch on a stick. Lost persons must always plan ahead.

The Big Fix

I had the opportunity the other day to ride in the perfect outdoor vehicle, namely one of those vehicles that belongs to somebody else.

In this case, the owner of the perfect outdoor vehicle was young Milt Thomas, a lad scarcely older than his car. Although I own a four-wheel-drive pickup, the road up to the mountain stream Milt and I intended to fish was so rough and terrible that I quickly realized that the only appropriate vehicle for such terrain was Milt's 1968 sedan. As he is still relatively inexperienced in outdoorsmanship, the lad was slow to perceive why his vehicle was the more appropriate one to meet the challenge.

"It's quite simple," I explained. "The Blue Creek Road is rough and dangerous, and requires a certain delicacy of motion to traverse. Your car just happens to possess that essential subtlety of traction provided by tires unencumbered by tread. See? Now shut up and drive."

Scarcely had we left the interstate and begun pounding up the Blue Creek Road than the wisdom of taking Milt's

142

vehicle became loudly apparent. A horrible sound began emanating from beneath the sedan: *WOPPITTY WOP-PITTY WOPPITTY WOPPITTY!*

"Aaaaigh!" Milt cried. "A flat! Do you know what this means?"

"Oh no," I said. "You don't have a spare?"

"Sure, I have a spare," Milt said. "But we still have to change the tire. Then if we have another flat, we won't have a spare."

"Yeah, I already worked that out on my fingers," I said.

"We better change the tire and then go get your pickup," Milt said.

"Let's not be too hasty," I said. "Going thirty miles back up into the mountains without a spare, that's the sort of risk the true outdoorsman thrives on. Remember, Milt, it's risk that whets the edge of a person's life."

"Really?"

"Yup. Now, you hurry up and get that tire changed, while I have a cup of coffee and peruse the fishing regs pamphlet one more time. I'll be over there in the shade of that tree if you need any advice."

I would like to point out here that I eschew making the pretense that I am helping someone change a tire by standing next to him and occasionally handing him a tool that is no more than six inches from his hand. Such a pretense allows the stander-by to lay claim to a share of the work of the actual tire-changer. *"We* had to change a tire," he can brag. But think how much better it is to remove oneself entirely from the workplace and allow all the honor and glory to fall intact upon the person who does the real work, traditionally the owner of the perfect outdoor vehicle.

Unschooled as he is in logic and ethics, Milt failed to perceive the favor I was doing him. He seemed irritated even by my words of encouragement, such as, "Let's speed it up, Milt. Fish don't bite all day, you know."

As Milt shaped his mouth into its whining mode, I quickly offered inspiration. "Milt, Milt, my boy, you should look upon this bit of adversity as an opportunity to build your character."

"I don't see you building your character none," he retorted clumsily.

"That's because you fail to realize the strenuous mental labor required to comprehend fishing regulations pamphlets these days. Build my character? Why, just trying to understand the possession limit has put up four walls, roofed, and added a porch to my character in the short time I've been sitting here. My character's overbuilt, anyway. But to return to my original point, you should consider having to change a tire as an uplifting experience. Now *fixing* a tire, as they used to do in the old days, that was a journey of the spirit, Milt, a journey of the spirit, fixing a tire."

"Gosh," Milt said, "for a moment there I thought I heard background music. You kidding me? How could they fix their own tires in the olden days? They didn't even have VCRs back then."

"Yes," I said, "we are talking ancient times—pre-Columbian, pre-VCR. I myself was but a small child when I first was witness to a tire-fixing."

Tire-fixings were to become a regular and enlightening occurrence during the years of my early youth. My father was a man who believed that a spare tire ranked as a shameless luxury, an accessory serving no other purpose than evidence of conspicuous consumption. He apparently felt the same way about tire tread, if not the thin film of rubber coating the cords of his tires.

The typical tire-fixing occurred on remote dirt roads, where my father frequently took us on Sunday drives. Deprived as I was of almost any form of entertainment in those days, I looked forward to the drives with great anticipation, largely because of the excitement and adventure promised by the inevitable flat.

That first flat tire remains one of my earliest and most cherished memories. We were driving happily along, my father and mother in the front seat singing the forty-ninth verse of "The Old Gray Mare," my sister (the Troll) and I enthusiastically slugging it out in the back seat, when suddenly the joyfulness of the moment was shattered by an ominous sound: *WOPPITTY WOPPITTY WOPPITTY!*

"Oh dear, a flat," my mother announced. "Well, you will just have to get out and fix it. You really should buy a spare."

Dad responded by banging his forehead up and down on the steering wheel. "Women!" he snapped, in a tone suggesting the flat was Mom's fault. I wasn't sure how she had made the tire go flat, but supposed she had driven a nail into it when no one was looking.

We all got out and gathered around the flat, staring at it as though it were some aberration of nature. Dad kicked the tire a few times. That effort failing to inflate it noticeably, he heaved a long sigh. Hoping to cheer him up, I suggested that we could all sing "The Old Gray Mare" while he fixed the tire. Dad stared at me as though I, too, were an aberration of nature. After that I kept my suggestions to myself and concentrated on learning how to fix a tire.

A car jack apparently fell into the same category in which my father placed spares and tread. In any case, we

never seemed to have a jack with us. Thus, Dad would go
off in search of what he termed a "pry pole," usually one
of the fenceposts a considerate farmer had stationed at intervals around his field for just such an emergency.

Dad returned with a pry pole and built a fulcrum out of
rocks and pieces of rotting wood, giving no indication that
he heard a word of Mom's lengthy lecture on the subject
of jacks. Once the car was levered up into the air, Dad
crawled under it and blocked up the axle, while the rest of
the family sat on the end of the pry pole, bouncing it up
and down to Dad's hearty cries of, "Steady! Steady! Stea-
deeeee!"

As soon as the car was precariously blocked up, Dad
remembered that he had forgotten to loosen the lug nuts
on the wheels, and so the whole process had to be repeated.
This was the first time I realized my father knew a foreign
language. "Sum glits um blotten putter fitzon mang fudder
dits!" he shouted, although I can no longer remember the
exact words.

Nowadays, lug nuts are welded to their bolts by fiends
in garages using pneumatic wrenches, in the expectation
that the tire might next be changed at the edge of a busy
expressway at night in the rain by a pudgy middle-aged
man using a hand-powered lug wrench. Pneumatic
wrenches being unknown in the old days, lug nuts were
held in place by rust, an early fixative possessing the qualities of both holding strength and cheapness.

Once the rust bond had been broken and the wheel removed from the axle, Dad set about separating the tire
from the rim. To accomplish this, he used a tire iron—an
instrument now unfamiliar to the average motorist—and a
screwdriver. The screwdriver substituted for a second tire
iron that was essential for removing the tire from the rim.

I studied Dad's technique carefully, to be ready for the day when I, too, would be old enough and lucky enough to fix tires on remote roads.

First, Dad shoved the tire iron between the lip of the tire and the wheel and pried a six-inch section of the tire up over the rim. Next, he stuck in the screwdriver and pried up a three-inch section of tire lip, leaving a gap about as wide as a man's hand between the screwdriver and the tire iron. Finally, holding the tire iron down with his knee, and the screwdriver down with his other hand, he thrust his fingers into the gap and attempted to jerk the rest of the tire lip up over the rim. That was when his knee slipped off the tire iron and the tire clamped shut on his fingers with kind of a slurping sound.

Mom gasped. The Troll emitted a frightened yelp. My father, not to be outdone in the dramatics of the moment, sprang to his feet and began to dance around in an impromptu impression of a foreign-speaking maniac, the tire swinging from his fingers like a vicious but toothless dog.

"Glop kitch feng dopper glitz!" Dad shouted, clasping the tire under one arm and wrenching his fingers free. His lighthearted antics had provoked me instantly to loud, delighted laughter, which was quickly smothered by Mom's hand over my mouth and a vague but ominous prediction as to my immediate fate should I persist. Nevertheless, I have long cherished the thoughtfulness of my father in taking time out from a dirty and difficult task to entertain his young son, a person generally regarded as somewhat peculiar by the family.

Eventually, Dad managed to eviscerate the tube from the tire. For those unacquainted with tubes in this day of the tubeless tire, I will explain that tubes consisted of a donut-shaped collection of patches held together by narrow margins of rubber. Dad hated tubes. The patching kit was equipped with a perforated lid used to roughen the tube surface so that a patch could be affixed to it. Muttering incoherently, Dad scraped the tube so vigorously as to make one think he was trying to torture out of it a confession of all its many crimes against him.

At last the tube was patched, reinserted in the tire, and inflated with a hand pump. Inflating a tire by hand pump, I learned from my father, is made easier by chanting a mantra as you pump: "Hennnn—UFF! Henn-nn-nn—UFF! Hennn-nn-nn-nn-n-n-n—UFF!" It works!

Two hours after the intrusion of the flat into our Sunday drive, we were back in the car heading home, Dad slumped behind the wheel in dense silence.

"There, there," Mom said consolingly, "that wasn't so bad, was it? Still, if we'd had a spare and a jack . . ."

"Women!" Dad barked, his tone speaking volumes in explanation. I knew then once and for all that women are responsible for flat tires.

Even to this day I am alert to any suspicious movements in the vicinity of my tires by my wife and daughters. Still, they manage to sneak by me from time to time and cause a flat. I guess they can't help themselves, and I try not to hold it against them.

"Hey," Milt called, rudely awakening me from a peaceful slumber. "Guess what caused the flat. A nail! How do you suppose a nail got in that tire?"

"Your wife put it there," I said.

"Wife? I'm not even married."

"Oh, that's right. It must have been your mother, then. Or your sister. If not her, possibly a neighbor lady. Women are responsible for all flat tires."

"But why?"

"Nobody knows, Milt, but they are."

I paused and shook my head for proper effect, just as my father had shown me so many decades ago, and then barked:

"Women!"

The Fine Art of Delay

Young Wally Whipple showed up at my house the other morning a whole hour late for the start of our hunting trip. The first thing he did was offer excuses.

"I'm sorry to be so late," he said, "but Retch wasn't ready when I got to his house." Here he jerked a thumb over his shoulder to indicate Retch Sweeney, who was grinning broadly and shaking his head in disbelief. "Retch wasn't even out of bed yet. Then, while he was making his lunch, he asked me if I would change a flat tire on his wife's car so we could get started sooner. After I got the tire changed, he still had to oil his boots and put new laces in them. So he asked me to pick up after the dogs that had knocked over his garbage can. Next he had to look for his sleeping bag, while I changed the bulb in his porch light. Geez, if I hadn't given him a hand, we wouldn't have got started on the hunt until noon. Now I see you ain't ready either."

"I suppose you are referring to the fact that I'm still in

my nightgown," I replied. "It just happens you guys were so late I thought you weren't coming, and I decided to go back to bed."

"You wear a nightgown?" Retch said, a note of suspicion in his tone.

"Of course," I replied. "Doesn't everyone?"

During the course of Wally's long harangue, I had scarcely been able to suppress a chuckle of appreciation at Retch's skilled performance. The man was a master of delay. I happened to know that Ernestine Sweeney's tire had been flat for three days, the garbage can had been the sport of dogs nearly a week earlier, and the porch light had been out for a year. Not bad, not bad at all. A delay of that quality and magnitude would be tough to top.

"I'll be ready in a jiff," I said. "Why don't you fellows sit down and have a cup of coffee while I get dressed? Oh, I nearly forgot!"

At this, Retch turned and headed for the door, mumbling that he didn't want any coffee and would wait in the car. As a master of delay, he can recognize one coming from a mile off.

"Hold it," I said. "We want to get this hunt under way as soon as possible, right?" Retch stopped, his shoulders sagging in surrender. "As I was saying, I nearly forgot that my wife asked me to perform an organ transplant for her before I left."

"Good grief!" Wally said.

"Yeah," I said. "The organ is in the basement rec room and she wants it transplanted up to the living room." I thought the joke pretty good, but it didn't get so much as a smile. "Just so we can get started a little sooner on the hunt, why don't you boys transplant the organ while I get dressed?"

As soon as they had disappeared into the basement, I whisked the nightgown off from over my hunting togs and started putting on my boots. A nightgown, for Pete's sake! I limited myself to a couple of brief chuckles as I listened to them grunting out what sounded like an off-color Gregorian chant as they hauled the organ up the stairs. An organ transplant beats a flat tire, a spilled garbage can, and a blown-out light bulb any day of the week. And Retch knew it, too, even if Wally didn't.

There are many reasons for hunting and fishing delays, other than getting help with a few chores around the house. Take, for example, my goose-hunting trip with two burly friends I'll call Keith and Gary.

I had been all but paralyzed by cold for the past hour, a particularly grim circumstance, since we were still in the car on our way out to the goose pits. Soon I would be crouched in one of the muddy pits, with icy rain rattling down on me like machine-gun fire. All I could think about was curling up under a nice warm electric blanket and dreaming that I had never heard of goose hunting. I needed to come up with a delay, one that would last until the rain at least eased up to a downpour.

"I love mornings like this," Keith said, throwing out his chest and beating on it with his fists. "It makes a man feel alive!"

"Yeah," Gary said. "It's invigorating. Grows hair on your chest. Some guys, all they could think about on a morning like this would be curling up under a nice warm electric blanket, the lily-livered sissies."

"Pardon?" I said. "You say something to me?"

"No, I was talking about lily-livered sissies."

"Oh," I said. "Hey, we're nearly to Greasy Gert's Gas

& Grub Truck Stop. Let's whip in there for a quick cup of
coffee before hitting the ol' goose pits. Just take a couple of
minutes. We can warm up a bit and give the hair follicles
on our chest a rest. What say, guys?''

"I guess we got time for a quick cup," Keith said. "But
just one, no refills.''

It is important to note here the skill with which I eased
my companions into the first stage of a delay. Both Gary
and Keith are experts at delay themselves, and had neatly
parried my utility delay back at my house, where I had tried
a thrust at getting them to put the snow tires on my truck.
Once on the road, however, they quickly relaxed their vig-
ilance, and I was able to take advantage of the element of
surprise.

As soon as we were seated in the restaurant, Gert herself
came over to take our orders. "What'll ya have, fellas?''

"Three coffees, Gert," Gary said.

"And an order of French toast," I blurted out.

"We don't have time for French toast!" Keith snarled.

"French toast takes hardly any time at all," I said. "Besides, on an empty stomach I can't get the full enjoyment
out of freezing off assorted parts of my anatomy in a flooded
goose pit.''

Twenty minutes and three coffee refills later, Gert returned with my French toast. I glanced out the window. Icy
rain still pounded down.

"What's this white stuff on my French toast?" I
asked Gert.

"Powdered sugar," she snapped. "What'd ya think?''

"I can't eat French toast with powdered sugar on it," I
said. "Cook me up a new batch, plain.''

"We don't have time!" Gary screamed. He reached

across the table, grabbed my slices of French toast, and wiped them across his pants leg. "There. Now your French toast doesn't have any powdered sugar on it. Eat!"

"Those pants clean? Okay, okay, put down the knife! I'll eat, I'll eat. Uh, say, Gert, you forgot my bacon."

"YOU DIDN'T ORDER BACON!"

"Did so!"

"Did not!"

I looked outside. The rain had stopped. Shafts of sunlight were breaking through the clouds. "Are we going to sit here and argue all morning, or are we going to hunt?" I said. "Let's go. Sometimes I think you guys would do anything to stay out of a goose pit for a few extra minutes."

Among the delaying tactics I've had pulled on me, the "roadside historical attraction" is the one I hate most, possibly because it is favored by my neighbor, Al Finley. We'll drive by a sign announcing HISTORICAL SITE ONE MILE.

"Historical site one mile," Finley says.

"I can read," I say. "But we're not stopping. Otherwise, we'll miss the peak feeding time."

"We're not talking fish here, we're talking history. Abe Lincoln, Thomas Jefferson . . ."

Knowing he'll give me no peace and probably even accuse me of being unpatriotic, I swerve into the turnout, where a rustic board sign hangs by chains from two posts. The printing on the sign tells us that at this very spot 150 years ago, the first white man to enter the region probably camped for the night, although it may have been a spot eighteen miles away, but it was easier to dig the postholes for the sign here.

"Isn't that interesting?" Finley says. "You can almost see him camped here, old Fletcher Malone. Hostile Indians finally did him in."

"Small wonder," I say. "I've never laid eyes on the man, and he's already made me hostile."

I have known many masters of the hunting and fishing delay, but none greater than Mr. Cranston, a tall, bald man who lived down the road from our place when Retch Sweeney and I were youngsters. Retch and I would be riding our bikes past his place and Mr. Cranston would call out, "Hey, you boys want to go fishing with me tomorrow? Be here at five in the morning sharp."

Retch and I would be at his place at five sharp. Mr. Cranston would stick his head out of his garage. "Be with you in a minute, boys. I've got to do a little work on my outboard motor's carburetor. Say, while you're waiting, would you mind pulling those nails out of the pile of boards by the barn? We can get away a little faster that way."

Mr. Cranston always had huge piles of old boards around his barn. Why the nails needed to be pulled out of them at this very moment, before we could go fishing, remained something of a mystery to us, but we never questioned him about it. About ten o'clock, Mr. Cranston would finish his carburetor work and relieve us of our five hours of free labor to go fishing with him.

We went fishing with Mr. Cranston several dozen times, but never once that he didn't first have to spend four or five hours tinkering with his carburetor.

"I sure wish Mr. Cranston would get a new motor," Retch would say, pulling his ten-thousandth rusty nail and tossing it into a coffee can. "Or at least a new carburetor."

"Me too," I would say. "He probably doesn't realize how much time he wastes fooling with that old thing."

After several years of pulling nails for Mr. Cranston, we finally caught on and found someone else with a boat to take us fishing. Mr. Cranston didn't seem to mind. Every so often, we would go by his place and see a couple of little boys out by his barn, enthusiastically pulling nails.

"What you guys doin'?" Retch would yell.

"Goin' fishin' with Mr. Cranston," one of them would yell back. "What does it look like?"

As I watched Retch and Wally stagger into the living room to complete the organ transplant, I thought once again of Mr. Cranston and what a fine old gentleman he had been, taking the time to teach Retch and me so much about fishing and, of course, the fine art of delay.

Gun-Trading

As my friends will be quick to tell you, I am normally this easygoing guy, practically brimming over with goodwill and love of humanity. It's only when I trade guns that I turn into a shrewd, hardhearted sharpie. Take last week, for example.

Gary Roedl called me up. "You want to go to the gun show tomorrow?" he asked. "Maybe we can trade a few guns."

"Sure," I said. "Sounds like fun."

I'm learning gun-trading from Roedl. Fifteen years ago he started out trading with a rusty single-shot .22 and has turned it into 47,000 guns. Roedl is shrewd.

The next morning when he picked me up in his truck, I was carrying my .48-caliber bolt-action, silver-inlaid, custom-checkered Thumlicker rifle with the digital readout sights.

"You going to sell your Thumlicker?" Roedl asked.

"Nope," I said. "This is my trading stock."

"Wow," Roedl said. "You're starting out in a big way."

157

"Right," I said.

"But you've got to be shrewd," Roedl said. "Let me see your shrewd look."

I gave him my shrewd look. Roedl shook his head.

"You've got to practice more," he said. "You still don't have the eyes right. Your squint is too tight. Well, forget that for now. Let me see your dumb look."

I gave him my dumb look. Roedl complimented me on it. He said it was so natural he would almost guess that I had been born with a dumb look, which pleased me. To trade guns successfully, you have to be able to do a good dumb look. Nobody wants to trade guns with somebody who looks smart.

Next, I did my yawn for Roedl, and he said that was pretty good, too. The yawn is one of the best weapons in the gun trader's arsenal. It works like this. You see a trader who is offering a deal so absolutely fantastic you want to leap in the air, click your heels, and give a rebel yell. Instead, you study the offered item with your look of casual disinterest—have I mentioned the look of casual disinterest?—and then you do your yawn. It should be a wide, slow, gaping yawn, the kind of yawn that implies that the deal being offered is so ordinary and boring that it's practically putting you to sleep on your feet.

Master gun traders like Roedl can even talk while yawning: "Hoooh-ah-you-ahh-hum-ever notice—yaaawph—that the barrel—ho-hummmm-on your gun there—unnnnh-ahhh—is badly warped—hummmm?"

I tried the talking-yawn once but it didn't come off the way I expected. A 300-pound gun trader snatched me off my feet, wrapped his arms around me, and began performing the Heimlich maneuver, almost crushing my ribs in the process. He stopped when a piece of meat shot eight inches out of my mouth, not realizing it was my tongue.

"What are you using for trading stock?" I asked Roedl.

"Four empty .30-30 shell casings and a brass belt buckle," he said. "I'm not in the mood to do any heavy trading today." He yawned.

The gun show was at the fairgrounds. We bought our tickets, got our hands stamped, and went into one of the buildings housing the show. A hundred or so tables had been covered with blankets. Artistically arranged on the blankets was every kind of gun I'd ever heard or read about. Tiny derringers rested in the shade of antitank guns. There were rifles, shotguns, revolvers, automatics, knives, hatchets, bows, arrows, shells, bullets, cartridges, shot . . . In short, just about every conceivable thing even slightly related to weaponry covered every flat surface as far as the eye could see. Actually, the eye couldn't see that far, because pressed shoulder-to-shoulder between the tables were hundreds of prospective gun traders, their trading stock in hand, all looking for that once-in-forever bargain. I jumped right in.

I stopped at a table where the trader, a grizzled old chap in a battered cowboy hat, had spread out his collection of fine old muzzle-loaders. He looked dumb.

"Is that an authentic Hawken rifle there?" I asked.

"Duh, I don't know fer sure. One gun looks about like another to me. All I knows is my great, great, great-grandpap owned it. I found it up in the attic. Think it's worth anything?"

The man obviously was so deficient I almost hated to take advantage of him. I yawned and stared off with my disinterested look. "Well, shucks, I don't know. I suppose I could take a chance on it." Then I put on my dumb look to set him up for the coup de grace. "I reckon I could trade you my Thumlicker here for it."

The trader yawned so long I thought he had forgotten I was standing there. "Oh, all right," he said. "I guess I could let you have this here gun, which might be an authentic Hawken for all I know, if you was to throw in a twenty-dollar bill with the Thumlicker."

Well, I could scarcely pull out my wallet and get the twenty-dollar bill, my hands were so slippery from the sweat on them. All the time I was afraid the trader would catch on to me and back out of the deal, but he didn't. He just sat there looking dumb and happy, without the slightest notion he was getting taken.

Shortly thereafter I made another fine swap, the Hawken for a knife once owned by Jim Bowie, with only one of the blades broken, and a nice little single-shot .22 rifle and a fine pump shot gun that some maniac had painted red, white, and blue. I calculated that a little paint remover would make it good as new, which is what I told the man I traded it to. By the end of the day, I'd made so many trades my jaws ached from yawning. But I felt exuberant and triumphant, and not a little shrewd. Gun-trading gets in a man's blood.

When I met Roedl back at his truck late in the afternoon, he seemed a little depressed.

"How'd you do?" I asked him.

"Not too well," he said. "I ended up with only three rifles, two shotguns, and a revolver. The stock on one of the shotguns has a small scratch on it, though. How'd you do?"

"Great!" I said. "I traded up from the Thumlicker to four empty .30-30 shell casings and a brass belt buckle!"

"Hey, all right!" Roedl said. "That's a whole lot better

than you did last time. You're starting to get the hang of gun-trading.''

"No kidding? You really think so?''

"Sure," Roedl said. "No doubt about it.''

Then he stared off at the horizon and yawned. Small wonder. Gun-trading can wear a person out.

Throwing Stuff

As far back as I can remember, I've had a compulsion to project objects through the air in the direction of a target of some sort. This compulsion peaked at about age eight and has been in slow decline ever since, although I still cannot pass up a good throwing rock.

My wife, Bun, and I were strolling along a beach the other day when I suddenly pointed in the direction of her feet and shouted, "Look!" She bounded into the air and performed a series of acrobatics usually associated with persons who have just stepped on a dead mouse with their bare feet. I admit to surprise at Bun's display of agility, something rarely found in a person of her years and demeanor.

"What! What! What!" she demanded in a voice not unlike the quacking of a startled duck. "What did you point at?"

"Why, nothing less than an absolutely incredible throwing stone, that's what," I replied, plucking the projectile from the sands. "Look at the way it fits perfectly the curve of my thumb and finger. Notice the texture, smooth but with just enough surface grain to provide good grip. The aerodynamics of its shape could scarcely be improved upon by aeronautical engineers. This is a throwing rock of rare quality, its equal not likely to be found anytime in the near future. Oh my gosh, there's another one! And another! Bun! Bun! We've struck the mother lode of throwing rocks!"

"Give me one of them," Bun said, blowing her hair out of her face and tucking her shirttail back in.

"Why?" I said. "There's nothing here to throw at."

"Let me be the judge of that!" she snapped.

Ever alert to possible marital pitfalls, I deposited the rocks in a pants pocket, safely out of the reach of persons unfamiliar with the dangers of accidentally discharging a throwing rock.

"Nope," I said. "Too dangerous. Gosh, that reminds me. I remember back when I was a kid . . ."

Bun rolled her eyes heavenward. "Please! Please! Spare me!" she cried.

I quickly assayed the area around us and, detecting no signs of threat to our well-being, concluded that Bun was merely a bit distraught from her recent fright. I hurried on with the little tale of my youthful experience with throwing things, hoping to distract her from the unfathomable horror that seemed to hold her in its grip.

As a boy of eight, I simply could not pass up a good throwing rock. I would pick it up, rub the dirt from it with my shirtsleeve, test it for heft and balance, and then deposit it in my pants pocket. At the end of the day, I would return home with my pockets so full of good throwing rocks that my pants would come slouching through the door a good five seconds behind me.

What did I do with the good throwing rocks? Well, I

saved them. I never wasted a good throwing rock by throwing it. Naturally, there was some expectation that one day I would come upon a target worthy of being thrown at with a good throwing rock. The problem was that every time I came upon such a target, all my good throwing rocks were stored in a box under my bed and unavailable. So I had to throw at the target with just any old rock that was handy. It was seldom if ever that a good target and a good throwing rock converged on the same point in space and time.

Thus it was that the rock collection under my bed grew and grew, until the floor joists under it creaked ominously, and any round object dropped anywhere in the house rolled in the direction of my bedroom. (I think it had something to do with Einstein's theory of relativity.) And then one day, I looked under my bed and the rock collection was gone!

"My rock collection's gone!" I shouted.

"Oh my gosh!" my mother exclaimed. "We must have been burgled! Is anything else missing? The furs, the jewelry, the silver?"

"We don't have any of that stuff," I pointed out.

"Thank goodness for that. I guess all the thieves made off with was your rock collection, terrible loss that it is."

There was something in her tone that aroused suspicion, but of course nothing could be proved.

Wonderful as rocks were to throw, there were things even more satisfying. Once my friend Crazy Eddie Muldoon and I found a nest of chicken eggs in a stump pile. We had no way of knowing how long the eggs had been abandoned by the hen who laid them, until, of course, we fired the first one against a tree. Then we were able to calculate that the eggs had been ripening anywhere from two months to two years. The rotten egg made an explosive *pop!* when it hit. The egg gunk splattered around the cottonwood and then began a slow slide down the trunk, eating away the bark as it went. The shock wave of poisonous gas arrived a few seconds later, smiting us almost to our knees. The odor was so potent and disgusting and nauseating that we could scarcely believe our good fortune.

"Wow *choke!*" Crazy Eddie said, wiping tears from his eyes. "This is *gag* great!"

"Yeah *rrretch!*" I exclaimed joyfully. "The smell almost *gasp* blinded me! Neato!"

We then set out to find targets of sufficient quality on which to expend our deadly ammunition. We blasted a few stumps, which seemed to shudder in revulsion upon impact. We defaced a large rock, probably for the remainder of its life. None of these targets, however, seemed truly deserving of being hit by such fine projectiles as rotten eggs. We looked around. Several of the Muldoon cows stared at us malevolently from the pasture. The thought crossed my mind that— But Crazy Eddie looked knowingly at me.

"No, we'd better not," he said, his voice tense from unaccustomed restraint. "My pa probably wouldn't like it."

"How about just one cow?" I said.

"Okay."

One of the nice things about Eddie was his willingness to compromise. But before we could execute our plan, the cows somehow got wind of it and galloped off.

"Hey, I know," Eddie exclaimed. "We only got six eggs left. You take three and I'll take three, and we'll play war. I'll hide over there in the woodlot, see, and you attack my position."

I stared at Crazy Eddie in disbelief. In all the years I had known him, he had come up with a lot of stupid and dangerous ideas, but this one . . . this one . . . Why, it was absolutely brilliant!

"Yeah!" I said. "Let's do it!"

As it turned out, I had the opportunity to charge Eddie's position only once. Crouching low, I ran along using some high brush for cover. Then I snapped a twig under my feet, and Eddie fired at the sound. An egg whizzed by my head and struck a limb three feet to my rear. The blast of odor lifted me off my feet and slammed me to the ground. I staggered out of the woodlot and collapsed behind a pile of brush, trying to collect my senses, although my sense of smell now seemed pretty well shot.

As I lay there recovering, I heard footsteps. Eddie! He was charging me! I snatched up an egg in my throwing hand and peeked over the brush pile. Much to my relief, I discovered that the footsteps weren't those of Eddie but his father. Mr. Muldoon stopped to fill his pipe, resting his double-bitted ax on the ground. I saw him sniff the air, turning his head this way and that, then holding his tobacco pouch to his nose and sniffing it. He shook his head, lit his pipe, put the ax on his shoulder, and strolled into the woodlot. I heard one of his big boots snap a twig.

Poor Eddie, I thought. If only Mr. Muldoon weren't carrying that double-bitted ax! I really didn't want to see this. Since I was already halfway home, however, it was highly unlikely I would.

I was somewhat surprised to see Eddie the next day, alive and in one piece. He said he had survived the disaster pretty well, considering, and figured that within a week or two he would be able to sit on hard surfaces again. He estimated it would be at least that long before his mother let his father back in the house, and in the meantime Eddie was enjoying the peace and quiet while he had the chance. His father, he said, got on his nerves a lot.

Certainly nothing was more exciting to throw than rotten

eggs, but dirt clods probably came in second in providing a satisfying throw. I think it must be at least twenty-five or thirty years since I've seen a really fine dirt clod, but when I was a kid we had trillions of them around. The road in front of the house, where we got the car stuck all the time in the spring, provided a sufficient supply of clods to last me all summer. The ruts would dry out and cake off into fine dirt clods, just the right size for throwing. The summer sun would bake them even harder. You could pick up one of these dirt clods and fire it at a tree, and it would explode into dust with a wonderfully satisfying *WHOP!*

One summer we had a chicken named Herbie, who was indistinguishable from all the other chickens, except he had a talent for getting out of the pen and digging in my mother's vegetable garden. One of the few chores I had consisted of running Herbie out of the garden. To do this, I would lob dirt-clod mortar rounds at him. Herbie would take off running as soon as he saw me, his neck stretched out and his feet churning like mad, and all around him the mortar shells would be going off, *WHOP! WHOP! WHOP!* I don't know if Herbie enjoyed the game as much as I did, but he continued to escape from the pen and raid the garden, so he must not have minded too much. Your average chicken leads a pretty dull life.

That summer my rich Aunt Alice came to visit from back east. My mother was particularly apprehensive about her visit, because, Mom said, Aunt Alice was a wealthy and genteel lady and unaccustomed to some of the rough ways of Westerners. Alice apparently held the opinion that gunplay still enjoyed a lot of popularity in our part of the country and that human life hereabouts was generally regarded as cheap.

Mom put on an elaborate welcoming dinner for Alice,

and we all sat around trying our best to act couth. In the middle of dinner, my sister, the Troll, went out to the well house for another jar of buttermilk. Upon returning, she reported disgustedly, "Herbie's out in the backyard again."

"Oh good," I said, sliding my chair back from the table. "I'll go have a little fun with him. Excuse me. I'll be right back."

"Oh, you have someone to play with way out here in the country," Aunt Alice said, smiling. "That's nice. I've always been partial to the name Herbert."

"Herbie's just a chicken," the Troll said.

Aunt Alice laughed genteelly. "My dear, don't be so quick to judge others. What we sometimes perceive to be cowardice often turns out to be wisdom."

Aunt Alice had a peculiar way of talking, so we all just smiled and tried not to look puzzled.

I excused myself and stepped out to the back porch. Herbie saw me immediately and made a dash for cover, his neck stretched out to its limit. Seeing I had only time for one shot, I snatched up a clod and, rather than mortaring it, rifled it at him, leading his beak by about six feet. Much to my astonishment, and probably even more to the chicken's, the sunbaked clod detonated right on Herbie's head. The chicken skidded along the ground in a cloud of clod dust, finally coming to a stop, with not so much as a feather twitching. I shrugged and walked back into the house, dusting off my hands.

"Guess what," I announced. "I just killed Herbie."

Aunt Alice's forkful of mashed potatoes stopped halfway to her mouth. "Wha—? Oh, I see, you're making a jest."

"Nope," I said. "I killed him deader than a doorknob."

"Are you sure?" Mom asked, buttering a roll. Do-it-yourself execution of chickens was a routine activity around our place, and not one to arouse much interest.

"Yeah, I'm sure," I said. "I hit him in the head with a dirt clod. He didn't even twitch."

"My gawwww . . . !" Aunt Alice said, turning whiter than her mashed potatoes.

I thought she must have a soft spot for chickens and decided to change the subject. "Boy, is it ever hot out!"

"Well, if you ask me," the Troll said, "it served Herbie right to get killed."

Aunt Alice's fork clattered into her dish, and Mom, too, noticed that she seemed ill, her eyes wild and blinking, her lips quivering as if she had unexpectedly found herself amid a band of cold-blooded killers.

"Enough talk about killing," Mom said. "This certainly isn't very pleasant dinner conversation. Alice, let me freshen that coffee for you, and then I'll serve the pie. Fresh huckleberry with homemade vanilla ice cream! Doesn't that sound good?"

Aunt Alice's head made a little jerking motion.

Reluctant to let go of the topic, the Troll asked, "You gonna bury Herbie?"

"B-bury?" Aunt Alice said.

"Naw," I said. "I thought I'd just chuck him on the manure pile."

"Enough!" Mom ordered. "Now go wash your hands before you eat your pie. You'll give Aunt Alice the impression we're nothing but a bunch of savages out here in the West. Right, Alice?"

"N-n-n-," Aunt Alice said.

About then, Herbie staggered by the living room window all goggled-eyed and grinning stupidly, which is about the only way a chicken can grin.

"Look, you didn't kill him after all," the Troll yelled. "Herbie's still alive!"

Aunt Alice gave a little jump and stared at the chicken. After a moment she whispered, "Thank you, thank you, thank you," although I wasn't aware that any of us had done her any particular favors.

Aunt Alice left a few days later, cutting short her visit by a week. She was a nice lady, if a little strange, but we weren't sad to see her go. We'd had about all the couth we could stand for one summer.

By the time Bun and I had finished our stroll on the beach, I had managed to collect a sizable arsenal of fine throwing stones. When we got back to our cabin, Bun still nursed a raging fit of feminism, merely because I had offered the opinion that women are incapable of appreciating the fine art of throwing stuff.

"Cramming all those dumb rocks in your pockets!" she raged. "That's the most infantile exhibition of macho . . . and your new pants, too . . . what about your new pants! Just tell me that! What about your new pants?"

"What about them?" I said. "We've only been home a few seconds. My pants will be along any time now."

Letter to Santa

Dear Santa:

For some time now, I have been in correspondence with one of your subordinates, a Mr. Elf Watson, Vice-President, Hunting and Fishing Gifts. As you are aware, most inquiries to your firm are now answered by computer. Thus it was with some relief that I finally received a reply from a real person, namely Elf Watson—assuming, of course, Mr. Watson is a person. (I confess my ignorance as to which species elves belong, if any.)

In the beginning of our rather lengthy correspondence, Mr. Watson impressed me as an amiable and ingratiating chap, and we soon arrived at a first-name basis. As time passed, however, Elf became increasingly surly and, in my opinion, even somewhat irrational. In his most recent letter to me, he lowered himself to outright insults, inquiring sarcastically, "What's a grown man like you doing writing letters to Santa for, anyway?" I am sure you don't approve of such belligerence shown toward your clientele by your employees and will take appropriate disciplinary action.

After my unhappy experience with Elf Watson, I decided to take my problem directly to the top, namely yourself. (I trust that by writing "personal" on the envelope, I have ensured that this letter will elude the computer and make its way to your desk.) Let me say, first of all, that I have generally been well pleased with my Christmas gifts for the past thirty or forty years, although there have been a few problems.

The insulated waders you brought me last Christmas were several sizes too small, prompting my children to laugh hysterically when I tried them on and my wife, Bun, to comment dryly that I looked like a roasted wiener about to burst its skin. I can understand how you and the elves might enjoy playing a little joke from time to time, but in the future I would appreciate a more serious attitude when it comes to filling my gift order.

You also made a minor error last Christmas in giving my wife a nice little side-by-side 20-gauge shotgun, since she doesn't hunt. But don't concern yourself about it. As I told Bun, even Santa can slip up on occasion, and there is no reason to hold a grudge against you. I think she is starting to come around, but I might suggest that this year, instead of entering through the chimney, perhaps you should just sling our presents on the porch as you go by. Okay?

Also, when I said I wanted fish scales for Christmas, I meant an instrument on which to weigh fish. Either there was a communications breakdown or Elf was pulling another of his practical jokes. True, Bun had a good laugh over the look on my face when I opened the package, but she stopped laughing when she had to vacuum the fish scales out of a shag carpet. So when you sling our presents on the porch, don't go "Ho, ho ho" or any of that stuff, and you'll probably be all right. It might be well to press the pedal to the metal on old Dancer and Prancer, even though Bun still isn't much of a wing shot.

But now to my point of contention with Elf. The Christmas in question was that of 1941. As you may recall—and I hope your memory's better than Elf's—I was six years old at the time and living with my folks in a small log cabin in a remote valley of the Rocky Mountains. The Great Depression was over by then, as I've since learned, but nobody had told my parents. They thought we were still poor. My father kept saying things like, "Well, it can't get any worse than this," and then it would get worse. "Now I know we have hit rock bottom," he would say, only to have the bottom drop out from under us once again. I had grown quite accustomed to my father's optimistic pronouncements and didn't pay much attention to them.

Then one December day over our breakfast gruel, he muttered something so ominous and frightening I forgot what I was doing and actually placed some of the gruel in my mouth.

"Pickings have got so slim," Dad said, "I kind of doubt whether Santa Claus will even be able to afford to show up this year. I expect he's busted just like the rest of us."

"Choke, petewweee, gag!" I said. "Wha—? What did you say?"

Dad repeated himself, staring at me glumly through the gruel steam. "But what the heck," he said, "you have lots of other Christmases ahead of you. You'll make up for it later. No presents one Christmas ain't gonna knock a big hole in your life, I guess."

Not knock a big hole in my life? It would kick down all four walls of it, that's what it would do, no presents for Christmas! If Santa Claus thought he could weasel out on me just because times were hard, he had another think coming. Why, I'd . . . I'd . . . Actually, there was nothing I could do, as you, Mr. Claus, are well aware. I probably could have given up believing in you, but I was only enraged, not crazy.

Now, you may think this is one of those maudlin stories where at the very last minute you, Santa Claus, do show up, and everyone stands around laughing and wiping away tears of joy and saying this was the best Christmas ever. Forget it. You, Mr. Claus, did not put in an appearance at our house that Christmas in 1941. I hope you are ashamed of yourself.

Sure, my father tried to get you off the hook by whittling me out a little toy boat and saying it had come from you. One reason I think he said it came from you was he didn't want to take the blame for the boat himself. Dad wasn't much of a whittler and lacked patience. The boat was a board with a point at one end, and a long nail pounded into it for a mast. The mast was too heavy for the boat and caused it to float upside down.

"This is the worst Christmas ever!" I complained.

"Shut up," my father said, "and go play with your boat."

So, the way I see it, Mr. Claus, you still owe me a Christmas, and I would like to collect. If you will check your records, you will see that in my letter to you in December 1941, I requested a tin boat that you put these little wax candles into and lit them and they generated steam and powered the little boat. Having computed the interest, compounded semiannually, on that little boat over a period of forty-five years, I find that it now amounts to a thirty-eight-foot sportfisher with twin diesels and a flying bridge. I would like you to pay up this Christmas, or I shall have to turn the matter over to a collection agency.

You needn't gift wrap the boat. Also, it would be best if you left it at the local marina, with my name on the gift tag. For gosh sakes, don't try to drop it off at the house! It might get peppered with stray birdshot.

Sincerely yours,

Pat

The Cabin at Spooky Lake

One dark and stormy night in 1953, I participated in a strange and frightening occurrence at Spooky Lake in the mountains of North Idaho. Although the exact cause of that inexplicable event remains unknown, Birdy Thompson and Retch Sweeney advanced the theory that we were attacked by an enraged ghost. I personally find that theory to be sheer nonsense and even laughable. Sure, the ghost may have been a little upset but he certainly wasn't enraged.

The three of us were college sophomores at the time, and had been granted an unexpected leave of absence from the university. Somehow—and this in itself is amazing—the mascot of a rival university got hold of a hacksaw, sawed the lock off its cage, and made its way over twenty-five miles of rough terrain, up the back stairs of the dormitory, and right into our room, where it managed to conceal itself from us for three days! As we told the Dean, it was a terrible shock for us to discover that we had been sleeping in the same room with a 200-pound mountain lion, old, moth-eaten and toothless as he might be. We could certainly sympathize with the fright given the dorm counselor when he investigated our room as a possible source of strange smells, a more or less routine practice of his. The man apparently possessed an insatiable curiosity.

The Dean said our shock was certainly understandable and that he was giving us the rest of the semester off, to let our nerves calm down. We replied that we appreciated his thoughtfulness but that our nerves were already much better. He insisted, however, and thus it was that we were released on short notice from our strenuous academic labors.

As we packed our belongings and cleaned up the room, no small task as the result of the brief visit of the runaway mountain lion, we debated over the most profitable use to make of our free time.

"Maybe we won't have all that much free time," I said. "When our folks get the letters from the Dean, they'll probably kill us right off. I think what we should do is write letters home ourselves, explaining the whole misunderstanding and telling our folks that we are going on a camping trip for a week or so. Then we head up into the mountains and camp out until everybody has time to cool down. How does that sound?"

"Good," Birdy said. "Where shall we camp out?"

"You ever hear of Spooky Lake? Rancid Crabtree told me about it. Claims it's haunted. Ha! He says nobody goes there because they're afraid of the place. So Spooky Lake never gets fished. Rancid says it's full of huge old trout just waiting to be caught. Boy, it's funny how people can be so stupid and uneducated as to believe in ghosts."

"Yeah," Birdy said. "I hear Elk Lake is nice this time of year."

"Or Mirror Lake," Retch said. "I been wantin' to get back to ol' Mirror Lake for some fishin'."

"Nope," I said. "It's settled. We'll go to Spooky Lake, unless you guys happen to believe in ghosts and are too chicken to—"

"Naw, sounds okay to me," Birdy said. "Educated men like us don't believe in spooks, right, Retch?"

"Right," Retch said. "I still think Mirror Lake would be nicer, though."

That settled, we wrote our letters home and finished up the packing. I checked to make sure we had all our stuff: three shotguns, three .22s, two .30-06s and a .30-30, six flyrods, six casting rods, twenty fishing reels, three back-packs, three sleeping bags. "I guess that's about it," I said.

"Wait," Birdy said. "Where's the book?"

"Oh, yeah," I said. "We did have a book, a history of something or other."

"What the heck," Retch said. "We can always get an-other book if we have to. Let's go. Man, what a relief to get away from studying all the time!"

We stopped in our hometown long enough to stock up on grub at the mercantile, and then headed out to Rancid Crabtree's shack to get directions to Spooky Lake.

"Spooky Lake?" Rancid said. "You sure you fellers want to go up thar?"

"Why not?" I said. "Don't tell me you believe that story about the ghost that haunts the lake?"

"Course Ah do."

"Well, we don't," I said. "We're college men now, Ran-cid. College men don't believe in all the superstitious non-sense about ghosts. The phenomena people call 'ghosts' are quickly revealed to be nothing other than natural occurrences, if investigated by means of objective and rational thought."

"Ah didn't know thet," Rancid said, "Ah guess the ghost Ah seen at Spooky Lake didn't know it neither."

"You're joshing us, Rance. You didn't see any ghost."

Birdy cracked his knuckles. "Know anybody else who claims to have seen the so-called ghost, Mr. Crabtree?"

"Oh, mebbe a couple dozen folks is all, most of them timid souls. Pinto Jack claims the ghost jumped him up near the old Spooky Lake cabin one day, but you fellers know Pinto. Can't believe a word he says. Swears the ghost gave him that white streak runs through his ha'r. Ah tells him, 'Good, It'll match the yeller streak runs down your back.' Ha! Well, thet riled him, and he comes back at me with—"

"Rance," I said, having heard about the exchange of witticisms many times before, "did you just mention a cabin?"

"Yup. Thar's a cabin thar all right, but Ah'd steer clear of it iffen Ah was yous. Got a bad feelin' about it, thet cabin. Belonged to an old trapper. B'ar broke both his legs. He drug hisself into the cabin, tied splints on his legs with some rawhide, climbed into his bunk, and died. Coulda saved hisself the trouble of makin' the splints. Now as Ah was sayin', Pinto comes back at me with . . ."

We spent the night at Rancid's shack and left early in the morning for Spooky Lake. I had asked Rancid if he wanted to go along, but he said his old legs weren't up to a hike like that anymore. He stood in the doorway and waved good-bye as we drove away. " 'Member what Ah told yous," he called after us. "Don't go n'ar the cabin!"

I laughed. "Rancid doesn't fool me. He's just as scared

of the Spooky Lake ghost as anybody. Did you hear that
malarkey about his tired old legs? Last summer I saw him
walk straight up Blacktail Mountain without even stopping
to rest. I was glad to hear about the cabin. We can stay
there. What say, guys?''

''I say we give Mirror Lake a try,'' Retch said, cracking
his knuckles.

We left the car at the end of a logging road and started
our climb up the mountain, according to the complicated
directions given us by Rancid. If there was a trail, it had
grown up with brush, and now was impossible to find. I
began to wonder about the reliability of Rancid's directions,
vaguely recalling a map of the area that showed a supply
trail that ran to a Forest Service fire lookout station. If I
remembered correctly, the trail offered a much shorter and
easier route to where Spooky Lake was supposed to be. Still,
Rancid knew this country like the back of his grubby hand,
and there was no reason I could think of that he would
deliberately give us bad directions. He did love a good practical joke, but this would be too cruel even for him.

After three hours of climbing through steep, thick woods,
we finally broke out into the open on a rocky ridge. There,
down below us, Spooky Lake sparkled like a blue jewel in
the sun. Even from that distance, we could see the rings of
feeding trout rippling out all over the surface of the water.
I instantly regretted all the mean thoughts I had begun to
harbor about Rancid.

At the far end of the lake stood a grove of massive cedars.
In the shadowy, parklike area beneath the cedars we could
make out the shape of the trapper's cabin. It didn't look the
least bit scary. ''The cabin seems fine from here,'' I said.
''I think we're going to need it, too.'' I pointed to a mass

of thunderheads looming over a distant range of mountains to the west.

"Yeah," Birdy said. "Looks like rain, all right."

"What are we standing here yacking for?" Retch said. "Let's go catch some of those fish for supper."

The fishing was fantastic, for half an hour. We hauled in one nice cutthroat trout after another, and soon had plenty for both supper and breakfast. Then, as is the case with most high mountain lakes, the bite ended abruptly. The lake grew still and glassy, and the rising thunderheads cast a soft, ominous light into the tiny valley. We headed for the cabin.

Up close, the cabin did not appear so fine. It looked as if it had been tucked away among the cedars for a hundred years, which probably was the case. The mud-and-moss chinking had cracked out of the spaces between many of the whitish-gray logs. Moss covered the thick shake roof. The door to the tiny cabin was massive, made out of split cedar logs. It leaned unhinged against the doorway, held in place by a stout limb someone had wedged against it. Retch kicked the limb out of the way and, grunting mightily, set the door aside, commenting that it was a good thing he was along, because Birdy and I between the two of us probably couldn't have moved it.

"Yeah, sure," Birdy said. "Well, give me brains over brawn any day. Yeeesh! Look in there!"

The cabin was a mess. Garbage, animal droppings, pieces of old clothes, a rusty tin plate, bones, and various other debris not easily identified cluttered the floor. "Looks almost as bad as our dorm room," Retch said.

"Well, at least a mountain lion hasn't been cooped up in here for three days," I said. "Let's get the place mucked out. We aren't at college now."

By evening, we had the place tidied up and a fire built in
the little tin-can stove, which, after Retch had set the heavy
door back in its opening, gave off the only light in the cabin.
The mixed aromas of sizzling trout and bacon and fried
potatoes with onions filled the air, as did the raucous sounds
of our mirth at recalling our surprise at finding the runaway
mountain lion in our dorm room. Quickly, the strain of
intense study vanished from our countenances, and a disinterested observer might never have guessed that we had
any college education at all, so quickly did the three of us
revert back to our true, carefree natures.

"Ah, this is the life," Retch said, munching a crisp trout
held in his fingers like an ear of corn. "You know what our
problem was at college? We was just getting too civilized,
that's what."

"Yeah," I said, blowing on a handful of fried potatoes.
"But a man needs an education. Now, you know, most folks
probably would be afraid to stay in this cabin, because of
all the ghost talk and all. We take the rational view, shrug
off all that superstitious nonsense, and we've got ourselves
a nice cozy cabin to spend the night in."

"Speaking of the ghost," Birdy said, "I wonder where
the old trapper was buried around here."

"What?" Retch said. "Buried? You don't suppose they
buried him around here, do you?"

"Probably wasn't much to bury," I said. "According to
Rancid, they didn't find him until ten or fifteen years after
he died. Found his skeleton in that bunk over there, with
the rawhide and splints still on his broken leg bones."

The three of us looked at the bunk. At that moment,
thunder shook the tiny cabin and slivers of light leaped
through the cracks between the logs. Big drops of rain began

splattering down on the shake roof. An eerie gloom filled the cabin as the fire sputtered lower in the tin stove.

"Throw another stick in the stove," Retch said.

"Good idea," I said. "It's, uh, starting to turn cool in here." I mopped sweat off my forehead with my sleeve. "By the way, who wants to sleep in the bunk?"

"Why, I think I'll roll my bag right out here on the floor," Birdy said.

"Me too," Retch said. "You take the bunk, Pat."

"Naw," I said. "Too cramped for me. I'll sleep on the floor."

Sleep evaded me. All my senses seemed to be standing guard in the darkness of the cabin, alert to every rustle and scratch. The fire died out. Minutes crept by like lame hours. Then I heard a strange thumping behind the cabin, as though some creature were trying to pound its way through the logs. A chill filled the inside of my sleeping bag. I wondered if I should disturb Retch and Birdy from their slumbers.

"Guys," I whispered.

"Yeah?"

"What?"

They seemed alert enough. "Do you hear that strange thumping sound?"

"Been listening to it," Retch said.

"What could make a sound like that?" Birdy whispered.

The sound stopped. We listened. All was still, except for the cracking of knuckles and dripping of beads of sweat. Then something climbed to the roof of the cabin. We stared up into the darkness, above which the unmistakable sounds of two feet crunched across the shake roof in the direction of the tin chimney.

"Something's on our roof," Retch said unnecessarily.

"Probably just a . . ." I said. I couldn't think of what it might be.

"Sure," Birdy said. "Th-that's all it is."

A hideous moaning came down our chimney: "Oooooooooahhhhhhhhhhh! Oooooooaahhhhhhhhh! Maw leeeeeeeeeeggggss! Oooooooahhhhhhhh! Mawwww leeeeeegggggggs! Ooooooooo . . ."

That at least was what the hideous moaning sounded like. It was difficult to hear it clearly because of all the hyperventilation going on inside the cabin. A few frantic moments passed. Slowly I began to collect my wits, even as my heart beat wildly.

"Let's calm down," I said.

"Good idea," Retch said. "No point in getting ourselves all worked up over nothin'."

"All we have to do is think this thing through," Birdy said.

"No need to panic," I said. "There has to be a rational explanation for this."

"Yeah," Retch said. "I got one for you. It's that old trapper's ghost!"

"Right," Birdy said. "It's his ghost."

"I know that," I said. "But what's the rational explanation for its wanting to bother us?"

At that moment we raced onto the rocky ridge above the lake and paused to see if we were being followed.

"You can drop the door now, Retch," I said.

"Well, shucks," Retch said. "So that's what was slowing me down!"

We got back to Rancid's cabin just before dawn, but he was already up. He was sitting in his underwear having a cup of coffee. His pants, shirt, and jacket were spread out around the stove, drying.

"What happened?" I asked.

"Fell in the crick," he said. "What brings you fellers back so soon? Thought yous was gonna stay up at Spooky Lake fer a week or so. You educated fellers run afoul of the ghost?" He wiped a big hand across his mouth, in a vain attempt to conceal his concern for us.

"Rain," I said. "Too much rain. We decided to risk going home early."

"I hate rain," Retch said.

"Me too," said Birdy. "Say, Mr. Crabtree, you know, that Spooky Lake is kind of, well, weird. I don't think I'd go up there ever again if I were you. Its name is pretty darn appropriate, if you ask me."

"It should be," Rancid said. "It was named after the trapper what built thet cabin—ol' Tom Spooky. Say, did Ah ever tell you boys about the turble thang what happened to poor ol' Tom? A b'ar broke his legs and—"

"Yeah," I said. "You told us."

Outdoor Burnout

I recently received a letter from a young fellow who has spent several months working in a state park. "It is a 27,000-acre park and wood reserve with three hundred head of American bison, deer, antelope, turkey, elk, and bighorn sheep, as well as nongame species such as coyotes, porcupines, coon, golden and bald eagles, and an assortment of ground critters." He went on to describe the beautiful lakes and streams stocked with brown, rainbow, and brook trout.

It seemed like a wonderful place to work, and I thought perhaps he was getting around to inviting me up for a visit. But then he said, "When I first arrived here I mentioned to my associates that 'it would take a lot of this to make me sick.' Well, I've reached my saturation point!"

In other words, he was fed up to the eyeballs with beautiful streams and lakes, forests, mountains, bison, bighorns, golden eagles, the whole sordid mess. I knew at once that he was suffering from a classic case of outdoor burnout.

Outdoor burnout, a term often used to describe camp

cooking, is actually a severe malady brought on by overexposure to beautiful scenery, wildlife, and wilderness in general. I have suffered from it myself.

By the time I was seven years old, I had spent most of my life in a log cabin surrounded by forest. Everywhere I looked there was nothing but trees—big trees, small trees, skinny trees, fat trees, green trees, brown trees, trees, trees, TREES! So many trees can drive a person mad, and very nearly did me.

Even the house was made of dead trees, trimmed and peeled but nevertheless retaining the unmistakable character of trees. At breakfast, I would glance up and there would be the trees, peering at me from all angles. "YAAAAAAAAAAAAAAH!" I would scream.

My father would give me a quizzical look and say, "Son, if you're not gonna eat the rest of your gruel, pass it on over here." Dad was not a man to coddle a person suffering from burnout.

Such was my hatred of trees that if we happened to drive by a logging camp, I would yell out the car window, "Cut 'em all down! All of them! You hear meeeee?"

I loved a good forest fire. My father would come in from fighting a forest fire off in the mountains somewhere, drop his smoke-blackened self into a chair, and say, "We couldn't hold her. Fire topped out and jumped the line. Went up the side of Wolf Mountain like a blowtorch. Wiped out a lot of timber."

Delighted, I would gleefully clap my little hands. "Tell me again, Dad, how the fire burned up all the trees!"

Dad would pull back from me and say to Mom, "I tell you, the boy ain't right. We get some money we better take him in and get his screws tightened."

Eventually, we moved into open farm country, broken

only by a woodlot here and there, with the forests off at a sensible distance. I was amazed and relieved to discover that trees didn't blanket the entire world. It made life seem worth living.

After a while, I didn't mind trees as decoration, a patch of them here, a row there. I even developed an affection for a huge old solitary cottonwood out in the middle of our pasture. One summer day I took a picnic lunch out and ate it in the cool shade of the tree, listening to the wind rustling softly through the leaves. The tree seemed nice. I smiled up at it. The tree dropped a huge limb and tried to squish me. So much for trying to start a meaningful relationship with a tree.

As I grew older, of course, I learned to love the woods and the great outdoors in general. This was because I didn't live there, but made only periodic visits, to fish, hunt, camp, pick berries and mushrooms, that sort of thing. When I got tired of the wilds—five days was, and still is, about my limit—I went home. Sure, just as much as the next outdoorsperson, I enjoy sleeping in a dirty, soggy sleeping bag, freezing one side of me and roasting the other at the campfire, choking on woodsmoke, eating green hash and granite biscuits, and so on. No matter how much fun it is, though, after about five days the enjoyment begins to wane. I start to long for the roar of traffic, the smell of exhaust fumes, the clamor of shopping malls, and the haunting, melodic wail of sirens in the night. Then I know that outdoor burnout is not far off.

Frequently, I run into people who spend their entire lives in the woods. As a general rule, I notice that their appreciation for their environment will have diminished. I spent a night recently with Sam Scuppers in his cabin up at High Meadows. In the morning, the first rays of sun softly illuminated the meadow, with patches of wildflowers dappling the delicate greens of the new grass. A rainbow hung faintly in the mist rising from the glistening steam, and standing in front of the rainbow were a beautiful whitetail doe and her twin fawns.

"Wow!" I said. "Come look at this, Sam!"

Sam got up stiffly, pulled his suspenders on over his underwear, and hobbled over to the doorway.

"Jeez cripes," he said. "It's just some fool deer." Grumbling, he hobbled over to the stove and put on the coffee. It occurred to me that Sam's outdoor burnout has been going on for about forty years now. I judged it to be terminal.

At the opposite extreme are some friends from Los Angeles whom I recently picked up at the airport and drove up to my lake cabin. As they were getting out of the car, Bert yelled at his wife, "Back in the car, Martha, back in the car or we'll suffocate! There's no air here!"

"Don't be silly, Bert," I said. "Of course there's air here."

"I don't see any," he said, panicky.

I explained to Bert that only in large cities can you see the air. In most other places, air tends to be invisible. Thrilled and amazed, Bert and Martha took pictures of the air to show their friends back in Los Angeles. "They wouldn't believe us if we just told them," Bert said.

I must confess that I myself have occasionally forgotten about outdoor burnout. Back in the days of my brief and unlamented career as a free-lance photojournalist, I came up with a great idea for a photo essay and queried a national magazine about it. "What would be the most wonderful place in the world for a boy to grow up in?" I wrote the editors. "Why a national park, of course! Just think of a youngster fortunate enough to grow up surrounded by beau-

tiful mountains, forests, lakes and streams, wildlife . . ."
And so on. The editors, no doubt looking at the air outside
their offices in a New York skyscraper, wrote back that the
idea sounded super to them and for me to go ahead and do
the photo essay.

My first problem was to find a boy about nine years old
who lived in a national park. I unearthed one, the son of a
park ranger, whose parents happily volunteered the kid to
be the subject of my photo essay. Terrific, I thought. This
essay is as good as sold. I'll go out and shoot a few dozen
rolls of film of the kid enjoying his wonderful and exciting
life among mountains, lakes, wildlife, etc. Nothing to it. My
reputation as a photojournalist would be made.

I drove a thousand miles or so to the park, found the
rustic house in the rustic compound provided for park employees, and knocked on the rustic door. The kid's rustic
mother answered. "Oh, Pithwood," she called to the kid.
"Guess what! The photographer is here to take pictures of
you enjoying your wonderful and exciting life growing up
in a national park. Doesn't that sound like fun?"

Pithwood, slumped in front of the TV with an unwaver-
ing stare, snarled, "How many times do I have to tell you!
I ain't going to do it!"

The free-lance photographer, who hadn't slept for days
and had just driven a thousand miles plus and whose fingers
were still frozen in the position of being clamped around a
steering wheel, laughed uneasily. "Ha ha. What does he
mean, he ain't going to do it?"

Wishing I had thought to bring along a power winch, I
finally managed to move the lad away from the TV and out
into the open air of the park.

Once outside and alone with the boy, I assumed that fake
cheerfulness adults use with children who refuse to believe

they are having fun. "Know what, Pithwood? We're going to hike over to 'Huge Billion-Year-Old Cedar Tree' and you get to climb up into one of its giant hollows and pretend it's your secret hideout while I photograph you! Hey? What say, guy?"

"You crazy? I ain't climbing no tree. I hate climbing trees. You can fall out of them. They're dangerous."

"Well, we can put that off until later. We'll start with something fun. You can sit on a rustic stone wall with the beautiful glacier in the background and feed some bread to the squirrels. Hey?"

"I hate squirrels, the dirty, fat, ugly little beasts, always nosing around for a handout. Forget the squirrels."

"I see, heh heh. Forget the squirrels. Well, Pithwood, perhaps you can tell me something you like to do in the park."

"Something I like to do in this crummy, stupid park? I can't think of nothing. Oh, wait! I got it!"

"Yes? Yes?"

"You could photograph me slurping down a milk shake at the Old Rustic Snack Bar, with a burger and fries. How does that sound?"

I told little Pithwood how that sounded, first checking to make sure his mother had gone back in the house, and then went on to explain that I would be happy to photograph him slurping at the snack bar as soon as we got the other photographs of him enjoying his wonderful and exciting life in the national park, photos by which my future fame and fortune hung in precarious balance. He reluctantly acquiesced.

After seemingly endless days of slogging about the park, shooting pictures, Pithwood and I one afternoon wearily made our way to the Old Rustic Snack Bar, as had become our custom after each day of shooting. We slumped down at a split-log table and ordered milk shakes and fries.

"Listen, Pithwood," I said. "I really appreciate your going through with this sham of letting me photograph you pretending to love your wonderful and exciting life in a national park."

"You're welcome," he said. "Just don't ask me to do it again. I hate this crummy park."

"No kidding, pal," I said. "What a rotten place for a kid to grow up in. By the way, if you could grow up anyplace in the world, where would it be?"

Pithwood's face brightened. "Disneyland!"

"Sounds good to me. Hey, smell that, Pithwood. Nice, huh?"

"Yeah," he said. "It comes from the parking lot. It's called car exhaust."

"I know. Back in the city where I live, you can smell car exhaust anytime you want. Especially in the morning, during rush-hour traffic, when the exhaust fumes come wafting over our neighborhood in nice thick blue-black clouds. And off in the distance you can hear the screech of tires and the blare of horns."

"Gee," Pithwood said, "I wish I lived there."

"I don't blame you, pal. Maybe someday, huh?"

I didn't bother to send the magazine my photos: Pithwood frowning at Bridal Veil Falls; Pithwood sneering at squirrel; Pithwood throwing rocks at deer; Pithwood littering patch of wildflowers; Pithwood yawning at Spectacular Canyon; Pithwood consulting his watch at Eternal Bliss Vista . . . .

Poor kid. You would think his parents would have had better sense than to raise him in a place like that.

Advanced
Duck-Hunting Techniques

Dave Lisaius is a great duck hunter, but very secretive about his techniques.

"C'mon, Dave," I pleaded with him the other day. "Tell me. Is it some little trick you do with the call?"

"Nope."

"Okay, it's the way you set up the decoys, isn't it?"

Dave shook his head.

"You'd better tell me," I threatened. "Otherwise I'm not going to give you any more fishing tips."

He was instantly unnerved, or so I judged by his attempt to distract me by holding his sides and making raucous, annoying sounds.

But I was not to be put off. "Furthermore, I won't give you any advice on how to hunt whitetail deer."

"Stop! Stop!" he cried, holding up his hands. "You're killing me!" Then he emitted a weird, loonish shriek and beat on his thighs with both fists.

"As for my instructing you on the best procedures for hunting elk—"

193

"Stop! Please stop! Have mercy! I'll tell! I'll tell!"

"Good," I said. "I really don't like having to use threats about withholding my fishing and hunting expertise but—"

"I said I'd tell! Now stop! I can't stand any more."

As soon as he had composed himself, Dave went on to explain his secret duck-hunting techniques in detail. I have not had the opportunity to field-test them, but they seem highly promising to me.

"Deception," Dave said. "Deception is the key to successful duck hunting. Master deception and you've mastered the sport."

"I know that," I said. "I know all about camouflage, decoys, duck blinds, and duck calls."

"That's all secondary," Dave said. "Now to begin with, here is a little trick that almost never fails to bring in ducks."

He held up one hand with the fingers straight but clustered tightly together. Then, with his other hand, he began to fold down the clustered fingers one by one, all the while smacking his lips.

"Know what I'm doing now?"

"Yes, irritating me."

"This gesture simulates peeling a banana," he said.

"Right, first you pretend to peel a banana, then you put out the decoys," I said, not without a trace of sarcasm.

"No, you've got it backwards. First you put out the decoys, then you pretend to peel the banana. Got it?"

I nodded my head affirmatively. "Sure. What could be simpler?"

"I haven't known the ol' banana ploy to fail yet," Dave continued. "Many years ago, I noticed that even when I hadn't caught so much as a glimpse of a duck in over four hours, the instant I started to eat lunch, a flight would go whistling directly over my head. I started doing some research. I'd set my gun down close at hand, begin to unwrap a sandwich, drop it, snatch up the gun, and usually nail a double as the ducks went over. I'd catch 'em totally by surprise."

But, Dave explained, using an actual lunch was messy. For one thing, until he became practiced in the maneuver, he used up as many sandwiches as shotgun shells. Other hunters would call out, "Hey, Dave, that's a big sack of decoys you got there," and he would reply, "No, this is my lunch. The sack with the decoys is the small one."

In the excitement of the moment, at first he had trouble keeping the procedure straight. Once he bit into a shotgun shell while trying to load a 10-gauge pickle into a 12-gauge gun.

Finally it occurred to him that ducks weren't all that smart. He tried just pretending to eat a lunch, and sure enough, here came the ducks. He eventually refined the technique down to the simple banana-peeling gesture. This alone provided him with the reputation of being a master duck hunter.

Not satisfied with mere mastery of the sport, Dave wanted to achieve greatness, and he went on to develop even more sophisticated techniques. Here are just a few of them:

The Long-Overcoat Trick—With this maneuver, the hunter wears a long overcoat, one that reaches nearly to his ankles. He makes a show of leaning his shotgun against a tree and walking away from it. The ducks will wait until he is about thirty feet from his gun. Then they will fly in and begin cavorting in the air above the hunter. At this point, he whips a second shotgun from beneath his overcoat and has at them.

Unloading the Gun—This bit of deception requires

sleight of hand, which should be practiced at home until the hunter becomes proficient at it. First the hunter shakes his fist at the duckless sky. Then he slumps his shoulders and hangs his head in the standard manner of skunked duck hunters the world over. He then makes a big pretense of unloading the gun and inserting the shells in his vest. But in fact the shells he inserts in his vest are shells he has palmed earlier. The gun is still loaded! Finally, the hunter walks in the traditional dejected manner back toward his car, occasionally kicking angrily at a rock or stick. He should remember to keep his head down so the ducks can't see his smile. Ducks can detect a smile on a hunter's face at six hundred yards, and even though they think his gun is empty, they will refrain from darkening the sky with their multitudes.

Toilet Tissue—It is a well-known scientific fact that a hunter scurrying out of a blind with a roll of toilet tissue in hand will bring in every duck within a ten-mile radius. The trick here is to have a second gun concealed some distance from the blind.

The Decoy—The hunter should obtain a mannequin from a department-store supply house and dress it in hunting togs identical to his own. An hour before dawn, he sets out his regular duck decoys, with the mannequin standing in the middle of them. While concealed in his blind, the hunter can pull a string that causes the mannequin's arms to move, as if it were still tossing out the duck decoys. As is well known, ducks will drop everything else they are doing in order to fly over a hunter while he is standing hip-deep in water arranging his decoys. Properly executed, the decoy ploy will provide excellent shooting.

On those days when absolutely nothing is moving, the

hunter may have to resort to drastic measures to bring the ducks over. Throwing the mannequin into the water and causing it to thrash around as though it were drowning brings fantastic results. Ducks will fly twenty miles out of their way to see a hunter fall out of his blind. If the weather is extremely cold and the hunter falls through a sheet of ice, ducks will *walk* twenty miles for a chance at such first-class entertainment.

The Cigarette Lighter—This is a simple but effective bit of deception. The duck hunter merely fakes the recommended procedure for thawing out his frozen trigger finger by holding it in a lighter flame. Since in this case the finger is already thawed, it is a good idea to use either a fake lighter or a fake finger. A fake finger is especially useful for veteran duck hunters whose real fingers have already been frozen down to nubbins. Finger nubbins are too hard for ducks to detect from a great distance. Ducks cannot resist coming in once they think a hunter's trigger finger has frozen up, and Dave recommends this ploy highly.

Fake Game Regulations—This device can be expensive, but Dave claims it is well worth the cost. You have a fake game regulations pamphlet printed up. In it you have set the official opening and closing times for the day's hunting fifteen minutes later and earlier respectively. Then you let the pamphlet appear to fall out of your pocket accidentally, making sure that it is open to the page where the ducks can see the times.

"During those fifteen-minute adjustments in the fake opening and closing times," Dave said, "you will have some of the best duck hunting you ever had in your life."

"C'mon, Dave!" I said, looking up from the pad on which I was scribbling notes. "You know good and well ducks can't read. Here you give me some good, sound, practical techniques for hunting ducks, and then you try to pull this on me."

"You don't think ducks can read opening and closing times?" Dave said. "Well, then, you're never going to master duck hunting, I can tell you that right now."